GETTING TO KNOW MASTER ZHU XI:
ENGLISH TRASLATION OF
SELECTIONS FROM ZHUZI YULEI

《朱子语类》

选译

王晓农　赵增韬　译

中国社会科学出版社

图书在版编目（CIP）数据

《朱子语类》选译 / 王晓农，赵增韬译 . —北京：中国社会科学
出版社，2018.10

ISBN 978 – 7 – 5203 – 3299 – 6

Ⅰ. ①朱… Ⅱ. ①王… ②赵… Ⅲ. ①朱熹(1130 – 1200)—
哲学思想②《朱子语类》—译文 Ⅳ. ①B244.74

中国版本图书馆 CIP 数据核字（2018）第 232985 号

出 版 人	赵剑英	
责任编辑	刘　艳	
责任校对	陈　晨	
责任印制	戴　宽	

出　　版	中国社会科学出版社
社　　址	北京鼓楼西大街甲 158 号
邮　　编	100720
网　　址	http://www.csspw.cn
发 行 部	010 – 84083685
门 市 部	010 – 84029450
经　　销	新华书店及其他书店

印　　刷	北京明恒达印务有限公司
装　　订	廊坊市广阳区广增装订厂
版　　次	2018 年 10 月第 1 版
印　　次	2018 年 10 月第 1 次印刷

开　　本	710 × 1000　1/16
印　　张	41.25
插　　页	2
字　　数	602 千字
定　　价	158.00 元

序

　　朱子是中国历史上著作形态最丰富的思想家和学问家。他写过学术专著如《周易本义》《太极图说解》《论孟精义》《资治通鉴纲目》等，也遍注群经如《诗集传》《四书章句集注》《楚辞集注》，还有考订类的著作如《昌黎先生集考异》《周易参同契考异》，又有问答体的著作如《四书或问》《延平答问》等，至于韵文如诗、词、赋、铭及散文如序、跋、奏、劄、状、记、箴、表、启、赞、祝文、祭文等更是数不胜数。《朱子语类》是属于语录体的著作，它是朱子的学生们听课和与老师讨论各种问题时的记录。《论语》是语录体著作鼻祖，孔子去世以后，他的学生们把自己所记忆或记录的孔子言行汇编成一本书，这就是《论语》。孔子以后，语录体的著作并不流行，倒是佛教很好地接过了这种生动活泼的文体，语录体的佛学著作层出不穷。以至于不少人误以为，宋代重又兴盛起来的语录体著作是宋儒照搬佛陀的结果。这就有点数典忘祖了。

　　胡适是现当代研究《朱子语类》比较早的学者。他的《〈朱子语类〉的历史》一文全面系统地梳理了《朱子语类》的编修历史。从他的叙述中我们可以看到《朱子语类》的编修是有一个从"语录"到"语类"的演变过程。朱子去世以后 15 年（1215），李道传在潘时举、叶贺孙、黄榦等朱子的学生们的协助下搜辑朱子的语录，编成了一部四十二卷的书，称"语录"。这以后又有了李性传编的《语续录》（1228）、王佖在婺州编的《语录》（1245）、蔡抗在饶州编的《语后录》（1249）。与李道传同时稍后（1219）黄士毅编成《语类》，1252年，王佖又在徽州编刊《朱子语续类》，这两种是以分类的方式编辑的朱子语录。直到1270年，黎靖德集大成，以黄士毅、王佖的分类为基础，删除重复、补录遗缺，编成了比较完整的《朱子语类》。① 这就是我们今天看到的流传最广、最常见、被使用最多的《朱子语类》。其实，《朱子语类》在形成过程中出现过很多版本，黎靖德在集成"语录""语类"的过程中不免会有所遗漏。1982年，韩国学者李乃扬在日本发现了《朝鲜古写徽州本朱子语类》，这就是一本从中国流传到韩国，又从韩国流传到日本，最后竟成为孤本的一种《朱子语类》。这本"语类"呈现出与黎靖德本不同的面貌。中国的青年学者胡秀娟对此本"语类"做了系统的研究，完成了博士学位论文《〈朝鲜古写徽州本朱子语类〉研究》。② 在她的博士后导师朱杰人的指导下，胡秀娟又在研究的基础上与导师合作，将黎靖德本"语类"与"朝鲜古写本"合刊，编成一种全新的"朱子语类"，名曰《朱子语类合刊本》，于2018年12月由华东师范大学出版社出版。

《朱子语类》成书以后，对于它的价值意义，一直就有不同的意见。比如朱子的学生兼女婿黄榦就批评说："记录之语，未必尽得师传之本旨。"③ 并强调"不可以随时应答之语易平生著述之书。"④ 但是，更多的人则竭力推崇"语类"，认为它保存了朱子的思想，具有极大的价值。吴坚说："朱子教人既有成书，又不能忘言者，为答问发也。天地之所以高厚，一物之所以然，其在成书引而不发者，《语录》所不可无也。"⑤ 李性传就曾引用朱子的话证明语录对理解一个人的思想和学术具有重要的意义。

确实，《朱子语类》对我们了解和研究朱子的思想、学说具有不可

---

① 参见胡适《〈朱子语类〉的历史》，《胡适全集》第八卷，安徽教育出版社2003年版，第397页。
② 胡秀娟：《〈朝鲜古写徽州本朱子语类〉研究》，华东师范大学出版社2013年版。
③ 朱熹：《朱子语类》（第一册），中华书局1986年版，第2页。
④ 同上，第3页。
⑤ 同上，第4页。

替代的作用。语类是朱子在对学生讲课和对话时的即兴之言，这些言论往往是脱口而出，最能真实地反映出朱子的思想。读朱子的语录，往往可以很感性地体现出朱子思想的细微与奥妙之处。语录记载的是当时的口语，所以它表现出与书面语不同的意蕴，有些只能意会不能言传的文字记载，到了"语类"中顿时变得清晰而明了了。加之朱子是个性情活泼的人，他的言论可爱而生动，也使他深刻的形而上思考变得具有了更大的可读性与亲和力。前文已经述及，《朱子语类》经历了从"语录"到"语类"的演变，并最终被定格为"语类"。这不是偶然的。黎靖德最大的贡献就在于他把朱子的语录以一种最具价值阈的形式呈现给了读者。这种形式既便于阅读又利于检索，他被广大的学者及普通读者所接受所喜爱，当然是自然而然的事了。"语类"的编者们，无论是最早的"语录"的收集者还是"语类"的编定者，无不秉承着一种严谨的科学态度。我们可以看到，每一条语录（极个别的除外）都记载了记录者的名字，而每一位记录者在朱子那里问学的时间又有年代的交代。同时听闻者的不同记录也以不同的形式予以保留。这就在最大的程度上保证了记录的可靠性，也使朱子思想的变化有迹可循。所以，我始终认为《朱子语类》是具有极大学术和历史价值的可靠文献。它对于我们真正理解和认识朱子其人、其学，对于我们认识朱子那个时代，具有不可替代的价值。

当然，诚如黄榦所言，《朱子语类》确实不能取代朱子的著作，引用《朱子语类》也不能断章取义。如上所述，语录是朱子的即兴所言，有时他的话未必和经过他深思熟虑的思想完全契合，所以我们在使用《朱子语类》时一定要兼顾朱子的有关著作、文本。如果语类和朱子的著作有矛盾，一般应该以著作为准。另外，朱子的思想是在发展的，他的很多话早期和后期会有所不同。所以我们在引用《朱子语类》时就应该有一个时间概念，不能断章取义，不能顾头不顾尾。但是，这些所谓"问题"，其实并不是"语类"的缺点，而恰恰是它的宝贵之处。用得好，可以有所发现、有所发明；用得不好，则可能走入歧途。所以，"问题"不在"语类"，而在用"语类"的人。

朱子的著作已有很多被翻译成外文，但是"语类"还没有被系统和成规模地被翻译成英文（日本和韩国早已有了"语类"的译本）。王晓农和赵增韬两先生填补了这一学术空缺，撰成《〈朱子语类〉选译》。[①] 虽曰"选译"，但已经囊括了《朱子语类》的基本门类，读了这本译著大致可以了解《朱子语类》的内容与精神，不失为一本对英语世界的读者们全面介绍这本在中国思想史和学术史上具有举足轻重价值的巨著的好读本。晓农先生不弃，要我为他们的译本写一个序，我的英文程度有限，不敢对他们的译作妄加评论，只能把自己多年来研读《朱子语类》的心得写出来，与英语世界的朋友们分享、讨论。

是为序。

朱杰人

2018 年 7 月 1 日于上海桑榆匪晚斋

---

① 由王晓农英译的《朱子语类》选译本《朱子语类选》（汉英对照）入选"大中华文库"，由广西师范大学出版社 2014 年出版。

Foreword

Zhu Xi (1130 – 1200), Zhuzi (Master Zhu) as he has been called respectfully, is a thinker and scholar who authored the most various forms of works in the intellectual history of dynastic China. His works include not only academic writings such as *Zhouyi Benyi* (Original Meaning of *Classic of Change*) , *Taiji Tu Shuo Jie* (Explanation of *Interpretation of the Great Ultimate Diagram*) , *Lun Meng Jingyi* (Collected Meanings of *Analects* and *Mencius*) , and *Zizhi Tongjian Gangmu* (Detailed Outline of *Comprehensive Mirror to Aid in Government*) and annotations of many classics such as *Shi Ji Zhuan* (Commentary on Explanations of *Classic of Poetry*) , *Sishu Zhangju Jizhu* (Interpretation of the Four Books with Collected Annotations) , and *Chuci Jizhu* (Collected Annotations of *Songs of the South*) , but also textual studies such as *Changli Xiansheng Ji Kaoyi* (Textual Study of *Collected Works of Han Yu*) and *Zhouyi Cantong Qi Kaoyi* (Textual Study of *The Kinship of the Three in Accordance with the Classic of Change*) , and dialogue style writings such as *Sishu Huowen* (Questions and Answers on the Four Books) and *Yanping Huowen* (Questions and Answers on Yanping's Discourses). In addition, he wrote numberless poems, rhapsodies, and inscriptions, as well as over ten styles of essays for various purposes.

Zhuzi Yulei (Classified Conversations of Master Zhu Xi) is a record of the conversations between Master Zhu and his disciples while discussing questions concerning wide-ranging topics. It belongs to the category of the conversational style works. The first ancient Chinese work in this style is *Lunyu* (the Analects of Confucius), a collection of sayings and ideas attributed to Confucius (551 – 479 BC) and his contemporaries, traditionally believed to have been compiled and written by his followers after he died. However, after the *Analects*, the conversational writing style did not get popular among Chinese intellectuals, and later it is Chinese Buddhists who inherited that lively style, as evidenced by Buddhist writings in the conversational style keeping on emerging. Consequently, when the conversational style revived in the Song Dynasty (960 – 1279), particularly among the Confucians in that period, quite a few people have taken it for a result of their borrowing the style from Buddhist writers. This misunderstanding indicates an ignorance of its own origin.

Hu Shi (1891 – 1962) is a pioneering modern Chinese scholar who studied *Zhuzi Yulei*. In his article "The History of *Zhuzi Yulei*," he gave a complete and systematic review of its compilation history, by which we know the development in its compilation from *yulu* (recorded conversations) to *yulei* (classified conversations). In 1215, fifteen years after Zhu passed away, Li Daochuan (1170 – 1271), with the help of Pan Shiju (dates unknown), Ye Hesun (dates unknown), Huang Gan (1152 – 1221), and some other disciples of Master Zhu, collected a number of his sayings and conversations and compiled them into a collection of forty two books entitled *Yulu* (Recorded Conversations). This work was continued by *Yuxulu* (Further Recorded Conversations) compiled by Li Xingchuan (1174 – 1255) in 1228, *Yulu* (Recorded Sayings) compiled by Wang Bi (dates unknown) in Wuzhou (what is now Jinhua, Zhejiang Province) in 1245, and *Yuhoulu* (Complement to Recorded Conversations) compiled by Cai Kang (dates unknown) in Raozhou (in Shangrao, Jiangxi Province today) in 1249. In 1219, Huang Shiyi (dates unknown) compiled *Yulei* (Classified

Conversations) and in 1252 Wang Bi published *Zhuzi Yuxulei* (Further Classified Conversations of Master Zhu) in Huizhou (in Anhui Province today). These two works were compiled by classifying the collected sayings and conversations of Master Zhu. The year 1270 saw the monumental publication of *Zhuzi Yulei* (Classified Conversations of Master Zhu Xi), Li Jingde's (dates unknown) synthetic compilation of the existent records on the basis of Huang Shiyi's and Wang Bi's work by deleting duplications and making up deficiencies. ① His *Zhuzi Yulei* with 140 *juan* (fascicles or books) is the most often seen and most widely read edition today.

Therefore, there appeared different editions of the classified conversations of Master Zhu. In spite of his synthetic compilation, Li Jingde's edition is not truly complete, for inevitably there are still some not covered in it. In 1982, Lee Nae-Yang, a Korean scholar, found and published in Japan the *Korean Manuscript of Zhuzi Yulei Huizhou Edition*. It is a Korean manuscript from the Huizhou edition of *Zhuzi Yulei* which was taken to Korea and later the copy found its way to Japan, which has become the only one of its kind available today. It takes on a different look from that work compiled by Li Jingde. Hu Xiujuan made a systematic study of the Korean manuscript and completed her doctoral dissertation *Research of the Korean Manuscript of Zhuzi Yulei (Classified Conversations of Master Zhu) Huizhou Edition*. ② Hu, now working on her post-doctoral program supervised by Zhu Jieren, has made efforts to further her study and in collaboration with Zhu Jieren, she has attempted to combine Li Jingde's edition and the Korean manuscript into a new edition entitled *Zhuzi Yulei Hekanben* (Combined Edition of *Zhuzi Yulei*), which will be published by East China Normal University Press this

---

① See Hu Shi, "The History of *Zhuzi Yulei*," Vol. 8 of *Complete Works of Hu Shi*, Anhui Education Press, 2003, p. 397.

② The dissertation was published with the same title by East China Normal University Press in 2013.

year.

After *Zhuzi Yulei* came out, with regard to its academic value and significance, there have been different opinions. For example, Huang Gan, disciple and son-in-law of Master Zhu, said critically, "Those so called recorded sayings are not necessarily completely accurate as far as our teacher's original ideas go,"[①] and he emphasized "What Master Zhu said in his daily conversations should not be taken in place of all the works he wrote in his life."[②] By contrast, more people heaped praises on it for its tremendous value in containing Master Zhu's thought. For example, Wu Jian (1213 – 1276) said, "Regarding Master Zhu's teachings, we can read his writings, yet we should not forget his sayings, for they were made in answering questions. Concerning the reason why the heaven and earth are so high and so thick and why a thing is what it is, since his writings are good at guiding the students while allowing them to make their own inferences, his recorded sayings, which can be more directly revealing, are indispensable."[③] To fortify his opinion, Li Xingchuan cited Master Zhu's own words to the effect that the recorded sayings of a scholar were of considerable importance to understanding his thought and scholarship.

Zhuzi Yulei is indeed irreplaceable when we try to study and understand Master Zhu's thought and doctrine. He made those sayings impromptu while lecturing to or conversing with his disciples, and since they flowed from his mouth naturally, they conveyed his mind most truly. While reading his sayings, we can get a perceptive understanding of what is deep and subtle in his idea. The spoken language recorded therein manifests different shades of meaning from the written language at that time. The meaning of some written

---

① Zhu Xi, *Classified Conversations of Master Zhu Xi*, Vol. 1, Zhonghua Book Company, 1986, p. 2.

② Ibid. p. 3.

③ Ibid. p. 4.

words in his writings is elusive, which can only be felt, but when expressed colloquially in *Zhuzi Yulei*, it became much more intelligible. In addition, Master Zhu was a lively and cheerful person, whose style of speaking was lovely and vivid, rendering the expression of his profound metaphysical thinking more accessible and amicable. As aforementioned, *Zhuzi Yulei* was the outcome of the formal development from "recorded conversations" to "classified conversations," and it is not accidental for the latter to be established as the ultimate form. Li Jingde made his major contribution by compiling all the available recorded sayings and conversations of Master Zhu and presenting them in a form most valuable to their readers, for it is both easy to read and convenient to search. It is only natural that his edition of *Zhuzi Yulei* has been accepted extensively among dedicated scholars and average readers. Actually, all those compilers, whether the early collectors of "recorded conversations" or the later compilation finalizer of *Classified Conversations of Master Zhu*, cherished a rigorous scholarly attitude towards their work. For example, almost every one in the overwhelming majority of the recorded conversations is provided with the recorder's name, and the information of the time period when he studied with Master Zhu is also clear. Meanwhile if there is disparity between two different disciples' records, both are retained in a marked manner, thus ensuring to the maximum extent the reliability of the records and making the changes in Master Zhu's thought traceable. Therefore, I have been of the opinion that *Zhuzi Yulei* is reliable literature with tremendous academic and historical value and its role is irreplaceable for our attempt to know and understand truly the person and scholarship of Master Zhu and see his time in perspective.

Of course, as Huang Gan said, *Zhuzi Yulei* can not take the place of Master Zhu's writings. When we quote some words from it, we should avoid ignoring their contexts. Since it records, as we mentioned above, what Master Zhu said improvisationally, sometimes his sayings are not necessarily in complete accordance with what he presents in his works which he wrote on a well-thought out basis. Therefore, when we try to grasp and understand his thought, we should take into account both *Zhuzi Yulei* and all his other works. If there is any discordance between them in his idea, usually we accept the latter as prevailing over the former. Additionally, as Master Zhu's thought was in the process of development, his idea about something in his early life was not necessarily the same as that in his later life. Therefore, when we quote even the same words from *Zhuzi Yulei*, we should be aware of that possibility of change and take into consideration the specific contexts where they were said. Nevertheless, these so called "problems" with it are the very place where much of its value lies. Whether one can give play to such value depends on whether he can make use of them well, for when used well, they can serve as a source of revelations and findings to him, but otherwise they may lead him astray. Thus whether those "problems" are problems depends on the user of *Zhuzi Yulei* rather than the work itself.

Many works of Master Zhu have been translated into other languages, and *Zhuzi Yulei* has already been rendered into Korean and Japanese, but a systematical and complete translation of *Zhuzi Yulei* into English has still been unavailable. Fortunately, Wang Xiaonong and Zhao Zengtao have selected from *Zhuzi Yulei* ten books and translated them into English, and their translation will be published as *Getting to Know Master Zhu Xi: English Translation of Selections from Zhuzi Yulei*, which will fill in the blank to some extent. ① Though it is "selections," their work involves the basic categories of conversations collected in *Zhuzi Yulei*, and can serve as an introduction to the English speaking world of *Zhuzi Yulei* which is of great value in the intellectual history of China. By reading their translation, English readers can

---

① In 2014, Wang Xiaonong's *Selections from Classified Conversations of Zhu Xi*, an English translation of nine books of *Zhuzi Yulei*, was published as a contribution to the bilingual series of "Library of Chinese Classics," a key state-sponsored publishing project of China.

get an idea of the content and spirit of the voluminous Chinese classic. Mr. Wang invited me to write a foreword for their translation and though my English is rather limited, I accepted, but I dared not to make comments on their work, so I just presented some of my understanding of *Zhuzi Yulei* I gained from reading it for many years so as to share and discuss it with friends in the English speaking world.

So much for my foreword to this translated work.

Zhu Jieren

July 1, 2018

"Twilight But Not of Work" Study

Shanghai, China

目　　录

CONTENTS

卷第四 Book 4

性理一
Nature and Principle I

人物之性气质之性
The Nature of Humankind and Things, and Physical Nature

1① 这几个字，自古圣贤上下数千年，呼唤得都一般。毕竟是圣学传授不断，故能如此。至春秋时，此个道理其传犹未泯。如刘定公论人受天地之中以生，郑子产论伯有为厉事，其穷理煞精。广。

These several sino-graphs② of *renwu zhi xing* 人物之性 (the nature of humankind and things) and *qizhi zhi xing* 气质之性 (physical nature)③, in the past few thousands of years since the remote ancient sages and worthies, have been understood in an invariable way. After all, that is because the transmission of the sages' learning of them has never been interrupted. Even in the Spring and Autumn Period (770 – 476 BC), an age with an overgrowth

---

① The translator marks the Chinese passages with numbers to indicate their sequence.

② The *zi* 字 or *hanzi* 汉字 is usually rendered into "character" or "Chinese character." In this translation, the more academically colored term "sino-graph" is employed to render it.

③ Where in the original Chinese text there appear Chinese terms and Chinese titles of books and essays, which have no correspondent expressions in English, a tripartite version will be provided when they are rendered for the first time in a chapter or a chapter-level part, which includes the transliteration (based on modern Chinese Pinyin), the original sino-graph (s), and sense translation (in round brackets). For Chinese personal names, only the transliteration and sino-graphs will be presented. Thereafter, when the titles, names, or terms re-appear in the original Chinese text, only transliteration or sense translation will be used.

of doctrines, the truth therein still continued being passed on. For example, Ji Xia 姬夏（？ −531 BC）, Duke Ding of the State of Liu, who articulated on the conception and birth of humankind between Heaven and Earth, and Zichan 子产（？ −522 BC）of the State of Zheng, who expounded the story of Boyou's 伯有（？ −543 BC）change into a ferocious ghost after he was persecuted to death. They were quite versed in enquiring into *li* 理 (principle). ① ［Guang］②

2 天之生物也，一物与一无妄。大雅。

As regards Heaven's production of *wu* 物 (thing［s］), it endows every one of them with its nature free from guile. ［Daya］③

3 天下无无性之物。盖有此物，则有此性；无此物，则无此性。若海。

In the world, there is no thing not endowed with *xing* 性 (nature). If there is this thing, it is endowed with this nature, and if there is not this thing, there is not this nature. ［Ruohai］④

4 问："五行均得太极否？"曰："均。"问："人具五行，物只得一行？"曰："物亦具有五行，只是得五行之偏者耳。"可学。

Question: Do the *wuxing* 五行 (Five Agents, i. e. Metal, Wood, Water, Fire, and Earth) each possess *Taiji* 太极 (Great Ultimate)?

Answer: Yes, they each do.

---

① In the translation, when no information is explicitly offered for marking the speaker or the source of a passage (e. g. Master Zhu said), the speaker is Zhu Xi.

② In the end of each conversation or passage of the Chinese text, there is appended the given name or the styled name of Zhu Xi's disciple who recorded it. In the English translation, the given name of the disciple is offered by transliteration. For example, this "Guang" means "Recorded by Guang. " Guang 广 is the given name of Fu Guang 辅广 (courtesy name Hanqing 汉卿), a disciple of Zhu Xi's. In most cases, a passage contains one or more conversations between Zhu Xi and a disciple of his, and if the recorder of a passage is the disciple conversing with Zhu Xi, the name of him as a speaker is rendered into "I" in the translated passage.

③ Yu Daya 余大雅 (courtesy name Zhengshu 正叔), a disciple of Zhu Xi's.

④ Yang Ruohai 杨若海 (courtesy name unknown).

Further question：Humankind embodies all the Five Agents. Do things embody only one of them?

Answer：Things also embody all the Five Agents, only that they embody them partially. ［Kexue］①

5 问："性具仁义礼智?" 曰："此犹是说'成之者性'。上面更有'一阴一阳'，'继之者善'。只一阴一阳之道，未知做人做物，已具是四者。虽寻常昆虫之类皆有之，只偏而不全，浊气间隔。"德明。

Question：Does the nature embody *ren* 仁 （benevolence）, *yi* 义 （righteousness）, *li* 礼 （propriety）, and *zhi* 智 （wisdom）?

Answer：Yes. That is just like saying "What brings it to its completeness is its nature. " Before these words, there are, still more important, "A *yin* 阴 and then a *yang* 阳② in successive movement is called *Dao* 道 （the Way）," and "What ensues after it （the Way） is *shan* 善 （good）."③ There is only the Way of a *yin* and then a *yang* in successive movement, and when something is brought into being, before whether it is a person or not is known, it is already endowed with those four. This is true of even insects and the like, only that what they get is partial rather than complete, because their turbid *qi* 气 （vital force；material force） obstructs them from getting the four complete. ［Deming］④

6 人物之生，其赋形偏正，固自合下不同。然随其偏正之中，又

---

① Zheng Kexue 郑可学 （courtesy name Zishang 子上）.

② *Yin* and *yang*：Transliterated from the sino-graph 阴 and 阳, literally, the former meaning the dark and the negative side, and the latter, the bright and the positive side. The *yang* and *yin* （the conventional order in saying the two terms is *yin-yang*）, which are regarded as the two material forces or cosmic forces, distinctive yet complementary, retain their phenomenological meanings in terms of our experiences of light and dark, motion and rest, and hardness and softness, day and night, male and female, etc. Although these two terms had appeared earlier in the Chinese history of philosophy, it was not until the third century BC that they achieved a great deal of influence.

③ The quotations are from "Xici" 系辞 （Appended Remarks） of *Yijing* 易经 （Classic of Change）.

④ Liao Deming 廖德明 （courtesy name Zihui 子晦）.

自有清浊昏明之异。偁。

When humankind and things are produced, it is true that *pian* 偏 (partiality) or *zheng* 正 (impartiality) of their endowment is different intrinsically, but with their endowment difference in terms of impartiality or partiality, there is also their difference between clearness and turbidity and between dimness and brightness. [Xian]①

7 物物运动蠢然，若与人无异。而人之仁义礼智之粹然者，物则无也。当时所记，改"人之""之"字为"性"字，姑两存之。节。

Other things than humankind are always moving and operating without rest, which seem the same as humankind. However, humankind is endowed with pure benevolence, righteousness, propriety, and wisdom, but other things are not. The record for this sentence made on the spot reads "However, humankind is endowed with pure nature and benevolence, righteousness, propriety, and wisdom, but other things are not." Both versions are presented here. [Jie]②

8 或问："人物之性一源，何以有异？"曰："人之性论明暗，物之性只是偏塞。暗者可使之明，已偏塞者不可使之通也。横渠言，凡物莫不有是性，由通蔽开塞，所以有人物之别。而卒谓塞者牢不可开，厚者可以开而开之也难，薄者开之也易是也。"又问："人之习为不善，其溺已深者，终不可复反矣。"曰："势极重者不可反，亦在乎识之浅深与其用力之多寡耳。"大雅。

Question: Since the nature of humankind and that of things originate from the same source, why are they different?

Answer: The nature of humankind can be spoken of in terms of brightness or benightedness, while for the nature of things it is only a matter of partiality and obstruction. The benighted can be made to become bright, but the partial and obstructed can not be made to become impartial and unobstructed. Hengqü

---

① Shen Xian 沈偁 (courtesy name Zhuangzhong 庄仲).
② Gan Jie 甘节 (courtesy name Jifu 吉父).

横渠 (i. e. Zhang Zai 张载 [1020–1077]), said, "A thing, whatever it is, has its own nature, which is obstructed or unobstructed, and that is why there is the difference between humankind and things. In the final analysis, the obstructed can not get unobstructed, whereas, in terms of the benightedness or brightness (on the part of humankind), relatively, though the thick is possible to get free from the obstruction, it is very difficult, and for the thin, it is easy."

Further question: If a person has got used to doing what is not good and ingrained deep therein, then he is impossible to return to his original state (of goodness) (, isn't he?)

Answer: Though it is almost impossible for him to cast off his extremely ingrained habits, it depends on how insightful his understanding of casting them off is and how much his effort to cast them off is. [Daya]

9 先生答黄商伯书有云："论万物之一原，则理同而气异；观万物之异体，则气犹相近，而理绝不同。"问："'理同而气异'，此一句是说方付与万物之初，以其天命流行，只是一般，故理同；以其二五之气有清浊纯驳，故气异。下句是就万物已得之后说，以其虽有清浊之不同，而同此二五之气，故气相近；以其昏明开塞之甚远，故理绝不同。中庸是论其方付之初，集注是看其已得之后。"曰："气相近，如知寒煖，识饥饱，好生恶死，趋利避害，人与物都一般。理不同，如蜂蚁之君臣，只是他义上有一点子明；虎狼之父子，只是他仁上有一点子明；其他更推不去。恰似镜子，其他处都暗了，中间只有一两点子光。大凡物事禀得一边重，便占了其他底。如慈爱底人少断制，断制之人多残忍。盖仁多，便遮了义；义多，便遮了那仁。"问："所以妇人临事多怕，亦是气偏了？"曰："妇人之仁，只流从爱上去。"僩。

In a letter to Huang Shangbo 黄商伯 (dates unknown, a disciple of Zhu's), the Master (i. e. Zhu Xi)[①] says, "As regards the one and only

---

[①] For the Chinese *xiansheng* 先生 in the text, which is used by the disciples of Zhu Xi mainly to refer to their teacher, it may be rendered into different versions in contexts in the translation, such as "The Master"; "The Teacher"; "sir."

origin of myriad things, their principles are the same, while their vital forces are different. Seeing from the different forms of myriad things, their vital forces are quire similar, whereas their principles are absolutely different."

Question: When you said that "Their principles are the same, while their vital forces are different," you meant that when at first the myriad things were endowed with the principle, since the operation of *tianming* 天命 (what Heaven has conferred) on every one of them was the same, their principles were also the same. But, as regards the *er-wu zhi qi* 二五之气 (two-five [i. e. *yin* and *yang*, and the Five Agents] vital forces), when they were embodied in the myriad things, there is difference in terms of their clearness or turbidity and their purity or impurity, and thus their vital forces are different. The next sentence concerns the state of the myriad things after getting their vital forces, and, despite their difference in purity, they were of the same two-five vital forces, so their vital forces are quite similar. However, due to their much difference in terms of being bright or not, or of being obstructed or not, their principles were absolutely different. What the book *Zhongyong* 中庸 (Doctrine of the Mean) refers to is the state when myriad things got the principle at first, while your *Jizhu* 集注 (Collected Annotations)[①] concerns the state after they got it. (Is my understanding right?)

Answer: Their vital forces are similar, as evidenced by sensing coldness and warmth, feeling hunger and satiation, liking life and disliking death, drawing on advantages and avoiding disadvantages, in all of which humankind and things are similar. Their principles, however, are different. For instance, the sovereign and its subjects in the world of bees or ants, who have got only an iota of brightness in terms of righteousness, and the father and its sons in the world of tigers or wolves, who have got only an iota of brightness

---

① Referring to *Zhongyong Zhangju* 中庸章句 (Interpretation of the *Doctrine of the Mean*) compiled by Zhu Xi.

in terms of benevolence. In other respects, they have got even less. It is just like the mirror which is dim all over except only one or two spots showing faint light in its central part. If a *wushi* 物事 (thing-event) is endowed dominantly with one aspect, it tends to push aside other aspects and occupy their space. For example, those kind and loving people tend to be less arbitrary, whereas those arbitrary people tend to be more cruel. It is probably because, when benevolence predominates, it overshadows righteousness, and vice versa.

Further question: Therefore, since women are liable to give up to fears when anything crops up, does that mean their vital force is partial?

Answer: The benevolence on the part of women only flows towards *ai* 爱 (love). [Xian]

10 问："人物皆禀天地之理以为性，皆受天地之气以为形。若人品之不同，固是气有昏明厚薄之异。若在物言之，不知是所禀之理便有不全耶，亦是缘气禀之昏蔽故如此耶？"曰："惟其所受之气只有许多，故其理亦只有许多。如犬马，他这形气如此，故只会得如此事。"又问："物物具一太极，则是理无不全也。"曰："谓之全亦可，谓之偏亦可。以理言之，则无不全；以气言之，士毅录作"以不能推言之"。则不能无偏。故吕与叔谓物之性有近人之性者，如猫相乳之类。温公集载他家一猫，又更差异。人之性有近物之性者。"如世上昏愚人。广。

Question: Humankind and things are all endowed with the principle of Heave and Earth as their nature, and receive the vital force of Heaven and Earth as their physical form. It is true that the difference in personality is due to the various degrees of purity and strength of the vital force. But in the case of things, are they as they are because of the incompleteness of the principle with which they are endowed? Or because of the impurity and beclouded character of the vital force endowed in them?

Answer: The principle received by things is precisely in the same degree as the vital force received by them. For example, dogs and horses, who, with their vital force and physical constitution being what they are, know only how to do certain things.

Further question: If each individual thing possesses its own Great Ultimate in its completeness, then its principle can never be incomplete. (In this case, how is it that things possess principle only to a limited degree?)

Answer: You may consider it complete or you may consider it partial. From the viewpoint of principle, it is always complete, but from the viewpoint of vital force Shiyi's[①] record reads "from the viewpoint of its being not admissive of deduction", it cannot help being partial. This is why Lü Yüshu 吕与叔 (i.e. Lü Dalin 吕大临 [1040 – 1092]) said that in certain cases the nature of things approximates to that of humankind. For example, the cat nursing the kittens of another cat.[②] The cat story[③] recorded in *Wengong Ji* 温公集 is more weird; in some other cases the nature of humankind approximates to that of things. For example, those stupid and muddleheaded people in the world.[④] [Guang]

11 问："气质有昏浊不同，则天命之性有偏全否？"曰："非有偏全。谓如日月之光，若在露地，则尽见之；若在蔀屋之下，有所蔽塞，有见有不见。昏浊者是气昏浊了，故自蔽塞，如在蔀屋之下。然在人则蔽塞有可通之理；至于禽兽，亦是此性，只被他形体所拘，生得蔽隔之甚，无可通处。至于虎狼之仁，豺獭之祭，蜂蚁之义，却只通这些子，

---

① Huang Shiyi 黄士毅 (courtesy name Zihong 子洪).

② For the story, see "Mao Xiangru" 猫相乳 (The Cat Nursing the Kittens of Another Cat), an essay written by Han Yu 韩愈 (768 – 824), a distinguished essayist of the Tang dynasty. According to the story, an ancient king raised some cats and of them two female cats gave birth to kittens on the same day. One of the mother cats died after delivery, and her two kittens, sucking her breast but getting no milk, mewed piteously. The other mother cat, who was nursing her kittens, seemed to have heard those two kittens' crying and she stood, went out of her box, and following the sound, found the two kittens. She held one of them in the mouth first, went back to her box, and put it there, and then did the same to the other. She nursed them just like her own kittens.

③ The story is carried in the essay "Mao Shu Zhuan" 猫虪传 (A Biography of Shu, My Cat) in *Wengong Ji* 温公集 (Collected Works of Duke Wen) by Duke Wen, i.e. Sima Guang 司马光 (1019 – 1086).

④ The translation of this passage is based on the version by Chan Wing-tsit (See Chan Wing-tsit. trans. and comp. *A Source Book in Chinese Philosophy*. Princeton: Princeton University Press, 1963, p. 620), with slight modification.

譬如一隙之光。至于猕猴，形状类人，便最灵于他物，只不会说话而已。到得夷狄，便在人与禽兽之间，所以终难改。"嚣。

Question: Physical nature differs in the degree of purity. Does the nature bestowed by Heaven differ in the degree of its completeness?

Answer: No, there is no difference in the degree of its completeness. It is like the light of the sun and moon. In a clear, open field, it is seen in its entirety. Under a mat-shed, however, some of it is obstructed so that part of it is visible and part of it is not. What is impure is due to the impurity of vital force. So the obstruction is caused naturally, like the mat-shed obstructing the light. However, humankind possesses the principle that can penetrate this obstruction, whereas in birds and animals, though they also possess this nature, it is, nevertheless, restricted by their physical constitution, which creates such a degree of obstruction as to be impenetrable. As regards the benevolence in tigers and wolves, the sacrificial rites in jackals and otters[1], and the righteousness in bees and ants, only the obstruction to a particular part of their nature can be penetrated, just as a crack through which only a little ray of light can penetrate. As to the monkeys, whose bodily form resembles that of humankind, it is the most intelligent among other creatures than human beings, except that it cannot talk. [2]When it comes to barbarians, they are between human beings and beasts, so it is ultimately difficult for them to change. [Xun][3]

---

[1] In remote ancient times, when people saw groups of jackals beginning preying other animals and otters beginning catching large amount of fish more than they could devour and their storing the preys for the winter, they thought the jackals and otters as conducting sacrificial rites devoutly and took it as a signal indicating the beginning of their own hunting season. Ancient Confucians drew a moral lesson from the behaviors of the jackals and otters. See "Wangzhi" 王制 (Royal Regulations) in the Chinese classic *Liji* 礼记 (Record of Rites) (An English version of the classic is *Record of Rites*, trans. by J. Legge).

[2] The translation of this passage is based on the version by Chan Wing-tsit, p. 621, with some modifications.

[3] Huang Xun 黄嚣 (courtesy name Zigeng 子耕).

12 性如日光，人物所受之不同，如隙窍之受光有大小也。人物被形质局定了，也是难得开广。如蝼蚁如此小，便只知得君臣之分而已。偲。

The nature is like sunlight and the difference between humankind and things in their nature is like the difference between the amount of light penetrating through a big crack and that through a small crack. Since both humankind and things are restrained by their physical constitutions, it is hard for them to broaden their range of nature. For example, small things like mole crickets and ants know nothing but the difference between a sovereign and its ministers. [Xian]

13 或说："人物性同。"曰："人物性本同，只气禀异。如水无有不清，倾放白椀中是一般色，及放黑椀中又是一般色，放青椀中又是一般色。"又曰："性最难说，要说同亦得，要说异亦得。如隙中之日，隙之长短大小自是不同，然却只是此日。"夔孙。

Someone said, "The nature of humankind and of things are the same." The Master responded, "The nature of humankind and of things are originally the same, and their difference lies only in their endowments of vital force. It is like water which is always clear, yet when the clear water is in a white bowl, it takes on a color; when in a black bowl, it displays another color; when in a blue bowl, it appears in yet another color." He added, "Actually, it is hardest to say whether the nature of humankind and that of things are the same, for you can say they are the same, yet you can also say otherwise. It is just like looking at the sun through different cracks, and though the cracks are different in their lengths or sizes, the sun is always the same." [Kuisun]①

14 人物之生，天赋之以此理，未尝不同，但人物之禀受自有异耳。如一江水，你将杓去取，只得一杓；将椀去取，只得一椀；至于一桶一

---

① Lin Kuisun 林夔孙 (courtesy name Ziwu 子武).

缸，各自随器量不同，故理亦随以异。侗。

Both humankind and things are endowed by birth with their principles, which are not different, but what they actually receive are different naturally. The principle is like the water in a river. When you take it by a ladle, you get only a ladle of it, and when you take it by a bowl, you get only a bowl of it. In the same vein, when you take it by a barrel or even a vat, you can get much more. Just as the amount of water you can get varies with the volume of the vessel you use to take it, so the principles of humankind and things differ correspondingly (in quantity but not in quality). [Xian]

15 问："人则能推，物则不能推。"曰："谓物无此理，不得。只是气昏，一似都无了。"夔孙。

Question: For humankind, deduction can be made, while for things, it can not. (What does this mean?)

Answer: It means things are devoid of such principle as that humankind is endowed with. But it is not right to say that. It is simply because their vital force is faint, for which they appear devoid of that completely. [Kuisun]

16 天地间非特人为至灵，自家心便是鸟兽草木之心，但人受天地之中而生耳。敬仲。

It is not only that humankind is the most intelligent between Heaven and Earth, but also that, though his *xin* 心 (mind)① is the same as those of birds and beasts, and of grasses and trees, it is at the center between Heaven and Earth that he is produced. [Jingzhong]②

17 某有疑问呈先生曰："人物之性，有所谓同者，又有所谓异者。知其所以同，又知其所以异，然后可以论性矣。夫太极动而二气形，二气形而万化生。人与物俱本乎此，则是其所谓同者；而二气五行，纲缊交感，万变不齐，则是其所谓异者。同者，其理也；异者，其气也。

---

① In traditional Chinese philosophy, *xin* is roughly regarded as referring to what is meant by both *heart* and *mind*. It is a usual practice to translate *xin* into "mind."

② You Jingzhong 游敬仲 (courtesy name Lianshu 连叔).

必得是理，而后有以为人物之性，则其所谓同然者，固不得而异也；必得是气，而后有以为人物之形，则所谓异者，亦不得而同也。是以先生于大学或问因谓'以其理而言之，则万物一原，固无人物贵贱之殊；以其气而言之，则得其正且通者为人，得其偏且塞者为物；是以或贵或贱而有所不能齐'者，盖以此也。然其气虽有不齐，而得之以有生者，在人物莫不皆有理；虽有所谓同，而得之以为性者，人则独异于物。故为知觉，为运动者，此气也；为仁义，为礼智者，此理也。知觉运动，人能之，物亦能之；而仁义礼智，则物固有之，而岂能全之乎！今告子乃欲指其气而遗其理，梏于其同者，而不知其所谓异者，此所以见辟于孟子。而先生于集注则亦以为：'以气言之，则知觉运动人物若不异；以理言之，则仁义礼智之禀，非物之所能全也。'于此，则言气同而理异者，所以见人之为贵，非物之所能并；于彼则言理同而气异者，所以见太极之无亏欠，而非有我之所得为也。以是观之，尚何疑哉！有以集注、或问异同为疑者，答之如此，未知是否？"先生批云："此一条论得甚分明。昨晚朋友正有讲及此者，亦已略为言之，然不及此之有条理也。"枅

I submitted to the Master the following statement concerning a problem still in my mind: The nature of humankind and the nature of things are in some respects the same and in other respects different. Only after we know wherein they are similar and wherein they are different can we discuss the nature of both. As the Great Ultimate begins its activity, the two vital forces (i. e. *yin* and *yang*) assume physical form, and as they assume physical form, the myriad transformations of things are brought about. Both humankind and things have their origin here. This is where they are similar. But the two vital forces and the Five Agents, in their fusion and intermingling, and in their interaction and mutual influence, produce innumerable changes and inequalities. This is where they are different. They are similar in regard to principle, but different in respect to vital force. There must be the principle before there can be that which constitutes the nature of humankind and things. Consequently, what makes them similar can not make them different. There must be the vital force before there can be that which constitutes their physical form. Consequently, what makes them different cannot make them similar. For this reason, in your *Daxue Huowen* 大学或问 (Questions and Answers on the *Great Learning*), you say, "From the viewpoint of principle, all things have one source, and of course humankind and things cannot be distinguished as higher and lower creatures. From the viewpoint of vital force, that which receives it in its perfection and is unimpeded becomes humankind, while those that receive it partially and are obstructed become things. Because of this, they cannot be equal, but some are higher and others are lower." However, while they are unequal in respect to vital force, they both possess it as the vital substance of life, and while they are similar in respect to principle, in receiving it to constitute his nature, humankind alone differs from things. This consciousness and movement proceed from their vital force, whereas benevolence, righteousness, propriety, and wisdom proceed from principle. Both humankind and things are capable of consciousness and movement, but though things possess benevolence, righteousness, propriety, and wisdom, they cannot have them completely. Now, Gaozi 告子 (c. 420 – c. 350 BC) pointed to vital force yet neglected principle, and was confined to what is similar and ignorant of what is different. That is why he was attacked by Mencius 孟子 (372 – 289 BC). In your *Jizhu* 集注 (Collected Annotations)[1] you maintain that "In respect to vital force, humankind and things do not seem to differ in consciousness and movement, but in respect to principle, the endowment of benevolence, righteousness, propriety, and wisdom are necessarily imperfect in things." Here you say that humankind and things are similar in respect to vital force but different in respect to principle, in order to show that humankind is higher and cannot be equaled

---

[1]　Referring to *Mengzi Jizhu* 孟子集注 (Collected Annotations on the *Mencius*) by Zhu Xi.

by things. In *Questions and Answers on the Great Learning*, you say that humankind and things are similar in respect to principle but different in respect to vital force, in order to show that the Great Ultimate is not deficient in anything, so it is not subject to any interference by any individual. Looked at in this way, there should t be no question. When someone is puzzled by the discrepancy between the *Questions and Answers on the Great Learning* and the *Collected Annotations*, if I explain it in this way, is it correct?

The Master commented: On this subject, you have discussed it very clearly. It happened that last evening a friend mentioned this matter of discrepancy and I explained it to him briefly, but not as systematically as you have done in this statement. ① [Ji]②

18 子晦问人物清明昏浊之殊, 德辅因问: "尧舜之气常清明冲和, 何以生丹朱商均?" 曰: "气偶然如此, 如瞽瞍生舜是也。" 某曰: "瞽瞍之气有时而清明, 尧舜之气无时而昏浊。" 先生答之不详。次日, 廖再问: "恐是天地之气一时如此?" 曰: "天地之气与物相通, 只借从人躯壳里过来。" 德辅。

Zihui 子晦 (the courtesy name of Liao Deming 廖德明 [dates unknown], a disciple of Zhu Xi's) asked about the disparity between humankind and things in purity or turbidity. After that, I asked the question, "The vital force of Yao 尧 and that of Shun 舜③ were constantly pure, bright, and harmonious, by why were both Danzhu 丹朱, the eldest son of Yao, and Shangjun 商均, the son of Shun, regarded as unworthy?" The Master answered, "That is an accidental case of the vital force, like Gusou 瞽瞍 (lit. a blind fortune-teller) who fathered Shun." I said, "The vital force of Gusou was sometimes pure and bright, while that of Yao and of Shun were

---

① The translation of this passage is based on the version by Chan Wing-tsit, pp. 621 – 622, with some alterations.

② Chen Ji 陈枅 (courtesy name Zixiu 自修).

③ "Shun" and "Yu" are the names of two legendary sage-monarchs in remote ancient China.

always free from turbidity. （Why?）" The Master did not give any definite answer. The next day, Liao (i. e. Liao Deming) asked the Master "Does the vital force of Heaven and Earth, I am afraid, operate that way only sometimes?" The Master answered, "The vital force of Heaven and Earth communicates with that of things, only that the communication is via the human body. " ［Defu］①

19 问："虎狼之父子，蜂蚁之君臣，豺獭之报本，雎鸠之有别，物虽得其一偏，然彻头彻尾得义理之正。人合下具此天命之全体，乃为物欲、气禀所昏，反不能如物之能通其一处而全尽，何也?"曰："物只有这一处通，便却专。人却事事理会得些，便却泛泛，所以易昏。"铢。

Question: There are the father and son feeling among wolves or tigers, the sovereign and minister awareness among ants or bees, the gratefulness among jackals or otters, and the male and female distinction among ospreys. Despite all of them are things with partial endowments, what they have got is the completely right righteousness and principle. Though human beings are endowed from the very beginning by Heaven completely with impartial *yili* 义理 (i. e. *li* 理 ［principle］), when some get beclouded by their material desires and thereby confined by their vital forces, they become unable to go like those things that are capable of understanding one aspect only, but that completely. What is the reason for this?

Answer: Though things are capable of understanding only one aspect, they focus on it. By contrast, though those men have got to know various aspects, their understanding is rather superficial and that is why they tend to be beclouded. ［Zhu］②

20 虎遇药箭而死，也直去不回。虎是刚劲之物，便死得也公

---

① Wang Defu 汪德辅 (courtesy name Changru 长孺).

② Dong Zhu 董铢 (courtesy name Shuzhong 叔重).

正。偶。

When a tiger, pressing forward, gets shot by a poisoned arrow, it still goes ahead before its death. Since the tiger is a thing of firmness and tenacity, even when it meets death, it faces it in a stern, upright, and impartial manner. [Xian]

21 有飞蚁争集于烛而死，指而示诸生曰："此飞而亡者，便是属阴，便是'成之者性'。庄子谓：'一受其成形，不亡以待尽。'"道夫。

When seeing flying ants vied and darted into the candle flame, the Master said to his disciples, "These ants are flying in excitement, indicating their pertaining to *yin* (negative cosmic force), which is a case of 'What brings it to its completeness is its nature' as stated in the *Classic of Change*. Zhuangzi 庄子 (c. 369 – c. 286 BC) says, 'When once we have received the bodily form complete, its parts do not fail to perform their functions till the end comes.'①" [Daofu]②

22 问："人与物以气禀之偏全而不同，不知草木如何？"曰："草木之气又别，他都无知了。"广。

Question: Owing to partial or impartial endowment in vital force, humankind and things are different. What about grasses and trees?

Answer: The vital force of grasses and trees is so different from that of humankind as to be devoid of consciousness. [Guang]

23 一草一木，皆天地和平之气。人杰。

Either a grass or a tree embodies the peaceful and tranquil vital force of Heaven and Earth. [Renjie]③

24 "天下之物，至微至细者，亦皆有心，只是有无知觉处尔。且如一草一木，向阳处便生，向阴处便憔悴，他有个好恶在里。至大而天

---

① The English translation of the sentence cited from Zhuangzi is based on James Legge, trans. *Zhuangzi* [庄子] (http://ctext.org/zhuangzi).

② Yang Daofu 杨道夫 (courtesy name Zhongyu 仲愚).

③ Wan Renjie 万人杰 (courtesy name Zhengchun 正淳).

地，生出许多万物，运转流通，不停一息，四时昼夜，恰似有个物事积踏恁地去。天地自有个无心之心。复卦一阳生于下，这便是生物之心。又如所谓'惟皇上帝降衷于下民'，'天道福善祸淫'，这便自分明有个人在里主宰相似。心是他本领，情是他个意思。"又问："如何见天地之情？"曰："人正大，便也见得天地之情正大。天地只是正大，未尝有些子邪处，未尝有些子小处。"又曰："且如今言药性热，药何尝有性，只是他所生恁地。"道夫。

All things under Heaven, even the minutest and the most delicate, each possess their mind, only that some of them are not sentient beings. For example, the grasses and trees on the sunny side of a place tend to thrive, whereas those on the other, to wither, for they have a sense of liking and disliking. The supremely great Heaven and Earth have produced the myriad things, which have kept operating with vigor and vim, never stopping for even an instant, and the four seasons and the days and nights have gone on as if there were something pedaling, driving them on and on. Heaven and Earth has its own mind with no intention. For example, in "Hexagram Fu" 复 (Return)①, the bottom unbroken line, called "Chujiiu" 初九 (Nine in the First Place) signifies the beginning of the process of return in which the positive energy becomes sufficient to go upwards. That indicates the very mind of producing things. For another example, the "The great *Shangdi* 上帝 (the Topmost Master or Supreme Being) has conferred (even) on the inferior people a moral sense," and "The way of Heaven is to bless the good, and make the bad miserable," as said in *Shangshu* 尚书 (Book of History). What these words say sound clearly as if there were a person as the dominator over there. The mind is that which he is capable of and the *qing* 情 (feeling) is what he intends.

---

① The "Hexagram Fu," with the image of ䷗, is the twenty-fourth hexagram of the sixty-four hexagrams of the *Classic of Change*.

Further question: How to find the feelings of Heaven and Earth?

Answer: If one is upright and large-minded, he will be able to find the upright and large-minded feelings of Heaven and Earth. Heaven and Earth are simply upright and large-minded and they are always free from anything vile and also from anything mean.

Further answer: It is like speaking of the hot nature of a certain medicine. It is not that the medicine possesses the hot nature but that it can produce the effect of that hotness. [Daofu]

25 徐子融以书问:"枯槁之中,有性有气,故附子热,大黄寒,此性是气质之性?"陈才卿谓即是本然之性。先生曰:"子融认知觉为性,故以此为气质之性。性即是理。有性即有气,是他禀得许多气,故亦只有许多理。"才卿谓有性无仁。先生曰:"此说亦是。是他元不曾禀得此道理。惟人则得其全。如动物,则又近人之性矣。故吕氏云:'物有近人之性,人有近物之性。'盖人亦有昏愚之甚者。然动物虽有知觉,才死,则其形骸便腐坏;植物虽无知觉,然其质却坚久难坏。"广。

Xu Zirong 徐子融 (i. e. Xu Zhaoran 徐昭然 [dates unknown], a disciple of Zhu Xi's) wrote to the Master and asked, "In the dry and withered things are both the nature and the vital force; therefore, in their nature, the medicine monkshood is hot, while the rheum officinale is cold. Is their nature the physical nature?" On this point, Chen Caiqing 陈才卿 (dates unknown) (a disciple of Zhu Xi's) said that it was the original nature. The Master responded, "Zirong took consciousness for the nature, so he regarded it as the physical nature. The nature is nothing but the principle. Possessing the nature is nothing but possessing the vital force, in the sense that if a thing is endowed with a certain amount of vital force, it possesses the same amount of principle."

Caiqing stated that a thing's possessing the nature did not mean its possessing benevolence. In response, the Master said, "What you said is also justifiable. It is because it was not endowed with that (amount of) principle originally. Only humankind gets the principle in its completeness. In the case of animals, they come close to humankind in their nature. Therefore, Lü 吕 (referring to Lü Dalin) said, 'The nature of things approximates to that of humankind, and the nature of humankind approximates to that of things.' It is probably because some persons are too much muddleheaded. However, in spite of an animal's consciousness, after it dies, its dead body will get rotten soon, while, though a plant does not have that consciousness, after its death, since its texture is hard, it will last very long and be not easy to rot away. " [Guang]

26 问："曾见答余方叔书，以为枯槁有理。不知枯槁瓦砾，如何有理？"曰："且如大黄附子，亦是枯槁。然大黄不可为附子，附子不可为大黄。"节。

Question: I once read the letter you wrote to Yu Fangshu 余方叔 (i. e. 余大犹, dates unknown, a disciple of Zhu Xi's), in which you said that even dry and withered things possess the principle. How can such things have their principle?

Answer: It is like the two medicines of monkshood and rheum officinale, which are both dry and withered things. However, the rheum can not serve as officinale monkshood, and vice versa. [Jie]

27 问："枯槁之物亦有性，是如何？"曰："是他合下有此理，故云天下无性外之物。"因行街，云："阶砖便有砖之理。"因坐，云："竹椅便有竹椅之理。枯槁之物，谓之无生意，则可；谓之无生理，则不可。如朽木无所用。止可付之爨灶，是无生意矣。然烧甚么木，则是甚么气，亦各不同，这是理元如此。"贺孙。

Question: How is it that dry and withered things also possess the nature?

Answer: Because from the very beginning they possess this principle. This is why we say so. There is not a single thing in the universe that is outside the nature.

Thereupon the Master walked up the steps, and said: "The bricks of these steps have the principle of bricks in them. " Then he sat down and said: "A bamboo chair has the principle of the bamboo chair in it. It is correct to say that dry and withered things have no spirit of life, but it is incorrect to say that they have no principle of life. For example, rotten wood is useless except as fuel and there is in it no spirit of life. But when a particular kind of wood is burned, a particular kind of material force is produced, each different from another. This is so because of the principle inherent originally in it. " [Hesun]①

28 问:"枯槁有理否?"曰:"才有物,便有理。天不曾生个笔,人把兔毫来做笔。才有笔,便有理。"又问:"笔上如何分仁义?"曰:"小小底,不消恁地分仁义。"节。

Question: Does the principle dwell in the dry and withered things?

Answer: The moment a thing comes into being, it is endowed with the principle. Heaven has never produced a ready made writing brush, and humankind produces it by using rabbits' hair. The moment the making of a writing brush is completed, it is endowed with its principle.

Further question: How can benevolence and righteousness be distinguished in a writing pen?

Answer: It is very small, so that it is needless to distinguish its benevolence and righteousness in the usual way. [Jie]

29 问:"理是人物同得于天者。如物之无情者,亦有理否?"曰:"固是有理,如舟只可行之于水,车只可行之于陆。"祖道。

Question: Principle is what is received from Heaven by both humankind and things. Do those things without feelings also possess principle?

Answer: They of course have principle. For example, a ship can go only on water, while a cart can go only on land. [Zudao]②

---

① Ye Hesun 叶贺孙 (courtesy name Weidao 味道).
② Zeng Zudao 曾祖道 (courtesy name Zezhi 择之).

30 季通云："在陆者不可以入水，在水者不可以居陆。在陆者阳多而阴少，在水者阴多而阳少。若出水入陆，则龟獭之类是也。"端蒙。

Jitong 季通① said, "The living things which are destined to live on land shall not enter water, while those destined to reside in water shall not live on land. The former's *yang* outweighs its *yin*, while the latter's *yin* outweighs its *yang*. As for those who leave water and get used to living on land, they are only such beings as tortoises and otters. " 〔Duanmeng〕②

31 草木都是得阴气，走飞都是得阳气。各分之，草是得阴气，木是得阳气，故草柔而木坚；走兽是得阴气，飞鸟是得阳气，故兽伏草而鸟栖木。然兽又有得阳气者，如猿猴之类是也；鸟又有得阴气者，如雉雕之类是也。唯草木都是得阴气，然却有阴中阳、阳中阴者。"端蒙。

All grasses and trees are endowed with more *yin* vital force, whereas all those that can run or fly are endowed with more *yang* vital force. Inside either type, their *yin* and *yang* are also different. Grasses possess more *yin* vital force than trees, and thus grasses are soft, while trees are hard; the beasts possess more *yin* vital force than birds, and thus beasts go in grasses, while birds perch on trees. However, among beasts there are also some that are endowed with more *yang* vital force, such as monkeys, and among birds there are also some endowed with more *yin* vital force, such as pheasants. Only all grasses and trees are dominated by *yin* vital force, but among them there are also some with *yin* in *yang*, or with *yang* in *yin*. 〔Duanmeng〕

32 问："物有夏秋间生者。"曰："生得较迟，他又自有个小四时。"方子。

---

① The courtesy name of Cai Yuanding 蔡元定 (1135 – 1198), a famous disciple of Zhu Xi's, who is one of the main contributors to the founding of Zhu's *Lixue* 理学 (Neo-Confucianism of Principle).

② Cheng Duanmeng 程端蒙 (courtesy name Zhengsi 正思).

Question：Some things are produced in the transition from summer to autumn. （How about them？）

Answer：They come into being rather late, yet they have their own four seasons on a lesser scale. ［Fangzi］①

33 问："动物有知，植物无知，何也？"曰："动物有血气，故能知。植物虽不可言知，然一般生意亦可默见。若戕贼之，便枯悴不复悦怿。亦似有知者。尝观一般花树，朝日照曜之时，欣欣向荣，有这生意，皮包不住，自迸出来；若枯枝老叶，便觉憔悴，盖气行已过也。"问："此处见得仁意否？"曰："只看戕贼之便雕瘁，亦是义底意思。"因举康节云，"植物向下，头向下。'本乎地者亲下'，故浊；动物向上，人头向上。'本乎天者亲上'，故清。猕猴之类能如人立，故特灵怪，如鸟兽头多横生，故有知、无知相半。"德明。铢录云："'本乎天者亲上'，凡动物首向上，是亲乎上，人类是也。'本乎地者亲下'，凡植物本向下，是亲乎下，草木是也。禽兽首多横，所以无智。此康节说。"

Question：Why do animals possess consciousness but plants not?

Answer：That is because animals have vital force of their blood. Though plants have no consciousness to speak of, usually they can also manifest in silence their spirit of living. If a plant is injured, it will wither, becoming not so vigorous as it was, and even perish. Actually, there are some plants which seem to possess a little consciousness. I once observed some blossoming trees. When the morning sun shined on them, they became thriving, displaying their intention of growing prosperously. Their barks could not confine that intense intention, so its sprouting gushed out. But when it comes to the withered branches and old leaves, they turned more devoid of vigor, probably because their vital force had been done for and been over.

Question：Then, is benevolence meant or manifested here?

Answer：From the fact that injure causes loss of vigor and withering, it is

---

① Li Fangzi 李方子（courtesy name Gonghui 公晦）.

also what is meant by righteousness.

Then, the Master quoted Kangjie 康节① as saying "(The heads of) plants grow downward, for 'Things that draw their origin from Earth cleave to what is below,' so they are more turbid (in vital force); (the heads of) animals grow upward, for 'Things that draw their origin from Heaven move towards what is above,'② so they are purer. Such animals as monkeys can stand as erect as humans, so they are extraordinarily more sentient than other animals; the heads of most birds and beasts grow transverse with their bodies, so they possess half-consciousness." 〔Deming〕 Zhu's (铢) record reads, "As 'Things that draw their origin from Heaven move towards what is above,' if an animal's head grows upward on its shoulders, it is towards what is above. This is the case of humankind. As 'Things that draw their origin from Earth cleave to what is below,' if a plant takes root downward, it is towards what is below. This is the case of grasses and trees. For most birds and beasts, since their heads grow transversely, they are devoid of wisdom. This quotation is from Kangjie."

34 纯叟言："枇杷具四时之气：秋结菩蕾，冬花，春实，夏熟。才熟后，又结菩蕾。"先生顾谓德明曰："如此看去。"意谓生理循环也。德明。

Chunsou 纯叟③ said, "The loquat embodies the vital force of the four seasons, for it buds in autumn, flowers in winter, fruits in spring, and ripens in summer. Soon after its fruit ripens, it buds again." The Master turned to me, saying "Look at it in that way." He meant that the four stages of the loquat constituted a cycle of growing. 〔Deming〕

35 冬间花难谢。如水仙，至脆弱，亦耐久；如梅花蜡梅，皆然。至春花则易谢。若夏间花，则尤甚矣。如葵榴荷花，只开得一日。必竟

---

① The posthumous tile of Shao Yong 邵雍 (1011 – 1077), with the courtesy name Yaofu 尧夫, who is one of the major founders of the Neo-Confucianism in Northern Song Dynasty (960 – 1127).

② The two quoted sentences are from the "Wenyan" 文言 (Special Explanation of the Texts of "Hexagram Qian" 乾卦 and "Hexagram Kun" 坤卦) in the *Classic of Change*.

③ The courtesy name of Liu Yaofu 刘尧夫 (1146 – 1189), a scholar-official in Southern Song Dynasty, who once studied with Zhu Xi.

冬时其气贞固，故难得谢。若春夏间，才发便发尽了，故不能久。又云："大凡花头大者易谢，果实亦然。如梨树，极易得衰，将死时，须猛结一年实了死，此亦是气将脱也。"广。

The Master said, "In winter, flowers tend to last long. For example, the narcissus which is extremely delicate yet durable. This is also true of winter sweets. The flowers in spring are liable to wither. Those in summer are more liable to die away. For example, the blooming lotus lasts only one day. After all, the winter flowers are firm in their vital force, for which their flowering period is long. For those in spring and summer, soon after they begin to bloom, they already consume all their vital force, so they can not last long." The Master added, "Usually those flowers with big heads tend to wither easily, so do the big fruits. For example, the pear tree is very likely to wither and in the year before it dies, it will bear a larger amount of fruits than ever, which indicates that its vital force will be exhausted." [Guang]

36 看茄子内一粒，是个生性。方。

A seed within an eggplant, though very small, is endowed with the nature of growing. [Fang]①

37 问："命之不齐，恐不是真有为之赋予如此。只是二气错综参差，随其所值，因各不齐。皆非人力所与，故谓之天所命否？"曰："只是从大原中流出来，模样似恁地，不是真有为之赋予者。那得个人在上面分付这个！诗书所说，便似有个人在上恁地，如'帝乃震怒'之类。然这个亦只是理如此。天下莫尊于理，故以帝名之。'惟皇上帝降衷于下民'，降，便有主宰意。"问："'大哉乾元！万物资始。乾道变化，各正性命。'万物盈乎两间，生生不穷，日往则月来，寒往则暑来，风雷之所以鼓动，山川之所以流峙，皆苍苍者实有以主其造化之权邪；抑只是太极为万化枢纽，故万物自然如此？"曰："此与前只一意。"淳。以下论气质之性。

---

① Yang Fang 杨方 (courtesy name Zizhi 子直).

Question: As for the inequality of the destines of living things, I am afraid, it is not that they are endowed with their unequal destines but that the operation of the *yin* and *yang* vital forces on them is complex and irregular, hence the inequality. It is not caused by the power of humankind, so the inequality is said as being endowed by Heaven. Isn't it?

Answer: Their inequality only flows from the great origin with a status like that. But it is not that there is a real endower of the unequal destines. How can it be possible for there to be an endower working for that? What *Shijing* 诗经 (Classic of Poetry) and the *Shujing* 书经 (Classic of History) say gives an impression that there is one person high up, doing that sort of thing. For example, "*Di* 帝 (i. e. *Shangdi* 上帝 [the Topmost Master or Supreme Being]) was consequently roused to furious anger," as said in the *Book of History*. Nevertheless, that is attributed to nothing but principle which operates in that way. Nothing is more lofty than the principle, so the principle is referred to as *Di*. In the book is also "The great *Shangdi* has conferred (even) on the inferior people a moral sense," where the word "conferred" implies the meaning of domination.

Further question: "How great is the fundamental nature of Qian! The myriad things are provided their beginnings by it… The way of Qian brings about changes and transformations of things, keeping the nature and destiny of each of them correct."[1] The myriad things are thriving between Heaven and Earth, which goes on unceasingly: When the sun passes, the moon comes and when one season departs, another arrives; The wind blows and the thunder peals; The mountains are still and the rivers flow. Does the blue heaven possess really the power of dominating over the creation and operation

---

[1] The English translation of the quotation from the "Tuanzhuan" 彖传 (Explanation of the Judgments) of "Hexagram Qian" in the *Classic of Change* is based on Richard Lynn, trans. *The Classic of Changes: A New Translation of the I Ching as Interpreted by Wang Bi* (New York: Columbia University Press, 1994), p. 127, with slight modification.

of things, or is it only because the Great Ultimate works as the pivot for all changes and transformations and thereby the myriad things operate that way naturally?

Answer: This question can be answered by my answer to your first question. [Chun (淳)]① The several passages below concern the physical nature. ②

38 语厚之:"昨晚说'造化为性',不是。造化已是形而下,所以造化之理是形而上。"蜚卿问:"'纯亦不已',是理是气?"曰:"是理。'天命之谓性',亦是理。天命,如君之命令;性,如受职于君;气,如有能守职者,有不能守职者。"某问:"'天命之谓性',只是主理言。才说命,则气亦在其间矣。非气,则何以为人物?理何所受?"曰:"极是,极是。子思且就总会处言,此处最好看。"可学。

The Master said to Houzhi 厚之 (i. e. Wang Houzhi 王厚之 [1131 – 1204], courtesy name 顺伯), "Yesterday evening, it was mentioned that 'zaohua 造化 (creations and transformations in nature) is the nature.' That is not right, for zaohua exists after physical form, while its principle exists before physical form." Feiqing 蜚卿 (i. e. courtesy name of Tong Boyu 童伯羽) asked, "(The Doctrine of the Mean says) 'Singleness is likewise unceasing.' Is it concerned with principle or vital force?" The Master answered, "It is principle. (As said in the same book,) 'What Heaven has conferred is called the nature' is also concerned with principle. 'What Heaven has conferred' is like the order given by a sovereign. The nature is like a minister serving the sovereign. As for the vital force, in some cases, it can fulfill its function well, while in some others, it can not." I asked, "The

---

① Chen Chun 陈淳 (courtesy name Anqing 安卿).

② In the Chinese text, such meta-textual notes are appended to some passages (or, sections). Though the original notes contain 以下 (literally, the following, or below), what they refer to include the passages under which they appear. In this section, "The several passages below concern the physical nature" refers to Passage 37 and the several passages below it.

'What Heaven has conferred is called the nature' is only mainly said of principle. When it speaks of what is conferred by Heaven, it also touches upon the vital force. Without the vital force, how could humankind and things come into being? What could be the receiver of principle?" The Master responded, "You are quite right! What Zisi 子思 (483 – 402, grandson of Confucius and author of the *Doctrine of the Mean*) says refers to the general point, and that is where he puts it best." [Kexue]

39　因看礜等说性，曰："论性，要须先识得性是个甚么样物事。必大录此下云："性毕竟无形影，只是心中所有底道理是也。"程子：'性即理也'，此说最好。今且以理言之，毕竟却无形影，只是这一个道理。在人，仁义礼智，性也。然四者有何形状，亦只是有如此道理。有如此道理，便做得许多事出来，所以能恻隐、羞恶、辞逊、是非也。譬如论药性，性寒、性热之类，药上亦无讨这形状处。只是服了后，却做得冷做得热底，便是性，便只是仁义礼智。孟子说：'仁义礼智根于心。'如曰'恻隐之心'，便是心上说情。"

又曰："邵尧夫说：'性者，道之形体；心者，性之郭郭。'此说甚好。盖道无形体，只性便是道之形体。然若无个心，却将性在甚处！须是有个心，便收拾得这性，发用出来。盖性中所有道理，只是仁义礼智，便是实理。吾儒以性为实，释氏以性为空。若是指性来做心说，则不可。今人往往以心来说性，须是先识得，方可说。必大录云："若指有知觉者为性，只是说得'心'字。"如有天命之性，便有气质。若以天命之性为根于心，则气质之性又安顿在何处！谓如'人心惟危，道心惟微'，都是心，不成只道心是心，人心不是心！"

又曰："喜怒哀乐未发之时，只是浑然，所谓气质之性亦皆在其中。至于喜怒哀乐，却只是情。"又曰："只管说出语言，理会得。只见事多，却不如都不理会得底。"又曰："然亦不可含糊，亦要理会得个名义着落。"礜。人杰、必大录少异。

After reading some essays by Xun 礜 and others on nature, the Master said, "In discussing the nature, it is important to know first of all what kind of entity it really is. In the record by Bida①are the following words after this, ' At bottom the nature has neither physical form nor shadow. It is merely the principle possessed by the mind. ' Master Cheng Yi 程颐 (1033 – 1107) put it best when he said ' Nature is the same as principle. ' Now if we regard it as principle, then surely it has neither physical form nor shadow. It is nothing but this very principle. In humankind, benevolence, righteousness, propriety, and wisdom are his nature, but what physical form or shape have they? All they have are the principles of benevolence, righteousness, propriety, and wisdom. As they possess these principles, they carry out many deeds, so humankind is capable of having the feelings of *ceyin* 恻隐 (sadness and commiseration), *xiuwu* 羞恶 (shame and dislike), *cixun* 辞逊 (deference and compliance), and *shifei* 是非 (right and wrong). Take for example the nature of medicines, such as their properties of increasing or decreasing heat (vigor, strength, vitality). There is no external form of this nature to be found in a medicine. Only after the medicine is taken, heat or cold will be produced: this is their nature. In humankind, the nature is merely benevolence, righteousness, propriety, and wisdom. According to Mencius, ' benevolence, righteousness, propriety, and wisdom are rooted in the mind. ' When, for example, he speaks of the feeling of sadness and commiseration, he attributes it to the mind. ”

The Master further said: " Yaofu (i. e. Shao Yong) said that ' Nature is the concrete embodiment of *Dao* (the Way) and the mind is the enclosure of the nature. ' This theory is very good, for the Way itself has no physical form or body, so it finds its form or body only in the human nature. But if there were no mind, where could nature dwell in? There must be mind where nature can be gotten hold of and put forth into operation, for the principles contained in the human nature are benevolence, righteousness, propriety, and wisdom, and these are concrete principles. We Confucianists regard

---

① Wu Bida 吴必大 (courtesy name Bofeng 伯丰).

nature as real, whereas Buddhists see it as empty. However, it is incorrect to equate nature with mind. Nowadays people often explain nature in terms of mind. They should first understand what nature means before talking about it. Bida's record reads, 'If they consider consciousness as nature, they are only talking about the mind.' For example, wherever there is the nature as endowed by Heaven, there is also the physical nature. If we regard the nature endowed by Heaven as rooted in the mind, then where will you place the physical nature? When, for example, it is said in the *Book of History* that 'The human mind is precarious (liable to make mistakes), the moral mind is subtle (the mind that follows *Dao*),' the word 'mind' is used in both cases. It is incorrect to say that the mind following the Way is mind, whereas the mind of humankind is not mind. "

On other occasions, the Master said the following, respectively. "Before joy, anger, sorrow, and pleasure are aroused, they are only an entirety undistinguished, where all the so called physical nature dwells. The joy, anger, sorrow, and pleasure are only all feelings. " "If one does simply nothing but coming out with some words about the physical nature, they may indicate his understanding it. But when one sees merely many matters, it would be better if he did not understand it at all. " "Nevertheless, one should dispel any ambiguity when he tries to understand what the name (of physical nature) actually means and what its meaning really is. " [Xun] The records by Renjie and by Bida are a little different from this record.

40 "'天命之谓性。'命，便是告札之类；性，便是合当做底职事。如主簿销注，县尉巡捕；心，便是官人；气质，便是官人所习尚，或宽或猛；情，便是当厅处断事，如县尉捉得贼。情便是发用处。性只是仁义礼智。所谓天命之与气质，亦相衮同。才有天命，便有气质，不能相离。若阙一，便生物不得。既有天命，须是有此气，方能承当得此理。若无此气，则此理如何顿放！必大录此云："有气质之性，无天命之性，亦做人不得；有天命之性，无气质之性，亦做人不得。"天命之性，本未尝偏。但气质所禀，却有偏处，气有昏明厚薄之不同。然仁义礼智，亦无阙一之理。但若恻隐多，便流为姑息柔懦；若羞恶多，便有羞恶其所不当羞恶者。且如言光：必有镜，然后有光；必有水，然后有光。光便是性，镜水便是气质。若无镜与水，则光亦散矣。谓如五色，若顿在黑多处，便都黑了；入在红多处，便都红了，却看你禀得气如何，然此理却只是善。既是此理，如何得恶！所谓恶者，却是气也。孟子之论，尽是说性善。至有不善，说是陷溺，是说其初无不善，后来方有不善耳。若如此，却似'论性不论气'，有些不备。却得程氏说出气质来接一接，便接得有首尾，一齐圆备了。"又曰："才又在气质之下。如退之说三品等，皆是论气质之性，说得尽好。只是不合不说破个气质之性，却只是做性说时，便不可。如三品之说，便分将来，何止三品？虽千百可也。若荀扬则是'论气而不论性'，故不明。既不论性，便却将此理来昏了。"又曰："皋陶谟中所论'宽而栗'等九德，皆是论反气质之意，只不曾说破气质耳。"伯丰曰："匡衡疏中说治性之道，亦是说气质。"僩谓："'宽而栗'等，'而'下一字便是功夫。"先生皆然之。或问："若是气质不善，可以变否？"曰："须是变化而反之。如'人一己百，人十己千'，则'虽愚必明，虽柔必强'。"僩。

The Master said, "(The book *Doctrine of the Mean* says) 'What Heaven has conferred is called the nature.' What is 'conferred' here refers to giving such commands as verbal orders and written decrees, and the 'nature,' to the duties which should be fulfilled. That is like, for example, the roles played by the officials in a county government. The Keeper of Records is in charge of registering and canceling, and the Magistrate is responsible for patrolling and policing in the county. The mind plays the role of the head official of the county and then the physical nature is what he manifests habitually, which is either lenient or impetuous. And feelings can be likened to his handling affairs in the court, such as interrogating the thieves caught by the Magistrate. The feelings are the functions carried out. The nature is only benevolence, righteousness, propriety, and wisdom. The nature Heaven confers and the physical nature are also integrated, for, as far as a thing is concerned, the moment Heaven confers nature on it, its physical nature occurs, so they are inseparable. If either was absent, things would not be produced. Since there is the nature endowed by Heaven, there must be the vital force which happens concurrently, without which the principle could not be borne. If there were not such vital force, where and how would the principle be put? Bida's record of these several sentences reads, 'If there were only physical nature but no nature conferred by Heaven, it would be impossible to create a person; if there were only the nature conferred by Heaven but no physical nature, it would be impossible to create a person, either.'

"The nature endowed by Heaven is originally free from partiality, but the endowment in physical nature is partial to some extent, so vital forces are different in terms of clearness or turbidity, and of abundance or meagerness. As for benevolence, righteousness, propriety, and wisdom, there is no absence of anyone of them in the principle. However, for a person, when the feeling of sadness and commiseration outweighs other three feelings, he will be easily subject to appeasing and cowardly inclinations. By contrast, when the feeling of shame and dislike outweighs others, he will be apt to have the feeling of unjustified shames.

"Let us take light for example. There must be such things as a mirror or some water before there occurs light. The light is the nature, while the mirror or the water is the physical nature. Without the mirror or the water, there would be nowhere to find the light. Another example is the five colors (i. e. blue, yellow, red, white, and black), which, when put where there is more black, would all become black, and when put where there is more red, would all become red. So what color they finally show depends on where they are put, that is, on what the vital forces they possess are. But their principle is only all good, and then how can they get evil! The so called evil is actually due to the vital force. Mencius's argumentation dwells only on the nature being good. As for the nature of one being not good, he saw it as resulting from the circumstances through which he allows his mind to be ensnared and drowned in evil. What Mencius meant here is that the nature of a person is originally good, only that it deviates from the original goodness later. If my understanding of him is right, he seems to have discussed the nature but not touched on the vital force, so what he said is not right completely. Fortunately, Master Cheng expounded the physical nature to further Mencius's argumentation. Thus, now the theory has got both its head and tail and become complete. "

He said further, "The talent is still subordinate to the physical nature. For example, when Tuizhi 退之 (courtesy name of Han Yu 韩愈 [768 – 824], a famous scholar-official and writer in Tang Dynasty) proposed his *sanpin* 三品 (three grades) theory of nature and feelings, what he actually discussed is concerned with the physical nature and in that regard his opinion was very well-grounded. But he should have made it clear that he was discussing physical nature. If what he concerned is the human nature only, then he was not right. As for the three grades as he proposed, why only three grades? It is justifiable to propose a hundred grades or even a thousand. In the case of Xun 荀 (i. e. Xunzi 荀子 [313 –238 BC]) and Yang 扬 (i. e. Yang Xiong 扬雄 [53 –18 BC]), they discussed only the vital force rather than the nature, so what they said is not clear, for, though they did not concern the nature, they confused it with the principle. "

He added, "The 'affability combined with dignity' and other eight virtues[1] stated in the 'Gao Yao Mo' 皋陶谟 (Gao Yao's Counsels) of the *Book of History* are all pairs of opposite embodiments of the physical nature,

---

[1] On the basis of the *Book of History* translated by James Legge, the nine virtues mentioned by Gao Yao include affability combined with dignity; mildness combined with firmness; bluntness combined with respectfulness; aptness for government combined with reverent caution; docility combined with boldness; straightforwardness combined with gentleness; an easy negligence combined with discrimination; boldness combined with sincerity; valour combined with righteousness. (See http: //ctext. org/shang-shu/counsels-of-gao-yao)

only that Gao Yao did not lay bare what he said was of physical nature. "

Bofeng 伯丰（courtesy name of Wu Bida）said, "When Kuang Heng 匡衡（dates unknown; a prime minister of Han Dynasty［206 BC-AD 220］）mentioned, in a memorial to the throne, the way of cultivating the nature, he was referring actually to the physical nature. " And I said, "In 'affability combined with dignity' and each of the other eight pairs, the word after the 'combined with' implies efforts. " The Master agreed with both Bofeng and me.

Someone else asked, "If one's physical nature is not good, can he change it?"

The Master answered, "He has to make efforts in pursuit of its change and transformation to the opposite side. 'If another person succeeds by one effort, he will use a hundred efforts, and if another person succeeds by ten efforts, he will use a thousand. ' Then, 'Though dull, he will surely become intelligent; though weak, he will surely become strong. ' "① ［Xun］

41　人之所以生，理与气合而已。天理固浩浩不穷，然非是气，则虽有是理而无所凑泊。故必二气交感，凝结生聚，然后是理有所附着。凡人之能言语动作，思虑营为，皆气也，而理存焉。故发而为孝弟忠信仁义礼智，皆理也。然而二气五行，交感万变，故人物之生，有精粗之不同。自一气而言之，则人物皆受是气而生；自精粗而言，则人得其气之正且通者，物得其气之偏且塞者。惟人得其正，故是理通而无所塞；物得其偏，故是理塞而无所知。且如人，头圆象天，足方象地，平正端直，以其受天地之正气，所以识道理，有知识。物受天地之偏气，所以禽兽横生，草木头生向下，尾反在上。物之间有知者，不过只通得一路，如乌之知孝，獭之知祭，犬但能守御，牛但能耕而已。人则无不知，无不能。人所以与物异者，所争者此耳。然就人之所禀而言，又有

---

① The two original quotations are from the *Doctrine of the Mean* and their English version is based on James Legge's（see http：//ctext. org/liji/zhong-yong），with slight modification.

昏明清浊之异。故上知生知之资，是气清明纯粹，而无一毫昏浊，所以
生知安行，不待学而能，如尧舜是也。其次则亚于生知，必学而后知，
必行而后至。又其次者，资禀既偏，又有所蔽，须是痛加工夫，"人一
己百，人十己千"，然后方能及亚于生知者。及进而不已，则成功一
也。孟子曰："人之所以异于禽兽者几希。"人物之所以异，只是争这
些子。若更不能存得，则与禽兽无以异矣！某年十五六时，读中庸
"人一己百，人十己千"一章，因见吕与叔解得此段痛快，读之未尝不
竦然警厉奋发！人若有向学之志，须是如此做工夫方得。侗。

    The reason why humankind was produced lies only in the combination of
principle with vital force. Though the heavenly principle is inexhaustible,
without vital force, there would be nowhere for it to dwell. Therefore, the two
vital forces (i. e. *yin* and *yang*) interact, and condense into an integrated
whole before the principle can adhere itself in it. Whatever a person speaks
and acts, thinks and performs, is attributed to his vital force, where his
principle dwells. Thus, all *xiao* 孝 (filial piety), *di* 弟 (fraternity), *zhong*
忠 (loyalty), and *xin* 信 (faithfulness) and all the benevolence,
righteousness, propriety, and wisdom are manifested to embody the principle.
However, since the two vital forces and the Five Agents interact in countless
ways, the production of humankind and things is subject to varying extent of
refinement or coarseness. From the viewpoint of the vital force itself, both
humankind and things are born of the same vital force. From the viewpoint of
refinement or coarseness, humankind gains the vital force which is impartial
and unobstructed, while things get that which is partial and obstructed. It is
because what humankind gains is impartial that the principle in him is
unimpeded, free from obstruction; it is because what things get is partial that
the principle in them is obstructed, denied access to the same consciousness
as that of humankind. For example, the top of the human head is round like
the vault of heaven and his feet are square like the earth, and both are shaped
upright and straight to receive the impartial vital force of Heaven and Earth.

That is why humankind is capable of making access to truth and knowledge. By contrast, receiving the partial vital force of Heaven and Earth, birds and beasts tend to be produced with their heads transversely positioned in their bodies, and grasses and trees, with their heads growing downwards and their tails upwards. Among things, those with some consciousness are only capable of being aware of one aspect, as evidenced by the grown-up crow's feeding its old mother filially, the otter's performing sacrificial rites, the dog's watching house loyally, and the ox's ploughing diligently. However, humankind is capable of knowing everything and doing everything. What distances humankind from things lies in this very difference between them in regard to their vital forces. As regards what different humans are endowed with, there is the difference in clearness or dimness, and in purity or turbidity. The topmost ones are those endowed with knowledge by birth, whose vital forces are clear, bright, and pure, unaffected by even an iota of turbidity. Thus, knowing by birth how to conduct themselves well, they do not need to learn for acquisition of that knowledge, as evidenced by Yao and Shun. Second to them are those who have to learn before obtaining that knowledge and to act before reaching that realm. Still second to these people are those who are both endowed with partial vital forces and beclouded in one way or another. They have to make determined and strenuous efforts. "If another person succeeds by one effort, he will use a hundred efforts, and if another person succeeds by ten efforts, he will use a thousand," as said in the *Doctrine of the Mean*. Only in this way can they attain the realm of those second to the topmost. If one keeps on exerting himself and pursuing progress unceasingly, he will surely make a success. Mencius says, "That whereby humankind differs from birds and beasts is but small." (*Mencius*, 4B: 47) What causes the difference between humankind and the lower animals is nothing but these aspects. If a person fails to preserve them, he will not be able to distance himself from birds and beasts at all. At the age of fifteen and sixteen, when I read the chapter with "If another person succeeds by one effort, he will use a hundred efforts, and if another person succeeds by ten efforts, he will use a thousand" in the *Doctrine of the Mean*, I found Lü Yushu's explanation of those words very thorough and insightful. How much my reading of it roused me to vigilance over myself and inspired me to exert myself! If one aspires for learning, he must make efforts in this way before making a success. [Xian]

42 问气质之性。曰："才说性时，便有些气质在里。若无气质，则这性亦无安顿处。所以继之者只说得善，到成之者便是性。"干。

When asked about physical nature, the Master answered, "The moment the nature is spoken of, there is some physical nature implied concurrently. Without such physical nature, there would be nowhere for the nature to be placed. That is why only the good is mentioned when the *Classic of Change* speaks of what ensues as the result of the successive *yang* and *yin* movement, while it is the nature that is mentioned when the book says of what brings it to its completeness." [Gan]①

43 性只是理。然无那天气地质，则此理没安顿处。但得气之清明则不蔽锢，此理顺发出来。蔽锢少者，发出来天理胜；蔽锢多者，则私欲胜，便见得本原之性无有不善。孟子所谓性善，周子所谓纯粹至善，程子所谓性之本，与夫反本穷源之性，是也。只被气质有昏浊，则隔了，故"气质之性，君子有弗性者焉。学以反之，则天地之性存矣。"故说性，须兼气质说方备。端蒙。

Nature is principle only. However, without the vital force and concrete stuff of the universe, principle would have nothing in which to be put. When the vital force is received in its state of clearness, there will be no obscurity or obstruction and the principle will emanate itself freely. If there is small obscurity or obstruction, then in its operation, the emanated principle of Heaven will dominate; if the obstruction or obstruction is great, the human

---

① Huang Gan 黄干 (courtesy name Zhiqing 直卿).

selfish desire will dominate. From this, we know that the original nature is perfectly good. This is the nature described by Mencius as "good," by Master Zhou Dunyi 周敦颐 (1017 – 1073) as "pure and perfectly good," and by Master Cheng Yi as "the fundamental character of nature" and "the nature which can be traced to the origin." However, it will be obstructed if physical nature contains impurity. Hence, [as Zhang Zai] "In physical nature, there is that which *junzi* 君子 (the Superior Man) denies to be his original nature," and "If one returns through learning to the original nature endowed by Heaven and Earth, then it will be preserved." Therefore, in discussing nature, we must include physical nature so that our discussion can be complete. [1] [Duanmeng]

44 天命之性，若无气质，却无安顿处。且如一勺水，非有物盛之，则水无归着。程子云："论性不论气，不备；论气不论性，不明，二之则不是。" 所以发明千古圣贤未尽之意，甚为有功。大抵此理有未分晓处，秦汉以来传记所载，只是说梦。韩退之略近似。千有余年，得程先生兄弟出来，此理益明。且如唐刘知几之子云："注述六经之旨，世俗陶陶，知我者希！" 不知其书如何说，想亦是担当不得。如果能晓得此理，如何不与大家知！贺孙。

The nature conferred by Heaven, without physical nature, would find no place to get put. It is like a ladle of water, and without something like the ladle, there would be nothing to contain the water in. Master Cheng Hao 程颢 (1032 – 1085, elder brother of Cheng Yi) said, "When discussing nature, if one does not consider vital force, his discussion will be incomplete; when discussing vital force, if one does not consider nature, his discussion will be not clear. If one separates nature and vital force, then his discussion will be not right." Thus, by revealing what the sages and worthies had not

---

① The translation of this passage is based on the version by Chan Wing-tsit, pp. 623 – 624, with some modifications.

made completely clear, he made great contribution. In the past, there had been some point not clarified in the question of nature. What was recorded in all those biographies written since Qin and Han dynasties (221 BC-AD 220) is, as it were, talk in a dream. Han Tuizhi 韩退之 (i. e. Han Yu) failed to go far from that. It is after over a thousand years that the two brothers, i. e. Master Cheng Hao and Master Cheng Yi, emerged eventually, who clarified that point well. The son of Liu Zhiji 刘知几 (661 – 721) in Tang Dynasty (618 –907) said, "I have annotated the purports of the Six Classics①and in the mass of people, few know what I mean. " I do not know what his writings said, but I am afraid, probably his opinions were also short of any new clarification. If he understood that point well, why did he keep it from others? [Hesun]

45 性只是理。气质之性，亦只是这里出。若不从这里出，有甚归着。如云"人心惟危，道心惟微"，道心固是心，人心亦心也。横渠言："心统性情。"人杰。

Nature is principle only. The physical nature also emanates from here. Or else, what can it inhere in? When it is said in the *Book of History* that "The human mind is precarious (liable to make mistakes), and the mind that follows the Way is subtle," it means that the mind following the Way is mind and the mind of humankind is also mind. As Zhang Zai says, "The mind commands (unites) nature and feelings. " [Renjie]

46 论天地之性，则专指理言；论气质之性，则以理与气杂而言之。未有此气，已有此性。气有不存，而性却常在。虽其方在气中，然气自是气，性自是性，亦不相夹杂。至论其遍体于物，无处不在，则又不论气之精粗，莫不有是理。

When we speak of the nature of Heaven and Earth, we refer to principle

---

① Referring to the six Confucian canonical works, i. e. the *Classic of Poetry* (诗经), the *Classic of History* (书经 or 尚书), the *Record of Rites* (礼记), the *Classic of Change* (易经), the *Spring and Autumn Annals* (春秋), and the *Record of Music* (乐记).

alone. When we speak of the physical nature, we refer to principle and vital force in combination. Before vital force exists, nature was already in existence. Vital force does not always exist, but nature is eternal. Although nature is implanted in vital force, vital force is still vital force and nature is still nature, without being confused or mixed up. As to its immanence in things and universal existence, regardless of whether vital force is refined or coarse, there is nothing without its principle. ①

47 性非气质，则无所寄；气非天性，则无所成。道夫。

Nature, without physical constitution, would have nothing to inhere in; Vital force, without the nature conferred by Heaven, would have nothing to make any accomplishment by. [Daofu]

48 蜚卿问气质之性。曰："天命之性，非气质则无所寓。然人之气禀有清浊偏正之殊，故天命之正，亦有浅深厚薄之异，要亦不可不谓之性。旧见病翁云：'伊川言气质之性，正犹佛书所谓水中盐味，色里胶清。'"又问："孟子言性，与伊川如何？"曰："不同。孟子是剔出而言性之本，伊川是兼气质而言，要之不可离也，所以程子云：'论性不论气，不备；论气不论性，不明。'而某于太极解亦云：'所谓太极者，不离乎阴阳而为言，亦不杂乎阴阳而为言。'"道夫。闵祖录云："气禀之偏难除。释氏云，'如水中盐，色中胶'，取不出也。病翁爱说此。"

Feiqing asked about physical nature. The Master answered, "The nature endowed by Heaven, without the physical nature, would have nowhere to dwell. However, the vital forces humans are bestowed on are different in terms of their purity and impartiality; therefore, as for as the impartiality of the Heaven's endowment is concerned, there is the difference in depth and profundity. Nevertheless, it should not be said as not being the nature. I once read a comment by Bingweng 病翁（Liu Zihui 刘子翚 [1101 – 1147]）

---

① The translation of this passage is based on the version by Chan Wing-tsit, p. 624, with some modifications.

on Yichuan 伊川 (courtesy name of Cheng Yi), that is, 'His clarification of the physical nature is like, as described in a piece of Buddhist literature, "If water tastes salty, only the mind-king can perceive its underlying clarity."'"① Feiqing further asked, "How is Mencius's exposition of nature compared with Yizhuan's?" The Master answered, "Different. Mencius singles out the origin of nature and elaborates on it, while Yichuan talks about nature in combination with physical nature, regarding them as inseparable. So Master Cheng Hao says, 'When discussing nature, if one does not consider vital force, his discussion will be incomplete.' I said also in my 'Taiji Jie' 太极解 (Explanation of the Great Ultimate) that, 'As regards the so called Great Ultimate, one should not speak of it without considering *yin* and *yang*, nor should one speak of it by confusing it with *yin* and *yang*.'" [Daofu] Hongzu's② record reads, "It is rather hard to get rid of the partiality of the endowed vital force. As put in a saying of Buddhism, 'It is like the salt in water and the glue in paint,' which are impossible to be taken out. This is an opinion Bingweng set store by."

49 性即理也。当然之理，无有不善者。故孟子之言性，指性之本而言。然必有所依而立，故气质之禀不能无浅深厚薄之别。孔子曰"性相近也"，兼气质而言。砥。

Nature is the very principle. There is no originally endowed principle which is not good. Therefore, when Mencius spoke of nature, he referred to the origin of nature. However, the originally endowed nature had to have something to dwell in, and thus the endowments of physical nature can not get free from differences in their depth and profundity. When Confucius said "By nature, men are nearly alike," he concerned also physical nature. [Di]③

50 天地间只是一个道理。性便是理。人之所以有善有不善，只缘

---

① Cited from "Xinwang Ming" 心王铭 (Mind-King Inscription), written by Fu Xi 傅翕 (497–569), referred to as "Mahasattva Fu," a famous lay Buddhist in Liang Dynasty (502–557) of the period of Northern and Southern Dynasties (420–589).

② Li Hongzu 李闳祖 (courtesy name Shouyue 守约).

③ Liu Di 刘砥 (courtesy name Lüzhi 履之).

气质之禀各有清浊。去伪。

Between Heaven and Earth, there is one and only principle. Nature is the principle. The reason why some humans are good while some others are not is only that their endowments in physical nature are different in terms of their purity or turbidity. [Quwei]①

51 人所禀之气，虽皆是天地之正气，但衮来衮去，便有昏明厚薄之异。盖气是有形之物。才是有形之物，便自有美有恶也。广。

The vital force with which humankind was endowed, though it was received originally from the impartial vital force of Heaven and Earth, after incessant abrasive grindings and rollings, got differentiated in clearness and profundity on different humans. Probably that is because the vital force is something with a form. Immediately when the form comes into being, there occurs some good or evil with it. [Guang]

52 气质之性，便只是天地之性。只是这个天地之性却从那里过。好底性如水，气质之性如杀些酱与盐，便是一般滋味。偶。

The physical nature is not different from the nature of Heaven and Earth. The point is that the nature of Heaven and Earth runs through the physical nature. For example, the good nature is like water. The physical nature is like the peculiar flavor the water acquires after you add some sauce and salt in it. ② [Xian]

53 问："天理变易无穷。由一阴一阳，生生不穷。'继之者善'，全是天理，安得不善！孟子言性之本体以为善者是也。二气相轧相取，相合相乖，有平易处，有倾侧处，自然有善有恶。故禀气形者有恶有善，何足怪！语其本则无不善也。"曰："此却无过。"丁复之曰，"先生解中庸大本"云云。曰："既谓之大本，只是理善而已。才说人欲，便是气也，亦安得无本！但大本中元无此耳。"大雅。

---

① Jin Quwei 金去伪 (courtesy name Jingzhi 敬直).

② The translation of this passage is based on the version by Chan Wing-tsit, p. 624, with some modifications.

Question: The heavenly principle undergoes countless changes. The interaction of *yin* and *yang* gives birth to things unceasingly. "What ensues after the Way is good." Since it is the heavenly principle all over, how can it be not good? According to Mencius, the nature is originally good. The two vital forces (i. e. *yin* and *yang*), by rolling each other and drawing on each other, and combining with each other and going against each other, are productive of both equilibriums and inclinations, which naturally cause the good and the evil aspects. Therefore, it is no wonder that whatever is formed by endowed vital force is subject either to the good or the evil. As far as its origin is concerned, there is nothing not good in it. (How do you think about what I said?)

Answer: There is nothing wrong with it.

Ding Fuzhi 丁复之 (dates unknown, a disciple of Zhu Xi's) said "You, sir, wrote about the great origin expounded in the *Doctrine of the Mean*" and some other things.

The Master responded, "Since it is referred to as the great origin, it means nothing but the goodness of principle. The human selfish desire is but an embodiment of the vital force, so how can it have no origin? However, in the great origin, there was originally no such vital force." [Daya]

54 问："理无不善，则气胡为有清浊之殊？"曰："才说着气，便自有寒有热，有香有臭。"儒用。

Question: Since principle is free from any non-goodness, how is vital force differentiated in terms of purity or turbidity?

Answer: The moment the vital force comes into being, there occurs in it the difference, for example, between coldness and hotness and between fragrance and stench. [Ruyong][1]

55 二气五行，始何尝不正。只衮来衮去，便有不正。如阳为刚燥，

---

① Li Ruyong 李儒用 (courtesy name Zhongbing 仲秉).

阴为重浊之类。士毅。

The two vital forces and Five Agents were originally never partial. It is after their incessant abrasive grindings and rollings for long that partiality happened. For example, *yang* became firm and dry, while *yin*, heavy and turbid. 〔Shiyi〕

56 气升降，无时止息。理只附气。惟气有昏浊，理亦随而间隔。德明。

Vital force keeps rising and declining and that unceasingly. Principle adheres only to vital force. Only vital force is subject to turbidity, but principle also varies along with the different turbidity degrees of vital force. 〔Deming〕

57 人性本善，无许多不美，不知那许多不美是甚么物事。振。

The nature of humankind is originally good, free from the various kinds of non-goodness. I do not know what things or affairs those various kinds of non-goodness are. 〔Zhen〕①

58 问："赵书记一日问浩：'如何是性？'浩对以伊川曰：'孟子言"性善"，是极本穷原之性；孔子言"性相近"，是气质之性。'赵云：'安得有两样！只有中庸说"天命之谓性"，自分明。'"曰："公当初不曾问他：'既谓之善，固无两般。才说相近，须有两样。'便自说不得！"因问："'天命之谓性'，还是极本穷原之性，抑气质之性？"曰："是极本穷原之性。天之所以命，只是一般；缘气质不同，遂有差殊。孟子分明是于人身上挑出天之所命者说与人，要见得本原皆善。"浩。

Question: One day, Zhao Shuji 赵书记 (dates unknown) asked me, "How is the nature?" In answering him, I quoted Yichuan as saying "Mencius's 'Nature is good' refers to the original nature, while Confucius's 'By nature, men are nearly alike' concerns physical nature." Zhao replied, "How can there be two different types of nature? The *Doctrine of the Mean* says 'What Heaven has conferred is called the nature.' That is clear."

---

① Wu Zhi 吴振 (courtesy name Boqi 伯起).

(How do you think of his opinion?)

Answer: Why did not you say to him "Since nature is regarded as good, then it should not be separated into two, and since it is said as being alike, there must be at least two sides." Then, he would have nothing to say against that.

Further question: In "What Heaven has conferred is called the nature," is the nature the original nature or the physical nature?

Answer: It is the nature at the extreme origin. What Heaven has conferred is free from difference, but due to difference of vital force, its difference occurs. It is obvious that Mencius singled out what Heaven conferred originally by which to talk with others about the nature of humankind, articulating to them that the original nature of all men was good. [Hao]①

59 人之性皆善。然而有生下来善底，有生下来便恶底，此是气禀不同。且如天地之运，万端而无穷，其可见者，日月清明气候和正之时，人生而禀此气，则为清明浑厚之气，须做个好人；若是日月昏暗，寒暑反常，皆是天地之戾气，人若禀此气，则为不好底人，何疑！人之为学，却是要变化气禀，然极难变化。

如"孟子道性善"，不言气禀，只言"人皆可以为尧舜"。若勇猛直前，气禀之偏自消，功夫自成，故不言气禀。看来吾性既善，何故不能为圣贤，却是被这气禀害。如气禀偏于刚，则一向刚暴；偏于柔，则一向柔弱之类。人一向推托道气禀不好，不向前，又不得；一向不察气禀之害，只昏昏地去，又不得。须知气禀之害，要力去用功克治，裁其胜而归于中乃可。濂溪云："性者，刚柔善恶中而已。故圣人立教，俾人自易其恶，自至其中而止矣。"责沈言："气质之用狭，道学之功大。"璘。

The nature of all persons is good, and yet there are those who are good

---

① Shao Hao 邵浩 (courtesy name Shuyi 叔义).

from their birth and those who are evil from their birth. This is because of the difference in vital force with which they are endowed. The revolving operations of the universe consist of countless variations which are endless. But these may be clear to see: If the sun and moon are clear and bright, and the climate temperate and amicable, the person born at such a time and endowed with such vital force, which is clear, bright, well blended, and strong, should be a good person. But if the sun and moon are darkened and gloomy, and the temperature abnormal, all these are indicative of morbid vital force. If a person is endowed with such vital force, he will, no doubt, be a bad person. The objective of one's pursuit of learning is to transform his endowment of vital force. [①]However, such transformation is very hard to realize.

For example, when Mencius spoke of nature being good, he did not touch the endowment of vital force, but only said, "Everyone may be a Yao or a Shun. " If one is able to forge ahead with valor and vigor, he will remove by himself the partial inclination in his endowed vital force and his efforts will pay off in due course. It seems that, since the nature of everyone of us is good, we each are capable of becoming a sage or a worthy, but what does harm to us is the endowed vital force. If one's endowed vital force is inclined to be firm, he tends to be abrasive and quick to anger; if one's vital force is inclined to be soft, he tends to be weak and fainthearted. Some people are always saying as an excuse that their endowed vital force is not good, yet they do not exert themselves, so it is impossible for them to turn for the better. Not aware of the harmfulness of their endowment of partial vital force, they muddle along day after day, so it is also impossible for them to correct themselves. One must be aware of the harmfulness of the partially endowed

---

①　The translation of this passage is based on the version by Chan Wing-tsit, pp. 624 – 625, with some alterations.

vital force and make strenuous efforts to rectify it, and if he is able to remove what is superfluous and reach the mean, he will be all right. Lianxi 濂溪 (i. e. Zhou Dunyi) said, "Nature is nothing but the mean between firmness and softness and between goodness and evil. That is why, when the sage set about teaching, he instructed his pupils to get rid of their evil aspects by their own efforts until reaching the mean status." Zeshen 责沈 (i. e. Chen Guan 陈瓘 with the style name Liaoweng 了翁) said, "The function of physical nature is narrow, while the effect of (leaning) *Daoxue* 道学 (lit. the learning of the Way, referring to the Neo-Confucianism in the Song dynasty [960 – 1279]) is great (in correcting the partiality of vital force)." [Lin][1]

60 问："孟子言'性善'，伊川谓是'极本穷原之性'；孔子言：'性相近'，伊川谓是'气质之性'；固已晓然。中庸所谓'天命之谓性'，不知是极本穷原之性，是气质之性?"曰："性也只是一般。天之所命，何尝有异? 正缘气质不同，便有不相似处，故孔子谓之'相近'。孟子恐人谓性元来不相似，遂于气质内挑出天之所命者说与人，道性无有不善，即子思所谓'天命之谓性'也。"浩。

Question: Mencius discoursed "The nature of humankind is good," and Yichuan clarified that the nature in Mencius' discourse referred to the original nature of humankind. Confucius claimed "By nature, men are nearly alike," and Yichuan explained the nature in Confucius's discourse as referring to the physical nature. I have already understood all these. The *Doctrine of the Mean* says "What Heaven has conferred is called the nature." Does the nature here refer to the original nature or the physical nature?

Answer: The nature of persons is simply the same. How can the nature conferred by Heaven be different? It is due to the difference in vital force that the nature of different persons seems different in one way or another.

---

[1] Teng Lin 滕璘 (courtesy name Decui 德粹).

Therefore, Confucius said of that as persons being nearly alike. Mencius was afraid that other people would take the nature of persons for being originally dissimilar and so he singled out the nature endowed by Heaven from physical nature and emphasized that the nature of persons was free from any non-goodness. That is what Zisi meant when he said "What Heaven has conferred is called the nature." [Hao]

61 问:"孔子已说'继之者善,成之者性',如何人尚未知性?到孟子方才说出,到周先生方说得尽?"曰:"孔子说得细腻,说不曾了。孟子说得麤,说得疏略。孟子不曾推原原头,不曾说上面一截,只是说'成之者性'也。"义刚。

Question: Confucius had said "What ensues after the Way is good and what brings it to its completeness is its nature." Why did others not understand nature? Why was its meaning not pointed out until Mencius and not clarified completely until Master Zhou (i. e. Zhou Dunyi)?

Answer: What Confucius said about it is detailed, yet not complete. What Mencius said is coarse, with some negligence, for he did not consider the ultimate origin and was only concerned with "What brings it to its completeness is its nature," yet not touching "What ensues after the Way is good" said before that. [Yigang]①

62 孟子言性,只说得本然底,论才亦然。荀子只见得不好底,扬子又见得半上半下底,韩子所言却是说得稍近。盖荀扬说既不是,韩子看来端的见有如此不同,故有三品之说。然惜其言之不尽,少得一个"气"字耳。程子曰:"论性不论气,不备;论气不论性,不明。"盖谓此也。力行。

When Mencius discoursed nature, he only referred to the original nature. he did likewise when talking about talent. Xunzi (i. e. Xun Kuang) saw only what was evil and Yangzi (i. e. Yang Xiong) saw what was between

---

① Huang Yigang 黄义刚 (courtesy name Yiran 毅然).

the good and the evil. What Hanzi（i. e. Han Yu）said is, by contrast, closer. Probably, Xunzi's and Yangzi's opinions were not right, and Hanzi's understanding was truly different from theirs, so he proposed the theory of three grades of nature and feelings. However, it is a pity that his clarification was still incomplete, for he did not touch upon vital force. That is probably what Chengzi（i. e. Cheng Hao）meant when he commented that "When discussing nature, if one does not consider vital force, his discussion will be incomplete; when discussing vital force, if one does not consider nature, his discussion will be not clear. " ［Lixing］①

63 孟子未尝说气质之性。程子论性所以有功于名教者，以其发明气质之性也。以气质论，则凡言性不同者，皆冰释矣。退之言性亦好，亦不知气质之性耳。人杰。

Mencius did not touch physical nature in his discourse. The reason why Chengzi made contribution to the doctrine of Neo-Confucianism by his discussion of nature lies in his clarification of physical nature. With his concept of physical nature, all the problematic opinions of seeing the nature of different persons as being different would be rectified with ease. Tuizhi's （i. e. Han Yu）discourse of nature, though fairly good, indicates his ignorance of the physical nature. ［Renjie］

64 道夫问："气质之说，始于何人?"曰："此起于张程。某以为极有功于圣门，有补于后学，读之使人深有感于张程，前此未曾有人说到此。如韩退之原性中说三品，说得也是，但不曾分明说是气质之性耳。性那里有三品来！孟子说性善，但说得本原处，下面却不曾说得气质之性，所以亦费分疏。诸子说性恶与善恶混。使张程之说早出，则这许多说话自不用纷争。故张程之说立，则诸子之说泯矣。"因举横渠："形而后有气质之性。善反之，则天地之性存焉。故气质之性，君子有弗性者焉。"又举明道云："论性不论气，不备；论气不论性，不明，

---

① Wang Lixing 王力行（courtesy name Jinsi 近思）.

二之则不是。"

　　且如只说个仁义礼智是性，世间却有生出来便无状底，是如何？只是气禀如此。若不论那气，这道理便不周匝，所以不备。若只论气禀，这个善，这个恶，却不论那一原处只是这个道理，又却不明。此自孔子曾子子思孟子理会得后，都无人说这道理。

　　谦之问："天地之气，当其昏明驳杂之时，则其理亦随而昏明驳杂否？"曰："理却只恁地，只是气自如此。"又问："若气如此，理不如此，则是理与气相离矣！"曰："气虽是理之所生，然既生出，则理管他不得。如这理寓于气了，日用间运用都由这个气，只是气强理弱。譬如大礼赦文，一时将税都放了相似，有那村知县硬自捉缚须要他纳，缘被他近了，更自叫上面不应，便见得那气麄而理微。又如父子，若子不肖，父亦管他不得。圣人所以立教，正是要救这些子。"时举。柄录云："问：'天地之性既善，则气禀之性如何不善？'曰：'理固无不善，才赋于气质，便有清浊、偏正、刚柔、缓急之不同。盖气强而理弱，理管摄他不得。如父子本是一气，子乃父所生；父贤而子不肖，父也管他不得。又如君臣同心一体，臣乃君所命；上欲行而下沮格，上之人亦不能一一去督责得他。'"

Daofu asked, "Who was the first to put forth the theory of physical nature?" The Master answered, "Zhang (i. e. Zhang Zai) and Cheng (i. e. Cheng Hao) were the first. In my opinion, they made tremendous contribution to the sage-wise learning. Their clarification is of great help to the later generations of scholars and, reading it, we feel obliged to them, for before them no one else had elucidated the physical nature as clear as they did. For example, Han Tuizhi, in his 'Yuan Xing' 原性 (The Origin of Nature), elaborated the three grades of nature, who, though not wrong, did not make it clear that his referred to the physical nature. How could nature consist of three grades? When Mencius discoursed nature, he dwelt only on its origin, not touching upon the physical nature, so what he said of nature is not easy to understand thoroughly. Other philosophers contemporary with Mencius either claimed nature as being evil or confused the good and the evil in regard to nature. If the theory of Zhang and Cheng had appeared earlier, all those disputes would not have cropped up. Therefore, when their theories were put forth, the various views proposed by those earlier philosophers came to vanish due to their influence. " Then, he cited Hengqü (i. e. Zhang Zai) as saying "With the existence of physical form, there exists physical nature. If one returns skillfully to the original nature endowed by Heaven and Earth, then he will preserve it. Therefore, in physical nature there is that which the Superior Man denies to be his original nature" and Mingdao (i. e. Cheng Hao) as saying "When discussing nature, if one does not consider vital force, his discussion will be incomplete; when discussing vital force, if one does not consider nature, his discussion will be not clear. If one separates nature and vital force, then his discussion will be not right. "

He added, " For example, when we regard only benevolence, righteousness, propriety, and wisdom as being nature, how should we understand that there are in the world some persons who, when they were born, were devoid of any one of the four? It is because they were endowed with that sort of vital force. If we did not consider the vital force, our reasoning would not be watertight and it would be incomplete. If we considered only the vital force, the good, and the evil, without seeing the principle at the origin, our argumentation would not be clear. Confucius, Zengzi (i. e. Zeng Shen 曾 参 [505 – 435 BC], a famous disciple of Confucius), Zisi, and Mencius understood this truth, but since them, no one else discoursed it for a long time. "

Qianzhi 谦之 (i. e. Pan Bing 潘柄, a disciple of Zhu Xi's) asked, " Concerning the vital force of Heaven and Earth, when it gets in a state of mixed clearness and dimness, does the principle which dwells therein also become mixed in clearness and dimness?" The Master answered, " The principle remains what it is and the vital force only is subject to that change. " Qianzhi further asked, " If vital force is subject to that change, yet principle is not, then aren't principle and vital force separable?" The Master answered, "Though vital force is born of principle, when it comes into being, it will get out of control by principle. Since principle dwells in vital force, its daily use goes with the operation of vital force, only that the latter is strong, while the former is weak. For example, a state conducts a grand ceremony and proclaims a general amnesty, carrying out tax-exemption across the state for a certain period of time, but the Magistrate of a county in the state does otherwise and still forces the local people to pay taxes. That is because the Magistrate controls immediately the local people, who can not lodge complaints to the superior government and get responses. This can illustrate the relationship between the strong vital force and the weak principle. For another example, in the case of a father and his son, if the son is unworthy, the father has no way to correct him. The reason why the sages advocate their doctrines lies in nothing but rectifying those shortcomings. " [Shiju][1] Bing's[2] record reads, "Question: Since the nature endowed by Heaven and Earth is good, why is the physical nature not good? Answer: Principle is always free from non-goodness and the moment it is conferred on vital force, there occurs the difference in clearness or turbidity, partiality or impartiality, firmness or softness, greater or lesser urgency in different cases. Probably it is because vital force is strong, while principle is weak, principle can not control vital force. It is just like a father and his son, who share originally the same vital force, for the father generates his son, but when the father is worthy, yet his son is not, he has no way to control his son. For another example, though a sovereign and his ministers share, as it were, the same mind and body, for the sovereign appoints his ministers, but when the sovereign desires to have something done, yet his ministers do not follow his mind, he has no way to supervise and urge everyone of them. "

65 问:"人之德性本无不备,而气质所赋,鲜有不偏。将性对'气'字看,性即是此理。理无不善者,因堕在形气中,故有不同。所谓气质之性者,是如此否?"曰:"固是。但气禀偏,则理亦欠阙了。"问:"'德不胜气,性命于气;德胜其气,性命于德。'所谓胜者,莫是

---

① Pan Shiju 潘时举(courtesy name Zishan 子善).
② Pan Bing 潘柄(courtesy name Qianzhi 谦之).

指人做处否?"曰:"固是。"又问:"'性命于气',是性命都由气,则性不能全其本然,命不能顺其自然;'性命于德',是性命都由德,则性能全天性,命能顺天理否?"曰:"固是。"又问:"横渠论气质之性,却分晓。明道'生之谓性'一章却难晓。"曰:"它中间性有两三说,须子细看。"问云:"'生之谓性',它这一句,且是说禀受处否?"曰:"是。性即气,气即性,它这且是衮说;性便是理,气便是气,是未分别说。其实理无气,亦无所附。"又问:"'人生气禀,理有善恶云云,善固性也,然恶亦不可不谓之性也。'看来'善固性也'固是。若云'恶亦不可不谓之性',则此理本善,因气而鹘突;虽是鹘突,然亦是性也。"曰:"它原头处都是善,因气偏,这性便偏了。然此处亦是性。如人浑身都是恻隐而无羞恶,都羞恶而无恻隐,这个便是恶德。这个唤做性邪不是?如墨子之心本是恻隐,孟子推其弊,到得无父处,这个便是'恶亦不可不谓之性也'。"又问:"'生之谓性,人生而静以上云云,便已不是性也。'看此几句,是人物未生以前,说性不得。'性'字是人物已生,方着得'性'字。故才说性,便是落于气,而非性之本体矣。"曰:"它这是合理气一衮说。到孟子说性,便是从中间斡出好底说,故谓之善。"又问:"'所谓"继之者善"者,犹水流而就下也。皆水也,有流而至海'云云。"曰:"它这是两个譬喻。水之就下处,它这下更欠言语,要须为它作文补这里,始得。它当时只是衮说了。盖水之就下,便是喻性之善。如孟子所谓过颡、在山,虽不是顺水之性,然不谓之水不得。这便是前面'恶亦不可不谓之性'之说。到得说水之清,却依旧是譬喻。"问:"它后面有一句说,'水之清则性善之谓也',意却分晓。"曰:"固是。它这一段说得详了。"又问:"'此理天命也。'它这处方提起以此理说,则是纯指上面天理而言,不杂气说。"曰:"固是。"又曰:"理离气不得。而今讲学用心着力,却是用这气去寻个道理。"夔孙。

Question: The moral nature of all persons is originally complete, yet almost all the endowments of vital force are partial to varying extent. When we try to understand nature in relation to vital force, the nature is the very principle. Principle is free from any non-goodness, but since it falls into the form of vital force, it is different in different cases. As regards the so called physical nature, is what I just said also true of it?

Answer: It is true. But when the vital force is partial, the principle will be inadequate.

Further question: Master Zhang (i. e. Zhang Zai) said, "When moral character does not overcome the vital force, one's nature and *ming* 命 (destiny) proceed from the vital force. But when moral character overcomes the vital force, our nature and destiny proceed from moral character. "[1] Does the word "overcome" refer to anything as the result of human efforts?

Answer: It does, of course.

Further question: The "One's nature and destiny proceed from the vital force" means that, when both nature and destiny are subject to vital force, the nature can not retain its originally complete state and the destiny can not take the course of its own. Then, does the "One's nature and destiny proceed from moral character" mean that, when both nature and destiny are subject to moral character, the nature can retain its original state completely and the destiny can take the course of its own?

Answer: It does, of course.

Further question: Hengqü's discourse on physical nature is easy to understand, but Mingdao's chapter on "What is inborn is called nature" in the *Mencius* is not. (Why?)

Answer: Underlying his clarification of nature, he meant two or three viewpoints, so you should be more careful in reading that.

Question[2]: Does the "What is inborn is called nature" refer to the endowment?

---

[1] Cited from Section Six in Zhang Zai's "Chengming" 诚明 (Enlightenment Resulting from Sincerity). The translation is based on the version by Chan Wing-tsit, p. 512, with slight modification.

[2] In the paragraph by the same recorder, when there appears a second "question," it indicates a second questioner who starts to engage in a new conversation with Zhu Xi.

Answer: Yes. If it is said that nature is the same as vital force and vital force is the same as nature, that is in the sense of taking them as an entirety, and since nature is principle and physical nature is physical nature, that saying does not make a distinction between them. Actually, without vital force, principle would have nowhere to adhere.

Further question: (Master Cheng Hao said,) "In the vital force with which humankind is endowed at birth, there are both good and evil in principle…The human nature is of course good, but it can not be said that evil is not his nature." It seems that it is right to say "The human nature is of course good." As for the "It can not be said that evil is not his nature," it means the nature is originally good, but due to vital force, it becomes confounded. Despite that confounded state, it still remains to be nature. (How do you think about this?)

Answer: It is good all over at its origin, but because of the partiality of the vital force, the nature gets also partial. However, it is still the nature. For example, if a person is full of feelings of commiseration yet devoid of those of any shame, or is otherwise, then either is a case of moral evil. It is still referred to as nature, isn't it? In the mind of Mozi 墨子 (c. 468 – c. 376 BC) was originally commiseration (advocating jian-ai 兼爱 [loving all equally]), but Mencius focused on the demerit with it and deduced ultimately that Mozi did not acknowledge the peculiar affection due to a father. This is a typical case indicating "it can not be said that evil is not his nature."

Further question: (Master Cheng Hao said,) "What is inborn is called nature. By nature humankind is tranquil. The state preceding this can not be discussed. As soon as we talk about nature, we already go beyond it." Reading these sentences, I understand them as meaning that, before the production of a person or a thing, their nature is not discussible, for only when a person or a thing is produced can they are endowed with their nature. Thus, the moment the nature is spoken of, it falls into vital force, which is not the original nature. (How do you think about this?)

Answer: What he said is concerned with principle and vital force as an entirety. By contrast, in Mencius' discourse, he singled out only what was the good and thus stated it as being good.

Further question: (Master Cheng Hao said,) "As regards the so called 'What ensues after the Way is good,' it is like water flowing always downwards. Water as such is the same in all cases. Some water flows onward to the sea without getting dirty." (How should I understand him here?)

Answer: Two metaphors are used here. As for "water flowing always downwards," he should have been more elaborate on the word "downwards." It needs some annotation to make up for the curtness here before it gets more accessible. He said that only as an entirety. Probably when he said "water flowing always downwards," he used the metaphor to mean nature being good. For example, Mencius said "by striking water and causing it to leap up, one may make it go over his forehead" and "by damming and leading it, one may force it up a hill," and in both cases, though the nature of water is not made use of, it should not be said that water does not possess that nature. This also illustrates the aforementioned "It can not be said that evil is not his nature." The "some water flows onward to the sea without being dirty" is also a metaphor.

Further question: The meaning of the sentence "The original good of nature is like the original clearness of water" which he said later is rather clear, isn't it?

Answer: It is true. The section where that sentence appears is more detailed.

Further question: It is not until he reached the sentence "This principle is the Mandate of Heaven" that he mentioned principle. Did he refer to the heavenly principle purely, without considering vital force?

Answer: Yes, of course.

Further answer：Principle can not be separated from vital force. Nevertheless，when we make mental efforts to pursue learning today，what we depend on in search of the truth is the vital force.① ［Kuisun］

66 先生言气质之性，曰："性譬之水，本皆清也。以净器盛之，则清；以不净之器盛之，则臭；以污泥之器盛之，则浊。本然之清，未尝不在。但既臭浊，猝难得便清。故'虽愚必明，虽柔必强'，也煞用气力，然后能至。某尝谓原性一篇本好，但言三品处，欠个'气'字，欠个来历处，却成天合下生出三般人相似！孟子性善，似也少个'气'字。"砥。伯羽录云："大抵孟子说话，也间或有些子不觑是处。只被他才高，当时无人抵得他。告子口更不曾得开。"

The Master discoursed physical nature，saying "Nature is like water，the original state of which is clear. If clear water is contained in a clean vessel，it is still clear，but if the vessel is unclean，it will get to stink；if the container is dirty，it will become turbid. The original clearness is still with the water，but when it gets smelly or turbid，it is extremely hard to become clear again. Therefore，as said in the *Doctrine of the Mean*，'Though dull，one will surely become intelligent；though weak，one will surely become strong，' a dull and weak person has to make tremendous effort before possibly reaching the state of being intelligent and strong. I once said，'Though the argumentation in "The Origin of Nature"（by Han Yu）is good，where the three grades of nature are discussed，there lacks a concept of vital force for clarification of their source.' Consequently，it seems as if the three grades of persons were produced straight by Heaven. When Mencius argued for nature being good，it seems also that he lacked the concept of vital force." ［Di］Boyu's②record reads，"Basically speaking，in Mencius's discourse，there are also some points not insightful enough. He was

---

① All the sayings of Cheng Hao are cited from *Er-cheng Yishu* 二程遗书（Surviving Works of Two Chengs）. Their translation is based on the version by Chan Wing-tsit，pp. 527 – 528，with slight modification.

② Tong Boyu 童伯羽（courtesy name Feiqing 蜚卿）.

so talented that his contemporaries were incapable of equaling him. Gaozi 告子①, as recorded in the *Mencius*, did not even touch on that. "

67 性如水，流于清渠则清，流入污渠则浊。气质之清者、正者，得之则全，人是也；气质之浊者、偏者，得之则昧，禽兽是也。气有清浊，人则得其清者，禽兽则得其浊者。人大体本清，故异于禽兽；亦有浊者，则去禽兽不远矣。节。

Nature is like water. If it flows in a clean channel, it is clear, but if it flows in a dirty channel, it becomes turbid. When physical nature that is clear and balanced is received, nature will be preserved in its completeness. This is true of humankind. When physical nature that is turbid and unbalanced is received, it will be obscured. This is true of animals. Vital force may be clear or turbid. That received by humankind is clear and that received by animals is turbid. Most human beings possess clear vital force; hence the difference between them and animals. There are also some whose vital force is turbid, and they are not far removed from animals.② [Jie]

68 有是理而后有是气，有是气则必有是理。但禀气之清者，为圣为贤，如宝珠在清冷水中；禀气之浊者，为愚为不肖，如珠在浊水中。所谓"明明德"者，是就浊水中揩拭此珠也。物亦有是理，又如宝珠落在至污浊处，然其所禀亦间有些明处，就上面便自不昧。如虎狼之父子，蜂蚁之君臣，豺獭之报本，雎鸠之有别，曰"仁兽"，曰"义兽"是也。儒用。

There existed this principle before this vital force comes into being and if there is this vital force, there must be this principle. However, those endowed with pure vital force are sages and worthies, who are like a precious

---

① Gaozi is a figure who appears in *Mencius* and engages in discussions and debates with Mencius with regard to humanity. Little is known about him and there have been several traditional opinions on who he is. One opinion identifies him as a disciple of Mencius, and another takes him as being a fictitious figure in *Mencius*.

② The translation of this passage is based on the version by Chan Wing-tsit, p. 625, with some modifications.

pearl in clear and cool water. Those endowed with turbid vital force are fools and unworthies, who are like a pearl in muddy water. The so called "illustrating illustrious virtue" said in *Daxue* 大学（Great Learning）means wiping clean the pearl in the muddy water. Though a thing is also endowed with the principle, it is like a precious pearl bogged down in somewhere dirty and filthy, but what it is endowed with may occasionally possess some clear points, where it is not obscured. For example, the father and son feeling among wolves or tigers, the sovereign and minister awareness among ants or bees, the gratefulness among jackals or otters, and the male and female distinction among ospreys. Those capable of all such are called "benevolent animals" or "righteous animals."［Ruyong］

69 "理在气中，如一个明珠在水里。理在清底气中，如珠在那清底水里面，透底都明；理在浊底气中，如珠在那浊底水里面，外面更不见光明处。"问："物之塞得甚者，虽有那珠，如在深泥里面，更取不出。"曰："也是如此。"胡泳。

Principle dwells in vital force, like a bright pearl in water. When principle dwells in clear and pure vital force, like the pearl in limpid water, it is clear all over. When principle dwells in turbid vital force, like the pearl in muddy water, its brilliance is invisible from the outside.

When asked "If a thing is obscured too much, though it contains principle, this principle is, as it were, a pearl bogged too deep in mud to be taken out. （Is my understanding right?）" The Maser answered, "Right."［Hu Yong］①

70 "敬子谓：'性所发时，无有不善，虽气禀至恶者亦然。但方发之时，气一乘之，则有善有不善耳。'偁以为人心初发，有善有恶，所谓'几善恶'也。初发之时本善而流入于恶者，此固有之。然亦有气禀昏愚之极，而所发皆不善者，如子越椒之类是也。且以中人论之，其

---

① This is the full name of the disciple, with the courtesy name Boliang 伯量.

所发之不善者，固亦多矣。安得谓之无不善邪?"曰："不当如此说，如此说得不是。此只当以人品贤愚清浊论。有合下发得善底，也有合下发得不善底，也有发得善而为物欲所夺，流入于不善底。极多般样。今有一样人，虽无事在这里坐，他心里也只思量要做不好事，如蛇虺相似，只欲咬人。他有甚么发得善! 明道说水处最好。皆水也，有流而至海，终无所污;有流而未远，固已渐浊;有流而甚远，方有所浊。有浊之多者，浊之少者。只可如此说。"僴。

I asked, "Jingzi 敬子 (courtesy name of Li Fan 李燔 [1163 – 1232]) said, 'When nature functions at first, it is originally free from any non-goodness, which is true of even those endowed with the worst vital force. As soon as the nature functions and adheres into the vital force, it gets differentiated and becomes good or not.' In my opinion, when the mind of humankind functions at first, it is already good or not, and this is what 'The subtle activates force giving rise to good and evil' (said by Zhou Dunyi) means. The reason why the original good when the nature functions at first turns out evil is that the evil is also inherent. However, there are also cases where the endowed vital force is extremely benighted and stupid and the nature when it functions at first is not good. For example, the Ziyue Jiao 子越椒 (i. e. Dou Jiao 斗椒 [? – 605 BC], with the courtesy name Ziyue, a notorious traitor) and the like. As far as ordinary people are concerned, those whose nature at first is not good are also many. How can nature be said as originally free from any non-goodness?"

The Master answered, "You should not say that, for it is not right. Those cases can only be discussed in regard to moral character, intelligence or ignorance, purity or turbidity. In these aspects (of vital force), originally, some are good and some others are otherwise. Still some others, though good at first, get manipulated by material desire and fall down to non-goodness. Actually, there are countless cases. There is a type of persons, who have nothing to do and sit there, keeping their minds busy with nothing but thinking up bad ideas. They are like venomous snakes desiring nothing but to bite other people. What good do they have originally in them at first? Mingdao explained that very well by the analogy of water. He said, 'Water is the same in all cases. Some water flows onward to the sea without getting dirty. Some flows only a short distance before growing turbid. Some travels a long distance before growing turbid. Some becomes extremely turbid, while some only slightly so. ' This is the right way to clarify that. " [Xian]

71 或问气禀有清浊不同。曰："气禀之殊，其类不一，非但'清浊'二字而已。今人有聪明，事事晓者，其气清矣，而所为未必皆中于理，则是其气不醇也。有谨厚忠信者，其气醇矣，而所知未必皆达于理，则是其气不清也。推此求之可见。"

Someone asked about the inequality in the clearness of the vital force endowment. The Master answered: "The differences in that endowment are not limited to one kind and are not described only in terms of clearness and turbidity. There are persons who are so bright that they understand everything. Their vital force is clear, but what they do may not all be in accord with principle. The reason is that their vital force is not pure. There are others who are respectful, generous, loyal, and faithful. Their vital force is pure, but in their knowledge they do not always penetrate principle. The reason is that their vital force is not clear. From this, you can deduce the rest."[1]

72 问："季通主张气质太过。"曰："形质也是重。且如水之气，如何似长江大河，有许多洪流！金之气，如何似一块铁恁地硬！形质也是重。被此生坏了后，理终是拗不转来。"又曰："孟子言'人所以异于禽兽者几希'，不知人何故与禽兽异。"又言："'犬之性犹牛之性，牛之性犹人之性与？'不知人何故与牛犬异。此两处似欠中间一转语。须着说是形气不同，故性亦少异，始得。恐孟子见得人性同处，自是分

---

① The translation of this passage is based on the version by Chan Wing-tsit, p. 625, with some modifications.

晓直截，却于这些子未甚察。"又曰："了翁云：'气质之用狭，道学之功大。'与季通说正相反。若论其至，不可只靠一边。如了翁之说，则何故自古只有许多圣贤？如季通之说，则人皆委之于生质，更不修为。须是看人功夫多少如何。若功夫未到，则气质之性不得不重。若功夫至，则气质岂得不听命于义理！也须着如此说，方尽。"闳祖。

I said to the Master, "Jitong (i. e. Cai Yuanding) emphasizes physical nature too much. "

He responded, "That is because the physical embodiment of vital force is too weighty. For example, the vital force of *shui* 水 (water) can be as torrential as a great river surging with many flood currents and that of *jin* 金 (metal) can be as hard as a piece of iron. If it is already spoiled at birth, it is impossible for principle to rectify it. "①

He said further, "Mencius said 'That whereby humankind differs from birds and beasts is but small,' but he did not make clear why humankind is different from birds and beasts. He also said, 'The nature of a dog is like the nature of an ox, and the nature of an ox is like the nature of a person,' but he did not make clear why humankind is different from oxen and dogs. Between these two sayings, there seems to lack a transition. It should be pointed out that, due to their difference in vital force, their nature is somewhat different. I am afraid that Mencius saw the commonality of the nature in different persons and discoursed that straight and clear, but he failed to observe their differences well. "

He added, "Liaoweng said, 'The function of physical nature is narrow, while the effect of learning of the Way is great,' which is opposite to what Jitong said. If we consider the point well, we should avoid leaning on either side of them. If we take what Liaoweng said as right, then why have there

---

① The *shui* (water) and *jin* (metal) are two of the Five Agents, the other three being *mu* (wood), *huo* (fire), and *tu* (earth).

been so small a number of sages and worthies since ancient times? If we take what Jitong said as right, then don't the ordinary people submit to vital force and make no effort for self-cultivation? What will predominate inevitably depends on one's effort. If his effort has been inadequate, his physical nature is sure to predominate; if his effort is enough, doesn't his physical nature have to be subject to principle? It should be elucidated in this way before its clarification can get complete." [Hongzu]

73 人性虽同，禀气不能无偏重。有得木气重者，则恻隐之心常多，而羞恶、辞逊、是非之心为其所塞而不发；有得金气重者，则羞恶之心常多，而恻隐、辞逊、是非之心为其所塞而不发。水火亦然。唯阴阳合德，五性全备，然后中正而为圣人也。闳祖。

Although nature is the same in all persons, it is inevitable that [in most cases] the various elements in their vital force endowment are unbalanced. In some people, the vital force of *mu* 木 (wood) predominates. In such cases, the feeling of commiseration is generally uppermost, but the feeling of shame, of deference and compliance, and of right and wrong are impeded by the predominating vital force and do not emanate into action. In some others, the vital force of metal predominates. In such a case, the feeling of shame is generally uppermost, but the other feelings are impeded and do not emanate into action. So are the cases when the vital forces of water and *huo* 火 (fire) predominate, respectively. It is only when *yin* and *yang* are harmonized and the five moral natures (of benevolence, righteousness, propriety, wisdom, and good faith) are all complete that a person can have the qualities of the Mean and correctness and become a sage. ① [Hongzu]

74 性有偏者。如得木气多者，仁较多；金气多者，义较多。扬。

The nature of some people is partial. If the vital force of wood

① The translation of this passage is based on the version by Chan Wing-tsit, p. 625, with some modifications.

predominates in one, he will manifest more benevolence, while if that of metal outweighs others in one, he will have more feeling of righteousness. [Yang]①

75 先生曰:"人有敏于外而内不敏,又有敏于内而外不敏,如何?"曰:"莫是禀气强弱?"曰:"不然。淮南子曰:'金水内明,日火外明。'气偏于内故内明,气偏于外则外明。"可学。

The Master said, "Some people are quick more outside than inside, while some others are otherwise." I asked, "How is that? Could it be attributed to the difference in the strength of their endowed vital forces?" He answered, "No. The book *Huainanzi* 淮南子 says, 'Metal and water (two of the Five Agents) are bright inside, while the sun and the fire are bright outside.' When one's vital force is inclined inward, he is bright inside, while when it is inclined outward, he is bright outside." [Kexue]

76 "气禀所拘,只通得一路,极多样:或厚于此而薄于彼,或通于彼而塞于此。有人能尽通天下利害而不识义理,或工于百工技艺而不解读书。如虎豹只知父子,蜂蚁只知君臣。惟人亦然,或知孝于亲而薄于他人。如明皇友爱诸弟,长枕大被,终身不变,然而为君则杀其臣,为父则杀其子,为夫则杀其妻,便是有所通,有所蔽。是他性中只通得一路,故于他处皆碍,也是气禀,也是利害昏了。"又问:"以尧为父而有丹朱,以鲧为父而有禹,如何?"曰:"这个又是二气、五行交际运行之际有清浊,人适逢其会,所以如此。如算命推五行阴阳交际之气,当其好者则质美,逢其恶者则不肖,又非人之气所能与也。"偲。

Restrained in the endowed vital force, persons may have access to only one unobstructed aspect and such cases are extremely various. Some are strong here yet weak there, unobstructed there yet obstructed here. Some people are versed in knowing all forms of gains and losses in the world yet ignorant of the principle, while some others are adept at various crafts and

---

① Bao Yang 包扬 (courtesy name Xiandao 显道).

skills, yet know nothing of reading. They are like tigers and leopards who are only aware of the father and son relationship and bees and ants who are only conscious of the sovereign and minister relationship. Some people may know only to treat their family relations well yet be harsh to others. For example, Minghuang 明皇 (i. e. Emperor Xuanzong of Tang [r. 712 – 756]) treated his younger brothers very well for life. However, as a monarch, he had some of his ministers killed; as a father, he had three sons of his killed in one day; as a husband, he had his wife killed. That is because he was unobstructed here and obstructed there. In his nature, he could make access to only one unobstructed aspect and get obstructed in all other aspects, which was caused by his endowed vital force, and he was beclouded in respect to the gains and losses.

I asked, "As fathers, Yao had Danzhu, while Gun 鲧 had Yu. What do you think about them?"

The Master answered, "That is because, when the two vital forces and Five Agents operated and interacted, the effects were either pure or turbid and the births of their sons were met with those different effects. It is like a fortune-teller deducing the vital forces which will occur when the two vital forces and Five Agents interact, and when the birth of a person is met with good vital force, he will be a worthy, while when it is bad vital force, he will be an unworthy. That is not what the vital force of humankind is capable of taking part in. " [Xian]

77 问:"人有强弱,由气有刚柔,若人有技艺之类,如何?"曰: "亦是气。如今人看五行,亦推测得些小。"曰:"如才不足人,明得 理,可为否?"曰:"若明得尽,岂不可为,所谓'克念作圣'是也, 然极难。若只明得一二,如何做得!"曰:"温公论才德如何?"曰: "他便专把朴者为德。殊不知聪明、果敢、正直、中和,亦是才,亦是 德。"可学。

Question: Some persons are strong, while some others are weak, and that is due to the difference of soft and hard vital forces. What about the crafts and skills mastered by some people?

Answer: They also result from different vital forces. Nowadays, when people apply the Five Agents, their deduction is rather narrow.

Further question: If one is not talented enough, but understands the principle well, is he capable of doing something?

Answer: If he understands it completely, why is he not capable? That is what is meant by "The foolish, by thinking, become wise" as said in the *Book of History*. But it is extremely difficult. If one can only understand one or two tenth, how is he capable?

Further question: How do you think of Duke Wen's (i. e. Sima Guang) discourse on talent and virtue?

Answer: He regarded only simplicity as indicative of virtue, yet hardly realized that ingenuity, courage and resolution, fair-mindedness, and equilibrium and harmony all manifest talent and virtue, too. [Kexue]

78 或问："人禀天地五行之气，然父母所生，与是气相值而然否？"曰："便是这气须从人身上过来。今以五行枝干推算人命，与夫地理家推择山林向背，皆是此理。然又有异处。如磁窑中器物，闻说千百件中，或有一件红色大段好者，此是异禀。惟人亦然。瞽鲧之生舜禹，亦犹是也。"人杰。

Someone asked, "A person is endowed with his vital force of Heaven and Earth and the Five Agents. When he was born by his parents, did that happen to encounter that vital force?" The master answered, "Yes, for that vital force had to come over via the human body. At present, in such cases as the Five Agents and the *Tiangan Dizhi* 天干地支 (Heavenly Stems and Earthly Branches) are applied to deducing the fate of a person and the geomancers decide on whether the position of a mountain or a forest is auspicious and advantageous, the principles at work are the same. For example, the wares undergoing sintering in a pottery kiln. It is said that, out of a thousand wares, there may appear a piece which is red and looks very nice. This piece represents a case of extraordinary endowment of vital force. This rarity is also true of persons, as evidenced particularly by Gu (i. e. Gusou) and Gun fathering Shun and Yu, respectively." [Renjie]

79 问："临漳士友录先生语，论气之清浊处甚详。"曰："粗说是如此。然天地之气有多少般。"问："尧舜生丹均，瞽叟生舜事，恐不全在人，亦是天地之气？"曰："此类不可晓。人气便是天地之气，然就人身上透过，如鱼在水，水入口出腮。但天地公共之气，人不得擅而有之。"德明。

I said to the Master: "In the record of what you said by a friend of mine from Linzhang (i. e. now Linzhang in Hebei), the section discoursing the clearness and turbidity of vital force is very detailed." He said, "But actually that is a rough exposition, for the types of vital force of Heaven and Earth are too many to be enumerated." I asked, "Yao and Shun fathered Danzhu and Shangjun respectively and Gusou fathered Shun. I am afraid, these affairs are not anything that can be determined completely by humankind. Are they attributed to the vital force of Heaven and Earth?" He answered, "That sort of affairs is not understandable. The vital force of humankind is the same as the vital force of Heaven and Earth, only that the latter has to work via the human body, just like the fish in water, where the water enters its fish mouth and then gets out from its gill. However, the vital force of Heaven and Earth is shared by all persons and things, so humankind should not appropriate it only to himself." [Deming]

80 亚夫曰："性如日月，气浊者如云雾。"先生以为然。节。

Yafu (courtesy name of Huan Yuan 晏渊, a disciple of Zhu Xi's) said to the Master "Nature is like the sun and moon, while those people with turbid vital force are like cloud and mist." He responded, "Right." [Jie]

81 人性如一团火，煨在灰里，拨开便明。椿。

The nature of humankind is like a ball of fire, yet covered by ashes, and when the ashes are poked aside, it will get bright. ［Chun（椿）］①

82 问气禀云云。曰："天理明，则彼如何着得！"可学。

When asked about the endowment of vital force and other questions, the Master answered，"If the heavenly principle is bright, then how can the partial vital force adhere to it?!"［Kexue］

83 问："人有常言，某人性如何，某物性如何，某物性热，某物性冷。此是兼气质与所禀之理而言否？"曰："然。"僩。

Question：It is often said that the nature of a certain person is such and such，the nature of a certain thing is such and such，and in nature a certain thing is hot and another thing is cold. Are all these said in regard to both physical nature and the endowed principle?

Answer：Right.

84 问指屋柱云："此理也；曲直，性也；所以为曲直，命也。曲直是说气禀。"曰："然。"可学。

Pointing to the pillars in a house，someone said，"They embody principle. Their being bent or straight manifests their nature. The reason why they are bent or straight is their destiny. Being bent or straight is concerned with their endowed vital force."The Master responded，"Right"［Kexue］

85 质并气而言，则是"形质"之"质"；若生质，则是"资质"之"质"。复举了翁责沈说，曰："他说多是禅。不知此数句如何怎说得好！"义刚。

The Master said，"The *zhi* 质 in *qizhi* 气质（physical nature）is the same as the *zhi* in *xingzhi* 形质（formal nature）；If *zhi* collocates with *sheng* 生 in *shengzhi* 生质（born quality），it is the same as the *zhi* in *zizhi* 资质（gifted quality）."Then he quoted some sentences from Liaoweng Zeshen（i. e. Chen Guan），saying "What he has discoursed is mostly about *Chan* 禅（the Chan sect of Buddhism），but I wonder why he put these several

---

① Wei Chun 魏椿（courtesy name Yuanshou 元寿）.

sentences so well. " ［Yigang］

86 性者万物之原，而气禀则有清浊，是以有圣愚之异。命者万物之所同受，而阴阳交运，参差不齐，是以五福、六极，值遇不一。端蒙。以下兼言命。

Nature is the original state of the myriad things, but their vital forces may be clear or turbid, which brings about the difference between sages and fools. Destiny is conferred on myriad things equally, but the interactive operations between *yin* and *yang* may produce different effects, which causes different encounters with the *wufu* 五福（five sources of happiness）and *liuji* 六极（six occasions of suffering）① . ［Duanmeng］ The several conversations below also concern destiny.

87 安卿问："'命'字有专以理言者，有专以气言者。"曰："也都相离不得。盖天非气，无以命于人；人非气，无以受天所命。"道夫。

Anqing 安卿（courtesy name of Chen Chun 陈淳）said to the Master, "Some people talked about 'destiny 命' exclusively in terms of principle, while some others, in terms of vital force. " He responded, "Principle and vital force should not be separated. Probably, that is because, without vital force, Heaven has no means by which to confer destiny on humankind, and humankind has no means by which to receive the destiny conferred by Heaven. " ［Daofu］

88 问："先生说：'命有两种：一种是贫富、贵贱、死生、寿夭，一种是清浊、偏正、智愚、贤不肖。一种属气，一种属理。'以僩观之，两种皆似属气。盖智愚、贤不肖、清浊、偏正，亦气之所为也。"曰："固然。性则命之理而已。"僩。

Question: You, sir, say that there are two kinds of destiny, one

---

① According to the *Classic of History*, trans. by J. Legge, the "five sources of happiness" refers to long life, riches, soundness of body and serenity of mind, the love of virtue, and fulfilling to the end the will（of Heaven）, and the "six occasions of suffering," to misfortune shortening the life, sickness, distress of mind, poverty, wickedness, and weakness. （See http：//ctext.org/shang-shu/great-plan） determining wealth or poverty, honor or humble station, life or death, and longevity or brevity of life, and the other determining clearness or turbidity, partiality or balance, the wise or the stupid, and the worthy or the unworthy. The former pertains to vital force, while the latter pertains to principle. As I see it, both seem to pertain to vital force, for the wise or the stupid, the worthy or the unworthy, clearness or turbidity, or partiality or balance are all caused by vital force.

Answer: That is of course true. However, nature consists of the principle of destiny (the principle underlying wisdom, stupidity, and so forth). ①

89 问："性分、命分、何以别?" 曰："性分是以理言之, 命分是兼气言之。命分有多寡厚薄之不同, 若性分则又都一般。此理, 圣愚贤否皆同。"淳。宇录少异。

Question: How to distinguish the portion of nature and that of destiny?

Answer: The portion of nature is discoursed in terms of principle, while that of destiny is, in terms of both principle and vital force. The portion of destiny is different in amount and abundance, while that of nature is the same in different cases. This is true of whether one is sagely or stupid, worthy or unworthy. [Chun (淳)] Yu's② record reads a little different.

90 "命" 之一字, 如 "天命谓性" 之 "命", 是言所禀之理也。"性也有命焉" 之 "命", 是言所以禀之分有多寡厚薄之不同也。伯羽。

What the sino-graph *ming* 命 says of, as the *ming* (conferred) in *tianming weixing* 天命谓性 (What is conferred by Heaven is called nature) as said in the *Doctrine of the Mean* does, is the endowed principle, while what the sino-graph *ming* 命 in *xing ye you ming yan* 性也有命焉 (In connection with nature, there is the appointment of Heaven) as said in the

---

① The translation of this passage is based on the version by Chan Wing-tsit, p. 626, with some modifications.

② Xu Yu 徐寓 (courtesy name Jufu 居父).

Mencius means is the difference of the endowed destiny in amount and abundance. [Boyu]

91 问："'天命谓性'之'命'，与'死生有命'之'命'不同，何也?"曰："'死生有命'之'命'是带气言之，气便有禀得多少厚薄之不同。'天命谓性'之'命'，是纯乎理言之。然天之所命，毕竟皆不离乎气。但中庸此句，乃是以理言之。孟子谓'性也，有命焉'，此'性'是兼气禀食色言之。'命也，有性焉'，此'命'是带气言之。性善又是超出气说。"淳。

Question: The sino-graph *ming* 命 in *tianming weixing* 天命谓性 (What is conferred by Heaven is called nature) and the *ming* 命 in *sisheng youming* 死生有命 (Death and life have their determined appointment) as said in the *Analects* (i. e. the *Analects of Confucius*, 12: 5) are different in their reference. Why is that?

Answer: The latter is said in terms of both principle and vital force, and thus the endowment of vital force is different in amount and abundance. By contrast, the former is said purely in terms of principle. Nevertheless, what is conferred by Heaven is, above all, inseparable from vital force. However, the statement in the *Doctrine of the Mean* is made in terms of principle. When Mencius said, "*xing ye you ming yan* (In connexion with nature, there is the appointment of Heaven)," his *ming* (appointment) concerns endowed principle and vital force as well as food and colors. In his "*ming ye you xing yan* 命也有性焉 (In one's appointment by Heaven, there is an adaptation of his nature)," the *ming* is said in terms of principle and vital force. His proposition of nature being good is made by touching on nothing of vital force. [Chun (淳)]

92 问："子罕言命。若仁义礼智五常皆是天所命。如贵贱死生寿夭之命有不同，如何?"曰："都是天所命。禀得精英之气，便为圣，为贤，便是得理之全，得理之正。禀得清明者，便英爽；禀得敦厚者，便温和；禀得清高者，便贵；禀得丰厚者，便富；禀得久长者，便寿；

禀得衰颓薄浊者，一本作："衰落孤单者，便为贫为贱为夭。"便为愚、不肖，为贫，为贱，为夭。天有那气生一个人出来，便有许多物随他来。"

又曰："天之所命，固是均一，到气禀处便有不齐。看其禀得来如何。禀得厚，道理也备。尝谓命，譬如朝廷诰敕；心，譬如官人一般，差去做官；性，譬如职事一般，郡守便有郡守职事，县令便有县令职事。职事只一般，天生人，教人许多道理，便是付人许多职事。别本云："道理只一般。"气禀，譬如俸给。贵如官高者，贱如官卑者，富如俸厚者，贫如俸薄者，寿如三两年一任又再任者，夭者如不得终任者。朝廷差人做官，便有许多物一齐趂。后来横渠云：'形而后有气质之性，善反之，则天地之性存焉，故气质之性，君子有弗性焉。'如禀得气清明者，这道理只在里面；禀得昏浊者，这道理也只在里面，只被昏浊遮蔽了。譬之水，清底里面纤毫皆见，浑底便见不得。孟子说性善，他只见得大本处，未说得气质之性细碎处。

程子谓：'论性不论气，不备；论气不论性，不明；二之则不是。'孟子只论性，不论气，但不全备。论性不论气，这性说不尽；论气不论性，性之本领处又不透彻。荀扬韩诸人虽是论性，其实只说得气。荀子只见得不好人底性，便说做恶。扬子见半善半恶底人，便说善恶混。韩子见天下有许多般人，所以立为三品之说。就三子中，韩子说又较近。他以仁义礼智为性，以喜怒哀乐为情，只是中间过接处少个'气'字。"宇。

Question: Seldom did Confucius touch on the subject of *ming* 命. It seems that benevolence, righteousness, propriety, and wisdom, and *wuchang* 五常 (Five Constant Virtues)[1] are all conferred（命）by Heaven. Is this *ming* different from the *ming* of life or death, long-living or short-living, and being noble or lowly?

Answer: Both are endowed by Heaven. If one is endowed with the pure

---

[1] The Five Constant Virtues are the father being righteousness, the mother being kind, the elder brother being friendly, the younger brother being respectful, and the son being filial.

and quintessential vital force, he will be a sage or a worthy, which indicates his possession of complete and balanced principle. One endowed with clear and bright vital force will be valiant and straightforward; one with profound vital force will be temperate; one with clear and lofty vital force will be noble; one with abundant vital force will be wealthy; one with lasting vital force will enjoy longevity; one with meager, decadent and turbid vital force will be foolish, unworthy, poor, lowly, or short-lived. For the last clause in these coordinated ones, another record reads "One endowed with decadent and solitary vital force will be poor, lowly, or short-lived." When Heaven operates with vital force and creates a person, there will be many things coming along with him.

Further answer: What is conferred by Heaven on persons is, naturally, equal, but when it gets integrated with the endowed vital force, inequality will occur. The principle varies with the vital force endowments and when one's endowment is profound, the principle therein is also more complete. I once said that, "The destiny 命 (what is conferred by Heaven) works like an imperial court issuing mandates; the *xin* 心 (mind) functions like officials appointed to offices; the nature 性 acts like the duties the government head of a province and that of a county are obliged to fulfill respectively. Their duties are similar, and Heaven produces persons and instructs them many aspects of truth, just like committing many duties to them which they should fulfill. Another record reads, 'The truth therein is the same.' The endowments of vital force can be compared to the official salaries. The noble, the lowly, the rich, and the poor, are respectively like superior officials, inferior officials, the highly paid, and the lowly paid. As for lifetime, the long-lived is like an official appointed to a post and working there for a couple of years and then re-appointed to another post and working there for more years, while the short-lived, like one failing to complete even one term of office. When the imperial court appoints one to an official post, there will be many things done to follow him to his office. " Later I read Hengqü (i. e. Zhang Zai) who said, " With the existence of physical form, there exists physical nature. If one is good at returning to the original nature endowed by Heaven and Earth, then in him it will be preserved. Therefore, in physical nature there is that which the Superior Man denies to be his original nature." If one is endowed with pure and clear vital force, the principle inheres there, and if one gets impure and turbid vital force, though the principle also inheres there, it is beclouded by that impurity and turbidity. It is like the water in a vessel, and if the water is clear an extremely minute thing on the bottom can be seen, but when the water is turbid it can not be seen. When Mencius discoursed nature being good, he saw only the great origin thereof, failing to expound the physical nature at length.

Master Cheng said, "When discussing nature, if one does not consider vital force, his discussion will be incomplete; when discussing vital force, if one does not consider nature, his discussion will be not clear. If one separates nature and vital force, then his discussion will be not right." Mencius, by contrast, talked about nature only, without mentioning anything of vital force, so his discussion is incomplete. That is because when nature is discussed without mentioning vital force, that discussion of nature will be not adequate, while when vital force is discussed without mentioning nature, that discussion will not be thorough with regard to the capability of nature. Though Xunzi (i. e. Xun Kuang), Yangzi (i. e. Yang Xiong), and Hanzi (i. e. Han Yu) dwelt on nature, what they said of are concerned only with vital force. Xunzi saw only the evil nature and came to the rash conclusion that the nature of humankind was evil. Yangzi saw only those persons who were half good and half evil. Hanzi saw the various types of persons in the world and thus proposed his theory of three grades of nature. Of them, Hanzi was closer. He regarded benevolence, righteousness, propriety, and wisdom as nature and pleasure, anger, sorrow, and joy as feelings, only that there lacks in his theory the concept of vital force as the bridge between them.

93 问："颜渊不幸短命。伯牛死，曰：'命矣夫！'孔子'得之不得曰有命。'如此之'命'，与'天命谓性'之'命'无分别否？"曰："命之正者出于理，命之变者出于气质。要之，皆天所付予。孟子曰：'莫之致而至者，命也。'但当自尽其道，则所值之命，皆正命也。"因问："如今数家之学，如康节之说，谓皆一定而不可易，如何？"曰："也只是阴阳盛衰消长之理，大数可见。然圣贤不曾主此说。如今人说康节之数，谓他说一事一物皆有成败之时，都说得肤浅了。"木之。

Question: (The disciple of Confucius) Yan Yuan 颜渊 (i. e. Yan Hui 颜回 [521 – 481 BC]) unfortunately lived a short life. When (another disciple) Bo Niu 伯牛 (i. e. Ran Geng 冉耕 [c. 544 – ? BC]) died, Confucius said, "Alas! It is *ming* 命." And in regard to his obtaining office or not, he said, "That depends on *ming*." Is there no difference between this *ming* (destiny) in these cases and the *ming* (conferred) in the sentence "What is conferred by Heaven is called nature"?

Answer: Correct destiny proceeds from principle, whereas modified destiny proceeds from physical nature. Essentially, in both cases it is conferred by Heaven. Mencius said, "That which happens without humankind's causing it to happen is the Mandate of Heaven." However, humankind ought to fulfill his duty, and then whatever mandate he meets with is correct mandate.

Thereupon the question: At present the school of occultism (divination and the use of numbers), such as that of Kangjie (i. e. Shao Yong), asserts that all is predetermined and cannot be changed. What do you say?

Answer: They can only show the general course in which the principle of the prosperity and decline and the augmentation and diminution of *yin* and *yang* is revealed. Such theories were not held by sages or worthies. At present people expounding Kangjie's [system based on] numbers assert that he said that everything and every event succeeds or fails at a predetermined point of time. Such exposition is superficial. ① ［Muzhi］②

94 或问：" '亡之，命矣夫！' 此 '命' 是天理本然之命否？" 曰：
"此只是气禀之命。富贵、死生、祸福、贵贱，皆禀之气而不可移易
者。" 祖道曰："'不知命无以为君子，'与'五十知天命'，两'命'
字如何？" 曰：" '不知命' 亦是气禀之命，'知天命' 却是圣人知其性
中四端之所自来。如人看水一般：常人但见为水流，圣人便知得水之发
源处。" 祖道。

Someone asked, "The *Analects* (6:10) says, 'It is killing him. Alas!
It is the *ming* 命 (appointment) of Heaven.' Does this *ming* refer to the
heavenly principle endowed originally?" The Master answered, "That is only
the *ming* of the endowed vital force. Life or death, weal or woe, being rich or
poor, noble or lowly, all these are resulted from the unchangeable
endowments of vital force."

Zudao asked, "In the 'Without recognizing *ming* (the ordinances of
Heaven), it is impossible to be a Superior Man' (*Analects*, 20:3) and the
'At the age of fifty, I knew *tian-ming* (the decrees of Heaven),'
(*Analects*, 2:4) do the two sino-graphs of *ming* mean the same?" The
Master answered, "In the former, the *ming* is also that of endowed vital
force, while in the latter the *ming* means the sage knew where the *siduan* 四
端 (four beginnings)③ in his nature had come from. It is like people looking
at a river. The ordinary people see only the water flowing, while the sages see
the flowing water and know where it comes from." ［Zudao］

95 闻一问：'亡之，命矣夫！' 此 '命' 字是就气禀上说？" 曰：
"死生寿夭，固是气之所禀。只看孟子说'性也，有命焉'处，便分

---

① The translation of this passage is based on the version by Chan Wing-tsit, pp. 626 – 627, with some modifications.

② Qian Muzhi 钱木之 (courtesy name Zishan 子山).

③ The "four beginnings" are the feelings of sadness and commiseration, shame and dislike, deference and compliance, and right and wrong. (See *Mencius*, 2A:6, trans. James Legge ［http://ctext. org/mengzi/gong-sun-chou-i］)

晓。"择之问："'不知命'与'知天命'之'命'如何?"曰："不同。
'知天命',谓知其理之所自来。譬之于水,人皆知其为水,圣人则知
其发源处。如'不知命'处,却是说死生、寿夭、贫富、贵贱之命也。
然孟子又说当'顺受其正'。若一切任其自然,而'立乎岩墙之下',
则又非其正也。"因言,上古天地之气,其极清者,生为圣人,君临天
下,安享富贵,又皆享上寿。及至后世,多反其常。衰周生一孔子,终
身不遇,寿止七十有余。其禀得清明者,多夭折;暴横者,多得志。旧
看史传,见盗贼之为君长者,欲其速死,只是不死,为其全得寿考之气
也。人杰。

Wenyi 闻一（courtesy name of Lin Ci 林赐［dates unknown］, a
disciple of Zhu Xi's）asked, "The *Analects*（6：10）says, 'It is killing him.
Alas! It is the *ming* 命（appointment）of Heaven. ' Is this *ming* said with
regard to endowed vital force?" The Master said, "Life and death, long-living
and short-living, are, of course, dependent on the endowment of vital force.
It is easy to understand that by reading only Mencius's ' In connection with
nature, there is the appointment of Heaven ' and his explanation of it. "

Zezhi 择之（courtesy name of Zeng Zudao 曾祖道［dates unknown］, a
disciple of Zhu Xi's）asked, "What about the *ming* in ' not recognizing *ming*
（ordinances of Heaven）'（*Analects*, 20：3）and ' knowing the *ming*
（decrees）of Heaven '（*Analects*, 2：4）?" The Master answered,
"Different. The ' knowing the *ming* of Heaven ' means knowing where the
principle comes from. Take water for example. All of us know water as water,
but the sage knows where water comes from. The ' not recognizing *ming*, ' by
contrast, concerns the destiny of life or death, long-living or short-living,
being rich or poor, and noble or lowly. However, the *Mencius*（7A：2）says
that one should ' receive submissively what may be correctly ascribed
thereto. ' If one lets everything go on their natural courses, and ' stands
beneath a precipitous wall, '（*Mencius*, 7A：2）then that is not correctly
ascribed to the appointment of Heaven. "

Thereupon he went on, "In the far remote ancient times, the extremely pure vital force of Heaven and Earth produced the sages to function as the sovereigns of the world, who enjoyed not only wealth and honor but also longevity. The later times went mostly against that trend. For example, Confucius, who was born in the declined period of Zhou Dynasty, was frustrated in his life time and passed away only at the age of seventy two. Most of those endowed with clear and bright vital force died young, while those with cruel and violent vital force tended to have successes thrust upon them. When I read histories in the past, I wished those thieves and brigands on thrones or at high positions recorded in them had all died as soon as possible, but they lived on and on. It is because they had got the long-life vital force." [Renjie]

96 履之说:"子温而厉,威而不猛,恭而安。"因问:"得清明之气为圣贤,昏浊之气为愚不肖;气之厚者为富贵,薄者为贫贱,此固然也。然圣人得天地清明中和之气,宜无所亏欠,而夫子反贫贱,何也?岂时运使然邪?抑其所禀亦有不足邪?"曰:"便是禀得来有不足。他那清明,也只管得做圣贤,却管不得那富贵。禀得那高底则贵,禀得厚底则富,禀得长底则寿,贫贱夭者反是。夫子虽得清明者以为圣人,然禀得那低底、薄底,所以贫贱。颜子又不如孔子,又禀得那短底,所以又夭。"

又问:"一阴一阳,宜若停匀,则贤不肖宜均。何故君子常少,而小人常多?"曰:"自是他那物事驳杂,如何得齐!且以扑钱譬之:纯者常少,不纯者常多,自是他那气驳杂,或前或后,所以不能得他恰好,如何得均平!且以一日言之:或阴或晴,或风或雨,或寒或热,或清爽,或鹘突,一日之间自有许多变,便可见矣。"又问:"虽是驳杂,然毕竟不过只是一阴一阳二气而已,如何会恁地不齐?"曰:"便是不如此。若只是两个单底阴阳,则无不齐。缘是他那物事错揉万变,所以不能得他恰好。"又问:"如此,则天地生圣贤,又只是偶然,不是有意矣。"曰:"天地那里说我特地要生个圣贤出来!也只是气数到那里,恰相凑着，所以生出圣贤。及至生出，则若天之有意焉耳。"又问：
"康节云：'阳一而阴二，所以君子少而小人多。'此语是否？"曰："也
说得来。自是那物事好底少而恶底多。且如面前事，也自是好底事少，
恶底事多。其理只一般。"偁。

Lüzhi 履之（courtesy name of Liu Di 刘砥）said，"The *Analects*（7：
38）says，'The Master（referring to Confucius）was mild yet dignified；
majestic yet not fierce；respectful yet easy.'"Thereupon，he asked，"It is
true that those who are conferred with clear and bright vital force are sages
and worthies，while those with dim and turbid vital force are stupid ones and
unworthies，and those with abundant vital force are rich and noble，while
those with meager vital force are poor and lowly. But since the sage possesses
the clear，bright，balanced and harmonious vital force of Heaven and Earth，
he should be free from any deficiency. Why Confucius was poor and lowly？"

Answer：It is because there is some deficiency in his endowment. The
clear and bright vital force he possessed made him a sage，but had nothing to
do with whether he was rich and noble. With lofty endowment，he will be
noble；with abundant endowment，he will be rich；with long-living
endowment，he will enjoy longevity. The endowment for a poor one，for a
lowly one，and for a short-lived one are opposite，respectively. Though a sage
due to his possessing clear and bright vital force，Confucius was conferred
with the low and meager vital force concurrently，so he was poor and lowly.
Yanzi 颜子（i. e. Yanhui）was conferred with still lower and more meager
vital force than Confucius and，worse than that，he was bestowed with the
short-living vital force，which is why he was short-lived.

Further question：*Yin* and *yang* are equal and therefore the number of
worthy and unworthy people should be equal. Why is it that there are always
fewer superior men and more petty men？

Answer：That is because，naturally，things and events are multifarious.
Then，how can they be equal？Take the casting of coins for example. The

metal for that purpose is more often impure than pure in different cases, because the vital force there is mixed, so it is hard to get the proper purity and the actual purity is either higher or lower. Thus how can the equality be gained? Take a day for another example, it may be clear or overcast, windy or rainy, hot or cold, cloudless or cloudy. One day sees so many changes, by which the reason for the inequality is easy to see.

Further question: Although things and events are multifarious, nevertheless, they are nothing but the successive movement of the two vital forces of *yin* and *yang*. How is it that they are not equal?

Answer: That is not the case as you say. If there were only a single *yin* and a single *yang*, everything would be equal. But because of the great complexity and infinite transformations of things, it is impossible to have everything just right equally.

Further question: If so, then Heaven produces sages and worthies only accidentally rather than with any intention.

Answer: When does Heaven say that it wants to produce a sage or a worthy purposely? The mere fact is that whenever the courses of vital force reach certain point and meet, a sage or a worthy is born. After he is born, it does seem that Heaven had such an intention. [1]

Further question: Kangjie said, "*Yang* is one and *yin* is two, so the number of superior men is small, while that of petty men is big." Is what he said right?

Answer: That makes some sense. Naturally, the number of good things and events is small, while that of those bad is big. The good events before us are also fewer than the bad ones. However, the principle in all these is the same. [Xian]

---

[1] The translation of this part in this passage is based on the version by Chan Wing-tsit, p. 627, with some modifications.

97 敬子问自然之数。曰："有人禀得气厚者，则福厚；气薄者，则福薄。禀得气之华美者，则富盛；衰飒者，则卑贱；气长者，则寿；气短者，则夭折。此必然之理。"问："神仙之说有之乎？"曰："谁人说无？诚有此理。只是他那工夫大段难做，除非百事弃下，办得那般工夫，方做得。"又曰："某见名寺中所画诸祖师人物，皆魁伟雄杰，宜其杰然有立如此。所以妙喜赞某禅师有曰：'当初若非这个，定是做个渠魁。'观之信然。其气貌如此，则世之所谓富贵利达，声色货利，如何笼络得他住！他视之亦无足以动其心者。"或问："若非佛氏收拾去，能从吾儒之教，不知如何？"曰："他又也未是那'无文王犹兴'底，只是也须做个特立独行底人，所为必可观。若使有圣人收拾去，可知大段好。只是当时吾道黑淬淬地，只有些章句词章之学。他如龙如虎，这些艺解都束缚他不住，必决去无疑。也煞被他引去了好人，可畏可畏！"侗。

Jingzi asked about the numerology concerned with destiny. The Master answered, "If one is endowed with the abundant vital force, he will be abundant in good fortune, while if one is with meager vital force he will be meager in good fortune. He who is endowed with resplendent vital force will be rich and flourish, while he who is with decaying and decrepit vital force will be humble and lowly. Endowed with long-stretched vital force, one will be long-lived, while with short-lasting vital force, one will be short-lived. This is an inevitable truth. "

Further question: Are there really immortals as said by some people?

Answer: Who says there are not? There is such truth indeed, only that it is very hard for one to make such efforts as to become an immortal, unless he is determined and gives up everything other than pursuing that end before possibly reaching it.

Further answer: I once visited a well-known Buddhist Temple and saw the portraits of those founding masters of the Sect of Buddhism. They all appeared strong built, imbued with heroism, who were so outstanding figures.

Therefore, an Abhirati inscription there eulogizes a master, the subject of a portrait, saying "But for his pursuit of Buddhism at first, he would have been a head of an armed rebellious group." Looking at the portrait, I believed it. With his magnificent air like that, how could he be confined by the worldly called riches and honors, looks and colors, benefits and gains? In the face of all such, he would not be moved at all.

Someone asked, "If he had not been attracted by Buddhism and had followed our Confucianism, what would he have been like?" The Master answered, "He would not necessarily have been one of those who, 'without (the favorable climate created by) King Wen of Zhou, rouse themselves' (*Mencius*, 7: 10), but he would have been surely a person of independent character and noteworthy conduct. Had he been a follower of a sage, he would have been accomplished with remarkable merits. However, at that time when Buddhism was introduced (in Eastern Han Dynasty [25 – 220]), Confucians were still stumbling in the darkness and what they did was only concerned with some explanations of the ancient classics. Since they (who started with learning Confucianism and wound up with Buddhism) were all as lively as dragons and tigers, how could that confine them? They would, no doubt, leave for somewhere else. What a pity it is that such good people as them were recruited by Buddhism! Isn't it awful?" [Xian]

98 问：“富贵有命，如后世鄙夫小人，富尧舜三代之世，如何得富贵？”曰：“当尧舜三代之世不得富贵，在后世则得富贵，便是命。”曰：“如此，则气禀不一定。”曰：“以此气遇此时，是他命好；不遇此时，便是有所谓资适逢世是也。如长平死者四十万，但遇白起，便如此。只他相撞着，便是命。”可学。

Question: Riches and honors have their determined appointment, but those vulgar and petty people in later times possessed more riches than Yao and Shun and other sages in the most ancient *sandai* 三代 (the Xia, Shang, and [Western] Zhou dynasties). How did that happen?

Answer: In the times of Yao and Shun and the three dynasties, that type of people had not got riches and honors but, in later times, they got them. That is what destiny brings about.

Further question: Then, the endowed vital force is not determined, isn't it?

Answer: When that vital force meets that time when one is born, his destiny is good, but when it does not meet that time, then there occurs the birth in a so called wrong time. For example, after the battle at Changping[①], the four hundred thousand soldiers who had given themselves up were buried alive. They could not escape because they encountered Bai Qi[②] and such encounter is the very result of destiny. [Kexue]

99 问："前日尝说鄙夫富贵事。今云富贵贫贱是前定，如何?"曰："恁地时节，气亦自别。后世气运渐乖，如古封建，毕究是好人在上。到春秋乃生许多逆贼。今儒者多叹息封建不行，然行着亦可虑。且如天子，必是天生圣哲为之。后世如秦始皇在上，乃大无道人，如汉高祖，乃崛起田野，此岂不是气运颠倒!"问："此是天命否?"曰："是。"可学。

Question: In the day before yesterday, you talked about the matter of vulgar men getting riches and honors. Now you say that whether one is rich or poor, noble or lowly, is predetermined. Why is that inconsistency?

Answer: In different times, the vital force is also naturally different. In the far remote ancient times, when the system of enfeoffment was practiced, those on the top ranks were, after all, good people. The later times saw the

---

① In c. 260 BC, the battle at Changping (in what is now Gaoping City, Shanxi Province) occurred between the state of Qin and the state of Zhao, two of the seven major powers in the Warring States period of dynastic China. It is a decisive one between the two states. The battle played a significant role in Qin's carrying out its strategy of conquering the other six major states before its establishing the Qin dynasty (221 – 206 BC).

② Bai Qi 白起 (?, –257) is a famous general of the state of Qin, who acted as the commander of the Qin troops in the decisive battle with the state of Zhao at Changping.

trend towards decadence of vital force, as evidenced by the Spring and Autumn Period (770 – 476 BC) when many treacherous ministers and traitors were produced. The Confucians today are liable to deplore the enfeoffment not in practice, but even if it was practiced, it would give rise to much anxiety. For example, the role of the *Tianzi* 天子 (Son of Heaven, i. e. Emperor) should be played by a born sage. In later times, for example, Emperor Shihuang of Qin (259 – 210 BC) was a notorious unprincipled and unscrupulous person and Emperor Gaozu of Han (256 – 195 BC) was one rising from the grassroots. Isn't this indicative of the inverted operation of vital force?

Further Question: Is it caused by the Mandate of Heaven?

Answer: Yes. [Kexue]

100 人之禀气，富贵、贫贱、长短，皆有定数寓其中。禀得盛者，其中有许多物事，其来无穷。亦无①盛而短者。若木生于山，取之，或贵而为栋梁，或贱而为厕料，皆其生时所禀气数如此定了。扬。

In the endowed vital force of humankind dwells the predetermined courses of being rich or poor, of being noble or lowly, and of being long-lived or short-lived. If one is endowed with magnificent vital force, it will bring about many things and events to him, the number of which can be countless. There is also the case where one is not endowed with magnificent vital force and short-lived. ②It is like the trees growing on a mountain, some of which can serve as ridgepoles and beams in building a house, while some others of which can only be used as materials for the lavatory in it. That is because their different functions were already determined by their vital forces they were endowed with at birth. [Yang]

---

① "無" 贺疑当做 "有"。

② Hesun suspected that a mistake had been made in the record of "one is not endowed with magnificent vital force and short-lived," which should have been "one is endowed with magnificent vital force yet short-lived."

卷第五 Book 5

性理二

Nature and Principle II

性情心意等名义

The Names and Meanings of Nature, Feelings, Mind, Intention, and Some Others

1 问："天与命，性与理，四者之别：天则就其自然者言之，命则就其流行而赋于物者言之，性则就其全体而万物所得以为生者言之，理则就其事事物物各有其则者言之。到得合而言之，则天即理也，命即性也，性即理也，是如此否？"曰："然。但如今人说，天非苍苍之谓。据某看来，亦舍不得这个苍苍底。"贺孙。以下论性命。

Question: As regards the distinction between *tian* 天 (Heaven, or Nature), *ming* 命 (destiny, or fate), *xing* 性 (nature, or humanity), and *li* 理 (principle), Heaven refers to being what it is; destiny refers to that which flows and is endowed in all things; nature refers to the total substance and that by which all things attain their being produced; and principle refers to the laws underlying all things and events. Taken together, Heaven is the same as principle, destiny is the same as nature, and nature is the same as principle. Is this understanding correct?

Answer: Yes. Nowadays, it is maintained that Heaven does not refer to the blue sky. In my view, the blue sky should not be left out of account. ① ［Hesun］The three conversations below discourse nature and destiny.

2 理者，天之体；命者，理之用。性是人之所受，情是性之用。道夫。

Principle is the substance of Heaven, while destiny is the function of principle. One's nature is what is received by him. And one's feelings are the function of his nature. ② ［Daofu］

3 命犹诰敕，性犹职事，情犹施设，心则其人也。贺孙。

Destiny is comparable to the imperial order; nature is to the duties of an official post; feelings are to the facilities of the post; and *xin* 心 (mind) is to the official occupying the post. ［Hesun］

4 天所赋为命，物所受为性。赋者命也，所赋者气也；受者性也，所受者气也。宇。

That which is endowed by Heaven is destiny; That which is received by things is nature. That which is endowed is destiny and that by which the endowment is made is vital force. That which is received is nature and that by which the reception is made is vital force. ［Yu］

5 道即性，性即道，固只是一物。然须看因甚唤做性，因甚唤做道。淳。以下论性。

Dao (the Way) is identical with the human nature of humankind and things, and the nature is identical with the Way. They are one and the same, but we must understand in what connection it is called the nature and in what connection it is called the Way. ③ ［Chun (淳)］The several conversations below concern nature.

6 性即理也。在心唤做性，在事唤做理。焘。

［Cheng Yi said,］"The nature is the same as principle." In relation to

---

① The translation of this passage is based on the version by Chan Wing-tsit, p. 612, with slight modification.

② Ibid.

③ Ibid. , p. 614, with slight modification.

the mind, it is called the nature. In relation to events, it is called principle. ① [Tao]②

7 生之理谓性。节。

The principle of life is called the nature. ③ [Jie]

8 性只是此理。节。

The nature is only the principle. [Jie]

9 性是合当底。同。

The nature is like the duties of an official post. [Jie]

10 性则纯是善底。同。

The nature is purely good. [Jie]

11 性是天生成许多道理。同。

The nature consists of innumerable principles produced by Heaven. ④ [Jie]

12 性是许多理散在处为性。同。

The nature is where innumerable principles dwell dispersedly, which constitute the nature. [Jie]

13 问:"性既无形,复言以理,理又不可见。"曰:"父子有父子之理,君臣有君臣之理。"节。

Question: The nature is formless, but when it is said further in relation to principle, the principle can not be seen, either. (How is that?)

Answer: Between a father and his son is the father-son principle and between a sovereign and his minister is the sovereign-minister principle. [Jie]

14 性是实理,仁义礼智皆具。德明。

The nature consists of concrete principle, complete with benevolence,

---

① The translation of this passage is based on the version by Chan Wing-tsit, p. 614, with slight modification.

② Lü Tao 吕焘 (courtesy name Dezhao 德昭).

③ The translation of this passage is based on the version by Chan Wing-tsit, p. 614.

④ Ibid. , with slight modification.

righteousness, propriety, and wisdom. ① ［Deming］

15 问：“性固是理。然性之得名，是就人生禀得言之否？”曰：“‘继之者善，成之者性。’这个理在天地间时，只是善，无有不善者。生物得来，方始名曰‘性’。只是这理，在天则曰‘命’，在人则曰‘性’。”淳。

Question: The nature is, of course, the principle. However, is the nature named in regard to what is endowed in one at birth?

Answer: Confucius said "What ensues after the Way is good and what brings it to its completeness is its nature." When the principle resides between Heaven and Earth, it is entirely good, free from any non-goodness. When it is endowed in a thing at its birth, it is referred to as its nature. The principle, when it resides in Heaven, is called destiny, while, when dwelling in man, it is called nature. ［Chun（淳）］

16 郑问：“先生谓性是未发，善是已发，何也？”曰：“才成个人影子，许多道理便都在那人上。其恻隐，便是仁之善；羞恶，便是义之善。到动极复静处，依旧只是理。”曰：“这善，也是性中道理，到此方见否？”曰：“这须就那地头看。‘继之者善也，成之者性也。’在天地言，则善在先，性在后，是发出来方生人物。发出来是善，生人物便成个性。在人言，则性在先，善在后。”或举“孟子道性善”。曰：“此则‘性’字重，‘善’字轻，非对言也。文字须活看。此且就此说，彼则就彼说，不可死看。牵此合彼，便处处有碍。”淳。

Zheng（i.e. Kexue）asked, "You, sir, say that the nature is（a state）not roused, whereas the good is（a state）roused. Why is that?" The Master answered, "As soon as a person begins to take shape, there are already many principles inhering in him. His feeling of sadness and commiseration is the good of benevolence and his feeling of shame and dislike is the good of

---

① The translation of this passage is based on the version by Chan Wing-tsit, with slight modification.

righteousness. Where the activity goes to its extreme and tranquility begins, there is still only principle. " Zheng further asked, "This good is also the principle in the nature. Can it be seen in this phase?" The Master answered, "You have to consider what is the final result. 'What ensues after the Way is good and what brings it to its completeness is its nature. ' In relation to Heaven and Earth, the good comes first before the nature. The good has to be emanated before a person is created. Thus, the good is roused so as to give birth to a person, which embodies the nature. By contrast, in regard to humankind, the nature comes first before the good. "

Someone else cited Mencius as saying nature being good. The Master responded, "In Mencius's discourse here, what the 'nature' means outweighs what the 'good' means. They are not opposites in the context. In reading something, you should be flexible, avoiding being too rigid. When you read a word in this context, you should understand it in this way, while when you read it in that context, you should understand it in that way. If you take this meaning of the word in this context for the meaning of it in that context, then you will find obstacles everywhere in your reading. " [Chun（淳）]

17　性不是卓然一物可见者。只是穷理、格物，性自在其中，不须求，故圣人罕言性。德明。

The nature is not something conspicuously tangible and visible. If one engages himself in nothing but investigating things to enquire the principle thoroughly, he will come naturally to be aware of the nature therein and it is not necessary for him to seek after it purposely. So the sages seldom spoke of the nature. [Deming]

18　诸儒论性不同，非是于善恶上不明，乃"性"字安顿不着。砥。

The Confucians' discourses on nature are different from one another. The reason for that is not that they failed to understand good and evil but that they did not get the right place for the nature to fit in. [Di]

19　圣人只是识得性。百家纷纷，只是不识"性"字。扬子鹘鹘突突，荀子又所谓隔靴爬痒。扬。

The sages saw the nature only right. However, all others, with all the disparity of their opinions, failed to understand the nature right. Yangzi (i. e. Yang Xiong) was rather confused and Xunzi (i. e. Xun Kuang) missed the essential point. [Yang]

20 致道谓"心为太极"，林正卿谓"心具太极"，致道举以为问。先生曰："这般处极细，难说。看来心有动静：其体，则谓之易；其理，则谓之道；其用，则谓之神。"直卿退而发明曰："先生道理精熟，容易说出来，须至极。"贺孙问："'其体则谓之易'，体是如何？"曰："体不是'体用'之'体'，恰似说'体质'之'体'，犹云'其质则谓之易'。理即是性，这般所在，当活看。如'心'字，各有地头说。如孟子云：'仁，人心也。'仁便是人心，这说心是合理说。如说'颜子其心三月不违仁'，是心为主而不违乎理。就地头看，始得。"又云："先生太极图解云：'动静者，所乘之机也。'蔡季通聪明，看得这般处出，谓先生下此语最精。盖太极是理，形而上者；阴阳是气，形而下者。然理无形，而气却有迹。气既有动静，则所载之理亦安得谓之无动静！"又举通书动静篇云："'动而无静，静而无动，物也；动而无动，静而无静，神也。动而无动，静而无静，非不动不静也。物则不通，神妙万物。'动静者，所乘之机也。"先生因云："某向来分别得这般所在。今心力短，便是这般所在都说不到。"因云："向要至云谷，自下上山，半涂大雨，通身皆湿，得到地头，因思着：'天地之塞，吾其体；天地之帅，吾其性。'时季通及某人同在那里。某因各人解此两句，自亦作两句解。后来看，也自说得着，所以迤逦便作西铭等解。"贺孙。以下论心。

Zhidao 致道 (courtesy name of Zhao Shixia 赵师夏 [dates unknown], a disciple of Zhu Xi's) said, "Mind is the Great Ultimate," while Zhengqing 正卿 (courtesy name of Lin Xuemeng 林学蒙 [dates unknown], a disciple of Zhu Xi's) thought, "Mind embodies the Great Ultimate." Zhidao asked about that. The Master answered, "In this regard, which is too minute, it is hard to say. It seems the mind is capable of both activity and tranquility. In relation to its *ti* 体 (body), the mind is called *yi* 易 (change); with respect to its principle, it is called the Way; concerning its function, it is called *shen* 神 (the inscrutable). " After leaving the Master's room, Zhiqing (i. e. Huang Gan) sighed with emotion, " Our Master is versed so well in learning on the principles as to clarify that with ease. One must be extremely learned before he can do like that. "

I asked, " In your ' In relation to its substance 体, it is called change, ' what do you mean by *ti*? " The Master answered, " The *ti* does not mean the same as the *ti* in *tiyong* 体用 (substance and function). In its reference, it is similar to the *ti* in *tizhi* 体质 (body-constitution) and saying ' In relation to its *ti*, it is called change ' is comparable to saying ' In relation to its constitution, it is called change. ' The principle is nature. In such regard, the words should be understood flexibly. For example, for the sino-graph of *xin* 心, there are different understandings with regard to their original references. In the ' Benevolence is the *xin* of humankind, ' (*Mencius*, 6A：11) the *xin* refers to the mind in the sense of principle. By contrast, in ' For three months there would be nothing in his (i. e. Yan Hui's 颜回) *xin* contrary to benevolence, ' (*Analects*, 6：7) the *xin* means the mind which predominates and does not go against principle. So you have to see its origin before you understand its reference truly well. "

I further said, " You, sir, said in your *Taiji Tu Jie* 太极图解 (Explanation of the Diagram of the Great Ultimate), that, ' The operation of activity and tranquility brings about opportunities that can be made use of. ' Cai Jitong, in a display of ingenuity, saw what it meant and spoke highly of what you said as the most insightful in that regard. Probably the Great Ultimate is the principle, which exists before physical form, whereas *yin* and *yang* are vital forces, which exist after physical form. The principle is formless, yet the vital force shows its shape. Since the vital force operates in activity and tranquility, how can the principle carried in it not operate in activity and tranquility?!" I went on and, citing the chapter "Dongjing" 动静 (Activity and Tranquility) in *Tongshu* 通书 (Penetrating the *Classic of Change*) by Zhou Dunyi as saying, "Things can not be tranquil while active or active while tranquil. Spirit, however, can be active without activity and tranquil without tranquility. Being active without activity and tranquil without tranquility does not mean that spirit is neither active nor tranquil. Things can not penetrate each other but spirit works wonders with all things."[1] Then I said, "That means indeed 'The operation of activity and tranquility brings about opportunities that can be made use of.'"

The Master, thereupon, said, "I used to be able to clarify such points well, but now that I have felt inadequate in making such mental effort as to elucidate that sort of things." He went on saying, "Once I climbed the Yungu Mountain. When I reached half way up it I was caught by a heavy rain and got wet all over. After arriving in my destination, I thought of 'That which fills the universe I regard as my body and that directs the universe I consider as my nature' (said by Zhang Zai in his 'Ximing' 西铭 [The Western Inscription])[2]. On that occasion, Jitong and someone else were with me. I asked them to explain this sentence and I myself also offered an explanation of it. When I considered its meaning later, I found my explanation at that time reasonable and then I set about writing a series of explanations for 'The Western Inscription' and some other treatises."

[Hesun] The several conversations below are concerned with mind.

21 心之理是太极，心之动静是阴阳。振。

The principle of the mind is the Great Ultimate. The activity and tranquility of the mind are the *yin* and *yang*.[3] [Zhen]

---

① The translation of this part in the passage is based on the version by Chan Wing-tsit, pp. 471 – 472.

② Ibid., p. 497, with slight modification.

③ Ibid., p. 628.

22 惟心无对。方子。

Mind alone has no opposite. [1] ［Fangzi］

23 问：“灵处是心，抑是性？”曰：“灵处只是心，不是性。性只是理。”淳。

Question：Where does the intelligence dwell? Mind or nature?

Answer：It is in the mind but not in the nature that the intelligence dwells. The nature is only principle. ［Chun（淳）］

24 问：“知觉是心之灵固如此，抑气之为邪？”曰：“不专是气，是先有知觉之理。理未知觉，气聚成形，理与气合，便能知觉。譬如这烛火，是因得这脂膏，便有许多光焰。”问：“心之发处是气否？”曰：“也只是知觉。”淳。

Question：Is consciousness what it is because of the intelligence of the mind or is it because of the operation of vital force?

Answer：Not vital force alone. （Before vital force existed）, there was already the principle of consciousness. But principle at this stage does not give rise to consciousness. Only when it comes into union with vital force is consciousness possible. Take, for example, the flame of this candle. It is because it has received this rich fat that there is so much light.

Question：Is that which emanates from the mind vital force?

Answer：No, that is simply consciousness. [2] ［Chun（淳）］

25 所知觉者是理。理不离知觉，知觉不离理。节。

What gives rise to consciousness is principle. The principle does not leave consciousness and consciousness does not leave principle. ［Jie］

26 问：“心是知觉，性是理。心与理如何得贯通为一？”曰：“不须去着实通，本来贯通。”“如何本来贯通？”曰：“理无心，则无着处。”节。

---

① The translation of this passage is based on the version by Chan Wing-tsit, p. 628.

② Ibid. , p. 628, with slight modification.

Question: Mind is consciousness and the nature is principle. How do the mind and principle pervade each other and become one?

Answer: They need not move to pervade each other, for from the very start they pervade each other.

Question: How do they pervade each other from the very start?

Answer: Without the mind, principle would have nowhere to inhere. ① [Jie]

27 所觉者，心之理也；能觉者，气之灵也。节。

What gives rise to consciousness is the principle of mind; what can be conscious is the intelligence of the vital force. [Jie]

28 心者，气之精爽。节。

The mind is the ingenuity of vital force. [Jie]

29 心官至灵，藏往知来。焘。

The faculty of mind is supremely intelligent, which is capable of remembering what is in the past and knowing what will come. [Tao]

30 发明"心"字，曰："一言以蔽之，曰'生'而已。'天地之大德曰生'，人受天地之气而生，故此心必仁，仁则生矣。"力行。

When revealing what "mind" means, the Master said, "To put it in a word, it means nothing but 'giving life (生).' As said in 'Xici' 系辞 (Appended Remarks) of the *Classic of Change*, 'The great virtue of Heaven and Earth is giving life.' Humankind is conceived by receiving the vital force of Heaven and Earth and thus given life to. Therefore, the mind of Heaven and Earth must be benevolent. With the benevolence, Heaven and Earth give life." [Lixing]

31 心须兼广大流行底意看，又须兼生意看。且如程先生言：'仁者，天地生物之心。'只天地便广大，生物便流行，生生不穷。端蒙。

---

① The translation of this passage is based on the version by Chan Wing-tsit, p. 628, with slight modification.

The "mind" (of Heaven and Earth) must be understood by considering both the meaning of vastness and flowing and that of giving life. As Master Cheng said, "The benevolence lies in the mind of Heaven and Earth which give life to myriad things." Since Heaven and Earth came into being, they have been vast, and since things came into being, they have been flowing. The process of giving life to things never ceases. [Duanmeng]

32 "心与理一，不是理在前面为一物。理便在心之中，心包蓄不住，随事而发。"因笑云："说到此，自好笑。恰似那藏相似，除了经函，里面点灯，四方八面皆如此光明粲烂，但今人亦少能看得如此。"广。

The Master said, "Mind is identical with principle. It is not that the principle is an entity in front of the mind. The principle is within the mind, and since the mind is hardly capable of confining it, the principle emanates whenever an event occurs." Thereupon, smiling, he went on saying "Speaking of this point, it is laughable. The mind is just like a depository of Buddhist sutras, where, besides the cases containing those sutras, there is a lamp (principle) illuminating the whole room so brightly. However, nowadays, few people are able to see all such." [Guang]

33 问："心之为物，众理具足。所发之善，固出于心。至所发不善，皆气禀物欲之私，亦出于心否？"曰："固非心之本体，然亦是出于心也。"又问："此所谓人心否？"曰："是。"子升因问："人心亦兼善恶否？"曰："亦兼说。"木之。

Question: Mind as an entity embraces all principles. The good that is roused, of course, proceeds from the mind. But the evil that is roused is all due to selfish material desires endowed by vital force. Does it also proceed from the mind?

Answer: It is certainly not the original substance of the mind, but it also emanates from the mind.

Further question: Is this what is called the mind of humankind?

Answer：Yes.

Thereupon Zisheng 子升（a disciple of Zhu Xi's）asked：Does the mind of humankind include both good and evil?

Answer：Both are included. ① ［Muzhi］

34 或问："心有善恶否？"曰："心是动底物事，自然有善恶。且如恻隐是善也，见孺子入井而无恻隐之心，便是恶矣。离着善，便是恶。然心之本体未尝不善，又却不可说恶全不是心。若不是心，是甚么做出来？古人学问便要穷理、知至，直是下工夫消磨恶去，善自然渐次可复。操存是后面事，不是善恶时事。"问："明善、择善如何？"曰："能择，方能明。且如有五件好底物事，有五件不好底物事，将来拣择，方解理会得好底。不择，如何解明？"谦。

Someone asked, "Is there good or evil mind?" The Master answered, "Since mind is something in activity, naturally there is good or evil mind. For example, the feeling of sadness and commiseration is good, so when one sees a child about to fall into a well yet without feeling sadness and commiseration, his mind is evil. Leaving from good is evil. However, the original state of mind is never not good, but it should not be said that evil is not mind at all. If it is not mind, what on earth makes it happen? When ancients pursued learning and strove to investigate things for acquiring complete knowledge[2], their purpose was to make those efforts to wear away the evil from their minds so that the good would be able to recover gradually. As for the moral integrity and fortitude, they are matters posterior to those of good and evil mind. " When asked "What about understanding the good and choosing the good?"

---

① The translation of this passage is based on the version by Chan Wing-tsit, pp. 628 – 629, with slight modification.

② When Zhu Xi（as well as other Neo-Confucians）mentioned "to investigate things for acquiring complete knowledge," he did not say it in the sense of the Western science or modern science, but in the sense of ethics and morality. In other words, it means pursuing what he called the heavenly principle, the human relations, the sages' messages, and so on, rather than the natural law and scientific truth.

the Master replied, "Only when one knows to choose can he understand truly. For example, there are five good things or events and five bad things or events, yet you do not know which is good and even what the good is like. When you gather all of them and try to make choices from them, then you will understand what is the good well. Without choosing, how can that understanding be possible?" [Qian]①

35 心无间于已发未发。彻头彻尾都是，那处截做已发未发！如放僻邪侈，此心亦在，不可谓非心。。

As regards mind, there is no distinction between being roused and being not roused to speak of, for it is uniform all over, so which part of it can be said as being roused or not? Even if it is full of what is evil and vile, the mind remains still there and it should not be said as being not mind. [Chun (淳)]

36 问："形体之动，与心相关否？"曰："岂不相关？自是心使他动。"曰："喜怒哀乐未发之前，形体亦有运动，耳目亦有视听，此是心已发，抑未发？"曰："喜怒哀乐未发，又是一般。然视听行动，亦是心向那里。若形体之行动心都不知，便是心不在。行动都没理会了，说甚未发！未发不是漠然全不省，亦常醒在这里，不恁地困。"淳。

Question: Does the activity of the physical form have something to do with the mind?

Answer: Doesn't it have to do with the mind? Naturally, it is the mind that causes its activity.

Further question: Before pleasure, anger, sorrow, and joy happen, there are the activities of the physical form and the seeing and hearing of ears and eyes. Does this mean the mind has been emanated or not?

Answer: Before these feelings happen, whether the mind is emanated or not is a different case. Nevertheless, when the seeing, hearing, and activities

---

① Liao Qian 廖谦（courtesy name Yizhong 益仲）.

occur, the mind is also roused towards them. If the mind did not know the activities of the physical form, that would mean the mind is absent. Then the mind would not be concerned with the activities. Can it be said that the mind is not emanated? The so called "not emanated" does not mean complete indifference. The mind is constantly awake there, not so sleepy. [Chun（淳）]

37 问："恻隐、羞恶、喜怒、哀乐，固是心之发，晓然易见处。如未恻隐、羞恶、喜怒、哀乐之前，便是寂然而静时，然岂得块然槁木! 其耳目亦必有自然之闻见，其手足亦必有自然之举动，不审此时唤作如何。"曰："喜怒哀乐未发，只是这心未发耳。其手足运动，自是形体如此。"淳。

Question: The feeling of sadness and commiseration and of shame and dislike and the feeling of pleasure, anger, sorrow, and joy, are of course the emanations of the mind, and that is easy to see. Before those feelings is a state of quiet. But can it be said that the physical form is, as it were, a piece of withered wood? Its ears and eyes also hear and see naturally and its hands and feet also have their natural activities. Then, is the mind at such time emanated?

Answer: That the pleasure, anger, sorrow, and joy are not emanated means only the mind does not emanate them. The activities of hands and feet are what the physical form is naturally capable of doing. [Chun（淳）]

38 问："先生前日以挥扇是气，节后思之：心之所思，耳之所听，目之所视，手之持，足之履，似非气之所能到。气之所运，必有以主之者。"曰："气中自有个灵底物事。"节。

Question: You, sir, likened vital force to waving a fan the day before yesterday. Then I think that the thinking of the mind, the hearing of the ears, the seeing of the eyes, the holding of the hands, and the walking of the feet seem to be all that the vital force does not control. There must be something that directs the operation of vital force. (How do you think about this?)

Answer：In the vital force, naturally, there dwells something intelligent. [Jie]

39 虚灵自是心之本体，非我所能虚也。耳目之视听，所以视听者即其心也，岂有形象。然有耳目以视听之，则犹有形象也。若心之虚灵，何尝有物！人杰。

The *xuling* 虚灵（void intelligence）is naturally the original being of the mind and it is not that we can cause it to be in a state of void. The reason why eyes and ears can see and hear lies in the mind. Can the mind have a visible shape? Nevertheless, when we hear something by our ears and see it by our eyes, there seems to be some visible shape of the mind. But there is never a concrete shape of the void intelligence of the mind. [Renjie]

40 问："五行在人为五脏。然心却具得五行之理，以心虚灵之故否？"曰："心属火，缘是个光明发动底物，所以具得许多道理。"僩。

Question：The Five Agents are embodied as the five internal organs①in a person, but the mind possesses all the principles of the Five Agents. Is it because of the void intelligence of the mind?

Answer：The mind pertains to fire, and because it is, as it were, something that gives light and offers dynamics, it possesses many principles. [Xian]

41 问："人心形而上下如何？"曰："如肺肝五脏之心，却是实有一物。若今学者所论操舍存亡之心，则自是神明不测。故五脏之心受病，则可用药补之；这个心，则非菖蒲、茯苓所可补也。"问："如此，则心之理乃是形而上否？"曰："心比性，则微有迹；比气，则自然又灵。"谦。

Question：Is the *xin* of humankind metaphysical or physical?

Answer：If it is the *xin* which refers to the heart, one of the five internal organs of a person, it is a thing, indeed. But the *xin* which scholars today

---

① The "five internal organs" refers to heart, liver, spleen, lungs and kidneys.

mention in their discourses such as "If one hold *xin* fast, it remains with him; if one lets it go, he loses it" refers to the mind, which is as inscrutable as spirits and deities. Therefore, if one's heart in his five internal organs is ill, he can remedy it by taking medicines. But if his mind is ill, it can by no means be remedied by calamus or tuckahoe or any other medicines. [Qian]

42 问："先生尝言，心不是这一块。某窃谓，满体皆心也，此特其枢纽耳。"曰："不然，此非心也，乃心之神明升降之舍。人有病心者，乃其舍不宁也。凡五脏皆然。心岂无运用，须常在躯壳之内。譬如此建阳知县，须常在衙里。始管得这一县也。"某曰："然则程子言'心要在腔子里'，谓当在舍之内，而不当在舍之外耶？"曰："不必如此。若言心不可在脚上，又不可在手上，只得在这些子上也。"义刚。

Question: You, sir, once said that the *xin* was not this piece (heart). In my humble opinion, all one's entire body is his *xin*, but isn't this *xin* (heart) only the pivot of the body?

Answer: No. That (body) is not the *xin* (mind) but the house where its spirit goes up and down. If there is something wrong with it, its house will get unquiet. This is also true of the five internal organs. The mind, of course, plays its function, but that has to be within the physical body. It can be comparable to the Magistrate of Jianyang County who has to work in his office. Or else, he would not be able to administer the county.

Further question: However, when Master Cheng said, "The mind must remain in the body," doesn't he mean that it should be within the house rather than outside it?

Answer: You do not necessarily understand him in that way. It is like saying that it can not be said that one's mind resides in his hands, or in his feet, for it only resides within all such. [Yigang]

43 性犹太极也，心犹阴阳也。太极只在阴阳之中，非能离阴阳也。然至论太极，自是太极；阴阳自是阴阳。惟性与心亦然。所谓一而二，二而一也。韩子以仁义礼智信言性，以喜怒哀乐言情，盖愈于诸子之言性。然至分三品，却只说得气，不曾说得性。砥。以下总论心性。

The nature is comparable to the Great Ultimate and the mind to *yin* and *yang*. The Great Ultimate exists only in the *yin* and *yang*, and cannot be separated from them. In the final analysis, however, the Great Ultimate is the Great Ultimate and *yin* and *yang* are *yin* and *yang*. So it is with regard to either nature or mind. They are one and yet two, two and yet one, so to speak. Master Han Yü discoursed nature as benevolence, righteousness, propriety, wisdom, and faithfulness and the feelings as pleasure, anger, sorrow, and joy. This is an advance over other philosophers on the problem of human nature. As to his division of human nature into three grades (superior, medium, and inferior), he only explained vital force but not nature. [①] [Di] The several conversations below are concerned with a general view of mind and nature.

44 问："天之付与人物者为命，人物之受于天者为性，主于身者为心，有得于天而光明正大者为明德否？"曰："心与性如何分别？明如何安顿？受与得又何以异？人与物与身又何间别？明德合是心，合是性？"曰："性却实。以感应虚明言之，则心之意亦多。"曰："此两个说着一个，则一个随到，元不可相离，亦自难与分别。舍心则无以见性，舍性又无以见心，故孟子言心性，每每相随说。仁义礼智是性，又言'恻隐之心、羞恶之心、辞逊、是非之心'，更细思量。"大雅。

Question: That which Heaven confers on humankind and things is destiny; that which humankind and things receive from Heaven is nature; what predominates the body is mind; what is gained from Heaven and is bright, upright, and great is the brilliant virtue. Are all these sayings right?

Answer (by asking questions): How to distinguish between mind and nature? Where to place the "bright"? What is the difference between

---

① The translation of this passage is based on the version by Chan Wing-tsit, p. 630, with slight modification.

"confer" and "receive"? How to differentiate humankind, thing, and body? Is the "brilliant virtue" said in regard to the mind or the nature?

The first questioner replied, "The nature is concrete. To put it in terms of the inductive response to vacuity and brightness, what the mind means is also much."

Further answer: Of them, when one is spoken of, the other has to be considered concurrently, for they are actually inseparable and also hard naturally to distinguish. Without considering the mind, the nature would by no means be seen, and without considering the nature, the mind would by no means be seen, either. That is why whenever Mencius discoursed mind and nature, he talked about one without losing sight of the other. When he said that the benevolence, righteousness, propriety, and wisdom constituted the nature, he also mentioned the feelings of sadness and commiseration, of shame and dislike, of deference and compliance, and of right and wrong, which indicates his more careful thought. [Daya]

45 或问心性之别。曰："这个极难说，且是难为譬喻。如伊川以水喻性，其说本好，却使晓不得者生病。心，大概似个官人；天命，便是君之命；性，便如职事一般。此亦大概如此，要自理会得。如邵子云："性者，道之形体。"盖道只是合当如此，性则有一个根苗，生出君臣之义，父子之仁。性虽虚，都是实理。心虽是一物，却虚，故能包含万理。这个要人自体察始得。"学蒙。方子录云："性本是无，却是实理。心似乎有影象，然其体却虚。"

Someone asked about the difference between mind and nature. The Master answered, "It is extremely hard to clarify and also difficult to find something proper by which to draw an analogy between them. When Yichuan (i. e. Cheng Yi) took water for example, though his analogy was good in itself, it was productive of trouble on the part of those who failed to see it right. The mind is probably comparable to a government official and the mandate of Heaven is, to the order of the sovereign. Then the nature is like the duties the official is obliged to fulfill. This analogy is basically right, yet you have to try to attain a personal understanding of the truth therein. As Master Shao (i. e. Shao Yong) said, 'Nature is the physical form of the Way. ' Probably he means only that the Way is only what it is, yet the nature has its source, which gives rise to the sovereign-minister righteousness and the father-son benevolence. Although nature is vacuous, it consists of concrete principles. Although the mind is a distinct entity, it is vacuous, and therefore embraces all principles. This truth will be apprehended only when people examine it by themselves. " [Xuemeng] For the last three sentences, the record by Fangzi reads, "The nature is originally non-being①, but consists of concrete principles. The mind seems to show itself in images and shapes, but its being is vacuous. "

46 旧尝以论心、论性处，皆类聚看。看熟，久则自见。淳。

You'd better collect my discourses on mind and those on nature and read them together. After some time, when you get very familiar with them, their meanings will present themselves to you clear in due course. [Chun (淳)]

47 性便是心之所有之理，心便是理之所会之地。下 "心" 字，饶录 作 "性"。升卿。

Nature consists of principles embraced in the mind, and the mind is where these principles are united. ②For the second "mind" in this record, the record in the Raozhou edition is "nature." [Shengqing]③

48 性是理，心是包含该载，敷施发用底。夔孙。

Nature is principle. The mind is its embracement and reservoir, and issues it forth into operation. ④ [Kuisun]

49 问心之动、性之动。曰："动处是心，动底是性。"宇。

When asked about the activity of the mind and that of the nature, the

---

① Hesun suspected that the part of the sentence had been "The nature is originally formless. "

② The translation of this passage is based on the version by Chan Wing-tsit, p. 631.

③ Huang Gao 黄㮚 (courtesy name Shengqing 升卿).

④ The translation of this passage is based on the version by Chan Wing-tsit, p. 631.

Master answered, "Where the activity occurs is the mind and what is in activity is the nature." [Yu]

50 心以性为体，心将性做馅子模样。盖心之所以具是理者，以有性故也。盖卿。

The mind takes the nature as its substance. The mind and nature are, as it were, the wrapper and filling. Probably the reason why the mind possesses its principle lies in the nature. [Gaiqing]①

51 心有善恶，性无不善。若论气质之性，亦有不善。节。

Mind may be good or evil, but nature is never not good. When it comes to physical nature, it may be not good. [Jie]

52 郑仲履问："先生昨说性无不善，心固有不善。然本心则元无不善。"曰："固是本心元无不善，谁教你而今却不善了！今人外面做许多不善，却只说我本心之善自在，如何得！"盖卿。

Zheng Zhonglü 郑仲履 (dates unknown, a disciple of Zhu Xi's) asked, "Yesterday, you mentioned, 'Nature is never not good, whereas certainly mind may be not good.' But mind is originally free from non-goodness, isn't it?" The Master answered, "It is true that mind is originally free from non-goodness, but who has taught you now that the mind has become not good? Nowadays, when some people have done a lot of bad things outside, they claim actually that their original good mind is always there inside them. How can that be possible?" [Gaiqing]

53 心、性、理，拈着一个，则都贯穿，惟观其所指处轻重如何。如"养心莫善于寡欲，虽有不存焉者寡矣"。"存"虽指理言，然心自在其中。"操则存"，此"存"虽指心言，然理自在其中。端蒙。

Whenever any one of mind, nature, and principle is mentioned in discourses, the meanings of them should be considered concurrently, yet what is important is to consider whether what it refers to in a specific context is

---

① Xi Gaiqing 奚盖卿 (courtesy name Mengxi 梦锡).

emphasized or not. For example, "To nourish the mind, there is nothing better than to make the desires few··· for some things, one may not be able to keep in his mind, but they will be few." (*Mencius*, 7B:81) Here the "keep" is said in regard to principle, but mind is also meant naturally therein. In the "Hold it fast, and it remains with you," (*Mencius*, 6A:8)① though the "remain" is said in relation to mind, principle is also involved naturally therein. [Duanmeng]

54 或问:"人之生,禀乎天之理以为性,其气清则为知觉。而心又不可以知觉言,当如何?"曰:"难说。以'天命之谓性'观之,则命是性,天是心,心有主宰之义。然不可无分别,亦不可太说开成两个,当熟玩而默识其主宰之意可也。"高。

Question: When a person is given life to, the principle he is endowed with by Heaven is his nature, and if the vital force is clear, it will be consciousness. But mind can not be equaled to consciousness. How to solve this problem?

Answer: It is hard to say. From the viewpoint of "What Heaven has conferred is called the nature," what is conferred by Heaven is nature and Heaven is mind in the sense that mind is the dominator. However, in discussing nature and mind, a distinction must be made between them and meanwhile they should not be separated too far from each other as two different sides. If you can ponder them and get familiar with them, and then understand in silence them in the sense of the dominator, that will be adequate. [Gao]②

55 说得出,又名得出,方是见得分明。如心、性,亦难说。尝曰:"性者,心之理;情者,性之动;心者,性情之主。"德明。

Only when one can speak it out and name it explicitly can he be said as

---

① The translation of the two citations from *Mencius* is based on a version by J. Legge, with slight modification (see http://ctext.org/mengzi).

② Shu Gao 舒高 (courtesy name unknown).

being clear about it. When it comes to such points as mind and nature, they are hard to clarify. I once said, "Nature is the principle of mind; feelings are the activities of nature; mind is the dominator of nature and feelings." [Deming]

56 性对情言，心对性情言。合如此是性，动处是情，主宰是心。大抵心与性，似一而二，似二而一，此处最当体认。可学。

Nature is opposite to feelings and mind is opposite to nature and feelings. That which is what it is is nature, where activity occurs is feelings, and what dominates is mind. Roughly speaking, mind and nature are one and yet two, two and yet one. This is a point most deserving one's effort to gain a personal understanding of it. [Kexue]

57 有这性，便发出这情；因这情，便见得这性。因今日有这情，便见得本来有这性。方子。

It is this nature that emanates these feelings; it is due to these feelings that manifest this nature. It is because of these feelings today that there being originally this nature is known. [Fangzi]

58 性不可言。所以言性善者，只看他恻隐、辞逊四端之善则可以见其性之善，如见水流之清，则知源头必清矣。四端，情也，性则理也。发者，情也，其本则性也，如见影知形之意。力行。

Nature is beyond words. Therefore, to talk about nature being good, one needs to observe the goodness of the four beginnings, i. e. the feeling of sadness and commiseration, of shame and dislike, of deference and compliance, and of right and wrong, which indicate nature being good. It is like, by seeing the limpid flow of water, knowing for sure that its source must be limpid. The four beginnings are feelings, while nature is principle. What is emanated is the feelings, whereas their root is in nature. This can be known, as, when we see a shadow, we know the form. [Lixing]

59 在天为命，禀于人为性，既发为情。此其脉理甚实，仍更分明易晓。唯心乃虚明洞彻，统前后而为言耳。据性上说"寂然不动"处是心，亦得；据情上说"感而遂通"处是心，亦得。故孟子说"尽其心者，知其性也"，文义可见。性则具仁义礼智之端，实而易察。知此实理，则心无不尽，尽亦只是尽晓得耳。如云尽晓得此心者，由知其性也。大雅。

What depends on Heaven is destiny and what humankind is endowed with is nature, which emanates as feelings. The conceptual sequence of these terms is explicit and more easily understandable. They are said only around the mind which is vacuous and bright, and clear to see. In regard to nature, it is also acceptable to say that where "It is still and without movement" is mind, and in regard to feeling, it is also intelligible to say that where "When acted on, it penetrates forthwith" is mind. [①]Therefore, *Mencius* (7 A: 1) said, "He who has exerted his mind to the utmost knows his nature," the meaning of which is obvious to see. Nature embraces the beginnings of benevolence, righteousness, propriety, and wisdom, so it is actually easy to observe. If one knows such substantial principle, he will be able to exert his mind to the utmost. The "to the utmost" means nothing but completeness in understanding. If one is said to have understood completely his mind, it means he has known his nature. [Daya]

60 景绍问心性之别。曰："性是心之道理，心是主宰于身者。四端便是情，是心之发见处。四者之萌皆出于心，而其所以然者，则是此性之理所在也。"道夫问："'满腔子是恻隐之心'，如何?"曰："腔子是人之躯壳。上蔡见明道，举经史不错一字，颇以自矜。明道曰：'贤却记得许多，可谓玩物丧志矣?'上蔡见明道说，遂满面发赤，汗流浃背。明道曰：'只此便是恻隐之心。'公要见满腔子之说，但以是观之。"问："玩物之说主甚事?"曰："也只是'矜'字。"道夫。

Jingshao 景绍 (courtesy name of Zheng Zhaoxian 郑昭先 [dates

---

① The two citations in the sentence are from "Xici Shang" 系辞上 (Appended Remarks I) of the *Classic of Change*.

unknown], a disciple of Zhu Xi's) asked about the difference between mind and nature. The Master answered, "Nature is the principle of mind and mind is the dominator of the body. The four beginnings are feelings, which are indicators of mind. The four beginnings are all originated from mind, while what causes them is that which the principle of the nature dwells in." I asked, "How do you think about 'The entire cavity is filled with the mind of sadness and commiseration' (said by Master Cheng Hao)?" The Master answered, "The 'cavity' refers to the human body. When Shangcai 上蔡 (i. e. 谢良佐 [1050 – 1103]) once visited Mingdao 明道 (i. e. Cheng Hao), he recited some classics and histories without any error and appeared very complacent. Mingdao said, 'You are a worthy man, yet you have only memorized so many. Haven't you paid excessive attention to such trivia but sapped your aspiration?' Hearing Mingdao's criticism, Shangcai blushed, with sweat streaming down his back. Mingdao went on saying 'This (blushing) can indicate your mind of sadness and commiseration.' You can draw on these words by Mingdao when you try to understand his 'The entire cavity is filled with the mind of commiseration'." I asked further, "What did Master Cheng mainly intend to say by 'excessive attention to such trivia'?" The Master replied, "It is nothing but what the sino-graph *jin* 矜 (complacency) means." [Daofu]

61 伯丰论性有已发之性，有未发之性。曰："性才发，便是情。情有善恶，性则全善。心又是一个包总性情底。大抵言性，便须见得是元受命于天，其所禀赋自有本根，非若心可以一概言也。却是汉儒解'天命之谓性'，云'木神仁，金神义'等语，却有意思，非苟言者。学者要体会亲切。"又叹曰："若不用明破，只恁涵养，自有到处，亦自省力。若欲立言示训，则须契勘教子细，庶不悖于古人！"大雅。

Bofeng talked about the aroused nature and the un-aroused nature. The Master said, "The moment the nature emanates, it gives rise to feeling. The feeling may be good or evil, but the nature is completely good. Mind is what embraces both nature and feeling. Generally, when discussing nature, one should understand that it is endowed originally by Heaven and it has its root in that endowment, so it should not be included in what mind means. The Confucians of the Han dynasty, when explaining 'What is conferred by Heaven is called nature,' tended to say 'The spirit of wood pertains to benevolence, the spirit of metal pertains to righteousness' and the like, which is interesting and not careless discourse. You learners should try to get a personal understanding of them. " He sighed with emotion, "If one depends only on self-cultivation, without resorting to others' explicit verbal explication, he will gain his personal understanding and that calls also for less mental effort. If one intends to write words for verbal explication, then he should make careful collation of the original texts, making sure that his explication does not go counter to what the ancients intended to mean. " [Daya]

62 履之问未发之前心性之别。曰："心有体用,未发之前是心之体,已发之际乃心之用,如何指定说得!盖主宰运用底便是心,性便是会恁地做底理。性则一定在这里,到主宰运用却在心。情只是几个路子,随这路子恁地做去底,却又是心。"道夫。

Lüzhi asked about the difference between mind and nature before emanating. The Master said, "Mind possesses substance and function. Before its emanation, it is the substance, while after that, it is its function. But how can they be said as something fixed at a certain time? Probably, it is the mind that controls the function and the nature is but the principle which makes that happen. The nature is certain to dwell here, while that which controls the function lies in the mind. The feelings are only several outlets, but it is again the mind that lets the outlets operate in their own ways. " [Daofu]

63 或问:"静是性,动是情?"曰:"大抵都主于心。'性'字从'心',从'生';'情'字从'心',从'青'。性是有此理。且如'天命之谓性',要须天命个心了,方是性。"汉卿问:"心如个藏,四方八面都恁地光明皎洁，如佛家所谓六窗中有一猴，这边叫也应，那边叫也应。"曰："佛家说心处，尽有好处。前辈云，胜于杨墨。"贺孙。

Someone asked, "Is tranquility nature 性 and is activity feeling 情?" The Master answered, "Basically, they are subject to mind 心 . The sinograph *xing* 性 is composed of the two components of *xin* 忄（i. e. variant of 心）and *sheng* 生（production）; the sino-graph *qing* 情 is composed of *xin* 忄 and *qing* 青（green）. The *xing* 性 means there being such principle. For example, as meant by 'What is conferred by Heaven is called nature,' Heaven has to confer a *xin* 忄 before there occurs *xing* 性 ." Hanqing（i. e. Fu Guang）asked, "The mind is comparable to a depository of Buddhist sutras, inside which everywhere is light, bright, and clear. It is as if, as said in Buddhist sutras, an ape living inside the house with 'six windows,'[1] who can respond to the call from this or that window. " The Master replied, "The discourse of Buddhism on mind is replete with insights. It was said by a previous Confucian that its exposition is better than that of Yangzi and Mozi. " [Hesun]

64 叔器问："先生见教，谓'动处是心，动底是性'。窃推此二句只在'底'、'处'两字上。如谷种然，生处便是谷，生底却是那里面些子。"曰："若以谷譬之，谷便是心，那为粟，为菽，为禾，为稻底，便是性。康节所谓"心者，性之郛郭"是也。包裹底是心，发出不同底是性。心是个没思量底，只会生。又如吃药，吃得会治病是药力，或凉，或寒，或热，便是药性。至于吃了有寒证，有热证，便是情。"义刚。

Shuqi 叔器（dates unknown, a disciple of Zhu Xi's）, said to the Master, "You, sir, instructed me that 'Where the activity occurs is the mind and what is in activity is the nature. ' In my humble opinion, the key words

---

① The "six windows," according to Buddhism, are also called the "six roots of sensations," i. e. eye, ear, nose, tongue, body, and mind.

here are 'where' and 'what.' That can be comparable to the growing grain, for where the kernel appears is the grain, but what makes that happen is something inside." The Master responded, "If we take the seed of grain for example, the grain is comparable to the mind, while that which makes the millet, the beans, the rice, the wheat, is the nature. That is what Kangjie meant when he said, 'The mind is the outer city walls of the nature.' What wraps the nature is the mind, while what makes difference is the nature. The mind, which does, as it were, nothing of thinking, can do nothing but giving rise to something. Taking medicine may serve as another example here. The reason why a certain medicine can cure a certain disease is its medicinal efficacy, while it may be cool, cold, or hot, which indicates its nature. When one takes a medicine, he may display a cold or hot syndrome, and this indicates feelings." [Yigang]

65 旧看五峰说，只将心对性说，一个情字都无下落。后来看横渠"心统性情"之说，乃知此话有大功，始寻得个"情"字着落，与孟子说一般。孟子言："恻隐之心，仁之端也。"仁，性也；恻隐，情也，此是情上见得心。又曰"仁义礼智根于心"，此是性上见得心。盖心便是包得那性情，性是体，情是用。"心"字只一个字母，故"性"、"情"字皆从"心"。偲。

Some time ago, I read some discourses by Wufeng 五峰 (Hu Hong 胡宏 [1100 – 1155]) in which he spoke of the mind only in contrast to nature, leaving the feelings unaccounted for. Later when I read Hengqü's (Zhang Zai's) doctrine that "The mind commands man's nature and feelings," I realized that it was a great contribution. Only then did I find a satisfactory account of the feelings. His doctrine agrees with that of Mencius. In the words of Mencius, "The feeling of commiseration is the beginning of benevolence." Now benevolence is nature, and commiseration is feeling. In this, the mind can be seen through the feelings. He further said, "Benevolence, righteousness, propriety, and wisdom are rooted in the mind. " In this, the mind is seen through nature. For the mind embraces both nature and the feelings. Nature is substance and feelings are function. [1] Of the three sino-graphs, i. e. *xin* (mind), *xing* (nature), and *qing* (feeling), *xin* was first coined and *xing* and *qing* were made on the basis of it. [Xian]

66 人多说性方说心，看来当先说心。古人制字，亦先制得"心"字，"性"与"情"皆从"心"。以人之生言之，固是先得这道理。然才生这许多道理，却都具在心里。且如仁义自是性，孟子则曰"仁义之心"；恻隐、羞恶自是情，孟子则曰"恻隐之心，羞恶之心"。盖性即心之理，情即性之用。今先说一个心，便教人识得个情性底总脑，教人知得个道理存着处。若先说性，却似性中别有一个心。横渠"心统性情"语极好。又曰："合性与知觉有心之名，则恐不能无病，便似性外别有一个知觉了！"

Many people discuss first nature and then mind, but I think mind should be discussed first. When ancients created graphs, they first coined *xin* and then on the basis of it, *xing* and *qing*. From the viewpoint of the production of humankind, the principle is certainly the first to be conferred. But as soon as the many principles are conferred, they come to dwell in the mind. For example, both benevolence and righteousness pertain to nature, yet Mencius said "the mind of benevolence and righteousness. " As regards the feelings of sadness and commiseration and of shame and dislike, Mencius also said "the mind of sadness and commiseration and of shame and dislike. " Probably nature is the principle of mind and feeling is the function of nature. Now if we discuss mind first, that will instruct learners to get some idea of the control center for the nature and feeling and let them know where the principle resides. Master Zhang Zai said very well, "The mind commands human nature and feelings. " But he also said that "In the unity of the nature and

---

[1] The translation of this passage is based on the version by Chan Wing-tsit, p. 631, with slight modification.

consciousness, there is the mind." I am afraid this idea is not free from error, for it is as though there were a consciousness outside nature.

67 或问心情性。曰："孟子说'恻隐之心，仁之端也'一段，极分晓。恻隐、羞恶、是非、辞逊是情之发，仁义礼智是性之体。性中只有仁义礼智，发之为恻隐、辞逊、是非，乃性之情也。如今人说性，多如佛老说，别有一件物事在那里，至玄至妙，一向说开去，便入虚无寂灭。吾儒论性却不然。程子云：'性即理也。'此言极无病。'孟子道性善'，善是性合有底道理。然亦要子细识得善处，不可但随人言语说了。若子细下工夫，子细寻究，自然见得。如今人全不曾理会，才见一庸人胡说，便从他去。尝得项平甫书云，见陈君举门人说：'儒释，只论其是处，不问其同异。'遂敬信其说。此是甚说话！元来无所有底人，见人胡说话，便惑将去。若果有学，如何谩得他！如举天下说生姜辣，待我吃得真个辣，方敢信。胡五峰说性多从东坡子由们见识说去。"谦。

Someone asked about mind, nature, and feelings. The Master answered, "The section with 'The feeling of sadness and commiseration is the beginning of benevolence' in the *Mencius* (2A: 6) clarifies them very explicitly. All the feelings of sadness and commiseration, shame and dislike, deference and compliance, and right and wrong are the emanated feelings, and benevolence, righteousness, propriety, and wisdom are the substance of nature. In the nature are only benevolence, righteousness, propriety, and wisdom, which are emanated as the feelings attributed to nature, i. e. the feelings of sadness and commiseration, shame and dislike, deference and compliance, and right and wrong. Today when people talk about nature, they tend to say, as Buddhists and Taoists have claimed, that there is a separate thing somewhere, which is supremely mysterious and wonderful and their floods of words end up with only nothingness and quietus. We Confucians are different. Master Cheng said, 'Nature is the same as principle,' which is completely free from error. Mencius regarded nature as being good, which means that the good is the principle which makes nature what it is. Nevertheless, you have to be careful and see where the good is, avoiding following blindly what others say. If you make strenuous effort and probe punctiliously in this regard, you will understand it naturally in due course. Nowadays, most people do not strive to attain a personal understanding, but merely accept blindly the nonsense a certain mediocre scholar drivels about. Years ago, I read a letter written by Xiang Pingfu 项平甫（i. e. 项安世 [1129 – 1208]）, which said that, when he heard a disciple of Chen Junju 陈君举（i. e. 陈傅良 [1137 – 1203]）state 'Whether it is Confucianism or Buddhism, we discuss only where it is right rather than the difference of one from the other,' he respected and believed that opinion. How could he do that? If one has nothing of his own, when hearing someone else talking about something, he is liable to believe it, unable to recognize it as nonsense. If one is learned, how can he be misled? For example, even if everyone else says the fresh ginger is hot, only when I taste it by myself dare I believe its being hot. Hu Wufeng's (Hu Hong's) discourse on nature drew basically from the opinions held by Dongpo 东坡（i. e. Su Shi 苏轼 [1037 – 1101]）and Ziyou 子由（i. e. Su Zhe 苏辙 [1039 – 1112], younger brother of Su Shi). " [Qian]

68 问性、情、心、仁。曰："横渠说得最好，言：'心，统性情者也。'孟子言：'恻隐之心，仁之端；羞恶之心，义之端。'极说得性、情、心好。性无不善。心所发为情，或有不善。说不善非是心，亦不得。却是心之本体本无不善，其流为不善者，情之迁于物而然也。性是理之总名，仁义礼智皆性中一理之名。恻隐、羞恶、辞逊、是非是情之所发之名，此情之出于性而善者也。其端所发甚微，皆从此心出，故曰：'心，统性情者也。'性不是别有一物在心里。心具此性情。心失其主，却有时不善。如'我欲仁，斯仁至'；我欲不仁，斯失其仁矣。'回也三月不违仁'，言不违仁，是心有时乎违仁也。'出入无时，莫知其乡。'存养主一，使之不失去，乃善。大要在致知，致知在穷理，理穷自然知至。要验学问工夫，只看所知至与不至，不是要逐件知过，因一事研磨一理，久久自然光明。如一镜然，今日磨些，明日磨些，不觉自光。若一些子光，工夫又歇，仍旧一尘镜，已光处会昏，未光处不复光矣。且如'仁'之一字，上蔡只说知仁，孔子便说为仁。是要做工夫去为仁，岂可道知得便休！今学问流而为禅，上蔡为之首。今人自无实学，见得说这一般好，也投降；那一般好，也投降。许久南轩在此讲学，诸公全无实得处。胡乱有一人入潭州城里说，人便靡然从之，此是何道理！学问只理会个是与不是，不要添许多无益说话。今人为学，多是为名，又去安排讨名，全不顾义理。说苑载证父者以为直，及加刑，又请代受以为孝。孔子曰：'父一也，而取二名！'此是宛转取名之弊。学问只要心里见得分明，便从上面做去。如'杀身成仁'，不是自家计较要成仁方死，只是见得此事生为不安，死为安，便自杀身。旁人见得，便说能成仁。此旁人之言，非我之心要如此。所谓'经德不回，非以干禄；哭死而哀，非为生也'。若有一毫为人之心，便不是了。南轩云：'为己之学，无所为而然。'是也。"谦。

When asked about nature, feelings, mind, and benevolence, the Master answered, "Hengqü said extremely well, 'Mind is that which commands nature and feelings.' Mencius discoursed very well on nature, feelings, and mind, 'The feeling of sadness and commiseration is the beginning of benevolence. The feeling of shame and dislike is the beginning of righteousness.' (*Mencius*, 2A: 6) Nature is all good. What is emanated from the mind is feelings, which may be not good. It should not be said that the mind is not good, for the original state of the mind is all good, yet after that it may become not good, because the feelings emanated from the mind are subject to outside things. The nature is the general name of principles and all the benevolence, righteousness, propriety, and wisdom are names of the principles in the nature. The sadness and commiseration, shame and dislike, deference and compliance, and right and wrong are names of the emanated feelings, all of which are attributed to the nature and are good. The beginnings of their emanations are very little, which all issue from the mind; hence 'Mind is that which commands nature and feelings.' As for the nature, it is not a separate entity in the mind. The mind embraces the nature and feelings. When the mind loses its master, it is not good sometimes. For example, 'I wish to be benevolent, and now the benevolence is at hand,' (*Analects*, 7: 30) and when 'I' wish to be not benevolent, now the benevolence is lost. 'Such was Hui (i.e. Yan Hui) that for three months he would not go against benevolence.' (*Analects*, 6: 7) Though it says 'not go against benevolence,' it actually means that in his mind he would have something contrary to benevolence sometimes. 'Its outgoing and incoming cannot be defined as to time or place.' (*Mencius*, 6A: 8) Either preservation or nourishment should be oriented to the same focus, avoiding losing it, and then that will be good. Essentially, one should make efforts to pursue knowledge by striving to inquire principle to the utmost and when the principle is inquired to the utmost, the complete knowledge will naturally come. To testify one's learning and accomplishment, it is enough to see whether his knowledge is complete or not. That means not that one has to experience everything and get knowledge of it, but that for a matter, he should ponder its principle, and then he can apply it to other matters of the same type. With the passage of time, he will be naturally enlightened. This process is comparable to making a copper mirror. When one polishes it today, continues polishing it further tomorrow, and keeps on polishing it day by day, then the mirror will be naturally more and more bright though he is not necessarily aware of it. If one polishes it for a few days but then discontinues, the mirror remains dusty, on which the polished spot will get less bright and the unpolished spot will never get bright again. Take benevolence for another example. Shangcai only mentioned knowing benevolence, while what Confucius advocated is practicing benevolence, who urged others to make efforts to practice it. How can it be said that one stops at only knowing it?

Nowadays, the learning of Confucian scholars is inclined downward to the Chan Buddhism and among them the most representative one is Shangcai. Devoid of solid scholarship, many scholars today, when finding this theory good, yield to it and, when finding that theory good, also yield to it. Some time ago when Nanxuan 南轩 (style name of Zhang Shi 张栻 [1133 - 1180]), an accomplished scholar, lectured on learning here, none of those scholars present on the occasion got any true understanding of him. But when someone entered the city of Tanzhou (present-day Changsha, Hunan Province) and preached some ridiculous opinions, they all went and followed him submissively. What reason drove them to do that? In pursuit of learning, what matters is only understanding what is right and what is not, and saying words to no avail should be avoided. Many people have gone in for learning for no other purpose than gaining some fame and some have even tried to get fame by any means, without considering anything about the principle. As recorded in the book *Shuoyuan* 说苑 (Garden of Anecdotes, by Liu Xiang 刘向 [77 - 6 BC]), a person bore witness against his father to show his uprightness, and when his father was sentenced, he offered to serve the sentence in stead of his father, by which he wanted to show his filial piety. Confucius said, 'He had one father, yet he gained two fames!' This case indicates the malpractice of gaining fame indirectly. In regard to learning, so long as one can see the truth clear in his mind, he needs only to practice it in person. For example, the saying of 'one sacrificing his life to preserve his benevolence complete.' That does not mean that one intended to kill himself to preserve his benevolence complete, but rather mean that he understood that, as regards something, if he lived on, he would feel no mental peace, and only his death would bring that peace to him, so he killed himself. But others saw it as his sacrificing his life to preserve his benevolence complete. Such words were said by others, but they did not mean what he had intended. Mencius said, 'Weeping for the dead should be from real sorrow and not for a show to the living. The regular path of benevolence is to be pursued without any bend, free from any aim at emolument. ' (*Mencius*, 7B: 79) If one harbors even an iota of intention to pursue learning for show to others, he is not correct. Nanxuan was right when he said 'One's pursuit of learning for no other purpose than himself will bring him success in learning. ' " [Qian]

69　性、情、心，惟孟子横渠说得好。仁是性，恻隐是情，须从心上发出来。"心，统性情者也。"性只是合如此底，只是理，非有个物事。若是有底物事，则既有善，亦必有恶。惟其无此物，只是理，故无不善。盖卿。

As regards nature, feeling, and mind, only Mencius and Hengqü discoursed them well. Benevolence pertains to nature, and sadness and commiseration, to feeling, both of which have to be emanated from mind. Hengqü said, "Mind commands nature and feelings. " Nature is only what it is and it is only principle, not being a concrete thing there. If there was such a thing, it would display both good and evil. But since there is no such a thing as that, nature is only principle, so it is all good. [Gaiqing]

70　伊川"性即理也"，横渠"心统性情"二句，颠扑不破！砥。

Both Yichuan's "Nature is the same as principle" and Hengqü's "Mind commands nature and feelings" are indisputably right. [Di]

71　"性是未动，情是已动，心包得已动未动。盖心之未动则为性，已动则为情，所谓'心统性情'也。欲是情发出来底。心如水，性犹水之静，情则水之流，欲则水之波澜，但波澜有好底，有不好底。欲之好底，如'我欲仁'之类；不好底则一向奔驰出去，若波涛翻浪；大段不好底欲则灭却天理，如水之壅决，无所不害。孟子谓情可以为善，是说那情之正，从性中流出来者，元无不好也。"因问："'可欲之谓善'之'欲'，如何?"曰："此不是'情欲'之'欲'，乃是可爱之意。"铢。

The Master said, "Nature is the state before activity begins, the feelings are the state when activity has started, and the mind includes both states.

Nature is the mind before it is aroused, while feelings are the mind after it is aroused, as is expressed in (Zhang Zai's) saying, 'The mind commands man's nature and feelings.' Desire emanates from feelings. The mind is comparable to water, nature is comparable to the tranquility of still water, feeling is comparable to the flow of water, and desire is comparable to its waves. Just as there are good and bad waves, so there are good desires, such as 'I desire benevolence,' and bad desires which rush out like wild and violent waves. When bad desires are substantial, they will destroy the principle of Heaven, as flood bursts a dam and damages everything. When Mencius said that 'Feelings enable people to do good,' (*Mencius*, 6A: 6) he meant that the correct feelings flowing from our nature are originally all good." Thereupon I asked, "What is meant by the *yu* 欲 in 'What deserves *yu* is called good' (*Mencius*, 7B: 71)?" The Master answered, "This *yu* is the same as the *yu* denoting feeling and desire, for it means 'to be loved.'" [1] [Zhu]

72 心，主宰之谓也。动静皆主宰，非是静时无所用，及至动时方有主宰也。言主宰，则混然体统自在其中。心统摄性情，非儱侗与性情为一物而不分别也。端蒙。

The mind means the dominator. It is the dominator whether in the state of activity or in the state of tranquility. It is not true that in the state of tranquility there is no need of a dominator and there is a dominator only when the state becomes one of activity. By the dominator is meant an all-pervading control and command existing in the mind by itself. The mind unites and commands nature and feelings, but it is not united with them as a vague entity without any distinction. [2] [Duanmeng]

73 性以理言，情乃发用处，心即管摄性情者也。故程子曰"有指

---

① The translation of this passage is based on the version by Chan Wing-tsit, p. 631, with some alterations.

② Ibid.

体而言者，'寂然不动'是也"，此言性也；"有指用而言者，'感而遂通'是也"，此言情也。端蒙。

Nature is the same as principle, feeling is the emanated function, and mind works as the commander of nature and feeling. Therefore, Master Cheng said, "Some words are said of the substance, that is, 'It is still and without movement.' Some other words are said of the function, that is, 'When acted on, it penetrates forthwith.'" The former refers to nature, while the latter, to feeling. [Duanmeng]

74 "心统性情"，故言心之体用，尝跨过两头未发、已发处说。仁之得名，只专在未发上。恻隐便是已发，却是相对言之。端蒙。

As Hengqü said, "Mind commands nature and feeling," so when I once talked about the substance and function of the mind, I covered both ends, that is, the state before the emanation starts and that after the emanation started. The naming of benevolence is solely attributed to the not emanated state of the mind. The feeling of sadness and commiseration is the state after the emanation, but it is said so as an opposite. [Duanmeng]

75 心者，主乎性而行乎情。故"喜怒哀乐未发则谓之中，发而皆中节则谓之和"，心是做工夫处。端蒙。

The mind is the master of nature and the practitioner of feelings. Therefore, "While there is no emanation of pleasure, anger, sorrow, or joy, the mind may be said to be in the state of *zhong* 中 (equilibrium). When those feelings have been emanated and act in their due degree, there ensues what may be called the state of *he* 和 (harmony)."[1] (*Doctrine of the Mean*, 1) The mind is that which calls for efforts for its cultivation. [Duanmeng]

76 心之全体湛然虚明，万理具足，无一毫私欲之间；其流行该遍，贯乎动静，而妙用又无不在焉。故以其未发而全体者言之，则性也；以

---

[1] The translation of this citation is based on the version by James Legge, with some modification (http: //ctext. org/liji/zhong-yong).

其已发而妙用者言之，则情也。然"心统性情"，只就浑沦一物之中，指其已发、未发而为言尔；非是性是一个地头，心是一个地头，情又是一个地头，如此悬隔也。端蒙。

The entire mind is vacuous and crystal-clear, replete with all principles and free from even an iota of selfish desire. Its operation is uniform all over, it is pervaded with activity and tranquility, and it is capable completely of all wonderful functions. Thus, its entirety in the state before any emanation is the nature and the wonderful functions in the state after any emanation are feelings. However, the "Mind commands nature and feeling" is said with regard to both the emanated and the not emanated state in the entire thing. It does not mean that nature, mind, and feeling are three different things separate and far apart. [Duanmeng]

77 问："人当无事时，其中虚明不昧，此是气自然动处，便是性。"曰："虚明不昧，便是心；此理具足于中，无少欠阙，便是性；感物而动，便是情。横渠说得好，'由太虚有"天"之名，由气化有"道"之名'，此是总说。'合虚与气，有"性"之名；合性与知觉，有"心"之名'，是就人物上说。"夔孙。

I asked: When a person is free from any cares, there is somewhere inside him which is vacuous, clear, and unobscured, and that is where vital force moves naturally. Isn't that nature?" The Master answered, "The somewhere which is vacuous, clear, and unobscured is the mind; when it embraces all principles, free from any deficiency, that is the nature; when it moves due to induction with things, that is feeling. Henqü said well 'From *taixu* 太虚 (Great Void), there is Heaven. From the transformation of vital force, there is the Way. In the unity of the Great Vacuity and vital force, there is the nature. And in the unity of the nature and consciousness, there is the mind. ' The former two sentences are a general opinion, while the latter two are said in regard to humankind and things. " [Kuisun]

78 问心性情之辨。曰："程子云：'心譬如谷种，其中具生之理是性，阳气发生处是情。'推而论之，物物皆然。"赘。

When asked about the distinction between nature and feeling, the Master answered, "Master Cheng Yi said, 'The mind is comparable to the seed of grain, inside which what possesses the principle of production is nature and where the *yang* vital force triggers the production is feeling. ' By deducing from it, that is true of all other things. "［Xun］

79 因言，心、性、情之分，自程子张子合下见得定了，便都不差。如程子诸门人传得他师见成底说，却一齐差！却或曰："程子张子是他自见得，门人不过只听得他师见成说底说，所以后来一向差。"曰："只那听得，早差了也！"偰。

The Master said thereupon, "As regards the difference among mind, nature, and feeling, when Master Chengs and Master Zhang clarified it at first, their understandings were both right. But, for example, though the disciples of Master Chengs have transmitted, as they have claimed, their teachers' opinions, none of their understandings has been right. " Someone else said, "Master Chengs and Master Zhang got their understandings by themselves, but those disciples heard their teachers' opinions and, without seeing their points truly, tried to relay them to others, so their understandings were inadequate. " The Master responded, "But what those disciples understood while hearing is not what their teachers intended to mean at all. "［Xian］

80 性主"具"字，"有"字。许多道理。昭昭然者属性；未发理具，已发理应，则属心；动发则情。所以"存其心"，则"养其性"。心该备通贯，主宰运用。吕云："未发时心体昭昭。"程云："有指体而言者，有指用而言者。"李先生云："心者贯幽明，通有无。"方。

The nature is the master of or embraces many principles. What is clear and bright pertains to nature; what is not roused is contained in the principles and what is roused is based on the principles, both of which pertain to the mind; what is roused and in activity is feelings. Therefore, Mencius said, "To

preserve one's mind and nourish one's nature (is the way to serve Heaven)."
(*Mencius*, 7A：1) The mind is sufficiently equipped and penetrating all
over, which is the master of functions. Lü (i. e. Lü Dalin) said, "Before the
state of being roused, the substance of the mind is clear and bright." Master
Cheng Yi said, "Some discourses are concerned with the substance of the
mind, while some others, with the function of it." Master Li (Li Tong 李侗
[1093 – 1163], Zhu Xi's teacher) said, "The mind links the world of the
living and that of the dead and penetrates both being and non-being."
[Fang]

81 心如水，情是动处，爱即流向去处。椿。

Mind is like water, feeling is where it moves, and love is that which it
flows towards. [Chun (椿)]

82 问："意是心之运用处，是发处？"曰："运用是发了。"问：
"情亦是发处，何以别？"曰："情是性之发，情是发出恁地，意是主张
要恁地。如爱那物是情，所以去爱那物是意。情如舟车，意如人去使那
舟车一般。"宇。以下兼论意。

Question：Is *yi* 意 (intention) where mind functions or emanates?

Answer：Emanating is the same as functioning.

Further question：Feeling is also where mind emanates. Then how to
distinguish them?

Answer：The feeling is the emanation of nature. It is what has been
emanated in a specific way, while the intention is the motivation for doing in
that specific way. For example, loving a thing is feeling and the reason why
the loving happens is intention. The feeling can also be likened to a boat or
carriage, and then the intention can be likened to one going to use the boat or
carriage. [Yu] The several conversations below also concern intention.

83 心、意犹有痕迹。如性，则全无兆朕，只是许多道理在这
里。砥。

Mind and intention are indicated by some signs, but nature gives completely no such sign, which only embraces many principles. [Di]

84 问："意是心之所发，又说有心而后有意。则是发处依旧是心主之，到私意盛时，心也随去。"曰："固然。"

Question: It is said that the intention is what is emanated by mind. At the same time, it is also said that there is the mind before there arises intention. Then, where the emanation occurs, the mind still remains the dominator, while when the private intention thrives, the mind also goes away following it. (Is this understanding right?)

Answer: Yes, of course.

85 李梦先问情、意之别。曰："情是会做底，意是去百般计较做底，意因有是情而后用。"夔孙录云："因是有情而后用其意。"义刚。

Li Menxian 李梦先 (a disciple of Zhu Xi's, whose dates are unknown) asked about the difference between feeling and intention. The Master answered, "Feeling is that which can do something, while the intention is that which does it by trying every means. The intention, attributable to there being the feeling, plays its function." For the last sentence, Kuisun's record says, "Since there occurs the feeling, then the intention plays its function." [Yigang]

86 问："情、意，如何体认？"曰："性、情则一。性是不动，情是动处，意则有主向。如好恶是情，'好好色，恶恶臭'，便是意。"士毅。

Question: How to distinguish feeling and intention?

Answer: Nature and feeling are in unity. Nature is not in activity, feeling is where activity happens, and intention is orientation. For example, liking and disliking are feelings, while "hating a bad smell, and loving what is beautiful" indicates intention. [Shiyi]

87 未动而能动者，理也；未动而欲动者，意也。若海。

That which is not in activity but is capable of causing activity is principle, while that which is not in activity but desires for activity is intention. [Ruohai]

88 性者，即天理也，万物禀而受之，无一理之不具。心者，一身之主宰；意者，心之所发；情者，心之所动；志者，心之所之，比于情、意尤重；气者，即吾之血气而充乎体者也，比于他，则有形器而较麄者也。又曰："舍心无以见性，舍性无以见心。"椿。以下兼论志。

The Master said, "Nature is the heavenly principle, which is conferred to and received by myriad things, and the nature of each of them embraces the principle. Mind is the master of the body. Intention is the emanation of the mind. Feeling is the activity of the mind. *Zhi* 志 (bent) is what the mind orients itself to, which outweighs feeling and intention. Vital force is the vigor of our blood which fills out bodies and, compared with other concepts, it is embodied as physical forms and concrete things yet relatively coarse. " He added, "Without considering the mind, the nature would by no means be seen, and without considering the nature, the mind would by no means be seen, either. " [Chun (椿)] The following conversations also discuss bent.

89 "心之所之谓之志，日之所之谓之时。'志'字从'之'，从'心'；'旹'字从'之'，从'日'。如日在午时，在寅时，制字之义由此。志是心之所之，一直去底。意又是志之经营往来底，是那志底脚。凡营为、谋度、往来，皆意也。所以横渠云：'志公而意私。'"问："情比意如何？"曰："情又是意底骨子。志与意都属情，'情'字较大，'性、情'字皆从'心'，所以说'心统性情'。心兼体用而言。性是心之理，情是心之用。"侃。

The Master said, "That which the mind orients itself to is called bent, and that which the sun orients itself to is called *shi* 时 (time). The sinograph *zhi* 志 consists originally of two components i. e. *zhi* 之 (going [towards]) and *xin* 心 (mind) and the sino-graph *shi* 旹 (time), a miswritten form of 时, is also composed of *zhi* 之 (going [towards]) and *ri* 日 (the sun). For example, the sun at the time of *wu* 午 or *yin* 寅[1], which

---

① According to the traditional Chinese system of timing, a day is divided into twelve periods. The *wu* time refers to the period of the day from 11 a. m. to 1 p. m. and the *yin* time, to the period of the day from 3 a. m. to 5 a. m.

is the basis for making the sino-graph in either case. The *zhi* 志 means what the mind orients itself to and goes towards it straight. The intention 意 is what operates the *zhi* 志 in coming or going, which serves as the feet of the latter. Whatever operates and performs, plans and schemes, comes and goes, manifests the intention. Therefore, Hengqü said, 'The bent 志 is impartial (public), while the intention 意 is partial (private).' " I asked him, "How is feeling in comparison with intention?" The Master answered, "The feeling is the bone of the intention. Both the bent and the intention pertain to the feeling, so the feeling is more inclusive. Both nature and feeling are based on mind and, therefore, 'The mind commands nature and feeling.' The mind is meant in terms of both substance and function. The nature is the principle of the mind and the feeling is the function of it." [Xian]

90 问意志。曰："横渠云：'以"意、志"两字言，则志公而意私，志刚而意柔，志阳而意阴。'"卓。

When asked about intention and bent, the Master replied, "As Hengqü said, 'As far as *yi* (intention) and *zhi* (bent) are concerned, the bent is impartial, while the intention is partial; the bent is firm, while intention is soft; the bent is positive *yang*, while the intention is negative *yin*.' " [Zhuo][1]

91 志是公然主张要做底事，意是私地潜行间发处。志如伐，意如侵。升卿。

The bent is comparable to what is claimed publicly to be done, while the intention is what is privately schemed to be done. The difference between the bent and the intention is like that between a sovereign dispatching publicly an expedition against his enemy and his infringing privately upon where the enemy is. [Shengqing]

92 问："情与才何别？"曰："情只是所发之路陌，才是会恁地去

---

① Huang Zhuo 黄卓 (courtesy name Xianzhi 先之).

做底。且如恻隐，有恳切者，有不恳切者，是则才之有不同。"又问："如此，则才与心之用相类？"曰："才是心之力，是有气力去做底。心是管摄主宰者，此心之所以为大也。心譬水也；性，水之理也。性所以立乎水之静，情所以行乎水之动，欲则水之流而至于滥也。才者，水之气力所以能流者，然其流有急有缓，则是才之不同。伊川谓'性禀于天，才禀于气'，是也。只有性是一定。情与心与才，便合着气了。心本未尝不同，随人生得来便别了。情则可以善，可以恶。"又曰："要见得分晓，但看明道云：'其体则谓之易，其理则谓之道，其用则谓之神。'易，心也；道，性也；神，情也。此天地之心、性、情也。"砥。以下兼论才。

Question: What is the difference between feeling and *cai* 才 (talent)?

Answer: Feelings are only the roads for emanations, while talent is the capability of doing along the roads. For example, as regards sadness and commiseration, one's feeling of it may be strong, while another's feeling of it may be not so strong. Therefore, different people possess different talents.

Further question: In that case, is talent similar to the function of mind?

Answer: Talent is the strength of mind, which means the strength by which mind is able to do something. The mind is the master for managing things and that is why the mind is predominant. The mind is comparable to water, while nature, the principle of water. Nature is that by which water is tranquil, feeling is that by which it moves, and desire is that by which it flows and even floods. Talent is that strength of water by which it can flow, yet the flowing may be slow or rapid, which manifests the difference in talents. Yichuan (i. e. Cheng Yi) was right when he said, "Nature is endowed by Heaven, while talent is conferred by vital force." Only the nature is certain, while the feeling, mind, and talent all are in conformity to the vital force. The original state of mind is not different to different persons, but when it is bestowed on different persons at birth, it becomes different. Feeling may be good or bad.

Further answer: To see all such clearly, please strive to understand Mingdao's (i. e. Cheng Hao's) "The substance 体 is called change 易; their principle, the Way 道; their function, the inscrutable 神 . " The change refers to the mind; the Way, to nature; the inscrutable, to the feeling. These are the mind, nature, and feeling of Heaven and Earth. " [Di] The following conversations are also concerned with talent.

93 性者，心之理；情者，心之动。才便是那情之会恁地者。情与才绝相近。但情是遇物而发，路陌曲折恁地去底；才是那会如此底。要之，千头万绪，皆是从心上来。道夫。

The nature is the principle of mind and the feeling is the activity of mind. The talent is that by which the feeling is what it is. The feeling and the talent are close to each other absolutely, but the feeling occurs due to the trigger by something, which goes towards an end along a tortuous path, while the talent is what drives that going along the path. In a nutshell, all the multitude of occurrences is ascribable to the mind. [Daofu]

94 问："性之所以无不善，以其出于天也；才之所以有善不善，以其出于气也。要之，性出于天，气亦出于天，何故便至于此？"曰："性是形而上者，气是形而下者。形而上者全是天理，形而下者只是那查滓。至于形，又是查滓至浊者也。"道夫。

Question: The reason why the nature is all good is that it is endowed by Heaven, and the reason why talent may be good or otherwise is that it is conferred by vital force. However, since the nature is from Heaven and vital force is also from Heaven, why is there such difference?

Answer: The nature exists before physical form, while vital force, after physical form. All that exists before physical form is heavenly principle, while all that exists after physical form is dross. As for the physical forms themselves, they are merely the most turbid part of the dross. [Daofu]

95 问："才出于气，德出于性？"曰："不可。才也是性中出，德也是有是气而后有是德。人之有才者出来做得事业，也是它性中有了，便出来做得。但温厚笃实便是德，刚明果敢便是才。只为他气之所禀者生到那里多，故为才。"夔孙。

Question: Does talent stem from vital force and does virtue stem from nature?

Answer: No. Talent also stems from nature and virtue also comes into being after there being vital force. The talented ones of people stand out and achieve merits. It is because they possess their talent in their nature by which they are capable of making that achievement. But if one is gentle and kind, honest and sincere, that is his virtue, while if one is firm and bright, courageous and resolute, that is his talent. When the firmness and brightness, courage and resoluteness brought forth by the vital force one is endowed with prevails in him, that becomes his talent. [Kuisun]

96 问："能为善，便是才。"曰："能为善而本善者是才。若云能为善便是才，则能为恶亦是才也。"人杰。

Question: Is being able to do good the talent?

Answer: What is able to do good and is originally good is talent. If being able to do good is said as talent, isn't being able to do evil also talent? [Renjie]

97 论才气，曰："气是敢做底，才是能做底。"德明。

When discussing talent and vital force, the Master said, "The vital force is that which dares to do something, while the talent is that which is able to do it." [Deming]

98 问："'天命之谓性'，充体谓气，感触谓情，主宰谓心，立趋向谓志，有所思谓意，有所逐谓欲。"答云："此语或中或否，皆出臆度。要之，未可遽论。且涵泳玩索，久之当自有见。"铢尝见先生云："名义之语极难下。如说性，则有天地之性，气质之性。说仁，则伊川有专言之仁，偏言之仁。此等且要默识心通。"人杰。

Question: "What is conferred by Heaven is called nature." What fills the body is called vital force. What is touching is called feeling. What is the master is called mind. What sets up orientation is called bent. That which one thinks about is intention. That which one pursues is called desire. Are all these right?

Answer: Of them, some are right, while others are only surmised. In brief, you should avoid making conclusions rashly. Rather, pore over them and chew them, and in due course you will digest them and get your personal understanding of them.

Zhu (i. e. Dong Zhu) once heard the Master say, "It is extremely difficult to define names and clarify their concepts. For example, as regards nature, there are the nature of Heaven and Earth and the physical nature; concerning benevolence, according to Yichuan, there are separately said benevolence and collectively said benevolence. [①]You should strive to bear all of them in mind and understand them thoroughly." [Renjie]

99 问：“知与思，于人身最紧要。”曰：“然。二者也只是一事。知与手相似，思是交这手去做事也，思所以用夫知也。”卓。

Question: Are *zhi* 知 (knowledge) and *si* 思 (thinking) the two aspects which matter most to a man?

Answer: Yes. Actually the two are only one thing. Knowledge is comparable to a hand, while thinking is comparable to having the hand to do something, so thinking is the function of knowledge. [Zhuo]

---

① According to Cheng Yi, the *wuchang* 五常 (Five Constant Virtues), i. e. benevolence, righteousness, propriety, wisdom, and faithfulness, can be spoken of separately or collectively. Thus, the benevolence can be said separately or as one situated in the entirety of the five constant virtues. (See Chan Wing-tsit, 570)

卷第六 Book 6

性理三
Nature and Principle III
仁义礼智等名义
The Names and Meanings of Benevolence, Righteousness, Propriety, Wisdom, and Some Others

1 道者，兼体、用，该隐、费而言也。节。以下道理。

Dao 道（the Way）embraces substance and function, which should be discoursed as being both secret and far-and-wide reaching. ［Jie］The several conversations below are concerned with the Way and principle.

2 道是统名，理是细目。可学。

The Way is a general name, while the principle 理 represents a detailed catalogue. ［Kexue］

3 道训路，大概说人所共由之路。理各有条理界瓣。因举康节云："夫道也者，道也。道无形，行之则见于事矣。如'道路'之'道'，坦然使千亿万年行之，人知其归者也。"阂祖。

The Master said, "The sino-graph *dao* 道 is explained originally as way, which roughly means the way taken by all people. As for the principle, it consists in various veins with delimited spheres. " Thereupon he cited Kangjie (i. e. Shao Yong) as saying in his *Huangji Jingshi Shu* 皇极经世书 (Supreme Principles Governing the World), "The *Dao* is the Way. Since it is formless, whether one conforms to the Way is manifested on what he does. It is comparable to what is referred to by the sino-graph *dao* 道（way）in *daolu* 道路 (ways), wide and straight, on which humankind has gone and will go for trillions of years, who knows where it leads. " 〔Hongzu〕

4 理是有条瓣逐一路子。以各有条，谓之理；人所共由，谓之道。节。

The principle in a generic sense consists of various veins, each of which is a defined way. Since each vein has its delimited sphere, it is called a principle. The principle shared by all people is called the Way. 〔Jie〕

5 问："道与理如何分?"曰："道便是路，理是那文理。"问："如木理相似?"曰："是。"问："如此却似一般?"曰："'道'字包得大，理是'道'字里面许多理脉。"又曰："'道'字宏大，'理'字精密。"胡泳。

Question: How to distinguish the Way and principle?

Answer: The Way is comparable to a way and the principle is its texture.

Further question: Is the texture like that of wood?

Answer: Yes.

Further question: If so, the Way and principle are similar, aren't they?

Answer: The Way is more inclusive, whereas the principle is the many veins in the Way.

Further answer: The Way is grand and magnificent, while the principle is fine and delicate. 〔Hu Yong〕

6 问："万物粲然，还同不同?"曰："理只是这一个。道理则同，其分不同。君臣有君臣之理，父子有父子之理。"节。

Question: The myriad things are bright and luxuriant. Are they different or not?

Answer: There is the same principle in them. In spite of the same principle, its manifestations are different. There is the sovereign-minister principle between a sovereign and his minister (s) and the father-son principle between a father and his son (s). 〔Jie〕

7 理者有条理，仁义礼智皆有之。节。

The principle possesses veins. So does benevolence, righteousness, propriety, or wisdom. [Jie]

8 问："既是一理，又谓五常，何也?"曰："谓之一理亦可，五理亦可。以一包之则一，分之则五。"问分为五之序。曰："浑然不可分。"节。

Question: Since there is one and the same principle, why are there Five Constant Virtues?

Answer: It can be called one principle and can also be called five principles. If it is regarded as a whole, it is one, but if it is divided into five, it is five.

Further question: What is the sequence of the five principles?

Answer: The principles constitute a complete entirety and their sequence is indefinable. [Jie]

9 只是这个理，分做四段，又分做八段，又细碎分将去。四段者，意其为仁义礼智。当时亦因言文路子之说而及此。节。

The one and same principle is divided into four portions, which are divided into eight sub-portions, which are divided further and further. The four portions are benevolence, righteousness, propriety, and wisdom. When I explained my viewpoint of the principle as a pattern of veins, I also mentioned this. [Jie]

10 理，只是一个理。理举着，全无欠阙。且如言着仁，则都在仁上；言着诚，则都在诚上；言着忠恕，则都在忠恕上；言着忠信，则都在忠信上。只为只是这个道理，自然血脉贯通。端蒙。

There is only one and the same principle. It is complete, free from any deficiency. For example, when it is said with reference to benevolence, it is all concerned with benevolence. When it is said in regard to *cheng* 诚 (sincerity), *zhong-shu* 忠恕 (loyalty-forbearance, which means one cultivating to the utmost the principles of his nature and exercises them on the guideline of reciprocity), or *zhong-xin* 忠信 (loyalty-faithfulness), it is all concerned with sincerity, loyalty-forbearance, and loyalty-faithfulness, respectively. Since there is one and only principle, naturally the veins are free from obstruction. [Duanmeng]

11 理是有条理，有文路子。文路子当从那里去，自家也从那里去；文路子不从那里去，自家也不从那里去。须寻文路子在何处，只挨着理了行。节。

The principle possesses a pattern of lines, showing veins. Where the veins go, we should follow them, but where they do not go, we should not go, either. We should seek after where the veins are, and go along the principles. [Jie]

12 "理如一把线相似，有条理，如这竹篮子相似。"指其上行篾曰："一条子恁地去。"又别指一条曰："一条恁地去。又如竹木之文理相似，直是一般理，横是一般理。有心，便存得许多理。"节。

The Master said, "The principles can be likened to a bundle of lines, with their orderliness similar to that of the neat strips in this bamboo basket." Pointing to those bamboo strips, he said, "Like these bamboo strips which run straight." Then pointing to a bamboo strip, he added, "Like such a bamboo strip running straight. They are also like the texture of the bamboo or wood. Crosswise, there is a principle, while lengthways, there is another principle. The mind contains many principles." [Jie]

13 季通云："理有流行，有对待。先有流行，后有对待。"曰："难说先有后有。"季通举太极说，以为道理皆然，且执其说。人杰。

Jitong said, "Principle is in both operation and opposition. The operation is prior to the opposition." The Master replied, "It is hard to say which comes first." Jitong, citing the theory of *Taiji* 太极 (the Great Ultimate), thought that the priority of operation to opposition is true of all principles and adhered to his opinion. [Renjie]

14 先生与人书中曰："至微之理，至著之事，一以贯之。"节。

The Master said in a letter he wrote to a friend that, "Through either the most subtle principle or the most obvious matter runs an all-pervading unity. ” [Jie]

15 理无事，则无所依附。节。

Without matters, the principle would have nothing to adhere to. [Jie]

16 问：“仁与道如何分别？”曰：“道是统言，仁是一事。如‘道路’之‘道’，千枝百派，皆有一路去。故中庸分道德曰，父子、君臣以下为天下之达道，智仁勇为天下之达德。君有君之道，臣有臣之道。德便是个行道底。故为君主于仁，为臣主于敬。仁敬可唤做德，不可唤做道。”干。以下兼论德。

Question: How to differentiate benevolence and the Way?

Answer: The Way is a general name, while benevolence is a matter. For example, though the ways on the ground are bifurcate and numberless, there is always the way as a general name of them. Therefore, the *Doctrine of the Mean* distinguishes the Way and *de* 德 (virtue), saying that the duties between sovereign and minister, between father and son, between husband and wife, between elder brother and younger, and between friends are the Way universally binding in the world, and wisdom, benevolence, and bravery indicate the virtues universally binding in the world, too. The sovereign abides by the principle governing being a sovereign and the minister abides by the principle governing being a minister. The virtue is that which carries out the principle. Thus, what dominates being a sovereign is benevolence and what dominates being a minister is *jing* 敬 (respectfulness). The benevolence and respectfulness can be called virtues rather than the Way. [Gan] The several conversations below are also concerned with virtue.

17 “至德、至道”：道者，人之所共由；德者，己之所独得。“盛德、至善”：盛德以身之所得而言，至善以理之极致而言。诚、忠、孚、信：一心之谓诚，尽己之谓忠，存于中之谓孚，见于事之谓信。端蒙。

As regards *zhide* 至德 (supreme virtue) and *zhidao* 至道 (the supreme

Way）, the Way is shared by all people, while the virtue is owned by oneself. As regards *shengde* 盛德（complete virtue）and *zhishan* 至善（supreme good）, the complete virtue is said in terms of what the body gains, whereas the supreme good is said in relation to what is the perfect state of principle. As regards sincerity 诚, loyalty 忠, *fu* 孚（confidence-inspiring）, and faithfulness 信, one-mindedness is called sincerity; devoting oneself to the greatest extent is loyalty; preserving equilibrium 中 is confidence-inspiring; proving oneself in events is faithfulness. [Duanmeng]

18 存之于中谓理，得之于心为德，发见于行事为百行。节。

What is preserved in equilibrium is principle, what is attained in the mind is virtue, and what is embodied in performing events is *baixing* 百行（hundred conducts or activities）. [Jie]

19 德是得于天者，讲学而得之，得自家本分底物事。节。

Virtue is that which is gained from Heaven. When one gains it seemingly by means of learning and lecturing, it is actually what is originally in him. [Jie]

20 问：“泛观天地间，‘日往月来，寒往暑来’，‘四时行，百物生’，这是道之用流行发见处。即此而总言之，其往来生化，无一息间断处，便是道体否?”曰：“此体、用说得是。但‘总’字未当，总，便成兼用说了。只就那骨处便是体。如水之或流，或止，或激成波浪，是用；即这水骨可流，可止，可激成波浪处，便是体。如这身是体；目视，耳听，手足运动处，便是用。如这手是体；指之运动提掇处便是用。”淳举论语集注曰：“往者过，来者续，无一息之停，乃道体之本然也。”曰：“即是此意。”淳。以下论体、用。

Question：From a general viewpoint of what is between Heaven and Earth, "The sun goes and the moon comes··· The cold goes and the heat comes" （"Appended Remarks II" of the *Classic of Change*, 5）and "The four seasons pursue their courses and all things are continually being produced." （*Analects*, 17：19）These are where the operation of the function of the Way manifests itself. Therefore, to sum up, the coming and going, and various changes, continue constantly. Are these the substance of the Way?

Answer: What you said about the substance and function is right, but your use of "to sum up" is improper, for that means what you said about the substance involves also the function. Only where there is the "bone," there is the substance. For example, water is still, flows or surges, and this is its function. Its "bone" is capable of being still, flowing, or surging, and this is its substance. Take the body for another example. The body is the substance, while the eyes seeing, the ears hearing, and the hands and feet moving are all its function. The hand is the substance, while its fingers' movement, their lifting or pulling something, are its function.

I cited the Master's *Lunyu Jizhu* 论语集注 (Collected Annotations of the *Analects*) as saying "What has passed is gone and what is coming continues coming. There is no stop for even an instant in that process. It is the natural being of the substance of the Way." The Master responded, "That's it." [Chun (淳)] The conversations below concern substance and function.

21 问："前夜说体、用无定所，是随处说如此。若合万事为一大体、用，则如何？"曰："体、用也定。见在底便是体，后来生底便是用。此身是体，动作处便是用。天是体，'万物资始'处便是用。地是体，'万物资生'处便是用。就阳言，则阳是体，阴是用；就阴言，则阴是体，阳是用。"宇。

Question: At the night before last, you, sir, said that neither substance nor function was certainly located, for they were said as being what they were only in relation to this thing or that. What about considering all things as a great whole with its own substance and function?

Answer: Actually, either substance or function can be certainly located. What is produced first is the substance and what is brought forth later is function. The body is its substance and its movements are its function.

Heaven is its substance and what "All things owe to Heaven their beginning"① refers to is its function. Earth is its substance and what "All things owe to it their birth"② refers to is its function. Viewed from *yang*, *yang* is the substance and *yin* is the function; viewed from *yin*, *yin* is the substance and *yang* is the function. [Yu]

22 体是这个道理，用是他用处。如耳听目视，自然如此，是理也；开眼看物，着耳听声，便是用。江西人说个虚空底体，涉事物便唤做用。节。

The substance is the principle and the function of it is its use. Take eyes and ears for example. Eyes and ears can naturally see and hear, respectively, and these are their principles. When eyes open and see things and ears erect and hear sounds, these are their functions. The scholar of Jiangxi (at present Jiangxi Province)③ regards the substance as being vacuous and, when it involves concrete things and events, calls it function. [Jie]

23 问："先生昔曰：'礼是体。'今乃曰：'礼者，天理之节文，人事之仪则。'似非体而是用。"曰："公江西有般乡谈，才见分段子，便说道是用，不是体。如说尺时，无寸底是体，有寸底不是体，便是用；如秤，无星底是体，有星底不是体，便是用。且如扇子有柄，有骨子，用纸糊，此便是体；人摇之，便是用。"杨至之问体。曰："合当底是体。"节。

Question: You, sir, once said "The propriety is substance. " Now you say, "The propriety is the definite regulations of the heavenly principle and the ritual rules of the human events. " Here it seems not concerned with substance but rather function, doesn't it?

---

① This is said in the "Tuanzhuan" 彖传 (Explanation of the Judgment) of "Qian Gua" 乾卦 (Hexagram Qian), the first hexagram in the *Classic of Change*.
② This is said in the "Tuanzhuan" of "Kun Gua" 坤卦 (Kun Hexagram), the second hexagram in the *Classic of Change*.
③ Referring to Lu Jiuyuan 陆九渊 (1139–1193), a contemporary of Zhu Xi, who is a famous Confucian scholar.

Answer: As the scholars in your Jiangxi①have done, as soon as they see the scale markings of something, they will say that they are its function rather than its substance. Here are several illustrative examples. According to them, as regards *chi* 尺 (a unit of length [1/3 meter]), the *chi* ruler without markings of *cun* 寸 (a unit of length [1/3 decimeter]) is its substance, while that with the *cun* markings is its function. And as regards a *cheng* (a portable balance consisting of a pivoted bar with two unequal arms, like a steelyard today), that without the gradation markings on the beam is its substance, while that with the markings is its function. Actually, take a fan for example, and its handle, framework, paper, paste, and the so on constitute its substance, while when someone waves the fan, that is its function.

When Yang Zhizhi 杨至之 (i. e. 杨至 Yang Zhi, with courtesy name Zhizhi, a disciple of Zhu Xi's) asked him about substance, the Master answered, "What a thing should be capable of is its substance." [Jie]

24 人只是合当做底便是体，人做处便是用。譬如此扇子，有骨，有柄，用纸糊，此则体也；人摇之，则用也。如尺与秤相似，上有分寸星铢，则体也；将去秤量物事，则用也。方子。

What one should do is his substance and what he does actually is his function. Take this fan for example. Its handle, framework, paper, paste, and the so on make its substance, and when someone waves it, it is its function. For the *chi* ruler or the *cheng* balance, that with *cun* or gradation markings is its substance, while when it is used to measure something, it is its function. [Fangzi]

25 问："去岁闻先生曰：'只是一个道理，其分不同。'所谓分者，莫只是理一而其用不同？如君之仁，臣之敬，子之孝，父之慈，与国人交之信之类是也。"曰："其体已略不同。君臣、父子、国人是体；仁敬慈孝与信是用。"问："体、用皆异？"曰："如这片板，只是一个道

---

① Referring to those scholars represented by Lu Jiuyuan in Jiangxi.

理，这一路子恁地去，那一路子恁地去。如一所屋，只是一个道理，有厅，有堂。如草木，只是一个道理，有桃，有李。如这众人，只是一个道理，有张三，有李四；李四不可为张三，张三不可为李四。如阴阳，西铭言理一分殊，亦是如此。"又曰："分得愈见不同，愈见得理大。"节。

Question: Last year, I heard you, sir, say "There is one and the same principle, but its manifestations are different." As for the manifestations, though their principle is the same, are their functions different? For example, such different functions as the benevolence of a sovereign, the respectfulness of a minister, the filial piety of a son, the kindness of a father, and the faithfulness with which one contacts his fellow countrymen.

Answer: They are a little different already in their substances. The sovereign and minister, the father and son, and the fellow countrymen are all substances, while benevolence, respectfulness, filial piety, kindness, and faithfulness are all functions.

Further question: Are the substances different? And the functions?

Answer: Here are some examples for its illustration. There is only one principle in this piece of board, where here its vein runs through this line and there it runs through that line. There is only one principle in a house, which has its hall, rooms, and so on. There is only one principle in grasses or trees, which include peach trees, plum trees, and so on. There is only one principle in this group of people, in whom are this person, that person, and others. This person can not be that person, and vice versa. In the case of *yin* and *yang*, the "Principle is one, while its manifestations are many," as meant in "Xi Ming" 西铭（Western Inscription）（by Zhang Zai）, is also applicable thereto.

Further answer: The more the manifestations are different, the more the principle can be manifested. [Jie]

26 诚者，实有此理。节。以下论诚。

Sincerity means there being really the principle. [Jie] The four conversations below discourse on sincerity.

27 诚只是实。又云："诚是理。"一作"只是理"。去伪。

The Master said, "Sincerity is only something real." He added, "Sincerity is principle." For the second quotation, another record reads "Sincerity is only principle." [Quwei]①

28 诚，实理也，亦诚悫也。由汉以来，专以诚悫言诚。至程子乃以实理言，后学皆弃诚悫之说不观。中庸亦有言实理为诚处，亦有言诚悫为诚处。不可只以实为诚，而以诚悫为非诚也。砥。

Sincerity is real principle and also said as *chengque* 诚悫 (honesty and guilelessness). Since the Han dynasty (202 BC – AD 220), sincerity had been explained as honesty and guilelessness before Master Cheng Yi who put forth an explanation of sincerity as real principle. All the scholars after him have dropped the explanation in terms of honesty and guilelessness. The *Doctrine of the Mean* says of real principle as sincerity in a section and honesty and guilelessness as sincerity in another. You should not only regard being real as sincerity, yet regard honesty and guilelessness not as sincerity. [Di]

29 问性、诚。曰："性是实，诚是虚；性是理底名，诚是好处底名。性，譬如这扇子相似；诚，譬则这扇子做得好。"又曰："五峰曰：'诚者，命之道乎！中者，性之道乎！仁者，心之道乎！'此语分得轻重虚实处却好。某以为'道'字不若改做'德'字，更亲切。'道'字又较疏。"植。

When asked about nature and sincerity, the Master answered, "The nature is the substantial, while sincerity is the unsubstantial. The nature is the name of principle, while sincerity is the name of merit. Take this fan for example. The nature is like the fan itself, while the sincerity is comparable to the fan being well done." He added, "Wufeng (i. e. Hu Hong) said, 'Isn't

---

① Jin Quwei 金去伪 (courtesy name Jingzhi 敬直).

sincerity the Way of destiny? Isn't equilibrium the Way of nature? Isn't benevolence the Way of mind?' He did well in distinguishing between heavy and light and between empty and full. However, in my opinion, if the 'Way' had been 'virtue,' what he said would have been closer, for the 'Way' is more distant. " [Zhi (植)]①

30　先生问诸友：" '诚、敬' 二字如何分？" 各举程子之说以对。先生曰："敬是不放肆底意思，诚是不欺妄底意思。" 过。以下诚敬。

The Master asked his disciples, "How to distinguish between sincerity and *jing* 敬 (seriousness)?" They all answered him by citing what Master Cheng had said about them. The Master told them, "The seriousness means not being wanton, and sincerity, not being deceptive. " [Guo]② The four conversations below are concerned with sincerity and seriousness.

31　诚只是一个实，敬只是一个畏。端蒙。

Sincerity means nothing but being real, while seriousness is nothing but being in awe. [Duanmeng]

32　妄诞欺诈为不诚，怠惰放肆为不敬，此诚敬之别。干。

Being absurd and deceptive is not sincerity, while being indolent and unscrupulous is not seriousness. That tells sincerity from seriousness. [Gan]

33　问诚、敬。曰："须逐处理会。诚若是有不欺意处，只做不欺意会；敬若是有谨畏意处，只做谨畏意会。中庸说诚，作中庸看；孟子说诚处，作孟子看。将来自相发明耳。" 夔孙。

When asked about sincerity and seriousness, the Master replied, "You should try to understand the different cases where they are mentioned one by one. If the sincerity seems to have a meaning of not cheating, you can just take it as meaning not cheating. If the seriousness seems to have a meaning of solemnly revering something, you can just regard it as meaning solemnly

---

① Pan Zhi 潘植 (courtesy name Li Zhi 立之).

② Wang Guo 王过 (courtesy name Youguan 幼观).

revering something. When you read the words on sincerity in the *Doctrine of the Mean*, understand them in their specific context. Likewise, when you read those words on sincerity in the *Mencius*, understand them in their specific context. In due course, their integrated meaning will dawn on you. "〔Kuisun〕

34 "谨"字未如敬，敬又未如诚。程子曰："主一之谓敬，一者之谓诚。"敬尚是着力。铢。以下杂论。

Jin 谨（being solemnly careful）is not as efficacious as seriousness, and seriousness is not as efficacious as sincerity. Master Cheng Yi said, "Being concentrated on one thing is called as seriousness, while oneness is called as sincerity. " Seriousness means still making efforts. 〔Zhu〕 The conversations below discourse on miscellaneous topics.

35 问诚、信之别。曰："诚是自然底实，信是人做底实。故曰：'诚者，天之道。'这是圣人之信。若众人之信，只可唤做信，未可唤做诚。诚是自然无妄之谓。如水只是水，火只是火，仁彻底是仁，义彻底是义。"夔孙。

When asked about the difference between sincerity and faithfulness, the Master answered, "Sincerity means being naturally real, while faithfulness means being artificially real. It is said, therefore, that 'Sincerity is the way of Heaven. ' (*Mencius*, 4A：12; *Doctrine of the Mean*, 22) This is the faithfulness of the sage. The faithfulness on the part of ordinary people can only be referred to as faithfulness but can not be called sincerity. By sincerity is meant being naturally free from deception. For example, water is simply water and fire is simply fire; Benevolence is thoroughly benevolence and righteousness is thoroughly righteousness. "〔Kuisun〕

36 叔器问："诚与信如何分?"曰："诚是个自然之实，信是个人所为之实。中庸说'诚者，天之道也'，便是诚。若'诚之者，人之道也'，便是信。信不足以尽诚，犹爱不足以尽仁。上是，下不是。"可学。

Shuqi asked, "How to distinguish sincerity and faithfulness?" The Master answered, "Sincerity means being naturally real, while faithfulness means being artificially real. The *Doctrine of the Mean*（22）says 'Sincerity is the way of Heaven,' which refers to sincerity, and 'The attainment of sincerity is the way of humankind,' which refers to faithfulness. The faithfulness is not enough for the attainment of sincerity, just as love is not enough for attainment of benevolence. The upper end of faithfulness can be enough, but the lower part of it can not." ［Kexue］

37 诚者实有之理，自然如此。忠信以人言之，须是人体出来方见。端蒙。

The sincerity is the principle really existing, which is naturally what it is. When it comes to loyalty and faithfulness, speaking from humankind, they can't be seen until they are manifested by humankind. ［Duanmeng］

38 "诚"字以心之全体而言，"忠"字以其应事接物而言，此义理之本名也。至曾子所言"忠恕"，则是圣人之事，故其忠与诚，仁与恕，得通言之。如恕本以推己及物得名，在圣人，则以己及物矣。端蒙。

The sincerity 诚 is said on the basis of the entire mind, while the loyalty 忠 is said in regard to the mind in handling affairs and dealing with things, which is the original name referring to the idea of what is right. When Zengzi（i. e. Zeng Shen）put forth *zhong-shu* 忠恕, meaning one cultivating to the utmost his loyalty 忠 and exercises them on the guideline of reciprocity 恕, it referred to what the sage did. Therefore, loyalty and sincerity, benevolence and reciprocity, all started to be discoursed in an interconnected way. For example, the name of *shu*（reciprocity）was originally intended to mean one considering a thing by placing himself in its position. When it comes to the sage, it means considering a thing by considering himself. ［Duanmeng］

39 问："仁与诚何别？"曰："仁自是仁，诚自是诚，何消合理会！理会这一件，也看到极处；理会那一件，也看到极处，便都自见得。"淳。

Question: What is the difference between benevolence and sincerity?

Answer: Naturally, benevolence is benevolence and sincerity is sincerity, and is there any need to understand them together? When trying to understand this, strive to see the most esoteric point of it, and when trying to understand that, strive also to see the most esoteric point of it. Then you will get to know what either means. [Chun (淳)]

40 或问:"诚是体,仁是用否?"曰:"理一也,以其实有,故谓之诚。以其体言,则有仁义礼智之实;以其用言,则有恻隐、羞恶、恭敬、是非之实,故曰:'五常百行非诚,非也。'盖无其实矣,又安得有是名乎!"植。

Someone asked, "Is sincerity the substance and benevolence the function?" The Master answered, "The principle is one and since it is something real, it is called sincerity. Viewed from its substance, there are the real four beginnings, i.e. benevolence, righteousness, propriety, wisdom; viewed from its function, there are the four real feelings of sadness and commiseration, shame and dislike, deference and compliance, right and wrong. Therefore, the *Tongshu* 通书 (Penetrating the *Classic of Change*) (by Zhou Dunyi) says, 'Without sincerity, the Five Constant Virtues and all activities will be wrong.'[①] That is probably because they do not have their realizations, and then how can they be referred to by those names?" [Zhi (植)]

41 或问:"诚是浑然不动,仁是此理流出否?"曰:"自性言之,仁亦未是流出,但其生动之理包得四者。"

Someone asked, "Does sincerity mean a complete existence of inactivity and does benevolence mean the outward flow of the principle?"

Answer: Viewed from nature, the benevolence does not mean the

---

① The translation of this citation is based on the version by Chan Wing-tsit, p. 466.

outward flow, but the principle of production and activity embraces the four (i. e. benevolence, righteousness, propriety, and wisdom).

42 问："一与中，与诚，浩然之气，为一体事否？"曰："一只是不杂，不可将做一事。中与诚与浩然之气，固是一事，然其分各别：诚是实有此理，中是状物之体段，浩然之气只是为气而言。"去伪。

Question: Are oneness and equilibrium, and sincerity, and *haoran zhi qi* 浩然之气 (flowing vast vital force) consist in the same one thing?

Answer: Oneness only means being free from impurity and they should not be taken as consisting in the same one thing. Though the equilibrium, sincerity, and the flowing vast vital force, consist in the same one thing, they are different from one another. The sincerity means the real existence of the principle; the equilibrium is a description of what something looks like; the flowing vast vital force is said only in reference to the vital force. [Quwei]

43 问："仁、义、礼、智、诚、中、庸，不知如何看？"曰："仁义礼智，乃未发之性，所谓诚。中庸，皆已发之理。人之性本实，而释氏以性为空也。"辉。

Question: I do not know how to see benevolence, righteousness, propriety, wisdom, sincerity, equilibrium, and *yong* 庸 (being ordinary①).

Answer: Benevolence, righteousness, propriety, and wisdom pertain to the state of nature before its emanation, all of which are regarded as aspects of sincerity. Equilibrium and *yong* both pertain to the emanated principle. The human nature is substantially real, while Buddhism sees it as void. [Hui]②

44 在天只是阴阳五行，在人得之只是刚柔五常之德。泳。以下五常。

Viewed from Heaven, only the *yin* and *yang* and the Five Agents operate, while viewed from a man, they are conferred on him as the firmness

---

① According to Zhu Xi's explanation of *yong* 庸, it means being ordinary; hence the translation offered in the brackets.

② Li Hui 李辉 (courtesy name Huifu 晦父).

and softness and the Five Constant Virtues. [Yong] The conversations below discuss the Five Constant Virtues.

45 大而天地万物，小而起居食息，皆太极阴阳之理也。又曰："仁木，义金，礼火，智水，信土。"祖道。

The Master said, "All things and events, big or small, ranging from Heaven and Earth and myriad things to the diet and daily life of a person, embody the principle of the Great Ultimate and *yin* and *yang*." He added, "Benevolence pertains to wood; righteousness, to metal; propriety, to fire; wisdom, to water; faithfulness, to earth." [Zudao]

46 或问："仁义礼智，性之四德，又添'信'字，谓之'五性'，如何？"曰："信是诚实此四者，实有是仁，实有是义，礼智皆然。如五行之有土，非土不足以载四者。又如土于四时各寄王十八日，或谓王于戊己。然季夏乃土之本宫，故尤王。月令载'中央土'，以此。"人杰。

Someone asked, "Benevolence, righteousness, propriety, wisdom are the four virtues of the nature. Now, how do you think about adding faithfulness to them and regarding them as *wuxing* 五性 (Five Natures)?" The Master answered, "The faithfulness means there being really the four virtues, that is, there being really benevolence, there being really righteousness, and so on. Faithfulness is comparable to earth in the Five Agents. Without earth, there would be nothing to carry the other four agents on. In the system, earth works in all four seasons, like a king, and prevails in eighteen days in each season. It can also be said as the king being *wu-ji* 戊己[①]. The last month of the summer season (the sixth month of the lunar calendar in Chinese tradition) is the zodiac palace owned by earth, so in that

---

① In the lunar calendar in Chinese tradition, the days of a year (also a month or a season) are numbered by the ten Heavenly Stems. The *wu* 戊 day pertains to *yang* (positive) earth, and the *ji* 己 day, to *yin* (negative) earth. Usually, the *wu-ji* 戊己 is used as another reference to earth, the agent in the central position of the Five Agents.

period it is more kingly. Therefore, it is recorded in 'Yueling' 月令 (Proceedings of Government in Different Months) of the *Liji* 礼记 (Record of Rites) that 'Right in the middle (between Heaven and Earth 地 and the other four agents) is earth 土'." [Renjie]

47 问："向蒙戒喻，说仁意思云：'义礼智信上着不得，又须见义礼智信上少不得，方见得仁统五常之意。'大雅今以树为喻：夫树之根固有生气，然贯彻首尾，岂可谓干与枝、花与叶无生气也?"曰："固然。只如四时：春为仁，有个生意；在夏，则见其有个亨通意；在秋，则见其有个诚实意；在冬，则见其有个贞固意。在夏秋冬，生意何尝息！本虽雕零，生意则常存。大抵天地间只一理，随其到处，分许多名字出来。四者于五行各有配，惟信配土，以见仁义礼智实有此理，不是虚说。又如乾四德，元最重，其次贞亦重，以明终始之义。非元则无以生，非贞则无以终，非终则无以为始，不始则不能成终矣。如此循环无穷，此所谓'大明终始'也。"大雅。

Question：The other day, you, sir, said that "When you have seen that benevolence does not adhere to righteousness, propriety, wisdom, and faithfulness at all, and at the same time righteousness, propriety, wisdom, and faithfulness would not do without benevolence, then you will understand that benevolence commands the other four in the Five Constant Virtues." Now let me take the tree for an analogy. The root of the tree is imbued with vigor for its growth, but the vigor pervades the whole tree from its root to its leaves. Can we say that its trunk and branches, its flowers and leaves, are not imbued with vigor?

Answer：They are, of course, imbued with vigor. It is also comparable to the four seasons. In spring, there originates the benevolence with the intention to produce; in summer, there arises the prevalence of prosperity; in autumn, there takes place the fruition; in winter, there comes the fortification for being firm. Thus, in summer, autumn, and winter, does the intention to produce ever cease? Though the body withers, the intention to produce exists constantly. Basically speaking, there is only one principle between Heaven and Earth, which is referred to by different names where it is manifested in different ways. The four (i. e. benevolence, righteousness, propriety, and wisdom) match the four of the Five Agents, respectively, and the last virtue faithfulness matches the last agent earth, which is to indicate that the benevolence, righteousness, propriety, and wisdom are real rather than empty. In the case of the four virtues of "Hexagram Qian," i. e. *yuan* 元 (origination), *heng* 亨 (prosperity), *li* 利 (advantage), and *zhen* 贞 (firmness)[①], the " origination " is the most significant and next is the "firmness," both of which make clear the meaning of beginning and ending. Without the "origination," there would be no production to speak of. Without the "firmness," there would not be anything by which the process comes to an ending. Without the end, there would be no beginning afresh. Without the beginning afresh, there would be no completion of an ultimate end. All these constitute a ceaseless cycling and that is what is meant by " Its brilliance permeates all from first to last. " (as said in the " Explanation of the Judgment " of "Hexagram Qian" in the *Classic of Change.*) [Daya]

48 得此生意以有生, 然后有礼智义信。以先后言之, 则仁为先; 以大小言之, 则仁为大。闳祖。

Owing to the intention to produce, production occurs and then there arise propriety, wisdom, righteousness, and faithfulness. In terms of their sequential order, the benevolence comes first; in terms of their greatness, the benevolence is the greatest. [Hongzu]

49 问: "先生以为一分为二, 二分为四, 四分为八, 又细分将去。程子说: '性中只有仁义礼智四者而已。' 只分到四便住, 何也?" 曰: "周先生亦止分到五行住。若要细分, 则如易样分。"节。以下仁义礼智。

① For what is meant by the four sino-graphs 元亨利贞 for the judgment of " Hexagram Qian" in the *Classic of Change*, there have been various explanations. Their translation in the text is based on what Zhu Xi explains them as in the context.

Question：You, sir, are of the opinion that one is divided into two; two into four; four into eight; and the division can be further made in that way. Master Cheng (i. e. Cheng Yi) said, "In the nature are only the four, i. e. benevolence, righteousness, propriety, and wisdom." Why did he stop at that division into four?

Answer：Master Zhou (i. e. Zhou Dunyi) stopped also at a division into five, i. e. the Five Agents. If further division is to be made, it can be made in the way illustrated by the *Classic of Change* (with sixty four hexagrams).

[Jie] The several conversations below are concerned with benevolence, righteousness, propriety, wisdom.

50 尝言仁义礼智，而以手指画扇中心，曰："只是一个道理，分为两个。"又横画一画，曰："两个分为四个。"又以手指逐一指所分为四个处，曰："一个是仁，一个是义，一个是礼，一个是智，这四个便是个种子。恻隐、羞恶、恭敬、是非便是种子所生底苗。"节。

The Master once spoke of benevolence, righteousness, propriety, and wisdom, and holding a fan in one hand and gesturing by moving the other hand to draw a vertical central line on it, he said, "There is only one principle and it is divided into two." Then, he gestured further by drawing a horizontal line cross the vertical one and said, "The two are divided further into four." Pointing to the four sections one by one, he said, "They are benevolence, righteousness, propriety, and wisdom, which are four seeds. The feelings of sadness and commiseration, shame and dislike, deference and compliance, and right and wrong, sprout from the four seeds." [Jie]

51 人只是此仁义礼智四种心。如春夏秋冬，千头万绪，只是此四种心发出来。铢。

Humankind possesses only four types of mind, that is, benevolence, righteousness, propriety, and wisdom. They are like the spring, summer, autumn, and winter, and despite the countless things, they are all brought forth from the four seasons. ［Zhu］

52 吉甫问：“仁义礼智，立名还有意义否？”曰：“说仁，便有慈爱底意思；说义，便有刚果底意思。声音气象，自然如此。”直卿云：“六经中专言仁者，包四端也；言仁义而不言礼智者，仁包礼，义包智。”方子。

Jifu 吉甫 (courtesy name of Gan Jie) asked, "As regards benevolence, righteousness, propriety, and wisdom, are there any meanings connoted in their names?" The Master replied, "Speaking of benevolence, it connotes kindness and affection; speaking of righteousness, it implies firmness and resoluteness. It is like sounds and images giving naturally such connotative meanings." Zhiqing (courtesy name of Huang Gan) said, "In the Six Classics, when benevolence is discoursed, it is meant to include all the Four Beginnings (i. e. benevolence, righteousness, propriety, and wisdom); when benevolence and righteousness are discoursed without mentioning propriety and wisdom, they are meant to include the latter two, that is, benevolence includes propriety and righteousness includes wisdom." ［Fangzi］

53 仁与义是柔软底，礼智是坚实底。仁义是头，礼智是尾。一似说春秋冬夏相似，仁义一作“礼”。是阳底一截，礼智一作“义智”。是阴底一截。渊。方子录云：“仁义是发出来嫩底，礼智是坚硬底。”

Benevolence and righteousness are soft and gentle, whereas propriety and wisdom are solid and firm. Benevolence and righteousness are comparable to the head, whereas propriety and wisdom, to the tail. Like spring, summer, autumn, and winter, benevolence and righteousness pertain to the *yang*-dominant section, while propriety and wisdom, to the *yin*-dominant section. Another record reads "Benevolence and propriety pertain to the *yang*-dominant section, while righteousness and wisdom, to the *yin*-dominant section." ［Yuan］[1] Fangzi's record reads, "Benevolence and righteousness are emanated tender, whereas propriety and wisdom are solid

---

① Huan Yuan 晏渊 (courtesy name Yafu 亚夫).

and firm. "

54 问仁义礼智体用之别。曰："自阴阳上看下来，仁礼属阳，义智属阴；仁礼是用，义智是体。春夏是阳，秋冬是阴。只将仁义说，则'春作夏长'，仁也；'秋敛冬藏'，义也。若将仁义礼智说，则春，仁也；夏，礼也；秋，义也；冬，智也。仁礼是敷施出来底，义是肃杀果断底，智便是收藏底。如人肚脏有许多事，如何见得！其智愈大，其藏愈深。正如易中道：'立天之道，曰阴与阳；立地之道，曰柔与刚；立人之道，曰仁与义。'解者多以仁为柔，以义为刚，非也。却是以仁为刚，义为柔。盖仁是个发出来了，便硬而强；义便是收敛向里底，外面见之便是柔。"僩。

When asked about the difference between the substance and function of benevolence, righteousness, propriety, and wisdom, the Master answered, "From the viewpoint of *yin* and *yang*, benevolence pertains to *yang*, while righteousness, to *yin*. Benevolence and propriety are the functions, while righteousness and wisdom are the substances. They are akin to the four seasons, of which spring and summer pertain to *yang*, while autumn and winter, to *yin*. Speaking of only benevolence and righteousness, then 'In spring the process of growth begins and in summer it matures,' which manifests benevolence; 'In autumn the gathering-in is done and in winter what has been gathered in is stored,' which manifests righteousness. If considering all the four seasons, then spring indicates benevolence; summer, propriety; autumn, righteousness; winter, wisdom. Benevolence and propriety are productive forth-bringing; righteousness is resolute gathering-in; wisdom is storing. It is like there being so many things in one's bosom, and how can they all be seen? The greater the wisdom is, the deeper it is stored. Just as said in the *Classic of Change*, 'With this view they exhibited (in them) the way of Heaven, calling (the lines) *yin* and *yang*; the way of Earth, calling (them) the weak (or soft) and the strong (or hard); and the way of humankind, under the names of benevolence and righteousness. '① Those annotators of this statement have tended to regard benevolence as being soft and righteousness as being hard, but this understanding is wrong. I think, benevolence should be seen as being hard and righteousness as being soft. That is because benevolence is that which has been emanated, thus being hard and strong, while righteousness is introvert, of which what can be seen outside is soft. " [Xian]

55 仁礼属阳, 义智属阴。袁机仲却说: "义是刚底物, 合属阳; 仁是柔底物, 合属阴。" 殊不知舒畅发达, 便是那刚底意思; 收敛藏缩, 便是那阴底意思。他只念得 "于仁也柔, 于义也刚" 两句, 便如此说。殊不知正不如此。又云: "以气之呼吸言之, 则呼为阳, 吸为阴, 吸便是收敛底意。乡饮酒义云: '温厚之气盛于东南, 此天地之仁气也; 严凝之气盛于西北, 此天地之义气也。'" 僩。

The Master said, "Benevolence and propriety pertain to *yang*, while righteousness and wisdom, to *yin*. Yuan Jizhong 袁机仲 (i. e. 袁枢 [1131 – 1205], courtesy name Jizhong), however, claimed, 'Righteousness is something hard, which should be regarded as pertaining to *yang*, whereas benevolence is something soft, which should be taken as pertaining to *yin*. ' But he did not know being extending and extroversive outward is what is meant by being hard and being retracting and contractive inward is what is meant by pertaining to *yin*. He read no more than 'In regard to benevolence, (the *junzi* 君子 [Superior Man]) is soft. In regard to righteousness, (he) is firm'② before getting that rash conclusion. He did not know that his opinion was not right. " He added, "Take breath for example. Exhaling is *yang* and inhaling is *yin*, for inhaling means taking-in. According to the meaning attached to the festivity of drinking in the country districts, 'The gentle and

---

① Cited from "Shuo Gua" 说卦 (Discussion of the Trigrams) in the *Classic of Change*. The English translation is based on the version by J. Legge (see http: //ctext. org/book-of-changes/yi-jing).

② Cited from *Fayan* 法言 (Exemplary Sayings) by Yang Xiong 扬雄 (53 – 18 BC).

kind scene flourishes in the south and east, which manifests the vital force of benevolence of Heaven and Earth; the grim and congealing scene flourishes in the north and west, which shows the vital force of righteousness of Heaven and Earth. ' " [Xian]

56 "仁礼属阳，属健；义知属阴，属顺。"问："义则截然有定分，有收敛底意思，自是属阴顺。不知智如何解？"曰："智更是截然，更是收敛。如知得是，知得非，知得便了，更无作用，不似仁义礼三者有作用。智只是知得了，便交付恻隐、羞恶、辞逊三者。他那个更收敛得快。"僴。

The Master said, "Benevolence and propriety pertain to *yang* and to vigorousness, while righteousness and wisdom, to *yin* and to compliance. " Someone asked, "Righteousness, which has sharply definite manifestations and implies the sense of restraint, bears naturally on *yin* and compliance. What about wisdom?" The Master answered, "Wisdom is more sharply definite in its manifestations and means more restraint. If wisdom knows well right or wrong, it will play little function and at least less function than benevolence, righteousness, or propriety. That is because wisdom only plays the function of knowing right or wrong, and when it knows it, it will leave it to the other three for the feelings of sadness and commiseration, of shame and dislike, and of deference and compliance, and thus it is faster to retract itself. " [Xian]

57 生底意思是仁，杀底意思是义，发见会通是礼，收一作"深"。藏不测是智。节。

The meaning of *sheng* 生 (growing) is benevolence; the meaning of *sha* 杀 (withering) is righteousness; that which is brought forth and together smoothly is propriety; that which is deep stored and inscrutable is wisdom. [Jie]

58 仁义礼智，便是元亨利贞。若春间不曾发生，得到夏无缘得长，秋冬亦无可收藏。泳。

Benevolence, righteousness, propriety, and wisdom are the very origination, prosperity, advantage, and firmness. If origination does not happen in spring, there will no growing in summer and then no gathering-in and storage to speak of in autumn and winter. 〔Yong〕

59 问："元亨利贞有次第,仁义礼智因发而感,则无次第。"曰："发时无次第,生时有次第。"佐。

Question: The origination, prosperity, advantage, and firmness have their sequential order. As for benevolence, righteousness, propriety, and wisdom, only after their emanations can they be felt. They do not have their sequential order, do they?

Answer: At the time of their emanations, they do not have their sequential order, but when they are produced, they will have their sequential order. 〔Zuo〕①

60 百行皆仁义礼智中出。节。

All activities come forth from benevolence, righteousness, propriety, and wisdom. 〔Jie〕

61 仁义礼智,性之大目,皆是形而上者,岂可分也! 人杰。

Since benevolence, righteousness, propriety, and wisdom are all the four major portions of human nature, all of which are metaphysical, how can they be separated? 〔Renjie〕

62 问："仁得之最先,盖言仁具义礼智。"曰："先有是生理,三者由此推之。"可学。

Question: The benevolence is attained earlier than the other three. Can it be said basically that benevolence embraces righteousness, propriety, and wisdom?

Answer: What comes first is the principle of production and the other three are deduced from it. 〔Kexue〕

---

① Xiao Zuo 萧佐 (courtesy name Dingfu 定夫).

63 仁，浑沦言，则浑沦都是一个生意，义礼智都是仁；对言，则仁与义礼智一般。淳。

To put it as a complete whole, benevolence is an intention to produce, and all righteousness, propriety, and wisdom are the same as benevolence. To put them as separate virtues, benevolence is akin to righteousness, propriety, or wisdom. [Chun（淳）]

64 郑问："仁是生底意，义礼智则如何？"曰："天只是一元之气。春生时，全见是生；到夏长时，也只是这底；到秋来成遂，也只是这底；到冬天藏敛，也只是这底。仁义礼智割做四段，一个便是一个；浑沦看，只是一个。"淳。

Zheng（Kexue）asked, "If benevolence is an intention to produce, what about righteousness, propriety, and wisdom?" The Master answered, "Heaven consists in only one vital force all over. When production occurs in spring, all things that are seen indicate production; when they thrive in summer, they all are also indicative of production; when they bear fruits in autumn, they all are also indicative of production; when they are stored in winter, they all are also indicative of production. When benevolence, righteousness, propriety, and wisdom are seen as separate parts, they are four, but when they are seen as a whole, they are one." [Chun（淳）]

65 问："仁是天地之生气，义礼智又于其中分别。然其初只是生气，故为全体。"曰："然。"问："肃杀之气，亦只是生气？"曰："不是二物，只是敛些。春夏秋冬，亦只是一气。"可学。

Question: Benevolence is the vital force of Heaven and Earth for production, which embraces righteousness, propriety, and wisdom as three separately defined virtues. However, at first they are all of the same vital force for production, so the four are an entirety, aren't they?

Answer: Yes.

Further question: Is the vital force at the time of withering also that for production?

Answer: They are not two things, only the vital force at the time of withering is contractive to some extent. The vital force in the four seasons are the same. [Kexue]

66 仁与智包得，义与礼包不得。方子。

Both benevolence and wisdom can include the other two, while neither righteousness nor propriety can. [Fangzi]

67 仁所以包三者，盖义礼智皆是流动底物，所以皆从仁上渐渐推出。仁智、元贞，是终始之事，这两头却重。如坎与震，是始万物、终万物处，艮则是中间接续处。

The reason why benevolence can embrace the other three lies probably in that all righteousness, propriety, and wisdom are in a flowing state of operation, all of which can be deduced one by one from benevolence. Benevolence and wisdom are a beginning and an end. So are origination and firmness. However, in either case, the beginning and the end are more significant. They are comparable to *Kan* 坎 and *Zhen* 震, which represent respectively where myriad things begin and end, with *Gen* 艮 serving as the transition between them. ①

68 味道问："仁包义礼智，恻隐包羞恶、辞逊、是非，元包亨利贞，春包夏秋冬。以五行言之，不知木如何包得火金水？"曰："木是生气。有生气，然后物可得而生；若无生气，则火金水皆无自而能生矣，故木能包此三者。仁义礼智，性也。性无形影可以摸索，只是有这理耳。惟情乃可得而见，恻隐、羞恶、辞逊，是非是也。故孟子言性曰：'乃若其情，则可以为善矣。'盖性无形影，惟情可见。观其发处既善，则知其性之本善必矣。"时举。

Weidao asked, "Benevolence includes righteousness, propriety, and

---

① *Kan* 坎, *Zhen* 震, and *Gen* 艮 are three of the eight trigrams used in Daoist cosmology to represent the fundamental principles of reality, seen as a range of eight interrelated concepts. The symbols of the three trigrams are water, thunder, and mountain respectively. The eight trigrams constitute the basis for the sixty four hexagrams in the *Classic of Change*.

wisdom; sadness and commiseration include shame and dislike, deference and compliance, and right and wrong; origination includes prosperity, advantage, and firmness; spring includes summer, autumn, and winter. Seen from the Five Agents, how can wood include fire, metal, and water?" The Master said, "Wood is the vital force for production. With it, things can be produced. Without it, fire, metal, or water can not bring forth anything by itself. In this sense, wood can include fire, metal, and water. Benevolence, righteousness, propriety, and wisdom bear on the nature, which is formless and intangible and can not be fumbled and in which only the principle dwells. What is visible are only the feelings of sadness and commiseration, shame and dislike, deference and compliance, and right and wrong. Therefore, *Mencius* (6A: 6) said of the nature, 'If the feelings are proper to it, what is good can be practiced. ' That is probably because the nature is formless and only feelings are visible. If one observes that the emanation of feelings is good, he will know that the nature is sure to be originally good. " [Shiju]

69 问: "孟子说仁义礼智, 义在第二; 太极图以义配利, 则在第三。" 曰: "礼是阳, 故曰亨。仁义礼智, 犹言东西南北; 元亨利贞, 犹言东南西北。一个是对说, 一个是从一边说起。" 夔孙。

Question: When Mencius discoursed benevolence, righteousness, propriety, and wisdom, he put righteousness in the second place, but in "Taiji Tu" 太极图 (Diagram of the Great Ultimate) righteousness is put in the third place to match advantage (after origination and prosperity). (Why is that difference?)

Answer: In the diagram, righteousness pertains to *yang* and thus is said as advantage (in the third place). Benevolence, righteousness, propriety, and wisdom are comparable to east, west, south, and north, whereas origination, prosperity, advantage, and firmness, to east, south, west, and north. The former indicates two pairs of opposites, while the latter follows an order in a circle. [Kuisun]

70 四端犹四德。逐一言之，则各自为界限；分而言之，则仁义又是一大界限，故曰："仁，人心也；义，人路也。" 如乾文言既曰 "四德"，又曰："乾元者，始而亨者也；利贞者，性情也。" 文蔚。

The Four Beginnings are comparable to the Four Virtues. Speaking of the Four Beginnings as four separate parts, they each have their well defined boundaries. Speaking of them as two separate virtues, benevolence and righteousness each have their greater spheres well delimited, so *Mencius* (6A：11) says "Benevolence is the human mind, and righteousness is the human path. " The "Wenyan" appended to "Hexagram Qian" discourses "Four Virtues," but also says "The 'origination' represented by Qian refers to it as (the symbol of) what gives their beginning (to all things) and (also) secures their prosperity. The advantage and the firmness refer to its nature and feelings (as seen in all the resulted things). "[1] [Wenwei][2]

71 正淳言："性之四端，迭为宾主，然仁智其总统也。'恭而无礼则劳'，是以礼为主也；'君子义以为质'，是以义为主也。盖四德未尝相离，遇事则迭见层出，要在人默而识之。" 曰："说得是。" 大雅。

Zhengchun 正淳 (courtesy name of Wan Renjie 万人杰) said, "Of the Four Beginnings of nature, in their sequential order, each pair of two can be in a host-guest relationship, yet benevolence and wisdom can command others. In 'Being respectful yet without the rules of propriety becomes a labor to no avail,' (*Analects*, 8：2) the propriety is the dominant, while in 'The Superior Man considers righteousness to be essential in everything,' (*Analects*, 15：18) the righteousness is the dominant. Probably that is because in the Four Virtues, one never distances from another and when meeting events, they will come up in alternation, which requires that we keep a treasuring-up of them in mind and understand their relationships. " The

---

① The English translation of the citation from the *Classic of Change* is based on a version by J. Legge (see http：//ctext. org/book-of-changes).

② Chen Wenwei 陈文蔚 (courtesy name Caiqing 才卿).

Master replied, "Right." ［Daya］

72 学者疑问中谓："就四德言之，仁却是动，智却是静。"曰："周子太极图中是如此说。"又曰："某前日答一朋友书云：'仁体刚而用柔，义体柔而用刚。'"人杰。

A scholar, a little puzzled, said, "Viewing from the Four Virtues (of 'Hexagram Qian'), benevolence is in activity, while wisdom is in tranquility." The Master responded, "So is said in Master Zhou's (Zhou Dunyi's) 'Diagram of the Great Ultimate.'" Then he added, "I said to a friend of mine in a letter to him the other day, 'Benevolence is firm in its substance and soft in its function, while righteousness is soft in its substance and firm in its function.'" ［Renjie］

73 问："仁义礼智四者皆一理。举仁，则义礼智在其中；举义与礼，则亦然。如中庸言：'舜其大智也欤。'其下乃云，'好问，好察迩言，隐恶而扬善'，谓之仁亦可；'执其两端，用其中于民'，谓之义亦可。然统言之，只是发明'智'字。故知理只是一理，圣人特于盛处发明之尔。"曰："理固是一贯。谓之一理，则又不必疑其多。自一理散为万事，则灿然有条而不可乱，逐事自有一理，逐物自有一名，各有攸当，但当观当理与不当理耳。既当理后，又何必就上更生疑！"大雅。

Question: Underlying all benevolence, righteousness, propriety, and wisdom is the same principle. When benevolence emerges, the righteousness, propriety, and wisdom are also embraced in it. This is also true of righteousness and propriety. The *Doctrine of the Mean* says "Shun was indeed great in wisdom!" Following this sentence is that "He loved to question others and study their words, though they might be shallow, and concealed what was bad and displayed what was good in them." It is reasonable to regard him as being benevolent. Then the book says "He took hold of their two extremes, determined the Mean, and employed it in his government of the people." Here he may be regarded as being righteous. However, to speak generally, all these discourses purport only to elucidate wisdom. Thus it can be known that the principle is the same, only the sage reveals it where it is salient. (Is this understanding right?)

Answer: The principle is, of course, the same principle pervading them all. Since it is one, it should not be doubted that it is many. Since the one and the same principle was allocated to myriad things and events, it has been brilliant and orderly, free from confusion. They each have been endowed with their principle and have been given their names, each being proper and adequate. What one should observe is whether they fit their allotments of principle. When he finds they fit them indeed, then why does he doubt in this regard? [Daya]

74 仁义礼智，才去寻讨他时，便动了，便不是本来底。又曰："心之所以会做许多，盖具得许多道理。"又曰："何以见得有此四者？因其恻隐，知其有仁；因其羞恶，知其有义。"又曰："伊川穀种之说最好。"又曰："冬饮汤，是宜饮汤；夏饮水，是宜饮水。冬饮水，夏饮汤，便不宜。人之所以羞恶者，是触着这宜，如两个物事样。触着宜便羞恶者，是独只是一事。"节。末数语疑有脱误。

The Master said, "As regards benevolence, righteousness, propriety, and wisdom, the moment you seek to find them, they have already moved and not been what they were." He went on and said, "The reason why the mind is capable of many doings is probably that it possesses many principles."

He continued, "Why can we find there being the four (benevolence, righteousness, propriety, and wisdom)? It is because, since there is the feeling of sadness and commiseration, we know there being benevolence, and since there is the feeling of shame and dislike, we know there being righteousness."

He then commented on Yichuan's (i. e, Cheng Yi's) analogy between the seed of grain and the mind, saying "Yichuan's metaphor of the seed of grain is to the point best."

He added, "Drinking (warm) soup in winter is due to the practice and

time being suitable to each other, and drinking (cool) water in summer is also due to their being suitable. Drinking soup in summer or drinking water in winter means the practice and the time being unsuitable to each other. The reason why a person feels shame and dislike of something is that it violates the suitability, that is, the person and the thing are not suitable to each other."①
[Jie]

75 "仁"字须兼义礼智看，方看得出。仁者，仁之本体；礼者，仁之节文；义者，仁之断制；知者，仁之分别。犹春夏秋冬虽不同，而同出于春：春则生意之生也，夏则生意之长也，秋则生意之成，冬则生意之藏也。自四而两，两而一，则统之有宗，会之有元，故曰："五行一阴阳，阴阳一太极。"又曰："仁为四端之首，而智则能成始而成终；犹元为四德之长，然元不生于元而生于贞。盖天地之化，不翕聚则不能发散也。仁智交际之间，乃万化之机轴。此理循环不穷，吻合无间，故不贞则无以为元也。"又曰："贞而不固，则非贞。贞，如板筑之有干，不贞则无以为元。"又曰："文言上四句说天德之自然，下四句说人事之当然。元者，乃众善之长也；亨者，乃嘉之会也。嘉会，犹言一齐好也。会，犹齐也，言万物至此通畅茂盛，一齐皆好。利者，义之和处也；贞者，乃事之桢干也。'体仁足以长人'，以仁为体，而温厚慈爱之理由此发出也。体，犹所谓'公而以人体之'之'体'。嘉会者，嘉其所会也。——以礼文节之，使之无不中节，乃嘉其所会也。'利物足以和义'，义者，事之宜也；利物，则合乎事之宜矣。此句乃翻转，'义'字愈明白，不利物则非义矣。贞固以贞为骨子，则坚定不可移易。"铢。

The Master said, "The benevolence is hardly understandable unless the four are accessed as a whole. Benevolence is the substance of itself; propriety is the definite regulations of the benevolence; righteousness is the

---

① The last sentence, which is unintelligible, of this paragraph in the original text is not translated. The compiler of the text adds a note to the paragraph, saying that he suspects that a few sino-graphs are missing in the sentence or there are several misrecorded sino-graphs therein.

determination and administration by the benevolence, and wisdom is the differentiation by the benevolence. They are comparable to the four seasons, which are different from one another, yet all stem from spring. In spring, the intention to produce occurs; in summer, it prospers; in autumn, it fruits; in winter, it is stored. The four become two and the two become one, and thus the unity has its source and the mutual penetration has its origin. Therefore, the 'Diagram of the Great Ultimate' says, 'The Five Agents constitute one system of *yin* and *yang*, and *yin* and *yang* constitute one Great Ultimate. '"

He went on and said, "Benevolence is the first of the Four Beginnings, while wisdom can complete both the beginning and ending. They are comparable to the Four Virtues of 'Hexagram Qian,' where origination is the first of them. However, origination comes into being not in itself but in the last, i. e. firmness. That is probably because the transformation by Heaven and Earth, without convergence, would be incapable of divergence. The interactive transition between benevolence and wisdom is where the pivot for the myriad transformations lies. This principle circulates ceaselessly, enabling beginnings and endings to meet each other perfectly. Thus, without firmness, there would be no origination at all. "

He continued, "Being firm without constancy is not truly being firm. Being firm and constant is comparable to making an earth wall reinforced with bars, and without firmness and constancy, there would be nothing by which origination occurs. "

He added, "In the 'Wenyan' concerning the judgment of 'Hexagram Qian,' the first sentence says of the naturalness of the heavenly virtue and the second sentence, of the oughtness of human events. 'The origination is the first and chief of all qualities of goodness; the prosperity is the assemblage of excellences. ' The 'assemblage of excellences' here means that all are good. The 'assemblage,' referring to everything, implies that the myriad things in this phase flourish with vigor and vim, all of which are good. The advantage is the harmony of all that is righteous; the firmness and constancy are the guarantee of doing affairs well. ① 'The Superior Man embodies benevolence and it is fit for him to preside over other people.' This means taking benevolence as what is embodied, which is the source where the principle of kindness and affection issues out. The meaning of the 'embody' here is comparable to that in 'Being impartial is embodied by humankind' said by Yichuan. As regards the assemblage of excellences, all the excellences are made to be subject to the patterns of propriety so that every one of them is fit to show the propriety. In 'Benefiting all things, the Superior Man is fit to exhibit the harmony of all that is righteous,' the 'righteous' refers to the appropriateness of affairs and the 'benefiting all things' means being suitable to the appropriateness of affairs. This sentence can be understood by turning it to a double negation and the clearer one sees the meaning of 'righteous,' the easier he sees that whatever does not benefit all things is not righteous. Being firm and constant, with firmness as its bone, means being steadfast and unmovable." ② [Zhu]

76 问仁。曰："将仁义礼智四字求。"又问："仁是统体底否？"曰："且理会义礼智令分明，其空阙一处便是仁。"又曰："看公时一般气象如何，私时一般气象如何。"德明。

When asked about benevolence, the Master replied, "You can try to understand it by taking the benevolence, righteousness, propriety, and wisdom as a whole." When asked further, "Is benevolence that which commands the other three?" He answered, "If you can understand righteousness, propriety, and wisdom well, then you will see some vacancy in them and that is what the very benevolence fills." He added, "See what it is

---

① In the original, *zhengan* 桢干 refers to, when an earth wall is made, the stanchions used as supports for it. In the translation, a sense translation "guarantee" is employed.

② The part introduced by "He added" in the passage is Zhu's interpretation of "Wenyan," an explanation of the judgment of "Hexagram Qian" in the *Classic of Change*. The quotations from the "Wenyan" are translated on the basis of the English version by J. Legge (see http://ctext.org/book-of-changes/qian), with some modifications.

like when it is impartial and what it is like when it is partial. "［Deming］

77 萋卿问："仁恐是生生不已之意。人唯为私意所汩，故生意不得流行。克去己私，则全体大用，无时不流行矣。"曰："此是众人公共说底，毕竟紧要处不知如何。今要见'仁'字意思，须将仁义礼智四者共看，便见'仁'字分明。如何是义，如何是礼，如何是智，如何是仁，便'仁'字自分明。若只看'仁'字，越看越不出。"曰："'仁'字恐只是生意，故其发而为恻隐，为羞恶，为辞逊，为是非。"曰："且只得就'恻隐'字上看。"道夫问："先生尝说'仁'字就初处看，只是乍见孺子入井，而怵惕恻隐之心盖有不期然而然，便是初处否？"曰："恁地靠着他不得。大抵人之德性上，自有此四者意思：仁，便是个温和底意思；义，便是惨烈刚断底意思；礼，便是宣著发挥底意思；智，便是个收敛无痕迹底意思。性中有此四者，圣门却只以求仁为急者，缘仁却是四者之先。若常存得温厚底意思在这里，到宣著发挥时，便自然会宣著发挥；到刚断时，便自然会刚断；到收敛时，便自然会收敛。若将别个做主，便都对副不着了。此仁之所以包四者也。"问："仁即性，则'性'字可以言仁否？"曰："性是统言。性如人身，仁是左手，礼是右手，义是左脚，智是右脚。"萋卿问："仁包得四者，谓手能包四支可乎？"曰："且是譬喻如此。手固不能包四支，然人言手足，亦须先手而后足；言左右，亦须先左而后右。"直卿问："此恐如五行之木，若不是先有个木，便亦自生下面四个不得。"曰："若无木便无火，无火便无土，无土便无金，无金便无水。"道夫问："向闻先生语学者：'五行不是相生，合下有时都有。'如何？"曰："此难说，若会得底，便自然不相悖，唤做一齐有也得，唤做相生也得。便虽不是相生，他气亦自相灌注。如人五脏，固不曾有先后，但其灌注时，自有次序。"久之，又曰："'仁'字如人酿酒：酒方微发时，带些温气，便是仁；到发得极热时，便是礼；到得熟时，便是义；到得成酒后，却只与水一般，便是智。又如一日之间，早间天气清明，便是仁；午间极热时，便是礼；晚下渐凉，便是义；到夜半全然收敛，无些形迹时，便是智。只如此看，甚分明。"道夫。

Feiqing said to the Master, "I am afraid benevolence means producing creatures unceasingly. It is only because men are submerged by selfish intentions that in them the intention to produce can not prevail. Thus, if men are able to get rid of their selfish intentions, then their substance will be complete and their function will be great, and their intentions to produce will be prevalent in them at any time. " The Master responded, "This refers to what is common among all men, but after all you fail to clarify what matters in that regard. If you want to see what is meant by benevolence, you should try to understand benevolence, righteousness, propriety, and wisdom as a whole, and then you will get it well. When you see clearly what benevolence, righteousness, propriety, and wisdom mean respectively, you will find it easy to understand benevolence. But if you focus on benevolence only, the more you grapple with it, the more confused you will get. " Feiqing further asked, "Benevolence, I am afraid, means only the intention to produce, and therefore it is emanated as feelings of sadness and commiseration, shame and dislike, deference and compliance, and right and wrong. " The Master replied, "You may focus on the feeling of sadness and commiseration and try to have a thorough understanding of what it means. "

I asked, "You, sir, once said that, to understand what is meant by benevolence, one should turn to where it originates first. When one suddenly sees a child about to fall into a well, he will without exception experience a feeling of alarm and distress, and that happens though he did not expect it. Is this happening where benevolence originates first?" The Master answered, "In that way, you can not approach it. Generally, the moral character of a person naturally embraces what the four mean respectively: benevolence means gentleness and kindness; righteousness, staunchness and resoluteness; propriety, emitting and effect-taking; wisdom, retracting and retreating without leaving any trace behind. Though these four virtues inhere in the human nature, the sage advocated that the pursuit of benevolence was the most urgent, for it is prior to the other three. If the gentleness and kindness meant by benevolence can be preserved constantly here, when there appears an occasion calling for its being emitted and given play to, it will naturally be emitted and given play to, and if the occasion calls for being staunch and resolute or being retracted and retreated, it will naturally be so respectively. If you take one of the other three for the dominant, you will miss the point. That is why benevolence includes itself and all the other three. " I further asked, "Benevolence is the same as nature, and then can benevolence be understood from the viewpoint of nature?" The Master answered, "Nature is the general name, which is comparable to the human body, with the left hand and the right hand, the left foot and the right foot, being benevolence and propriety, righteousness and wisdom, respectively. "

Feiqing asked, "Benevolence embraces all the four, and does this mean the left hand can embrace all the four limbs?" The Master answered, "That is only a metaphor. It is true that the left hand can not embrace all the four limbs, but when speaking of the limbs, we mention first hands and then feet, and when speaking of the two sides, we say first left and then right. "

Zhiqing said, "That is, I am afraid, like the wood in the Five Agents. If there was no wood first, the other four would not be able to be produced. " The Master responded, "Without wood, there would be no fire, without which, there would be no earth, without which, there would be no metal, without which, there would be no water. "

I asked, "I once heard you, sir, tell to a student 'It is not that the Five Agents are in an inter-promoting relationship, but that when they should rise, they all rise simultaneously. ' (How do you think of that?)" The Master answered, "It is hard to say. When they happen to rise at the same time, naturally they will not contradict one another, so they can be regarded either as all rising simultaneously or as being in an inter-promoting relationship. Even though they do not inter-promote one another, they have themselves imbued with vital force in an sequential order. They are comparable to the five internal organs of a person, of which there is no inherently sequential order to speak of, but there is naturally an sequential order when they receive something. ”

After some time, the Master went on and said, “ Benevolence is comparable to brewing wine. When fermentation begins and produces some raw wine with some warmth, that is benevolence; when the fermentation reaches the hottest degree, that is propriety; when the fermentation ends, that is righteousness; when finished wine is made, which is water-like, that is wisdom. Benevolence is also akin to the daytime. The clear and bright morning is benevolence; the hottest noon is propriety; the cool evening is righteousness; the midnight when the retracting reaches the greatest extent, showing few active signs, is wisdom. With such analogy, what benevolence and the other three mean is very clear to see. ” [Daofu]

78 “今日要识得仁之意思是如何。圣贤说仁处最多，那边如彼说，这边如此说，文义各不同。看得个意思定了，将圣贤星散说体看，处处皆是这意思，初不相背，始得。集注说：‘爱之理，心之德。’爱是恻隐，恻隐是情，其理则谓之仁。心之德，德又只是爱。谓之心之德，却是爱之本柄。人之所以为人，其理则天地之理，其气则天地之气。理无迹，不可见，故于气观之。要识仁之意思，是一个浑然温和之气，其气则天地阳春之气，其理则天地生物之心。今只就人身己上看有这意思是如何。才有这意思，便自恁地好，便不恁地干燥。将此意看圣贤许多说仁处，都只是这意。告颜子以‘克己复礼’，克去己私以复于礼，自然都是这意思。这不是待人旋安排，自是合下都有这个浑全流行物事。此意思才无私意间隔，便自见得人与己一，物与己一，公道自流行。须是如此看。孔门弟子所问，都只是问做工夫。若是仁之体段意思，也各各自理会得了。今却是这个未曾理会得，如何说要做工夫！且如程先生云：‘偏言则一事，专言则包四者。’上云：‘四德之元，犹五常之仁。’恰似有一个小小底仁，有一个大大底仁。‘偏言则一事’，是小小底仁，只做得仁之一事；'专言则包四者'，是大大底仁，又是包得礼义智底。若如此说，是有两样仁。不知仁只是一个，虽是偏言，那许多道理也都在里面；虽是专言，那许多道理也都在里面。"致道云："如春是生物之时，已包得夏长、秋成、冬藏意思在。"曰："春是生物之时，到夏秋冬，也只是这气流注去。但春则是方始生荣意思，到夏便是结里定了，是这生意到后只渐老了。"贺孙曰："如温和之气，固是见得仁。若就包四者意思看，便自然有节文，自然得宜，自然明辨。"曰："然。"贺孙。

The Master said, "Today, you should know what benevolence means. The sages and worthies discoursed benevolence the most often, but here it was expounded this way, while there it was discussed that way, resulting in different explanations. You should try to get an understanding of its original meaning for sure and then chew the explanations scattered in the discourses by the sages and worthies. Only when you find that all those explanations conform to its original meaning, not going against it, can you attain a truly accurate understanding of it. I say in *Lunyu Jizhu* 论语集注 (Collected Annotations of the *Analects*) that benevolence is 'the principle of love and the virtue of mind.' Love is sadness and commiseration, which is a feeling, and its principle is called benevolence. The virtue of mind is only love. Though benevolence is called the virtue of mind, this virtue is the original basis (i. e. principle) of love. The reason why a man is what he is is that his principle is that of Heaven and Earth and his vital force is that of Heaven and Earth. The principle is formless, showing no trace of its own, so it can only be observed via the vital force. To understand the meaning of benevolence, you should know that it is undifferentiated mild vital force, its vital force is the vital force of Heaven and Earth for spring, and its principle is the mind of Heaven and Earth for producing things. Now please consider its meaning by yourselves. As soon as you see its meaning, you will find it so clear and fresh and not that dull and dry. With your understanding of that meaning, when you read those different explanations of benevolence by ancient sages and worthies, you will see only that meaning running through them. When Confucius told Yanzi 'To subdue one's self and return to propriety is benevolence,' what he meant is naturally that meaning, too. It does not mean that it awaits any arrangement made by humankind, but that there is originally something inhering in humankind, complete and undifferentiated. The moment you get this understanding free from any obstruction caused by your bias, you will see naturally the unity between others and yourself and the unity between things and yourself, in which the impartial Way penetrates and circulates. That is the way to understand it. What the disciples of Confucius asked him about was only how to make efforts to progress in learning, for they each had already gained their personal understanding of what benevolence meant. Nowadays, however, you have still not gained an adequate understanding of it. Then, how can you make efforts in pursuit of learning? Just as Master Cheng Yi said of the Five Constant Virtues, 'The separately said benevolence refers to the benevolence separate from the other four, while the collectively said benevolence embraces the other four to be an entirety.' Before this sentence, he said, 'The origination in the Four Virtues (of "Hexagram Qian") is comparable to the benevolence in the Five Constant Virtues.' It is as if there were a very small benevolence and a very large benevolence. The 'separately said benevolence' is the former, while the 'collectively said benevolence,' the latter, which includes propriety, righteousness, and wisdom. Thus, there would be two cases of benevolence. He did not know that there is actually only one benevolence, and, though the benevolence is said of separately, the many principles dwell in it, and though it is said of collectively, the many principles dwell in it, too."

Zhidao 致道 (courtesy name of Zhao Shixia 赵师夏 [dates unknown], a disciple of Zhu's) said, "For example, spring, which is the season when things are produced, already connotes what is meant by summer, autumn, and winter. " The Master responded, "Spring is the time when things are produced and in summer, autumn, and winter, it is the same vital force that flows and imbues them. But spring means the beginning of prosperity, which will mature in summer, and the intention to produce wanes in the later seasons. " I said, "It is true that benevolence can be seen in the gentle and kind vital force, but if we try to understand benevolence from the viewpoint of its embracing others, there are naturally the definite regulations of propriety, naturally the suitability, and naturally the clarity and accessibility. " The Master agreed with him. 〔Hesun〕

79 或问论语言仁处。曰:"理难见,气易见。但就气上看便见,如看元亨利贞是也。元亨利贞也难看,且看春夏秋冬。春时尽是温厚之气,仁便是这般气象。夏秋冬虽不同,皆是阳春生育之气行乎其中。故'偏言则一事,专言则包四者'。如知福州是这个人,此偏言也;及专言之,为九州岛安抚,亦是这一个人,不是两人也。故明道谓:'义礼智,皆仁也。若见得此理,则圣人言仁处,或就人上说,或就事上说,皆是这一个道理。'正叔云:'满腔子是恻隐之心。'"曰:"仁便是恻隐之母。"又曰:"若晓得此理,便见得'克己复礼',私欲尽去,便纯是温和冲粹之气,乃天地生物之心。其余人所以未仁者,只是心中未有此气象。论语但云求仁之方者,是其门人必尝理会得此一个道理。今但问其求仁之方,故夫子随其人而告之。"赵致道云:"李先生云:'仁是天理之统体。'"先生曰:"是。"南升。疑与上条同闻。

Someone asked about the discourse of benevolence in the *Analects*. The Master answered, "Principle is difficult to see, but vital force is easy. So you can understand what is meant by benevolence in regard only to vital force, in the same way as you see origination, prosperity, advantage, and firmness. If you find it not easy to see what the Four Virtues mean, you may turn to the four seasons. Spring is replete with the mild and temperate vital force and that is what benevolence is like. In all the other three seasons, though different, pervades the same productive vital force as spring is imbued with. So Master

Cheng Yi said, 'The separately said benevolence refers to the benevolence separate from the other four, while the collectively said benevolence embraces the other four to be an entirety.' For example, if the prefect of Fuzhou is said to be a person, that is the separately said person; and when he is said collectively as one of the pacification commission in Jiuzhoudao, he is still the same person. Therefore, Mingdao (i. e. Cheng Hao) said, 'Righteousness, propriety, and wisdom are all benevolence. If one sees this truth, when he reads the discourses of the sages on benevolence, he will understand that, though some of them refer to humankind and some others, to things, the same truth underlies both of them.' Zhengshu said, 'The entire cavity is filled with the mind of commiseration.' Benevolence is the mother of sadness and commiseration.'"

He added, "If you have understood this point, you will see what is meant by 'To subdue one's self and return to propriety is benevolence.' If one removes all his selfish desires, what remains in him is only the temperate and pure vital force, which is nothing but the mind of Heaven and Earth to produce things. If one has not reached such realm of benevolence, it is because there has not appeared that state of purity in his mind. The *Analects* records Confucius's disciples enquiring how to pursue benevolence, because they already understood that truth. So they asked about the way of seeking for benevolence, and Confucius answered them one by one." Zhao Zhidao said to the Master, "Mr. Li (Li Tong, Zhu's teacher) said, 'Benevolence is the commander of all heavenly principles.'" The Master replied, "Yes."
[Nansheng][1] This recorded passage may have been based on the conversations on the same occasion as the last one.

80 "仁有两般：有作为底，有自然底。看来人之生便自然如此，不待作为。如说父子欲其亲，君臣欲其义，是他自会如此，不待欲也。

---

① Zheng Nansheng 郑南升 (courtesy name Wenxiang 文相).

父子自会亲，君臣自会义，既自会恁地，便活泼泼地，便是仁。"因举手中扇云："只如摇扇，热时人自会恁地摇，不是欲他摇。孟子说'乍见孺子入井时，皆有怵惕恻隐之心'，最亲切。人心自是会如此，不是内交、要誉，方如此。大凡人心中皆有仁义礼智，然元只是一物，发用出来，自然成四派。如破梨相似，破开成四片。如东对着西，便有南北相对；仁对着义，便有礼智相对。以一岁言之，便有寒暑；以气言之，便有春夏秋冬；以五行言之，便有金木水火土。且如阴阳之间，尽有次第。大寒后，不成便热，须是且做个春温，渐次到热田地。大热后，不成便寒，须是且做个秋凉，渐次到寒田地。所以仁义礼智自成四派，各有界限。仁流行到那田地时，义处便成义，礼、智处便成礼、智。且如万物收藏，何尝休了，都有生意在里面。如谷种、桃仁、杏仁之类，种着便生，不是死物，所以名之曰'仁'，见得都是生意。如春之生物，夏是生物之盛，秋是生意渐渐收敛，冬是生意收藏。"又曰："春夏是行进去，秋冬是退后去。正如人呵气，呵出时便热，吸入时便冷。"明作。

The Master said, "There are two types of benevolence, one of which is artificial and the other, natural. It seems that the production of humankind is something natural, calling for no artificial benevolence. A father and his son desire closeness to each other and a sovereign and his minister desire righteousness between them. In either case, that state between the two sides is natural, which does not need anything artificial. So there are naturally father-son closeness and sovereign-minister righteousness, which are what they are. Such lively state indicates benevolence." Thereupon, raising the fan in his hand, he said, "It is like waving a fan. When one feels hot, he will wave it naturally rather than be desired by someone else to do it. Mencius was to the point best when he said, 'If men suddenly see a child about to fall into a well, they will without exception experience a feeling of alarm and distress.' (*Mencius*, 2A: 6) That is because the mind of humankind will experience that feeling on that occasion naturally rather than for gaining the favor of the child's parents or seeking the praise of their neighbors and friends. Generally speaking, in the mind of humankind dwells benevolence, righteousness, propriety, and wisdom, but originally there is only one, which is brought forth to become four naturally, like cutting one pear into four pieces. As east is opposite west, which gives rise to north being opposite south, benevolence is opposite righteousness and then propriety gets opposite to wisdom. It is also comparable to a year, with winter-cold and summer-heat; to vital force in a year, with spring, summer, autumn, and winter; to the Five Agents, with metal, wood, water, fire, and earth. In the case of *yin* and *yang*, there are also gradients between them. After the Great Cold (the last one of the 24 Solar Terms for a lunar year), the summer-heat will not come immediately, for it has to wait until the earth experiences spring warmth and gets hot gradually. Similarly, after the Great Heat (the 12th of the 24 Solar Terms), the winter-cold has to wait to come until the earth experiences autumn coolness and gets cold gradually. Therefore, benevolence, righteousness, propriety, and wisdom, are naturally separate, each with a delimited sphere. Whenever and wherever benevolence flows and operates, righteousness will be fully righteousness, and propriety and wisdom will fully be propriety and wisdom, respectively. It is like the myriad things being stored and preserved. There is not a moment of cessation in such an operation, for in all of these things there is the intention to produce. Take for example such things as seeds of grain or the peach and apricot kernels. When sown, they will grow, so they are not dead things. For this reason, they are called *ren* (the word *ren* meaning both kernel and benevolence). This shows that benevolence implies the intention to produce. In spring things begin to be produced; in summer, they prosper; in autumn, the intention to produce begins to be retracted by degrees; in winter, it is stored. " He added, "Spring and summer are advancing, while autumn and winter, retreating. It is like one breathing, and the exhaling feels warm, but the inhaling feels cool. " [Mingzuo]①

81 百行万善，固是都合着力，然如何件件去理会得！百行万善摠于五常，五常又摠于仁，所以孔孟只教人求仁。求仁只是"主敬"，"求放心"，若能如此，道理便在这里。方子。

It is ideal that we make efforts to understand all the activities embodying good, but we are impossible to investigate everyone of them. All those activities boil down to the Five Constant Virtues, which boil further down to benevolence. Thus, Confucius and Mencius taught others only to pursue benevolence. Pursuing benevolence is nothing but seeking for "the ruling of seriousness" (*Mencius*, 2B：11) and "the lost mind. " (*Mencius*, 6A：11) If one is able to accomplish that, he will see the truth therein. [Fangzi]

82 学者须是求仁。所谓求仁者，不放此心。圣人亦只教人求仁。盖仁义礼智四者，仁足以包之。若是存得仁，自然头头做着，不用逐事安排。故曰："苟志于仁矣，无恶也。"今看大学，亦要识此意，所谓"顾諟天之明命"，"无他，求其放心而已"。方子。

It is necessary for a scholar to exert himself in pursuit of benevolence. The so called "pursuit of benevolence" means not losing the mind. The sages instructed others to seek for benevolence only, for it embraces all benevolence, righteousness, propriety, and wisdom. If one is able to preserve benevolence, he will be capable of all things naturally and need not to make arrangement of them one by one purposely. Therefore, Confucius said, "If the will be set on virtue, there will be no practice of wickedness. " (*Analects*, 4：4) Now when you read *Daxue* 大学 (Great Learning) you should know this point, which it expresses as "He contemplated and studied the illustrious decrees of Heaven. " (*Great Learning*, 5) and "The great end of learning is nothing else but to seek for the lost mind. " (*Mencius*, 6A：11) [Fangzi]

83 问求仁。曰："看来'仁'字只是个浑沦底道理。如大学致知、

---

① Zhou Mingzuo 周明作 (courtesy name Wenxing 文兴).

格物，所以求仁也；中庸博学、审问、慎思、明辨、力行，亦所以求仁也。"又问："诸先生皆令人去认仁，必要人体认得这仁是甚物事。"曰："而今别把仁做一物事认，也不得；衮说鹘突了，亦不得。"焘。

I asked about seeking for benevolence. The Master answered, "It seems that benevolence is only an undifferentiated principle. For example, the aim of 'pursuing perfection of knowledge' and 'investigating things' advocated in the *Great Learning* is to seek for benevolence. In the *Doctrine of the Mean*, the purpose of making 'extensive study,' 'accurate inquiry,' 'careful reflection,' 'clear discrimination,' and 'earnest practice,' is also to seek for benevolence." I said thereupon, "All the teachers have instructed their students to ponder over benevolence and require that they attain a thorough understanding of what it means." The Master responded, "Now it will not do to understand benevolence as a concrete thing, nor it will do to regard it as something devoid of definite meaning." [Tao]

84 或问："存得此心，便是仁。"曰："且要存得此心，不为私欲所胜，遇事每每着精神照管，不可随物流去，须要紧紧守着。若常存得此心，应事接物，虽不中不远。思虑纷扰于中，都是不能存此心。此心不存，合视处也不知视，合听处也不知听。"或问："莫在于敬否？"曰："敬非别是一事，常唤醒此心便是。人每日只鹘鹘突突过了，心都不曾收拾得在里面。"又曰："仁虽似有刚直意，毕竟本是个温和之物。但出来发用时有许多般，须得是非、辞逊、断制三者，方成仁之事。及至事定，三者各退，仁仍旧温和，缘是他本性如此。人但见有是非、节文、断制，却谓都是仁之本意，则非也。春本温和，故能生物，所以说仁为春。"明作。

Someone asked, "The preservation of the mind means the attainment of benevolence. (Is it right?)" The Master replied, "The preservation of the mind means taking care of it and sticking to it with devotion and ardency no matter what happens, and avoiding being overcome by selfish desire and floating along with currents. If one can keep on making efforts to preserve his mind, when he handles affairs and copes with things, though not necessarily being the best in doing them, he will be not far from it. When one always feels anxieties disturbing his mind, it is because he fails to preserve his mind. With that failure, he will be ignorant of seeing what he ought to see and hearing what he ought to hear. " Someone else asked, "Does it depend on *jing* 敬 (being serious; seriousness)?" The Master answered, "Being serious is not anything different and what often awakens the mind is the very seriousness. Many people only live each day in confusion, never making any effort to take back their mind from outside. " He added, " Though benevolence seems to display some firmness and straightforwardness, it is actually mild and temperate. When it plays its function, it gives rise to many different orientations, requiring that the three others, i. e. the feeling of right and wrong, of deference and compliance, and the power of making decisions and enactments, play their roles before it can do anything. After it accomplishes something, all the three others will retire and benevolence will remain still mild and temperate, indicating its original state. If one observes there being the feeling of right and wrong, the implementing of definite regulations, and the making of decisions and enactments, and says all these are what benevolence has intrinsically, he is wrong. The inherent nature of spring is mild and temperate, by which it is able to produce things, so benevolence is manifested by spring. " [Mingzuo]

85 或曰：“存得此心，即便是仁。”曰：“此句甚好。但下面说‘合于心者为之，不合于心者勿为’，却又从义上去了，不干仁事。今且只以孟子‘仁，人心也；义，人路也’，便见得仁义之别。盖仁是此心之德；才存得此心，即无不仁。如说‘克己复礼’，亦只是要得私欲去后，此心常存耳，未说到行处也。才说合于心者行之，便侵过义人路底界分矣。然义之所以能行，却是仁之用处。学者须是此心常存，方能审度事理，而行其所当行也。此孔门之学所以必以求仁为先。盖此是万理之原，万事之本，且要先识认得，先存养得，方有下手立脚处耳。”

Someone said to the Master, "'The preservation of the mind is the attainment of benevolence.' How do you think of it?" He responded, "This sentence is said very well, but what follows it is 'Do what conforms to the mind and do not do what does not conform to the mind,' which is said in regard to righteousness and thus has nothing to do with benevolence. Now read 'Benevolence is the human mind, and righteousness is the human path,' said by *Mencius* (6A: 11), and you will see the difference between benevolence and righteousness. Probably it is because benevolence is the virtue of the mind, and the moment the preservation of the mind is accomplished, it is benevolence all over. When Confucius said 'To subdue one's self and return to propriety,' he meant only the constant preservation of the mind after getting rid of selfish desires, without touching upon the practice of it. As soon as the 'Do what conforms to the mind' is said, transgression is already made of the boundary of the righteousness as the human path. However, the reason why righteousness can be conducted is the function of benevolence. Only by preserving constantly his mind can a scholar be able to examine and assess the principle of things and do what he should do. That is why Confucians must prioritize the pursuit of benevolence. It is probably because benevolence is the source of all principles and the basis of all affairs. Therefore, one should make effort to seek for a personal understanding of it first and to preserve it first before he can gain a foothold for pursuing something more."

86 夫仁，亦在乎熟之而已矣！文蔚。

What matters for getting a thorough understanding of benevolence also lies in nothing but getting familiar with it. [Wenwei]

87 耳之德聪，目之德明，心之德仁，且将这意去思量体认。○将爱之理在自家心上自体认思量，便见得仁。○仁是个温和柔软底物事。老子说："柔弱者，生之徒；坚强者，死之徒。"见得自是。看石头上如何种物事出！"蔼乎若春阳之温，泛乎若醴酒之醇。"此是形容仁底意思。〇当来得于天者只是个仁，所以为心之全体。却自仁中分四界子：一界子上是仁之仁，一界子是仁义，一界子是仁之礼，一界子是仁之智。一个物事，四脚撑在里面，唯仁兼统之。心里只有此四物，万物万事皆自此出。〇天之春夏秋冬最分晓：春生，夏长，秋收，冬藏。虽分四时，然生意未尝不贯；纵雪霜之惨，亦是生意。〇以"生"字说仁，生自是上一节事。当来天地生我底意，我而今须要自体认得。〇试自看一个物坚硬如顽石，成甚物事！此便是不仁。〇试自看温和柔软时如何，此所以"孝悌为仁之本"。若如顽石，更下种不得。俗说"硬心肠"，可以见。硬心巷肠，如何可以与他说话！〇恻隐、羞恶、辞逊、是非，都是两意：恻是初头子，隐是痛；羞是羞己之恶，恶是恶人之恶；辞在我，逊在彼；是、非自分明。〇才仁，便生出礼，所以仁配春，礼配夏；义是裁制，到得智便了，所以配秋，配冬。〇既认得仁如此分明，到得做工夫，须是"克己复礼"；"出门如见大宾，使民如承大祭；己所不欲，勿施于人"，方是做工夫处。先生令思"仁"字。至第三夜，方说前三条。以后八条，又连三四夜所说。今依次第，不敢移动。泳。

〇 As the virtue of the ear is hearing and the virtue of the eye is seeing, the virtue of the mind is benevolence. Please ponder over what this means.

〇 Pore over the principle of love in your mind, and you will see what benevolence means.

〇 Benevolence is a temperate and soft thing. Laozi was right when he said, "What is firm and strong is the concomitant of death; what is soft and weak, the concomitant of life. " (*Laozi*, 76) How can one sow a seed on a rock and make it grow? "It is as temperate as the warm spring sun and as fine as mellow wine. " This is a description of what benevolence means.

〇 What is bestowed by Heaven is only benevolence, so it is the entire mind itself, but delimited in it are four spheres, which are respectively the benevolence of benevolence, the righteousness of benevolence, the propriety of benevolence, and the wisdom of benevolence, like four feet supporting it, with benevolence as their commander. Therefore, in the mind are only those four respects from which the myriad things and affairs stem.

○ The four seasons of Heaven are the most evident to see, for things are produced in spring, exuberant in summer, harvested in autumn, and stored in winter. In spite of the division into four, the intention to produce runs through all of them without any interruption. Even when there are freezing snow and frost, they contain the spirit of life.

○ To discourse benevolence from the viewpoint of production, production is, of course, the first thing for benevolence to do. With regard to the original intention of Heaven and Earth to produce me, I have to attain a personal understanding of it.

○ Try and look at something as hard as a rock. What can it be good for? That is devoid of benevolence.

○ Try and look at something mild and soft. Isn't it indicative of "Filial piety and fraternal submission are the root of all benevolent actions"? (*Analects*, 1:2) If it is as hard as a rock, it is impossible to sow seeds in it. It can be seen from the idiomatic expression "hard heart." How can you talk with a person with a hard heart?

○ Each of the four feelings contains two respects: The "sadness and commiseration" contains sorrowfulness and compassion; the "shame" is for one's own evil and the "dislike" points to the evil of someone else; the "deference" concerns me, while "compliance" concerns him; the "right" and "wrong" are clearly opposite to each other.

○ The moment there is benevolence, it gives rise to propriety. Therefore, benevolence matches spring and propriety matches summer. Righteousness is decision and enactment and wisdom represents ending. Thus, they match autumn and winter respectively.

○ If you have understood benevolence so well, when you set about making efforts, you should do by "subduing your self and return to propriety." "When you go out, behave to every one as if you were receiving a great guest; employ the people as if you were assisting at a great sacrifice; Do not do to others what you would not like them to do to yourself. " (*Analects*, 12: 2) Only in this way can you make efforts effectively.

The Master asked us to think over what benevolence means. It was not until the third night that he told us the first three pieces. The other eight pieces were what he said at the following three or four nights. Their sequential order in which they were recorded is not changed. [Yong]

88 仁兼义言者，是言体；专言仁者，是兼体用而言。节。

When benevolence is discoursed in combination with righteousness, that concerns its substance, while, when it is discussed without involving others, that refers to both its substance and function. [Jie]

89 孔子说仁，多说体；孟子说仁，多说用。如"克己复礼"，"恻隐之心"之类。闳祖。

Confucius's discourse on benevolence is mostly concerned with its substance, such as "To subdue one's self and return to propriety. " (*Analects*, 12: 1) By contrast, Mencius's discourse on benevolence has to do mainly with its function, such as "the feeling of sadness and commiseration. " (*Mencius*, 2B: 6) [Hongzu]

90 直卿云："圣贤言仁，有专指体而言者，有包体、用而言者。"先生曰："仁对义、礼、智言之，则为体；专言之，则兼体、用。此等处，须人自看，如何一一说得。日日将来看，久后须会见得。"佐。

Zhiqing said, "In the discourses of the sages and worthies on benevolence, some are exclusively concerned with its substance, while some others cover both its substance and function. " The Master responded, "When benevolence is discoursed in regard to righteousness, propriety, and wisdom, that refers to its substance; When it is discussed exclusively, that concerns both its substance and function. As for such points as in those discourses, it is impossible to explain them one by one. When you meet some in your reading, you should ponder them by yourself. Study them day by day, and in due course you will see the point. " [Zuo]

91 周明作问仁。曰：“圣贤说话，有说自然道理处，如‘仁，人心’是也；有说做工夫处，如‘克己复礼’是也。”雉。

Zhou Mingzuo asked about benevolence. The Master answered, "In the discourses of the sages and worthies, some are concerned with what natural principles mean, such as ' Benevolence is the mind of humankind,' (*Mencius*, 6A：11) while some others, with how to make efforts in practice, such as 'To subdue one's self and return to propriety.' (*Analects*, 12：1)" [Zhi（雉）]①

92 前辈教人求仁，只说是渊深温粹，义理饱足。干。

When previous scholars instructed others to seek for benevolence, they said only that it was profound, mild, and pure, imbued with universal principle. [Gan]

93 仁在事。若不于事上看，如何见仁。方。

Benevolence is manifested by affairs. If one does not observe affairs, how can he see benevolence? [Fang]

94 做一方便事，也是仁；不杀一虫，也是仁；‘三月不违’，也是仁。节。

One doing something beneficial to others is benevolence; Not killing even one insect is also benevolence. "For three months there would be nothing in his mind contrary to perfect virtue" (*Analects*, 6：7) is benevolence, too. [Jie]

95 “仁则固一，一所以为仁。”言所以一者是仁也。方。

Master Cheng Yi said, "With benevolence, there will be intrinsic unity, and unity is the reason why benevolence is what it is." Here he explained why unity caused benevolence. [Fang]

96 熟底是仁，生底是恕；自然底是仁，勉强底是恕；无计较、无睹当底是仁，有计较、有睹当底是恕。道夫。

---

① Wu Zhi 吴雉（courtesy name Hezhong 和中）.

Benevolence is spontaneous, reciprocity 恕 is cultivated. Benevolence is natural, reciprocity is by effort. Benevolence is uncalculating and has nothing in view, reciprocity is calculating and has an object in view. [Daofu]

97 公在前，恕在后，中间是仁。公了方能仁，私便不能仁。可学。

Impartiality is in the fore, reciprocity is in the rear, and benevolence is in the middle. Only if there is impartiality can there be benevolence, for partiality makes it impossible for there to be benevolence. [Kexue]

98 仁是爱底道理，公是仁底道理。故公则仁，仁则爱。端蒙。

Benevolence is the principle of love, and impartiality is the principle of benevolence. Therefore, if there is impartiality, there is benevolence and if there is benevolence, there is love. [Duanmeng]

99 公是仁之方法，人身是仁之材料。铢。

Impartiality is the means of benevolence and the human body is the material of it. [Zhu]

100 公却是仁发处。无公，则仁行不得。可学。

Impartiality is the means by which benevolence takes effect. Without impartiality, benevolence can by no means be feasible. [Kexue]

101 仁，将"公"字体之。及乎脱落了"公"字，其活底是仁。季通语。方。

Benevolence makes impartiality as its embodiment. When the impartiality falls off, what lives on is benevolence. (Said by Jitong) [Fang]

102 或问仁与公之别。曰："仁在内，公在外。"又曰："惟仁，然后能公。"又曰："仁是本有之理，公是克己工夫极至处。故惟仁然后能公，理甚分明。故程子曰：'公而以人体之。'则是克尽己私之后，只就自身上看，便见得仁也。"

Someone asked about the difference between benevolence and impartiality. The Master said, "Benevolence is in, while impartiality is out." He continued, "Only when there is benevolence can impartiality be possible." He added, "Benevolence is but the inherent principle, whereas impartiality results from one making effort to restrain his selfishness to the utmost. Therefore, only when there is benevolence can impartiality be possible, and then the principle will be manifested explicitly. Thus Master Cheng Yi said, 'Impartiality displays itself via the human embodiment of it (i. e. benevolence).' This means that if one gets completely free from selfishness, what remains in himself is benevolence. "

103 公不可谓之仁，但公而无私便是仁。敬不可谓之中，但敬而无失便是中。道夫。

Impartiality should not be referred to as benevolence, but being impartial and free from selfishness manifests benevolence. Seriousness should not be referred to as equilibrium, but being serious and free from fault manifests equilibrium. [Daofu]

104 无私以闲之则公，公则仁。譬如水，若一些子碍，便成两截，须是打并了障塞，便滔滔地去。从周。

Being free from selfishness and keeping it at bay means impartiality, and by impartiality benevolence will be manifested. It is comparable to a river, and if it is blocked by some obstacle, it can not flow smoothly, but if the obstacle is removed, it will run torrentially. [Congzhou]①

105 做到私欲净尽，天理流行，便是仁。道夫。

If one is able to get rid of his selfish desire completely, the heavenly principle will circulate in him and that is the very benevolence. [Daofu]

106 余正叔尝于先生前论仁，曰："仁是体道之全。"曰："只是一个浑然天理。"文蔚。

Yu Zhengshu 余正叔 (i. e. Yu Daya 余大雅) once talked about benevolence before the Master and said, "Benevolence is the complete embodiment of the Way. " The Master responded, " It is only an undifferentiated heavenly principle. " [Wenwei]

---

① Dou Congzhou 窦从周 (courtesy name Wenqing 文卿).

107 王景仁问仁。曰："无以为也。须是试去屏送了私欲，然后子细体验本心之德是甚气象，无徒讲其文义而已也。"壮祖。

Wang Jingren 王景仁 (dates unknown, a disciple of Zhu's) asked about benevolence. The Master said, "It is of little use talking about it only. One should try to get himself shielded as much as possible from selfish desire and then carefully experience and try to know what the virtue of his original state of mind is like. It is to not much avail only to talk about the meaning of benevolence." [Zhuangzu]

108 周明作谓："私欲去则为仁。"曰："谓私欲去后，仁之体见，则可；谓私欲去后便为仁，则不可。譬如日月之光，云雾蔽之，固是不见。若谓云雾去，则便指为日月，亦不可。如水亦然。沙石杂之，固非水之本然。然沙石去后，自有所谓水者，不可便谓无沙无石为水也。"雉。

Zhou Mingzuo said to the Master, "The state made free from selfish desire is benevolence." The Master responded, "It is right to say that the state made free from selfish desire manifests the substance of benevolence, but it is not right to say the state made free from selfish desire is benevolence itself. For example, the light of the sun or the moon. When its light is shielded by clouds, it can not be seen, but when the clouds clear away, it is not right to say that the state free from clouds is the sun or the moon itself. This is also true of water. When the water contains sands and stones, that is not the original state of water, indeed, and when the sands and stones are all removed, the water remains, but the state free from sands and stones should not be said as water itself." [Zhi (雉)]

109 余正叔谓："无私欲是仁。"曰："谓之无私欲然后仁，则可；谓无私便是仁，则不可。盖惟无私欲而后仁始见，如无所壅底而后水方行。"方叔曰："与天地万物为一体是仁。"曰："无私，是仁之前事；与天地万物为一体，是仁之后事。惟无私，然后仁；惟仁，然后与天地万物为一体。要在二者之间识得毕竟仁是甚模样。欲晓得仁名义，须并

'义、礼、智'三字看。欲真个见得仁底模样，须是从'克己复礼'做工夫去。今人说仁，如糖，皆道是甜；不曾吃着，不知甜是甚滋味。圣人都不说破，在学者以身体之而已矣。"闳祖。

Yu Zhengshu said to the Master, "The state free from selfish desire is benevolence. " The Master replied, "You would be right to say 'Benevolence ensues when selfish desire is eradicated. ' The state free from selfish desire should not be referred to as benevolence. That is probably because only after selfish desire is eradicated can benevolence appear, as only when the obstruction of water is removed can it flow. " Fangshu said, "The state in oneness with Heaven and Earth and the myriad things is benevolence. " The Master responded, "Getting free from selfish desire is that which is prior to benevolence and entering oneness with Heaven and Earth and the myriad things is that which is posterior to benevolence. Only when there is the state free from selfish desire can benevolence occur and only with benevolence can a person become one with Heaven and Earth and the myriad things. What benevolence means should be understood by situating it between the two sides. If one wants to know the name and meaning of benevolence, he should consider it together with righteousness, propriety, and wisdom. If one wants to see what benevolence is truly like, he should start from 'subduing one's self and return to propriety' and make efforts in practice. Nowadays, it is as if, when many people talked about benevolence, all said that it was sweet like sugar, but since they had never tasted anything sweet by themselves, they did not know what sweetness was really like. In their discourses on benevolence, the sages did not lay it bare, so the students in later ages have had to experience it in person by themselves. " [Hongzu]

110 或问："仁当何训?"曰："不必须用一字训，但要晓得大意通透。"

Someone asked, "Can *ren* 仁 be explained by another sino-graph?" The Master answered, "It is not necessary to explain it by using another sino-graph, but you should understand its basic meaning thoroughly. "

111 "仁"字说得广处,是全体。恻隐、慈爱底,是说他本相。高。

In a broad sense, benevolence refers to its entirety. Commiseration and kindness refer to its true state. [Gao]

112 仁是根,恻隐是萌芽。亲亲、仁民、爱物,便是推广到枝叶处。夔孙。

Benevolence is the root and commiseration is the germination. Being affectionate to parents, disposed lovingly to people generally, and kind to creatures is what is extended to the branches and leaves. [Kuisun]

113 仁固有知觉;唤知觉做仁,却不得。闳祖。

Though benevolence possesses consciousness, consciousness should not be referred to as benevolence. [Hongzu]

114 以名义言之,仁自是爱之体,觉自是智之用,本不相同。但仁包四德。苟仁矣,安有不觉者乎!道夫。

Viewed from its name and meaning, benevolence is, of course, the substance of love and consciousness is, of course, the function of wisdom, which are different originally. However, benevolence embraces the Four Virtues. If there is benevolence, how can there be no consciousness of it? [Daofu]

115 问:"以爱名仁,是仁之迹;以觉言仁,是仁之端。程子曰:'仁道难名,惟公近之,不可便以公为仁。'毕竟仁之全体如何识认?'克己复礼,天下归仁',孟子所谓'万物皆备于我',是仁之体否?"先生曰:"觉,决不可以言仁,虽足以知仁,自属智了。爱分明是仁之迹。"浩曰:"恻隐是仁情之动处。要识仁,须是兼义、礼、智看。有个宜底意思是义,有个让底意思是礼,有个别白底意思是智,有个爱底意思是仁。仁是天理,公是天理。故伊川谓:'惟公近之。'又恐人滞着,随即曰:'不可便以公为仁。''万物皆备'固是仁,然仁之得名却不然。""浩曰"二字可疑。浩。

Question: When love is used to name benevolence, it refers but to the trace of benevolence; when consciousness is used to discourse benevolence, it refers but to the beginning of benevolence. Master Cheng Yi said, "The way of benevolence is hard to describe. Only impartiality is close to it. But impartiality is not identical with benevolence." After all, how to understand the entire substance of benevolence? Confucius said, "If one subdues himself and returns to propriety, all under heaven will ascribe benevolence to him." (*Analects*, 12:1) Mencius said, "All things are already complete in us." (*Mencius*, 7A:4) Did they refer to the substance of benevolence?

Answer: Consciousness can never be applied to discoursing benevolence, for, though consciousness is enough to let benevolence be known, it pertains to wisdom. Obviously, love can be said as the trace of benevolence.

Further answer: The commiseration indicates where the feelings of benevolence stir. To see the meaning of benevolence, one should understand it in combination with righteousness, propriety, and wisdom. The meaning in regard to appropriateness pertains to righteousness; that in regard to comity, to propriety; that in regard to discrimination, to wisdom; that in regard to love, to benevolence. Benevolence represents heavenly principle, so does impartiality. Therefore, Yichuan said, "Only impartiality is close to it." For fear that misunderstanding cropped up therein on the part of others, he added immediately, "But impartiality is not identical with benevolence." It is true that the "All things are already complete in us" is said of benevolence, but that is not why benevolence is named as it is. [Hao]

116 问:"先生答湖湘学者书,以'爱'字言仁,如何?"曰:"缘上蔡说得'觉'字太重,便相似说禅。"问:"龟山却推'恻隐'二字。"曰:"龟山言'万物与我为一'云云,说亦太宽。"问:"此还是仁之体否?"曰:"此不是仁之体,却是仁之量。仁者固能觉,谓觉为仁,不可;仁者固能与万物为一,谓万物为一为仁,亦不可。譬如说屋,不论屋是木做柱,竹做壁,却只说屋如此大,容得许多物。如万物为一,只是说得仁之量。"因举禅语是说得量边事云云。德明。

Question: In your letter replying the several scholars of Huxiang (at present, Hunan), sir, you explained benevolence by mentioning love. Why?

Answer: That is because Shangcai (i. e. Xie Liangzuo) emphasized consciousness so much that he sounded like talking about Chan 禅 (Dhyana) as preached by Buddhism.

Further question: But Guishan 龟山 (style name of Yang Shi 杨时 [1053 – 1135]) was emphatic of commiseration. (How do you think about that?)

Answer: In his discourses such as "The myriad things and me are one," he said that in too broad a sense.

Further question: Is that still concerned with the substance of benevolence?

Answer: That is not the substance of benevolence, but is the capacity of it. Though benevolence is capable of consciousness, the consciousness should not be called benevolence. Though benevolence is capable of being in oneness with myriad things, the myriad things being one should not be called benevolence. For example, as regards a house, whether its pillars are made from wood or its walls are from bamboo, when speaking of its capacity, we only say it is so capacious as to contain many things. The so called myriad things being one refers to the capacity of benevolence. The Master mentioned thereupon some Chan discourses and said that they were concerned with something on the verge of the capacity. [Deming]

117 问："程门以知觉言仁，克斋记乃不取，何也？"曰："仁离爱不得。上蔡诸公不把爱做仁，他见伊川言：'博爱非仁也，仁是性，爱是情。'伊川也不是道爱不是仁。若当初有人会问，必说道'爱是仁之情，仁是爱之性'，如此方分晓。惜门人只领那意，便专以知觉言之，于爱之说，若将浼焉，遂蹉过仁地位去说，将仁更无安顿处。'见孺子匍匐将入井，皆有怵惕恻隐之心'，这处见得亲切。圣贤言仁，皆从这处说。"又问："知觉亦有生意。"曰："固是。将知觉说来冷了。觉在知上却多，只些小搭在仁边。仁是和底意。然添一句，又成一重。须自看得，便都理会得。"淳。

Question：Master Cheng and his disciples discussed benevolence in terms of consciousness, but in your "Kezhai Record"（克斋记），you do not accept their opinions. Why?

Answer：Benevolence is inseparable from love. Shangcai and other scholars did not regard love as concerning benevolence. He heard Yichuan say "Universal love is not benevolence, for benevolence pertains to nature, while love, to feelings." Actually Yichuan did not mean that love was not benevolence. If someone else had asked him, he would have said "Love is the feeling of benevolence, while benevolence is the nature of love," which would have clarified the point well. It is a pity that his disciples failed to see his point and consequently began to discuss benevolence only in terms of consciousness. In their discourses on love, as if to contaminate it, they explained it in the place of benevolence and consequently had nowhere to put benevolence. Mencius was to the point when he said "When one suddenly sees a child about to fall into a well, he will without exception experience a feeling of alarm and distress." (*Mencius*, 2A：6) That is where the sages and worthies started to talk about benevolence.

Further question：Does consciousness possess the spirit of life?

Answer：Yes, of course. But the consciousness is not very close. Consciousness means knowing and sensing, yet is more on the side of knowing and only touches benevolence a little. Benevolence means basically harmoniousness. But when you add such a sentence in its explanation, it gets extended with yet another meaning. You have to strive to see it clearly and will attain a personal understanding of it in due time. [Chun（淳）]

118 余景思问仁之与心。曰："'仁'字是虚，'心'字是实。如水之必有冷，'冷'字是虚，'水'字是实。心之于仁，亦犹水之冷，火之热。学者须当于此心未发时加涵养之功，则所谓恻隐、羞恶、辞逊、是非发而必中。方其未发，此心之体寂然不动，无可分别，且只恁混沌养将去。若必察其所谓四者之端，则既思便是已发。"道夫。

Yu Jingsi 余景思（i. e. Yu Yuanyi 余元一, with courtesy name Jingsi, a disciple of Zhu's）asked about benevolence and its relation to mind. The Master answered, "Benevolence is vacuous, while mind is substantial. Their relation is comparable to coolness and water, in which coolness is vacuous, while water is substantial. Mind is to benevolence what water is to coolness or what fire is to heat. You students should strive to nourish the state of your mind before it emanates. If you do it well, your feelings of sadness and commiseration, shame and dislike, deference and compliance, right and wrong, will be adequate whenever they are emanated. Only before such emanation occurs can the mind be still and tranquil, complete and undifferentiated, and that is the state you should keep on nourishing. If you insist on observing the so called Four Beginnings, then the moment you think of them, they will already have been emanated. "［Daofu］

119 仁。

The sayings in the passage below concern benevolence.

○鸡雏初生可怜意与之同。

A newborn chick is fresh and tender, so is the meaning of benevolence.

○意思鲜嫩。

The meaning of benevolence is tender and delicate.

○天理著见，一段意思可爱，发出即皆是。

The heavenly principle displays itself palpable with its meaning lovely, so is every manifestation of it.

○切脉同体。说多不能记，盖非言语可喻也。

The feeling of impulse is indicative of the entire body. The words said in this regard were to many to be recorded on the spot, and actually what the Master meant was beyond words.

○孟子便说个样子。今不消理会样子，只如颜子学取。

Mencius only gave some rough idea of it. Today, people do not need to go into what he meant, but should turn to Yanzi (i. e. Yan Hui) only and learn from him.

○孔子教人①仁，只要自寻得了后自知，非言可喻。

Confucius taught others benevolence②, telling them that they should seek to understand it by themselves, for its meaning is beyond words.

○只是天理，当其私欲解剥，天理自是完备。只从生意上说仁。

To attain the heavenly principle, one should get rid of his selfish desire, and thus the heavenly principle will become naturally complete in him. The benevolence can be discoursed only in terms of the spirit of life.

○其全体固是仁，所谓专言之也。又从而分，则亦有仁义分言之仁。今不可于名言上理会，只是自到便有知得。

All the four as an entirety is embraced in benevolence, so benevolence in this sense is a collective concept. When the entirety is divided into four, benevolence can be a concept differentiated from those of righteousness and others, and then the benevolence in this sense is a separate concept. Now it will not do only to try and get a superficial understanding of its name and word, for only when you have made sufficient effort will you be able to attain a true understanding of it.

○上蔡所谓"饮食知味"也。方。

That is what Shangcai meant when he said, "Only after one eats and drinks something personally can he know what its taste is really like." [Fang]

120 湖南学者说仁，旧来都是深空说出一片。顷见王日休解孟子

---

① "人"下，贺疑脱"求"字。

② Hesun suspected that the part of the sentence had been "Confucius taught others to pursue benevolence."

云："麒麟者，狮子也。"仁本是恻隐温厚底物事，却被他们说得抬虚打险，瞠眉弩眼，却似说麒麟做狮子，有吞伏百兽之状，盖自"知觉"之说起之。麒麟不食生肉，不食生草；狮子则百兽闻之而脑裂。謇

When the group of Hunan scholars talked about benevolence, they were liable to fetch something from what is empty and groundless. The other day I read something written by Wang Rixiu 王日休 for explanation of the *Mencius*, who said, "Kylin 麒麟 refers to the lion." Benevolence is originally something commiserative and temperate, but they distorted it as something fierce and dangerous, with staring eyes and cross-bowed eyebrows. So the Kylin was claimed as the lion who was able to subdue and even devour other beasts. Probably their approach of explanation started with their theory of consciousness. The Kylin does not eat raw meat or grass, while the lion is a beast so fierce and powerful that when other beasts hear its roar, their brains break up. [Xun]

121 若说得本源，则不犯"仁"字。禅家曹洞有"五位法"，固可笑。以黑为正位，白为偏位。若说时，只是形容个黑白道理，更不得犯"黑白"二字。皆是要从心中流出，不犯纸上语。从周。

When it comes to origin, it does not deviate from benevolence. The Caodong Sect of Buddhism proposed "Doctrine of Five Approaches," which is really absurd. In the central-biased approach, the black is the central position, while the white is the biased position. In its discourse, the description of them is only metaphoric, touching nothing of what "black" and "white" really mean. The understanding of benevolence should flow from the mind rather than be obsessed with the sino-graphs on paper. [Congzhou]

122 义，便作"宜"字看。洽。

The righteousness can be understood by taking it as what is meant by appropriateness. [Qia]①

---

① Zhang Qia 张恰 (courtesy name Yuande 元德).

123 不可执定，随他理去如此，自家行之便是义。节。

Keep from being rigid with it, but rather follow the principle of it wherever it goes, and what you practice accordingly is righteousness. [Jie]

124 义是个毅然说话，如利刀着物。季札。

Righteousness is, as it were, a resolute action, like a sharp knife cutting something. [Jizha]①

125 义如利刀相似，都割断了许多牵绊。祖道。

Righteousness is akin to a sharp knife, which cuts all the entanglements off. [Zudao]

126 义如利刀相似，胸中许多劳劳攘攘，到此一齐割断了。圣贤虽千言万语，千头万项，然一透都透。如孟子言义，伊川言敬，都彻上彻下。

Righteousness, like a sharp knife, cuts all those disturbances in the mind off. Despite all those discourses by the sages and worthies, with all their complexities, when you understand the point thoroughly, all others will become easy to make access to. For example, Mencius's explanation of righteousness and Yichuan's explanation of seriousness 敬, either of which will become clear thoroughly.

127 "义"字如一横剑相似，凡事物到前，便两分去。"君子义以为质"，"义以为上"，"义不食也"，"义弗乘也"，"精义入神，以致用也"：是此义十分精熟，用便见也。

The righteousness, which is comparable to a keen sword, cuts whatever meets it into two parts. "The Superior Man considers righteousness to be essential in everything." (*Analects*, 15：18) "(The Superior Man) holds righteousness to be of highest importance." (*Analects*, 17：23)② "(The Superior Man) feels it righteous not to eat." ("Hexagram Mingyi" 明夷 in

① Li Jizha 李季札 (courtesy name Jizi 季子).

② The translation of the two citations from *Analects* is based on a version by J. Legge (see http：//ctext. org/analects).

Classic of Change）"（ He can discard a carriage and walk on foot, for）righteousness requires that he should not ride. "（ "Hexagram Bi" 贲 in *Classic of Change*）"When we minutely investigate the nature and reasons（of things）till we have entered into the inscrutable and spirit-like in them, we attain to the largest practical application of them. "（ "Appended Remarks II" in *Classic of Change*）① All these discourses are insightful, and whenever you apply them in practice, you will know their incisiveness.

128 "克己复礼为仁"，善善恶恶为义。骧。

"Subduing one's self and returning to propriety is benevolence," and regarding what is good as being good and what is evil as being evil ıs righteousness［Xiang］②

129 仁义，其体亦有先后。节。

In regard to their substances, benevolence is prior to righteousness.［Jie］

130 仁对义为体、用。仁自有仁之体、用，义又有义之体、用。伯羽。

Benevolence is the substance of righteousness, which is the function of benevolence. Benevolence has its own substance and function, so is righteousness.［Boyu］

131 赵致道问："仁义体用、动静何如？"曰："仁固为体，义固为用。然仁义各有体用，各有动静，自详细验之。"贺孙。

Zhao Zhidao asked, "How about the substance and function and the activity and tranquility of benevolence and righteousness?"

The Master answer："Benevolence is the substance of righteousness and righteousness is the function of benevolence. However, either has its own substance and function, and its own activity and tranquility. You should

---

① The translation of the three citations from *Analects* is based on a version by J. Legge（see http：//ctext. org/book-of-changes）.

② Yang Xiang 杨骧（courtesy name Zi'ang 子昂）.

ponder over this regard carefully. " ［Hesun］

132 仁义互为体用、动静。仁之体本静，而其用则流行不穷；义之用本动，而其体则各止其所。

Benevolence and righteousness are each other's substance and function as well as activity and tranquility. The substance of benevolence is tranquil in nature, while its function is operating unceasingly; the function of righteousness is active in nature, while its substance is where it should rest.

133 义之严肃，即是仁底收敛。淳。

When righteousness becomes stern, that means the recessing of benevolence. ［Chun（淳）］

134 以仁属阳，以义属阴。仁主发动而言，义主收敛而言。若扬子云："于仁也柔，于义也刚。"又自是一义。便是这物事不可一定名之，看他用处如何。

Benevolence pertains to *yang*, while righteousness, to *yin*. They are said so because benevolence is in charge of initiation, whereas righteousness is in charge of recession. When Yangzi（i. e. Yang Xiong）said, "The Superior Man is flexible in matters of benevolence, while firm in matters of righteousness," what he meant is something different. Therefore, a thing or an event should not be given a name to once and for all, for its naming depends on what it is put to use for.

135 问"于仁也柔，于义也刚"。曰："仁体柔而用刚，义体刚而用柔①。"铢曰："此岂所谓'阳根阴，阴根阳'邪?"曰："然。"铢。

Someone asked the Master："What do you think of 'being flexible in matters of benevolence, while firm in matters of righteousness'?" The Master answered, "The substance of benevolence is soft and its function is firm, while the substance of righteousness is firm and its function is soft. "② I said

---

① 贺疑"体柔"以下，刚柔互误。

② Hesun suspected that what Zhu had said was "The substance of benevolence is firm and its function is soft, while the substance of righteousness is soft and its function is firm. "

to the Master, "Isn't it the so called 'Yang roots in yin, while yin, in yang'?" The Master replied, "Yes. " [Zhu]

136 先生答叔重疑问曰: "仁体刚而用柔, 义体柔而用刚。" 广请曰: "自太极之动言之, 则仁为刚, 而义为柔; 自一物中阴阳言之, 则仁之用柔, 义之用刚。" 曰: "也是如此。仁便有个流动发越之意, 然其用则慈柔; 义便有个商量从宜之义, 然其用则决裂。" 广。

When answering Shuzhong's (Dong Zhu's) question, the Master said, "The substance of benevolence is firm and its function is soft, while the substance of righteousness is soft and its function is firm. " I said to him, "From the viewpoint of the activity of the Great Ultimate, benevolence is firm, while righteousness is soft; from the viewpoint of the ying-yang in a thing, the function of benevolence is soft, while that of righteousness is firm. " The Master replied, "That is right. Benevolence has the intention to start up something, whereas its function is soft and gentle. By contrast, righteousness has the intention to consult for what is appropriate, whereas its function is firm and resolute. " [Guang]

137 "寻常人施恩惠底心, 便发得易, 当刑杀时, 此心便疑。可见仁属阳, 属刚; 义属阴, 属柔。" 直卿云: "即将'舒敛'二字看, 便见: 喜则舒, 怒则敛。" 方子。

The Master said, "Ordinary people are liable to grant a boon to others, while they tend to be dubious to mete out a punishment. Thus, benevolence bears on yang and on firmness, while righteousness, on yin and to softness. " Zhiqing responded, "Seeing from relaxing and retracting, it is obvious that pleasure is relaxing, while anger is retracting. " [Fangzi]

138 仁义如阴阳, 只是一气。阳是正长底气, 阴是方消底气; 仁便是方生底义, 义便是收回头底仁。要之, 仁未能尽得道体, 道则平铺地散在里, 仁固未能尽得。然仁却是足以该道之体。若识得阳, 便识得阴; 识得仁, 便识得义。识得一个, 便晓得其余个。道夫。

Benevolence and righteousness are, like yin and yang, of one vital *force.* *Yang* is the vital force on the increase, while *yin* is the vital force on the decline. Benevolence is the righteousness just produced, whereas righteousness is the benevolence already withdrawn. In a word, benevolence is unable to gain the complete substance of the Way, for the Way lies scattered in them. Despite its failure to gain it completely, benevolence is sufficient to manifest the substance of the Way. If one understands *yang*, he will naturally understand *yin*, and if he understands benevolence, he will naturally understand righteousness. In such cases, the understanding of one will lead to that of the other. [Daofu]

139 问：“义者仁之质？”曰：“义有裁制割断意，是把定处，便发出许多仁来。如非礼勿视听言动，便是把定处；‘一日克己复礼，天下归仁’，便是流行处。”淳。

Question: Is righteousness the *zhi* 质 (essence) of benevolence?

Answer: Righteousness has the meaning of measuring, tailoring and cutting-off, and it is like guarding a pass, via which many portions of benevolence are emanated. For example, "looking not at, listening not, and speaking not what is contrary to propriety, and making no movement which is contrary to propriety," (*Analects*, 12:1) which are all dependent on the results of pass-guarding; "If one subdues himself and returns to propriety, all under heaven will ascribe benevolence to him," (*Analects*, 12:1) indicates where benevolence flows. [Chun (淳)]

140 问：“孟子以恻隐为仁之端，羞恶为义之端。周子曰：‘爱曰仁，宜曰义。’然以其存于心者而言，则恻隐与爱固为仁心之发。然羞恶乃就耻不义上反说，而非直指义之端也。‘宜’字乃是就事物上说。不知义在心上，其体段如何。”曰：“义之在心，乃是决裂果断者也。”柄。

Question: Mencius regarded the feeling of sadness and commiseration as the beginning of benevolence and the feeling of shame and dislike as the beginning of righteousness. Master Zhou (i. e. Zhou Dunyi) said, "Love is benevolence and appropriateness is righteousness. " However, from the viewpoint of their being preserved in mind, it is true that the feeling of commiseration and love is the emanation of benevolence, but the feeling of shame and dislike is said actually as feeling shameful of non-righteousness, which does not refer straightly to the beginning of righteousness. The "appropriateness" is said with regard to things and events. How about the role of righteousness in mind?

Answer: The righteousness in mind plays the role of one who is determined and resolute to do something. [Bing]

141 天下之物, 未尝无对: 有阴便有阳, 有仁便有义, 有善便有恶, 有语便有默, 有动便有静。然又却只是一个道理。如人行出去是这脚, 行归亦是这脚。譬如口中之气, 嘘则为温, 吸则为寒耳。雉。

None of the things in the world has no opposite, as evidenced by *yin* and *yang*, benevolence and righteousness, good and evil, speaking and being silent, and activity and tranquility. However, there is only one principle. It is like a person walking out and in by the same pair of feet and also like breathing with exhaling warmth and inhaling coolness [Zhi (雉)].

142 礼者, 节文也。礼数。节。

Propriety is definite regulations (for the feelings). There are grades of ceremonial rites. [Jie]

143 直卿曰: "五常中说知有两般: 就知识处看, 用着知识者是知; 就理上看, 所以为是为非者, 亦知也。一属理, 一属情。" 曰: "固是。道德皆有体有用。" 宇。

Zhiqing said to the Master, "In the discourses on the Five Constant Virtues, there are two types of wisdom: From the viewpoint of knowledge, that which uses knowledge is wisdom; from the viewpoint of the principle, what causes right or wrong is also wisdom. The former pertains to principle, while the latter, to feeling." The Master responded, "That is, of course, right. All virtues each have their substances and functions." [Yu]

144 礼者，仁之发；智者，义之藏。且以人之资质言之：温厚者多谦逊，通晓者多刻剥。焘。

Propriety is the emanation of benevolence; wisdom is the storage of righteousness. To put it simply with regard to the human endowment, the people who are gentle and kind tend to be modest, while those who are strong in understanding things tend to be acerb. [Tao]

145 问仁、敬。曰："上蔡以来，以敬为小，不足言，须加'仁'字在上。其实敬不须言仁，敬则仁在其中矣。"方，以下兼论恭敬忠信。

When asked about benevolence and seriousness, the Master answered, "Shangcai and some others have regarded seriousness too insignificant to be spoken of, so it has to be joined by benevolence. Actually, in discoursing seriousness, it is unnecessary to call for mentioning benevolence, for, with seriousness, benevolence dwells therein." [Fang] The following conversations also concern respectfulness, seriousness, loyalty, and faithfulness.

146 恭主容，敬主事。有事着心做，不易其心而为之，是敬。恭形于外，敬主于中。自诚身而言，则恭较紧；自行事而言，则敬为切。淳。

Gong 恭 (respectfulness) is the master of looks, while seriousness, of affairs. To be devoted to doing affairs and never change mind therein is what is meant by seriousness. Respectfulness manifests in the outside, while seriousness works in the inside. Respectfulness has more to do with cultivating sincerity in oneself, whereas seriousness, with doing things. [Chun (淳)]

147 初学则不如敬之切，成德则不如恭之安，敬是主事。然专言，则又如"修己以敬"，"敬以直内"。只偏言是主事。恭是容貌上说。端蒙。

In the beginning of learning, one's seriousness is more urgent, while in completing virtue respectfulness is more significant, for seriousness is more concerned with doing things. However, though seriousness as a separate concept concerns doing things, when it is taken as a collective concept, for example, in "cultivating oneself in seriousness" (*Analects*, 14：42) and "maintaining the inward correctness by seriousness," ("Hexagram Kun" in the *Classic of Change*) its meanings are different. Only when seriousness is meant as a separate concept does it refer to doing things. By contrast, respectfulness concerns looks. [Duanmeng]

148 问："'恭敬'二字，以谓恭在外，功夫犹浅；敬在内，功夫大段细密。"曰："二字不可以深浅论。恭敬，犹'忠信'两字。"文蔚曰："恭即是敬之发见。"先生默然良久，曰："本领虽在敬上，若论那大处，恭反大如敬。若不是里面积盛，无缘发出来做得恭。"文蔚。

Someone asked "As regards respectfulness and seriousness, respectfulness is concerned with the external side, calling for only shallow effort, while seriousness concerns the internal side, calling for much deeper effort. (Can we think so?)" The Master answered, "The two aspects should not be compared in terms of the depth of the required effort. They are comparable to loyalty and faithfulness." I said to him, "Respectfulness is the very manifestation of seriousness." He was silent for some time and then said, "The essential point is with respectfulness, but when it comes to the more significant point, respectfulness is greater than seriousness. Without the flourishing accumulation inside, it would be impossible for seriousness to manifest itself as respectfulness outside." [Wenwei]

149 吉甫问恭敬。曰："'恭'字软，'敬'字硬。"直卿云："恭似低头，敬似抬头。"至。

Jifu asked about respectfulness and seriousness. The Master answered, "Respectfulness is soft, while seriousness is hard." Zhiqing said, "Respectfulness is like lowering the head, while seriousness, like raising the head. " ［Zhi（至）］①

150 因言"恭敬"二字如忠信，或云："敬，主于中者也；恭，发于外者也。"曰："凡言发于外，比似主于中者较大。盖必充积盛满，而后发于外，则发于外者岂不如主于中者！然主于中者却是本，不可不知。"偰。

The Master mentioned thereupon that respectfulness and seriousness are comparable to loyalty and faithfulness. Someone said to him, "Seriousness is that which prevails in the inside, while respectfulness is that which is manifested in the outside. " The Master responded, "Whatever is said as being manifested in the outside is greater than that which prevails in the inside. That is probably because only when it accumulates to the full will it be able to manifest itself outside. Thus, how can't what is manifested externally be greater than what prevails in the inside? But one should know it well that what prevails in the inside is the source. " ［Xian］

151 忠信者，真实而无虚伪也；无些欠阙，无些间断，朴实头做去，无停住也。敬者，收敛而不放纵也。祖道。

Loyalty and faithfulness refer to what is actual and true and not unreal and false. With no deficiency and no interruption, in a loyal and faithful manner, one should engage himself in doing something perseveringly. Seriousness means restraining rather than indulging oneself. ［Zudao］

152 忠自里面发出，信是就事上说。忠，是要尽自家这个心；信，是要尽自家这个道理。

Loyalty emanates from inside, while faithfulness is concerned with affairs. Loyalty is the devotion of all one's mind, while faithfulness is the utmost conformity to the principle one is endowed with.

---

① Yang Zhi 杨至 (courtesy name Zhizhi 至之).

卷第七 Book 7

学一
Learning I
小学
Primary Learning[①]

1 古者初年入小学，只是教之以事，如礼乐射御书数及孝弟忠信之事。自十六七入大学，然后教之以理，如致知、格物及所以为忠信孝弟者。骧。

In ancient times, when the young pupils started schooling in *xiaoxue* 小学（primary school）, they were taught only some affairs, such as the *liuyi* 六艺（six arts）of *li* 礼（rites）, *yue* 乐（music）, *she* 射（archery）, *yu* 御（driving a chariot）, *shu* 书（writing）, and *shu* 数（mathematics）, and the rules of filial piety, fraternal submission, loyalty, and faithfulness. When they entered *daxue* 大学（imperial academy）at the age of sixteen or seventeen, they were taught with some pursuits and reasons, such as the extension of knowledge and investigation of things and the reasons for filial piety, fraternal submission, loyalty, and faithfulness. ［Xiang］

2 古人自入小学时，已自知许多事了；至入大学时，只要做此工

---

① In this book, the *xiaoxue* 小学 is rendered into three versions in contexts, i. e. into "primary school," referring to the ancient primary educational institution; into "primary learning," referring to the initial stage of learning; into "Primary Learning," referring to the book with that name, which was compiled by Zhu Xi and his disciple Liu Qingzhi 刘清之（1134 – 1190）.

夫。今人全未曾知此。古人只去心上理会，至去治天下，皆自心中流出。今人只去事上理会。泳。

In ancient times, when pupils entered the primary schools, they had got to know many events. When they entered the imperial academy, what they did was only to make efforts to put their knowledge into practice. Nowadays, however, people are completely ignorant of those events. The ancients strove to understand the events by their mind and when they engaged themselves in the rule of the country, what they did all flowed from their mind. Today, in contrast, people try to understand them only as events but nothing more. [Yong]

3 古者小学已自养得小儿子这里定，已自是圣贤坯璞了，但未有圣贤许多知见。及其长也，令入大学，使之格物、致知，长许多知见。节。

The ancient primary schools nourished the mind of the pupils, and they had already in themselves, as it were, the bases or uncut jades for their growing to be sages and worthies, though they were still in want of the intelligence and insights marking sages and worthies. When they grew up, they would be taught in the imperial academy, where they would grow in intelligence and insights through investigating things and extending knowledge. [Jie]

4 古人小学养得小儿子诚敬善端发见了。然而大学等事，小儿子不会推将去，所以又入大学教之。璘。

In ancient times, the primary school nourished the pupils so that their beginnings of sincerity, seriousness, and goodness occurred. However, they could not infer by themselves that which would be taught in the imperial academy, so they would be instructed there. [Lin]

5 小学是直理会那事；大学是穷究那理，因甚恁地。宇。

In the primary school, pupils sought for understanding events straight, while in the imperial academy, they made thorough enquiries into the

principle underlying them and the reasons why they were what they were.
[Yu]

6 小学者，学其事；大学者，学其小学所学之事之所以。节。

The primary school aimed to teach the pupils many events, while the imperial academy was intended to teach them the reasons why those events were what they were. [Jie]

7 小学是事，如事君，事父，事兄，处友等事，只是教他依此规矩做去。大学是发明此事之理。铢。

What the primary school concerned were events such as serving the sovereign, serving the father, serving the elder brother, and getting along with friends. The pupils were instructed to conduct them by following certain rules. The imperial academy aimed to reveal the principle underlying those events. [Zhu]

8 古人便都从小学中学了，所以大来都不费力，如礼乐射御书数，大纲都学了。及至长大，也更不大段学，便只理会穷理、致知工夫。而今自小失了，要补填，实是难。但须庄敬诚实，立其基本，逐事逐物，理会道理。待此通透，意诚心正了，就切身处理会，旋旋去理会礼乐射御书数。今则无所用乎御。如礼乐射书数，也是合当理会底，皆是切用。但不先就切身处理会得道理，便教考究得些礼文制度，又干自家身己甚事！贺孙。

In ancient times, since pupils had learned the events they should have known in their primary schools, when they grew up, it was not hard for them to practice them. For example, as regards the rites, music, archery, driving a chariot, writing, and mathematics, they had learned their basics and when they grew up they did not need to work hard to learn them any more but rather make concentrated effort to inquire the principle to the utmost for extension of knowledge. Nowadays, since pupils do not get that sort of teaching, when they grow up, it will be truly hard for them to make up for what they fall short of. But they can, in a display of seriousness and sincerity, lay their foundation by which to investigate things and events one by one in pursuit of their inherent principles. When they have got a thorough understanding of the approach and made their will sincere and their mind correct, they will be in a position to examine what is of immediate concern to themselves, and then strive to understand gradually the rites, music, archery, driving a chariot, writing, and mathematics. Today, though driving a chariot is out of use, they should get a personal understanding of the rites, music, archery, writing, and mathematics, for they are all of immediate concern to themselves. If they do not strive to understand the principles of those things immediately concerned with them but only focus on those ritual patterns and systems, what do those things have to do with them? [Hesun]

9 古者，小学已自暗养成了，到长来，已自有圣贤坯模，只就上面加光饰。如今全失了小学工夫，只得教人且把敬为主，收敛身心，却方可下工夫。又曰："古人小学教之以事，便自养得他心，不知不觉自好了。到得渐长，渐更历通达事物，将无所不能。今人既无本领，只去理会许多闲汩董，百方措置思索，反以害心。"贺孙。

The Master said, "In ancient times, the pupils were nourished mentally in their primary schools and when they grew up, since they had already got the moulds for becoming sages and worthies, what they needed to do was only embellish the moulds. Nowadays, since the primary effort of that sort has been lost completely, what can be done is only teaching learners to set store by seriousness as the dominant attitude and to converge the body and mind before making efforts." He added, "The ancient primary school taught the pupils events, whereby their mind was nourished, so they got on the right track without knowing it. When they grew up gradually, they became more and more conversant with things and events and ultimately capable of everything. Today, people not only are devoid of that capability but also know only to get familiar with those useless antique things and rack their brains to pore over them, which, on the contrary, does harm to their mind." [Hesun]

10 问："大学与小学，不是截然为二。小学是学其事，大学是穷其理，以尽其事否？"曰："只是一个事。小学是学事亲，学事长，且直理会那事。大学是就上面委曲详究那理，其所以事亲是如何，所以事长是如何。古人于小学存养已熟，根基已深厚，到大学，只就上面点化出些精彩。古人自能食能言，便已教了，一岁有一岁工夫。至二十时。圣人资质已自有十分。宇作"三分"。大学只出治光彩。今都蹉过，不能转去做，只据而今当地头立定脚做去，补填前日欠阙，栽种后来合做底。宇作"根株"。如二十岁觉悟，便从二十岁立定脚力做去；三十岁觉悟，便从三十岁立定脚力做去。纵待八九十岁觉悟，也当据见定札住硬寨做去。"淳。

Question: The *xiaoxue* 小学 (primary learning) and the *daxue* 大学 (great learning) are not completely separate. The former aims for learning the events themselves, while the latter, for investigating the principle underlying them to the utmost. Is this distinction between them right?

Answer: They are concerned with the same thing. By the primary learning, the learners learn how to serve their parents and their elders, and how to know those events as what they are. By the great learning, they probe the principles over those events carefully and thoroughly and get to know the reasons why they should serve their parents and elders in that way. In the primary school, ancients had attained mature preservation and nourishment of their mind, and in the imperial academy, they needed only to reveal some brilliant splendor therefrom. In ancient times, when a baby was able to take his own food and able to speak, his education began, and in each year he would make efforts required for that year. When he was at the age of twenty, he already got ten tenth Yu's record reads "three tenth" of the intelligence for becoming a sage. In the imperial academy, he needed only to bring forth his splendor. Nowadays, however, since people have idled their time away when young and could not start once again, they can only try to stand firm on the basis of what they have had now and make efforts in the hope of filling up their gaps and cultivating Yu's record reads "planting" what is attainable for them. If, at the age of twenty, one gets aware of that truth, he can try to stand firm and do it from that age. If, at the age of thirty, one gets aware of that truth, he can try to stand firm and do it from that age. Even if one gets aware of it when he is already eighty or ninety years of old, he should also try to stick to his foothold and make up his mind to do it from that age. [Chun（淳）]

11 器远前夜说："敬当不得小学。"某看来，小学却未当得敬。敬已是包得小学。敬是彻上彻下工夫。虽做得圣人田地，也只放下这敬不得。如尧舜，也终始是一个敬。如说"钦明文思"，颂尧之德，四个字独将这个"敬"做擗初头。如说"恭己正南面而已"，如说"笃恭而天下平"，皆是。贺孙。

Qiyuan said the night before last, "Seriousness is not worthy of the primary learning." In my opinion, on the contrary, the primary learning is inadequate in pursuing seriousness, for seriousness covers the pursuit in the primary learning. Seriousness means making efforts unceasingly from the very beginning to the very ultimate. Even when one attains the realm of the sage, the only thing that he can not put aside is seriousness. For example, Yao and Shun, who stuck to seriousness throughout their lifetimes. In "He was reverential, intelligent, accomplished, and thoughtful,"[1] which praises the virtue of Yao, all the meanings of the four words begin from seriousness. This is also true of both "He did nothing but gravely and reverently occupying his royal seat." (*Analects*, 15：5)[2] and "The *junzi* 君子 (Superior Man) being sincere and reverential, the whole world is conducted to a state of

---

① The citation is from "Yaodian" 尧典 (Canon of Yao) in the ancient Chinese classic *Shangshu* 尚书 (Book of History), also called *Shujing* 书经 (Classic of History). The translation is based on a version by J. Legge (see http：//ctext. org/shang-shu).

② The translation of the citation from the *Analects* is based on J. Legge's version (see http：// ctext. org/analects).

happy tranquility. " (*Doctrine of the Mean*)① [Hesun]

12 陆子寿言:"古者教小子弟,自能言能食,即有教,以至洒扫应对之类,皆有所习,故长大则易语。今人自小即教做对,稍大即教作虚诞之文,皆坏其性质。某当思欲做一小学规,使人自小教之便有法,如此亦须有益。"先生曰:"只做禅苑清规样做,亦自好。"大雅。

Lu Zishou 陆子寿 (i. e. Lu Jiuling 陆九龄 [1132 – 1180]) said to the Master, "In ancient times, when a child began to be able to take his own food and speak, his education also began. He would learn various aspects, such as sprinkling and sweeping the ground and answering and replying. Therefore, when he grew up, he was easy to talk to. Nowadays, the education of a child began with learning how to compose antitheses and when he grew in age, he was taught how to make writings ostentatious yet devoid of substance, to the detriment of his character. I have desired to set up a set of rules and regulations for children's education at the primary stage, so that since childhood they can be taught by good ways. Thus their education can be expected to bring about good results. " The Master said, "It will be also good if you model on the monastic rules stipulated in *Chanyuan Qinggui* 禅苑清规 (Rules in the Buddhist Monasteries)② . " [Daya]

13 天命,非所以教小儿。教小儿,只说个义理大概,只眼前事。或以洒扫应对之类作段子,亦可。每尝疑曲礼"衣毋拨,足毋蹶;将上堂,声必扬;将入户,视必下" 等叶韵处,皆是古人初教小儿语。列女传孟母又添两句曰:"将入门,问孰存。"淳。

The Mandate of Heaven is not something proper for the teaching of children. Their teaching can be limited only to the rough idea of what principle means and the events which take place daily before their eyes. It is

---

① The translation of the citation from the *Doctrine of the Mean* is based on J. Legge's version (see http://ctext.org/ http://ctext.org/liji/zhong-yong).

② A book of the rules in the Buddhist monasteries, compiled by Zongze 宗赜 (dates unknown), a Song dynasty Buddhist monk.

also proper to teach them with such daily activities as sprinkling and sweeping the ground and answering and replying. I used to suspect that those rhyming sentences of "Qüli" 曲礼（Summary of Ritual Rules）in *Liji* 礼记（Record of Rites）were utterances which ancients made to teach children first with, such as "His clothes should not hang loosely, nor should his feet move hurriedly," "When about to go up to the hall, he must raise his voice," "When about to enter the door, he must keep his eyes cast down." A more sentence "When about to enter the gate, he should first knock at it and ask if there is someone inside" was added to them in the story about the mother of Mencius in the *Lienü Zhuan* 列女传（Biographies of Famous Women）.① ［Chun（淳）］

14 教小儿读诗，不可破章。道夫。

When children are taught to read the *Classic of Poetry*, the stanza of a poem should not be broken. ［Daofu］

15 先生初令义刚训二三小子，见教曰："授书莫限长短，但文理断处便住。若文势未断者，虽多授数行，亦不妨。盖儿时读书，终身改口不得。尝见人教儿读书限长短，后来长大后，都念不转。如训诂，则当依古注。"问："向来承教，谓小儿子读书，未须把近代解说底音训教之。却不知解与他时如何？若依古注，恐他不甚晓。"曰："解时却须正说，始得。若大段小底，又却只是粗义，自与古注不相背了。"义刚。

When the Master instructed me to teach two or three children for the first time, he told me, "When you teach them something from an ancient book, do not limit its length at a time, but stop only at where its thread of thought comes to a halt temporarily. Where the thread of thought does not pause, it does not matter to teach them a few more lines. Probably, it is hardly possible

---

① The cited rhyming sentences in the original Chinese text are rendered into English only semantically.

for one to change his habit of reading he developed in his childhood. In the past, I saw some people set up limits on how long a part should have been for children to read at a time, but, unfortunately, when the children grew up, they found it difficult to do well in reading. As regards the explanation of words, you should follow the ancient annotations. "

I asked, "You, sir, told me, 'When teaching children to read books, you do not have to instruct them by the sound-teaching way developed in the past scores of years.' But how to explain the ancient words to them? If I follow the ancient annotations, I am afraid they are hardly intelligible to the students." The Master answered, "When making explanations, you should follow the orthodox interpretation and that is the right way. If you give only some rough explanations of them largely, you naturally do not go against the ancient annotations." [Yigang]

16 余正叔尝言:"今人家不善教子弟。"先生曰:"风俗弄得到这里,可哀!"文蔚。

Yu Zhengshu once said to the Master, "Nowadays, families are not good at teaching their children." The Master replied, "The mores have got into such situation. How deplorable!" [Wenwei]

17 小童添炭,拨开火散乱。先生曰:"可拂杀了,我不爱人恁地,此便是烧火不敬。所以圣人教小儿洒扫应对,件件要谨。某外家子侄,未论其贤否如何,一出来便齐整,缘是他家长上元初教诲得如此。只一人外居,气习便不同。"义刚。

When a child fed some charcoals to a stove, he poked the fire clumsily and some firing charcoals fell to the ground. Seeing that, the Master said, "Put them out. I dislike one doing things like that. It is indicative of lacking respectfulness to handling fire. That is why the sages taught children to be careful in doing everything, such as sprinkling and sweeping the ground and answering and replying. A nephew of mine on my wife's side, no matter whether he is worthy or not, is dressed neatly whenever he goes out. That is because he was taught by his elders that way when young. If one lives alone in a place far away from his family, his habits will be different." [Yigang]

18 问: "女子亦当有教。自孝经之外，如论语，只取其面前明白者教之，何如？"曰: "亦可。如曹大家女戒、温公家范，亦好。"义刚。

Question: Women should also receive education. Besides *Xiaojing* 孝经 (Classic of Filial Piety), the *Analects*, for example, can be taught to them, but what is taught should only be limited to the parts more easily understandable to them. What do you think about it?

Answer: It is also advisable. Others such as Cao Dagu's 曹大家 (i. e. Ban Zhao 班昭 [c. 49 – c. 20], a lady scholar) *Nüjie* 女戒 (Lessons for Women) and Duke Wen's *Jiafan* 家范 (Family Precepts) are also good options. [Yigang]

19 后生初学，且看小学之书，那是做人底样子。广。

When young pupils make first efforts in learning, they should read the book *Xiaoxue* 小学 (Primary Learning), for it tells them how to conduct themselves. [Guang]

20 先生下学，见说小学，曰: "前贤之言，须是真个躬行佩服，方始有功。不可只如此说过，不济事。"淳。

When the class was over, the Master heard the students discussing *Primary Learning*, and he said "As regards what the ancient worthies said, one should truly admire it and put it into practice in person before he may accomplish something. It is no use paying only lip service to it." [Chun (淳)]

21 和之问小学所疑。曰: "且看古圣人教人之法如何。而今全无这个。'天佑下民，作之君，作之师'，盖作之君，便是作之师也。"时举。

Hezhi 和之 (courtesy name of You Ni (游倪), dates unknown, a disciple of Zhu's) asked about his doubt concerning *Primary Learning*. The Master answered, "Just read something about the way the ancient sages adopted to teach others. Nowadays, it is completely lost. In 'Heaven, for the help of the earthly people, made for them rulers and made for them teachers,' (*Book of History*) the 'rulers' means probably the very 'teachers.' " [Shiju]

22 或问："某今看大学，如小学中有未晓处，亦要理会。"曰："相兼看亦不妨。学者于文为度数，不可存终理会不得之心。须立个大规模，都要理会得。至于其明其暗，则系乎人之才如何耳。"人杰。

Someone said to the Master, "Now I am reading the *Great Learning*, but when I have got anything hard to understand in the book of *Primary Learning*, I also try to figure it out. " The Master replied, "You may as well read them both concurrently. Pursuing words as their goal, learners should not bear in their mind the idea that they will never understand them. One should establish for himself a great sphere, and strive to understand everything within it. As for whether he can see it clearly or dimly, that depends on his talent. " [Renjie]

23 问："小学载乐一段，不知今人能用得否？"曰："姑使知之。古人自小皆以乐教之，乃是人执手提诲。到得大来涵养已成，稍能自立便可。今人既无此，非志大有所立，因何得成立！"可学。

Question: As regards the citation from *Yueji* 乐记 (Book of Music) in your *Primary Learning*, can what it describes be applied by people today?

Answer: They may as well be made to know it. In ancient times, since childhood, all were taught with music and that through taking them by the hand. When they grew up, with ripe mental cultivation, and were able to stand just by their own feet, they could continue by themselves. Nowadays, people do not undergo such and, unless one cherishes great aspiration, what can he stand firm by? [Kexue]

24 因论小学，曰："古者教必以乐，后世不复然。"问："此是作乐使之听，或其自作？"曰："自作。若自理会不得，自作何益！古者，国君备乐，士无故不去琴瑟，日用之物，无时不列于前。"问："郑人赂晋以女乐，乃有歌钟二肆，何故？"曰："所谓'郑声'，特其声异耳，其器则同。今之教坊乐乃胡乐。此等事，久则亡。欧阳公集古录载寇莱公好舞柘枝，有五十曲。文忠时，其亡已多，举此可见。旧见升朝官以上，前导一物，用水晶为之，谓之'主斧'，今亦无之。"某云："今之籍妓，莫是女乐之遗否？"曰："不知当时女乐如何。"通老问"左手执钥，右手秉翟"。曰："所谓'文舞'也。"又问："古人舞不回旋？"曰："既谓之'舞'，安得不回旋？"某问："'汉家周舞'，注云：'此舜舞'。"曰："遭秦之暴，古帝王乐尽亡，惟韶乐独存，舜舞乃此舞也。"又问通老，大学祭孔子乐。渠云："亦分堂上堂下，但无大钟。"曰："竟未知今之乐是何乐。"可学。

The Master thereupon discoursed on the primary learning. He said, "In ancient times the teaching was carried out with music, but in later times that practice discontinued. " Someone asked, "Do you mean the music was performed to let students hear or let them compose music by themselves?" The Master answered, "They composed by themselves. They must have got their understanding of music, or else what avail could that practice be to? In ancient times, a ruler of a state was prepared for music. Unless for some reason, a scholar would play on the *qin-se* 琴瑟 (ancient Chinese plucked music instruments, like zithers and lutes) every day, which were his objects of daily use, always put in front of him. " When asked further "The State of Zheng bribed the State of Jin[1] with female musicians, which carried thirty two song bells. Why?" The Master said, "The so called 'Songs of Zheng' means their sounds were particularly licentious, but their music instruments were not different. Today the music played by the imperial music house is the music of Hu 胡 .[2] After a long period of time such things would be lost. For example, according to the ancient records carried in *Ouyang Gong Ji* 欧阳公集

---

① Both are vassal states in the Eastern Zhou dynasty (770 – 256 BC), usually referred to as the Spring and Autumn and the Warring States period in Chinese history.

② The Hu 胡 is a collective term referring to the regions roughly in Central Asia at present.

(Collected Works of Ouyang Xiu 欧阳修［1007 – 1072］), Duke Lai 莱公 (posthumous title of Kou Zhun 寇准［961 – 1023］) was keen on Zhezhi (柘枝) Dance①, which included fifty pieces of music. In the days of Wenzhong 文忠 (posthumous title of Su Shi 苏轼［1037 – 1101］), most of them were lost. I once saw there being something made of crystal used for leading those senior officials who went to the imperial court. It was called *zhufu* 主斧 (Dominating Axe), but now it has disappeared." I asked, "Are the singing girls today the vestige of ancient female musicians?" The Master said, "I do not know what ancient female musicians were like." Tonglao 通老 (courtesy name of Yang Ji 杨楫, a disciple of Zhu's) said, "The *Classic of Poetry* says 'In my left hand I grasp a flute; In my right I hold a pheasant's feather.'" The Master responded, "That describes the *Wenwu* 文舞 (Refined Dance)." Tonglao asked, "Was that ancient dance performed without spins?" The Master answered, "Since it is called a dance, how can it be performed without spins?" I said to the Master, "The note of 'The Dance of Zhou in the Han Imperial Court' says 'This refers to the *Shunwu* 舜舞 (Dance of Shun).'" The Master replied, "All ancient kings' music pieces were lost due to the tyranny of Qin (221 – 206 BC) except the *Shaoyue* 韶乐 (Shao Music). It is the dance of Shun." He turned to Tonglao and asked him about the performance of music on memorial ceremonies for Confucius as recorded in the *Great Learning*. Tonglao replied, "It was divided into the part for performing inside the hall and that for outside, but it did not employ the big bell." The Master responded, "After all we do not know what the music performed on such occasions today is." [Kexue]

25 元兴问："礼乐射御书数。书，莫只是字法否?"曰："此类有数法：如'日月'字，是象其形也;'江河'字，是谐其声也;'考老'

---

① A dance introduced from Xiyu 西域 (Western Regions), which refers to the area west of Yumen Gate, Gansu, China, including what is now China's Xinjiang and parts of Central Asia (the oasis states bordering the Taklamakan desert and areas further to the west).

字，是假其类也。如此数法，若理会得，则天下之字皆可通矣。"时举。

Yuanxing 元兴 (courtesy name of Zhou Mingzuo) asked, "In the six arts of rites, music, archery, driving a chariot, writing, and mathematics, does the writing refer only to the ways of forming sino-graphs?"

Answer: It refers to a lot of ways. For example, the two sino-graphs *ri* 日 (the sun) and *yue* 月 (the moon) are made by the pictographic way. The *jiang* 江 and *he* 河 (either of these two means river) are made by the pictophonetic way. The *kao* 考 (father, esp. deceased father) and *lao* 老 (old) are mutually explanatory sino-graphs. If you understand such ways of making sino-graphs, you will be able to know the formation of every sino-graph. [Shiju]

26 弟子职一篇，若不在管子中，亦亡矣。此或是他存得古人底，亦未可知。或是自作，亦未可知。窃疑是他作内政时，士之子常为士，因作此以教之。想他平日这样处都理会来。然自身又却在规矩准绳之外！义刚。

The piece of writing entitled "Dizi Zhi" 弟子职 (Pupils' Rules and Regulations), if not contained in *Guanzi* 管子 (Writings of Master Guan)[①], would have been lost. Perhaps it was written by someone else before Guanzi in the more ancient times and collected by him into the book, or it was written by himself. It is hardly possible to know which case is true. I suspect that, when Guanzi served as the chancellor of the State Qi, the sons of those scholars usually aspired to be scholars and so he wrote that piece to educate them with. I think at ordinary times he conducted those rules and regulations as stipulated in that writing. However, he kept himself out of the control by those rules and regulations. [Yigang]

---

① Guanzi 管子 (723 – c. 645) was a chancellor and reformer of the State of Qi during the Spring and Autumn period (771 – 476 BC) in Chinese history. He has been claimed as the author of the book *Guanzi*, which is actually a much later compilation of works from the scholars of "Jixia Xuekong" 稷下学宫 (Jixia Academy) located in the capital of the State of Qi.

27 弟子职"所受是极",云受业去后,须穷究道理到尽处也。"毋骄恃力",如恃气力欲胡乱打人之类。盖自小便教之以德,教之以尚德不尚力之事。"卓。

The *suoshou shiji* 所受是极 in "Pupils' Rules and Regulations" means that after a pupil finishes schooling and leaves his school, he should continue to inquire into the truth to the utmost. The *wujiao shili* 毋骄恃力 in it says something to the effect that a pupil should not use his strength to hit others indiscriminately. That probably purported to educate the pupils with virtues since their childhood and instructed them to set store by virtues rather than resort to strength. [Zhuo]

卷第八 Book 8

学二

Learning II

总论为学之方

General Discussion of Methods for Pursuing Learning

1 这道体，饶本作"理"。浩浩无穷。

This substance of *Dao* 道（the Way）The Rao edition is "*li* 理（principle）" is vast and boundless.

2 道体用虽极精微，圣贤之言则甚明白。若海。

Though the substance and function of the Way are extremely subtle and profound, what the sages and worthies said of them are very clear, plain, and definite. [Ruohai]

3 圣人之道，如饥食渴饮。人杰。

The way of the sage is comparable to what we eat when hungry and what we drink when thirsty. [Renjie]

4 圣人之道，有高远处，有平实处。道夫。

In the way of the sage manifest both what is far and lofty and what is plain and unadorned. [Daofu]

5 夫道若大路然，岂难知哉！人病不由耳。道夫。

The Way is like the broad road. How can it be hard to understand? It is due to the disease with men that they do not abide by it. [Daofu]

6 道未尝息，而人自息之。非道亡也，幽厉不由也。道夫。

The Way has never rested and it is men who have it "at rest" by themselves. It is not that the Way perished but that King You of Zhou and King Li of Zhou①refused to abide by it. [Daofu]

7 圣人教人，大概只是说孝弟忠信日用常行底话。人能就上面做将去，则心之放者自收，性之昏者自着。如心、性等字，到子思孟子方说得详。因说象山之学。儒用。

When the sages taught others, probably they said only something about filial piety, fraternal submission, loyalty, and faithfulness, and some practices in daily use. If others could do as they said and hold on to it, then of them those with indulgent mind would restrain it by themselves and those with benighted nature would get it bright by themselves. As regards mind, nature, and the like, it was not until Zisi and Mencius that they were clarified with considerable elaboration. Thereupon the Master went on and talked about the learning on the part of Xiangshan 象山 (style name of Lu Jiuyuan 陆九渊 [1139 – 1193]). [Ruyong]

8 圣人教人有定本。舜"使契为司徒，教以人伦：父子有亲，君臣有义，夫妇有别，长幼有序，朋友有信"。夫子对颜渊曰："克己复礼为仁。""非礼勿视，非礼勿听，非礼勿言，非礼勿动。"皆是定本。人杰。

The sages taught others with their fundamental tenets. Shun 舜 "appointed Xie 契 the Minister of Instruction in charge of teaching the relations of humanity: how, between father and son, there should be affection; between sovereign and minister, righteousness; between husband and wife, attention to their separate functions; between old and young, a proper order; and between friends, faithfulness." (*Mencius*, 3A: 4)②

---

① King Li of Zhou (r. 878 – 841 BC) and King You of Zhou (r. 782 – 771 BC) are two despotic kings of the Western Zhou Dynasty (c. 11th century – 771 BC).

② The translation of the citation from *Mencius* is based on a version by J. Legge (see http: // ctext. org/mengzi), with slight modification.

Confucius said to Yan Yuan "To subdue one's self and return to propriety is benevolence," and "Look not at what is contrary to propriety; listen not to what is contrary to propriety; speak not what is contrary to propriety; make no movement which is contrary to propriety." (*Analects*, 12：1)[①] All these are fundamental tenets. [Renjie]

9 圣门日用工夫，甚觉浅近。然推之理，无有不包，无有不贯，及其充广，可与天地同其广大。故为圣，为贤，位天地，育万物，只此一理而已。常人之学，多是偏于一理，主于一说，故不见四旁，以起争辨。圣人则中正和平，无所偏倚。人杰。

What the sages advocated for daily efforts sounds very simple and plain. However, when inferring the principle therefrom, we will find it covers everything and penetrates everything, and its range can be as vast as Heaven and Earth. Therefore, being a sage, being a worthy, and being identified with Heaven and Earth for nourishing the myriad things are all governed by nothing but the same one principle.

Ordinary people's pursuit of learning is usually inclined to sticking to one theory or one doctrine, and since they fail to see the four sides around it, that is provocative of debates. By contrast, the sages personify equilibrium, correctness, harmoniousness, and placidity, free from partiality. [Renjie]

10 圣贤所说工夫，都只一般，只是一个"择善固执"。论语则说："学而时习之"，孟子则说"明善诚身"，只是随他地头所说不同，下得字来，各自精细。其实工夫只是一般，须是尽知其所以不同，方知其所谓同也。侗。

The efforts the sages and worthies advocated are similar, which boil down to "choosing what is good and firmly holding it fast." (*Doctrine of the Mean*, 22) The *Analects* (1：1) says, "To learn and practice frequently

---

① The translation of the two citations from *Analects* is based on a version by J. Legge (see http：//ctext. org/analects), with slight modification.

what one has learned," and *Mencius* (4A: 12) says "To understand what is good and attain sincerity in oneself." With their different purposes, what the two sages say are different, but both use words which are delicate and exquisite. The efforts they call others to make are similar. Only by knowing well why their words are different can we see clearly their common ground. [Xian]

11 这个道理，各自有地头，不可只就一面说。在这里时是恁地说，在那里时又如彼说，其宾主彼此之势各自不同。侗。

This same truth is discoursed with orientations to different destinations, so you should not see only one of them and lose sight of others. It may be said this way here, while it may be said that way there. Thus, in different contexts, the guest and the host it involves have different momentums. [Xian]

12 学者工夫，但患不得其要。若是寻究得这个道理，自然头头有个着落，贯通浃洽，各有条理。如或不然，则处处窒碍。学者常谈，多说持守未得其要，不知持守甚底。说扩充，说体验，说涵养，皆是拣好底言语做个说话，必有实得力处方可。所谓要于本领上理会者，盖缘如此。谟。

When a learner makes learning efforts, what troubles him most is his possibility of failing to grasp the key point. If he can seek and find the truth therein, naturally he will see the points in all other respects, which will be coherently interconnected and mutually penetrated, each with its own orderliness. Otherwise, he will be obstructed everywhere. It is often said among learners that a certain learner, when striving to stick to something, fails to hold on to the key point and to know what should be held on to. When it comes to extension, experience, or self-cultivation, they always pick out those words which sound good and talk about them. But it will not do unless one can truly gain something therefrom. So the reason why we stress that the most important is to pursue first understanding of the fundamental point lies therein. ［Mo］①

13 为学须先立得个大腔当了，却旋去里面修治壁落教绵密。今人多是未曾知得个大规模，先去修治得一间半房，所以不济事。僴。

To pursue learning is comparable to building an edifice. One should establish first an overall well-structured framework, and then turn to its inside and replenish and substantiate it, so that the entire edifice will become fine, tight and complete. On the contrary, nowadays, many people did not get any idea of their basic framework before they start to build one or two rooms. Thus, that is of no use. ［Xian］

14 识得道理原头，便是地盘。如人要起屋，须是先筑教基址坚牢，上面方可架屋。若自无好基址，空自今日买得多少木去起屋，少间只起在别人地上，自家身己自没顿放处。贺孙。

One's good understanding of the source where the truth originates constitutes, as it were, his foundation on which to build a house, for one has to lay a solid foundation before starting to work on it. Without a solid foundation of one's own, no matter how much wood he buys to build his house with today, what he builds it on is the site owned by someone else, and he ends up with going nowhere to settle himself. ［Hesun］

15 须就源头看教大底道理透，阔开基，广开址。如要造百间屋，须着有百间屋基；要造十间屋，须着有十间屋基。缘这道理本同，甲有许多，乙也有许多，丙也有许多。贺孙。

A leaner should turn to the source and strive to get a thorough understanding of the fundamental truth and thereby he should lay a broad foundation on a large site. For example, to build a hundred rooms, one has to prepare the foundation large enough for those rooms, while, to build ten rooms, one has to lay a foundation big enough for them. That is because the reason holds true for all the cases: when there is the proper amount allotted

---

① Zhou Mo 周谟 (courtesy name Shunbi 舜弼).

for A, there should be the proper amount for B and also the proper amount for C. [Hesun]

16 学须先理会那大底。理会得大底了，将来那里面小底自然通透。今人却是理会那大底不得，只去搜寻里面小小节目。植。

A learner should strive to understand the fundamental truth first. With a thorough understanding of it, in due course he will see naturally in perspective the lesser points covered by it. Nowadays, many people, who have not gained an adequate understanding of the fundamental truth, are busy with going inside it and seeking for the insignificant points. [Zhi (植)]

17 学问须是大进一番，方始有益。若能于一处大处攻得破，见那许多零碎，只是这一个道理，方是快活。然零碎底非是不当理会，但大处攻不破，纵零碎理会得些少，终不快活。"曾点漆雕开已见大意"，只缘他大处看得分晓。今且道他那大底是甚物事？天下只有一个道理，学只要理会得这一个道理。这里才通，则凡天理、人欲、义利、公私、善恶之辨，莫不皆通。

In pursuing learning, only when one has taken great pains and gained a big stride forward can he begin to feel the benefit therefrom. If one has been able to break through a major barrier and has seen that underlying all those secondary and fragmentary points is the same truth, he will be truly joyful. It is not that the fragmentary points need not to be understood, but that when the major point is not seen through, the fragmentary points will not be understood deeply and thoroughly, and then that will not bring about true joy. Zeng Dian (dates unknown) and Qidiao Kai (c. 540BC – ?)[1] already grasped the principal meaning of Confucius's doctrine. That is because they saw the major point clearly. Now, what is the major point of Confucius's doctrine? There is only one truth in the world and the purpose of learning is to get access to the

---

① Both were disciples of Confucius. Zeng Dian was the father of Zeng Shen 曾参 (505 – 435 BC), a famous disciple of Confucius.

truth. As soon as one understands it thoroughly, he will see clearly through all such debates as on the heavenly principle, human selfish desire, righteousness and benefit, impartiality and partiality, and good and evil.

18 或问："气质之偏，如何救得?"曰："才说偏了，又着一个物事去救他偏，越见不平正了，越讨头不见。要紧只是看教大底道理分明，偏处自见得。如暗室求物，把火来，便照见。若只管去摸索，费尽心力，只是摸索不见。若见得大底道理分明，有病痛处，也自会变移不自知，不消得费力。"贺孙。

Someone asked, "How to rectify the partiality of physical nature?" The Master answered, "You just said the partiality, yet you now try to find something to rectify it. Thus you will have it to be further away from being balanced and upright and then make it more difficult to find either head or tail of it. What counts is to strive to see the major point of the truth clearly, and when you do well in it, you will naturally see those secondary points. It is like searching for something in a dark room, and when you get a light, you will see everything clearly. If you do nothing but groping, despite strenuous efforts, you end up with finding nothing. So long as you can understand the major point of the truth thoroughly, even if there is something troubling you somewhere, it will go away without your knowing it, calling for no effort from you." [Hesun]

19 成己方能成物，成物在成己之中。须是如此推出，方能合义理。圣贤千言万语，教人且从近处做去。如洒扫大厅大廊，亦只是如洒扫小室模样；扫得小处净洁，大处亦然。若有大处开拓不去，即是于小处便不曾尽心。学者贪高慕远，不肯从近处做去，如何理会得大头项底！而今也有不曾从里做底，外面也做得好。此只是才高，以智力胜将去。中庸说细处，只是谨独，谨言，谨行；大处是武王周公达孝，经纶天下，无不载。小者便是大者之验。须是要谨行，谨言，从细处做起，方能克得如此大。又曰："如今为学甚难，缘小学无人习得。如今却是从头起。古人于小学小事中，便皆存个大学大事底道理在。大学，只是推将开阔去。向来小时做底道理存其中，正似一个坯素相似。"明作。

The Master said, "Completing oneself is the precondition for completing other people and things and completing other people and things dwells in completing oneself. Only by inferring it in this way can it conform to the principle. No matter how much the sages and worthies said, what they taught others boils down to starting with things at hand. For example, sprinkling and sweeping a big hall or a long gallery are like sprinkling and sweeping a small room. When one can sweep the small room clean, he can sweep a big one clean in the same way. If there is a big room one can not sweep clean, that is surely because he did not devote himself to sweeping a small one. If a learner is greedy for only the lofty and distant, unwilling to start from the things at hand, how can he attain a good understanding of the major point? Of course, there are also some people who, though never starting from inside, do very well in the outside, but they depend on nothing but their extraordinary talent and make it by their intelligence. As regards the lesser points, the *Doctrine of the Mean* dwells on being watchful over oneself when he is alone and being careful in speaking and acting, while as regards the major point it focuses on King Wu of Zhou's and Duke Zhou's far-extending filial piety and ordering and adjusting the great relations of humankind, with nothing that they did not sustain. The lesser is the testifier of the major. One should be cautious in his speaking and acting and start from insignificant things. Only in this way can it be possible for him to attain the ultimate greatness. " He added, "Nowadays it is very hard to pursue learning, for the learners have not started from the primary learning. But now learning has to be started from the first. In the primary leaning and insignificant events, the ancients found the stored truth for the great learning and the significant events. The great learning is only extended and broadened from the primary learning. In what one did in his childhood inheres the truth, quite like an embryo. " [Mingzuo]

20 学者做工夫，莫说道是要待一个顿段大项目工夫后方做得，即今逐些零碎积累将去。才等待大项目后方做，即今便蹉过了！学者只今便要做去，断以不疑，鬼神避之。"需者，事之贼也！"至。

As regards learners' making efforts in pursuit of learning, they should avoid only waiting for an occasion for doing something remarkable for that purpose, but rather set about handling fragmentary things at hand and accumulate their small achievements. If they do nothing until an occasion may appear in future, they will waste the time at present. For the time being, a learner should start and engage himself in making efforts, big or small, and that without any doubt. Then even ghosts and spirits keep away from him. "Waiting is the cause of failure to do anything." (*Zuozhuan* 左传 [Zuo's Explanation of the *Spring and Autumn Annals*]) [Zhi (至)]

21 "如今学问未识个入路，就他自做，倒不觉。惟既识得个入头，却事事须着理会。且道世上多多少少事！"江文卿云："只先生一言一语，皆欲为一世法，所以须着如此。"曰："不是说要为世法。既识得路头，许多事都自是合着如此，不如此不得。自是天理合下当然。"贺孙。

The Master said, "Nowadays, when pursuing learning, if one does not know anything about the approach but rather goes in for it only intuitively, he will not be conscious of that. Only when he has known the approach will he be able to pay attention to it when dealing with every thing or event. How many things and events there are in the world!" Jiang Wenqing 江文卿 (dates unknown, a disciple of Zhu's) said to the Master, "Every word of what you have said, sir, can be desired applicable universally, so a learner should do as you have said." He responded, "It is not intended to be applied universally. If one gets to know the approach to the pursuit of learning, he will be aware that many events have been done as a matter of course and if not, they would not have happened. They are naturally so because they conform to the heavenly principle." [Hesun]

22 若不见得入头处，紧也不可，慢也不得。若识得些路头，须是莫断了。若断了，便不成。待得再新整顿起来，费多少力！如鸡抱卵，看来抱得有甚暖气，只被他常常恁地抱得成。若把汤去荡，便死了；若抱才住，便冷了。然而实是见得入头处，也自不解住了，自要做去，他自得些滋味了。如吃果子相似：未识滋味时，吃也得，不消吃也得；到识滋味了，要住，自住不得。贺孙。

If a leaner has not seen where the entry is, whether he is rapid or slow in making efforts, he will go nowhere. If one has got to know the approach, he should ensure its continuation, for when it interrupts, his efforts will be to no avail. In the case, he would have to start afresh and try to get on the track again, and how much more effort that would call for! It is akin to a hen's brooding eggs. When a hen sits on her eggs, the eggs get warm gradually and it has to keep them warm for some time before they hatch. If one puts the eggs in hot water in the hope of getting chicks to emerge from them, they will never. If the hen sits on her eggs for a while and then leaves them, they will never get warm. Therefore, if one sees truly where the entry to the pursuit of learning is and holds on to it unremittingly of his own accord, he will get some true taste in due course. It is like eating a fruit. Before one knows its taste, he may want to eat it or not, but when you have known its taste, even if you want to stop eating, you can not help eating it up. [Hesun]

23 "待文王而后兴者，凡民也。若夫豪杰之士，虽无文王犹兴。"豪杰质美，生下来便见这道理，何用费力。今人至于沉迷而不反，圣人为之屡言，方始肯来，已是下愚了。况又不知求之，则终于为禽兽而已！盖人为万物之灵，自是与物异。若迷其灵而昏之，则与禽兽何别？大雅。

"The mass of men wait for a King Wen of Zhou, and then they will receive a rousing impulse. Scholars distinguished from the mass, without a King Wen, rouse themselves." (*Mencius*, 7A: 10)[①] The distinguished

---

① The translation is based on a version by J. Legge (see http://ctext.org/mengzi), with slight modification.

scholars, endowed with fine qualities, knew the truth by birth and needed not to make efforts to know it. Today, many people have refused to come to their senses and mend their ways, and they have begun to come willingly only after they were taught repeatedly what sages had said, but they have already bogged themselves down in foolishness. In spite of that, they do not know how to make strenuous efforts to elevate themselves, so they end up with a status hardly different from that of birds and beasts. Humankind is the most intelligent of all living things and naturally different from other things. But if one loses his intelligence and gets benighted, then how can he differentiate himself from birds and beasts? [Daya]

24 学问是自家合做底。不知学问，则是欠阙了自家底；知学问，则方无所欠阙。今人把学问来做外面添底事看了。广。

Learning is what one should pursue for himself. If one does not know learning, he owes himself something that he should have. Only with knowledge of learning can one be said as in want of nothing. People today see the pursuit of learning as merely something imposed on them from outside. [Guang]

25 圣贤只是做得人当为底事尽。今做到圣贤，止是恰好，又不是过外。祖道。

The sages and worthies did only what men should do completely. Nowadays, to attain the realm of sages and worthies, what one should do is nothing but what he should do adequately and there is nothing more than that requirement. [Zudao]

26 "凡人须以圣贤为己任。世人多以圣贤为高，而自视为卑，故不肯进。抑不知，使圣贤本自高，而己别是一样人，则早夜孜孜，别是分外事，不为亦可，为之亦可。然圣贤禀性与常人一同。既与常人一同，又安得不以圣贤为己任？自开辟以来，生多少人，求其尽己者，千万人中无一二，只是衮同枉过一世！诗曰：'天生烝民，有物有则。'今世学者，往往有物而不能有其则。中庸曰：'尊德性而道问学，极高明而道中庸。'此数句乃是彻首彻尾。人性本善，只为嗜欲所迷，利害所逐，一齐昏了。圣贤能尽其性，故耳极天下之聪，目极天下之明，为子极孝，为臣极其忠。"某问："明性须以敬为先？"曰："固是。但敬亦不可混沦说，须是每事上检点。论其大要，只是不放过耳。大抵为己之学，于他人无一毫干预。圣贤千言万语，只是使人反其固有而复其性耳。"可学。

The Master said, "Ordinary people should take following the examples set by the sages and worthies as their own duty. Common people tend to see the sages and worthies too lofty to reach and themselves as too humble, so they are unwilling to make efforts for progress. They should know that the sages and worthies are originally lofty and they are a different group of men. So, for them, making earnest efforts day and night is something out their duties that they may choose to do it or not. However, in regard to the endowed nature, the sages and worthies are the same as ordinary people. Given this sameness, how can ordinary people not take following their examples as their duty? Since the world came into being, it has produced multitudes of people, but, among them, only one or two out of ten millions complete themselves, while all others are similar, who have lived their lives in vain. The *Classic of Poetry* says, 'Heaven, in giving birth to the multitudes of the people, / To every one of the things annexed its law.'[1] The learners today tend to know the things but not the law. The *Doctrine of the Mean* says '(The *junzi* 君子 [Superior Man]) honors his virtuous nature, and maintains constant inquiry and study, ··· to raise it to its greatest height and brilliancy, so as to pursue the course of the Mean.' What these several sentences tell is true most thoroughly. The human nature is originally good, but when it is obstructed by selfish desires and by calculating of losses and gains, it gets completely benighted. The sages and worthies are able to give full development to their nature, so in the world they

---

[1] The translation of the citation from the *Classic of Poetry* is based on a version by Jame Legge (see http://ctext.org/book-of-poetry), with some modification.

are the ablest to see and hear, the most filial to their parents, and the most loyal to their sovereigns." I asked him, "Should we give priority to seriousness in our attempt to bring brilliance back to our nature?" He answered, "Yes, of course. However, you should not take seriousness indiscriminately, for it has to be examined with regard to every event. As regards its essential point, it means only that any event should not be let go by. Generally, one's pursuit of learning is purely for his own sake, which has nothing to do with others at all. Though so many words have been said by the sages and worthies, they convey only one point that one should return to what he had originally and to his nature." [Kexue]

27 学者大要立志。所谓志者，不道将这些意气去盖他人，只是直截要学尧舜。"孟子道性善，言必称尧舜。"此是真实道理。"世子自楚反，复见孟子。孟子曰：'世子疑吾言乎？夫道一而已矣。'"这些道理，更无走作，只是一个性善可至尧舜，别没去处了。下文引成覸颜子公明仪所言，便见得人人皆可为也。学者立志，须教勇猛，自当有进。志不足以有为，此学者之大病。谟。

A leaner should cherish a high aspiration. The so called aspiration does not mean the desire to outshine others by that will and spirit but rather the determination to follow the examples set by Yao and Shun. "Mencius discoursed how the human nature is good, and when speaking, always made laudatory reference to Yao and Shun." (*Mencius*, 3A: 1) This sentence tells some solid truth. "When the prince①was returning from the State of Chu, he again visited Mencius. Mencius said to him, 'Prince, do you doubt my words? The path is one and only one.'" (*Mencius*, 3A: 1)② The truth expressed here is free from any distortion, which says nothing more than the

---

① Referring to the prince who became later Duke Wen of Teng. He had to go to the State of Chu and, when he went by way of the State of Song, visited Mencius.

② The translation of the two citations from *Mencius* is based on a version by Jame Legge (see http: //ctext. org/menzi), with slight modification.

good nature leading to Yao and Shun. After that sentence, the *Mencius* cited what, Cheng Jian 成覵 (dates unknown, a warrior of the state of Qi), Yanzi (i. e. Yan Yuan), and Gongming Yi 公明仪 (dates unknown, a musician in the Warring States period) said, which indicates that everyone is capable of following Yao and Shun as examples. When a learner aspires to pursue something, he should be brave and valiant and thus he will certainly make progress. If a learner's aspiration does not call for strenuous efforts, it will be a serious trouble with him. [Mo]

28 世俗之学，所以与圣贤不同者，亦不难见。圣贤直是真个去做，说正心，直要心正；说诚意，直要意诚；修身齐家，皆非空言。今之学者说正心，但将正心吟咏一晌；说诚意，又将诚意吟咏一晌；说修身，又将圣贤许多说修身处讽诵而已。或掇拾言语，缀缉时文。如此为学，却于自家身上有何交涉？这里须要着意理会。今之朋友，固有乐闻圣贤之学，而终不能去世俗之陋者，无他，只是志不立尔。学者大要立志，才学，便要做圣人是也。谟。

The reason why the learning conducted by common people is different from that by the sages and worthies is not difficult to see. The sages and worthies meant what they said. When saying rectifying the mind, they strove to rectify their mind truly; when saying making the will sincere, they stove to make their will sincere truly. When they claimed to foster their persons and regulate their families, they did not make mere empty talk. However, nowadays, when learners speak of rectifying the mind, they merely recite some words concerned with that from ancient books, and when they speak of making the will sincere, they merely recite some words concerned with that from ancient books. When turning to self-cultivation, they also only recite many discourses which sages and worthies made about it. Besides, they toil themselves in picking out fine-sounding words and phrases from here or there and put them together to make writings in a popular style. What does such learning have to do with themselves? You should pay some attention to understanding this point. Among the friends of mine, there are some who have taken delight in hearing of what sages and worthies said in regard to their learning, yet still have been unable to get rid of their worldly weaknesses. The reason for their failure lies in nothing but their failure to have any aspiration. A learner should cherish an aspiration and as soon as he sets about learning, he should make up his mind to and try his best to be a sage. [Mo]

29 学者须是立志。今人所以悠悠者，只是把学问不曾做一件事看，遇事则且胡乱恁地打过了。此只是志不立。雉。

A learner must have an aspiration. The reason why many learners at present idle away and make no progress is that they do not regard learning as a cause and, whatever challenge they meet, muddle along. The serious trouble with them is their lack of definite aspiration for learning. [Zhi（雉）]

30 问："人气力怯弱，于学有妨否？"曰："为学在立志，不干气禀强弱事。"又曰："为学何用忧恼，但须令平易宽快去。"宇举圣门弟子，唯称颜子好学，其次方说及曾子，以此知事大难。曰："固是如此。某看来亦有甚难，有甚易！只是坚立着志，顺义理做去，他无跷欹也。"宇。

I asked, "Does the weakness of one's physical endowment hamper his pursuit of learning?" The Master answered, "The pursuit of learning depends on firm aspiration and it has nothing to do with whether one is strong or weak in his physical endowment." He further answered, "In pursuing learning, why worry about this or that? Just take it easy and go it in a relaxed way." I cited some disciples of Confucius as examples. I said that, of them, only Yanzi (i. e. Yan Yuan) was keen on learning and the next one was Zengzi (i. e. Zeng Shen), so it indicated that learning was really difficult. The Master replied, "It is, indeed, but as I see it, there is no difficulty or easiness about it to speak of, for what counts is, with determined aspiration, setting about it along with the principle, and then you will find that there is nothing odd about it." [Yu]

31 英雄之主所以有天下，只是立得志定，见得大利害。如今学者只是立得志定，讲究得义理分明。贺孙。

The main reason why a hero could conquer a country is in his firm determination and full consciousness of the relevant major advantage and disadvantage. Now, for a scholar, what he needs is to have firm aspiration and clear consciousness of what idea is right. [Hesun]

32 立志要如饥渴之于饮食。才有悠悠，便是志不立。祖道。

Aspiration is to a learner what food and drink are to hanger and thirst. If a learner starts to muddle along, that indicates his failure to hold on to any aspiration. [Zudao]

33 为学须是痛切恳恻做工夫，使饥忘食，渴忘饮，始得。砥。

To pursue learning, one should make strenuous and earnest efforts, and only when he becomes forgetful of food when hungry and of drink when thirsty can he get really devoted to it. [Di]

34 这个物事要得不难。如饥之欲食，渴之欲饮，如救火，如追亡，似此年岁间，看得透，活泼泼地在这里流转，方是。偰。

It is not hard to gain this thing-event 物事. It is like the desire to eat when one feels hungry and to drink when he feels thirsty, and the urgency for fighting fire or for looking for what gets lost. It is also like the passage of time from one year to another, which flows so lively before us. If one can see it thoroughly in this way, one can get a right understanding of it. [Xian]

35 学者做工夫，当忘寝食做一上，使得些入处，自后方滋味接续。浮浮沉沉，半上落下，不济得事。振。

When making efforts in pursuing learning, a learner should struggle hard with one-mindedness for some time to the extent of forgetting sleep and food and when he has got some substantial progress, he will know the taste therein gradually and can not help continuing his pursuit. It is to no avail if one always sways to the left and right and gets subject to ups and downs. [Zhen]

36 "而今紧要且看圣人是如何，常人是如何，自家因甚便不似圣人，因甚便只是常人。就此理会得透，自可超凡入圣。淳。

What is crucial for a leaner now is to see what the sages were like and what ordinary people are like, and why he is different from the sages and why he is only an ordinary person. If he is able to gain a thorough understanding in this regard, naturally he can elevate himself and ultimately attain the realm of the sages. [Chun（淳）]

37 为学，须思所以超凡入圣。如何昨日为乡人，今日便为圣人！须是辣拔，方始有进！砥。

In pursuing learning, one should consider how he can transcend himself and attain the realm of the sages, and how an ordinary person yesterday can turn sage today. Only by holding dear such lofty ideal can one begin to make real progress. [Di]

38 为学须觉今是而昨非，日改月化，便是长进。砥。

In striving for learning, one should be always aware that he is right today but not yesterday and thus with daily improvement and monthly transformation, he will experience true advance in learning. [Di]

39 今之学者全不曾发愤。升卿。

All those learners today have never made determined efforts. [Shengqing]

40 为学不进，只是不勇！焘。

The reason why a learner has pursued learning yet not got advance is his want of courage. [Tao]

41 不可倚靠师友。方子。

A learner should not depend on his teacher and friends. [Fangzi]

42 不要等待。方子。

Don't wait. [Fangzi]

43 今人做工夫，不肯便下手，皆是要等待。如今日早间有事，午间无事，则午间便可下手，午间有事。晚间便可下手，却须要待明日。今月若尚有数日，必直待后月，今年尚有数月，不做工夫，必曰，今年岁月无几，直须来年。如此，何缘长进！因康叔临问致知，先生曰：
"如此说得，不济事。"盖卿。

The Master said, "Those learners, when trying to make efforts to pursue learning, are reluctant to set about doing; rather, they only wait. Today, if one is occupied by something in the morning but free at noon, he can make some effort, and if he is occupied at noon, he can do it in the evening. Why does one wait for tomorrow? When there are still some days before this month ends, he does nothing but waiting for the next month, and when there are still several months before this year closes, he does nothing, and is sure to say that, since there are few months left before this year ends, he will wait for the next year. Thus, how can he make any advance?" When Kang Shulin 康叔临 (dates unknown, a disciple of Zhu's) said something about the way for extension of knowledge and asked him about it, the Master replied, "That way you said just now is of no help." [Gaiqing]

44 道不能安坐等其自至，只待别人理会来，放自家口里！淳。

One should not sit there and wait for the coming of the Way to him, nor should he only keep waiting for some understanding of it gained by others in the hope of taking it over and putting it into his own mouth. [Chun (淳)]

45 学者须是奈烦，奈辛苦。方子。

A learner should be patient and endure toil and moil. [Fangzi]

46 必须端的自省，特达自肯，然后可以用力，莫如"下学而上达"也。去伪。

One must examine himself conscientiously and thoroughly and then he will be in a position to exert himself. He had better do in a way as indicated by "My learning lies low but my penetration rises high." (*Analects*, 14：35) [Quwei]

47 凡人便是生知之资，也须下困学、勉行底工夫，方得。盖道理缜密，去那里捉摸！若不下工夫，如何会了得！敬仲。

An ordinary person, even if born with the possession of knowledge, also has to make efforts as those who are dull and stupid do in pursuing learning, and has to exert himself in his endeavor. That is probably because the truth is subtle and elusive, which is really hard to get access to. If one does not make efforts, how can he gain a true understanding of it? [Jingzhong]

48 今之学者，本是困知、勉行底资质，却要学他生知、安行底工夫。便是生知、安行底资质，亦用下困知、勉行工夫，况是困知、勉行底资质！文蔚。

The learners today are born with the aptitude which is low in knowledge and requires hard work, but when making efforts they just choose to follow as their examples those born with the possession of knowledge and unnecessary to do hard work. Even those born with the possession of knowledge and unnecessary to do hard work will make efforts as those dull and stupid do in pursuing learning and exert themselves, let alone those born with the aptitude low in knowledge and calling for hard work. [Wenwei]

49 大抵为学虽有聪明之资，必须做迟钝工夫，始得。既是迟钝之资，却做聪明底样工夫，如何得！伯羽。

Generally, when pursuing learning, a learner, despite his intelligent aptitude, has to make efforts as one with stupid aptitude does. However, some learners, despite their stupid aptitude, choose to do as those with intelligent aptitude. [Boyu]

50 今人不肯做工夫。有先觉得难，后遂不肯做；有自知不可为，公然逊与他人。如退产相似，甘伏批退，自己不愿要。盖卿。

People today are unwilling to make efforts for the purpose of learning. Some feel it difficult to pursue learning and then become reluctant to do it. Some others know that it is beyond their power and admit themselves as inferior to others. What these people do is like a pregnant woman having an abortion, willing to suffer it, for she does not want the fetus of her own accord. [Gaiqing]

51 "为学勿责无人为自家剖析出来，须是自家去里面讲究做工夫，要自见得。"道夫。

A learner should keep from complaining about no one else isolating the truth out and giving it to him straight, for he has to probe into things and events and make efforts to see it by himself. [Daofu]

52 小立课程,大作工夫。可学。

Spend less time and energy on receiving teaching but more on making efforts for learning. [Kexue]

53 工夫要趱,期限要宽。从周。

Making efforts should be hurried up and the time range for it should be wide. [Congzhou]

54 且理会去,未须计其得。德明。

Just keep on doing it and keep from calculating the gain therefrom. [Deming]

55 才计于得,则心便二,头便低了。至。

As soon as you calculate what you will gain, you mind gets distracted and your head gets lowered more. [Zhi(至)]

56 严立功程,宽着意思,久之,自当有味,不可求欲速之功。道夫。

Be strict in making efforts and conducting the learning schedule, be broad in understanding the meaning, and you will relish the true taste in due time. Never seek to find any short cut. [Daofu]

57 自早至暮,无非是做工夫时节。道夫。

The time from morning to evening is nothing but the period for making efforts in pursuit of learning. [Daofu]

58 人多言为事所夺,有妨讲学,此为"不能使船嫌溪曲"者也。遇富贵,就富贵上做工夫;遇贫贱,就贫贱上做工夫。兵法一言甚佳:"因其势而利导之"也。人谓齐人弱,田忌乃因其弱以取胜,今日三万灶,明日二万灶,后日一万灶。又如韩信特地送许多人安于死地,乃始得胜。学者若有丝毫气在,必须进力!除非无了此气,只口不会说话,方可休也。因举浮屠语曰:"假使铁轮顶上旋,定慧圆明终不失!"力行。

Many learners complain that their time is occupied by various affairs, which impedes them from making efforts for learning. That is a classic case of "One who can not paddle his boat straight ahead complains that the river is tortuous." With one's lot being rich and honored, he can make efforts in regard to being rich and honored, while with one's lot being poor and lowly, he can make efforts in regard to being poor and lowly. It is said well in a book of military strategy and tactics that "One should exploit a given situation to benefit from all its possible favorable factors."[①] The Qi troops were said weaker than their enemy, but Tian Ji 田忌 (c. 4th century BC), their commander, made use of their weakness and won the battle. The tactic he adopted was ordering his soldiers to make fewer stoves (cookfires) day by day. On the first day, the stoves were enough for 100, 000 people; on the second day, the stoves were for only 50, 000 people; on the third day, the stoves were only for an army of 20, 000.[②]Another example is Han Xin's 韩信 (? – 196BC) purposely deployment of his troops in a situation where they were confronted with the danger of death, who fought desperately and won their victory. A learner, as long as he lives, should exert himself for advance. Unless he loses all his vigor and vim and can not speak any longer, he should not give up. Thereupon he cited Buddhist discourse as saying "However the burning iron ring revolves around my head, I, with bright completeness of dhyana and prajna, never lose my equanimity."[③] [Lixing]

59 圣贤千言万语，无非只说此事。须是策励此心，勇猛奋发，拔

① Said by Sun Bin 孙膑 (? – 316BC), a military strategist of the State of Qi, which is cited from "Sunzi Wu Qi Liezhuan" 孙子吴起列传 (Biographies of Sunzi [i. e. Sun Bin] and Wu Qi) in *Shiji* 史记 (Records of the Grand Historian).

② Referring to the Battle of Maling (马陵之战) between State of Qi, who fought on behalf of the State of Han, and the State of Wei. This battle is well recorded in history texts and is famous for Tian Ji's employment of the tactics proposed by Sun Bin, known as the "Tactic of Missing Stoves," in which one side was led to underestimate the other by creating an illusion of soldiers running away from the army. (See https://en. wikipedia. org/wiki/Battle_ of_ Maling)

③ Cited from the Buddhist poem of "Zhengdao Ge" 证道歌 (The Song of Enlightenment).

出心肝与他去做！如两边擂起战鼓，莫问前头如何，只认卷将去！如此，方做得工夫。若半上落下，半沉半浮，济得甚事！佣。

What the thousands of words said by the sages and worthies mean boil down to nothing but one point. A learner should spur himself on, rouse himself with courage, and make up his mind to fight for gaining it. It is as if, with war drums beaten on both flanks, a fighter, no matter what happened in front of him, forged ahead fearlessly. Only in this way can one's efforts truly pay off. If one is of two minds and always sways to the left and right, what avail can it be to? [Xian]

60 又如大片石，须是和根拔。今只于石面上薄削，济甚事！作意向学，不十日五日又懒，孟子曰："一日暴之，十日寒之！"可学。

Another example is cutting a large stone. One has to cut it at its root, but if he cuts here and there only on the surface of it, what use can it be of? If one determines to pursue learning, yet after five or ten days he gets dispirited, that is what Mencius said as "Letting it have genial heat for one day, yet then exposing it to cold for ten days. " (*Mencius*, 7A: 9) [Kexue]

61 宗杲云："如载一车兵器，逐件取出来弄，弄了一件又弄一件，便不是杀人手段。我只有寸铁，便可杀人！"瞽。

Zong Gao 宗杲 (1089 - 1163, an eminent monk) said, "It is like a carriage of weapons. If one takes them out one by one and plays with them one by one, he is hard to master any way of killing. But if I have got an inch of iron, I will be able to kill. " [Xun]

62 且如项羽救赵，既渡，沈船破釜，持三日粮，示士必死，无还心，故能破秦。若瞻前顾后，便做不成。瞽。

An example is the story of Xiang Yu 项羽 (232 - 202BC, a famous general) rescuing the State of Zhao. In the battle against the Qin forces[①],

---

① Referring to the Battle of Julu, an important battle in the revolution against the Qin dynasty (see https: //en. wikipedia. org/wiki/Xiang_ Yu#Battle_ of_ Julu).

after crossing a river, Xiang Yu ordered his men to sink their boats and destroy all but three days worth of rations, in order to force his men to choose between prevailing against overwhelming odds within three days or die trapped before the walls of the city with no supplies or any hope of escape. Despite being heavily outnumbered, Xiang's troops scored a great victory. So if one is indecisive and hesitant, he will accomplish nothing. [Xun]

63 如居烧屋之下！如坐漏船之中！可学。

It is like staying under a burning roof. It is like sitting in a leaking boat. [Kexue]

64 为学极要求把篙处着力。到工夫要断绝处，又更增工夫，着力不放令倒，方是向进处。为学正如上水船，方平稳处，尽行不妨。及到滩脊急流之中，舟人来这上一篙，不可放缓。直须着力撑上，不一步不紧。放退一步，则此船不得上矣！洽。

The pursuit of learning extremely requires making efforts, so to speak, at where the punt-pole works when punting a boat. When one's effort is about to discontinue, he should add strength so that it keeps going on, and that is where progress can be made. Pursuing learning is akin to punting a boat against the currents. When the boat is now going on some slack currents, one may as well let it go ahead steadily, not necessarily making much effort, but when it reaches some rapids near a shoal ridge, he must punt the boat, preventing it from getting slow. One should make effort and punt it so that it keeps going ahead. If it got a step back, it would not be able to go upstream any more. [Qia]

65 学者为学，譬如炼丹，须是将百十斤炭火锻一饷，方好用微微火养教成就。今人未曾将百十斤炭火去锻，便要将微火养将去，如何得会成！恪。

A learner's pursuit of learning is akin to *liandan* 炼丹 (Daoist external alchemy), which requires burning dozens of kilograms of charcoals first for tempering in a high firing for some time, before refining slowly in a low firing. Nowadays, learners have not burned dozens of kilograms of charcoals for tempering first in a high firing, yet they want to start refining slowly in a low firing. How can that do? [Ke][1]

66 今语学问，正如煮物相似，须爇猛火先煮，方用微火慢煮。若一向只用微火，何由得熟？欲复自家元来之性，乃恁地悠悠，几时会做得？大要须先立头绪。头绪既立，然后有所持守。书曰："若药弗瞑眩，厥疾弗瘳。"今日学者皆是养病。可学。

In my opinion, pursuing learning is comparable to stewing something, for which one should set a high fire for stewing it first for some time and then keep a low fire to finish it slowly. If one starts with a low fire, how can he stew it thoroughly? If one wants to restore his original nature but idles along in a way like that, when will he make it? The first important thing to do is set up a start-up and then, insisting on it, keep going on. As said in the *Classic of Poetry*, "(You should be) like medicine, which, if it does not distress the patient first, will not cure his sickness." Actually, the learners today are all necessary to cure their sickness and regain their health. [Kexue]

67 譬如煎药：先猛火煎，教百沸大衮，直至涌坌出来，然后却可以慢火养之。

It is like boiling herbal medicine in water. You have to set a high fire and let it boil to the extent that the water surges and spills before keeping on decocting it in a low fire slowly.

68 须磨砺精神去理会。天下事，非燕安暇豫之可得。淳。

A learner should spirit up with courage to seek for understanding of things and events in the world, for he can not get it merely with ease and comfort. [Chun (淳)]

69 万事须是有精神，方做得。振。

As regards all events in the world, one must pick oneself up first and

---

① Lin Ke 林恪 (courtesy name Shugong 叔恭)

then he will be capable of doing any of them. ［Zhen］

70 阳气发处，金石亦透。精神一到，何事不成！骧。

Where *yang*（positive comic force）emanates, even metal or stone can be penetrated by it. Where spirit is picked up, everything can be done by it. ［Xiang］

71 凡做事，须着精神。这个物事自是刚，有锋刃。如阳气发生，虽金石也透过！贺孙。

One should spirit up in doing whatever it is. This spirit is the very firmness, which has its sharp blade. It is like the vital force of *yang*, and where it occurs, it can penetrate even metal and stone. ［Hesun］

72 人气须是刚，方做得事。如天地之气刚，故不论甚物事皆透过。人气之刚，其本相亦如此。若只遇着一重薄物事，便退转去，如何做得事！从周。方子录云："天地之气，虽至坚如金石，无所不透，故人之气亦至刚，盖其本相如此。"

One's vital force should be firm, or else he is incapable of things. For example, when the vital force of Heaven and Earth is firm, it can penetrate whatever it is. So is the original state of the firm vital force of humankind. If one meets only something that can not even be said as a challenge and he feels dispirited and backs out, how can he do anything? ［Congzhou］ Fangzi's record reads, "The vital force of Heaven and Earth is able to penetrate what is as hard as metal and stone, and that of humankind is also firm to that extent, for that is its original state."

73 "学者识得个脉路正，便须刚决向前。若半青半黄，非惟无益。"因举酒云："未尝见有衰底圣贤。"德明。

The Master said, "So long as a learner has known his approach right, he should keep on making efforts and forging ahead with resolution. If he discontinues efforts only halfway, that will be of no use to him." Raising a cup of wine, he added, "I have never heard of any sage or worthy who slackened his efforts." ［Deming］

74 学者不立，则一齐放倒了！升卿。

If a learner does not brace himself up, everything of him will fall down.
[Shengqing]

75 不带性气底人，为僧不成，做道不了。方。

Whoever is devoid of aspiration is incapable of being a monk or a Daoist.
[Fang]

76 因言，前辈也多是背处做几年，方成。振。

The Master thereupon said, "Most of the preceding generations of scholars had insisted on making efforts in adversity before they were able to accomplish something." [Zhen]

77 进取得失之念放轻，却将圣贤格言处研穷考究。若悠悠地似做不做，如捕风捉影，有甚长进！今日是这个人，明日也是这个人。季札。

A learner should not think too much of gain or loss but rather pore over the maxims said by the sages and worthies to the utmost. If one keeps idling about, seeming to do something but actually not, isn't he doing like catching at the shadow? Can he make any progress? Today he is the person, and tomorrow he will remain the same person. [Jizha]

78 学者只是不为己，故日间此心安顿在义理上时少，安顿在闲事上时多，于义理却生，于闲事却熟。方子。

Since learners do not think they do learning for themselves, they spend little time settling their mind on studying the principle but rather much time on trivial matters, and thus what they are familiar with is those matters but not the sagely ideas. [Fangzi]

79 今学者要紧且要分别个路头，要紧是为己为人之际。为己者直拔要理会这个物事，欲自家理会得；不是漫恁地理会，且恁地理会做好看，教人说道自家也曾理会来。这假饶理会得十分是当，也都不阙自身己事。要须先理会这个路头。若分别得了，方可理会文字。贺孙。

What counts for learners today is that they should strive to see the right starting point and think out whether he pursues learning for themselves or for others. To pursue learning for themselves, they should make efforts straight for their own understanding of the thing-events. It is not intended that they get an understanding for no other purpose than showing to others and gaining some self-satisfaction when hearing others say they have got that understanding. Even if their understanding is rather right, it has nothing to do with themselves. One should rectify his understanding of the starting point, and when he has got it right, he can begin to make efforts to understand the words (said by the sages and worthies). [Hesun]

80 学者须是为己。譬如吃饭，宁可逐些吃，令饱为是乎？宁可铺摊放门外，报人道我家有许多饭为是乎？近来学者，多是以自家合做底事报与人知。又言，此间学者多好高，只是将义理略从肚里过，却翻出许多说话。旧见此间人做婚书，亦说天命人伦。男婚女嫁，自是常事。盖有厌卑近之意，故须将日用常行底事装荷起来。如此者，只是不为己，不求益；只是好名，图好看。亦聊以自诳，如南越王黄屋左纛，聊以自娱尔。方子。

The Master said, "A learner should pursue learning for himself. It is like having a meal. Does one get anything and eat it only for satisfying his hunger? Does one only put what he has outside his gate and show to others that he has so much for meal? Learners today are liable to show to others what they ought to do for themselves. " He continued, "Many a learner at present aims too high and, only by having some words said by the sages and worthies to pass his chest rashly, he churns out actually so many discourses from that. I once saw someone composing a marriage contract, piling words on the Mandate of Heaven and human relationships on it. A man taking a wife and a woman taking a husband are only ordinary matters. Probably that indicates some feeling of loathing what is humble or near, so what is daily used and practiced is wrapped by something decorative and showy. The purpose of one doing that is not for himself and for any true benefit but for earning some fame and for some good-looking display, which is done also for some self-deception. That is what was done by the King of South Yue Kingdom①by sitting in a carriage built with yellow-silked roof and decorated with yak tails on the left, by which just to entertain himself." [Fangzi]

81 近世讲学不着实，常有夸底意思。譬如有饭不将来自吃，只管铺摊在门前，要人知得我家里有饭。打迭得此意尽，方有进。振。

In recent years, many learners have tended to be ostentatious rather than pragmatic. What they have done is like one getting food not for eating it for a meal but for putting it outside his gate so that others know he has food. Only when one gets rid of such idea can he gain true advance. [Zhen]

82 今人为学，多只是谩且恁地，不曾真实肯做。方子。

Many learners at present are inclined to deceive themselves, who have never been willing to make conscientious efforts in pursuit of learning. [Fangzi]

83 今之学者，直与古异，今人只是强探向上去，古人则逐步步实做将去。广。

Learners today are diagonally different from the ancient scholars, for the former only force themselves in the vain hope of touching the sky by one step, but the latter made solid efforts to gain progress step by step. [Guang]

84 只是实去做工夫。议论多，转闹了。德明。

Do nothing but making substantial efforts. If one always indulges himself in empty talk, that will result in nothing but a waste of time and energy. [Deming]

85 每论诸家学，及己学，大指要下学着实。方。

Every time I consider the various schools of learning as well as my own learning, I become more convinced that the most important point for the pursuit of learning is to make solid efforts for learning. [Fangzi]

---

① Referring to Zhao Mei 赵眜 (r. 137 – 122 BC), King of South Yue Kingdom in the Western Han Dynasty.

86 为学须是切实为己，则安静笃实，承载得许多道理。若轻扬浅露，如何探讨得道理？纵使探讨得，说得去，也承载不住。铢。

If one understands well that his pursuit of learning is truly for himself, he will be placid and conscientious and thus be capable of accepting and carrying many truths. How can one who is shallow and showy make any achievement in probing truths? Even if he can probe them and utter them, he is incapable of accepting and carrying them. [Zhu]

87 入道之门，是将自家身己入那道理中去。渐渐相亲，久之与己为一。而今入道理在这里，自家身在外面，全不曾相干涉。侗。

To enter the gate of the realm of truth means to gain access into the truth and, by keeping close contact with it for a long time, identify oneself ultimately with it. But now the truth is here, while one stays there, and thus one side has nothing to do with the other. [Xian]

88 或问为学。曰："今人将作个大底事说，不切己了，全无益。一向去前人说中乘虚接渺，妄取许多枝蔓，只见远了，只见无益于己。圣贤千言万语，尽自多了。前辈说得分晓了，如何不切己去理会！如今看文字，且要以前贤程先生等所解为主，看他所说如何，圣贤言语如何，将己来听命于他，切己思量体察，就日用常行中着衣吃饭，事亲从兄，尽是问学。若是不切己，只是说话。今人只凭一己私意，瞥见些子说话，便立个主张，硬要去说，便要圣贤从我言语路头去，如何会有益。此其病只是要说高说妙，将来做个好看底物事做弄。如人吃饭，方知滋味；如不曾吃，只要摊出在外面与人看，济人济己都不得。"谦。

When asked about the pursuit of learning, the Master answered, "People today tend to say it as a thing so high as to have nothing to do with themselves and consequently it is to no avail. They have gone to the doublespeak made by others and got submerged there, and emerged with many insignificant stuffs, which are far-fetched and also meaningless to themselves. There are thousands of words said by the sages and worthies, and some preceding scholars offered insightful explanations. Why not turn to them and strive for personal understandings? Today, when you read the classics, remember to resort to their explanations made by such previous worthies as Master Cheng Hao and Master Cheng Yi, and consider how they explained in comparison with what the classics say. Submitting yourself to them, you should examine their words in regard to yourself. Actually, what is daily used and practiced such as having meals, getting dressed, serving parents, and obeying elder brothers, is all occasions calling for inquiry into learning. However, if it is not concerned with yourself, it will be nothing but words. Some people today, from their own private viewpoints, glimpse some words in the classics and then concoct an opinion out of them and importune others to accept it. They attempt to bend the sages to mean what they claim the sages meant. Can such doing be to any avail? Their trouble is their intentions to make what they have concocted sound high and impressive in the hope of producing something with good look and then working further on it. Take having a meal for example. After one has had it, he has known its taste, but if he did not have it and only put it outside for show, is that of any use to himself or to others?" [Qian]

89 或问："为学如何做工夫？"曰："不过是切己，便的当。此事自有大纲，亦有节目。常存大纲在我，至于节目之间，无非此理。体认省察，一毫不可放过。理明学至，件件是自家物事，然亦须各有伦序。"问："如何是伦序？"曰："不是安排此一件为先，此一件为后，此一件为大，此一件为小。随人所为，先其易者，阙其难者，将来难者亦自可理会。且如读书：三礼春秋有制度之难明，本末之难见，且放下未要理会，亦得。如书诗，直是不可不先理会。又如诗之名数，书之盘诰，恐难理会。且先读典谟之书，雅颂之诗，何尝一言一句不说道理，何尝深潜谛玩，无有滋味，只是人不曾子细看。若子细看，里面有多少伦序，须是子细参研方得。此便是格物穷理。如遇事亦然，事中自有一个平平当当道理，只是人讨不出，只随事衮将去，亦做得，却有掣肘不中节处。亦缘卤莽了，所以如此。圣贤言语，何曾误天下后世，人自学不至耳。"谦。

Someone asked, "How to make efforts in pursuit of learning?" The Master answered, "It is adequate by nothing but keeping it concerned with yourself. This pursuit has its outline and detailed catalogue. Bear the outline in your mind, and in the detailed catalogue is indicated nothing but the same principle. You should strive to cognize and examine it and not overlook even an iota of it. When the principle becomes clear to you and learning begins to dawn on you, you will understand that every one of thing-events is of your concern, but you should know the human relation order manifested in them." The questioner asked further, "What does the human relation order mean?" The Master replied, "It does not mean that you rigidly prioritize one to another or let one outweigh another, but rather you, depending on your conditions, approach what is easy first and the difficult may become understandable automatically in due time. When you read books, for example, since the three books on rites[①]and the *Chunqiu* 春秋 (Spring and Autumn Annals) all contain descriptions of ancient ritual institutions not easy to understand, whose ins and outs are hard to clarify, you may as well put them aside temporally. As for the *Classic of Poetry* and the *Book of History*, you have to strive to understand them first. But the names and numbers in the former and the announcements and admonitions in the latter are also difficult to understand. You may as well read first the odes in the former and the canons and counsels in the latter. Whatever word or sentence is said in them conveys the truth, and so long as you chew them, you will find them tasteful. But their readers are usually careless. If they were careful in reading them, how many human relation orders would they be able to see! So you should study-read those parts in the hope of seeing them. This is what is meant by

---

① Referring to the three ancient books of *Zhouli* 周礼 (The Rites of Zhou), *Yili* 仪礼 (Ceremonial Etiquettes) and *Liji* 礼记 (Record of Rites).

investigating things for inquiring into the principle to the utmost. This is also true of handling affairs, and in each of them dwells a truth still and steady. But many learners can not find it out, so they let it go like that. Though this failure does not matter much, it sometimes can be a drag on them, causing their missing the point. That is also due to their recklessness when reading. When has what the sages and worthies said misled the later generations? If there is any misleading, that is because of the inadequacy of learning on the part of the later generations themselves. " [Qian]

90 佛家一向撤去许多事，只理会自身己；其教虽不是，其意思却是要自理会。所以他那下常有人，自家这下自无人。今世儒者，能守经者，理会讲解而已；看史传者，计较利害而已。那人直是要理会身己，从自家身己做去。不理会自身己，说甚别人长短！明道曰："不立己后，虽向好事，犹为化物。不得以天下万物挠己，己立后，自能了当得天下万物。"只是从程先生后，不再传而已衰。所以某尝说自家这下无人。佛家有三门：曰教，曰律，曰禅。禅家不立文字，只直截要识心见性。律本法甚严，毫发有罪。如云不许饮水，才饮水便有罪过。如今小院号为律院，乃不律之尤者也！教自有三项：曰天台教，曰慈恩教，曰延寿教。延寿教南方无传，有些文字，无能通者。其学近禅，故禅家以此为得。天台教专理会讲解。慈恩教亦只是讲解。吾儒家若见得道理透，就自家身心上理会得本领，便自兼得禅底；讲说辨讨，便自兼得教底；动由规矩，便自兼得律底。事事是自家合理会。颜渊问为邦。看他陋巷箪瓢如此，又却问为邦之事，只是合当理会，看得是合做底事。若理会得入头，意思一齐都转；若不理会得入头，少间百事皆差错。若差了路头底亦多端：有才出门便错了路底，有行过三两条路了方差底，有略差了便转底，有一向差了煞远，终于不转底。贺孙。

Buddhists have isolated themselves from many affairs and thus focused on understanding themselves. Though their religion is not right, it requires the Buddhists to strive for an understanding of their own and therefore there are always many believers of Buddhism. By contrast, there have been fewer followers of Confucianism. Nowadays, of the Confucians, those who have stuck to the Confucian classics have only cared explanation of them; those who have focused on histories and biographies have been interested only in calculating gains and losses. The Buddhists have gone straight to seeking to understand themselves and started with themselves. Without a personal understanding of oneself, how can he comment on another's merits and demerits? Mingdao (i. e. Cheng Hao) said, "If one has not established oneself, though he may turn to good affairs later, he will still be subject to the transformation of things. One should not let the myriad things in the world disturb himself, and when he has established himself, he will naturally be able to carry those myriad things in him. " It is only since Master Cheng that Confucianism began to be transmitted more widely and ceased to decline. That is why I said once that there had been few followers of Confucianism. Buddhism has three schools, i. e. Teachings, Vinaya, and Chan (or Dhyana). The Chan School, not resorting to establishment of words, requires understanding the mind and seeing the nature straight. The Vinaya is a system of rather strict disciplines, and a Buddhist may commit a sin by doing something trivial against it. For example, when it does not allow a Buddhist to drink water on a certain occasion, if he drinks, he commits a sin. The "Small Temple" today is referred grandly to as Vinaya Monastery, which is a place where the disciplines are not abided by to the greatest extent. The Teachings include three, i. e. Tiantai 天台 (lt. Heavenly Platform), Ci'en 慈恩 (lt. Thanks-Giving), and Yanshou 延寿 (lt. Extension of Longevity). The Yanshou Teaching is not transmitted in the south and some words from it are already incomprehensible now. Its doctrine is close to that of the Chan Sect, so the Chan Buddhists set store by it. The Tiantai Teaching is specialized in understanding explanations and the Ci'en Teaching is also focused on explanations. If we Confucians can comprehend the truth thoroughly, as regards our capability of understanding by our own mind and body, it means we can gain the essence of Chan; as regards our ability to lecture, discourse, debate, and discuss, it means we can take in the strength of the Teachings; as regards our self-conduct and self-discipline, it means we can draw on what the Vinaya requires. Everything calls for one's own understanding of it. Yan Yuan once asked Confucius how a state should be administered. [1]Yan was a man who lived by only a single bamboo dish of rice and a single gourd dish of drink, and in a mean narrow lane, yet he asked that question. That is because the question is concerned with something that he should understand, so he was doing what he should have done. If one's understanding is right at its outset, he will understand all the meanings right, but if one's starting point is wrong, his understandings of meanings will all get wrong. But in the case of wrong starting, there are several possibilities. Some people get wrong the moment they go out the door or after crossing several roads; some others get back to the right track before they go astray too far; still some others never turn to the right direction after making a wrong starting. [Hesun]

91 不可只把做面前物事看了，须是向自身上体认教分明。如道家存想，有所谓龙虎，亦是就身上存想。士毅。

Don't see the thing-events before you as mere thing-events. You should understand them well with regard to yourself. The *cunxiang* 存想 (keeping thinking) of Daoism, which can be activated by the so called *long-hu* 龙虎 (lt. dragon and tiger, referring metaphorically to spirit and essence), is also a practice in regard to the thinker himself. [Shiyi]

92 为学须是专一。吾儒惟专一于道理，则自有得。砥。

To pursue learning, one must be single-minded. We Confucians are concentrated on the principle and then will naturally gain advance in learning. [Di]

---

① See *Analects*, 15:11.

93 既知道自家患在不专一，何不便专一去！逍遥。

When you have known you are troubled for lack of single-mindedness, so why not be single-minded? [Xiaoyao]①

94 须是在己见得只是欠阙，他人见之却有长进，方可。偁。

It will do only when what you see in yourself is all shortcomings but in others' eyes what you have got is advance. [Xian]

95 人白睚不得，要将圣贤道理扶持。振。

Never stare others angrily, but rather assist them with the truth advocated by the sages and worthies. [Zhen]

96 为学之道，须先存得这个道理，方可讲究事情。

As called for by the way of doing learning, one should preserve this principle first, or else he is not in a position to delve into things.

97 今人口略依稀说过，不曾心晓。淳。

Currently, the learners have been talking about it briefly and vaguely, yet they have not got a true understanding of it. [Chun (淳)]

98 发得早时不费力。升卿。

If one is enlightened early, his pursuit of learning does not call for so strenuous effort. [Sehngqing]

99 有资质甚高者，一了一切了，即不须节节用工。也有资质中下者，不能尽了，却须节节用工。振。

Whoever is highly gifted, when having understood the crucial point, sees all other points with ease, so he does not need to make efforts at every point. By contrast, there are those with middle or lower aptitude, who can not understand all in that way, so they have to make efforts at every point. [Zhen]

100 博学，谓天地万物之理，修己治人之方，皆所当学。然亦各有次序，当以其大而急者为先，不可杂而无统也。

---

① Guo Xiaoyao 郭逍遥 (courtesy name unknown).

Extensive learning means that all thing-events ranging from the principles of Heaven and Earth and the myriad things to the methods of self-cultivation and governing others should enter the scope of learning. Of course, they should be studied in their sequential orders. The significant and urgent ones should be prioritized and disorderliness should be avoided.

101 今之学者多好说得高，不喜平。殊不知这个只是合当做底事。节。

Nowadays, in regard to learning, many learners take to talking big, disliking speaking frankly. They do not know that their pursuit of learning is only what they should do. [Jie]

102 譬如登山，人多要至高处。不知自低处不理会，终无至高处之理。德明。

Take climbing a mountain for example. Climbers tend to try only to reach its summit, unaware that if they do not start well from the foot of the mountain they will by no means be able to ascend to its summit. [Deming]

103 于显处平易处见得，则幽微底自在里许。德明。

What is seen where things are obvious, simple, and ordinary manifests naturally what dwells in them subtly and profoundly. [Deming]

104 且于切近处加功。升卿。

Intensify your efforts on things close at hand. [Shengqing]

105 着一些急不得。方子。

Never rush in pursuing learning. [Fangzi]

106 学者须是直前做去，莫起计获之心。如今说底，恰似画卦影一般。吉凶未应时，一场鹘突，知他是如何。到应后，方始知元来是如此。广。

A learner should go straight in for learning and not consider what he will gain therein. This is akin to the drawing prepared for confirming a divination for someone. Before the divinatory result of auspiciousness or not is confirmed, he is in confusion, ignorant of what will happen. It is not until the result is confirmed that he knows what it is. ［Guang］

107 某适来，因澡浴得一说：大抵揩背，须从头徐徐用手，则力省，垢可去。若于此处揩，又于彼处揩，用力杂然，则终日劳而无功。学问亦如此，若一番理会不了，又作一番理会，终不济事。盖卿。

Just now I have got a metaphor after I had a bath. Generally, when one helps someone else rubbing down the back, if he starts from the head and goes downward step by step, his efforts will be the least and the effect is the best. But, if he rubs here for a while and then there for some time, despite his long time and much toil, his disorderly efforts will end up with little effect. This is also true of doing learning. If one works now here for some time but fails to get a thorough understanding and then does it there but still fails, he will wind up with going nowhere. ［Gaiqing］

108 学者须是熟。熟时，一唤便在目前；不熟时，须着旋思索。到思索得来，意思已不如初了。士毅。

A learner should get familiar with what he is learning. With such familiarity, whenever he calls it in his mind, it will come immediately. But without such familiarity, one should spend time thinking of it, yet when he has got it, the meaning of it has already not been so fresh as ever. ［Shiyi］

109 道理生，便缚不住。淳。

When the truth emerges, it is impossible to be bound up. ［Chun（淳）］

110 见，须是见得确定。淳。

When one sees it, he should make sure that he sees it truly. ［Chun（淳）］

111 须是心广大似这个，方包裹得过，运动得行。方子。

A learner should be large-minded so as to embrace it（i. e. the truth）all and allow its free movement in his mind. ［Fangzi］

112 学者立得根脚阔，便好。升卿。

When a learner stands firm on a broad ground, he will be well grounded. ［Shengqing］

113 须是有头有尾，成个物事。方子。

One should make effort complete from its beginning to its end, so as to accomplish an entire thing-event. ［Fangzi］

114 彻上彻下，无精粗本末，只是一理。赐。

Inhering in everything, from top to bottom, whether it is refined or coarse, and whether it is the root or the branch, is one principle. ［Ci］①

115 最怕粗看了，便易走入不好处去。士毅。

The most worrying is that a learner starts with carelessness, for which he is liable to go astray. ［Shiyi］

116 学问不只于一事一路上理会。振。

The pursuit of learning does not mean that one strives only for understanding with regard to individual things or approaches. ［Zhen］

117 贯通，是无所不通。

Penetrating thoroughly means that there is nothing that one does not understand.

118 "未有耳目狭而心广者。"其说甚好。振。

"There is no one who is narrow-earshoted and short-sighted, yet large-minded." What this says is truly right. ［Zhen］

119 帖底谨细做去，所以能广。振。

Go ahead and do it with care, rigor, and prudence, and you will reach far and wide. ［Zhen］

120 大凡学者，无有径截一路可以教他了得；须是博洽，历涉多，方通。振。

Generally, a learner who engages in doing learning should not expect to get a short cut from his teacher, and only by doing wide-ranging studies and getting rich experiences can he be enlightened. ［Zhen］

121 不可涉其流便休。方子。

---

① Lin Ci 林赐（courtesy name Wenyi 闻一）

Never stop at only getting to know its flow (but not its source).
[Fangzi]

122 天下更有大江大河，不可守个土窟子，谓水专在是。力行。

There are great rivers and lakes in the world. Never get attached to the small pond before you and say all water of the world is here in it. [Lixing]

123 学者若有本领，相次千枝万叶，都来凑着这里，看也须易晓，读也须易记。方子。

If a learner is truly capable, when reading books, despite the thousands of branches and leaves layer upon layer, as it were, they all get together here towards him, which become simple to understand and easy to remember.
[Fangzi]

124 大本不立，小规不正。可学。

If the primary foundation is not laid right, the secondary rules are impossible to be upright. [Kexue]

125 刮落枝叶，栽培根本。可学。

Cut off the branches and leaves, and foster the root. [Kexue]

126 大根本流为小根本。举前说。因先说："钦夫学大本如此，则发处不能不受病。"方。

The Master said, "There may be a fall from the primary root down to a secondary root." He cited something he had said before to illustrate it. He thereupon said, "When Qinfu studied the primary root, he had a fall like that, and thus he was troubled inevitably where he had begun." [Fang]

127 学问须严密理会，铢分毫析。道夫。

In doing learning with regard to something, one should make efforts for a rigorous understanding, without losing sight of even an iota of it. [Daofu]

128 因论为学，曰："愈细密，愈广大；愈谨确，愈高明。"偶。

Thereupon the Master discussed the pursuit of learning. He said, "The more meticulous, the more extensive; the more prudent, the more brilliant."
[Xian]

129 开阔中又着细密，宽缓中又着谨严。广。

Be broad-sighted and meanwhile careful and cautious; be leisurely-paced and meanwhile precise and rigorous. [Guang]

130 如其窄狭，则当涵泳广大气象；颓惰，则当涵泳振作气象。方子。

If one is narrow-minded now, he should begin making efforts to nourish his mien of large-mindedness; if one is indolent and dejected now, he should begin striving and fostering his mien of spiriting up and vigorousness. [Fangzi]

131 学者须养教气宇开阔弘毅。升卿。

A learner should nourish himself so as to be imposing in his bearing and fortitude. [Shengqing]

132 常使截断严整之时多，胶胶扰扰之时少，方好。德明。

If one usually experiences much more occasions when his thinking is clear cut and neat than those when he feels muddled and confused, then he is on the right track. [Deming]

133 只有一个界分，出则便不是。广。

There is only one demarcation, beyond which is going astray. [Guang]

134 义理难者便不是。振。

If one feels the idea carried by classics difficult to understand, that is not the true idea. [Zhen]

135 体认为病，自在即好。振。

If a learner feels troubled when identifying it, take it easy and he will overcome that trouble. [Zhen]

136 须是玩味。方子。

A learner should relish the taste of it. [Fangzi]

137 咬得破时，正好咀味。文蔚。

When you are able to bite just into it, it is the right time when you chew its taste. [Wenwei]

138 若只是握得一个鹘仑底果子，不知里面是酸，是咸，是苦，是涩。须是与他嚼破，便见滋味。㽫。

If you only hold a whole fruit, you are impossible to know whether its inside tastes sour, salty, bitter, or astringent. So you have to bite it to know its taste. [Xun]

139 易曰："学以聚之，问以辨之，宽以居之，仁以行之。"语曰："执德不弘，信道不笃，焉能为有！焉能为亡！"学问之后，继以宽居。信道笃而又欲执德弘者，人之为心不可促迫也。人心须令着得一善，又着一善，善之来无穷，而吾心受之有余地，方好。若只着得一善，第二般来又未便容得，如此，无缘心广而道积也。洽。

The *Classic of Change* says "(The Superior Man) learns and accumulates the results of his learning; puts questions and discriminates among those results; dwells magnanimously in what he has attained; and carries it into practice with benevolence. "① The *Analects* (19: 2) says, "When a person holds fast to virtue, but without seeking to enlarge it, and believes in right principles, but without firm sincerity, what account can be made of his existence or non-existence?"② A learner should dwell magnanimously in what he has attained in his learning. To cultivate one's mind for the belief in right principles with firm sincerity and the desire for holding fast to virtue and seeking to enlarge it, he should not rush into rash actions. He should let his mind attain some goodness and then more, and it will be a good state when it is able to keep accepting endless arrivals of goodness, and that with some leeway. If one accepts some goodness but when more goodness arrives he can not take it in, then he has no luck to

---

① Cited from the "Wenyan" 文言 (Special Explanation of the Texts) for "Hexagram Qian" in the *Classic of Change*. The translation is based on a version of James Legge (see http://ctext.org/book-of-changes/yi-jing), with some alteration.

② The translation is based on a version of James Legge (see http://ctext.org/analects), with slight modification.

accumulate the right principles in a broad mind. 〔Qia〕

140 自家犹不能快自家意，如何他人却能尽快我意！要在虚心以从善。升卿。

When even you can not discontent your own intention by yourself, how can others discontent your intention? The important is to keep your mind open and accept goodness. 〔Shengqing〕

141 "虚心顺理"，学者当守此四字。人杰。

"Keep the mind open and abide by the principle. " A learner should stick to this as a motto. 〔Renjie〕

142 圣人与理为一，是恰好。其它以心处这理，却是未熟，要将此心处理。可学。

A sage is identical with the principle to the most proper extent. Others treat the principle also with their mind, but their mind is not ripe. The principle should be treated with a ripe mind. 〔Kexue〕

143 今人言道理，说要平易，不知到那平易处极难。被那旧习缠绕，如何便摆脱得去！譬如作文一般，那个新巧者易作，要平淡便难。然须还他新巧，然后造于平淡。又曰："自高险处移下平易处，甚难。"端蒙。

The Master said, "When many people today talk about the principle, they try to turn it into plain and easy discourse, but they do not know that it is extremely difficult to reach the state where the principle can be presented that way. How can they get rid of the conventional practices wrapping them? That is like writing an essay, where it is easy to produce something novel and exquisite, but hard to compose something in a plain and simple style. However, one has to experience novelty and exquisiteness before reaching plainness and simplicity once more. " He added, "It is rather difficult to move from a perilous height down to a plain and simple level. " 〔Duanmeng〕

144 人之资质有偏，则有缝罅。做工夫处，盖就偏处做将去。若资质平底，则如死水然，终激作不起。谨愿底人，更添些无状，便是乡原。不可以为知得些子便了。焘。

If one's aptitude is partial, it means there being a gap with it. In this sense, when he makes efforts, he should focus on where the gap is and strive to fill it out. But when his aptitude is ordinary, which is like a pond of stagnant water, it is eventually hard to activate it. Besides that, if he is timid and over-cautious, it makes that more difficult, and thus he is no more than a hypocrite. Never think that it is enough to get to know only a little. [Tao]

145 只闻"下学而上达",不闻"上达而下学"。德明。

I have heard only "My learning lies low but my penetration rises high," (*Analects*, 14：35) but never heard "My penetration rises high but my learning lies low." [Deming]

146 今学者之于大道,其未及者虽是迟钝,却须终有到时。唯过之者,便不肯复回来耳。必大。

Currently, when pursuing the learning of the great Way, though some learners have not made access to it due to their stupidity, they will attain it some day. But those who have got beyond it tend to be reluctant to return. [Bida]

147 或人性本好,不须矫揉。教人一用此,极害理。又有读书见义理,释书,义理不见,亦可虑。可学。

There are some people who are originally good in nature and so need not rectification of it through straightening or crooking. To teach them with such straightening or crooking would do utter harm to the principle. There are also some who can see the principle when reading a Confucian classic, but can not see it when putting it down, so they are worrying. [Kexue]

148 学者议论工夫,当因其人而示以用工之实,不必费辞。使人知所适从,以入于坦易明白之域,可也。若泛为端绪,使人迫切而自求之,适恐资学者之病。人杰。

When discussing with students the way of pursuing learning, don't do more than considering the different conditions with different students and instructing them correspondingly with suitable ways of making substantial efforts. It is enough to let them know what they should do so as to enter a field flat and easy and go in for understanding. If a teacher shows them too many general clues and urges them to start from them urgently and seek for more by themselves, I'm afraid that will add to the trouble they have already endured. [Renjie]

149 师友之功，但能示之于始而正之于终尔。若中间三十分工夫，自用吃力去做。既有以喻之于始，又自勉之于中，又其后得人商量是正之，则所益厚矣。不尔，则亦何补于事。道夫。

To a student, the merit of a teacher lies in nothing but instructing him how to begin and correcting him when he comes to an end. Between his beginning and his end, the student should make strenuous efforts by himself for the best learning result. If a student can get a teacher who can explain to him how to begin, keep encouraging him in the middle, and have what he achieves corrected through consulting with him in the end, then the benefit he can gain therein will be much indeed. Or else, what benefit can he get from the teaching in regard to his learning? [Daofu]

150 或论人之资质，或长于此而短于彼。曰："只要长善救失。"或曰："长善救失，不特教者当如此，人自为学亦当如此。"曰："然。"焘。

Someone said of the aptitudes of a person, which may be strong here, yet weak there. The Master responded, "What matters is only giving full play to the strong point and make up for the weak point." The former said further, "Your 'giving full play to the strong point and making up for the weak point' is applicable not only to the teacher but also to the learner when he teaches himself." The Master replied, "Right." [Tao]

151 凡言诚实，都是合当做底事；不是说道诚实好了方去做，不诚实不好了方不做。自是合当诚实。偶。

Whenever being sincere is mentioned, it means something that one should do. It does not mean that one should not set about pursuing learning until he becomes sincere and, without becoming sincere, one would not be able to do it. It is natural that one should be sincere. [Xian]

152 "言必忠信"，言自合着忠信，何待安排。有心去要恁地，便不是活，便不能久矣。若如此，便是剩了一个字在信见边①自是着不得。如事亲必于孝，事长必于弟，孝弟自是道理合当如此。何须安一个"必"字在心头，念念要恁地做。如此，便是辛苦，如何得会长久？又如集义久，然后浩然之气自生。若着一个意在这里等待气生，便为害。今日集得许多，又等待气生，却是私意了。"必有事焉而勿正"，正，便是期必也。为学者须从穷理上做工夫。若物格、知至，则意自诚；意诚，则道理合做底事自然行将去，自无下面许多病痛也。"扩然而大公，物来而顺应。"

"Whenever saying something, one should be determined to keep faithful and sincere."② Since whatever one says should be faithful and sincere, why does it await determination? If one intends to do in such way, that will not be living and can not last long. Thus, it seems that there are two more words in the cited sentence, which do not get visible. ③When one serves his parents, he must be filial and when he serves his elder brother, he must be respectful. His being filial and respectful is naturally what he should be. Why should one bear the "should be determined" in his mind, trying constantly to do things as it requires? With so much moil, how can one make efforts for long? Likewise, if one has accumulated righteous deeds for a long time, he will naturally feel the vast and profound vital force in him. If one keeps an intention here to await the production of that vital force, this will be harmful.

---

① 贺疑"在信见边"有误。

② Cited from *Kongzi Jiayu* 孔子家语 (Confucius's Family Discourse).

③ A note in the original text says "Hesun suspected that the there had been a mistake made in the record of the sentence, for which it did not make sense." The translation is rendered to make some sense in the context, and thus the cited sentence, according to Zhu's analysis, should be "Whenever saying something, one should not be determined to keep faithful and sincere intentionally."

If one has accumulated so many today and then he turns to waiting for the production of that vital force, it is his selfish intention. "Always be doing something without expectation." (*Mencius*, 2A: 2)① The "expectation" means always expecting something. To pursue learning, one should make efforts to inquire the principle to the utmost. If one can investigate things for extension of knowledge sufficiently, his intention will be sincere, and with such sincerity, he will do naturally what the principle requires him to do, free from that many troubles he endured before. "(The Superior Man should) become broad and extremely impartial and respond spontaneously to all things as they come."②

153 切须去了外慕之心！力行。

Be sure to get rid of your yearning for external things. [Lixing]

154 有一分心向里，得一分力；有两分心向里，得两分力。文蔚。

The more you orient your mind to the internal, the more benefit you will gain. [Wenwei]

155 须是要打迭得尽，方有进。从周。

Only by getting rid of all distractions can a learner gain progress. [Congzhou]

156 看得道理熟后，只除了这道理是真实法外，见世间万事，颠倒迷妄，耽嗜恋着，无一不是戏剧，真不堪着眼也。又答人书云："世间万事，须臾变灭，皆不足置胸中，惟有穷理修身为究竟法耳。" 僩。

The Master said, "When one has understood the principle thoroughly, to him, only the principle is true. None of the myriad affairs in the world, whether perverse or confusing, whether addictive or captivating, is not a

---

① The translation of the citation is based on the version by Chan Wing-tsit (See Chan Wing-tsit. trans. and comp. *A Source Book in Chinese Philosophy*. Princeton: Princeton University Press, 1963, p. 63).

② Cited from Cheng Hao's "Da Hengqu Xiansheng Shu Lun Ding Xing" 答横渠先生书论定性 (Reply to Master Hengqü's Letter on Calming Human Nature). The translation is based on the version by Chan Wing-tsit (p. 525).

drama, which is really intolerable to the eye. " In his reply to the letter from a friend of his, he said, "The myriad things in the world undergo, in an instant, changing and perishing, and none of them is worthwhile to be put in the mind, except the probe into the principle to the utmost and self-cultivation, which represent the only ultimate realities. "① [Xian]

157 大凡人只合讲明道理而谨守之，以无愧于天之所与者。若乃身外荣辱休戚，当一切听命而已。襄。

Generally, what one should do is clarify the truth and stick to it with caution, so as to live up to what Heaven endowed him with. As for the worldly honors or disgraces, joys or sorrows, he should follow the arrangement of his destiny. [Xiang]

158 因说索面，曰："今人于饮食动使之物，日极其精巧。到得义理，却不理会，渐渐昏蔽了都不知。"广。

Thereupon, the Master touched on *suomian* 索面 (a special hand-pulled noodle). He said, "Nowadays, the food and drink, and the utensils in daily life, have become more and more fine and delicate. However, when it comes to the universal principle, people today have paid little attention to it and consequently got benighted gradually yet without knowing it. " [Guang]

---

① In the original text, Zhu Xi uses the Buddhist terms *zhenshi fa* 真实法 (sacca-dhamma) and *jiujing fa* 究竟法 (paramattha dhamma), which means "truths" and "ultimate realities (The 'paramattha' denotes the exposition that is true in the highest or ultimate sense)," respectively. They are sense-translated into "true" and "ultimate realities" in the contexts.

卷第九 Book 9

学三
Learning III
论知行
Knowledge and Action

1 知、行常相须，如目无足不行，足无目不见。论先后，知为先；论轻重，行为重。闳祖。

Knowledge and action always require each other. It is like a person who cannot walk without legs, although he has eyes, and who cannot see without eyes, although he has legs. With respect to their order of priority, knowledge comes first, and with respect to their importance, action is more important. ①
[Hongzu]

2 论知之与行，曰："方其知之而行未及之，则知尚浅。既亲历其域，则知之益明，非前日之意味。"公谨。

As regards knowledge and action, the Master said, "When one knows something but has not yet acted on it, his knowledge is still shallow. After he has experienced it, his knowledge will be increasingly clear, and different

① The translation of this passage is based on the version by Chan Wing-tsit (See Chan Wing-tsit. trans. and comp. *A Source Book in Chinese Philosophy*. Princeton: Princeton University Press, 1963, p. 609), with some alterations.

from what it was before. "① ［Gongjin］②

3 圣贤说知，便说行。大学说"如切如磋，道学也"；便说"如琢如磨，自修也"。中庸说"学、问、思、辨"，便说"笃行"。颜子说"博我以文"，谓致知、格物；"约我以礼"，谓"克己复礼"。泳。

In the discourses of the sages and worthies, knowledge is always coupled with action. For example, in the *Great Learning* (4), when "The expression of ' As we cut and then file ' describes the work of learning" is said, following it is "The expression of ' As we chisel and then grind ' indicates that of self-cultivation. " In the *Doctrine of the Mean* (22), the "extensive study of what is good, accurate inquiry about it, careful reflection on it, clear discrimination of it" is followed by the "earnest practice of it. " In the *Analects* (9：11), Yanzi (i. e. Yan Hui) says "He (Confucius) enlarged my mind with learning," which concerns investigation of things and extension of knowledge, and then "(He) taught me the restraints with propriety," which bears on "subduing one's self and returning to propriety. " (*Analects*, 12：1)③ ［Yong（泳）］

4 致知、力行，用功不可偏。偏过一边，则一边受病。如程子云："涵养须用敬，进学则在致知。"分明自作两脚说，但只要分先后轻重。论先后，当以致知为先；论轻重，当以力行为重。端蒙。

In making efforts for the attainment of knowledge and practice of action, one should refrain from leaning towards one side, for the inclination would be at the cost of the other side. Master Cheng Yi said, "The progress of self-cultivation should be made with seriousness and the purpose of pursuing advance in learning is to extend knowledge. " It is obvious that he said of them as two separate things, but different in terms of priority or importance.

---

① The translation of this passage is based on the version by Chan Wing-tsit, p. 609.

② Li Wezi 李文子, with the courtesy name Gongjin 公谨.

③ The English translation of the citations in the passage is based on J. Legge's relevant versions (see http：//ctext. org).

In regard to their priority, the extension of knowledge comes first, while, with respect to their importance, the practice of action is more important. [Duanmeng]

5 问:"南轩云:'致知、力行互相发。'"曰:"未须理会相发,且各项做将去。若知有未至,则就知上理会,行有未至,则就行上理会,少间自是互相发。今人知不得,便推说我行未到,行得不是,便说我知未至,只管相推,没长进。"因说一朋友有书来,见人说他说得不是,却来说我只是践履未至,涵养未熟,我而今且未须考究,且理会涵养。"被他截断,教人与他说不得,都只是这个病。"胡泳。

When asked about Nanxuan's (i. e. Zhang Shi) saying "The attainment of knowledge and the practice of action are mutually enlightening," the Master answered, "It is unnecessary to pay attention to their mutually enlightening. You just make efforts for both sides. If you feel inadequate in knowledge, exert yourself more for knowledge, and if you feel weak in action, exert yourself more for action. Soon both sides will be mutually enlightening in you. Today, many learners, when feeling inadequate in knowledge, say that they have not made adequate efforts for action, while, when feeling weak in action, say that their knowledge has not got sufficient. Consequently, such excuses are productive of no progress at all." Thereupon, he mentioned what a friend of his had said in his letter to him. The friend, when someone else criticized him by saying what he had said was not right, claimed that the reason for his problem lay in his deficiency in action due to unripe self-cultivation and that what he would have to do next was nothing but making efforts for his self-cultivation. The Master commented, "The reason why he (the friend) fell victim to the criticism which interrupted him, and why he was vulnerable to that criticism are both in the trouble with him who failed to understand right the relation between the two sides." [Hu Yong]

6 汪德辅问:"须是先知,然后行?"曰:"不成未明理,便都不持守了!且如曾点与曾子,便是两个样子:曾点便是理会得底,而行有不揜；曾子便是合下持守，旋旋明理，到一唯处。"德明。

Wang Defu asked, "Should we attain knowledge before engaging in action?" The Master answered, "When one has not got his personal understanding of the truth, what does he stick to? It is like Zeng Dian and his son Zengzi (i. e. Zeng Shen), both disciples of Confucius, who set two different examples. Zeng Dian had first got his personal understanding of the truth and was also sufficient in his action, while Zengzi preserved and stuck to the knowledge he had been endowed with and became gradually aware of the truth, and thus attained the realm free from doubts."① [Deming]

7 圣贤千言万语，只是要知得，守得。节。

The thousands of words said by the sages and worthies boil down to one point that one should strive to be capable of understanding and preserving. [Jie]

8 只有两件事：理会，践行。节。

There are only two pursuits: the pursuit of understanding and that of practicing. [Jie]

9 学者以玩索、践履为先。道夫。

A learner should prioritize contemplative rumination and earnest practice. [Daofu]

10 某与一学者言，操存与穷格，不解一上做了。如穷格工夫，亦须铢积寸累，工夫到后，自然贯通。若操存工夫，岂便能常操。其始也，操得一霎，旋旋到一食时；或有走作，亦无如之何。能常常警觉，久久自能常存，自然光明矣。人杰。

I said to a learner that he should make untiring efforts to adhere to his personal integrity so that it never leaves him and to investigate things for

---

① In the original text, *yiwei* 一唯 refers to the conversation between Confucius and Zeng Shen recorded in *Analects*, which is: "The Master said, 'Shen, my doctrine is that of an all-pervading unity (*yi* 一).' The disciple Zeng replied, 'Yes (*wei* 唯).'" The *yiwei* is used by later scholars to refer to one reaching the realm free from doubts.

inquiring the principle to the utmost concurrently. With regard to the effort to investigate things for inquiring the principle to the utmost, one should accumulate it little by little and when his accumulation is enough, he will attain a thorough understanding of the principle. As for the effort for adhering to his personal integrity, how can one hold onto it always in the same manner? At the beginning, one may be able to adhere to it only for an instant and step by step he reaches the time needed for having a breakfast. Sometimes it gets distorted, but he is unable to remedy that. If one can keep alert constantly, in due time he will get able to hold onto it fast and will naturally be brilliant. [Renjie]

11 操存涵养，则不可不紧；进学致知，则不可不宽。祖道。

One's effort to foster his personal integrity should have to be intensified as soon as possible, while his effort to advance his learning for extending his knowledge should have to be made little by little. [Zudao]

12 所谓穷理，大底也穷，小底也穷，少间都成一个物事。所谓持守者，人不能不牵于物欲，才觉得，便收将来。久之，自然成熟。非谓截然今日为始也。夔孙。

By the so called inquiring the principle to the utmost is meant that things and events, whether big or small, should be inquired to the utmost and before long they become of the same thing-event to the inquirer. In the so called treasuring up and preserving something, one can not but be subject to selfish desire for materials, but the moment he feels that, he should quell it. After a long time, he will be mature. It does not mean that one starts up today and can make it completely tomorrow. [Kuisun]

13 千言万语，说得只是许多事。大概在自家操守讲究，只是自家存得些在这里，便在这里。若放去，便是自家放了。道夫。

What those thousands of words say is concerned only with a lot of events. Probably, for one who makes efforts to treasure up and hold onto his personal integrity, when he preserves it here, it will dwell here in himself, but when he lets it go, he has it leave by himself. [Daofu]

14 思索义理，涵养本原。儒用。

Ponder over the principle and nourish its original state. [Ruyong]

15 涵养中自有穷理工夫，穷其所养之理；穷理中自有涵养工夫，养其所穷之理，两项都不相离。才见成两处，便不得。贺孙。

When one is striving for self-cultivation, it means naturally that he is making efforts to inquire the principle to the utmost, that is, the principle he is cultivating; when one is striving for inquiring the principle to the utmost, it also means naturally that he is making efforts for self-cultivation, that is, cultivating the principle he is inquiring to the utmost. Thus, the two sides are inseparable. They should not be seen as two separate sides for even an instant. [Hesun]

16 择之问："且涵养去，久之自明。"曰："亦须穷理。涵养、穷索，二者不可废一，如车两轮，如鸟两翼。如温公，只恁行将去，无致知一段。"德明。

Zezhi asked, "One should keep on his efforts for self-cultivation and in due time he will get enlightened. (Is it right?)" The Master answered, "He should inquire the principle to the utmost concurrently, for his effort should not be inclined to only one side. They are like the two wheels of a cart or the two wings of a bird. The Duke of Wen (i.e. Sima Guang) is one-sided, for he emphasized only keeping on practicing, yet ignored extending knowledge. " [Deming]

17 人之为学，如今雨下相似：雨既下后，到处湿润，其气易得蒸郁。才略晴，被日头略照，又蒸得雨来。前日亢旱时，只缘久无雨下，四面干枯；纵有些少，都滋润不得，故更不能蒸郁得成。人之于义理，若见得后，又有涵养底工夫，日日在这里面，便意思自好，理义也容易得见，正如雨蒸郁得成后底意思。若是都不去用力者，日间只恁悠悠，都不曾有涵养工夫。设或理会得些小道理，也滋润他不得，少间私欲起来，又间断去，正如亢旱不能得雨相似也。时举。

One's pursuit of learning is akin to the raining today. After the rain, the ground is wet everywhere and the rain water is liable to evaporate. Thus, when it is clear a little and the sun shines for a while, the evaporated water will turn into rain again. Some time ago, severe drought prevailed and things withered, which was caused by not raining for a long time. In spite of some rain, it was too little to moisten things, let alone be evaporated for more rain. As regards the principle, if one has been able to see it and made daily efforts for self-cultivation, he will feel affinity with it naturally and also is liable to understand it well. This state is just like that when the rain water can be evaporated well. If one fails to make those efforts and idle away day by day, he is impossible to attain any progress in self-cultivation. Even though he may have got some understanding of some lesser principles, he can never be moistened by them, and soon when his selfish desire stirs up, he will discontinue, just like the shortage of rainfall in a severe drought. [Shiju]

18 学者工夫，唯在居敬、穷理二事。此二事互相发。能穷理，则居敬工夫日益进；能居敬，则穷理工夫日益密。譬如人之两足，左足行，则右足止；右足行，则左足止。又如一物悬空中，右抑则左昂，左抑则右昂，其实只是一事。广。

The efforts made by a scholar are to pursue two events, that is, treasuring up seriousness 敬 in doing things and inquiring the principle to the utmost. The two events are mutually promoting. One making effort to inquire the principle to the utmost promotes his advance in his effort to cherish seriousness, and his capability of making effort to cherish seriousness promotes his effort to inquire the principle to the utmost. It is like the two feet of a person, of which when one moves a step ahead, the other stops and then when one stops, the other moves a step ahead. Thus he can go further and further by their moving alternately. It is also like something hanging in the air. When it is pressed on the right side, its left side rises up and when it is pressed on the left side, its right side rises up, both of which are, in essence, of the same event. [Guang]

19 人须做工夫，方有疑。初做工夫时，欲做此一事，又碍彼一事，便没理会处。只如居敬、穷理两事便相碍。居敬是个收敛执持底道理，穷理是个推寻究竟底道理。只此二者，便是相妨。若是熟时，则自不相碍矣。广。

A person must make efforts (for learning) and it is in that process that his doubt occurs. When one makes his initial effort, he desires to do this thing, but is obstructed by that thing, and thus he ends up with no understanding of either. Consequently, for him, treasuring up seriousness and inquiring the principle to the utmost seem two things that hinder each other. The treasuring-up of seriousness represents the principle for retracting and keeping, while inquiring the principle to the utmost means deducting and seeking for the ultimate principle. At the beginning when one makes efforts, he finds these two respects hampering each other, but as he gets more and more mature, he will naturally find them free from that hampering. [Guang]

20 主敬、穷理虽二端，其实一本。

Though cherishing seriousness and inquiring the principle to the utmost are two ends, they are actually of the same origin.

21 持敬是穷理之本；穷得理明，又是养心之助。夔孙。

The treasuring-up of seriousness is the basis for inquiring the principle to the utmost; the enlightening in regard to the principle is conducive to nourishing the mind. [Kuisun]

22 学者若不穷理，又见不得道理。然去穷理，不持敬，又不得。不持敬，看道理便都散，不聚在这里。淳。

If a scholar does not strive to inquire the principle to the utmost, he can not see the truth. However, when he strives to inquire the principle to the utmost, yet does not cherish seriousness, he will go nowhere. Without holding on to seriousness, even though he may see some truths, they are scattered and do not come together to form an entirety. [Chun (淳)]

23 持敬观理，如病人相似。自将息，固是好，也要讨些药来服。泳。

The process of cherishing seriousness and observing the principle is like that of treating the sickness with a person. Though it is good indeed that he gets to recover from it by himself, he should take some medicine. 〔Yong（泳）〕

24 文字讲说得行，而意味未深者，正要本原上加功，须是持敬。持敬以静为主。此意须要于不做工夫时频频体察，久而自熟。但是着实自做工夫，不干别人事。"为仁由己，而由人乎哉!"此语的当，更看有何病痛。知有此病，必去其病，此便是疗之之药。如觉言语多，便用简默；意思疏阔，便加细密；觉得轻浮浅易，便须深沉重厚。张先生所谓"矫轻警惰"，盖如此。谟。

When a scholar can do a good job in interpreting words yet fails to go deep and touch their profound significance, he should make more efforts in regard to their origin and that by cherishing seriousness. In cherishing seriousness, being tranquil is the most important. He should keep on experiencing and observing this meaning when he rests himself from making efforts, and in due course after a long time, he will get mature naturally. However, one should be aware that the efforts are something that he must do by himself and that has nothing to do with other people. "Is the practice of benevolence from a man himself, or is it from others?" (*Analects*, 12：1) This question asked by Confucius is to the point. Furthermore, one should try to know what sickness troubles him. After knowing it, he should try to overcome it and, to this end, what Confucius says is the very medicine for it. If one feels too talkative, he can start to set store by silence and talk less; if his way of conveying ideas is loose, he can make conscious effort to put it in a well-knit manner; if his style is frivolous and shallow, he can deepen it so that it will be profound. This is probably what Master Zhang (i.e. Zhang Zai) meant when he said "Rectifying frivolousness and keeping vigilant against idleness. ”［Mo］

25 或问：“致知必须穷理，持敬则须主一。然遇事则敬不能持，持敬则又为事所惑，如何”？曰：“孟子云：‘操则存，舍则亡。’人才一把捉，心便在这里。孟子云‘求放心’，已是说得缓了。心不待求，只警省处便见。‘我欲仁，斯仁至矣。’‘为仁由己，而由人乎哉？’其快如此。盖人能知其心不在，则其心已在了，更不待寻。”祖道。

Someone asked, "To extend knowledge, one must inquire the principle to the utmost; to hold onto seriousness, he must be concentrated mentally. However, when one is caught by an event, he can not hold onto seriousness, and when he tries to hold onto seriousness, he is distracted by the event. How do you think about it?" The Master answered, "Mencius said, 'Hold it fast, and it remains with you. Let it go, and you lose it. ' (*Mencius*, 6A：8) As soon as one holds it, his mind goes to it already. But when Mencius said, '(The great end of learning is nothing else but) to seek for the lost mind,' (*Mencius*, 6A：11), his words mean the already delayed arrival of the mind. The mind does not wait for one seeking for it, for it is present wherever he reflects on himself. 'The moment I wish to be benevolent, it is already at hand. ' (*Analects*, 7：30) 'Is the practice of benevolence from a man himself, or is it from others?' (*Analects*, 12：1) So quick is the arrival of the mind like that. Probably, when one knows his mind is absent, his mind is already present, so it does not wait for his seeking for it. "[1]［Zudao］

26 致知、敬、克己，此三事，以一家譬之：敬是守门户之人，克己则是拒盗，致知却是去推察自家与外来底事。伊川言：“涵养须用敬，进学则在致知。”不言克己。盖敬胜百邪，便自有克，如诚则便不消言闲邪之意。犹善守门户，则与拒盗便是一等事，不消更言别有拒盗底。若以涵养对克己言之，则各作一事亦可。涵养，则譬如将息；克

---

① The English translations of the citations in the passage are based on J. Legge's versions of *Analects* and *Mencius* (see http：//ctext. org), with some alterations.

己，则譬如服药去病。盖将息不到，然后服药。将息则自无病，何消服药。能纯于敬，则自无邪僻，何用克己。若有邪僻，只是敬心不纯，只可责敬。故敬则无己可克，乃敬之效。若初学，则须是功夫都到，无所不用其极。端蒙。

The relations among the three affairs, i. e. extending knowledge, cherishing seriousness, and subduing oneself, are comparable to a household: cherishing seriousness is like gate-keeping; subduing oneself is like guarding against burglary; extending knowledge is like deducting and observing the domestic and the external events. Yichuan (i. e. Cheng Yi) said, "The progress of self-cultivation should be made with seriousness and the purpose of pursuing advance in learning is to extend knowledge. " He did not mention subduing oneself. That is probably because seriousness overcomes all sorts of depravity, so it implies already subduing oneself. It is just as when sincerity is mentioned there will be no need to speak of guarding against depravity. It is true of the case that when one is said as good at gate-keeping, there will be no need to mention his good at guarding against burglary, for they are of the same event. If self-cultivation is mentioned in relation to subduing oneself, they can also be treated as two separate events. Self-cultivation is akin to an ill person recovering from the illness by oneself, while subduing oneself is like taking medicine against the illness. Probably, when the self-recovery does not work, he has to take medicine, but when he recovers by himself from the illness, he does not need to take medicine. If one can cherish seriousness purely, since he is free from evil and depravity, he does not need to subdue himself. Whenever he is troubled by evil and depravity, that is only due to his impure mind in cherishing seriousness, and then what he can do is nothing but resorting to seriousness. Therefore, with seriousness, one has no self to subdue, and this is the effect of cherishing seriousness. For a beginner in learning, he must make efforts in every respect to the greatest extent. [Duanmeng]

27 学者吃紧是要理会这一个心，那纸上说底，全然靠不得。或问："心之体与天地同其大，而其用与天地流通"云云。先生曰："又不可一向去无形迹处寻，更宜于日用事物、经书指意，史传得失上做工夫。即精粗表里，融会贯通，而无一理之不尽矣。"

The Master said, "What matters to a learner is to strive to understand the mind, yet for this those words on paper are completely undependable." Someone asked about the statement that the substance of the mind was as great as Heaven and Earth and its function flows in resonance with Heaven and Earth. The Master responded, "One should not go and seek for it where no trace of things can be found, but rather make efforts to work on events and things of daily life, the meanings of Confucian classics, and the gain and loss of the histories and biographies. That is, when one has gained a thorough understanding of things and events with regard to what is the fine and the coarse and what is the outside and the inside of them, he will see every one of the principles."

28 为学先要知得分晓。泳。以下论知为先。

To pursue learning, one should strive first to know things well. [Yong（泳）] The following several conversations discourse on the priority of gaining knowledge.

29 问致知涵养先后。曰："须先致知而后涵养。"问："伊川言：'未有致知而不在敬。'如何？"曰："此是大纲说。要穷理，须是着意。不着意，如何会理会得分晓。"文蔚。

When asked about the extension of knowledge and self-cultivation in regard to their priority, the Master answered, "You have to give priority to the extension of knowledge to self-cultivation." The questioner asked further, "As Yichuan said, 'There is no extension of knowledge which does not depend on seriousness.' How do you think of it?" The Master replied, "He said that as a cardinal guideline. To inquire the principle to the utmost, one should act with care and effort. Without acting with care and effort, how can he reach a thorough understanding?" [Wenwei]

30 尧卿问："穷理、集义孰先？"曰："穷理为先。然亦不是截然有先后。"曰："穷是穷在物之理，集是集处物之义否？"曰："是。"淳。

Yaoqing 尧卿（courtesy name of Li Tangzi 李唐咨, a disciple of Zhu's, who was Chen Chun's father-in-law）asked, "Of inquiring the principle to the utmost and *jiyi* 集义（accumulating righteousness）, which comes first?" The Master answered, "Inquiring the principle to the utmost comes first. However, they should not be separated completely in terms of priority." The questioner asked further, "Does the 'inquiring' mean inquiring the principle dwelling in things and the 'accumulating' mean accumulating the righteousness inherent in things?" The Master answered, "Yes." ［Chun（淳）］

31 万事皆在穷理后。经不正，理不明，看如何地持守，也只是空。道夫。

Only by one's inquiring the principle underlying the myriads of events to the utmost can they become significant to him. If one does not rectify his understanding of the classics and get clear about the principle, no matter how he strives to adhere to them, what he gains is but nothing at all. ［Daofu］

32 痛理会一番，如血战相似，然后涵养将去。因自云："某如今虽便静坐，道理自见得。未能识得，涵养个甚！"德明。

The Master said, "A scholar should pitch in for understanding for some time, just like going all out fighting in a bloody battle, before engaging in self-cultivation." Thereupon he remarked, "Now, even when I sit quietly here, I see the principles before me effortlessly. If a learner has not got any understanding of something, what will he cultivate in his self-cultivation?" ［Deming］

33 有人专要理会躬行，此亦是孤。去伪。

Someone set about nothing but practicing, yet what he did is one-sided. ［Quwei］

34 王子充问："某在湖南，见一先生只教人践履。"曰："义理不明，如何践履？"曰："他说：'行得便见得。'"曰："如人行路，不见，便如何行。今人多教人践履，皆是自立标致去教人。自有一般资质好底人，便不须穷理、格物、致知。圣人作个大学，便使人齐入于圣贤之域。若讲得道理明时，自是事亲不得不孝，事兄不得不弟，交朋友不得不信。"于。

Wang Zichong 王子充（dates unknown, a disciple of Zhu's）asked, "When in Hunan, I saw a teacher teaching his students only to practice. （How do you think of that?）" The Master answered, "When uninformed of the principle, how can one practice?" Wang added, "That teacher said that they could see the principle while engaging in practice." The Master replied, "It is like walking. When one does not know the road, how can he start to walk? Nowadays, many teachers have preached nothing but practicing, yet what they have taught is their own standards. There are, of course, some people good in their endowment, who are unnecessary to make efforts to investigate things, extend knowledge, and inquire the principle to the utmost. The purpose of the sage who composed the *Great Learning* is to help other people enter the realm of sages and worthies. Thus, when one can clarify the principle clear, he can not but be filial in serving his parents, be respectful in serving his elder brother, and be faithful in making friends." [Gan]

35 而今人只管说治心、修身。若不见这个理，心是如何地治？身是如何地修？若如此说，资质好底便养得成，只是个无能底人；资质不好，便都执缚不住了。傅说云："学于古训乃有获。事不师古，以克永世，匪说攸闻。"古训何消读他做甚？盖圣贤说出，道理都在里，必学乎此，而后可以有得。又云："惟学逊志，务时敏，厥修乃来。允怀于兹，道积于厥躬。惟敩学半。念终始典于学，厥德修罔觉。"自古未有人说"学"字，自傅说说起。他这几句，水泼不入，便是说得密。若终始典于学，则其德不知不觉自进也。夔孙。义刚录云："人如何不博学得！若不博学，说道修身行己，也猛撞做不得。大学'诚意'，只是说'如好好色，如恶恶臭'。及到说修身处时，已自宽了。到后面也自无甚事。其大本只是理会致知、格物。若是不致知、格物，便要诚意、正心、修身；气质纯底，将来只便成一个无见识底呆人。若是意思高广底，将来遏不下，便都颠了，如刘淳叟之徒。六经说'学'字，自傅说方说起来：'王，人求多闻，时惟建事。学于古训，乃有获。'先生至此，讽诵'念终始典于学，厥德修罔觉'，曰：'这数句，只恁地说，而其曲折意思甚密。便是学时自不知不觉，其德自修。而今不去讲学，要修身，身如何地修！'"

Nowadays, people preach only regulating the mind and cultivating oneself. However, when one has failed to see the principle, how can he regulate his mind and how can he cultivate himself? If that was right, then those good in their aptitudes could complete the regulating and cultivating, but they would turn out persons capable of no practice; those not so good in their aptitudes could not even be confined (merely by the regulating and cultivating). Fu Yue 傅说 (c. 1335 – c. 1246 BC, a famous worthy minister in the Shang dynasty) said, "To learn the lessons of the ancients is the way to attainment. That the affairs of one, who does not make the ancients his masters, can be perpetuated for generations is what I have not heard of. " (*Book of History*) Why necessary to read those lessens of the ancients? That is probably because what the ancient sages and worthies said is where the truth dwells and one has to read them before he is able to gain something. Fu Yue also said, "In learning, there should be a humble mind and the maintenance of a constant earnestness; in such a case (the learner's) improvement will surely come. He who sincerely cherishes these things will find all truth accumulating in his person. Teaching is the half of learning; when a man's thoughts from first to last are constantly fixed on learning, his virtuous cultivation comes unperceived. " (*Book of History*) In the remote ancient times there had been no mentioning of learning before Fu, who was the first to advocate it. The above several sentences he said are water-tight, for his idea is well-knit. It is indeed right to say that when a man's thoughts from first to last are constantly fixed on learning, his virtuous cultivation comes unperceived. [Kuisun] For this passage, the record by Yigang reads, "How can one not pursue wide learning? Without wide learning, even if one claims to cultivate himself and tries to conduct himself, he will not make it only by some rash actions. When the *Great Learning* says 'making the thoughts sincere,' it means only allowing no self-deception, as when we hate a bad smell, and as when we love what is beautiful. Where it mentions self-cultivation, it already naturally admits of no urgency. And after that, there is also naturally no trouble. The basic tenet of it is only for an understanding of the investigation of things and extension of knowledge. If people do not pursue them, yet they engage in only making his thoughts sincere, rectifying his mind, and cultivating himself, then those of them with pure physical nature will turn out only persons slow-witted and devoid of insights and those with high and broad aim and intention will not be confined and consequently get lost in other doctrines, such as Liu Chunsou 刘淳叟 (dates unknown) and his like. In the Six Confucian Classics, the first mention of *xue* 学 (learning) was made by Fu Yue, who said, 'O king, a ruler should seek to learn much, with a view to establish his affairs; but to learn the lessons of the ancients is the way to attain this.' (*Book of History*)① With this, the Master recited from the *Book of History* 'When a man's thoughts from first to last are constantly fixed on learning, his virtuous cultivation comes unperceived,' saying 'These several sentences, though seemingly plain, contain well-knit meanings, implying that when a learner is devoted to learning, his virtue is cultivated naturally and unknowingly. Nowadays, if one does not engage in learning, yet wants to attain self-cultivation, how can he cultivate himself?'"

36　见，不可谓之虚见。见无虚实，行有虚实。见只是见，见了后却有行，有不行。若不见后，只要硬做，便所成者窄狭。瞽

Seeing should not be regarded as seeing emptily. In regard to seeing, there is no emptiness or actuality to speak of, but with respect to acting, there are acting emptily and acting actually. Seeing is only seeing, but following seeing may be acting or not acting. Even when one, though failing to see, insists on acting, what he will gain will be rather limited. [Xun]

---

① The English translation of the citations from the *Book of History* is based on the version by J. Legge (see http://ctext.org/shang-shu), with some alterations.

37 学者须常存此心，渐将义理只管去灌溉。若卒乍未有进，即且把见成在底道理将去看认。认来认去，更莫放着，便只是自家底。缘这道理，不是外来物事，只是自家本来合有底，只是常常要点检。如人一家中，合有许多家计，也须常点认过。若不如此，被外人蓦然提将去，也不知。又曰："'温故而知新'，不是离了故底别有一个新，须是常常将故底只管温习，自有新意：一则向时看与如今看，明晦便不同；一则上面自有好意思；一则因这上面却别生得意思。伊川云：'某二十以前读论语，已自解得文义。到今来读，文义只一般，只是意思别。'"贺孙。

The Master said, "A learner should preserve constantly the mind and irrigate it gradually with his understanding of the principles. If he fails to gain advance shortly, he may turn to see and understand the principles close at hand and keep on doing that, never neglecting them. Thus he will recognize them as something of his own. That is because the principles, which are not acquired from outside, are what he possesses originally, only that they need inspecting often. It is like the belongings of a family. The family should inspect and check up them frequently, or else when one or two of them are stolen, it will probably not know that." He added, "Confucius says, 'One can acquire new knowledge by reviewing the old.' He does not mean that one can get something completely new that has nothing to do with the old, but rather one should keep on reviewing the old frequently and acquire something new therefrom naturally. For one thing, it is like an object which, when seen at different moments of the day, looks dim or clear; for another, naturally, there is some good meaning in them; for a third, some fresh meaning can be found dwelling in the old. As Yichuan said, 'When I read the *Analects* twenty years ago, I was able to comprehend what the words in it refer to by myself. When I read it today, to me, though what those words refer to has not changed, their meaning has changed.'" [Hesun]

38 学聚、问辨，明善、择善，尽心、知性，此皆是知，皆始学之功也。道夫。以下专论知。

The accumulation of learning, the inquiry and discrimination, the clarifying and choosing of what is good, and the exerting of the mind to the utmost and understanding of humanity, all bear on knowledge and all are what a learning beginner should make efforts to pursue. [Daofu] The following two sections are concerned only with knowledge.

39 人为学，须是要知个是处，千定万定。知得这个彻底是，那个彻底不是，方是见得彻、见得是，则这心里方有所主。且如人学射：若志在红心上，少间有时只射得那帖上；志在帖上，少间有时只射得那垛上；志在垛上，少间都射在别处去了！卓。

Whoever pursues learning should know there being a truth, by which the myriads of things and events can be determined. Only when one knows this as completely true and that as completely not true can he see the truth thoroughly and that right, and can he have what serves as the master in his mind. It is comparable to one learning how to shoot arrows. If the learner aims to hit the center of the target, after some time of learning he actually hits only the area around the center of the target; if he aims to hit that area around the center, after some time of learning he actually hits the mound where the target stands; if he aims to hit the mound, after some time of learning he actually hits some other place than the mount. [Zhuo]

40 只争个知与不知，争个知得切与不切。且如人要做好事，到得见不好事，也似乎可做。方要做好事，又似乎有个做不好事底心从后面牵转去，这只是知不切。贺孙。

What one should strive for is only knowing or not, and knowing pertinently or not. It is like one who wants to do something good, but who, when he sees something not good, seems also to take to it. The moment he wants to do something good, there seems to crop up an idea for doing something not good, which drags him and even turns him around. The reason for such being of two minds is his not knowing pertinently. [Hesun]

41 许多道理，皆是人身自有底。虽说道昏，然又那曾顽然恁地暗！也都知是善好做，恶不好做。只是见得不完全，见得不的确。所以说穷理，便只要理会这些子。贺孙。以下穷理。

Many principles are possessed by a person originally by birth. Despite the benightedness, is it ever incorrigible? It is known to all that for one to do what is good is easy, while for one to do what is evil is not. It is only because what one has seen is not complete and not pertinent. Therefore, to inquire the principle to the utmost means to gain understanding of such respects. [Hesun] The following sections are on inquiring the principle.

42 这个道理，与生俱生。今人只安顿放那空处，都不理会，浮生浪老，也甚可惜！要之，理会出来，亦不是差异底事。不知如何理会个得恁少，看他自是甘于无知了。今既要理会，也须理会取透；莫要半青半黄，下梢都不济事。道夫。

This principle is what one is born with. Nowadays, people put it in where there is vacancy and, paying no attention to it at all, they idle away their lifetime. What a pity, indeed! In a word, attaining understanding of it is not something weird. I wonder why few of them have paid attention to it. Most of them appear willing to be ignorant. Now, if one wants to seek for an understanding of it, he must do it thoroughly for a complete understanding, refraining from leaving it incomplete, for in that case he will go nowhere. [Daofu]

43 人生天地间，都有许多道理。不是自家硬把与他，又不是自家凿开他肚肠，白放在里面。贺孙。

Humankind is born between Heaven and Earth, endowed with many principles. It is not that they impose themselves on him, nor is it that they cut his belly open and get into it for nothing. [Hesun]

44 一心具万理。能存心，而后可以穷理。季札。

One mind possesses ten thousands of principles. If one can preserve his mind, then he can inquire the principles to the utmost. [Jizha]

45 心包万理，万理具于一心。不能存得心，不能穷得理；不能穷得理，不能尽得心。阳。

The mind embraces ten thousands of principles and the ten thousands of principles dwell in the one mind. If unable to preserve his mind, one will be unable to inquire the principle to the utmost; if unable to inquire the principle to the utmost, one will be unable to exhaust his mind. ［Yang（阳）］

46 穷理以虚心静虑为本。淳。

The fundamental to the efforts to inquire the principle to the utmost is making the mind vacuous and considering in tranquility. ［Chun（淳）］

47 虚心观理。方子。

Keep the mind vacuous and observe the principle. ［Fangzi］

48 或问："而今看道理不出，只是心不虚静否？"曰："也是不曾去看。会看底，就看处自虚静，这个互相发。"义刚。

Someone asked, "Now, I can not see the principle. Is this due to my wanting of mental vacuity and tranquility?" The Master answered, "You have not tried to see in the true sense of seeing. If one knows how to see, he will get vacuous and tranquil where he tries to see it. Seeing and being vacuous and tranquil are mutually promoting. " ［Yigang］

49 而今看道理不见，不是不知，只是为物塞了。而今粗法，须是打迭了胸中许多恶杂，方可。张子云："义理有疑，则濯去旧见，以来新意。"人多是被那旧见恋不肯舍。除是大故聪明，见得不是，便翻了。夔孙。

If one can not see the principle, it is not that he does not possess knowledge of it but that his knowledge is obstructed by things. To apply a rough way to getting rid of the obstruction, he has to remove those many irrelevant and evil conceptions from his bosom. Master Zhang（i. e. Zhang Zai）said, "When one gets doubt about the principle, he should wash off his old opinions, so as to usher in fresh meanings. " People are attached to their old opinions, reluctant to discard them, except those who are so intelligent as to see what troubles them and are resolute to throw the old away. [Kuisun]

50 理不是在面前别为一物，即在吾心。人须是体察得此物诚实在我，方可。譬如修养家所谓铅汞、龙虎，皆是我身内之物，非在外也。广。

The principle does not mean that there is something discrete before us, for it dwells in our mind. A learner should ponder and examine it so as to reach the belief that it really inheres in him. It is like what are referred to as *qiangong* 铅汞 (lit. lead and mercury; fig. destiny and nature) and *longhu* 龙虎 (lit. dragon and tiger; fig. spirit and essence) by Daoists, who believe that they dwell inside rather than outside their own bodies. [Guang]

51 "穷理，如性中有个仁义礼智，其发则为恻隐、羞恶、辞逊、是非。只是这四者，任是世间万事万物，皆不出此四者之内。"黄问："有可一底道理否？"曰："见多后，自然贯。"又曰："会之于心，可以一得，心便能齐。但心安后，便是义理。"卓。

The Master said, "To illustrate inquiring the principles to the utmost, in human nature dwell benevolence, righteousness, propriety, and wisdom, which are emanated as the feelings of sadness and commiseration, of shame and dislike, of deference and compliance, and of right and wrong. They are only four, but every one of the myriads of things and events in the world is confined by them. " I asked, "Is there a principle penetrating all?" The Master answered, "When you see many enough, you will understand there being one principle penetrating all. " He added, "When all converge in the mind, they can be understood by virtue of one principle and then the mind is capable of equalizing them. But when peace prevails in the mind, it indicates the emergence of the principle. " [Zhuo]

52 器远问："穷事物之理，还当穷究个总会处，如何？"曰："不消说总会。凡是眼前底，都是事物。只管恁地逐项穷教到极至处，渐渐多，自贯通。然为之总会者，心也。"贺孙。

Qiyuan asked: "In investigating the principles of things and affairs to the utmost, should one investigate exhaustively the point where all principles converge? What do you think?" The Master answered, "There is no need to talk about the converging point. All that is before our eyes is things and affairs. Just investigate one item after another somehow until the utmost is reached. As more and more is done, one will naturally achieve a far and wide penetration. That which serves as the converging point is the mind."[1] [Hesun]

53 凡看道理，要见得大头脑处分明。下面节节，只是此理散为万殊。如孔子教人，只是逐件逐事说个道理，未尝说出大头脑处。然四面八方合聚凑来，也自见得个大头脑。若孟子，便已指出教人。周子说出太极，已是太煞分明矣。且如恻隐之端，从此推上，则是此心之仁；仁即所谓天德之元；元即太极之阳动。如此节节推上，亦自见得大总脑处。若今看得太极处分明，则必能见得天下许多道理条件皆自此出，事事物物上皆有个道理，元无亏欠也。铢。

Whenever one tries to understand the principles, he should strive to see clear where the most essential principle is. The secondary principles are only the many different manifestations of the most essential principle. When Confucius conducted teaching, he clarified the principles with regard only to a specific thing or event, and did not state clear where the most essential principle was. However, when the principles converge from all quarters, there emerges naturally the most essential one. In the case of Mencius, he pointed out it and taught it to others. Master Zhou (i. e. Zhun Dunyi) was the first to introduce the Supreme Ultimate, who made that crystal clear, indeed. For example, the beginning of the feeling of sadness and commiseration. From that, the benevolence of the mind can be deduced. Thus, benevolence is what is called the origination of *tiande* 天德 (heavenly virtue); that origination is the movement of the *yang* of the Supreme Ultimate. In this way, the deduction can be made step by step towards the

---

[1] The translation of this passage is based on the version by Chan Wing-tsit, p. 610.

most important point. If now one can see clear where the Supreme Ultimate is, he will understand that many principles in the world come forth from it and that there inheres a principle in every one of the myriad of things or events, which is never absent originally. [Zhu]

54 今之学者自是不知为学之要。只要穷得这道理，便是天理。虽圣人不作，这天理自在天地间。"天高地下，万物散殊；流而不息，合同而化"，天地间只是这个道理流行周遍。不应说道圣人不言，这道理便不在。这道理自是长在天地间，只借圣人来说一遍过。且如易，只是一个阴阳之理而已。伏羲始画，只是画此理；文王孔子皆是发明此理。吉凶悔吝，亦是从此推出。及孔子言之，则曰："君子居其室，出其言善，则千里之外应之；出其言不善，则千里之外违之。言行，君子之枢机；枢机之发，荣辱之主也。言行，君子之所以动天地也，可不谨乎！"圣人只要人如此。且如书载尧舜禹许多事业，与夫都俞吁咈之言，无非是至理。恪。

Today the scholars themselves do not get to know what the key to learning is. So long as they understand the principle by inquiring it to the utmost, it is the very heavenly principle. Though it was not created by the sage, the heavenly principle fills up between Heaven and Earth. "There are Heaven above and Earth below, and between them are distributed all the (various) beings with their different (natures and qualities)," and "(The influences of) Heaven and Earth flow forth and never cease; and by their united action (the phenomena of) production and change ensue. "[①] (*Book of Music*) So, everywhere between Heaven and Earth flows only the principle. It should not be said that, since the sage does not utter any word, the principle does not exist. It is what it is between Heaven and Earth, only that it is told once via the sage. For example, *yi* 易 (change) manifests nothing but the principle

---

① The translation of these two citations from the *Book of Music* is based on the version by J. Legge (see http: //ctext. org/liji/yue-ji).

represented by *yin* and *yang* in interaction. When Fu Xi created the trigrams, he conveyed only the principle, and both the King Wen of Zhou and Confucius gave further expression to the principle. The "auspicious," 吉 "inauspicious," 凶 "regret," 悔 and "trouble" 吝 were all deducted from it. When Confucius expressed it, he said, "The *junzi* 君子 (Superior Man) occupies his room and sends forth his words. If they be good, they will be responded to at a distance of more than a thousand miles; … If they be evil, they will awaken opposition at a distance of more than a thousand miles; … Words and actions are the hinge and spring of the Superior Man. The movement of that hinge and spring determines glory or disgrace. His words and actions move Heaven and Earth. May he be careless in regard to them?"[1] (the *Classic of Change*) That is what the sage requires. The many deeds accomplished by Yao, Shun, and Yu, the three remote ancient sage-kings, and the words indicating rapport between sovereign and minister in their exchange of ideas, which are recorded in the *Book of History*, are nothing but manifestations of the supreme principle. [Ke]

55 这道理，若见得到，只是合当如此。如竹椅相似：须着有四只脚，平平正正，方可坐；若少一只脚，决定是坐不得。若不识得时，只约摸恁地说，两只脚也得，三只脚也得；到坐时，只是坐不得。如穿牛鼻，络马首，这也是天理合当如此。若络牛首，穿马鼻，定是不得。如适来说克己，伊川只说个敬。今人也知道敬，只是不常如此。常常如此，少间自见得是非道理分明。若心下有些子不安稳，便不做。到得更有一项心下习熟底事，却自以为安；外来卒未相入底，却又不安。这便着将前圣所说道理，所做样子，看教心下是非分明。贺孙。

As regards the principle, when one sees it, he will know it is what he possesses originally. It is akin to a bamboo chair: when it is level and upright

---

[1] The translation of the citation from "Xici I" (Appended Remarks, Part I) in the *Classic of Change* is based on a version by J. Legge (see http://ctext.org/book-of-changes), with slight modification.

on its four feet, one can sit on it, but when one of its feet gets missing, it is not in a position for sitting on. If one does not know it, he can only guess that it will do with only two feet or three feet, but when he tries to sit on it, he will know it impossible to sit on. An ox is led by a terret through its snout, while a horse is by a net on its head, and that is the ways of leading them required by the heavenly principle. It will not do if the ox is led by a net on its head and the horse by a terret through its snout. When discoursing on subduing oneself, Yichuan only mentioned seriousness. People are now aware of being serious, yet they are not constantly serious. If one can adopt that attitude constantly, before long he will be able to distinguish right and wrong clear by himself. But if his mind is somewhat not secure, he will not. When he meets something he is familiar with, he feels at ease, but when he faces something alien, he feels disturbed. In this case, he should strive to make out the principles stated and the examples set by the sages so that he can see clear what is right and what is wrong. [Hesun]

56 人见得义理熟时，自然好。振。

When one sees the principle with familiarity, he feels naturally good. [Zhen]

57 心熟后，自然有见理处。熟则心精微。不见理，只缘是心粗。① 辞达而已矣。去伪。

With familiarity in his mind, one will naturally read out where the principle is. Familiarity indicates the subtlety of the mind. If one fails to see the principle, it is because he still falls short of mental subtlety. ② "One's words are good enough as long as they can help get his ideas across." ③ (*Analects*, 15: 41)

---

① 贺疑有阙文。

② Hesun suspects that one or more words were left out when the passage was recorded.

③ The translation of the citation from *Analects* is based on a version by Lin Wusun (*Getting to Know Confucius: A New Translation of the Analects*, Beijing: Foreign Language Press, 2010, p. 281).

58 今人口略依稀说过，不曾心晓。淳。

Nowadays, they only take to some talk about it, without a true understanding in their mind. ［Chun（淳）］

59 学者理会道理，当深沉潜思。从周。

When a learner tries to understand the principle, he should go deep and ponder on it. ［Congzhou］

60 义理尽无穷，前人恁地说，亦未必尽。须是自把来横看竖看，尽入深，尽有在。士毅。

Moral principles are quite inexhaustible. No matter what past scholars said, they did not necessarily exhaust the subject. We must examine them this way and that way ourselves. The more deeply we go into them, the more we shall discover. [1] ［Shiyi］

61 道理既知缝罅，但当穷而又穷，不可安于小成而遽止也。焘。

When one gets to know there being still gaps in his understanding of the principle, he should strive to inquire and inquire it to the utmost, avoiding discontinuing abruptly, with mere content with some small attainments. ［Tao］

62 今只是要理会道理。若理会得一分，便有一分受用；理会得二分，便有二分受用。理会得一寸，便是一寸；一尺，便是一尺。渐渐理会去，便多。贺孙。

What should be done now is to understand the principle. With a step closer to the principle, it brings about a step's enjoyment, and with two steps closer, it brings about two steps' enjoyment. When one gets an inch of advance in his understanding, he gains a solid inch of attainment, and when he gets a foot of advance there, he gains a solid foot of attainment. Thus, when one advances step by step in his understanding, he will draw nearer and

---

① The translation of this passage is based on the version by Chan Wing-tsit, p. 610, with slight modification.

nearer to the principle. [Hesun]

63 看得一件是，未可便以为是，且顿放一所，又穷他语。相次看得多，相比并，自然透得。德明。

When you read a section and think your understanding of it is right, you should know that your understanding is not necessarily right. You may as well put it aside temporally, and turn to another section and then still another. Then you can compare your understandings of them and naturally attain a coherent and thorough understanding. [Deming]

64 道理无穷。你要去做，又做不办；极力做得三五件，又倦了。盖是不能包括得许多事。人杰。

The principles are inexhaustible. When you want to do something, yet you do not go in for it; when you have tried your best and done a couple of events, yet you begin to feel tired. That is probably because you are hardly capable of embracing many events. [Renjie]

65 太凡义理积得多后，贯通了，自然见效。不是今日理会得一件，便要做一件用。譬如富人积财，积得多了，自无不如意。又如人学作文，亦须广看多后，自然成文可观。不然，读得这一件，却将来排凑做。韩昌黎论为文，便也要读书涵味多后，自然好。柳子厚云，本之于六经云云之意，便是要将这一件做那一件，便不及韩。端蒙。

Generally, only with sufficient accumulation of the understanding of the principles can one feel able to penetrate them all and thus naturally that his efforts have taken effect. It is not that, since one has got an understanding of a principle today, he should apply it for some purpose. It is like a man accumulating riches, who, after having got a big accumulation, will naturally feel free from discontents. It is also comparable to a man learning how to write essays. He must read widely the good essays by others, before he starts to be able to write his own essays impressively. Otherwise, after reading a piece of writing, he turns rashly to writing his own by following it, and this way of learning is of no use. When Han Changli 韩昌黎 (i. e. Han Yu) discoursed on how to write an essay, he also emphasized that only after one had read more books and tasted them sufficiently could he do well naturally in writing. By contrast, Liu Zihou 柳子厚 (i. e. Liu Zongyuan 柳宗元〔773 – 819〕),① who advocated learning the way of writing essays from the Six Confucian Classics, encouraged learners to write a type of essay after examining a classic as their model. Therefore, Liu's opinion in this regard is inferior to Han's.〔Duanmeng〕

66 只守着一些地,做得甚事!须用开阔看去。天下万事都无阻碍,方可。从周。

If one keeps merely watching a narrow piece of field, what else can he do? One should take a broad and wide view, and aim to see all the myriad of events in the world in a way free from any obstruction.〔Congzhou〕

67 大着心胸,不可因一说相碍。看教平阔,四方八面都见。方子。

Keep large-minded and large-hearted, and do not get hindered by a certain opinion. When looking, you should take a broad and wide view and thus can see everything in all quarters.〔Fangzi〕

68 理会道理,到众说纷然处,却好定着精神看一看。骧。

In attempting to understand the principles, when encountering a place where opinions vary, one should concentrate on them and have a good look at them.〔Xiang〕

69 看理到快活田地,则前头自磊落地去。淳。

In trying to understand the principle, when one begins feeling joy, then naturally he will make easy access to what will come next.〔Chun (淳)〕

70 道理有面前底道理。平易自在说出来底,便说;说得出来崎岖底,便不好。节。

Of the principles, some are close at hand. As for those that can be expressed with ease, one should just say them out, but if he has a hard time

---

① Han and Liu are both famous essay writers in the Tang dynasty.

to say them with ease, his understanding of them is still inadequate. [Jie]

71 今日且将自家写得出、说得出底去穷究。士毅。

Today, just investigate to the utmost what you can write out and speak out. [Shiyi]

72 今人凡事所以说得恁地支离，只是见得不透。

Nowadays, whenever one can only say it out in a fragmented way, the reason is nothing but that he has not understood it thoroughly.

73 看道理，须是见得实，方是有功效处。若于上面添些玄妙奇特，便是见他实理未透。道夫。

When trying to see the principle, one should ensure that what he has seen is substantial, and then he will get some solid progress. If one chooses to add something odd and weird to it, this indicates that he has still fallen short of a thorough understanding of the substantial principle. [Daofu]

74 理只要理会透彻，更不理会文辞，恐未达而便欲已也。去伪。

What the principle calls for is nothing but a thorough understanding of it. One should avoid being confined by the words. I am afraid, when the words were still unable to help put their writers' ideas across, yet they thought they were good enough. [Quwei]

75 或问："如何是反身穷理?"曰："反身是着实之谓，向自家体分上求。"广。

Someone asked, "What is meant by 'turning to self-examination for inquiring the principle to the utmost'?" The Master answered, "The 'turning to self-examination' refers to making substantial efforts, meaning resorting to oneself for seeking for the principle." [Guang]

76 今之学者不曾亲切见得，而臆度揣摸为说，皆助长之病也。道理只平看，意思自见，不须先立说。僴。

Nowadays learners have never seen personally the principle, but rather formed their opinions merely by speculating and surmising, which adds to their sickness which has already troubled them. To see the principle, one needs only to make fair observation of it and in due time its meaning will naturally emerge. So he should not form an opinion first before seeing it. [Xian]

77 便是看义理难，又要宽着心，又要紧着心。这心不宽，则不足以见其规模之大；不紧，则不足以察其文理—作"义"。之细密。若拘滞于文义，少间又不见他大规模处。

It is really difficult to see the principle, for it calls for both a broadened mind and a tightened mind. Without a broadened mind, one would not be able to see its largeness in scale, and without a tightened mind, one would not be able to examine its fineness in texture. Another record reads "in meaning." If one constrains his understanding to what the specific words say, he will soon lose sight of the large scale of the principle.

78 以圣贤之意观圣贤之书，以天下之理观天下之事。人多以私见自去穷理，只是你自家所见，去圣贤之心尚远在！祖道。

The books written by the sages and worthies should be read from the viewpoint of what they intended to mean and the events in the world should be seen from the viewpoint of the world's principle. People tend to inquire the principle to the utmost from the viewpoint of their private opinions, but as these opinions are only private, they are still far from the mind of the sages and worthies. [Zudao]

79 自家既有此身，必有主宰。理会得主宰，然后随自家力量穷理格物，而合做底事不可放过些子。因引程子言："如行兵，当先做活计。"铢。

The Master said, "Since we have our bodies, we must have our masters inhering in ourselves. With a good understanding of the masters, we should give play to our own strength and investigate things for inquiring the principle to the utmost, never ignoring what we should do." Thereupon, he cited Master Cheng as saying "It is like dispatching troops, for which the first thing to be considered is how to supply logistic support for them." [Zhu]

80 万理洞开。○众理参会。如说"思事亲"至"不可不知天",又事亲乃能事天之类,无不互备。方。

The myriad of principles are wide open. ○ The many principles converge. This is what is meant by the words from "In order to serve his parents" to "he may not dispense with a knowledge of Heaven"① in the *Doctrine of the Mean*. Thus, there is nothing lacking with regard to serving one's parents and further serving Heaven, and the like. 〔Fang〕

81 不可去名上理会。须求其所以然。方子。

Pay no attention to names. We must investigate into the reason why things are as they are.② 〔Fangzi〕

82 "事要知其所以然。"指花斛曰:"此两个花斛,打破一个,一个在。若只恁地,是人知得,说得。须知所以破,所以不破者如何。"从周。

The Master said, "You should know the reason why events are what they are." Pointing to two flower vases, he went on, "Here are two flower vases, and suppose one of them is broken and the other is not. That is only the fact you know and say. But you should know why one is broken, while the other is not." 〔Congzhou〕

83 思索譬如穿井,不解便得清水。先亦须是浊,渐渐刮将去,却自会清。贺孙。

Pondering is like digging a well. If one keeps on digging, he will gain clear water some day. But he will get muddy water first and, after some more effort, he will gain clear water. 〔Hesun〕

84 这个物事广录作"道理"。密,分毫间便相争。如不曾下工夫,

---

① Those words in the *Doctrine of the Mean* (20) read, as translated by J. Legge, "In order to serve his parents, he may not neglect to acquire knowledge of men. In order to know men, he may not dispense with a knowledge of Heaven." (see http://ctext.org/liji/zhong-yong)

② The translation of this passage is based on the version by Chan Wing-tsit, p. 610, with slight modification.

一时去旋揣摸他，只是疏阔。真个下工夫见得底人，说出来自是胶粘。旋揣摸得，是亦何补！士毅。

This thing-event _{Guang's record reads "principle"} is thick and every detail of it calls for much effort. If one has made no effort, yet tries to think over it rashly on the spur of the moment, what he can get can only be something thin and coarse. For one who has made strenuous efforts and fathomed the truth, what he says of it will naturally be cohesive and coherent. What use is the result of thinking on the spur of the moment for? [Shiyi]

85 只是见不透，所以千言万语，费尽心力，终不得圣人之意。大学说格物，都只是要人见得透。且如"杨氏为我，墨氏兼爱"，他欲以此教人，他岂知道是不是，只是见不透。如释氏亦设教授徒，他岂道自不是，只是不曾见得到，但知虚，而不知虚中有理存焉。此大学所以贵穷理也。贺孙。

When one's trouble is his failure to penetrate the truth, then though he has racked his brains in reading thousands of words, he has still been unable to get access to what the sages intended to mean. The purpose of the *Great Learning* when advocating investigating things is to help learners to penetrate the truth. "Yang Zhu's principle is 'each one for himself,'" and "Mozi's principle is 'to love all equally.'" (*Mencius*, 3B: 14) Either of them wanted to teach others his principle, but he did not know whether it was right or not, for he failed to see through it. Similarly, Buddhists have also established their religion and instructed their disciples, but they would not admit they are not right, for they have failed to see it. Though they know vacuity, they do not know that the principle dwells in the very vacuity. That is why the *Great Learning* treasures up inquiring the principle to the utmost. [Hesun]

86 知，只有个真与不真分别。如说有一项不可言底知，便是释氏之误。士毅。

With regard to knowledge, there is only the distinction between truth and falsehood. If Buddhists say there being some unspeakable knowledge, they are wrong. [Shiyi]

87 若曰，须待见得个道理然后做去，则"利而行之，勉强而行之"，工夫皆为无用矣！顿悟之说，非学者所宜尽心也，圣人所不道。人杰。

If the saying that a learner should see such and such principle before setting about practicing was right, then, all efforts for "practicing them from a desire for their advantages and practicing them by strenuous effort" (*Doctrine of the Mean*, 20) would be useless. The theory of *dunwu* 顿悟 (sudden enlightenment) is not something that a learner is proper to devote himself to, and therefore the sages did not mention it. [Renjie]

88 务反求者，以博观为外驰；务博观者，以内省为狭隘，堕于一偏。此皆学者之大病也！道夫。

Those who pursue only self-examination take wide-ranging observation for sticking rigidly to the external, while those who pursue only wide-ranging observation take internal examination for being narrow-minded. Either of them is one-sided. Both represent serious troubles with learners. [Daofu]

卷第十四 Book 14

大学一
Great Learning I ①

纲领

Guideline

1 学问须以大学为先，次论语，次孟子，次中庸。中庸工夫密，规模大。德明。

The *Great Learning* should be read first in the pursuit of learning, and then the *Analects*, then the *Mencius*, and then the *Doctrine of the Mean*. Reading the *Doctrine of the Mean* requires much strenuous and concentrated effort, for its scope is broad-ranging. [Deming]

2 读书，且从易晓易解处去读。如大学中庸语孟四书，道理粲然。人只是不去看。若理会得此四书，何书不可读！何理不可究！何事不可处！盖卿。

When reading, a learner should start with something easy to understand and explain. For example, the Four Books, that is, the *Great Learning*, the *Doctrine of the Mean*, the *Analects*, and the *Mencius*, which are resplendent with their abundant truths. However, nowadays, learners have not turned to them. With understanding them thoroughly, what other books can't they read,

---

① The English translation of the citations from *Daxue* 大学 in the text of this book is based on J. Legge's version entitled "The Great Learning", with some alterations in contexts (see http://ctext.org/liji/da-xue).

what principles can't they inquire, and what events can't they handle?
〔Gaiqing〕

3 某要人先读大学,以定其规模;次读论语,以立其根本;次读孟子,以观其发越;次读中庸,以求古人之微妙处。大学一篇有等级次第,总作一处,易晓,宜先看。论语却实,但言语散见,初看亦难。孟子有感激兴发人心处。中庸亦难读,看三书后,方宜读之。宇。

In regard to learning, I suggest to the beginners that they read the *Great Learning* first, so as to decide their scope of learning; then read the *Analects*, so as to lay their fundamental foundation; then read the *Mencius*, so as to manifest their aspiration; and lastly read the *Doctrine of the Mean*, so as to make access to the subtlety of the ancients. With its explicitly sequential presentation of ideas gathered there, the text of the *Great Learning* is easy to understand and should be read first. The *Analects*, by contrast, is substantial, but its language is loosely organized, so it is difficult for a beginner to read. The *Mencius* contains sections which inspire and stimulate the mind. The *Doctrine of the Mean* is also difficult to read. So, it is appropriate to turn to it after reading well the other three of the Four Books.
〔Yu〕

4 先看大学,次语孟,次中庸。果然下工夫,句句字字,涵泳切己,看得透彻,一生受用不尽。只怕人不下工,虽多读古人书,无益。书只是明得道理,却要人做出书中所说圣贤工夫来。若果看此数书,他书可一见而决矣。谦。

Read the *Great Learning* first before the *Analects* and the *Mencius*, and finally the *Doctrine of the Mean*. If one makes conscientious effort to read them, understands each word and each sentence of them thoroughly, and chews them in regard to himself, he will benefit from them ceaselessly in his lifetime. I am afraid, learners do not exert themselves hard and thus, though reading through many ancient books, they gain no benefit from that. The books purport only to make clear the truths, but require their reader to make as much effort as said in them, effort which enables him to become a sage or worthy. Provided that he reads the Four Books well, he can understand other books at a glance of them. [Qian]

5 论孟中庸，待大学贯通浃洽，无可得看后方看，乃佳。道学不明，元来不是上面欠却工夫，乃是下面元无根脚。若信得及，脚踏实地，如此做去，良心自然不放，践履自然纯熟。非但读书一事也。

As for the *Analects*, the *Mencius*, and the *Doctrine of the Mean*, a learner had better read them after he understands the *Great Learning* coherently and cohesively and can not read out anything more from it. If one does not do well in the learning of *Dao* 道（the Way）, it is not because he does not make efforts on the level of branches and leaves, but because he fails to foster the roots well first. If a learner believes in what I say, he should make conscientious efforts in a down-to-earth style and thus naturally he will not lose his original mind. In due time, he will become mature in his practice of action. Actually, it is not only a matter of reading.

6 "人之为学，先读大学，次读论语。大学是个大坯模。大学譬如买田契，论语如田亩阔狭去处，逐段子耕将去。"或曰："亦在乎熟之而已。"曰："然。"去伪。

The Master said, "In pursuing learning, a learner should read the *Great Learning* first, and then read the *Analects*. The *Great Learning* presents a large mould. If the *Great Learning* is comparable to the contract for buying a piece of field, the *Analects* is like the wide and the narrow parts in it, each of which needs ploughing." Someone asked, "Does it also call for the learner's familiarity with each of them?" He answered, "Yes." [Quwei]

7 问："欲专看一书，以何为先?"曰："先读大学，可见古人为学首末次第。且就实处理会却好，不消得专去无形影处理会。"淳。

Question: I want to focus on a book. What should I read first?

Answer: You should read the *Great Learning* first, by reading which you can know the beginning and end and the sequence of the ancients in pursuit of learning. You had better strive to gain a personal understanding of what is the substantial and there is no need to concentrate on those places where neither form nor shadow is visible for an understanding. ［Chun（淳）］

8　可将大学用数月工夫看去。此书前后相因，互相发明，读之可见，不比他书。他书非一时所言，非一人所记。惟此书首尾具备，易以推寻也。力行。

You may spend several months reading the *Great Learning*. In this book，its beginning and its ending are causes of each other，which reveal each other mutually，and you will see that and know it is different from other three books. Each of the other three books is a collection of words neither said on the same occasion nor recorded by the same hand. Only the *Great Learning* is complete from its beginning to its end，so it is easy to deduce and seek its meaning. ［Lixing］

9　今且须熟究大学作间架，却以他书填补去。如此看得一两书，便是占得分数多，后却易为力。圣贤之言难精。难者既精，则后面粗者却易晓。大雅。

At present，you should read the *Great Learning*，get versed in it，and set up a skeleton from it，and then provide it with flesh and blood you fetch from other books. If you can read a book or two in this way，you will own more shares of all learning，which facilitates your efforts to understand more books. It is difficult to gain an accurate and insightful comprehension of what the sages and worthies said，but when you gain such comprehension of the difficult，it will be easy for you to see the meaning of other books which are not that subtle and profound. ［Daya］

10　亚夫问大学大意。曰："大学是修身治人底规模。如人起屋相似，须先打个地盘。地盘既成，则可举而行之矣。"时举。

Yafu asked about the basic idea of the *Great Learning*. The Master answered，"The book elucidates the scale on which the learning for the cultivation of personal character and the governing of people can be pursued. It is comparable to building a house, for which a foundation has to be laid first. With the completed foundation, the building of the house can be started." [Shiju]

11 或问："大学之书，即是圣人做天下根本？"曰："此譬如人起屋，是画一个大地盘在这里。理会得这个了，他日若有材料，却依此起将去，只此一个道理。明此以南面，尧之为君也；明此以北面，舜之为臣也。"

Someone asked, "Was the book of the *Great Learning* written by the sage to clarify what is the fundamental for doing events in the world?" The Master answered, "It is like, before a house is built, demarcating an area as the foundation for it. If one has understood it well, when he has got building materials, he can build the house on that foundation step by step. The book conveys nothing but this principle. That is why Yao, who, with his understanding of it, faced to the south, served as the sovereign of Shun, and Shun, who, with his understanding of it, faced to the north, served as the minister of Yao."

12 大学一书，如行程相似。自某处到某处几里，自某处到某处几里。识得行程，须便行始得。若只读得空壳子，亦无益也。履孙。

The book of the *Great Learning* tells, so to speak, its readers about the distances of their travels. It is this number of miles to this destination, and that number of miles to that destination. With such information of the distances, they can start their travels. If one reads out merely an empty shell, it is to no avail. [lüsun]

13 大学如一部行程历，皆有节次。今人看了，须是行去。今日行得到何处，明日行得到何处，方可渐到那田地。若只把在手里翻来覆去，欲望之燕，之越，岂有是理！自修。

The *Great Learning* is comparable to a calendar for a travel, which makes clear the definite arrangement of the steps to be taken. Now, when a learner has read it, what he should do is put it into practice. He has to travel a number of miles today and another number of miles tomorrow, and thus, as the calendar indicates, he will arrive at the destination. If one does nothing but turning it over and over again in his hands, yet desires to reach the far state of Yan and then to the farther state of Yue, he will actually end up with going nowhere at all. [Zixiu][1]

14 大学是一个腔子，而今却要去填教实着。如他说格物，自家是去格物后，填教实着；如他说诚意，自家须是去诚意后，亦填教实着。节。

The *Great Learning* provides the learners with only a framework, who should add materials to it so that it can be completely substantial. For example, when it states investigating things, a leaner should engage in investigating things and then substantiate the statement; when it advocates making thought sincere, he should strive to make his thought sincere and then substantiate the advocacy. [Jie]

15 大学重处都在前面。后面工夫渐渐轻了，只是揩磨在。士毅。广录云："后面其失渐轻，亦是下揩磨底工夫在。"

What weighs more in the *Great Learning* is all stated in the beginning parts of its text. The effort which the parts after its text require the learner to make becomes less and less, and they call for only some wiping and polishing work. [Shiyi] Guang's record reads, "The effort required by the later parts decreases gradually, which is only some wiping and polishing."

16 看大学前面初起许多，且见安排在这里。如今食次册相似，都且如此呈说后，方是可吃处。初间也要识许多模样。贺孙。

When one reads the *Great Learning*, he will find that many ideas are stated in the beginning parts, clarifying the overall arrangement of the text. It is read like a menu today, where what is stated first is some introduction and

---

① Sun Zixiu 孙自修 (courtesy name Jingfu 敬父).

then the dishes are listed. This means that the first thing for a learner to do is to get some rough idea of it. [Hesun]

17 大学一字不胡乱下，亦是古人见得这道理熟。信口所说，便都是这里。淳。

In the *Great Learning* there is no indiscriminate use of any word. That is because the ancients were up on the truths. Even when they said of something casually, their words were rich in truth. [Chun（淳）]

18 大学总说了，又逐段更说许多道理。圣贤怕有些子照管不到，节节觉察将去，到这里有恁地病，到那里有恁地病。节。

The *Great Learning* presents a general exposition first and then elucidates many principles section by section. The sage who wrote the book stated the many respects one by one for fear that learners might neglect them, pointing out that they might be troubled by this problem in this respect and by that problem in that respect. [Jie]

19 明德，如八窗玲珑，致知格物，各从其所明处去。今人不曾做得小学工夫，一旦学大学，是以无下手处。今且当自持敬始，使端悫纯一静专，然后能致知格物。椿。

The *mingde* 明德（illustrious virtue）is akin to eight windows spacious and bright, and *zhizhi gewu* 致知格物（extension of knowledge and investigation of things）means that each of them can be the starting point. Nowadays, since learners have not ever made efforts with regard to the primary learning（小学, for children）, when they want to pursue the great learning（大学, for adults）, they do not know where to start. Now they should begin with *chijing* 持敬（cherishing seriousness）so as to be sincere and conscientious, purely minded and placidly concentrated, before they can engage in their extension of knowledge through investigation of things. [Chun（椿）]

20 而今无法。尝欲作一说，教人只将大学一日去读一遍，看他如何是大人之学，如何是小学，如何是"明明德"，如何是"新民"，如何是"止于至善"。日日如是读，月去日来，自见所谓"温故而知新"。须是知新，日日看得新方得。却不是道理解新，但自家这个意思长长地新。义刚。

There seems no good way for turning things around for the better. I once wanted to write something and instruct the learners to read the *Great Learning* once a day so that they could know what was meant by the adults-oriented great learning and by the children-oriented primary learning, what was meant by *ming mingde* 明明德 (to illustrate illustrious virtue), by *xinmin* 新民 (to renovate the people), and by *zhiyu zhishan* 止于至善 (to rest in the highest excellence). If one reads it day by day in this way, in due time, he will naturally see what is meant by "One can acquire new knowledge by reviewing the old." It has to be "new knowledge." That means that he should know something new each day with the passage of time. The "new" does not refer to seeing new truths, but rather to keeping his understanding of the truths being renewed constantly. [Yigang]

21 才仲问大学。曰："人心有明处，于其间得一二分，即节节推上去。"又问："小学、大学如何？"曰："小学涵养此性，大学则所以实其理也。忠信孝弟之类，须于小学中出。然正心、诚意之类，小学如何知得。须其有识后，以此实之。大抵大学一节一节恢廓展布将去，然必到于此而后进。既到而不进，固不可；未到而求进，亦不可。且如国既治，又却絜矩，则又欲其四方皆准之也。此一卷书甚分明，不是滚作一块物事。"可学。

Caizhong 才仲 (i. e. Wei Caizhong 魏才仲, dates unknown) asked about the *Great Learning*. The Master answered, "There is some bright area in the human mind, where one is endowed with one or two tenths. Then from that he makes deduction step by step towards the highest state." He asked further, "Is the primary learning different from the great learning?" The Master replied, "The primary learning purports to cultivate humanity, while the great learning is the means by which to substantiate the principles.

Faithfulness and sincerity, filial piety and fraternity, and the like, all have to be known from the primary learning. But as for rectifying the mind, making thought sincere, and the like, how can they be known from that? Only when a learner has got that knowledge from the primary learning can he substantiate it by the great learning. Generally, in the *Great Learning*, the primary is extended and expanded step by step to an extent, and one has to start from that extent for further progress. He should not seek no progress when he has reached that extent, nor should he seek progress when he has not reached it. It is like ruling a state. The ruler sets up a principle with which, as with a measuring square, he regulates his conduct, and furthermore he expects all people in the state to follow his practice. This book is very definite in its different parts, which should not be taken as only one piece of thing-event. ”
［Kexue］

22 大学是为学纲目。先通大学，立定纲领，其他经皆杂说在里许。通得大学了，去看他经，方见得此是格物、致知事；此是正心、诚意事；此是修身事；此是齐家、治国、平天下事。

The *Great Learning* serves as the guideline for the pursuit of learning. A learner should strive first to understand it thoroughly and fix up the guideline, and the clues of all other classics are merged into it to some extent. If he has understood the *Great Learning* well, when he reads other classics, he will know what pertains to investigating things for extension of knowledge, what to rectifying the mind and making thought sincere, and what to cultivating oneself, governing a state, and making the whole empire peaceful and happy.

23 问：“大学一书，皆以修身为本。正心、诚意、致知、格物，皆是修身内事。”曰：“此四者成就那修身。修身推出，做许多事。”椿。

Question：In the *Great Learning*, everything is based on self-cultivation. Rectifying the mind, making thought sincere, extension of knowledge, and investigation of things are all matters within the confines of self-cultivation. (How do you think of that?)

Answer: The self-cultivation is accomplished by the four aspects. From the self-cultivation are deduced many events which should be done. [Chun (椿)]

24 致知、格物，大学中所说，不过"为人君，止于仁；为人臣，止于敬"之类。古人小学时都曾理会来。不成小学全不曾知得。然而虽是"止于仁，止于敬"，其间却有多少事。如仁必有所以为仁者，敬必有所以为敬者，故又来大学致知、格物上穷究教尽。如入书院，只到书院门里，亦是到来，亦唤做格物、致知得。然却不曾到书院筑底处，终不是物格、知至。僩

The extension of knowledge and investigation of things as said in the *Great Learning* are concerned no more than with such as "As a sovereign, he (the King Wen of Zhou) rested in benevolence. As a minister, he rested in reverence" and the like. The ancients, when they engaged themselves for the primary learning, already read such things. They knew them all completely by their primary learning. But despite the seemingly simple "He rested in benevolence" and "He rested in reverence," how many events they imply! For example, his benevolence must imply the reason for benevolence and his reverence must imply the reason for reverence. So learners need to turn to the *Great Learning* and inquire to the utmost in regard to the extension of knowledge and investigation of things. Take the entry to an academy for example. If a learner only steps across its threshold, it also means his going into the academy and also can be said that he does some investigation of things and extension of knowledge. However, he never reaches the recesses of the academy and never does investigation of things and extension of knowledge in their true sense. [Xun]

25 人多教践履，皆是自立标置去教人。自有一般资质好底人，便不须穷理、格物、致知。此圣人作今大学，便要使人齐入于圣人之

域。干。

Many teachers have taught others to set about practicing, yet what they taught is some standards they set by themselves. There are some people endowed with good aptitudes, by which they are unnecessary to make efforts for inquiring the principle to the utmost, investigating things, and extending knowledge. The purpose of the sage for writing the book of the *Great Learning* is to help all others attain the realm of the sages. [Gan]

26 大学所载，只是个题目如此。要须自用工夫做将去。贺孙。

What is carried in the *Great Learning* is only a guideline. A learner should go and exert himself in the light of it. [Hesun]

27 大学教人，先要理会得个道理。若不理会得，见圣人许多言语都是硬将人制缚，剩许多工夫。若见得了，见得许多道理，都是天生自然铁定底道理，更移易分毫不得。而今读大学，须是句句就自家身上看过。少间自理会得，不待解说。如语孟六经，亦须就自家身上看，便如自家与人对说一般，如何不长进！圣贤便可得而至也。贺孙。

The purpose of the *Great Learning* is to instruct the learners to understand the principle for pursuing learning. Without such understanding, when they read the many discourses from the sages, they would take them for something binding them rigidly, not worth their efforts. With such understanding, they will find that many principles are true innately, naturally, and indisputably, which are like bedrocks, admitting of no changeability. When a learner reads the *Great Learning* today, he should ponder over every sentence of it in regard to himself. Before long he will attain his personal understanding of it, needing no explanation. As for the *Analects*, the *Mencius*, and the Six Confucian Classics, he should also read them with regard to himself. If he can do it as if he talked with them in a conversation, how can he not gain advance? Thus, he can get close to the sages and, ultimately, attain the realm of them. [Hesun]

28 今人都是为人而学。某所以教诸公读大学，且看古人为学是如何，是理会甚事。诸公愿为古人之学乎？愿为今人之学乎？敬仲。

Nowadays, the learners tend to do learning all for others. When I instruct you to read the *Great Learning*, I want you to know how the ancients pursued learning and what they strove to understand. Then, do you want to pursue learning as the ancients did or as those at present are doing? [Jingzhong]

29 读大学，且逐段捱。看这段时，似得无后面底。看第二段，却思量前段，令文意联属，却不妨。干。

When you read the *Great Learning*, ponder over it paragraph by paragraph. When reading this paragraph, you should treat it as if there was nothing more after it, while when reading the paragraph after it, you may as well consider both paragraphs together so that their meanings can be associated. [Gan]

30 看大学，固是着逐句看去。也须先统读传文教熟，方好从头仔细看。若全不识传文大意，便看前头亦难。贺孙。

When you read the *Great Learning*, it is true that you should read it sentence by sentence, but you had better read through the entire explanation appended to its text and get familiar with it before poring over every sentence from the beginning. Without knowing the rough idea of the explanation, you will feel it difficult to understand the beginning part while reading its text. [Hesun]

31 或问读大学。曰："读后去，须更温前面，不可只恁地茫茫看。须'温故而知新'。须是温故，方能知新。若不温故，便要求知新，则新不可得而知，亦不可得而求矣。"贺孙。

Someone asked about the *Great Learning*. The Master answered, "When you read the latter parts, you must review the parts before them. That is a process of 'acquiring new knowledge by reviewing the old.' So you have to review the old before acquiring something new. If you do not review the old yet desire to acquire something new, it is impossible for you to acquire new knowledge, nor is it possible for you to have any way for that. " ［Hesun］

32 读大学，初间也只如此读，后来也只如此读。只是初间读得，似不与自家相关；后来看熟，见许多说话须着如此做，不如此做自不得。贺孙。

When reading the *Great Learning*, you begin with reading it in a manner and later do it in the same manner. However, at first, what you read out from it seems to have nothing to do with yourself, while later when you get familiar with it you will find you have to do by following what it says, or else you will not do. ［Hesun］

33 谓任道弟读大学，云："须逐段读教透，默自记得，使心口相应。古时无多书，人只是专心暗诵。且以竹简写之，寻常人如何办得竹简如此多。所以人皆暗诵而后已。伏生亦只是口授尚书二十余篇。黄霸就狱，夏侯胜受尚书于狱中，又岂得本子。只被他读得透彻。后来著述，诸公皆以名闻。汉之经学所以有用。"贺孙。

Instructing Rendao 任道（dates unknown, a disciple of Zhu's）, a younger brother, to read the *Great Learning*, the Master said, "Read it paragraph by paragraph and make sure that you understand them thoroughly. Then learn them by heart so that they resonate with each other. In ancient times, there were few books, so learners had to depend on memory work. Those few books were in the form of bamboo slips, so how could an ordinary reader get and manage that many bamboo slips? They did nothing but trying their best to memorize the texts. Fu Sheng 伏生[1] passed on only twenty-odd pieces of literature in the *Book of History*. When Huang Ba 黄霸[2] was in imprisonment, he learned the way of reading the *Book of History* from Xiahou

---

① Fu Sheng（dates unknown）, a reputed scholar of Confucian classics in Western Han Dynasty （206 BC – AD 24）.

② Huang Ba（? –51 BC）, a senior official in the Western Han dynasty, was famous for his intelligence and perceptiveness.

Sheng 夏侯胜①, but how could he get the text? What he depended on is but learning by heart. Later, it is by writings that scholars earned their fames. So the learning of Confucian classics in Han Dynasty is of much use. " [Hesun]

34　或问大学。曰:"大概是如此。只是更要熟读,熟时,滋味自别。且如吃果子,生时将来吃,也是吃这果子;熟时将来吃,也是吃这果子,只是滋味别。"胡泳。

When asked about the *Great Learning*, the Master answered, "What you said is basically right. But you should make more efforts to read it carefully over and over again, and then you will get a unique taste. It is like eating a fruit. When you eat it unripe and when you eat it ripe, you will get different tastes, though the fruit is the same. " [Hu Yong]

35　问贺孙:"读大学如何?"曰:"稍通,方要读论语。"曰:"且未要读论语。大学稍通,正好着心精读。前日读时,见得前未见得后面,见得后未接得前面。今识得大纲统体,正好熟看。如吃果实相似,初只恁地硬咬嚼。待嚼来嚼去,得滋味,如何便住却!读此书功深,则用博。昔和靖见伊川,半年方得大学西铭看。今人半年要读多少书,某且要人读此,是如何?缘此书却不多,而规模周备。凡读书,初一项须着十分工夫了,第二项只费得九分工夫,第三项便只费六七分工夫。少刻读渐多,自贯通他书,自不着得多工夫。"贺孙。

The Master asked me, "How has your reading the *Great Learning* been going?" I answered, "I have understood it a little. Now I am about to read the *Analects*." He said, "Don't turn to the *Analects* now. Since you have got some understanding of the *Great Learning*, it is the right moment for you to make more efforts to read it carefully. When you read the first parts of it with some understanding, you might not have known what its latter parts convey,

---

　　①　Xiahou Sheng (dates unknown), a distinguished scholar in the Western Han dynasty, who founded "The Grand Xiahou School," a school of learning on the *Book of History*.

and when you reached the latter parts, you might not have associate them with the first parts. Now that you have known its outline as a whole, you are in a better position to read it carefully over and over again. It is comparable to eating a fruit. At first, you have simply a bite of it and after chewing it for some time, you know its taste, but how can you stop at that? Reading the *Great Learning* requires much effort, and its use is wide-ranging. When Hejing 和靖 (i. e. Yin Tun 尹焞 [dates unknown]) became a disciple of Yichuan (i. e. Cheng Yi), he spent half a year reading *Western Inscription* (by Zhang Zai). By contrast, the learners today read many books in half a year. Why have I asked you to read the *Great Learning*? It is not long, yet with a complete system in content. Generally, with regard to reading books, if one makes full effort to read the first book, he needs to make nine tenth of the effort to read the second, and for the third, he needs only six or seven tenth. Before long he will read others at a fast speed without making much effort and that with a coherent and thorough understanding." [Hesun]

36 诸生看大学未晓，而辄欲看论语者，责之曰："公如吃饭一般，未曾有颗粒到口，如何又要吃这般，吃那般！这都是不曾好生去读书。某尝谓人看文字晓不得，只是未曾着心。文字在眼前，他心不曾着上面，只是恁地略绰将过，这心元不曾伏杀在这里。看他只自恁地豹跳，不肯在这里理会，又自思量做别处去。这事未了，又要寻一事做，这如何要理会得！今之学者看文字，且须压这心在文字上。逐字看了，又逐句看；逐句看了，又逐段看，未有晓不得者。"贺孙。

Some disciples of his have still not attained an adequate understanding of the *Great Learning*, yet they wanted to turn to the *Analects*. Critical of them, the Master said, "It is like eating a meal. Though you have not yet touched a grain of rice, how can you be eager to eat this or that! The reason for this is that you have not settled yourselves down and concentrated on reading. I once said that the reason why one, when reading something, failed to understand it was that he did not devote himself truly to his reading. Despite the words before his eyes, he only looked through them cursorily but did not think over them, for his mind was not with them. Impetuous like a leopard jumping here and there, he was unwilling to set his mind at the words; instead, he was always distracted by some thought of doing something else. He did not finish doing this matter, yet wanted to turn to that matter. Then how could he gain an understanding of those words? When a learner reads a book, he should concentrate his mind on it and read it word by word and then sentence by sentence and then paragraph by paragraph. In this way, I am sure, he will gain a personal understanding of it." [Hesun]

37 子渊说大学。曰:"公看文字,不似味道只就本子上看,看来看去,久之浃洽,自应有得。公便要去上面生意,只讨头不见。某所成章句或问之书,已是伤多了。当初只怕人晓不得,故说许多。今人看,反晓不得。此一书之间,要紧只在'格物'两字,认得这里看,则许多说自是闲了。初看须用这本子,认得要害处,本子自无可用。某说十句在里面,看得了,只做一句说了方好。某或问中已说多了,却不说到这般处。看这一书,又自与看语孟不同。语孟中只一项事是一个道理。如孟子说仁义处,只就仁义上说道理;孔子答颜渊以'克己复礼',只就'克己复礼'上说道理。若大学,却只统说。论其功用之极,至于平天下。然天下所以平,却先须治国;国之所以治,却先须齐家;家之所以齐,却先须修身;身之所以修,却先须正心;心之所以正,却先须诚意;意之所以诚,却先须致知;知之所以至,却先须格物。本领全只在这两字上。又须知如何是格物。许多道理,自家从来合有,不合有。定是合有。定是人人都有。人之心便具许多道理:见之于身,便见身上有许多道理;行之于家,便是一家之中有许多道理;施之于国,便是一国之中有许多道理;施之于天下,便是天下有许多道理。'格物'两字,只是指个路头,须是自去格那物始得。只就纸上说千千万万,不济事。"贺孙。

Ziyuan 子渊 (i. e. Lin Ziyaun 林子渊, dates unknown, a disciple of Zhu's) talked about the *Great Learning*. The Master said, "When you read it, you are unlike Weidao who has read only the explanation of its text and, after a long time, will attain a coherent personal understanding of it. If you try to understand it by turning to its words themselves at first, you end up failing to see where its original meaning is. The explanations of it in my *Daxue Zhangju* 大学章句 (Interpretation of the *Great Learning*; hereafter *Interpretation* for short in Book 14) and *Daxue Huowen* 大学或问 (Questions and Answers on the *Great Learning*; hereafter *Questions and Answers* for short in Book 14) already leave its original meaning to a considerable extent. I said much for fear that readers did not understand the *Great Learning*. But now the explanation seems to be not so intelligible to the learners. In the *Great Learning* what counts is the investigation of things and if you strive to read it therefrom, many ideas in it will be easy to see. When you try to understand the *Great Learning*, you must read that explanation of it at first and when you get to know where it counts, the explanation will naturally become useless. For ten sentences given for explaining, if you can see their meaning, you had better summarize them as one sentence. Though I said much in my explanation, I did not mention such thing. Reading the *Great Learning* is different from reading the *Analects* and the *Mencius*, for the latter two mention one event to illustrate one principle. For example, in the *Mencius*, when mentioning benevolence and righteousness, it elucidates the principle with regard only to them. In the *Analects*, when Confucius replies Yan Yuan with 'subduing one's self and returning to propriety,' he illustrated the principle only therein. By contrast, the *Great Learning* only gives a general statement. As far as its use goes, it extends itself to the issue of bringing peace to the empire. But the precondition for that is governing a state, which depends on regulating a family, which depends on cultivating oneself, which depends on rectifying the mind, which depends on making thought sincere, which depends on extending knowledge, which depends on investigating things. Therefore, the pivot lies in investigating things and one must know what is meant by it. Many principles are what one is endowed with originally, aren't they? They are surely, and this is true of every person. The human mind possesses many principles: If they are manifested on one's body, they can be seen on his body; if they are practiced in a family, they can be seen in the family; if they are performed in a state, they can be seen in the state; if they are enforced in the empire, they can be seen in the empire. Investigating things serves as a guide for the way, so one must follow it personally and investigate things by himself. It is to no avail if he only knows what is said on paper." [Hesun]

38 答林子渊说大学,曰:"圣人之书,做一样看不得。有只说一个下工夫规模,有首尾只说道理。如中庸之书,劈初头便说'天命之谓性'。若是这般书,全着得思量义理。如大学,只说个做工夫之节目,自不消得大段思量,才看过,便自晓得。只是做工夫全在自家身心上,却不在文字上。文字已不着得思量。说穷理,只就自家身上求之,都无别物事。只有个仁义礼智,看如何千变万化,也离这四个不得。公且自看,日用之间如何离得这四个。如信者,只是有此四者,故谓之信。信,实也,实是有此。论其体,则实是有仁义礼智;论其用,则实是有恻隐、羞恶、恭敬、是非,更假伪不得。试看天下岂有假做得仁,假做得义,假做得礼,假做得智!所以说信者,以言其实有而非伪也。更自一身推之于家,实是有父子,有夫妇,有兄弟;推之天地之间,实是有君臣,有朋友。都不是待后人旋安排,是合下元有此。又如一身之中,里面有五脏六腑,外面有耳目口鼻四肢,这是人人都如此。存之为仁义礼智,发出来为恻隐、羞恶、恭敬、是非。人人都有此。以至父子兄弟夫妇朋友君臣,亦莫不皆然。至于物,亦莫不然。但其拘于形,拘于气而不变。然亦就他一角子有发见处:看他也自有父子之亲;有牝牡,便是有夫妇;有大小,便是有兄弟;就他同类中各有群众,便是有朋友;亦有主脑,便是有君臣。只缘本来都是天地所生,共这根蒂,所以大率多同。圣贤出来抚临万物,各因其性而导之。如昆虫草木,未尝不顺其性,如取之以时,用之有节:当春生时'不殀夭,不覆巢,不杀胎；草木零落，然后入山林；獭祭鱼，然后虞人入泽梁；豺祭兽，然后田猎'。所以能使万物各得其所者，惟是先知得天地本来生生之意。"贺孙。

In answering Lin Ziyuan's question on the *Great Learning*, the Master said, "The books written by the sages should not be read in the same manner. One book may purport only to make clear the scope for making efforts, while another, from beginning to end, may be concerned only with principles. For example, at the very beginning of the *Doctrine of the Mean* is 'What Heaven has conferred is called the nature.' If you read such a book, you should devote all yourself to pondering the principle it conveys. As for the *Great Learning*, it presents only a program for making efforts in pursuit of learning, which does not call for much attention paid to pondering. As soon as you read it, you will understand that. Nevertheless, a learner should make efforts by dedicating all himself mentally and physically rather than by reading only the words, for words do not require much consideration of themselves. In regard to inquiring the principle to the utmost, a learner should seek for it in himself, for that has nothing to do with other things. All boil down to benevolence, righteousness, propriety, and wisdom, and no matter how multifarious the changes things undergo are, they do not deviate from the four principles. You think over that by yourself and, in your daily life, see whether things and events can deviate from those four. As regards faithfulness, since there are the four principles, they are referred to as faithfulness. It means actuality and actually there are the four. With respect to their substance, there are actually benevolence, righteousness, propriety, and wisdom, and with respect to their function, there are actually the feelings of sadness and commiseration, shame and dislike, deference and compliance, and right and wrong, all of which brooks no falsehood. Who in the world is capable of false benevolence, false righteousness, false propriety, or false wisdom? Therefore, when one speaks of faithfulness, he means its actual being rather than its falsehood. When it is deduced to a family, there are actually father and son, husband and wife, and brothers; when it is deduced to between Heaven and Earth, there are actually sovereign and minister, and friends. All these are not the result of arrangement by some people later, for there are their beings originally. They are like a human body with its internal five viscera and six entrails[1]and the external eras, eyes, mouth, nose, and four limbs, which is true of every person. Preserved, they are benevolence, righteousness, propriety, and wisdom, while, emanated, they are the feelings of sadness and commiseration, shame and dislike, deference and compliance, and right and wrong. This is also true of every person, of father and son, brothers, husband and wife, friends, and sovereign and minister, and of all things, but they always are subject to their forms and their vital forces. However, the revealing can be made by one aspect: since there are father and son, there is naturally the father and son relationship; there are male and female, there is naturally the husband and wife relationship; since there are elder and younger, there is naturally fraternal relationship; since there are different members in the same type, there is naturally friendship; since there are the dominant and the secondary, there is naturally the sovereign and minister relationship. That is only because all are created by Heaven and Earth, they share the same root, and thus have more commonality than difference. When the sages and worthies came down to the myriad things in the world, they guided their growths according to their natures. For example, the insects, grasses, and trees, which are led to take their courses conforming to their natures and are taken in proper seasons and used with restraints. In the spring time, 'They did not kill those which had not attained to their full growth. They did not throw down nests. They did not

---

① In the tradition of Chinese medicine, the five viscera and six entrails of a human body refer to the five organs of heart, liver, spleen, lungs and kidneys and the six hollow organs of gallbladder, stomach, large intestine, small intestine, bladder and *sanjiao* 三焦 (triple energizer).

kill pregnant animals. When the plants and trees began to drop their leaves, they entered the hills and forests (with the axe). When the otter sacrificed its fish, the foresters entered the meres and dams. When the wolf sacrificed its prey, the hunting commenced. ' [Hesun]

39 问大学。曰："看圣贤说话，所谓坦然若大路然。缘后来人说得崎岖，所以圣贤意思难见。"贺孙。

When asked about the *Great Learning*, the Master answered, "Reading what the sages and worthies said, we feel the so called smoothness like a broad road. But due to the complication of it caused by later scholars, their original meaning is made hard to access. " [Hesun]

40 圣贤形之于言，所以发其意。后人多因言而失其意，又因注解而失其主。凡观书，且先求其意，有不可晓，然后以注通之。如看大学，先看前后经亦自分明，然后看传。可学。

The sages and worthies conveyed their meanings by forming them into words, but later people have tended to obsess themselves with their words only to lose their meanings and to annotate their words only to lose their tenets. Whoever reads a book should try to make out what it is intended for and when meeting something hard to understand, he may turn to its annotation given by later scholars. For example, in reading the *Great Learning*, one can see its idea by studying its first parts and latter parts coherently and then read those explanations of it by later scholars. [Kexue]

41 大学诸传，有解经处，有只引经传赞扬处。其意只是提起一事，使人读着常惺惺地。道夫。

Of the various explanations of the *Great Learning*, some are intended to

---

① The translation of the citation from the *Record of Rites* is based on a version by J. Legge (see http：//ctext. org/liji).

interpret its text, while some others only cite phrases and sentences from the book itself and other explanations in praise of it. In the latter case, the purpose is to mention something bearing on it so that, when reading it, people will often feel the goodness of its wording. [Daofu]

42 伊川旧日教人先看大学，那时未有解说，想也看得鹘突。而今看注解，觉大段分晓了，只在子细去看。贺孙。

When Yichuan instructed his disciples to read the *Great Learning* first, since there was no explanation available then, I am afraid, they were confused while reading it. Now, you can read the annotations of it and when you feel you can understand its basic idea, you should continue reading it carefully over and over again. [Hesun]

43 "看大学，且逐章理会。须先读本文，念得，次将章句来解本文，又将或问来参章句。须逐一令记得，反复寻究，待他浃洽。既逐段晓得，将来统看温寻过，这方始是。须是靠他这心，若一向靠写底，如何得。"又曰："只要熟，不要贪多。"道夫。

The Master said, "While reading the *Great Learning*, you should try to understand it paragraph by paragraph. You should read the text itself and, when you have seen its rough idea, read my *Interpretation* for explanation of it and then consult my *Questions and Answers* for cross reference. Learn them by heart and chew them over and over again for a coherent understanding. Thus, when you have understood all its paragraphs, read it as an entirety for a deeper understanding. That is the right way of reading it. You should count on its author's mind, for if you count on only the words, how can you see its truth?" He added, "You had better seek familiarity with it and refrain from being greedy for too much. " [Daofu]

44 圣人不令人悬空穷理，须要格物者，是要人就那上见得道理破，便实。只如大学一书，有正经，有注解，有或问。看来看去，不用或问，只看注解便了；久之，又只看正经便了；又久之，自有一部大学在我胸中，而正经亦不用矣。然不用某许多工夫，亦看某底不出；不用圣贤许多工夫，亦看圣贤底不出。大雅。

The sages did not require people to inquire the principle to the utmost from nothing. The reason for the necessity of investigating things is that the principle can only be understood by that, and only the understanding thus obtained is substantial. For example, as regards the *Great Learning*, learners can read the text, the *Interpretation*, and the *Questions and Answers* on it. In reading them, in due time, a learner will find it is enough to read *Interpretation* only for understanding of it and *Questions and Answers* can be dropped, and then it is enough to read the text itself and both *Interpretation* and *Questions and Answers* can be dropped. Ultimately there will be a *Great Learning* in his mind and the text will be of no use. However, if one does not make much effort, he will not understand my *Interpretation* and *Questions and Answers* and if he does not make the effort called for by the sages and worthies, he will not understand what they mean. [Daya]

45 或问："大学解已定否？"曰："据某而今自谓稳矣。只恐数年后又见不稳，这个不由自家。"问中庸解。曰："此书难看。大学本文未详者，某于或问则详之。此书在章句，其或问中皆是辨诸家说理未必是。有疑处，皆以'盖'言之。"淳。

Someone asked: "Is your understanding of the *Great Learning* determined now?" The Master answered, "As I see it at present, it is determined. But I am afraid some years later my understanding of it may change somewhat and this indeterminacy is not up to me." When asked about his understanding of the *Doctrine of the Mean*, the Master answered, "It is hard to read. When I found some points in the *Great Learning* hard for learners to understand, I gave some detailed explanations in my *Questions and Answers*. As for the *Doctrine of the Mean*, the explanations in my *Zhongyong Zhangju* 中庸章句 (Interpretation of the *Doctrine of the Mean*) are more helpful, for those in my *Zhongyong Huowen* 中庸或问 (Questions and Answers on the *Doctrine of the Mean*) aim to distinguish the various opinions held by different scholars on it and point out their inadequate points. When I was not sure of a point, I used 'probably' to indicate that. " [Chun（淳）]

46 大学章句次第得皆明白易晓，不必或问。但致知、格物与诚意较难理会，不得不明辨之耳。人杰。

The content of *Interpretation* easy to understand makes the *Questions and Answers* almost unnecessary. But since the words on extending knowledge, investigating things, and making thought sincere in the text were not so easy to read, I had to explain them in the latter. [Renjie]

47 子渊问大学或问。曰："且从头逐句理会，到不通处，却看章句。或问乃注脚之注脚，亦不必深理会。"贺孙。

Ziyuan asked about *Questions and Answers*. The Master answered, "You should try to understand it sentence by sentence from the beginning and when you meet any obstruction, you can turn to *Interpretation* for help. *Questions and Answers* serves as the footnote of a footnote, so it does not call for much effort for its understanding. " [Hesun]

48 "学者且去熟读大学正文了，又子细看章句。或问未要看，俟有疑处，方可去看。"又曰："某解书不合太多。又先准备学者，为他设疑说了。他未曾疑到这上，先与说了，所以致得学者看得容易了。圣人云：'不愤不启，不悱不发。举一隅不以三隅反，则不复也。'须是教他疑三朝五日了，方始与说他，便通透。更与从前所疑虑，也会因此触发，工夫都在许多思虑不透处。而今却是看见成解底，都无疑了。吾儒与老庄学皆无传，惟有释氏常有人。盖他一切办得不说，都待别人自去敲磕，自有个通透处。只是吾儒又无这不说底，若如此，少间差异了。"又曰："解文字，下字最难。某解书所以未定，常常更改者，只为无那恰好底字子。把来看，又见不稳当，又着改几字。所以横渠说命辞为难。"贺孙。

The Master said, "A learner should read the text of the *Great Learning* carefully and get familiar with it first before scrutinizing the *Interpretation*. He does not need to turn to the *Questions and Answers*, only when he gets any doubt he may take it up. " He continued, "When I explained the book, I thought it proper to avoid saying too much. And I supposed myself as a learner, and standing in his shoes, I posed some questions and then answered them myself. But if a learner has not got so deep as to doubt about a certain point, yet found my explanation of it, then he may think it is easy to read. As Confucius said, 'I do not open up the truth to one who is not eager to get knowledge, nor help out any one who is not anxious to explain himself. When I have presented one corner of a subject to anyone, and he cannot from it learn the other three, I do not repeat my lesson. '① (*Analects*, 7: 8) A learner should be kept in doubt of something for several days and then when he is provided with an explanation, it is easy for him to understand it thoroughly. This understanding will probably trigger the doubts he had before and thus solve them. Where there are points he can not see through, his efforts are more productive of positive effects. If he can easily get access to some ready-made explanations now, he will be deprived of the doubts. There have been few followers of Confucianism and Daoism, but many believers of Buddhism. It is probably because, since it resorts to no word for understanding its doctrine, they need to think over it by themselves and naturally reach a thorough understanding of it. But our Confucianism has not got that sort of thing that can resort to no word, and if it had, soon there would crop up differences in understanding. " He added, "In explaining something of the Confucian canonical works, I have felt it the most difficult to find a proper word for explaining it. The reason why I was often uncertain and made changes in my explanation is nothing but my failure to find the proper words for it. When I gave a second thought to something in my explanation, I would find it insecure and then change a few sino-graphs. That is why

---

① The translation of the citation from *Analects* is based on a version by J. Legge (see http: // ctext. org/analects).

Hengqü sighed that it was truly hard to find proper words in writing. ”〔Hesun〕

49　某作或问，恐人有疑，所以设此，要他通晓。而今学者未有疑，却反被这个生出疑！贺孙。

The reason why I wrote *Questions and Answers* is for fear that learners may be obstructed by doubts when reading the *Great Learning*, which may be solved by resorting to my explanation. However, today, learners have not got doubts concerning the *Great Learning*. On the contrary they have found my explanation doubtful. 〔Hesun〕

50　或问朱敬之：“有异闻乎？”曰：“平常只是在外面听朋友问答，或时里面亦只说某病痛处得。”一日，教看大学，曰：“我平生精力尽在此书。先须通此，方可读书。”贺孙。

One day, the Master asked Zhu Jingzhi 朱敬之（dates unknown, a disciple of Zhu's）, “Have you heard of something new?” The disciple answered, “In these days, outside I have usually heard my friends questioning and answering, and inside I have sometimes talked only about the problems troubling me. ” In another day, while instructing him to read the *Great Learning*, the Master said, “I have spent all my life on that book, and you should strive to understand it well before reading other books. ” 〔Hesun〕

51　某于大学用工甚多。温公作通鉴，言：“臣平生精力，尽在此书。”某于大学亦然。论孟中庸，却不费力。友仁。

I have made quite many efforts to pore over the *Great Learning*. In his *Zizhi Tongjian* 资治通鉴（Comprehensive Mirror for Aid in Government）, Duke of Wen（i. e. Sima Guang）said, “I have spent the energy of all my life on this book. ” That is true of my work on the *Great Learning*. As for the *Analects*, the *Mencius*, and the *Doctrine of the Mean*, I have spent much less energy on them. 〔Youren〕①

---

①　Guo Youren 郭友仁（courtesy name Deyuan 德元）.

52 大学一日只看二三段时，便有许多修处。若一向看去，便少。不是少，只是看得草草。

If a learner reads only two or three paragraphs of the *Great Learning* in a day, he will gain perception of many points. But if he reads on and on, he will see few. It is, actually, not seeing few, but only looking through the text cursorily, with no deep understanding.

53 某解注书，不引后面说来证前说，却引前说去证后说。盖学者方看此，有未晓处，又引他处，只见难晓。大学都是如此。僩。

When I annotated a book, I did not cite what appears in the later parts to evidence something in the first parts, but rather cite what appears in the first parts to evidence something in the later parts. Probably, while learners begin to read a part here and meet something hard to understand, if they have to deal with something else cited from there in another part, it will only add to their confusion. This is true of all the parts in the *Great Learning*. [Xian]

54 说大学启蒙毕，因言："某一生只看得这两件文字透，见得前贤所未到处。若使天假之年，庶几将许多书逐件看得恁地，煞有工夫。"贺孙。

Having finished talking about the *Great Learning* and *Yixue Qimeng* 易学启蒙（Rudimentary Knowledge of Learning on the *Classic of Change*）, the Master said thereupon, "In my life I have understood these two works most thoroughly and seen much that the predecessors failed to see. If I am blessed with enough years more to live, I will spend all of them reading many other books one by one in the same way, and such strenuous efforts will be much productive." [Hesun]

序
Preface（of *Interpretation of Great Learning*）

55 亚夫问："大学序云：'既与之以仁义礼智之性，又有气质之禀．'所谓气质，便是刚柔、强弱、明快、迟钝等否？"曰："然。"又云："气，是那初禀底；质，是成这模样了底。如金之矿，木之萌芽相似。"又云："只是一个阴阳五行之气，滚在天地中，精英者为人，渣滓者为物；精英之中又精英者，为圣，为贤；精英之中渣滓者，为愚，为不肖。"恪。

Yafu asked, "The preface of *Interpretation* says 'They（people）were endowed not only with the nature of benevolence, righteousness, propriety, and wisdom, but also with their physical nature. ' Is the so called physical nature the hardness or softness, strength or weakness, rapidity or slowness, and the like?" The Master answered, "Right. " Then he said, "Vital force 气 is that which is endowed with originally, while *zhi* 质 form is that which is formed actually. Their relation is like that between gold and the gold mine or that between tree and the sprout of a tree. " He added, "There was the vital force of *yin* and *yang* and the Five Agents, and it underwent revolving and grinding between Heaven and Earth, by which the quintessence of it became human beings and the dross turned to be other things. The most quintessential in the quintessence became sages and worthies, while the least quintessential in the quintessence, fools and unworthies. " [Ke]

56 问："'一有聪明睿智能尽其性者，则天必命之以为亿兆之君师'，何处见得天命处？"曰："此也如何知得。只是才生得一个恁地底人，定是为亿兆之君师，便是天命之也。他既有许多气魄才德，决不但已，必统御亿兆之众，人亦自是归他。如三代已前圣人都是如此。及至孔子，方不然。然虽不为帝王，也闲他不得，也做出许多事来，以教天下后世，是亦天命也。"偰。

Question: "The moment there is one born with brightness and intelligence, who can give fullest play to his nature, he must be mandated by Heaven as a sovereign and teacher for the multitudes of people. " Where can the "mandated by Heaven" be seen?

Answer: How can that be known? It only means that as soon as a man of that sort is born, he must be a sovereign and teacher for the multitudes of people and that indicates his being mandated by Heaven. Since he is gifted with bold vision and with superb talent and virtue, he will never bring benefit from them only for himself. Thus he will be a ruler over the multitudes of people, who are willing to be subject to him. For example, that is true of the sages in the *sandai* 三代 (Three Dynasties, i. e. the Xia, Shang, and Zhou dynasties). That did not change until the time of Confucius, who, though not a sovereign, was occupied and did many deeds, which taught all the people later in the world. His is also a case of being mandated by Heaven. [Xian]

57 问:"'天必命之以为亿兆之君师',天如何命之?"曰:"只人心归之,便是命。"问:"孔子如何不得命?"曰:"中庸云:'大德必得其位',孔子却不得。气数之差至此极,故不能反。"可学。

Question: "He must be mandated by Heaven as a sovereign and teacher for the multitudes of people." How can Heaven mandate him?

Answer: It means only that the minds of people are for him.

Further question: Why was Confucius not mandated?

Answer: As said in the *Doctrine of the Mean*, "It could not but be that he, having such great virtue, should obtain the throne." But Confucius did not obtain the throne. In the time he lived, the fortune was so extremely deteriorated that even he could not overturn it. [Kexue]

58 问"继天立极。"曰:"天只生得许多人物,与你许多道理。然天却自做不得,所以生得圣人为之修道立教,以教化百姓,所谓'裁成天地之道,辅相天地之宜'是也。盖天做不得底,却须圣人为他做也。"僩。

When asked about "continuing the work of Heaven and obtaining the throne," the Master answered, "What Heaven could do is only create human beings and endow them with many principles. Heaven could not do by itself beyond that, so it created the sages, who would, in stead of Heaven, cultivate the Way and found the doctrine for education and transformation of all the ordinary people. That is what is meant by 'The (sage) sovereign fashions and completes (his regulations) after the courses of Heaven and Earth, and assists the application of the adaptations furnished by them.'① (*Classic of Change*) Probably, that is because Heaven has the sages to do what it can not do." [Xian]

59 问："'各俛焉以尽其力。'下此'俛'字何谓？"曰："'俛'字者，乃是刺着头，只管做将去底意思。"友仁。

Question: You said, "Each should be *fu* 俛 (diligent) and try his best to do it." What do you mean by *fu*?

Answer: That word means that one should head on and, without any hesitation, throw himself in doing it. [Youren]

60 问："外有以极其规模之大，内有以尽其节目之详。"曰："这个须先识得外面一个规模如此大了，而内做工夫以实之。所谓规模之大，凡人为学，便当以'明明德，新民，止于至善'，及'明明德于天下'为事，不成只要独善其身便了。须是志于天下，所谓'志伊尹之所志，学颜子之所学也'。所以大学第二句便说'在新民'。"偶。

When asked about "In the outside is so extremely large a scope and in the inside is so extremely detailed a program," the Master answered, "You should first understand the extremely large scope in the outside before making efforts inside yourself to substantiate it. By the extremely large scope is meant that whoever pursues learning should aim 'to illustrate illustrious virtue; to renovate the people; and to rest in the highest excellence,' (*Great Learning*, 1) and 'to illustrate illustrious virtue throughout the empire,' (*Great Learning*, 2) rather than pay attention to his own moral uplift without

---

① Cited from "Xiangzhuan" 象传 (Explanation of Divinatory Symbol) of "Tai Guan" 泰卦 (Tai Hexagram) in the *Classic of Change*. The translation of the citation is based on a version by J. Legge (see http://ctext.org/book-of-changes), with slight modification.

any thought of others. Hence, he must cherish the aspiration to embrace the entire empire, 'desiring what Yi Yin desired and learning what Yanzi (i. e. Yan Hui) learned. ' ① Therefore, ' to renovate the people ' is said after ' to illustrate illustrious virtue ' in the outset of the *Great Learning*. " [Xian]

61 明德，新民，便是节目；止于至善，便是规模之大。道夫。

Both " to illustrate illustrious virtue " and " to renovate the people " are parts of the program, while " to rest in the highest excellence " (*Great Learning*, 1) is indicative of the large scope for the pursuit of learning. [Daofu]

62 仁甫问："释氏之学，何以说为'高过于大学而无用？'"曰："吾儒更着读书，逐一就事物上理会道理。他便都扫了这个，他便恁地空空寂寂，恁地便道事都了。只是无用。德行道艺，艺是一个至末事，然亦皆有用。释氏若将些子事付之，便都没奈何。"又曰："古人志道，据德，而游于艺：礼乐射御书数，数尤为最末事。若而今行经界，则算法亦甚有用。若时文整篇整卷，要作何用耶！徒然坏了许多士子精神。"贺孙。

Renfu 仁甫 (i. e. Wu Renfu 吴仁甫, dates unknown, a disciple of Zhu's) asked, " Why did you say that the learning of Buddhism ' is higher than the *Great Learning* yet to no avail ' ? " The Master answered, " We Confucians set store by reading books and understanding each of the principles in regard to things. Dropping all such, Buddhism takes to emptiness and silence and treats all things in that way. But that is only to no avail. Of virtue, conduct, the Way, and the six arts, the arts are the least significant, yet they are all to some avail. If Buddhists are asked to deal with such things, they are at a loss. " He added, " The ancients aspired to pursue

---

① Cited from the tenth chapter of Zhou Dunyi's *Penetrating the Classic of Change*. The translation of the citation is based on the version by Chan Wing-tsit, p. 470, with slight modification. Yi Yin 伊尹 (dates unknown) is a minister of early Shang Dynasty and one of the most honored officials of the era.

the Way, cultivated their virtue as the foundation, and entertained themselves in the six arts, i. e. rites, music, archery, driving a chariot, writing, and mathematics, of which mathematics was the least significant. If the measurement of farmland boundaries is carried out at present, it will be very useful. If one is only good at making *shiwen* 时文 (prescribed essay for the imperial examinations) and can produce long pieces or even rolls of it, what use can that be of? That has spoiled the spirit of many scholars for nothing."
[Hesun]

经上

The Text (of the *Great Learning*), Part I

63 大学首三句说一个体统，用力处却在致知、格物。端蒙。

The first sentence[①] in the outset of the text of the *Great Learning* says of a system, yet what one should make effort for to the utmost lies in the extension of knowledge and investigation of things. [Duanmeng]

64 天之赋于人物者谓之命，人与物受之者谓之性，主于一身者谓之心，有得于天而光明正大者谓之明德。敬仲。以下明明德。

What is conferred to humankind and things is called *ming* 命 (destiny), what is received by humankind and things is called *xing* 性 (nature), what works as the master of the body is called *xin* 心 (mind), and what is obtained from Heaven and is bright, upright, and great is called *mingde* 明德 (illustrious virtue). [Jingzhong] The following conversations concern illustrating illustrious virtue.

65 或问："明德便是仁义礼智之性否？"曰："便是。"

Someone asked, "Does illustrious virtue mean the nature of

---

① The firest sentence, the *sanjù* 三句 said in the original, is 大学之道，在明明德，在新民，在止于至善。

benevolence, righteousness, propriety, and wisdom?" The Master answered, "Yes, it is."

66 或问:"所谓仁义礼智是性,明德是主于心而言?"曰:"这个道理在心里光明照彻,无一毫不明。"

Someone asked, "The so called benevolence, righteousness, propriety, and wisdom pertain to nature. Is illustrious virtue spoken of in regard to the master of the mind?" The Master answered, "This principle is bright and shiny in the mind, where there is no iota which is not light."

67 明德是指全体之妙,下面许多节目,皆是靠明德做去。

Illustrious virtue refers to the subtleness of the entirety and many items of it are conducted by depending on illustrious virtue.

68 "明明德",明只是提撕也。士毅。

In "to illustrate illustrious virtue," the "to illustrate" only means to remind one of something. [Shiyi]

69 学者须是为己。圣人教人,只在大学第一句"明明德"上。以此立心,则如今端己敛容,亦为己也;读书穷理,亦为己也;做得一件事是实,亦为己也。圣人教人持敬,只是须着从这里说起。其实若知为己后,即自然着敬。方子。

A learner should pursue learning for his own sake. What the sage teaches lies only in "to illustrate illustrious virtue" in the first sentence. With his mind set on that, the learner makes himself upright and assume a serious expression, which is also for his own sake. His reading books and inquiring the principle to the utmost is also for his own sake. His doing one thing with some real result is also for his own sake. In regard to the sage's teaching of cherishing seriousness, it must start from here. Actually, if one knows that he does all those for his own sake, he will naturally adhere to seriousness. [Fangzi]

70 "明明德"乃是为己工夫。那个事不是分内事?明德在人,非是从外面请入来底。盖卿。

The "to illustrate illustrious virtue" represents effort to be made for one's own sake. Which event is not what one should do? Illustrious virtue lies intrinsically with a person and it is not something invited in from outside. [Gaiqing]

71 为学只"在明明德"一句。君子存之，存此而已；小人去之，去此而已。一念辣然，自觉其非，便是明之之端。儒用。

The pivot of pursuing learning lies in "to illustrate illustrious virtue." The *junzi* 君子（Superior Man）preserves it and does no more than that, while *xiaoren* 小人（petty man）casts it away and does no more than that. To one, when that idea becomes clear, he will be conscious of what is right and what is wrong, which indicates the beginning of illustrating illustrious virtue. [Ruyong]

72 大学"在明明德"一句，当常常提撕。能如此，便有进步处。盖其原自此发见。人只一心为本。存得此心，于事物方知有脉络贯通处。季札。

One should often remind himself of the "to illustrate illustrious virtue" in the *Great Learning*. With this, he will make progress. It is probably because that is where progress starts to be made primordially. It is fundamental for one to be single-minded. Only by preserving that mind can he get to know that there are veins penetrating things and events. [Jizha]

73 "在明明德"，须是自家见得这物事光明灿烂，常在目前，始得。如今都不曾见得。须是勇猛着起精神，拔出心肝与它看，始得！正如人跌落大水，浩无津涯，须是勇猛奋起这身，要得出来，始得！而今都只泛泛听他流将去。

As regards "to illustrate illustrious virtue," a learner should see it brilliant and resplendent constantly before his eyes. However, nowadays, people have failed to see it that way. One should, by mustering up courage and keeping his spirit up, devote himself, heart and soul, to seeing it. It is like a man who falls into the flood which is torrential and boundless. He can not get out of it unless he goes all out and fights against it bravely. But now they only let themselves flow with the currents.

74 或以"明明德"譬之磨镜。曰："镜犹磨而后明。若人之明德，则未尝不明。虽其昏蔽之极，而其善端之发，终不可绝。但当于其所发之端，而接续光明之，令其不昧，则其全体大用可以尽明。且如人知己德之不明而欲明之。只这知其不明而欲明之者，便是明德，就这里便明将去。"僩。

Someone likened "to illustrate illustrious virtue" to grinding and polishing a copper mirror. The Master commented, "The mirror has to undergo grinding before it can be bright. When it comes to the illustrious virtue of humankind, it is always bright. Even if it is beclouded extremely, ultimately the occurrence of the beginning of the good can not be suffocated. At the beginning of the good, if it can be furthered so as to get brightened up, then the entire great function of it can be bright all over. It is like one who is aware of his virtue not bright and desires to make it bright. This awareness of not bright virtue and therefore desire of making it bright are the very illustrious virtue, which indicates the starting point of regaining illustrious virtue. " [Xian]

75 "明明德"，如人自云，天之所与我，未尝昏。只知道不昏，便不昏矣。僩。

What "to illustrate illustrious virtue" means is comparable to one who says to himself "It is what Heaven confers on me and has never got benighted. " If only he knows that it has never got benighted, then it will not get benighted. [Xian]

76 "明明德"，是明此明德，只见一点明，便于此明去。正如人醉醒，初间少醒，至于大醒，亦只是一醒。学者贵复其初，至于已到地位，则不着个"复"字。可学。

The "to illustrate illustrious virtue" means one's awareness of there being the illustrious virtue in himself and that, with that little bright point, he should further its brightness. It is like a man sobering up from drunkenness. Soon he gets a little sober and then gets completely sober, but all soberness is the same. To a learner, what is treasurable is to return to his original state, and as for the extent of his returning, it has nothing to do with the returning itself. ［Kexue］

77 问"明明德"。曰："人皆有个明处，但为物欲所蔽，剔拨去了。只就明处渐明将去。然须致知、格物，方有进步处，识得本来是甚么物。"季札。

Asked about "to illustrate illustrious virtue," the Master replied, "Every man possesses a bright point, but it is benighted by his selfish desire for materials. To get rid of the benightedness, one should strive to brighten up that point. What he must do is extension of knowledge through investigation of things so that he can make gradual progress and get to know what its original status is like." ［Jizha］

78 明德未尝息，时时发见于日用之间。如见非义而羞恶，见孺子入井而恻隐，见尊贤而恭敬，见善事而叹慕，皆明德之发见也。如此推之，极多。但当因其所发而推广之。侗。

The illustrious virtue has never rested and it reveals itself in daily life. For example, one feels shame and dislike when seeing something unrighteous, commiserates when seeing a child about to fall into a well, is respectful when seeing a worthy, and is full of praise when seeing something meritorious, all of which embody the illustrious virtue. Deduced in this way, we can get countless similar cases. But this deduction should be based on the embodiments of it. ［Xian］

79 明德，谓得之于己，至明而不昧者也。如父子则有亲，君臣则有义，夫妇则有别，长幼则有序，朋友则有信，初未尝差也。苟或差焉，则其所得者昏，而非固有之明矣。履孙。

The "illustrious virtue" means what one is conferred with, which is supremely bright and originally free from benightedness. For example, the affection between father and son, the righteousness between sovereign and minister, the discrimination between husband and wife, the order between elder and younger, and the faithfulness between friends, all of which are free from deterioration in their original state. If there occurs some deterioration, it is due to the acquired benightedness over it but not due to the intrinsic brightness of it. [Lüsun]①

80　人本来皆具此明德，德内便有此仁义礼智四者。只被外物汩没了不明，便都坏了。所以大学之道，必先明此明德。若能学，则能知觉此明德，常自存得，便去刮剔，不为物欲所蔽。推而事父孝，事君忠，推而齐家、治国、平天下，皆只此理。大学一书，若理会得这一句，便可迎刃而解。椿。

All persons possessed originally that illustrious virtue, where dwelt the four of benevolence, righteousness, propriety, and wisdom. However, the illustrious virtue with the four was spoiled due to its illustriousness being submerged and benighted by external things. Therefore, what the *Great Learning* teaches is to illustrate the illustrious virtue first. If one is able to pursue learning, he will be conscious of the illustrious virtue and constantly strive to preserve it so as to get rid little by little of the benightedness caused by selfish desires for materials. Taking that as the starting point, one can deduce the same principle over the filial piety in serving parents and the loyalty in serving the sovereign, and over regulating the family, governing the state, and bringing peace to the empire. If one can understand the first sentence of the *Great Learning* well, he can understand the whole book readily. [Chun（椿）]

81　明德，也且就切近易见处理会，也且慢慢自见得。如何一日便都要识得！如出必是告，反必是面，昏定晨省，必是昏定晨省，这易见。"徐行后长者谓之弟，疾行先长者谓之不弟"，这也易见，有

---

① Pan Lüsun 潘履孙（courtesy name Tanweng 坦翁）.

甚不分明。如"九族既睦",是尧一家之明德;"百姓昭明",是尧一国之明德;"黎民于变时雍",是尧天下之明德。如"博弈好饮酒,不顾父母之养",是不孝;到能昏定晨省,冬温夏清,可以为孝。然而"从父之令",今看孔子说,却是不孝。须是知父之命当从,也有不可从处。盖"与其得罪于乡党州闾,宁熟谏"。"谕父母于道",方是孝。贺孙。

As regards the illustrious virtue, a learner should strive for understanding it by considering the things and events close at hand and easy to see and thus he will see it gradually. How can he know it all in one day? For instance, as said in the *Record of Rites*, "When a son is going out, he must inform (his parents where he is going); when he returns, he must present himself before them," and "in the evening, he must adjust everything (for their repose), and must inquire (about their health) in the morning." Such things are easy to see. As said in the *Mencius*, "To walk slowly, keeping behind his elders, is to perform the part of a younger. To walk quickly and precede his elders is to violate the duty of a younger brother." Such is also easy to see. As said in the *Book of History*, "The nine classes of his (Yao's) kindred (thus) became harmonious," displaying the illustrious virtue of Yao's family; "The people (of his domain) all became brightly intelligent," indicating the illustrious virtue of Yao's state; "He united and harmonized the myriad states; and so the black-haired people were transformed, with the result of (universal) concord," which manifests the illustrious virtue of Yao's empire. As for "One plays chess and gambles, and is fond of wine, without attending to the nourishment of his parents," (*Mencius*) it shows his unfiliality. When he can adjust everything (for the repose of his parents), and must inquire (about their health) in the morning, and in winter, he can warm (the bed for his parents) and cool it in summer, then he shows filiality. However, one's "obedience to the orders of his father," said in *Xiaojing* 孝经 (Book of Filial Piety), according to Confucius's explanation, is not necessarily indicative of filial piety. He should know whether an order of his father is proper to obey or not. Probably, "Rather than allow him to commit an offence against any one in the neighborhood or countryside, (the son) should strongly remonstrate with him." (*Record of Rites*). Then, the "instruction of his parents in the path of duty" (*Record of Rites*) is a display of filial piety. ① [Hesun]

82 曾兴宗问:"如何是'明明德'?"曰:"明德是自家心中具许多道理在这里。本是个明底物事,初无暗昧,人得之则为德。如恻隐、羞恶、辞让、是非,是从自家心里出来,触着那物,便是那个物出来,何尝不明。缘为物欲所蔽,故其明易昏。如镜本明,被外物点污,则不明了。少间磨起,则其明又能照物。"又云:"人心惟定则明。所谓定者,非是定于这里,全不修习,待他自明。惟是定后,却好去学。看来看去,久后自然彻。"又有人问:"自觉胸中甚昧。"曰:"这明德亦不甚昧。如适来说恻隐、羞恶、辞逊、是非等,此是心中元有此等物。发而为恻隐,这便是仁;发而为羞恶,这便是义;发而为辞逊、是非,便是礼、智。看来这个亦不是甚昧,但恐于义理差互处有似是而非者,未能分别耳。且如冬温夏清为孝,人能冬温夏清,这便是孝。至如子从父之令,本似孝,孔子却以为不孝。与其得罪于乡间,不若且谏父之过,使不陷于不义,这处方是孝。恐似此处,未能大故分别得出,方昧。且如齐宣王见牛之觳觫,便有不忍之心,欲以羊易之。这便见恻隐处,只是见不完全。及到'兴甲兵,危士臣'处,便欲快意为之。是见不精确,不能推爱牛之心而爱百姓。只是心中所见所好如此,且恁地做去。又如胡侍郎读史管见,其为文字与所见处甚好,到他自做处全相反。不知是如何,却似是两人做事一般,前日所见是一人,今日所行又是一人。是见不真确,致得如此。"卓。

Zeng Xingzong 曾兴宗 (1146 – 1212, courtesy name Guangzu 光祖, a disciple of Zhu's) asked, "What is meant by 'to illustrate illustrious

---

① The English translations of the citations from the *Record of Rites*, the *Book of History*, *Mencius*, and the *Book of Filial Piety* are based on the relevant versions by J. Legge (see http://ctext.org), with some alterations.

virtue'?" The Master answered, " One's ' illustrious virtue ' means there
being many principles in one's own mind. It is bright originally and free from
benightedness at first. A person, endowed with it, is capable of being
virtuous. For example, all the feelings of sadness and commiseration, shame
and dislike, deference and compliance, and right and wrong, emanate from
his own mind, and when the illustrious virtue is triggered, it will emerge,
always bright. But if it is benighted by material desires, its illustriousness is
liable to be covered. For example, if a mirror, which is bright originally, is
smeared by something dirty, it loses its brightness. But when it is polished
up, it can be so bright as to reflect things. " He added, " Only when the
human mind is determined can it become illustrious. The ' determined ' does
not mean that, having had it fixed here, one makes no effort for learning and
practicing, waiting for its becoming illustrious by itself, but means that,
having had it set up, one throws himself into learning, and thus, after a long
time, in due course, he will return to his original brightness all over. "
Someone else asked, " I have felt much benightedness in my mind. (Why is
that?)" The Master replied, "The illustrious virtue is not benighted at first.
For example, the feelings of sadness and commiseration, shame and dislike,
deference and compliance, and right and wrong, which I have just talked
about, are what dwell in the mind originally. That which emanates as the
feeling of sadness and commiseration is benevolence, that which emanates as
the feeling of shame and dislike is righteousness, and those which emanate as
the feeling of dereference and compliance and that of right and wrong are
propriety and wisdom, respectively. So it seems not very benighted, but I am
afraid that, since there is some paradoxical confusion of principles, the
indiscrimination of them is caused. For example, the sage says that a man
who can, in winter, warm (the bed for his parents) and cool it in summer is
filial, so whoever does that displays filial piety. However, though a son who
obeys the orders of his father seems filial, Confucius thought it otherwise, and

thus, rather than allow him to commit an offence against any one in the neighborhood or countryside, he should strongly remonstrate so as to prevent him from committing unrighteousness, which manifests his true filial piety. So in such points as this, if one fails to make basic discrimination, he will feel benighted. For another example, the King Xuan of Qi 'could not bear the frightened appearance of an ox whose blood would be used to consecrate a bell' and wanted 'to change it for a sheep.' (*Mencius*, 1A: 7) This indicates his feeling of commiseration, only that it is incomplete. When he 'collects his equipments of war and endangers his soldiers and officers,' he felt pleasure in his mind. This shows his inaccurate understanding of commiseration and failure to deduce his love for an ox to his love for his people. The reason for that is his allowing what he saw and what he liked in his mind to go as he pleased. Another example is Assistant Minister Hu (Hu Yin 胡寅 [1098 – 1156]). Both his writings and opinions in his *Dushi Guanjian* 读史管见 (Humble Opinions on Histories) were rather good, but his conducts were quite opposite. I wonder why what he did is like the things done by two different persons. When he aired his opinions yesterday, he is a person, but when he did things today, he was another person. He was two-faced because he failed to see truly the illustrious virtue."[Zhuo]

83 或问:"'明明德',是于静中本心发见,学者因其发见处从而穷究之否?"曰:"不特是静,虽动中亦发见。孟子将孺子将入井处来明这道理。盖赤子入井,人所共见,能于此发端处推明,便是明。盖人心至灵,有什么事不知,有什么事不晓,有什么道理不具在这里。何缘有不明?为是气禀之偏,又为物欲所乱。如目之于色,耳之于声。口之于味,鼻之于臭,四肢之于安佚,所以不明。然而其德本是至明物事,终是遮不得,必有时发见。便教至恶之人,亦时乎有善念之发。学者便当因其明处下工夫,一向明将去。致知、格物,皆是事也。且如今人做得一件事不是,有时都不知,便是昏处;然有时知得不是,这个便是明处。孟子发明赤子入井。盖赤子入井出于仓猝,人都主张不得,见之者莫不有怵惕恻隐之心。"又曰："人心莫不有知，所以不知者，但气禀有偏，故知之有不能尽。所谓致知者，只是教他展开使尽。"又曰："看大学，先将经文看教贯通。如看或问，须全段相参酌，看教他贯通，如看了只手，将起便有五指头，始得。今看或问，只逐些子看，都不贯通，如何得。"子蒙。

Someone asked, "Does the 'to illustrate illustrious virtue' mean the emanation of the original true mind in tranquility and that a learner starts from that and thereupon inquires the mind to the utmost?" The Master answered, "It is not only in tranquility, for it also emanates in activity. The *Mencius* uses the scene of an innocent child about to fall into a well to clarify the principle. Probably that scene is something everyone may see and if one can deduce from that feeling of commiseration as the beginning of benevolence to the illustrious virtue, it is the illustriousness itself at work. Probably, the human mind is the supremely intelligent, and what event can't it know? What principle doesn't it possess in itself? But why is it benighted? The reasons are the partial endowment of vital force and the confusion due to material desires, such as the eye's desire for good look, the ear for good sound, the mouth for good taste, the nose for good smell, and the four limbs for ease and comfort. That is why it is benighted. However, the original virtue is supremely illustrious. Ultimately, nothing can cover it up and sometimes it is bound to reveal itself. Even the evilest person feels some goodwill sometimes. A learner should make effort to expand its bright point and then keep on furthering towards its illustriousness. Extension of knowledge and investigation of things are both what he should strive to do. Nowadays, when many people do something not right, sometimes they even do not know it, and this indicates their benightedness. Sometimes they know what they did is not right, and this manifests their brightness. As for the scene of a child about to fall into a well the *Mencius* uses as an analogy, probably when one sees the child about to fall into the well, it is too late for him to do anything to prevent his fall, and whoever sees it feels sorrowful and commiserative. " He continued, "No human mind does not possess the power of knowledge. The reason why one is incapable of knowledge is the partial endowment of vital force with him, so his knowledge can not be complete. Thus, the so called extension of knowledge aims only to give full play to his power and attain complete knowledge. " He added, "When reading the *Great Learning*, a learner should read the text carefully to get a coherent understanding of it. If he reads my *Questions and Answers*, he should make cross reference to all the paragraphs for a thorough understanding. It is like seeing a hand, and from the beginning one should know it has five fingers. If one reads some words in this paragraph and then turns to other words in another paragraph, it is hard for him to understand them well, let alone gain a coherent understanding of the entire text. " [Zimeng]①

84 或问"明明德"云云。曰:"不消如此说,他那注得自分晓了。只要你实去体察,行之于身。须是真个明得这明德是怎生地明,是如何了得它虚灵不昧。须是真个不昧,具得众理,应得万事。只恁地说,不济得事。"又曰:"如格物、致知、诚意、正心、修身五者,皆'明明德'事。格物、致知,便是要知得分明;诚意、正心、修身,便是要行得分明。若是格物、致知有所未尽,便是知得这明德未分明;意未尽诚,便是这德有所未明;心有不正,则德有所未明;身有不修,则德有所未明。须是意不可有顷刻之不诚,心不可有顷刻之不正,身不可有顷刻之不修,这明德方常明。"问:"所谓明德,工夫也只在读书上?"曰:"固是在读书上。然亦不专是读书,事上也要理会。书之所载者,固要逐件理会。也有书所不载,而事上合当理会者;也有古所未有底事,而今之所有当理会者极多端。"侗。

Someone asked about "to illustrate illustrious virtue" and some other points. The Master answered, "There is no need to say that way. The

---

① Lin Zimeng 林子蒙 (courtesy name unknown)

annotations of them make their meaning clear already. What you should do is experience and observe it practically and conduct it personally. You should get to know truly why the illustrious virtue is illustrious and originally how it is vacuous, intelligent, and free from obscurity. You should know that it is truly free from obscurity, and embraces all the principles, ready for dealing with the myriad things. Mere talk about it is of little use." He added, "For example, the five events of investigating things, extending knowledge, making thought sincere, rectifying the mind, and cultivating oneself are all for illustrating illustrious virtue. The purpose of investigating things and extending knowledge is for knowing clearly and that of making thought sincere, rectifying the mind, and cultivating oneself is for practicing definitely. If one's investigation of things and extension of knowledge are incomplete, that means his knowing the illustrious virtue unclearly. Incomplete sincerity of thought, incomplete rectification of the mind, and incomplete cultivation of oneself, they each indicate knowing the virtue unclearly. Efforts should be made to keep the thought from being not sincere even in a moment, to keep the mind from being not rectified even in a moment, and to keep the self from being not cultivated even in a moment. Only in this way can the illustrious virtue be constantly illustrious." The questioner further asked, "Does the illustrious virtue imply making efforts to read books only?" The Master replied, "You should make efforts, of course, to read books, but that is not the only thing you should do, for you must understand them with respect to events. The events carried in the books should be read carefully one by one, but there are also those events which are not carried in the books, yet should be understood. Besides, the events which never happened in ancient times but currently occur and should be understood are extremely multifarious." [Xian]

85 问:"或谓'虚灵不昧',是精灵底物事;'具众理',是精灵中有许多条理;'应万事',是那条理发见出来底。"曰:"不消如此解说。但要识得这明德是甚物事，便切身做工夫，去其气禀物欲之蔽。能存得自家个虚灵不昧之心，足以具众理，可以应万事，便是明得自家明德了。若只是解说'虚灵不昧'是如何，'具众理'是如何，'应万事'又是如何，却济得甚事！"又问："明之之功，莫须读书为要否？"曰："固是要读书。然书上有底，便可就书理会；若书上无底，便着就事上理会；若古时无底，便着就而今理会。盖所谓明德者，只是一个光明底物事。如人与我一把火，将此火照物，则无不烛。自家若灭息着，便是暗了明德；能吹得着时，又是明其明德。所谓明之者，致知、格物、诚意、正心、修身，皆明之之事，五者不可阙一。若阙一，则德有所不明。盖致知、格物，是要知得分明；诚意、正心、修身，是要行得分明。然既明其明德，又要功夫无间断，使无时而不明，方得。若知有一之不尽，物有一之未穷，意有顷刻之不诚，心有顷刻之不正，身有顷刻之不修，则明德又暗了。惟知无不尽，物无不格，意无不诚，心无不正，身无不修，即是尽明明德之功夫也。"焘。

Question: Is it right to say that the "It is vacuous, intelligent, and free from obscurity" refers to the spirit of a thing-event; the "(it) embraces all the principles" means there being many sequential principles in the spirit; the "(it is) ready for dealing with the myriad things" is what emanates from the sequential principles?

Answer: You need not say it that way, but you should know what the illustrious virtue is and then make efforts in person so as to get rid of the cover over it caused by the partial endowment of vital force and material desires. If you can preserve your mind which is vacuous, intelligent, and free from obscurity, that will be enough for it to embrace all the principles and deal with the myriad things, which means that you will have illustrated your illustrious virtue. If you do nothing but explain "It is vacuous, intelligent, and free from obscurity," "(it) embraces all the principles," and "(it is) ready for dealing with the myriad things," it is of no use.

Further question: Is reading books the most important of the efforts called for by illustrating illustrious virtue?

Answer: Reading books is, of course, necessary. As for what is carried in the books, you can try to understand it by reading them; as for what is not carried in them, you can try to understand it by considering the events in practice; as for the events which did not exist in ancient times, you can try to understand them by considering the current times. Probably, the so called illustrious virtue is nothing but a bright thing-event. It is comparable to a torch given to me by someone else, which, when I shine it over things, lightens all of them. But when I let the torch die, I let my illustrious virtue be benighted. If I have the torch to be rekindled, I bring my illustrious virtue bright again. The so called illustrating illustrious virtue entails investigating things, extending knowledge, making thought sincere, rectifying the mind, and cultivating oneself. None of the five events should be absent. If one of them is absent, the virtue will not be bright completely. Probably, extending knowledge and investigating things are intended to know it clearly and making thought sincere, rectifying the mind, and cultivating oneself aim to conduct it definitely. Nevertheless, to illustrate one's illustrious virtue, he must make uninterrupted effort so that it remains constantly illustrious. If there is any incompleteness in his knowledge, any thing uninvestigated to the utmost, any moment of insincere thought, any instant of being devoid of upright mind, or any period of time of wanting self-cultivation, the illustrious virtue will be benighted again. Only with no knowledge left incomplete, no thing left uninvestigated, no thought left insincere, no mind left not rectified, and no self left not cultivated, can we say one has made effort to the utmost to illustrate his illustrious virtue. [Tao]

86 问："大学注言：'其体虚灵而不昧；其用鉴照而不遗。'此二句是说心，说德?"曰："心、德皆在其中，更子细看。"又问："德是心中之理否?"曰："便是心中许多道理，光明鉴照，毫发不差。"宇。

Someone asked, "Your annotation of the *Great Learning* says 'Its substance is vacuous, intelligent, and free from obscurity and its function is like a mirror reflecting things, leaving none of them unreflected.' Does this sentence refer to mind or virtue?" The Master answered, "Both mind and virtue are included. Please read it more carefully." The questioner further asked, "Is virtue the principle which dwells in the mind?" He replied, "It means that there dwell in the mind many principles, which are as bright and clear as a mirror, reflecting things exactly without the least distortion." [Yu]

87 "明德者，人之所得乎天，而虚灵不昧，以具众理而应万事者也。"禅家则但以虚灵不昧者为性，而无以具众理以下之事。僩。

"Conferred on humankind by Heaven, the illustrious virtue is vacuous, intelligent, and free from obscurity, which embraces all the principles and is ready to deal with the myriad events." (*Interpretation*) The Chan Buddhism only takes that which is vacuous, intelligent, and free from obscurity as nature, which does not touch upon its embracing all the principles and being ready to deal with the myriad events. [Xian]

88 问："'学者当因其所发而遂明之'，是如何?"曰："人固有理会得处，如孝于亲，友于弟；如水之必寒，火之必热，不可谓他不知。但须去致极其知，因那理会得底，推之于理会不得底，自浅以至深，自近以至远。"又曰："因其已知之理而益穷之，以求至乎其极。"广。

Question: What do you mean when you say "A learner should start from its emanation and further make it be illustrious (in your *Interpretation*)?"

Answer: It is true that there are many events one can understand, such as being filial to his parents and fraternal to his younger brother, and as water being cold and fire being hot, and it should not be said that he does not know such events. However, he should extend his knowledge to the utmost and deduce what he has not understood by considering what he has understood, from the shallow to the deepest and from the near to the farthest.

He added, "From the principles he has known, he should inquire more and more principles in pursuit of knowing them to the utmost. " [Guang]

89 问：" '大学之道，在明明德'。此'明德'，莫是'天生德于予'之'德'？"曰："莫如此问，只理会明德是我身上甚么物事。某若理会不得，便应公'是"天生德于予"之"德"'，公便两下都理会不得。且只就身上理会，莫又引一句来问。如此，只是纸上去讨。"又曰："此明德是天之予我者，莫令污秽，当常常有以明之。"襄。

Question: In "What the *Great Learning* teaches is to illustrate illustrious virtue," (*Great Learning*, 1) does this "illustrious virtue" mean the same as the virtue in "Heaven produced the virtue that is in me" (*Analects*, 7:23)?

Answer: Do not ask such a question. Try only to understand what the illustrious is in yourself. If I did not understand it, I would answer you, "Yes, it is the same as the virtue in 'Heaven produced the virtue that is in me. '" But in that case you would not understand either side. Just strive to understand it in regard to yourself and do not cite another sentence and ask a question like that. Or else, you would have to look for its meaning by depending on what is on paper.

Further answer: The illustrious virtue is conferred on humankind by Heaven and one should prevent it from being contaminated and make constant efforts to keep it illustrious as ever. [Xiang]

90 问：" '明明德' 意思，以平旦验之，亦见得于天者未尝不明。"曰："不要如此看。且就明德上说，如何又引别意思证？读书最不要如此。"贺孙遂就明德上推说。曰："须是更仔细，将心体验。不然，皆是闲说。"贺孙。

I asked, "As regards the meaning of 'to illustrate illustrious virtue,' by drawing an analogy between it and the daybreak, I can also know that what is conferred by Heaven is never benighted. (What do you think about it?)" The Master answered, "Do not read it that way. You just try to understand it by the 'illustrious virtue' itself, and do not fetch something else to verify it. You should avoid that way of reading books." Then I tried to deduce from the 'illustrious virtue' itself. He said, "You should be more careful and experience it with your mind. Otherwise, all is empty talk." [Hesun]

91 敬子说"明明德"。曰:"大纲也是如此。只是说得恁地孤单,也不得。且去子细看。圣人说这三句,也且大概恁地说,到下面方说平天下至格物八者,便是明德新民底工夫。就此八者理会得透彻,明德、新民都在这里。而今且去子细看,都未要把自家言语意思去搀他底。公说胸中有个分晓底,少间捉摸不着,私意便从这里生,便去穿凿。而今且去熟看那解,看得细字分晓了,便晓得大字,便与道理相近。道理在那无字处自然见得。而今且说格物这个事理,当初甚处得来? 如今如何安顿它? 逐一只是虚心去看万物之理,看日用常行之理,看圣贤所言之理。"夔孙。

Jingzi 敬子 (courtesy name of Li Fan 李燔 [1163 – 1232], a disciple of Zhu's) talked about an explanation (in *Interpretation*) of "to illustrate illustrious virtue." The Master said, "It is similar to the guideline informed by book of the *Great Learning*. But it will not do if it is just discoursed in too isolated and simplified a way. Read it carefully. The sage says the beginning sentence of the text only in a general manner and in a later part he dwells on the eight events from bringing peace to the empire to investigating things, which call for efforts to illustrate illustrious virtue and renovate the people. If you can understand the eight clearly, you will know they are all concerned with illustrating illustrious virtue and renovating the people. Now, read it carefully and do not mix your private opinion with its meaning. You said that, though you had gained some understanding in your mind, you soon had nowhere to find it. That is because you got some private opinion by which to impose on its meaning something farfetched. Now, just read carefully the explanation and when you can see the smaller sino-graphs clearly, you will be able to understand the bigger ones①and that will be close to the truth. The truth which dwells where there are no words will naturally dawn on you. You should consider, for example, where the principle underlying the event of investigating things comes from originally and now where it should be put. Thus, with a vacuous mind, concentrate on seeing the principles underlying the myriad things and the events in daily life and the truths conveyed by the sages and worthies. " [Kuisun]

92 明德，谓本有此明德也。"孩提之童，无不知爱其亲；及其长也，无不知敬其兄。"其良知、良能，本自有之，只为私欲所蔽，故暗而不明。所谓"明明德"者，求所以明之也。譬如镜焉：本是个明底物，缘为尘昏，故不能照；须是磨去尘垢，然后镜复明也。"在新民"，明德而后能新民。德明。以下明德新民。

The "illustrious virtue" means there being originally the illustrious virtue. "Children carried in the arms all know to love their parents, and when they are grown a little, they all know to love their elder brothers. " (*Mencius*, 7A: 15) Their *liangzhi* 良知 (intuitive knowledge) and *liangneng* 良能 (intuitive ability) are what they possess originally, but later due to their selfish desires the two are benighted. The so called "to illustrate illustrious virtue" purports to bring illustriousness back to them. It is like a mirror, which is originally bright but later due to dust can not reflect things brightly. So the dust must be removed by polishing it, which will be bright once more. As for the "to renovate people," it can only be done after the illustrious virtue is illustrated. [Deming]

---

① This refers to the fact with *Interpretation of Great Learning* that, the words in the annotations and explanations are printed with a smaller size, while those in the text of *Great Learning*, bigger size.

93 或问："明德新民，还须自家德十分明后，方可去新民?"曰："不是自家德未明，便都不管着别人，又不是硬要去新他。若大段新民，须是德十分明，方能如此。若小小效验，自是自家这里如此，他人便自观感。'一家仁，一国兴仁；一家让，一国兴让'，自是如此。"子蒙。

Someone asked, "Does the 'to illustrate illustrious virtue and to renovate people' mean that one's virtue has to be illustrious to the full before he sets about renovating people?" The Master answered, "It does not mean that, since one's own virtue has not been illustrious, he just ignores others, nor does it mean that he is forced to renovate others. With regard to renovating people on a large scale, it requires that the renovator's virtue should be illustrious to the full. But in the case of a person, if his virtue is illustrious, naturally he will make a positive image to others. That is what is meant by 'From the loving example of one family, a whole state becomes loving, and from its courtesies, the whole state becomes courteous.' (*Great Learning*, 11)" [Zimeng]

94 问："明德新民，在我有以新之。至民之明其明德，却又在它?"曰："虽说是明己德，新民德，然其意自可参见。'明明德于天下'，自新以新其民，可知。"宇。

Someone asked, "'To illustrate illustrious virtue and to renovate people' means renovating them with what one has, but when you say the people's illustrating their illustrious virtues, do you mean renovating them with something else?" The Master answered, "Though it is said to illustrate one's own virtue and to renovate people's virtues, their meanings are mutually revealing. It can be known that '(The ancients who wished) to illustrate illustrious virtue throughout the empire' means renovating themselves and thereby renovating the people at large." [Yu]

95 蜚卿问："新民，莫是'修道之谓教'，有以新之否?"曰："'道之以德'，是'明明德'；'齐之以礼'，是以礼新民，也是'修道之谓教'。有礼乐、法度、政刑，使之去旧污也。"骧。

Feiqing asked, "In regard to 'to renovate people,' as said in the *Doctrine of the Mean*, 'The cultivation of the Way is called instruction,' and thereby will there be anything by which to renovate them?" The Master answered, "'Lead them by virtue' (*Analects*, 2：3) means illustrating illustrious virtue and 'make them uniform by the rules of propriety' (*Analects*, 2：3) means renovating people with the rules of propriety, which is also implied by 'The cultivation of the Way is called instruction.' By means of the rites and music, the laws, and the punishments for violation of the laws, their blemishes can be removed from them." [Xiang]

96 至善，只是十分是处。贺孙。以下止至善。

"The highest excellence" means nothing but the good to the greatest extent. [Hesun] The following conversations are concerned with the highest excellence.

97 至善，犹今人言极好。方子。

"The highest excellence" is equivalent to the extremely good we say today. [Fangzi]

98 凡曰善者，固是好。然方是好事，未是极好处。必到极处，便是道理十分尽头，无一毫不尽，故曰至善。僩。

Whatever is said as excellence refers to, of course, the good, but not the extremely good. Only when it reaches the extreme where the principle is in the perfect state, free from an iota of imperfection, can it be said as the highest excellence. [Xian]

99 至善是极好处。且如孝：冬温夏清，昏定晨省，虽然是孝底事，然须是能'听于无声，视于无形'，方始是尽得所谓孝。履孙。

"The highest excellence" refers to the state of being extremely good. For example, as regards filial piety, it is true that, if one can adjust everything (for his parents' repose) in the evening, and inquire (about their health) in the morning, his is a case of being filial, but only when he can "hear (his parents) when there is no voice from them and see them when they are not actually there" (*Record of Rites*) can he be said as being filial to the greatest extent. 〔Lüsun〕

100 至善是个最好处。若十件事做得九件是，一件不尽，亦不是至善。震。

By "the highest excellence" is meant that which the perfect is in. For ten events, if one can do nine of them perfectly yet fails to do one that way, he does not reach the state of the highest excellence. 〔Zhen〕①

101 说一个"止"字，又说一个"至"字，直是要到那极至处而后止。故曰：'君子无所不用其极'也。德明。

In "to rest in the highest excellence" (*zhiyu zhishan* 止于至善), the *zhi* 止 (to rest) is used and, after it, the *zhi* 至 (highest) appears. They mean not resting until the highest is reached. Therefore, it is said that "The Superior Man in everything uses his utmost endeavors." (*Great Learning*, 6). 〔Deming〕

102 善，须是至善始得。如通书"纯粹至善"，亦是。泳。

The pursuit of excellence should not rest until attaining the highest excellence. The *chuncui zhishan* 纯粹至善 (pure and perfectly good) mentioned in *Penetrating the Classic of Change* (by Zhou Dunyi) means also the same. 〔Yong (泳)〕

103 问："'必至于是而不迁'，如何？"曰："未至其地，则求其至；既至其地，则不当迁动而之它也。"德明。

Question: "It must be attaining the highest excellence and holding onto it, never subject to movability." How is that?

Answer: When one has not attained that realm, he has kept on pursuing that attainment, and when he has attained it, he should not make any moving elsewhere. 〔Deming〕

104 问："'止于至善'，向承教，以为君止于仁，臣止于敬，各止

---

① Zhong Zhen 钟震 (courtesy name Chunbo 春伯)

其所而行其所止之道。知此而能定。今日先生语窦文卿，又云：'"坐如尸"，坐时止也；"立如齐"，立时止也。'岂以自君臣父子推之于万事，无不各有其止？"曰："固然。'定公问君使臣，臣事君。子曰："君使臣以礼；臣事君以忠。"'君与臣，是所止之处；礼与忠，是其所止之善。又如'视思明，听思聪，色思温，貌思恭'之属，无不皆然。"德明。

Question：With respect to "to rest in the highest excellence," you, sir, taught me that the sovereign rests in benevolence and the minister rests in respectfulness, so that they each rest in where they should rest and conduct themselves by obeying the rule which requires them to rest therein. Knowing that, they each are able to settle themselves down properly. Today, when you taught Dou Wenqing 窦文卿 (i. e. Dou Congzhou 窦从周), you said, "The 'If a man be sitting, let him do so as a personator of the deceased' (*Record of Rites*) means the stillness of one when he is seated; the 'If he be standing, let him do so (reverently), as in sacrificing,'[1] (*Record of Rites*) the stillness of one when he is standing. " Could it be said that, when where the myriad events each rest is deduced from where the sovereign and minister and the father and son rest, we know that they each have their state in which to rest?

Answer：Yes, of course. For example, " The Duke Ding asked Confucius how a sovereign should employ his ministers and how ministers should serve their sovereign. Confucius replied, 'A sovereign should employ his minister according to the rules of propriety and ministers should serve their sovereign with loyalty. '" (*Analects*, 3：19) The sovereign and the ministers represent where they should rest, respectively, and the rules of propriety and loyalty are the goodness in which they rest in, respectively. For another

---

[1] The English translation of the two citations from the *Record of Rites* is based on the version by J. Legge (http：//ctext. org/liji).

example, "In regard to the use of his eyes, he is anxious to see clearly. In regard to the use of his ears, he is anxious to hear distinctly. In regard to his countenance, he is anxious that it should be benign. In regard to his demeanor, he is anxious that it should be respectful. "[1] (*Analects*, 16: 10) Such things as these all have their places where they rest. [Deming]

105 问至善。先生云: "事理当然之极也。" "恐与伊川说 '艮其止, 止其所也' 之义一同。谓有物必有则, 如父止于慈, 子止于孝, 君止于仁, 臣止于敬, 万物庶事莫不各有其所。得其所则安, 失其所则悖。所谓 '止其所' 者, 即止于至善之地也。" 曰: "只是要如此。" 卓。

Someone asked about "the highest excellence. " The Master replied, "It means the matter-of-course extreme with regard to the principles underlying events. " The questioner responded, "I am afraid your explanation means the same as Yichuan's when he interpreted 'Resting in one's resting-point is resting in his proper place. '[2] According to him, events and things must entail rules over them, as manifested by the father who rests in kindness, the son who rests in filial piety, the sovereign who rests in benevolence, and the minister who rests in respectfulness. Thus, there is none of the myriad events and things but has a place in which to rest. Getting the place means complying with the principle, while losing the place means going counter to it. The so called 'resting in his proper place' implies resting in the place of the highest excellence. (How do you think?)" The Master answered, "It is only what they should be. " [Zhuo]

106 或问: "何谓明德?" 曰: "我之所得以生者, 有许多道理在

---

[1] The English translation of the two citations from the *Analects* is based on the version by J. Legge (http: //ctext. org/analects).

[2] Cited from "Tuanzhuan" 彖传 (Explanation of the Hexagram Judgment) of "Gen Gua" 艮卦 (Hexagram Gen) in the *Classic of Change*. The English translation is based on J. Legge's version (see http: //ctext. org/book-of-changes).

里，其光明处，乃所谓明德也。'明明德'者，是直指全体之妙。下面许多节目，皆是靠明德做去。"又问："既曰明德，又曰至善，何也?"曰："明得一分，便有一分；明得十分，便有十分；明得二十分，乃是极至处也。"又曰："明德是下手做，至善是行到极处。"又曰："至善虽不外乎明德，然明德亦有略略明者，须是止于那极至处。"铢。以下明德止至善。

Someone asked, "What is meant by the illustrious virtue?" The Master answered, "It is that which is endowed to humankind and in which there dwell many principles. As it is bright, so it is referred to as illustrious virtue. The 'to illustrate illustrious virtue' means the subtleness of it as an entirety, and the many items it involves are all conducted by depending on illustrious virtue." The questioner asked further, "Why 'illustrious virtue' and 'the highest excellence' are mentioned side by side?" The Master answered, "If one illustrates one tenth of the illustriousness, he gains one tenth of it and if he illustrates five tenth of it, he gains five tenth of it. When he illustrates ten tenth of it, he reaches the highest plane." He continued, "The 'illustrious virtue' means setting about doing, while 'the highest excellence,' reaching the extreme." He added, "Though the highest excellence bears on nothing but illustrious virtue, as far as virtue goes, one's virtue may be far from being illustrious, so one should not rest until he attains the highest excellence."

[Zhu] The following concerns the words from "illustrious virtue" to "the highest excellence."

107 大学只前面三句是纲领。如"孩提之童，无不知爱其亲；及其长也，无不知敬其兄"，此良心也。良心便是明德，止是事事各有个止处。如"坐如尸，立如齐"，坐立上须得如此，方止得。又如"视思明"以下，皆"止于至善"之意。大学须自格物入，格物从敬入最好。只敬，便能格物。敬是个莹彻底物事。今人却块坐了，相似昏倦，要须提撕着。提撕便敬；昏倦便肆，肆便不敬。德明。

Only the first sentence in the text of the *Great Learning* serves as the guideline. The *Mencius* (7A: 15) says "Children carried in the arms all know to love their parents, and when they are grown a little, they all know to love their elder brothers. " This indicates *liangxin* 良心 (intuitive mind), which is the illustrious virtue. The "to rest" means that every event or thing has a place where it should rest. As said in the *Record of Rites*, "If a man be sitting, let him do so as a personator of the deceased; if he be standing, let him do so (reverently), as in sacrificing," which manifests the way by which one should sit and stand so that he can rest in (the highest excellence of) sitting and standing. For another example, what the section beginning with "In regard to the use of his eyes, he is anxious to see clearly" in the *Analects* (16:10) conveys is what is meant by "to rest in the highest excellence. " In pursuing what the *Great Learning* teaches, one should enter for it from investigating things, for which he had better enter from seriousness (*jing* 敬). Only by seriousness is he able to investigate things. The seriousness is a thing-event which is lustrous and transparent. Now, learners just sit there like dull pieces, who seem sleepy and weary. They should keep brains sober. Being sober is indicative of seriousness, while being sleepy and weary manifests its opposite. [Deming]

108 问:"明德、至善,莫是一个否?"曰:"至善是明德中有此极至处。如君止于仁,臣止于敬,父止于慈,子止于孝,与国人交止于信,此所谓'在止于至善'。只是又当知如何而为止于仁,如何而止于敬,如何而止于慈孝,与国人交之信。这里便用究竟一个下工夫处。"景绍曰:"止,莫是止于此而不过否?"曰:"固是。过与不及,皆不济事。但仁敬慈孝,谁能到得这里?闻有不及者矣,未闻有过于此者也。如舜之命契,不过是欲使'父子有亲,君臣有义,夫妇有别,长幼有序,朋友有信',只是此五者。至于后来圣贤千言万语,只是欲明此而已。这道理,本是天之所以与我者,不为圣贤而有余,不为愚不肖而不足。但其间节目,须当讲学以明之,此所以读圣贤之书,须当知他下工夫处。今人只据他说一两字,便认以为圣贤之所以为圣贤者止此而已,都不穷究着实,殊不济事。且如论语相似:读'学而时习之',须求其所谓学者如何？如何谓之时习？既时习，如何便能说？'有朋自远方来'，朋友因甚而来自远方？我又何自而乐？须着一一与他考究。似此用工，初间虽觉得生受费力，久后读书甚易为工，却亦济事。"道夫。

Someone asked, "Does the illustrious virtue the same as the highest excellence?" The Master answered, "The highest excellence refers to the acme in the illustrious virtue. For example, the sovereign rests in benevolence, and the minister rests in respectfulness, the father rests in kindness, the son rests in filial piety, and one's association with his fellow countrymen rests in faithfulness. All these illustrate what is meant by 'to rest in the highest excellence.' But one should know what the sovereign should do to rest in benevolence, what the minister should do to rest in respectfulness, what the father should do to rest in kindness, what the son should do to rest in filial piety, and what one should do so that his association with his fellow countrymen rests in faithfulness, all of which bear on where it is to make efforts." Jingshao asked, "Does 'to rest' mean stopping somewhere and not getting beyond it?" The Master answered, "Yes, of course. Both to go beyond and to fall short are of no use. But who can reach benevolence, respectfulness, kindness, and filiality? Falling short has been often heard, but going beyond, never. For example, when Shun gave the details of his task to Xie, he said, 'Between father and son there should be affection; between sovereign and minister, righteousness; between husband and wife, attention to their separate functions; between old and young, a proper order; between friends, faithfulness,' (*Mencius*, 3A: 4) which are only five aspects. Later, the thousands of words said by the sages and worthies were intended to do nothing but elucidating those aspects. The principle is originally what is conferred by Heaven to human beings. Heaven does not confer more of it to a person because he is a sage or worthy, nor does it confer less of it to a person because he is a fool or unworthy. Nevertheless, the details of it should be clarified by pursuing learning. That is why a learner should read the books by the sages and worthies so as to know where to make efforts. Nowadays, people tend, only by reading a few words said by a sage, to think that the reason why he is a sage is no more than that. They do not exert themselves to see what the sage really means and consequently this is of no help at all to them. Take the *Analects* for example. When you read Confucius's 'to learn and to practice frequently what one has learned,' you should try to know what 'to learn' refers to and why 'to practice frequently' is said of 'what one has learned.' Since it is 'to practice frequently,' why can it be spoken of? As regards his 'to have friends coming from afar,' for what do his friends come from afar? For what does he feel delighted? You should pore over such questions one by one. If you make efforts in this way, despite the toil you endure at first, after a long time, you will feel it easy to read books well, which will be of much help to you." [Daofu]

109 "明明德"是知,"止于至善"是守。夫子曰:"知及之,仁能守之。"圣贤未尝不为两头底说话。如中庸所谓"择善固执",择善,便是理会知之事;固执便是理会守之事。至书论尧之德,便说'钦明',舜便说'浚哲文明,温恭允塞'。钦,是钦敬以自守;明,是其德之聪明。'浚哲文明',便有知底道理;'温恭允塞',便有守底道理。道夫。

"To illustrate illustrious virtue" pertains to knowing, while "to rest in the highest excellence," to holding. Confucius said, "By his knowledge, he is sufficient to attain it, and by his benevolence, he is able to hold onto it fast." (*Analects*, 15:33) The sage did not refrain from discourses with two ends. Another example is "choosing what is good and sticking to it firmly" said in the *Doctrine of the Mean* (22). The "choosing what is good" pertains to attaining knowledge, while "sticking to it firmly," to holding unto it fast. When the *Book of History* praises the virtue of Yao and that of Shun, it says "reverential and bright" and "profound, wise, accomplished, and intelligent; mild and courteous, and truly sincere," respectively. As regards the former, the "reverential" pertains to his holding, while the "bright," to his intelligence in knowing. As for the latter, the "profound, wise, accomplished, and intelligent" implies the principle of knowing, while "mild and courteous, and truly sincere" refers to the principle of holding. [Daofu]

110 问："新民如何止于至善?"曰："事事皆有至善处。"又曰："'善'字轻，'至'字重。"节。以下新民止至善。

Question: How can renovating the people rest in the highest excellence?

Answer: There is a place of the highest excellence in every event or thing.

Further answer: In terms of their reference, "the highest" outweighs "excellence." [Jie] The following conversations discourse on "to renovate the people" and "to rest in the highest excellence."

111 问："新民止于至善，只是要民修身行己，应事接物，无不曲当?"曰："虽不可使知之，亦当使由之，不出规矩准绳之外。"节。

Question: Does the "to renovate the people and to rest in the highest excellence" mean having the people to cultivate themselves and conduct themselves appropriately in coping with events and handling things?

Answer: Though the people may not be made to understand it, they may be made to follow the path of action, without transgressing what is right. [Jie]

112 "止于至善"，是包"在明明德，在新民"。己也要止于至善，人也要止于至善。盖天下只是一个道理，在他虽不能，在我之所以望他者，则不可不如是也。道夫。以下明德、新民、至善。

The "to rest in the highest excellence" includes "to illustrate illustrious virtue and to renovate the people." One should rest himself in the highest excellence and others also should rest in the highest excellence. Probably the same principle prevails across the world, and though on their part they are not able to do that, on his part, he should have to expect them to do that.

[Daofu] The following conversations concern illustrious virtue, renovating the people, and resting in the highest excellence.

113 明德、新民，二者皆要至于极处。明德，不是只略略地明德便了；新民，不是只略略地新得便休。须是要止于极至处。贺孙。

Both illustrating illustrious virtue and renovating the people should aim to reach their acmes. Illustrating illustrious virtue does not mean doing it cursorily, nor does renovating the people mean stopping at renewing them roughly. Both should aim to rest in the highest level. [Hesun]

114 问："至善，不是明德外别有所谓善，只就明德中到极处便是否？"曰："是。明德中也有至善，新民中也有至善，皆要到那极处。至善，随处皆有。修身中也有至善，必要到那尽处；齐家中也有至善，亦要到那尽处。至善，只是以其极言。不特是理会到极处，亦要做到极处。如'为人君，此于仁'，固是一个仁，然仁亦多般，须是随处看。如这事合当如此，是仁；那一事又合当如彼，亦是仁。若不理会，只管执一，便成一边去。如'为人臣，止于敬'，敬亦有多少般，不可只道擎跽曲拳便是敬。如尽忠不欺，陈善闭邪，纳君无过之地，皆是敬，皆当理会。若只执一，亦成一边去，安得谓之至善！至善只是些子恰好处。韩文公谓'轲之死不得其传'。自秦汉以来岂无人！亦只是无那至善，见不到十分极好处，做亦不做到十分极处。"淳。

Question: Does "the highest excellence" not mean there being something called good beyond the illustrious virtue, but mean that it is the acme of the illustrious virtue?

Answer: Yes. In the illustrious virtue dwells the highest excellence and in the renovating of the people dwells also the highest excellence, both being their acmes. Actually, there is the highest excellence everywhere. In cultivating oneself, its highest excellence means ascending to the loftiest plane, and in regulating one's family, it means doing that to the best extent. The highest excellence is said only with reference to the acme. It does not only mean the acme of understanding, but also that of practicing. For example, "As a sovereign, he rested in benevolence." (*Great Learning*, 7)

Though it is the same benevolence, it manifests itself in many forms, so one should observe them everywhere. If this event is what it should be, it manifests benevolence, and if that event is what it should be, it also manifests benevolence. If he does not observe and understand such manifestations but sticks rigidly to the one meaning, he will be one-sided. Likewise, in "As a minister, he rested in reverence," (*Great Learning*, 7) the reverence also takes many forms, so one should not take only "carrying (the memorandum tablet to court), kneeling, and bending the body reverentially" (*Zhuangzi*) as reverence. Being loyal and true to the sovereign, remonstrating with him so that he is free from faults, and carrying forward the good and avoiding the evil, these are all manifestations of reverence, which one should observe and understand. If he sticks rigidly to the one meaning, he will be one-sided and how can he be said as knowing the highest excellence? The highest excellence refers only to what is the most properly good. Han, (Han Yu, with the posthumous title) Duke Wen, said, "After Meng Ke (Mencius) passed away, the Way was not passed down." ("Yuan Dao" 原道 [Origin of the Way]) Could it be said that there were not men since Qin and Han dynasties? But since there was no embodiment of the highest excellence and they were not able to observe the extremely good, they could not make it to the best extent. [Chun (淳)]

115 明德，是我得之于天，而方寸中光明底物事。统而言之，仁义礼智。以其发见而言之，如恻隐、羞恶之类；以其见于实用言之，如事亲、从兄是也。如此等德，本不待自家明之。但从来为气禀所拘，物欲所蔽，一向昏昧，更不光明。而今却在挑剔揩磨出来，以复向来得之于天者，此便是"明明德"。我既是明得个明德，见他人为气禀物欲所昏，自家岂不恻然欲有以新之，使之亦如我挑剔揩磨，以革其向来气禀物欲之昏而复其得之于天者，此便是"新民"。然明德、新民，初非是人力私意所为，本自有一个当然之则，过之不可，不及亦不可。且以孝言之，孝是明德，然亦自有当然之则。不及则固不是，若是过其则，必有刲股之事。须是要到当然之则田地而不迁，此方是"止于至善"。泳。

The illustrious virtue is that which humankind receives from Heaven and which is the bright event-thing in his *fangcun* 方寸（heart［thought as the human organ of thinking］）. Overall speaking, it is benevolence, righteousness, propriety, and wisdom. In regard to its expressions, it manifests itself as the feeling of sadness and commiseration, shame and dislike, and the like. As regards its function in practice, it shows itself as a son serving his parents with filial piety, a younger brother complying with his elder brother, and the like. For one, originally, such virtue did not need his illustrating, but it has been restrained by his partial endowment of vital force and clouded by his material desires so much so that it has been benighted, giving no brightness at all. Now, he strives to wipe and polish it up so as to bring it back to its state conferred originally by Heaven? That is what is meant by illustrating the illustrious virtue. When I have illustrated my own illustrious virtue, if I see someone else be benighted by his endowed vital force and material desires, how can I not feel grieved and not long to renovate him so that he is willing to wipe and polish it up, get free from the benightedness caused by his endowed vital force and material desires, and restore its state conferred originally by Heaven? That is meant by renovating the people. However, initially, both illustrating the illustrious virtue and renovating the people are not what men intend privately to do by their efforts, so there is naturally a matter-of-course rule, which one should not go beyond or fall short of. Take filial piety for example. Filial piety is an illustrious virtue, yet it is governed by its matter-of-course rule. It is true that falling short of it is not right, but going beyond it would entail such an absurdity as one cutting flesh from his thigh for curing his parents' disease. What "to rest in the highest excellence" means is that one should strive to reach where the matter-of-course rule governs and observe it unswervingly. ［Yong（泳）］

116 明德、新民，皆当止于至善。不及于止，则是未当止而止；当止而不止，则是过其所止；能止而不久，则是失其所止。儡。

Both illustrating illustrious virtue and renovating the people should aim to rest in the highest excellence. If they fail to rest in that, they rest where they should not rest. If they should rest but they do not, they go beyond where they should rest. If they can rest yet can not last, they lose that in which they rest. [Xian]

117 "明德新民，皆当止于极好处。止之为言，未到此便住，不可谓止；到得此而不能守，亦不可言止。止者，止于是而不迁之意。" 或问："明明德是自己事，可以做得到极好处。若新民则在人，如何得他到极好处？" 曰："且教自家先明得尽，然后渐民以仁，摩民以义。如孟子所谓'劳之，来之，匡之，直之，辅之，翼之，又从而振德之'。如此变化他，自然解到极好处。" 铢。

The Master said, "Both illustrating the illustrious virtue and renovating the people should rest in the extremely good. As regards the 'rest,' if one stops doing them before reaching that acme, that is not what is referred to as 'rest.' The 'rest' means resting there without any movability." Someone asked, "One's illustrating the illustrious virtue is his own business and he can try his best to attain its acme. As for renovating the people, it involves other people, so how to have them to pursue and reach the extremely good?" The Master answered, "The first thing one should do is to illustrate his own illustrious virtue to the fullest extent. Then he will be in a position to enhance them with benevolence gradually and rub them with righteousness little by little. As the *Mencius* (3A: 4) said, 'Encourage them, lead them on, rectify them, straighten them, help them, and give them wings, thus causing them to become possessors of themselves. Then follow this up by stimulating them, and conferring benefits on them.'① In this way, they can be

---

① The translation of the citation from *Mencius* is based on a version by J. Legge (see http://ctext.org/mengzi).

transformed and naturally they will exert themselves to pursue the extremely good. " 〔Zhu〕

118 或问："明德可以止于至善，新民如何得他止于至善?" 曰："若是新民而未止于至善，亦是自家有所未到。若使圣人在上，便自有个处置。" 又问："夫子非不明德，其历诸国，岂不欲春秋之民皆止于至善? 到他不从，圣人也无可奈何。" 曰："若使圣人得位，则必须绥来动和。" 又云："此是说理，理必须是如此。且如'致中和，天地位，万物育'。然尧有九年之水，想有多少不育之物。大德必得名位禄寿，也岂个个如此! 只是理必如此。" 胡泳。

Question: Illustrating illustrious virtue can ultimately rest in the highest excellence. How can the renovating people be accomplished so that it rests in the highest excellence?

Answer: If the renovating people fails to rest in the highest excellence, that means the renovator's failure to reach the acme of illustrating his illustrious virtue. If the renovator was the sage, he would be able to handle it well.

Further question: Confucius is not a sage who failed to illustrate his illustrious virtue. Didn't he, who travelled in the various states, desire to have the people renovated so that they all could rest in the highest excellence? But when they did not follow him, sage as he was, he had no way to renovate them. (What do you think?)

Answer: If the sage was bestowed the position, he would surely be able to bring about peace, "make them happy, and forthwith multitudes would resort to his dominions," and "stimulate them, and forthwith they would be harmonious. " (*Analects*, 19: 25)

Further answer: That is said with regard to the principle. In principle, that must go that way. As said in the *Doctrine of the Mean* (1), "Let the states of equilibrium and harmony exist in perfection, and a happy order will prevail throughout Heaven and Earth, and all things will be nourished and flourished. " However, Yao suffered nine years of floods, for which we can imagine how many things had not been nourished and flourished. Whoever is great in virtue should be conferred with fame and position, emolument and longevity, but how can it be possible that each of them is conferred with them? However, in principle, they should be conferred with them. [Hu Yong]

119 明明德，便要如汤之日新；新民，便要如文王之"周虽旧邦，其命维新"。各求止于至善之地而后止也。德明。

To illustrate illustrious virtue is to renovate oneself from day to day as Tang, the founder of Shang Dynasty, did. To renovate the people is to do as the King Wen of Zhou, whose state, "although an ancient one, was conferred with the ordinance which was new. " (*Great Learning*, 6) Either means pursuing attainment of the realm of the supremely good before resting there. [Deming]

120 欲新民，而不止于至善，是"不以尧之所以治民者治民"也。明明德，是欲去长安；止于至善，是已到长安也。拱寿。

To renovate the people, yet not to aim to rest in the highest excellence, is a case of "He who does not rule his people as Yao ruled his. " (*Mencius*, 4A：2) Illustrating the illustrious virtue is comparable to wishing to reach Chang'an①, while resting in the highest excellence, to arriving actually at that destination. [Gongshou]②

121 刘源问"知止而后有定"。曰："此一节，只是说大概效验如此。'在明明德，在新民，在止于至善'，却是做工夫处。"雉。以下知止有定。

Liu Yuan 刘源 (dates unknown, a disciple of Zhu's) asked about

---

① Chang'an 长安, literally meaning lasting peace and stability, is the name of an ancient capital for thirteen dynasties and political regimes in feudal China. It was located roughly in what is now Xi'an, Shaanxi province, China.

② Dong Gongshou 董拱寿 (courtesy name Renshu 仁叔).

"Knowing the point where to rest, one's object of pursuit is then *ding* 定 (determined)." (*Great Learning*, 1) The Master answered, "This part only means that, basically speaking, that is the desired result. By contrast, the 'to illustrate illustrious virtue, to renovate the people, and to rest in the highest excellence' before it in the text means where efforts should be made." ［Zhi］The following discourses on "The point where to rest being known, the object of pursuit is then determined."

122 "在止于至善"。至者，天理人心之极致。盖其本于天理，验于人心，即事即物而无所不在。吾能各知其止，则事事物物莫不各有定理，而分位、界限为不差矣。端蒙。

As regards "to rest in the highest excellence," "the highest" implies the supreme realm of heavenly principle and human mind. Probably the highest excellence is originated in the heavenly principle and testified by the human mind, which dwells in every one of events and things. If I know that they each rest where they should rest, then there is no one of them which has not its own determined principle, with its extent and boundary free from faults. ［Duanmeng］

123 须是灼然知得物理当止之处，心自会定。砥。

Only after one knows brilliantly where a thing, as its principle requires, should rest will one's mind be naturally determined (with regard to it). ［Di］

124 问："'知止而后有定'，须是物格、知至以后，方能如此。若未能物格、知至，只得且随所知分量而守之否？"曰："物格、知至也无顿断。都知到尽处了，方能知止有定。只这一事上知得尽，则此一事便知得当止处。无缘便要尽底都晓得了，方知止有定。不成知未到尽头，只恁地鹘突呆在这里，不知个做工夫处！这个各随人浅深。固是要知到尽处方好，只是未能如此，且随你知得者，只管定去。如人行路，今日行得这一条路，则此一条路便知得熟了，便有定了。其它路皆要如此知得分明。所以圣人之教，只要人只管会将去。"又曰："这道理无它，只怕人等待。事到面前，便理会得去做，无有不得者。只怕等待，所以说：'需者，事之贼也！'"又曰："'需者，事之贼也！'若是等待，终误事去。"又曰："事事要理会。便是人说一句话，也要思量他怎生如此说；做一篇没紧要文字，也须思量他怎生如此做。"偰。

Someone asked, "With respect to 'Knowing the point where to rest, one's object of pursuit is then determined,' that is possible only after things have been investigated and knowledge has been extended to the utmost. If one has not investigated things and has not extended his knowledge to the utmost, then he has no alternative but to hold onto the extent to which he has extended his knowledge. (Is this right?)" The Master answered, "The investigation of things and extension of knowledge should not be made subject to interruption. Only when one has extended his knowledge to the utmost can he know the point where to rest and the object of pursuit which is determined. In regard to a specific thing, when he has extended his knowledge of it to the utmost, he will know the point where to rest in it. It does not mean that one can not know the object of pursuit which is determined until he gains knowledge of everything. Could it be that, having not extended his knowledge to the utmost, now one does nothing but staying here, unaware of making more efforts? The extent marking the extension of knowledge to the utmost varies with different persons. It is of course good that one can reach where his knowledge is extended to the utmost, but when he has not been able to do that, he should, by what he has known, determine unhesitatingly the object of his pursuit. It is like a man walking. When he walks along this road today, he will get familiar with it and thus have his determined destination. For other roads, he can also get familiar with them in the same way. That is why the sages taught others to do nothing but seeking for understanding of things and events." He continued, "The principle is simple, but what one should avoid is waiting. When facing events, just try to do them for understanding them, and there will be no one who does not gain it. What causes anxiety is waiting, so it is said 'Waiting is a thief of events.'"① He went on, "As meant by 'Waiting is a thief of events,' if waiting only, one would end up going nowhere." He added, "Every thing or event should be understood. Even if it is an event of someone saying something, it should be considered that why he said that. For a piece of writing which is insignificant, it should be considered also that why its writer wrote it."[Xian]

125 "知止而后有定"，须是事事物物都理会得尽，而后有定。若只理会得一事一物，明日别有一件，便理会不得。这个道理须是理会得五六分以上，方见得这边重，那边轻，后面便也易了。而今未理会到半截以上，所以费力。须是逐一理会，少间多了，渐会贯通，两个合做一个，少间又七八个合做一个，便都一齐通透了。伊川说"贯通"字最妙。若不是他自会如此，如何说出这字！贺孙。

By "Knowing the point where to rest, one's object of pursuit is then determined" is meant that one should understand all things and events to the utmost before his object of pursuit is determined. If he has only understood one thing or one event, when there occurs something new tomorrow, he will be unable to understand it. As regards the principle, one can not know that this aspect outweighs that until he understands things and events to the five or six tenth extent to the utmost. Then the other things and events will become easy for him to understand. Now that he has not reached that much, he has felt hard naturally. He should try to understand them one by one and before long he will be familiar with more and more and get a coherent understanding of them. After that, he will be in a position to deal with two as one and soon seven or eight as one, and finally attain a thorough understanding of all. Yichuan said, "The word 'thorough' is the most wonderful." If he had not had a coherent understanding of things, how could he have said that word?

---

① Recorded in "Aigong Shisi Nian" 哀公十四年 (Duke Ai, Fourteenth Year) of *Zuozhuan* 左传 (Zuo's Explanation of the *Spring and Autumn Annals*).

［Hesun］

126 "知止而后有定"，必谓有定，不谓能定，故知是物有定说。振。

In "Knowing the point where to rest, one's object of pursuit is then determined," it is the "object of pursuit is then determined," but not the "object of pursuit can then be determined." Thus, we know that it is a theory of there being something determined in a thing. ［Zhen］

127 未知止，固用做工夫，但费把捉。已知止，则为力也易。僩。

Before knowing the point where to rest, one should, of course, make efforts, but it is not easy for the efforts to take effect. After knowing the point where to rest, it becomes easy to make efforts effectively. ［Xian］

128 定亦自有浅深：如学者思虑凝定，亦是定；如道理都见得彻，各止其所，亦是定。只此地位已高。端蒙。

The "determinedness" varies naturally in terms of depth. For example, a scholar, while contemplating something, concentrates on it, which is a determined state; while seeing the principles thoroughly and knowing the points where to rest also point to a determined state. But the latter is higher that the former. ［Duanmeng］

129 问"定而后能静"。曰："定，是见得事事物物上千头百绪皆有定理；静，只就自家一个心上说。"贺孙。以下定静。

When asked about "With that determinedness, a calm *jing* 静 (unperturbedness) can be attained," (*Great Learning*, 1) the Master replied, "The 'determinedness' means seeing determined principles underlying all manifestations of the myriad things and events, while 'unperturbedness' is meant only in regard to one's own mind." ［Hesun］
The following is concerned with determinedness and unperturbedness.

130 定以理言，故曰有；静以心言，故曰能。义刚。

The "determinedness" is concerned with the principles, so it is said as "is (determined)," whereas the "unperturbedness" is concerned with the mind, so it is said as "can (be attained). " [Yigang]

131 定是理，静在心。既定于理，心便会静。若不定于理，则此心只是东去西走。泳。

The "determinedness" concerns the principles, while the "unperturbedness" lies in the mind. Now that there is determinedness with regard to the principles, the mind will become unperturbed. Otherwise, the mind can only be wandering hither or thither. [Yong (泳)]

132 问："章句云：'外物不能摇，故静。'旧说又有'异端不能惑'之语。窃谓将二句参看，尤见得静意。"曰："此皆外来意。凡立说须宽，方流转，不得局定。"德明。

Question: Your *Interpretation* says, "Since it can not be swayed by external things, it is said as being unperturbed. " In an older explanation, you mentioned "It is free from puzzlement caused by heretic doctrines. " In my humble opinion, by reading the two sentences and making cross reference to each other, a learner can see better what is meant by the "unperturbedness. " (How do you think?)

Answer: Both are outside explanations of it. Generally, the formation of a doctrine should allow for a broad room, where its constituents can fit one another in a coherent way, and thus get free from restriction and stagnation. [Deming]

133 问："大学之静与伊川'静中有动'之'静'，同否？"曰："未须如此说。如此等处，未到那里，不要理会。少顷都打乱了，和理会得处，也理会不得去。"士毅。

Question: Is the *jing* (unperturbedness) discoursed in the *Great Learning* the same as that *jing* Yichuan said in his "There is activity in *jing* (tranquility)"?

Answer: There is no need to compare them. It is far-fetched and should be avoided, or else you will soon feel puzzled and confused. Though there should be some point which needs understanding in that regard, in this stage of learning, you will find it hardly understandable. 〔Shiyi〕

134 问"静而后能安"。曰:"安,只是无巇嵬之意。才不纷扰,便安。"问:"如此,则静与安无分别。"曰:"二字自有浅深。"德明。以下静安。

Question: What is meant by the *an* 安 (tranquil repose) in "To that unperturbedness there will succeed a tranquil repose"? (*Great Learning*, 1)

Answer: The "tranquil repose" means being free from disturbance. As soon as one gets free from disturbance, he enters a tranquil repose.

Further question: Then, is there any difference between the unperturbedness and the tranquil repose?

Answer: They are different in terms of depth. 〔Deming〕 The following discourses on "unperturbedness" and "tranquil repose."

135 问:"'安,谓所处而安。'莫是把捉得定时,处事自不为事物所移否?"曰:"这个本是一意。但静是就心上说,安是就身上说。而今人心才不静时,虽有意去安顿那物事,自是不安。若是心静,方解去区处,方解稳当。"义刚。

Question: You, sir, said "The tranquil repose means that one feels tranquil where he is." Does the tranquil repose mean that when one has grasped the principle in a determined way he will naturally not be moved by things and events when dealing with them?

Answer: Essentially, it means the same as unperturbedness, but the tranquil repose is said of the body, while unperturbedness is said of the mind. When one's mind has still not reached the unperturbed state, though desiring to set his mind on a certain thing or event, he can not feel that tranquil repose. If his mind gets unperturbedness, he will be able to handle a thing or event and do it in a secure way. 〔Yigang〕

136 既静,则外物自然无以动其心;既安,则所处而皆当。看打做那里去,都移易他不得。道夫。

Now that one reaches the unperturbed state, the external things can naturally by no means move his mind; now that he attains a tranquil repose, the ways by which he deals with things are all proper. No matter how things go, he will not be movable. [Daofu]

137 问："'静而后能安'，是在贫贱，在患难皆安否？"曰："此心若不静，这里坐也坐不得，那里坐也坐不得。"宇。

Question: Does "To that unperturbedness there will succeed a tranquil repose" mean that one can attain a tranquil repose even when he is poor and lowly and suffers trials and tribulations?

Answer: It means that if one's mind has not entered the unperturbed state, he will not be able to sit calmly here or there. [Yu]

138 能安者，以地位言之也。在此则此安，在彼则彼安；在富贵亦安，在贫贱亦安。节。

One's attainment of a tranquil repose is said in regard to where he is. Here in this place, he attains his tranquil repose here, while there in that place he attains it there. He can attain his tranquil repose in wealth and rank, and he can also attain it in poverty and lowliness. [Jie]

139 问："知止章中所谓定、静、安，终未深莹。"曰："知止，只是识得一个去处。既已识得，即心中便定，更不他求。如求之彼，又求之此，即是未定。'定而后能静，静而后能安'，亦相去不远，但有深浅耳。与中庸动、变、化相类，皆不甚相远。"问："先生于此段词义，望加详数语，使学者易晓。"曰："此处亦未是紧切处，其它亦无可说。"德明。定、静、安。

Question: In the part concerned with knowing the point where to rest, I have still not understood in an in-depth way what the determinedness, unperturbedness, and tranquil repose mean. (Could you explain them to me?)

Answer: Knowing the point where to rest means only that one should know where he should go. If he has known that, he has got a determined object for his pursuit in his mind so that he would not seek after something else. If he seeks for this and meanwhile for that, it indicates his indeterminacy in regard to that object. What is meant by "that being determined, a calm unperturbedness may be attained. To that unperturbedness there will succeed a tranquil repose" is not far from that, but is different in terms of depth. Their meanings are close to those of *dong* 动 (activity), *bian* 变 (change) and *hua* 化 (transformation) said in the *Doctrine of the Mean.*

Further question: I hope that you, sir, add several more sentences to the existent ones explaining that part by which learners may find it more readily understandable.

Answer: This is not the very important part and actually I have nothing more to say. 〔Deing〕The following is concerned with "determinedness," "unperturbedness," and "tranquil repose."

140 定、静、安颇相似。定，谓所止各有定理；静，谓遇物来能不动；安，谓随所寓而安，盖深于静也。去伪。

Conceptually, the determinedness, unperturbedness, and tranquil repose are quite similar. For one, the determinedness means that the points where to rest each have their determined principles; the unperturbedness, that with the in-coming of things he can not be moved by them; the tranquil repose, that he can settle himself down in a tranquil repose, which is probably deeper in its reference than unperturbedness. 〔Quwei〕

141 定、静、安三字大略相类。然定是心中知"为人君止于仁，为人臣止于敬"。心下有个定理，便别无胶扰，自然是静。如此，则随所处而安。碏。

The determinedness, unperturbedness, and tranquil repose are quite similar in their basic meanings. Nevertheless, the determinedness means knowing "As a sovereign, he rests in benevolence; as a minister, he rests in reverence" (*Great Learning*, 7) in the mind. If there is a determined principle in the mind, naturally he can not be unperturbed, free from obsessing from other things. Therefore, wherever he is, he can have a tranquil repose. [Xun]

142 知止而后有定，如行路一般。若知得是从那一路去，则心中自是定，更无疑惑。既无疑惑，则心便静；心既静，便贴贴地，便是安。既安，则自然此心专一，事至物来，思虑自无不通透。若心未能静安，则总是胡思乱想，如何是能虑！贺孙。知止、定、静、安、虑。

What is meant by "Knowing the point where to rest, one's object of pursuit is then determined" is comparable to walking to a destination. If one knows well the path to that destination, his mind is naturally determined, free from any puzzlement. With the freedom from puzzlement, his mind will be in a state of unperturbedness; with the unperturbedness, he will feel placid, which is a tranquil repose. With the tranquil repose, his mind will naturally be concentrated on things and events. When things and events come up, he will naturally penetrate them with a thorough understanding. Without mental placidity, he will go off into wild flights of fancy, and then how can he focus his mind on careful deliberation of things and events? [Hesun] Knowing the point where to rest, determinedness, unperturbedness, tranquil repose, and deliberation.

143 定，对动而言。初知所止，是动底方定，方不走作，如水之初定。静则定得来久，物不能挠，处山林亦静，处廛市亦静。安，则静者广，无所适而不安。静固安，动亦安，看处甚事皆安然不挠。安然后能虑。今人心中摇漾不定迭，还能处得事否？虑者，思之精审也。人之处事，于丛冗急遽之际而不错乱者，非安不能。圣人言虽不多，推出来便有许多说话，在人细看之耳。侗。

The "determinedness" is said in relation to activity. When one knows at first the point where to rest, that means his activity is initially determined and just begins to get immune from contortions, which is like the surging water just calming down. The "unperturbedness" means that his determinedness has been fortified after a long time so that external things can not disturb him. Thus, while in a wooded mountain, he is able to be in an unperturbed state, and when in a market of hustle and bustle, he is also able to be in an unperturbed state. The "tranquil repose" means his extensive unperturbedness, and that wherever he is, he can be in a tranquil repose. With unperturbedness, he can, of course, be in a tranquil repose, and with activity, he can also be in it. Thus, whatever events he deals with, he can be in the tranquil repose, free from any disturbance. With the tranquil repose, he will be able to engage in deliberation. Nowadays, with their mind subject to vacillation and undeterminedness, can people cope with events? The "deliberation"（lü 虑）refers to the thinking which is punctilious. On occasions requiring urgent efforts to deal with complex events, only those in a tranquil repose are able to keep composed and be competent of doing it. Though the sages did not say much, from their few words can be deducted much, which calls for learners to read them carefully.［Xian］

144 问"安而后能虑"。曰："先是自家心安了，有些事来，方始思量区处得当。今人先是自家这里鹘突了，到事来都区处不下。既欲为此，又欲若彼；既欲为东，又欲向西，便是不能虑。然这也从知止说下来。若知其所止，自然如此，这却不消得工夫。若知所止，如火之必热，如水之必深，如食之必饱，饮之必醉。若知所止，便见事事决定是如此，决定着做到如此地位，欠阙些子，便自住不得。如说'事父母能竭其力，事君能致其身'，人多会说得。只是不曾见得决定着竭其力处，决定着致其身处。若决定见得着如此，看如何也须要到竭其力处，须要到致其身处。且如事君，若不见得决定着致其身，则在内亲近，必不能推忠竭诚，有犯无隐；在外任使，必不能展布四体，有殒无二。'无求生以害仁，有杀身以成仁。'这若不是见得到，如何会恁地！"贺孙。知止、安、虑。

Asked about "In that tranquil repose, there can be careful deliberation," the Master answered, "Only when your own mind gets tranquil can you think well how to handle things properly when they come up. Nowadays, many people bog themselves in confusion before things come up, and then how can they handle them properly? While wishing to do this, they desire to do that, and while wishing to go westward, they desire to go eastward. This confusion indicates their failure to settle themselves in careful deliberation. But this can also be seen from knowing the point where to rest. If one knows the point where to rest, he follows the natural course of things, and that does not need effort by him. If one knows the point where to rest, he must conduct himself and business in the same way as the fire must be hot and the water must be deep and as eating must alleviate hunger and drinking wine must cause drunkenness. If one knows the point where to rest, he will see it clear that a certain thing should be done in a determined way to a determined extent, and when he has not reached that extent he will never cease by himself his effort. For example, many know the teaching of Confucius that 'One should exert his utmost strength in serving his parents and he should devote his life in serving his sovereign,' (*Analects*, 1:7) but they have never been seen determined to try their best to that ends. Even if they have determined to do them, it is by their exerting their utmost strength and devoting their lives that the actual effects can be brought about. In serving his sovereign, if one has not been determined to devote himself, then when he serves him in his proximity, he will be impossible to be loyal to him completely and, though running the risk of offending him, to remonstrate with him, and when appointed as an envoy to a place far away from him, he will be impossible to go all out to fulfill his duties and, though running the risk of death, to be steady in his allegiance to him. 'They will not seek to live at the expense of injuring their benevolence, yet will even sacrifice their lives to preserve their benevolence complete.' (*Analects*, 15:9) If one has never seen such people, how can he believe that a man should conduct himself that way?" [Hesun] The following conversations concern "knowing where to rest," "tranquil repose," and "deliberation."

145 李德之问："'安而后能虑。'既首言知止矣，如何于此复说能虑?"曰:"既知此理,更须是审思而行。且如知孝于事亲,须思所以为事亲之道。"又问:"'知至而后意诚',如何知既尽后,意便能实?"先生指灯台而言:"如以灯照物,照见处所见便实;照不见处便有私意,非真实。"又问:"持敬、居敬如何?"曰:"且如此做将去,不须先安排下样子,后却旋求来合。"盖卿。

Li Dezhi 李德之 (dates unknown, a disciple of Zhu's) asked, "'In that tranquil repose, there can be careful deliberation.' Since it is already said to know the point where to rest, why 'there can be careful deliberation' is said here again?" The Master answered, "Since one has known that principle, he should be more careful in conducting himself and his business. For example, when one has known to be filial in serving his parents, he should think over the reason why a man should be filial in serving his parents." Li asked further, "'Their knowledge being complete, their thoughts were sincere.' (*Great Learning*, 2) Why, when one's knowledge is complete, will his thought be sincere?" The Master, pointing to a lamp stand, replied, "It can be comparable to lighting things with a lamp. Where its light reaches, what one sees is truly sincere, while where it does not reach, what he sees is adulterated with his private intention and thus not sincere." Li asked further, "What about cherishing seriousness and adhering to seriousness?" The Master answered, "Just go and do as required by them. It is not necessary to have some scheme arranged first and then try to do to conform to it." [Gaiqing]

146 子升问:"知止与能虑,先生昨以比易中深与几。或问中却兼下'极深研几'字,觉未稳。"曰:"当时下得也未仔细。要之,只着得'研几'字。"木之。

Zisheng 子升 (dates unknown, a disciple of Zhu's) said to the Master, "As for knowing the point where to rest and there being careful deliberation, yesterday, you, sir, compared them to *shen* 深 (the deep) and *ji* 几 (the minutest [springs of things]) as said in the *Classic of Change*. In your *Questions and Answers*, besides them, you also mentioned *jishen yanji* 极深研

几（searching out exhaustively what was deep, and investigating the minutest springs [of things]）. I feel they seem inconsistent. " The Master replied, "While giving that explanation in that book, I did not consider it carefully enough. In short, they are concerned only with investigating the minutest springs (of things). " [Muzhi]

147 李约之问"安而后能虑"。曰："若知至了，及临时不能虑，则安顿得不恰好。且如知得事亲当孝，也知得恁地是孝。及至事亲时不思虑，则孝或不行，而非孝者反露矣。"学蒙。安、虑。

Li Yuezhi 李约之（dates unknown, a disciple of Zhu's）asked about "In that tranquil repose, there can be careful deliberation. " The Master answered, "If one's knowledge reaches completeness, yet he fails to make careful deliberation of it, he will not be able to have it settled well. For example, if one knows that a man should be filial in serving his parents and also knows how to do to that end, but when he serves his parents practically, he does not deliberate on it, then what he does in pursuit of filial piety may be ineffective, while that may end up with betraying something unfilial. " [Xuemeng] The following is concerned with tranquil repose and deliberation.

148 问"安而后能虑"。曰："若不知此，则自家先已纷扰，安能虑！"德明。

Asked about "In that tranquil repose, there can be careful deliberation," the Master answered, "If one does not know this point, he himself will fall victim to disturbance before any deliberation. How can he make careful deliberation?" [Deming]

149 能安者，随所处而安，无所择地而安。能虑，是见于应事处能虑。节。

Whoever is capable of a tranquil repose can be in a tranquil repose wherever he is. One's ability to make careful deliberation is manifested in his dealing with events. [Jie]

150 虑，是思之重复详审者。方子。

Deliberation means the reiterative, comprehensive, and cautious thought. [Fangzi]

151 虑，是研几。闳祖。

Deliberating means investigating the minutest springs (of things) [Hongzu]

152 问："到能得处，学之工夫尽否？"曰："在己之功亦备矣。又要'明明德于天下'，不止是要了自家一身。"淳。得。

Question: When one has got *de* 得 (the attainment [of the desired end]), does it mean that his efforts for learning have become complete?

Answer: As far as he himself is concerned, his efforts have become complete. But, as required by "illustrating illustrious virtue throughout the empire," (*Great Learning*, 2) his efforts should not be limited to his own attainment alone. [Chun] The following is on "attainment."

153 因说知止至能得，上云"止于至善"矣，此又提起来说。言能知止，则有所定；有所定，则知其理之确然如是。一定，则不可移易，任是千动万动，也动摇他不得。既定，则能静；静，则能安；安，则能虑；虑，则能得其所止之实矣。卓。知止至能得。

Thereupon, the Master discoursed on the part from "knowing the point where to rest" to "the attainment of the desired end." (i.e. the second sentence in the first paragraph of the text of the *Great Learning*) He said, "In the preceding sentence, 'to rest in the highest excellence' is already said, here that is reiterated in another way. The part means that if one is able to know the point to rest, the object of his pursuit will be determined; with that determinedness, he will know the principle is truly the principle. Once determined, his object should not be moved and changed, and no matter what occurs, it should not be subject to any swaying. With the determinedness, one will be imperturbable. With the imperturbability, he will be able to be in a tranquil repose. With the tranquil repose, he will be able to make careful deliberation. With the careful deliberation, he will be able to attain substantially the point where to rest. " ［Zhuo］ The part from "knowing the point where to rest" to "the attainment of the desired end"

154 知止至能得，盖才知所止，则志有定向；才定，则自能静；静，则自能安；安，则自能虑；虑，则自能得。要紧在能字。盖滔滔而去，自然如此者。虑，谓会思量事。凡思天下之事，莫不各得其当，是也。履孙。

As regards the part from "knowing the point where to rest" to "the attainment of the desired end," it probably conveys the message that once one gets to know the point where to rest, the object of his pursuit will be determined; as soon as his object is determined, he will naturally be able to get calm unperturbedness; with his calm unperturbedness, he will be naturally able to enter into a tranquil repose; with his tranquil repose, he will be naturally able to make careful deliberation; By careful deliberation, he will be naturally able to attain (the desired end). What counts is the word of "able." It is like a surging river, which is naturally able to flow ahead torrentially. The "deliberation" pertains to the capability of pondering over events. It means that, with that capability, whenever pondering over each of the events in the world, one can be to the point of it. ［Lüsun］

155 知止，只是先知得事理如此，便有定。能静，能安，及到事来，乃能虑。能字自有道理。是事至物来之际，思之审，处之当，斯得之矣。夔孙。

Knowing the point where to rest means only that if one has known what the principle underlying events is, then he will be in a determined state. If he is capable of unperturbedness and of tranquil repose, when events come up, he will be able to deliberate carefully on them. The word "able" here is naturally reasonable. When things occur and events come up, if one thinks over them cautiously and deals with them properly, that means he has got that "able." ［Kuisun］

156 问："据知止，已是思虑了，何故静、安下复有个'虑'字？

既静、安了，复何所虑?"曰:"知止，只是先知得事理如此，便有定。能静能安，及到事至物来，乃能虑。'能'字自有意思。谓知之审而后能虑，虑之审而后能得。"赐。

Question: Since knowing the point where to rest already implies making deliberation, why is "deliberation" reiterated after saying "unperturbedness" and "tranquil repose"? Since there are unperturbedness and tranquil repose, what needs deliberating?

Answer: Knowing the point where to rest only means that if knowing the principle of events first, one will then have the object of his pursuit determined. If one is capable of unperturbedness and tranquil repose, when things occur and events come up, he will be able to deliberate carefully on them. Here the word "able," which naturally has its own reference, means that knowing cautiously entails the ability to make deliberation and deliberating cautiously entails the ability to attain (the desired end). [Ci]

157 或问定静安虑四节。曰:"物格、知至，则天下事事物物皆知有个定理。定者，如寒之必衣，饥之必食，更不用商量。所见既定，则心不动摇走作，所以能静。既静，则随所处而安。看安顿在甚处，如处富贵、贫贱、患难，无往而不安。静者，主心而言;安者，主身与事而言。若人所见未定，则心何缘得静。心若不静，则既要如彼，又要如此，身何缘得安。能虑，则是前面所知之事到得，会行得去。如平时知得为子当孝，为臣当忠，到事亲事君时，则能思虑其曲折精微而得所止矣。"胡泳。

Someone asked about the four parts concerning determinedness, unperturbedness, tranquil repose, and deliberation. The Master answered, "When one has investigated things and gained complete knowledge, he will know that every thing or event in the world possesses a determined principle. What the 'determined' means is like coldness calling for clothing, and hunger, for food, which does not need any consultation. With such determinedness in regard to what one has seen, his mind will be subject to no wavering and distraction, which is why he is able to be unperturbed. With such unperturbedness, he will be able to enter a tranquil repose wherever he is. No matter where he is put, rich or poor, with weal or woe, he will be in a tranquil repose. The unperturbedness is said in regard to the mind, while the tranquil repose, to his body and the events he is faced with. If one is undetermined about what he has seen, what can his mind get unperturbable by? Without mental unperturbedness, he will want to go this way and then that way, what can his body get a tranquil repose by? The ability to make deliberation means that when those events he has already known occur actually, he is able to deal with them properly. For example, if one knows at ordinary times that a son should be filial and a minister should be loyal, thus when he serves his parents and his sovereign personally, he is able to deliberate on the indirect and subtle aspects of those events and then to attain the point where to rest. " 〔Huyong〕

158 琼曰："上面已自知止，今虑而得者，依旧是知底意思"云云。先生曰："只上面是方知，下面是实得耳。"问："如此，何用更过定、静、安三个节目？"曰："不如此，不实得。"曰："如此，上面知止处，其实未有知也。通此五句，才做得'致知在格物'一句。"曰："今人之学，却是敏底不如钝底。钝底循循而进，终有得处。敏底只是从头呼扬将去，只务自家一时痛快，终不见实理。"琼。

I said to the Master "The preceding sentence already says 'to know the point where to rest,' what the 'attainment' means is still the same as knowing," as well as some of my other understandings of the *Great Learning*. The Master replied, "But the former implies knowing only, while the latter, substantial attainment. " I asked further, "Thus, why are the three steps necessary?" He answered, "Without them, the attainment would not be substantial. " I said then, "In that case, the 'to know the point where to rest' in the preceding sentence, actually, does not imply knowing. What the five sentences mean is simply what the one sentence ' The extension of

knowledge lies in the investigation of things' (*Great Learning*, 2) means."
The Master responded, "Nowadays, of the scholars in pursuit of learning,
those acute ones do not do so well as those not so acute, for the latter advance
step by step and will surely gain some substantial progress, yet the former
only choose to roar away from the beginning for their own momentary
satisfaction, yet end up with ignorance of the substantial truth." [Cong]①

159 问:"定,即心有所向,不至走作,便静;静,便可以虑,何
必待安?"曰:"安主事而言,不安便不能思。譬如静坐,有件事来挠,
思便不得专一。定、静、安都相似。未到安处,思量未得。知止,是知
个慈,知个孝。到得时,方是得个慈,得个孝底道理。虑,是虑个如何
是慈,如何是孝。"又问:"至于安时,无勉强意思否?"曰:"在贫贱
也安,在富贵也安,在这里也安,在那里也安。今人有在这里不安了,
在那里也不会安。心下无理会,如何会去思虑?"问:"章句中'虑谓
思无不审',莫是思之熟否?"曰:"虑是思之周密处。"芝。

Question: Determinedness is the orientation of the mind, free from
distraction, which entails unperturbedness. With this unperturbedness, one
can make careful deliberation. Why is a tranquil repose necessary?

Answer: This tranquil repose is spoken of mainly in regard to events, for
without it, one will be unable to deliberate. For example, when you sit in an
attempt to contemplate, yet something comes up, if you were not in a tranquil
repose, you would hardly be possible to concentrate your mind and get free
from its disturbance. Determinedness, unperturbedness, and tranquil repose
all are similar. Without reaching a tranquil repose, you can not enter
contemplation. Knowing the point where to rest means only, for example,
one's knowing what is meant by kindness or by filial piety. When he attains
it, what he gets is the principle of kindness or filial piety. To make
deliberation is to consider how to be kind or filial.

---

① Wu Cong 吴琮 (courtesy name Zhongfang 仲方)

Further question：As for a tranquil repose, does it mean anything difficult one should force himself to do?

Answer：It means that one settles himself in a tranquil repose whether he is poor and lowly, or wealthy and high-ranked, and whether he is here or there. If one can not have a tranquil repose here, he can not have it there, either. Without such tranquil repose in his mind, how can he make careful deliberation?

Further question：In your *Interpretation*, does the "Deliberation means thought free from incaution" refer to the maturity of thought?

Answer：Deliberation means the water-tightness of thought. ［Zhi（芝）］①

160 王子周问知止至能得。曰："这数句，只是要晓得知止。不知止，则不能得所止之地。如'定、静、安'数字，恰如今年二十一岁，来年二十二岁，自是节次如此来，自不可遏。如'在明明德，在新民，在止于至善'这三句，却紧要只是'在止于至善'；而不说知止，则无下工夫处。"震。

Wang Zizhou 王子周 (dates unknown, a disciple of Zhu's) asked about the part from "knowing the point where to rest" to "attainment (of the desired end)." The Master answered, "This several sentences are meant to let one know the point where to rest. Without knowing it, he will be unable to attain the point where to rest. The words of 'determinedness,' 'unperturbedness,' and 'tranquil repose' come up one by one just like the twenty-one years of age after the twenty years of age, which is something naturally unstoppable. Like the 'to illustrate illustrious virtue; to renovate the people; and to rest in the highest excellence' preceding them, where the most important is 'to rest in the highest excellence,' if 'knowing the point where to rest' is not said first, one would not know where to make efforts."

---

① Chen Zhi 陈芝（courtesy name Tingxiu 庭秀）

[Zhen]

161 游子蒙问："知止，得止，莫稍有差别否？"曰："然。知止，如射者之于的；得止，是已中其的。"问："定、静、安矣，如之何而复有虑？"曰："虑是事物之来，略审一审。"刘淮叔通问："虑与格物致知不相干。"曰："致知，便是要知父止于慈，子止于孝之类。虑，便是审其如何而为孝，如何而为慈。至言仁则当如尧，言孝则当如舜，言敬则当如文王，这方是得止。"子蒙言："开欲以'明德'之'明'为如人之失其所有，而一旦复得，以喻之。至'虑'字，则说不得。"曰："知止而有定，便如人撞着所失，而不用终日营营以求之。定而静，便如人既不用求其所失，自尔宁静。静而安，便如人既知某物在甚处，某物在甚处，心下恬然无复不安。安而虑，便如自家金物都自在这里，及人来问自家讨甚金物，自家也须将上手审一审，然后与之。虑而得，则称停轻重，皆相当矣。"或又问："何故知止而定、静、安了，又复言虑？"曰："且如'可以予，可以无予；可以取，可以无取；可以死，可以无死'，这上面有几许商量在。"道夫。

You Zimeng 游子蒙 (dates unknown, a disciple of Zhu's) asked, "Is there a little difference between 'knowing the point where to rest' and 'attainment (of the desired end)'?" The Master answered, "Yes. The former means, for example, the target for a bowman before he shoots, while the latter, the target his arrow hits." The questioner continued, "Since there are already determinedness, unperturbedness, and tranquil repose, why is there the need for deliberation?" The Master replied, "Making deliberation means thinking a little over events or things when they come up." Liu Huai 刘淮, courtesy name 叔通 Shutong (dates unknown, a disciple of Zhu's) asked, "Making deliberation has nothing to do with investigating things and extending knowledge, hasn't it?" The Master answered, "Extending knowledge means only knowing that, for example, a father rests in kindness and a son rests in filial piety. But making deliberation means pondering over how to be kind and how to be filial. Only when one is like Yao in regard to benevolence, like Shun in regard to filial piety, and like King Wen of Zhou in regard to respectfulness can he be said as attaining the desired end." Zimeng said, "In the beginning (of the text of the *Great Learning*), 'to illustrate illustrious virtue' implies metaphorically one's regaining of what he lost, though he had originally possessed it. But this can not be said of the 'deliberation.'" The Master responded, "Having known the point where to rest, one's object of pursuit is determined, and this is like coming across what he has lost, which does not call for his striving daily for seeking it. Being determined and unperturbed is comparable to there being no need of one seeking for what he has lost, yet there being his placidity. Being unperturbed and in a tranquil repose is like one knowing this thing is here and that thing is there, who is calm and free from anxiety. Making deliberation in a tranquil repose is like one having all his gold and treasures in his own hands and, when someone else comes to him and asks for some, considering it over before giving him what he asks for. Making deliberation and attainment refers to weighing one thing against another and considering their equivalence." Someone else asked, "Why is deliberation said after there being determinedness, unperturbedness, and tranquil repose?" The Master replied, "As said in the *Mencius*, (4B: 51), 'It appears proper to take a thing, and also proper not to take it; It appears proper to give a thing, and also proper not to give it; It appears proper to sacrifice one's life, and also proper not to sacrifice it.' As for those sayings, there is some consultation which dwells in them." [Daofu]

162 问"知止而后有定"。曰:"须是灼然知得物理当止之处,心自会定。"又问:"上既言知止了,何更待虑而后能得?"曰:"知止是知事事物物各有其理。到虑而后能得处,便是得所以处事之理。知止,如人之射,必欲中的,终不成要射做东去,又要射做西去。虑而后能得,便是射而中的矣。且如人早间知得这事理如此,到晚间心里定了,便会处置得这事。若是不先知得这道理,到临事时便脚忙手乱,岂能虑而有得!"问:"未格物以前,如何致力?"曰:"古人这处,已自有小学了。"砥。

Asked about "Knowing the point where to rest, one's object of pursuit is then determined," the Master answered, "One needs to know brilliantly the points where things should rest as required by their principles before his mind is naturally determined." When further asked "Since knowing the point where to rest has been said in the preceding sentence, why is it necessary to say making deliberation before the attainment (of the desired end)?" the Master answered, "Knowing the point where to rest means knowing there being a principle for each of things and events. Making deliberation and attainment refers to obtaining the principles for handling things and events. The former is comparable to a bowman shooting an arrow, who must desire to hit the target rather than to shoot at the west and meanwhile at the east. The latter, by contrast, refers to hitting the target. For another example, if one gets to know what the principle of a thing is in the morning and his mind gets determined in the evening, then he will be able to deal with the thing properly. However, without knowing the principle first, when the thing comes up, he will be in a muddle. Then, how can he deliberate it and attain his desired end?" When asked further "Before investigating things, how to make efforts in pursuit of learning?" The Master answered, "In this regard, the ancients had already undergone the primary learning before that." [Di]

163 子升问知止、能虑之别。曰:"知止,是知事物所当止之理。到得临事,又须研几审处,方能得所止。如易所谓'惟深也故能通天下之志',此似知止;'惟几也故能成天下之务',此便是能虑。圣人言语自有不约而同处。"木之说:"如此则知止是先讲明工夫,能虑是临事审处之功。"曰:"固是。"再问:"'知止而后有定',注谓'知之则志有定向'。或问谓'能知所止,则方寸之间,事事物物皆有定理矣'。语似不同,何也?"曰:"也只一般。"木之。

Zisheng asked about the difference between knowing the point where to rest and making deliberation. The Master answered, "The former means knowing the principle of something with regard to the point where he should rest. When it actually comes up, one should investigate the minutest springs of it and deliberate on it carefully before he can attain the point where he should rest. For example, the 'It is due to its depth that it can penetrate to the intents of all under the heaven,' as said in 'Appended Remarks I' of the *Classic of Changes*, seems to mean the same as knowing the point where to rest, while the 'It is due to its investigating the minutest springs of (things) that it can bring to a completion all undertakings under the heaven,' said after that in the same book, seems to mean the same as making deliberation. So, naturally, what was said by different sages happens to coincide." I said, "Thus, knowing the point where to rest is to make clear what efforts should be made, while making deliberation refers to the efforts actually made to think over and handle things when they come up." The Master responded, "Yes, of course." I asked further, "As regards 'Knowing the point where to rest, one's object of pursuit is then determined,' you said in your *Interpretation* 'Having known that, one's object of pursuit will be oriented determinedly,' while in your *Questions and Answers*, it is 'If one can know the point where to rest, he will be aware that dwelling in his mind are the determined principles of all things and events.' The meanings of these two explanations seem different. Why?" The Master answered, "They mean basically the same." [Muzhi]

164 知止，只是知有这个道理，也须是得其所止方是。若要得其所止，直是能虑方得。能虑却是紧要。知止，如知为子而必孝，知为臣而必忠。能得，是身亲为忠孝之事。若徒知这个道理，至于事亲之际，为私欲所汩，不能尽其孝；事君之际，为利禄所汩，不能尽其忠，这便不是能得矣。能虑，是见得此事合当如此，便如此做。道夫。

Knowing the point where to rest is only knowing there being such and such a principle, but it is not complete unless one attains to the point where to rest as required by it. To attain to that point, one has to be able to make deliberation, which matters more. If one knows the point where to rest, it means, for example, he is familiar with the principle that a son should be filial and a minister should be loyal, while attaining to the point means his personal behavior in serving his parents with filial piety and his sovereign with loyalty. If, though one knows those principles, when he serves his parents, he fails to be filial due to his submerging into selfish desires and when he serves his sovereign, he fails to be loyal due to his succumbing to wealth and position, he falls short of that attainment. By the ability to make deliberation is meant that, when one knows something should be done in a certain way, he throws himself into doing it in that way. [Daofu]

165 人本有此理，但为气禀物欲所蔽。若不格物、致知，事至物来，七颠八倒。若知止，则有定，能虑，得其所止。节。

A person possesses the principle by birth, but it is beclouded by his partial endowment of vital force and selfish material desires. If he does not engage in investigating things for extension of knowledge, when things and events come up to him, he will be in confusion, at a loss how to deal with them. But if he knows the point where to rest, his object of pursuit will be determined and he will be able to make deliberation and attain that point. [Jie]

166 问知止至能得。曰："真个是知得到至善处，便会到能得地位。中间自是效验次第如此。学者工夫却在'明明德，新民，止于至善'上。如何要去明明德，如何要去新民，如何要得止于至善，正当理会。知止、能得，这处却未甚要紧。圣人但说个知止、能得样子在这里。"宇。

Asked about the part from "knowing the point where to rest" to "attainment (of the desired end)," the Master answered, "If one truly knows how to pursue the highest excellence, he will surely reach the attainment (of his desired end). Between them are naturally those sequential steps of intended effects. However, a learner's efforts should be mainly made 'to illustrate illustrious virtue, to renovate the people, and to rest in the highest excellence.' He should strive to understand how to illustrate illustrious virtue, how to renovate the people, and how to rest in the highest excellence. As for 'knowing the point where to rest' and 'attainment,' they are not that essential, for they are only said by the sage to demonstrate what the above mentioned three hows should be like." [Yu]

167 陈子安问: "知止至能得, 其间有工夫否?" 曰: "有次序, 无工夫。才知止, 自然相因而见。只知止处, 便是工夫。" 又问: "至善须是明德否?" 曰: "至善虽不外乎明德, 然明德亦有略略明者。须是止那极至处。" 铢。

Chen Zian 陈子安 (dates unknown, a disciple of Zhu's) asked, "From knowing the point where to rest to reaching attainment (of the desired end), do the steps require effort?" The Master answered, "They are sequential, but call for no effort. The moment one knows the point where to rest, he will see the others thereupon one by one. But to know the point where to rest requires efforts to be made." Chen further asked, "Has the highest excellence have to call for illustrious virtue?" The Master replied, "Though the highest excellence calls for nothing but illustrious virtue, the cases of the illustriousness are different, of which some are only slightly illustrious. The point where illustrious virtue should rest has to be that where it is supremely illustrious." [Zhu]

168 真知所止, 则必得所止, 虽若无甚间隔, 其间亦有少过度处。健步勇往, 势虽必至, 然移步亦须略有渐次也。

Truly knowing the point where to rest must mean ultimately reaching attainment (of the desired end). Though there is little severance between them, there exist some transitions from the former to the latter. It is like one striding vigorously towards a goal, who, though he will surely reach the goal, has to take steps one after another in a slightly definite order.

169 林子渊问知止至能得。曰："知与行，工夫须着并到。知之愈明，则行之愈笃；行之愈笃，则知之益明。二者皆不可偏废。如人两足相先后行，便会渐渐行得到。若一边软了，便一步也进不得。然又须先知得，方行得。所以大学先说致知，中庸说知先于仁、勇，而孔子先说'知及之'。然学问、慎思、明辨、力行，皆不可阙一。"贺孙。

Lin Ziyuan asked about the part from "knowing the point where to rest" to "the attainment (of the desired end)." The Master answered, "The efforts of both knowledge and action must be exerted to the utmost. As one knows more clearly, he acts more earnestly, and as he acts more earnestly, he knows more clearly. Neither of the two should be unbalanced or discarded. It is like a person's two legs. If they take turns to walk, one will be able gradually to arrive at the destination. If one leg is weak and soft, then not even one forward step can be taken. However, we must first know before we can act. This is why the *Great Learning* first talks about the extension of knowledge, the *Doctrine of the Mean* puts wisdom ahead of benevolence and courage, and Confucius first of all spoke of knowledge being sufficient to attain its objective. But none of extensive study, accurate inquiry, careful thinking, clear sifting, and vigorous practice can be omitted."[①] [Hesun]

170 问"知止能得"一段。曰："只是这个物事，滋长得头面自各别。今未要理会许多次第，且要先理会个知止。待将来熟时，便自见得。"先生论看文字，只要虚心濯去旧闻，以来新见。时举。

Asked about the part from "knowing the point where to rest" to "the attainment (of the desired end)," the Master answered, "That is the same thing-event which manifests itself in different faces. Now you need not to turn to those many steps, but rather try first to understand knowing the point where to rest. When you have got familiar with it, you will naturally see others."

---

① The translation of the answer by Zhu is based on the version rendered by Chan Wing-tsit, p. 609, with some alterations.

Thereupon he continued talking about reading books and emphasized that learners should be modest and washed away their old hearsays so as to welcome new insights. [Shiju]

171 黄去私问知止至能得。曰："工夫全在知止。若能知止，则自能如此。"人杰。

Huang Qùsi 黄去私 (dates unknown, a disciple of Zhu's) asked about the part from "knowing the point where to rest" to "the attainment (of the desired end)." The Master answered, "All efforts are to be made to know the point where to rest. If one has known the point where to rest, he can achieve all others naturally and effortlessly." [Renjie]

172 知止至能得，譬如吃饭，只管吃去，自会饱。德明。

What is meant by the part from "knowing the point where to rest" to "the attainment (of the desired end)" is comparable to eating a meal. Just do nothing but eating, and one will eat his fill naturally. [Deming]

173 问知止至能得。曰："如人饮酒，终日只是吃酒。但酒力到时，一杯深如一杯。"儒用。

Asked about the part from "knowing the point where to rest" to "the attainment (of the desired end)," the Master answered, "It is akin to drinking wine, which is but drinking wine in the same way all day long. But when one drinks near his capacity for wine, he feels one more cup is deeper than the previous one to him." [Ruyong]

174 知止至能得，是说知至、意诚中间事。闳祖。

The part from "knowing the point where to rest" to "the attainment (of the desired end)" pertains to those matters between extending knowledge completely and making thought sincere. [Hongzu]

175 大学章句说静处，若兼动，即便到"得"地位，所以细分。方。

Where unperturbedness is explained in *Interpretation*, if activity is also considered, that will mean leaping immediately to the attainment (of the

desired end）. That is why the process between them is segmented further.
［Fang］

176 问：“知与得如何分别？”曰：“知只是方知，得便是在手。”
问：“得莫是行所知了时？”曰：“也是如此。”又曰：“只是分个知与
得。知在外，得便在我。”士毅。

Question：How to distinguish knowing and attaining?

Answer：Knowing something is but knowing it, but attaining it means
having it in hands.

Further question：Does attaining mean performing what has been known?

Answer：That is also right.

Further answer：There is but the distinction between knowing and
attaining, of which knowing pertains to something outside me, while
attaining, to it in my possession. ［Shiyi］

卷第十九 Book 19

论语一

Analects I[①]

语孟纲领

Guideline for Reading *Analects* and *Mencius*

1 语孟工夫少，得效多；六经工夫多，得效少。大雅。以下六经四子。

In studying the *Analects* (i. e. the *Analects of Confucius*) and the *Mencius*, a learner makes less effort yet more gain; by contrast, in reading the Six Confucian Classics, he has to make more effort yet less gain. [Daya]
The following sections are concerned with the Six Confucian Classics and Four Books.

2 语孟用三二年工夫看，亦须兼看大学及书诗，所谓"兴于诗"。诸经诸史，大抵皆不可不读。德明。

A learner should spend two or three years studying the *Analects* and the *Mencius*, and meanwhile, reading *Great Learning*, the *Book of History*, and the *Classic of Poetry*, for as Confucius says, "It is by the *Poetry* (i. e. *Classic of Poetry*) that the mind is aroused. " (*Analects*, 8：8) As for the other Confucian classics and histories, generally, he should also read through them

---

① The English translation of the citations from *Lunyu* 论语 in the text of this book is, unless indicated otherwise, based on J. Legge's version entitled "*The Analects*," (also known as *The Analects of Confucius* or *The Confucian Analects*) with some alterations in contexts (see http：//ctext. org/analects).

all in that period. ［Deming］

3 某论语集注已改，公读令大学十分熟了，却取去看。论语孟子都是大学中肉菜，先后浅深，参差互见。若不把大学做个匡壳子，卒亦未易看得。贺孙。

I have revised my *Lunyu Jizhu* 论语集注（Collected Annotations of the *Analects*）and after you read *Great Learning* and get conversant with it, you can read it. Both the *Analects* and the *Mencius* are the substances for the framework built up by the *Great Learning*, and, when they are put in contrast, which should be read first and which is deeper are clear to see. If one does not read the *Great Learning* first to set up a framework for his learning, he will end up failing to see what the former two truly mean. ［Hesun］

4 或云："论语不如中庸。"曰："只是一理，若看得透，方知无异。论语是每日零碎问。譬如大海也是水，一勺也是水。所说千言万语，皆是一理。须是透得，则推之其它，道理皆通。"又曰："圣贤所说只一般，只是一个'择善固执之'。论语则说'学而时习之'，孟子则说'明善诚身'，下得字各自精细，真实工夫只一般。须是知其所以不同，方知其所谓同也。而今须是穷究得一物事透彻方知。如入个门，方知门里房舍间架。若不亲入其门户，在外遥望，说我皆知得，则门里事如何知得。"僴。

Someone said, "The *Analects* is inferior to the *Doctrine of the Mean*." The Master responded, "The truths they convey are the same and only when you understand them thoroughly can you see their sameness. In the *Analects* are daily questions and answers, but just as both the water in the sea and the water taken from it in a ladle are the same, what those thousands of words convey is the one and the same truth. You have to understand that thoroughly before starting from it to deduce for others, and then you will find all penetrate one another." He continued, "What the sages and worthies said are all similar, which boils down to 'choosing what is good and firmly holding onto it fast. ' (*Doctrine of the Mean*, 22) That is expressed as ' learning with a constant perseverance and practicing frequently what is learned' in the *Analects* (1 : 1) and ' understanding what is good and seeking for the attainment of sincerity in one's self' in the *Mencius* (4A : 12). In spite of different wordings, they each are exquisite, which imply the same truth. One has to know the reason why they are different in wording before knowing what they share. But at present, a learner should make efforts first to investigate things to the utmost in order to know them thoroughly and in due time he will know that. It is just as one has to enter the gate of a house before knowing what the interior layout of it is like. If he does not enter the gate but rather looks only outside and claims he knows well all inside, how can it be possible for him to know it?" [Xian]

5 论语只说仁，中庸只说智。圣人拈起来底便说，不可以例求。泳。

What the *Analects* says is only of benevolence, while the *Doctrine of the Mean* says is only of wisdom. The sage (Confucius) would illustrate the truths by whatever he picked up, but what he meant goes beyond those specific cases. [Yong (泳)]

6 论语易晓，孟子有难晓处。语孟中庸大学是熟饭，看其它经，是打禾为饭。节。

The *Analects* is easy to understand, but in the *Mencius* there are difficult points. The Four Books, i. e. the *Analects*, the *Mencius*, the *Great Learning* and the *Doctrine of the Mean* are cooked rice, while reading other classics is but reaping rice and cooking it. [Jie]

7 古书多至后面便不分晓。语孟亦然。节。

The later sections in an ancient book tend to become hard to understand, and this is true of the *Analects* and the *Mencius*. [Jie]

8 夫子教人，零零星星，说来说去，合来合去，合成一个大物事。节。以下孔孟教人。

When Confucius taught others, he gave odd scraps of saying and touched upon this or that, but what he said would combine eventually and a grand thing-event would emerge therefrom. [Jie] The following sections are on how Confucius and Mencius instructed their disciples.

9 且如孔门教人，亦自有等。圣人教人，何不都教他做颜曾底事业？而子贡子路之徒所以止于子贡子路者，是其才止于此。且如"克己复礼"，虽止是教颜子如此说，然所以教他人，亦未尝不是"克己复礼"底道理。卓。

For example, when Confucius instructed his disciples, he also considered their different grades. Why didn't he teach others in the same manner as he taught Yan Hui and Zeng Shen so that they all could attain what the latter two accomplished? The reason why Zigong, Zilu and their like were only able to attain what Zigong, Zilu and their like could attain is that their extent of attainment was subject to their talents. However, as regards "subduing one's self and returning to propriety," (*Analects*, 12：1) for example, though Confucius said that only to Yan Hui while instructing him, when he instructed other disciples of his, what he said is never not the same principle as that of "subduing one's self and returning to propriety." [Zhuo]

10 孔门教人甚宽，今日理会些子，明日又理会些子，久则自贯通。如耕荒田，今日耕些子，明日又耕些子，久则自周匝。虽有不到处，亦不出这理。节。

Confucius's approach to instructing his disciples is very relaxed. Thus, today they understood something, and tomorrow, something else. After a long time, they were able to understand many things thoroughly and coherently. It is like ploughing an uncultivated land. Today one ploughs it here and tomorrow there, and after some days the land will get ploughed. Though there may be a small part or two of the land left untouched, they are also covered by the principle. [Jie]

11 问："孔子教人就事上做工夫，孟子教人就心上做工夫，何故不同？"曰："圣贤教人，立个门户，各自不同。"节。

Question：Confucius instructed his disciples to make efforts in regard to events, while Mencius instructed his disciples to make efforts in regard to the mind. Why were they different?

Answer：When the sages and worthies instructed their disciples, they would apply their own approaches, each of which was different from another. ［Jie］

12 孟子教人多言理义大体，孔子则就切实做工夫处教人。端蒙。

Mencius's teachings are mostly concerned with the basic meaning of the principles, while Confucius's emphasize those respects where solid efforts should be made. ［Duanmeng］

13 孔子教人只从中间起，使人便做工夫去，久则自能知向上底道理，所谓"下学上达"也。孟子始终都举，先要人识心性着落，却下功夫做去。端蒙。

In his teaching, Confucius guided his disciples to rise from only the middle and keep on making efforts so that after a long time they would naturally be able to know the principle for pursuing upwards. That is what is meant by "learning from the lower and aiming for the higher." (*Analects*, 14：35) By contrast, Mencius always taught from the higher, instructing others to strive to know truly the human mind and nature before their setting about making efforts for their cultivation. ［Duanmeng］

14 论语不说心，只说实事。节录作："只就事实上说。"孟子说心，后来遂有求心之病。方子。

The *Analects* does not discourse the mind but only says actual events Jie's record for the words after "but" in this sentence reads "only says of facts," whereas Mencius dwelt on the mind and later he turned to probing the trouble with the mind. ［Fangzi］

15 孟子所谓集义，只是一个"是"字；孔子所谓思无邪，只是一个"正"字。不是便非，不正便邪。圣贤教人，只是求个是底道理。

夔孙。

The *jiyi* 集义（the accumulation of righteous deeds）said by Mencius（*Mencius*, 2B：2）means nothing but "rightness." The *si wuxie* 思无邪（having no depraved thoughts）said by Confucius（*Analects*, 2：2）means nothing but "uprightness." Being not right is but being wrong, and being not upright is but being depraved. Therefore, what the sages and worthies taught is but the pursuit of the principle of rightness. ［Kuisun］

16 孔子教人极直截，孟子较费力。孟子必要充广。孔子教人，合下便有下手处。问："孔子何故不令人充广?"曰："'居处恭，执事敬'，非充广而何?"节。

The Master said, "Confucius was very straightforward when teaching others, while Mencius was rather painstaking, for he insisted on being far-reaching. When instructed by Confucius, his disciples would know there were things close at hand which they could make efforts on." Someone asked, "Why didn't Confucius insist on being far-reaching?" He answered, "When he said, ' in retirement, to be sedately grave; in the management of business, to be reverently attentive,'（*Analects*, 13：19）isn't he far-reaching?" ［Jie］

17 孔子教人只言"居处恭，执事敬，与人忠"，含畜得意思在其中，使人自求之。到孟子便指出了性善，早不似圣人了。祖道。

In his teaching, though Confucius only said " in retirement, to be sedately grave; in the management of business, to be reverently attentive; in exchange with others, to be strictly sincere,"（*Analects*, 13：19）what he wanted to teach is implied therein, by which he set his disciples to seek for it by themselves. By contrast, Mencius pointed out human nature being originally good directly, so his manner is quite unlike that of the sage（Confucius）. ［Zudao］

18 孔子只说"忠信笃敬"，孟子便发出"性善"，直是漏泄! 德明。

Confucius mentioned only "（When one conducts himself）, let his words be sincere and truthful and his actions honorable and careful," (*Analects*, 15:6) whereas Mencius said plainly "The nature is good," (*Mencius*, 6A:6) which is simply a practice of disclosing (the secret). [Deming]

19 孟子言存心、养性，便说得虚。至孔子教人"居处恭，执事敬，与人忠"等语，则就实行处做功夫。如此，则存心、养性自在。端蒙。

When Mencius talked about preserving the mind and nourishing the nature, he said of what is empty, while when Confucius taught others "in retirement, to be sedately grave; in the management of business, to be reverently attentive; in exchange with others, to be strictly sincere," (*Analects*, 13:19) he urged them to make efforts on what is substantial, by which preserving the mind and nourishing the nature would take care of themselves. [Duanmeng]

20 孔子之言，多且是泛说做工夫，如"居处恭，执事敬"，"言忠信，行笃敬"之类，未说此是要理会甚么物。待学者自做得工夫透彻，却就其中见得体段是如此。至孟子，则恐人不理会得，又趱进一着说，如"恻隐之心"与"学问之道，求放心"之类，说得渐渐亲切。今人将孔孟之言都只恁地草率看过了。雉。

What Confucius said is mostly general instructions on how to make efforts, such as his "in retirement, to be sedately grave; in the management of business" (*Analects*, 13:19) and "(When one conducts himself), let his words be sincere and truthful and his actions honorable and careful." (*Analects*, 15:6) He did not mention what things and events his disciples should handle for their understanding. When the disciples made efforts enough by themselves, they would see the truth which dwells in things and events. However, Mencius went a step further in his teachings for fear that others could not understand them. For example, his sayings such as "the feeling of sadness and commiseration" (*Mencius*, 2A:6) and "seeking for the lost mind" (*Mencius*, 6A:11) were more and more close explicitly to the principles. Nowadays, learners looked only cursorily through what Confucius and Mencius said. [Zhi (雉)]

21 问:"论语一书未尝说一'心'字。至孟子,只管拈'人心'字说来说去:曰'推是心',曰'求放心',曰'尽心',曰'赤子之心',曰'存心'。莫是孔门学者自知理会个心,故不待圣人苦口;到孟子时,世变既远,人才渐渐不如古,故孟子极力与言,要他从个本原处理会否?"曰:"孔门虽不曾说心,然答弟子问仁处,非理会心而何。仁即心也,但当时不说个'心'字耳。此处当自思之,亦未是大疑处。"枅。

Question: The *Analects* never mentions the mind, but what the *Mencius* says never leaves the mind, for example, "examination of the mind," (*Mencius*, 2A: 9) "seeking for the lost mind," (*Mencius*, 6A: 11) "exhausting the mind," (*Mencius*, 7A: 1) "infant's mind," (*Mencius*, 4B: 40) and "preserving the mind." (*Mencius*, 4B: 56) Could it be that since Confucius's disciples were able to understand by themselves what was meant by the mind, they did not wait for their teacher's painstaking teaching, but in the time of Mencius, which was far later, since human minds became gradually unlike what they had been, he had to exert himself strenuously to explain it to others so that they could understand what it was in the source?

Answer: Though Confucius did not mention the mind, when he answered the question asked by a disciple of his about benevolence, didn't he mean implicitly to instruct him to understand the mind? Benevolence is nothing but the mind, though he did not say anything of it explicitly. For this, think it over further by yourself and you will know it will not make a major doubtful point. [Ji]

22 蜚卿问:"论语之言,无所不包,而其所以示人者,莫非操存涵养之要;七篇之指,无所不究,而其所以示人者,类多体验充广之端。"曰:"孔子体面大,不用恁地说,道理自在里面。孟子多是就发见处尽说与人,终不似夫子立得根本住。所以程子谓'其才高,学之无可依据'。要之，夫子所说包得孟子，孟子所言却出不得圣人疆域。且如夫子都不说出，但教人恁地去做，则仁便在其中。如言'居处恭，执事敬，与人忠'，果能此，则心便在。到孟子则不然，曰：'恻隐之心，仁之端也。今人乍见孺子将入井，皆有怵惕、恻隐之心。'都教人就事上推究。"道夫问："如孟子所谓'求放心'，'集义所生'，莫是立根本处否？"曰："他有恁地处，终是说得来宽。"曰："他莫是以其所以做工夫者告人否？"曰："固是。也是他所见如此。自后世观之，孔颜便是汉文帝之躬修玄默，而其效至于几致刑措。孟子便如唐太宗，天下之事无所不为，极力做去，而其效亦几致刑措。"道夫。

Feiqing asked, "What the *Analects* says is inclusive of everything, but the essential of what it intends to instruct people with is holding fast personal integrity and self-cultivation, whereas, though what the seven pieces of writing (i. e. *Mencius*) purport is concerned with everything, what it intends to instruct people with lies mostly in the beginnings of experiencing and enlarging the mind. (Is this understanding right?)" The Master answered, "Confucius was large-minded, and he needed not to resort to explicit expressions, for all the truths he intended to teach dwelt naturally in his words. By contrast, Mencius tended to tell others exhaustively what he found, so eventually he did not seem to stand as firmly as Confucius. Therefore, Chengzi (i. e. Cheng Yi) said, 'Mencius was so high in talent that there was nothing on which learners were able to depend to reach him.' In short, as far as their teachings are concerned, Confucius covers Mencius, and What Mencius said does not go beyond the domain demarked by Confucius. Confucius did not lay bare the truths, but rather instructed others to make effort to do things, for they would be able to understand the truth of benevolence which inheres therein in due course. For example, he taught others 'in retirement, to be sedately grave; in the management of business, to be reverently attentive; in exchange with others, to be strictly sincere.'

(*Analects*, 13：19) If a leaner can do really as the sage said, he will be able to know what was meant by the mind and how to cultivate it. But Mencius applied a quite different teaching way. When he said, 'The feeling of sadness and commiseration is the beginning of benevolence,' and 'Even nowadays, if men suddenly see a child about to fall into a well, they will without exception experience a feeling of alarm and distress,' (*Mencius*, 2A：6) he instructed others to deduce from specific events." Daofu asked, "Do 'seeking for the lost mind,' (*Mencius*, 6A：11) '(It is) produced by the accumulation of righteous deeds,' (*Mencius*, 2A：2) and the like make clear where the base should be founded?" The Master answered, "He had that in himself and so eventually his teaching was broad-ranging." Daofu asked further, "Did he tell others why they should make efforts?" The Master replied, "Yes, of course. That is also what he thought it was. Seen from later generations, Confucius and Yan Hui were comparable to Emperor Wen of Han (r. 180 – 157 BC)[①], famous for his cultivating himself in keeping quiet, who produced effect almost equivalent to putting aside penal laws, while Mencius, to Emperor Taizong of Tang (r. 626 – 649), famous for conducting everything under heaven and trying his best to have it done, who also produced effect almost equivalent to putting aside penal laws." [Daofu]

23　看文字，且须看其平易正当处。孔孟教人，句句是朴实头。"人能充无受尔汝之实"，"实"字将作"心"字看。须是我心中有不受尔汝之实处，如仁义是也。祖道。

When reading a book, pay more attention to those words in it which read plain, easy, and upright. In the teachings of Confucius and Mencius, every one of their sentences is simple and unadorned. For example, in "(If) a man can give full development to the real feeling of dislike with which he receives

---

① Emperor Wen of Han was considered one of the most benevolent rulers in Chinese history. His reign and that of his son Emperor Jing were often collectively known together as the "Rule of Wen and Jing," renowned for general stability and relaxed laws.

the salutation 'er（尔）' or 'ru（汝）,'"① (*Mencius*, 7B：77) the "real feeling of dislike" can be seen as meaning "the mind." The sentence should be understood as meaning that there dwells in the human mind such as benevolence and righteousness that do not receive the salutation "er" or "ru." ［Zudao］

24 孟子比孔子时说得高。然"孟子道性善，言必称尧舜"，又见孟子说得实。因论南轩奏议有过当处。方子。

Mencius sounded a higher note than Confucius. However, "Mencius discoursed how the nature of humankind is good and, when speaking, always made laudatory reference to Yao and Shun," (*Mencius*, 3A：1) and this indicates the substantiality of Mencius's saying. Thereupon, the Master continued to discuss the improper points with Nanxuan's (i. e. Zhang Shi's) memorial to the throne. ［Fangzi］

25 或问："孟子说'仁'字，义甚分明，孔子都不曾分晓说，是如何？"曰："孔子未尝不说，只是公自不会看耳。譬如今沙糖，孟子但说糖味甜耳。孔子虽不如此说，却只将那糖与人吃。人若肯吃，则其味之甜，自不待说而知也。"广。

Someone asked, "Mencius made himself very clear in his explanation of what benevolence meant, but Confucius never said that clear. Why?" The Master answered, "Confucius also said it, yet you have not known how to read him. Let us take granulated sugar for example. Mencius would tell others only that it tastes sweet, but Confucius, without saying that, would give it to others. If they are willing to taste it, they will know its sweetness, so it is unnecessary to tell them what it tastes like." ［Guang］

26 圣人说话，磨棱合缝，盛水不漏。如云"一言丧邦"，"以直报怨"，自是细密。孟子说得便粗，如云"今乐犹古乐"，"太王好色"，

---

① The "er（尔）" and "ru（汝）" were both used originally in ancient Chinese by elders to refer to the person or people that they were talking to. Later, either was tinted with some color of disdain towards its receiver.

"公刘好货"之类。横渠说："孟子比圣人自是粗。颜子所以未到圣人处，亦只是心粗。"夔孙。

What the sage (Confucius) said is closely woven and water-tight. For example, his "A single sentence can ruin a country" (*Analects*, 13：15) and "Recompense injury with justice" (*Analects*, 14：14) are fine and well-knit. In contrast, Mencius's discourse is coarse, such as "The music of the present day is just like the music of antiquity," (*Mencius*, 1B：8) "King Tai was fond of beauty," (*Mencius*, 1B：12) and "Gong Liu was fond of wealth." (*Mencius*, 1B：12) Hengqü (i. e. Zhang Zai) said, "Mencius is naturally coarse compared with the sage (Confucius) and the reason why Yanzi (i. e. Yan Hui) failed to reach the status like that of the sage is also his mental coarseness." [Kuisun]

27 孟子要熟读，论语却费思索。孟子熟读易见，盖缘是它有许多答问发扬。贺孙。读语孟。

The *Mencius* needs reading over and over again, while the *Analects* calls for much pondering. The *Mencius* is easily accessible through reading it repeatedly. It is probably because it contains many questions and answers, which clarify what is meant to convey. [Hesun] The following concerns how to read the *Analects* and the *Mencius*.

28 看孟子，与论语不同，论语要冷看，孟子要熟读。论语逐文逐意各是一义，故用子细静观。孟子成大段，首尾通贯，熟读文义自见，不可逐一句一字上理会也。雉。

The way for reading the *Mencius* is different from that for reading the *Analects*, for the latter needs reading with cool contemplation, while the former needs reading over and over again. In the *Analects*, every passage conveys a meaning and those meanings are separate and therefore it calls for careful and sedate reading. The *Mencius* is different, for it contains many long paragraphs, each with a coherent expression of idea. When a leaner reads them over and over again, what those ideas are will become clear to him gradually. He should avoid trying to understanding them by poring over the text word by word and sentence by sentence. [Zhi（雉）]

29 沉浸专一于论孟，必待其自得。

Submerge yourself into the *Analects* and the *Mencius* with single-mindedness, and in due time you will emerge with your personal understanding of them.

30 读论语，如无孟子；读前一段，如无后一段。不然，方读此，又思彼，扰扰于中。这般人不惟无得于书，胸中如此，做事全做不得。

When you read the *Analects*, do it as if there were no book of the *Mencius*. When you read the first passage of it, do it as if there were no passage to come. Otherwise, when one touches this and meanwhile thinks of that, his mind will be never free from those disturbances. If you are such a man, you will go nowhere in reading books and, what is more, when your mind is always in that state, you will be incapable of making it whatever you do.

31 大凡看经书，看论语，如无孟子；看上章，如无下章；看'学而时习之'未得，不须看'有朋自远方来'。且专精此一句，得之而后已。又如方理会此一句未得，不须杂以别说相似者。次第乱了，和此一句亦晓不得。振。

When reading classics and books, for example, the *Analects*, you should read it as if the *Mencius* did not exist. When reading the first chapter, you should read it as if the next chapter did not exist. For instance, when you have not gained an adequate understanding of the first sentence with "learning with a constant perseverance and practicing frequently what is learned," do not turn to "having a friend coming to visit you from afar" (*Analects*, 1：1) after it. Just focus on that one sentence and strive for a thorough understanding of it before turning to another. When you have not understood it well, avoid mixing it by fetching some other sayings seemingly like it, for if your understandings of them get out of order, you will never gain a complete understanding of it. ［Zhen］

32 人有言，理会得论语，便是孔子；理会得七篇，便是孟子。子细看，亦是如此。盖论语中言语，真能穷究极其纤悉，无不透彻，如从孔子肚里穿过，孔子肝肺尽知了，岂不是孔子！七篇中言语，真能穷究透彻无一不尽，如从孟子肚里穿过，孟子肝肺尽知了，岂不是孟子！淳。

It is said that whoever understands the *Analects* is a Confucius and whoever understands the seven pieces of writing is a Mencius. Think over it carefully, and you will know it is true. That is probably because if one can truly inquire into the minutest of the words in the *Analects* and penetrate everything in it, which means he can, as it were, pass through the abdomen of Confucius and know his liver and lung all over. Isn't he a Confucius? Similarly, if one can truly inquire into everything of the words in the seven pieces of writing to the utmost, which means he can, as it were, pass through the abdomen of Mencius and know his liver and lung all over, isn't he a Mencius? ［Chun（淳）］

33 讲习孔孟书。孔孟往矣，口不能言。须以此心比孔孟之心，将孔孟心作自己心。要须自家说时，孔孟点头道是，方得。不可谓孔孟不会说话，一向任己见说将去。若如此说孟子时，不成说孟子，只是说"王子"也！又若更不逐事细看，但以一个字包括，此又不可。此名"包子"，又不是孟子也！力行。

The Master lectured on the *Analects* and the *Mencius*. He said, "Both Confucius and Mencius passed away long ago, and they could not say any more words. You should compare your mind with theirs and regard theirs as yours. You should try to make sure that, if they were alive, they would give a nod of assent to you when you told them your understandings of their words. Do not say that, since Confucius and Mencius are no more, you can allow yourself to understand their words as you please. If one explains what Mencius said in that way, it is not Menzi（i. e. Mencius）but rather a

'Wangzi' (literally, prince; figuratively, one's self-willed self) that he explains. Furthermore, if he does not strive to read Mencius's words carefully but rather attempts to wrap their meanings by only a word of his own, it will not do, either. That is the word of the 'wrapper' but not of Mencius. " [Lixing]

34 论语多门弟子所集，故言语时有长长短短不类处。孟子，疑自着之书，故首尾文字一体，无些子瑕疵。不是自下手，安得如此好! 若是门弟子集，则其人亦甚高，不可谓"轲死不传"。

Since the *Analects* was compiled by Confucius's many disciples and followers, those sayings and conversations in it are quite different in terms of their length. However, the *Mencius*, I suspect, is a book Mencius wrote by himself, so its text, from its beginning to its end, is an organic whole, which is almost flawless. If it had not been out of his own hand, how could it have been written so well? If it was complied by one or more of his disciples, they were surely very talented and, if this is the case, it should not be said that, after Meng Ke (name of Mencius) passed away, the Confucian orthodox was not inherited.

35 孔门问答，曾子闻得底话，颜子未必与闻；颜子闻得底话，子贡未必与闻。今却合在论语一书，后世学者岂不幸事! 但患自家不去用心。儒用。读论语。

Of the conversations between Confucius and his disciples, those heard by Zengzi (i.e. Zeng Shen) were not necessarily heard by Yanzi (i.e. Yan Hui) and those heard by Yanzi were not necessarily heard by Zigong, but all of them were collected into one book. Isn't this something fortunate to later scholars? What I worry about is only that you do not exert yourself to read it conscientiously. [Ruyong] The following is concerned with how to read the *Analects*.

36 问："论语近读得如何? 昨日所读底，今日再读，见得如何?"干曰："尚看未熟。"曰："这也使急不得，也不可慢。所谓急不得者，功效不可急；所谓不可慢者，工夫不可慢。"干。

The Master asked me, "How are you going in reading the *Analects*? When you read today what you had read yesterday, did you get anything new?" I answered, "I've been reading it, but still not got familiar with it." He said, "That is something you should not rush, but you should not slow down in doing it, either. It should not be rushed in the sense that the effect of reading it should not be expected to come soon, and it should not be slowed down in the sense that making efforts should not be decelerated." [Gan]

37 问叔器："论语读多少?"曰："两日只杂看。"曰："恁地如何会长进! 看此一书，且须专此一书。便待此边冷如冰，那边热如火，亦不可舍此而观彼。"淳。

The Master asked Shuqi, "How much have you read the *Analects*?" He answered, "In these two days, I have only chosen some other books, besides it, and read them." The Master told him, "How can you gain progress in that way? When you read the *Analects*, you must concentrate on it alone. Even if this is as cold as ice and that, as hot as fire, you should not leave this and turn to that." [Chun (淳)]

38 问林恭甫："看论语至何处?"曰："至述而。"曰："莫要恁地快，这个使急不得。须是缓缓理会，须是逐一章去搜索。候这一章透彻后，却理会第二章，久后通贯，却事事会看。如吃饭样，吃了一口，又吃一口，吃得滋味后，方解生精血。若只恁地吞下去，则不济事。"义刚。

The Master asked Lin Gongfu 林恭甫 (dates unknown, a disciple of Zhu's), "Which part have you reached in reading the *Analects*?" He answered, "I have reached Book 7." The Master said, "Don't go that fast, for reading it is something you should not rush. You should read it slowly by chewing the books of it one by one. Don't start to read the second book unless you have got a thorough understanding of the first book. After a long time, you will gain a coherent understanding of them and thereby know how to see things and events. It is just like having a meal. You have to eat it by having one mouthful after another, and only when you know well its taste can you get it digested for generating the essence and blood for your body. If you finished having the meal at one swallow, it would be to no avail. " [Yigang]

39 论语难读。日只可看一二段，不可只道理会文义得了便了。须是子细玩味，以身体之，见前后晦明生熟不同，方是切实。贺孙。

The *Analects* is difficult to read. A learner can only read one or two passages in one day, and it is not enough to get only an understanding of the surface meaning of the words. He should ruminate on them and experience them personally. Only when he feels the difference between his initial reading and his further rumination of them in terms of his enlightenment and conversancy can he be said as understanding them substantially. [Hesun]

40 论读书之法。择之云："尝作课程，看论语日不得过一段。"曰："明者可读两段，或三段。如此，亦所以治躁心。近日学者病在好高，读论语，未问学而时习，便说一贯；孟子，未言梁王问利，便说尽心；易，未看六十四卦，便先读系辞。"德明。

The Master talked about the way of reading books. Zezhi said, "I once made a schedule of reading the *Analects*, requiring that my reading go not beyond a passage in one day. " The Master replied, "For those passages not very difficult, you may as well read two or three of them in one day. Thus, this restraint of reading is curative of a rash mind. Nowadays, the trouble with learners in reading books is their aiming too high. When reading the *Analects*, before they understand 'learning with a constant perseverance and practicing frequently what is learned' (*Analects*, 1：1) well, they turn to 'an all-pervading unity (*yiguan* 一贯）' (*Analects*, 4：15）; when reading the *Mencius*, before they pore over 'King Hui of Liang asked "What counsels do you have to profit my kingdom," ' (*Mencius*, 1A：1) they pick up 'King Hui of Liang said, "I do indeed exert my mind to the utmost," ' (*Mencius*, 1A：3）; when reading the *Classic of Change*, before they touch the sixty four hexagrams, they read the appended remarks ('Xici' 系辞). " [Deming]

41 人读书，不得挥前去，下梢必无所得。如理会论语，只得理会论语，不得存心在孟子。如理会里仁一篇，且逐章相挨理会了，然后从公冶长理会去，如此便是。去伪。

While reading a book, one should not read another book, for they will get mixed up and he will end up gaining nothing. For example, when reading the *Analects*, he should concentrate on it and avoid being distracted by the *Mencius*. When reading the third book of the *Analects*, he should ponder over the passages in it one by one in their sequential order. After that he will be in a position to turn to the fourth book and then the next. [Quwei]

42 论语一日只看一段，大故明白底，则看两段。须是专一，自早至夜，虽不读，亦当涵泳常在胸次，如有一件事未了相似，到晚却把来商量。但一日积一段，日日如此，年岁间自是里面通贯，道理分明。干。

While reading the *Analects*, you should focus on one passage a day and for those not very hard to understand, read two passages. You must be concentrated on that one or two passages and from morning to evening, even when you do not read them in person, you should also bear them in your mind and think over them, just as in the day you have something yet to be finished and in the evening you take up it and put it to an end through consultation. When you focus on reading one passage a day and accumulate by doing that day by day, then you will, after a year, get a coherent understanding of them all and see what they mean clearly. [Gan]

43 问："看论语了未？"广云："已看一遍了。"曰："太快。若如此看，只是理会文义，不见得他深长底意味。所谓深长意味，又他别无说话，只是涵泳久之自见得。"广。

The Master asked me, "Have you finished reading the *Analects*?" I answered, "I have read through it once." He replied, "Too fast. If you read it that way, you can only get what it says on the surface rather than its profound meaning underlying that. As regards the so called profound

meaning, the *Analects* does not express it explicitly through its words, but it will dawn on you after you ponder over those words for a long time. "
[Guang]

44 论语，愈看愈见滋味出。若欲草草去看，尽说得通，恐未能有益。凡看文字，须看古人下字意思是如何。且如前辈作文，一篇中，须看它用意在那里。举杜子美诗云："更觉良工用心苦。"一般人看画，只见得是画一般；识底人看，便见得它精神妙处，知得它用心苦也。宇。

The Master said, "As regards the *Analects*, the more you read it, the more taste you get from it. If you look through the words of it hastily, though your explanation of them may make some sense, eventually that is not necessarily of some benefit. Whenever reading an ancient classic, you should consider what its writer intended to mean by choosing to use a certain word. It is like reading an essay written by a scholar preceding you, for which you have to read out why he wrote it. " Thereupon, he cited a line from a poem by Du Zimei 杜子美 (i. e. Du Fu 杜甫 [712 – 770], one of the most famous Tang dynasty poets), which reads "More felt is the well-thought out intention of the excellent painter. " (*Gengjue lianggong yong xin ku* 更觉良工用心苦) When ordinary viewers look at a brilliant painting, they see it no more than an ordinary painting, but when a discerning viewer looks at it, he sees its spirit and ingenuity and understands its painter's well-thought out intention. [Yu]

45 王子充问学。曰："圣人教人，只是个论语。汉魏诸儒只是训诂，论语须是玩味。今人读书伤快，须是熟方得。"曰："论语莫也须拣个紧要底看否？"曰："不可。须从头看，无精无粗，无浅无深，且都玩味得熟，道理自然出。"曰："读书未见得切，须见之行事方切。"曰："不然。且如论语，第一便教人学，便是孝弟求仁，便戒人巧言令色，便三省，也可谓甚切。"干。

Wang Zichong asked about learning. The Master answered, " The teachings of the sage are presented only in the *Analects*. The Confucians in the Han and Wei dynasties were more interested in explanation of its words, but what counts in reading the *Analects* is to taste it. The trouble with its readers today is their fast reading of it. The right way is to read it carefully over and over again. " The questioner asked further, "Should I choose some sections from the *Analects* and read them first?" The Master answered, "Never do that. You should read from the very beginning, and whether a part of it is fine or coarse, deep or shallow, it is worth reading carefully and tasting much. Thereby, the principles it implies will dawn on you naturally. " The questioner said, "Only by reading books, one can not gain personal understanding of the principles, for they can only be understood truly by seeing them practiced in doing things. " The Master responded, "Not so. For example, the *Analects* purports first to instruct learners in their learning to be filial to their parents and respectful to their elders and seek for benevolence, to abstain from fine words and an insinuating appearance, and to examine myself daily on three points. These can be said well as being very easily accessible for a personal understanding. " [Gan]

46 莫云论语中有紧要底，有泛说底，且要着力紧要底，便是拣别。若如此，则孟子一部，可删者多矣！圣贤言语，粗说细说，皆着理会教透彻。盖道理至广至大，故有说得易处，说得难处，说得大处，说得小处。若不尽见，必定有窒碍处。若谓只"言忠信，行笃敬"便可，则自汉唐以来，岂是无此等人，因甚道统之传却不曾得？亦可见矣。僭。

Don't say that there are some sections which matter and some others which are presented only generally in the *Analects*, and only the former deserves efforts. That would mean making selections. If that made any sense, then you could say the *Mencius* contains many sections that can be deleted. As regards the discourses from the sages and worthies, whether finely or coarsely presented, a learner should strive to read them for a thorough understanding. That is probably because the truths and principles are supremely great and broad-ranging and, therefore, some of them are discoursed in an easy manner, while some others in a difficult manner, and some are elaborated, while some others are mentioned briefly. If a learner fails to understand all of them, it means there must be obstructions with him. If one says that "(When one conducts himself,) let his words be sincere and truthful and his actions honorable and careful" (*Analects*, 15: 6) is enough, then, since the Han and Tang dynasties, weren't there the people whose words were sincere and truthful and whose actions honorable and careful? Why was the *daotong* 道统 (Transmission of the Way) not able to be continued? Therefore, the reason why one should not say that is obvious to see. [Xun]

47 先生问："论语如何看？"淳曰："见得圣人言行，极天理之实而无一毫之妄。学者之用工，尤当极其实而不容有一毫之妄。"曰："大纲也是如此。然就里面详细处，须要十分透彻，无一不尽。"淳。

The Master asked me, "How have you read the *Analects*?" I answered, "I have known the words and conducts of the sage, which embody supremely the substantial content of the heavenly principles, free from an iota of falsehood. When a learner makes efforts, he should particularly pursue that substantial content to its supreme extent in his learning, allowing of no iota of falsehood." The Master commented, "It is also what its basic content means. Nonetheless, as regards the particulars inside it, you should try to understand them thoroughly, leaving none of them unchewed." [Chun (淳)]

48 或讲论语，因曰："圣人说话，开口见心，必不只说半截，藏着半截。学者观书，且就本文上看取正意，不须立说别生枝蔓。唯能认得圣人句中之意，乃善。"必大。

Someone talked about the *Analects*. The Master said thereupon, "Whenever the sage wanted to say something, the moment he opened his mouth, he would display his mind, and would never say only half of it and hide the other half. While reading the book, a learner should strive to read out the right meaning intended by the text itself and avoid attempting to concoct into it a private opinion which ramifies from that. Only one who can identify what the sage meant in his words can be said as being a good reader. ” [Bida]

49 圣人之言，虽是平说，自然周遍，亭亭当当，都有许多四方八面，不少了些子意思。若门人弟子之言，便有不能无偏处。如夫子言"文质彬彬"，自然停当恰好。子贡"文犹质也，质犹文也"，便说得偏。夫子言"行有余力，则以学文"，自然有先后轻重。而子夏"虽曰未学，吾必谓之学"，便有废学之弊。端蒙。

The words of the sage, though said in an ordinary way, are naturally well-thought out, which are well-balanced in all respects, with nothing short in their meanings. By contrast, what his disciples said fall inevitably short of this or that. For example, Confucius's "Attention to *wen* 文（form and beauty）and to *zhi* 质（substance）are equally blended"（*Analects*, 6：18）is naturally conveyed, well-balanced to the just right extent, while Zixia's "Form and beauty are the same as substance and substance is the same as form and beauty"（*Analects*, 12：8）is partial；when Confucius said "If he still has energy to spare, let him devote himself to studying the historical documents and the six arts,"[①]（*Analects*, 1：6）he made naturally clear the sequence in terms of priority and importance, while Zixia's "Although men say that he has not learned, I will certainly say that he has,"（*Analects*, 1：7）is troubled by the possibility of abolishing learning. [Duanmeng]

50 人之为学，也是难。若不从文字上做工夫，又茫然不知下手处；若是字字而求，句句而论，不于身心上着切体认，则又无所益。且如说"我欲仁，斯仁至矣"，何故孔门许多弟子，圣人竟不曾以仁许之？虽以颜子之贤，而尚不违于三月之后，圣人乃曰"我欲斯至"！盖亦于日用体验，我若欲仁，其心如何？仁之至不至，其意又如何？又如说非礼

---

① The translation of the citation from *Analects* is based on a version by Lin Wusun（*Getting to Know Confucius: A New Translation of the Analects*, Beijing: Foreign Language Press, 2010, p. 29）.

勿视听言动，盍亦每事省察何者为非礼，而吾又何以能勿视勿听？若每日如此读书，庶几看得道理自我心而得，不为徒言也。壮祖。

It is truly hard for one to pursue learning. If he does not make efforts to study the words, he will feel at a loss how to do it, but if he sticks only to the words themselves one by one and sentence by sentence, without understanding them in regard to his own body and mind, he ends up gaining nothing. For example, Confucius said "The moment I wish for benevolence, it comes to me," (*Analects*, 7：30) but why didn't he, who had so many disciples, say such and such disciple was up to benevolence? Despite Yan Hui's worthiness, it is not until after three months during which "There would be nothing in his mind contrary to benevolence" (*Analects*, 6：7) that Confucius would say "The moment I wish for benevolence, it comes to me." In one's learning, why not read the words of the sage and experience what they mean in his daily life? He should ask, "If I wish for benevolence, what should my mind be like?" "What does the difference between 'It comes to me' and 'It does not come to me' mean to me?" For another example, as for the "Look not at what is contrary to propriety; listen not to what is contrary to propriety; speak not what is contrary to propriety; make no movement which is contrary to propriety," (*Analects*, 12：1) why not daily examine himself on what is contrary to propriety and how he can look not at it and listen not to it? If a learner can read the book in this way, eventually he will attain the principles by his mind and know that all those words from the sage are not vain indeed. [Zhuangzu]

51 德先问孟子。曰："孟子说得段段痛切，如检死人相似，必有个致命痕。孟子段段有个致命处，看得这般处出，方有精神。须看其说与我如何，与今人如何，须得其切处。今一切看得都困了。"扬。读孟子。

Dexian 德先 (dates unknown, a disciple of Zhu's) asked about the *Mencius*. The Master answered, "In the *Mencius*, every paragraph is cogent, reading which is comparable to conducting a postmortem examination to look for the trace of what causes the death. In each of the paragraphs of the *Mencius* is a key point, the 'trace of what causes the death,' so to speak, and only when a learner can read it out will he feel spirited. He should think what its doctrines have to do with him and with the people today and do that with regard to their key points. However, nowadays, learners feel drowsy when reading everything in the book." [Yang] The following several passages are on how to read the *Mencius*.

52 "'学问之道无它，求其放心而已。'又曰：'有是四端于我者，知皆扩而充之。'孟子说得最好。人之一心，在外者又要收入来，在内者又要推出去。孟子一部书皆是此意。"又以手作推之状，曰："推，须是用力如此。"又曰："立天之道，曰阴与阳；立地之道，曰柔与刚；立人之道，曰仁与义。"又曰："世间只有个阖辟内外，人须自体察取。"祖道。人杰录云："心在外者，要收向里；心在内者，却推出去。孟子云，学问求放心，四端扩而充之。一部孟子皆是此意。大抵一收一放，一阖一辟，道理森然。"赐录云："因说仁义，曰：'只有孟子说得好。如曰："学问之道无他，求其放心而已。"此是从外面收入里来。如曰："人之有是四端，知皆扩而充之。"又要从里面发出去。凡此出入往来，皆由个心。'又曰：'所谓"立天之道，曰阴与阳；立地之道，曰柔与刚；立人之道，曰仁与义"，都是恁地'。"

The Master said, "'The ultimate end of learning is nothing else but to seek for the lost mind,' (*Mencius*, 6A: 11) says the *Mencius*. 'Since all men have these four principles in themselves, let them know to give them all their development and completion.' (*Mencius*, 2A: 6) In these regards, the *Mencius* is the best to clarify them. As far as the human mind goes, what is outside should be taken in and what is inside should be pushed outwards. This is what is meant by the whole book of *Mencius*." Gesturing in a manner of pushing, he went on, "To push, you have to exert your strength like this." He continued, "(As the *Classic of Change* says,) '(The ancient sages) exhibited (in the hexagrams) the way of heaven, calling (the lines) *yin* and *yang*; the way of earth, calling (them) the weak (or soft) and the strong (or hard); and the way of men, under the names of benevolence and righteousness. '"① He added, "There is nothing but the opposition between opening and closing and that between inside and outside in the world, which men should experience, observe, and understand by themselves." [Zudao] Renjie's record: "The mind extended outside should be retracted inwards, while the mind restrained inside should be pushed outwards. As the *Mencius* says, 'The ultimate end of learning is nothing else but to seek for the lost mind' and 'Since all men have these four principles in themselves, let them know to give them all their development and completion.' Largely, the whole book of it expresses those ideas. Basically, the retracting inwards and the pushing outwards, one closing and one opening, these clarify the principle brilliantly." Ci's record: "Thereupon the Master talked about benevolence and righteousness, and said, 'The *Mencius* clarifies it best. For example, when it says, "The ultimate end of learning is nothing else but to seek for the lost mind," it means retracting the mind from outside, and when it says, "Since all men have these four principles in themselves, let them know to give them all their development and completion," it means extending the mind outside. Thus, retracting and extending, inside and outside, all is up to the mind.' He continued, 'What is meant by "(The ancient sages) exhibited (in the hexagrams) the way of heaven, calling (the lines) *yin* and *yang*; the way of earth, calling (them) the weak (or soft) and the strong (or hard); and the way of men, under the names of benevolence and righteousness," is similar.'"

53 读孟子，非惟看它义理，熟读之，便晓作文之法：首尾照应，血脉通贯，语意反复，明白峻洁，无一字闲。人若能如此作文，便是第一等文章！侗。

When reading the *Mencius*, you should not only try to understand its thought. If you read it carefully over and over again, you will also know how to compose a piece of writing. With its beginning and end resonating with each other, the text of the *Mencius* conveys its idea by emphatic repetitions,

---

① Cited from "Shuo Gua" 说卦 (Explanation of Hexagrams) in the *Classic of Change*. The translation is based on the version rendered by J. Legge (see http://ctext.org/book-of-changes).

through which a vein runs coherently. Stylistically, it is manifest, neat, and stern, without a single word useless. If you can write in such manner, your writing will be the first-rate. [Xian]

54 孟子之书，明白亲切，无甚可疑者。只要日日熟读，须教它在吾肚中先千百转，便自然纯熟。某初看时，要逐句去看它，便觉得意思浅迫。至后来放宽看，却有条理。然此书不特是义理精明，又且是甚次第文章。某因读，亦知作文之法。植。

The book of the *Mencius* is intelligible and approachable all over, with little subject to suspicion. So long as you read it carefully day by day to the extent that it gets rolled hundreds of times in your mind, you will naturally become well versed in it. When I took it up at first, I tried to read it sentence by sentence only to feel that what it meant was shallow. Later when I saw it in a broad view, I got to know that it had its own well-organized veins in itself. Then I was further aware that it was not only manifest and penetrating in presenting ideas, but also an excellent piece of writing. Therefore, I read it more consciously and thereby knew the way of writing. [Zhi (植)]

55 孟子，全读方见得意思贯。某因读孟子，见得古人作文法，亦有似今人间架。淳。

As regards the *Mencius*, only when you finish reading its whole text can you know it conveys its idea with unity and coherence. When I read the *Mencius*, thereupon, I saw the ancient way of writing, which employed a framework similar to that used by writers today. [Chun (淳)]

56 "孟子文章妙不可言。"文蔚曰："他每段自有一二句纲领，其后只是解此一二句。"曰："此犹是浅者，其它自有妙处。惟老苏文深得其妙。"文蔚。

The Master exclaimed, "How fantastic the writing of Mencius is!" I responded, "In each of his paragraphs, he began it with one or two sentences which serve as its guiding and what he said after them is only their elaboration." He said then, "That is merely the superficial, for it manifests more indescribable fortes, to which only those of the writings by Old Su (i. e. Su Xun 苏洵 [1009 – 1066]) can be comparable. " [Wenwei]

57 孟子之文，恐一篇是一人作。又疑孟子亲作，不然，何其妙也！岂有如是人出孟子之门，而没世不闻耶！方。

As regards the seven pieces of writing the text of the *Mencius* comprises, I'm afraid, they were composed by seven writers respectively, but at the same time I also suspect that they were out of Mencius's own hand, or else, why was it written so wonderfully? Could it be said that there was a disciple of Mencius who wrote the seven pieces but never was known to the world? [Fang]

58 集注且须熟读，记得。方子。集注。

You must peruse the *Jizhu* 集注 (Collected Annotations, referring to *Lunyu Jizhu* 论语集注 [Collected Annotations of the *Analects*] and *Menzi Jizhu* 孟子集注 [Collected Annotations of the *Mencius*]). Remember! [Fangzi] The following several passages are concerned with both *Collected Annotations of the Analects* and *Collected Annotations of the Mencius*.

59 语吴仁父曰："某语孟集注，添一字不得，减一字不得，公子细看。"又曰："不多一个字，不少一个字。"节。

The Master said to Wu Renfu 吴仁父 (dates unknown, a disciple of Zhu's), "As regards what I said in my *Collected Annotations of the Analects* and *of the Mencius*, there is no adding a more word to it, nor is there deleting a word from it. " He added, "It does not have a single superfluous word, nor does it want a more word. " [Jie]

60 论语集注如称上称来无异，不高些，不低些。自是学者不肯用工看。如看得透，存养熟，可谓甚生气质。友仁。

My words in *Collected Annotations of the Analects* were chosen, as it were, by weighing them on a scale so that they did not mean more or less than required. Unfortunately, you learners do not exert yourselves to peruse them. If you see them through and thereby make enough efforts to preserve your mind and cultivate your nature, it will be very productive of your physical nature. [Youren]

61 “某于论孟，四十余年理会，中间逐字称等，不教偏些子。学者将注处，宜子细看。”又曰：“解说圣贤之言，要义理相接去，如水相接去，则水流不碍。”后又云：“中庸解每番看过，不甚有疑。大学则一面看，一面疑，未甚惬意，所以改削不已。”过。

The Master said, “I spent forty years reading the *Analects* and the *Mencius* for a through understanding and in the period, I weighed every word in them and tried to make sure that my understanding of it was accurate and free from deviation. You learners should read carefully my annotations of the two books.” He continued, “To explain the words said by the sages and worthies, one should ensure that his explanation connects well with their thoughts. It is like this waterway getting to connect with that waterway, and if the connection is made well, the water will run smoothly from one to the other, free from any obstruction.” After some time, he said, “Every time I read my interpretation of the *Doctrine of the Mean*, I have felt little suspicion. As for my interpretation of the *Great Learning*, while reading it, I can not help feeling suspicion of this or that, and have not been satisfied with it completely. Thus, I have been making change of it verbally.” [Guo]

62 读书别无法，只管看，便是法。正如呆人相似，捱来捱去。自家都未要先立意见，且虚心只管看。看来看去，自然晓得。某那集注都详备，只是要人看无一字闲。那个无紧要闲底字，越要看。自家意里说是闲字，那个正是紧要字。上蔡云“人不可无根”，便是难。所谓根者，只管看，便是根，不是外面别讨个根来。僩。

There is no other way of reading books than simply going ahead in reading them. A reader should look like a fool in reading this here or that there. He should prevent himself from any preoccupations, but rather keep on reading and reading. Thus, he will understand naturally what he has read. My *Collected Annotations* is complete and detailed in its explanations, where, a reader of it should know, not a single word is useless. If a word seems to mean little to him, it calls for his more attention. If according to his understanding a word is of no use, it is the very word which matters. Shangcai (i. e. Xie Liangzuo) said, "A man can not be rootless," but it is truly difficult. The so called root can be understood as doing nothing but reading, and it does not mean asking for a root from outside. [Xian]

63 前辈解说，恐后学难晓，故集注尽撮其要，已说尽了，不须更去注脚外又添一段说话。只把这个熟看，自然晓得，莫枉费心去外面思量。

I summarized those preceding scholars' explanations and made clear all their key points in my *Collected Annotations*, for fear that learners today may find them hard to understand. So do not go out of the way and fetch something elsewhere to add to those footnotes. It is enough only to read carefully those offered in my *Collected Annotations* and naturally you will gain your understanding, so you should avoid trying in vain to consider outside them.

64 问："集注引前辈之说，而增损改易本文，其意如何？"曰："其说有病，不欲更就下面安注脚。"又问："解文义处，或用'者'字，或用'谓'字，或用'犹'字，或直言，其轻重之意如何？"曰："直言，直训如此。犹者，犹是如此。"又问"者"、"谓"如何。曰："是恁地。"节。

Question: You, sir, in your *Collected Annotations*, cited those preceding scholars' opinions, yet increased words to, or decreased words from, or even changed their texts, what was your purpose in doing that?

Answer: Because there were troubles with their opinions and I did not want to use too many footnotes under them.

Further question: In your explanations of the meanings of the Four Books, you used *zhe* 者 (an auxiliary) and *wei* 谓 (a verb), or *you* 犹 (a verb), or gave an explanation without using them. Is there any difference between them in terms of their importance?

Answer：To give an explanation without using them is to annotate directly. The *you* means "to be just like. "

Further question：What about the *zhe* and *wei*?

Answer：They together mean "this or that means such and such. " ［Jie］

65 集注中有两说相似而少异者，亦要相资。有说全别者，是未定也。淳。

In my *Collected Annotations*, there are some cases where two opinions are largely similar to each other, and you should read them by cross reference. If two opinions are completely different, which one is right is yet to be determined. ［Chun（淳）］

66 或问："集注有两存者，何者为长?"曰："使某见得长底时，岂复存其短底? 只为是二说皆通，故并存之。然必有一说合得圣人之本意，但不可知尔。"复曰："大率两说，前一说胜。"拱寿。

Someone asked, "In some places in your *Collected Annotations*, there are two opinions presented side by side for explaining the same point of the Four Books, then which one is more important?" The Master answered, "If I had been clear which one is more important, would I have had the less important one stay there? The two are cited there because both are reasonable. However, of them, there must be one closer to what the sage originally intended to mean, but we have no way of knowing which one is. " He added, "If two opinions are juxtaposed there, probably, the first one is a little more advisable. " ［Gongshou］

67 问："语解胡氏为谁?"曰："胡明仲也。向见张钦夫殊不取其说，某以为不然。他虽有未至处，若是说得是者，岂可废!"广。

Question：In your *Collected Annotations of the Analects*, you mention Hu. Who is he?

Answer：He is Hu Mingzhong 胡明仲 (dates unknown, a Southern Song scholar). Zhang Qinfu 张钦夫 (i. e. Zhang Shi) refused to adopt his opinion, but I didn't think he could be neglected. Despite his weak points, he had some opinions advisable, so how could they be ignored? [Guang]

68 集注中曾氏是文清公，黄氏是黄祖舜，晁氏是晁以道，李氏是李光祖。广。

In the *Collected Annotations*, Zeng is Duke Wenqing (posthumous title of Zeng Ji 曾几 [1085 – 1166], courtesy name Jifu 吉甫); Huang is Huang Zushun 黄祖舜 (1100 – 1165, courtesy name Jidao 继道); Chao is Chao Yidao 晁以道 (i. e. Chao Yuezhi 晁说之 [1059 – 1129], courtesy name Yidao); Li is Li Guangzu 李光祖 (i. e. Li Yu 李郁 [1086 – 1150], courtesy name Guangzu). [Guang]

69 程先生经解，理在解语内。某集注论语，只是发明其辞，使人玩味经文，理皆在经文内。易传不看本文，亦是自成一书。杜预左传解，不看经文，亦自成一书。郑笺不识经大旨，故多随句解。

As regards Master Cheng Yi's interpretation of the *Analects*, his understandings of the principles are elucidated in his explanatory words. By contrast, in my *Collected Annotations of the Analects*, what I purport to do is to clarify what the words of its text mean so as to help learners to taste them, and the principles are still contained in the text itself. Without reading the text proper of the *Classic of Change*, we can also take *Yizhuan* 易传 (Explanations of the *Classic of Change*) as a separate book. This is also true of Du Yu's 杜预 (222 – 285) annotation of *Zuozhuan* 左传 (Zuo's Explanation of the *Spring and Autumn Annals*), which can also stand by itself. However, when Zheng Xuan's 郑玄 (127 – 200) made interpretation of *Mao Shi* 毛诗 (Maos' Edition of the *Classic of Poetry*), since he failed to understand the basic purport of the *Classic of Poetry*, he explained the poems line by line.

70 论语集注盖某十年前本，为朋友间传去，乡人遂不告而刊。及知觉，则已分裂四出，而不可收矣。其间多所未稳，煞误看读。要之，圣贤言语，正大明白，本不须恁地传注。正所谓"记其一而遗其百，得其粗而遗其精"者也。道夫。

That first edition of *Collected Annotations of the Analects* is probably a version of mine ten years ago. At first, that version was spread among the friends of mine and, without informing me, some townsmen published it. When I was given a copy, I found the collected annotations were full of ramifications, but then they were already uncorrectable. Included in the version were many opinions (by preceding scholars), some of which were not well-grounded, and thus led their readers rather astray. In a word, what the sages and worthies said is right, great, and clear, for which there is no need of making those annotations. That is the very meaning of "One is recorded, yet a hundred are lost; the coarse is gained, yet the quintessence is lost."
[Daofu]

71 或述孟子集注意义以问。曰："大概如此，只是要熟，须是日日认过。"述大学以问。曰："也只如此，只是要日日认过。读新底了，反转看旧底，教十分熟后，自别有意思。"又曰："如鸡伏卵，只管日日伏，自会成。"贺孙。

Someone asked about the meaning of something in *Collected Annotations of the Mencius*. The Master answered, "Largely that is it. You should strive to get conversant with it by reading it daily." The questioner continued asking about the meaning of something in *Interpretation of the Great Learning*. The Master replied, "Also that is nothing but it. You should also read it daily. While you read some new part, think over what you have already read in relation to it. When you become very familiar with everything in the book, you will get to taste something different from it." He added, "It is like a hen hatching her eggs. So long as it keeps on hatching them day by day, it will succeed in due time." [Hesun]

72 初解孟子时，见自不明。随着前辈说，反不自明，不得其要者多矣。方。

When I made my first efforts to interpret the *Mencius*, I could not see its meanings clear. While following those preceding scholars' opinions, I felt even more confused, and there were many places where I did not see the point. [Fang]

73 集注乃集义之精髓。道夫。集注、集义。

The *Collected Annotations* is a collection of quintessence from *Jiyi* 集义 (i. e. *Lunyu Jiyi* 论语集义 [Collected Meanings of the *Analects*]) . [Daofu] The following several passages are about the *Collected Annotations of the Analects* and *Collected Meanings of the Analects*.

74 问：“孟子比论语却易看，但其间数段极难晓。”曰：“只尽心篇语简了，便难理会。且如‘养气’一章，被它说长了，极分晓，只是人不熟读。”问：“论语浩博，须作年岁间读，然中间切要处先理会，如何？”曰：“某近来作论语略解，以精义太详，说得没紧要处，多似空费工夫，故作此书。而今看得，若不看精义，只看略解，终是不浃洽。”因举五峰旧见龟山，问为学之方。龟山曰：“且看论语。”五峰问：“论语中何者为要？”龟山不对。久之，曰：“熟读。”先生因曰：“如今且只得挨将去。”干。

Someone asked, "The *Mencius* is easier to read than the *Analects*, but some sections of it are extremely difficult to understand. (How do you think?)" The Master answered, "Only the seventh piece of the seven is simple in language, which, however, makes it hard to understand. As for the others, for example, the second piece concerned with nourishing the vital force, which is elaborated at length, is very easy to understand, only learners have not perused it enough. " The questioner further asked, "Since the *Analects* is extensive and broad-ranging, a learner should spend one year or more reading it. Nevertheless, what about reading first those more essential passages which are in the middle of it?" The Master answered, "Lately, I wrote *Lunyu Luejie* 论语略解 (Brief Explanation of the *Analects*). Since the *Collected Meanings* (of the *Analects*) is too detailed, much of it does not concern the important points. So when a learner reads it, it seems largely a waste of time and energy. That is why I wrote the *Brief Explanation*. But as I consider it now, if a learner reads only the *Brief Explanation* but not the *Collected Meanings*, what he will get is eventually inadequate and incomplete." Then he cited a conversation between Wufeng 五峰 (i. e. Hu Hong) and Guishan 龟山 (i. e. Yang Shi) when the former visited the latter for advice on the way of learning: "Guishan said to Wufeng, 'Just read the *Analects*.' Wufeng asked, 'What is the essential in the *Analects*?' Guishan did not give him an immediate answer and after some time he said, 'Read it carefully over and over again.' My teacher (Zhu Xi once pursued learning with Hu Hong) had no choice but say 'Now I have to exert myself to read (the *Analects*).'" [Gan]

75 诸朋友若先看集义，恐未易分别得，又费工夫。不如看集注，又恐太易了。这事难说。不奈何，且须看集注教熟了，可更看集义。集义多有好处，某却不编出者，这处却好商量，却好子细看所以去取之意如何。须是看得集义，方始无疑。某旧日只恐集义中有未晓得义理，费尽心力，看来看去，近日方始都无疑了。贺孙。

If you, my friends, read *Collected Meanings* first, I am afraid, it is not easy for you to discriminate those many opinions, and also reading it is rather time-consuming. It is better to read *Collected Annotations*, but perhaps it is a little too easy. It is a hard choice. You may read *Collected Annotations* first and get familiar with it before turning to *Collected Meanings*. There are many merits within *Collected Meanings*, but when I compiled it I did not make them clear, the reason for which is easy to see. It calls for your careful reading and thinking over what my taking and dropping mean. You have to read and understand *Collected Meanings* before you can get free from doubts. In those days, I spent very much mental effort reading it over and over again, for fear that there might be still some meanings and principles I failed to have understood. It is only recently that I have resolved all my doubts. [Hesun]

76 因说"吾与回言"一章，曰："便是许多紧要底言语，都不曾说得出。且说精义是许多言语，而集注能有几何言语！一字是一字。其间有一字当百十字底，公都把做等闲看了。圣人言语本自明白，不须解说。只为学者看不见，所以做出注解与学者省一半力。若注解上更看不出，却如何看得圣人意出！"又曰："凡看文字，端坐熟读，久久于正文边自有细字注脚迸出来，方是自家见得亲切。若只于外面捉摸个影子说，终不济事。圣人言语只熟读玩味，道理自不难见。若果曾着心，而看他道理不出，则圣贤为欺我矣！如老苏辈，只读孟韩二子，便翻绎得许多文章出来。且如攻城，四面牢壮，若攻得一面破时，这城子已是自家底了，不待更攻得那三面，方入得去。初学固是要看大学论孟。若读得大学一书透彻，其它书都不费力，触处便见。"喟然叹者久之，曰："自有这个道理，说与人不信！"

Thereupon the Master talked about the passage introduced by "I have talked with Hui for a whole day" (*Analects*, 2: 9). He said, "There were many important words in my mind about that passage, but I did not say them (in *Collected Annotations*). Though *Collected Meanings* is lengthy, *Collected Annotations* is pithy, where one word is one word. Of those words I used in it, there are some ones very rich in meaning, each worth a hundred words, but unfortunately you treat them as merely ordinary words. What the sage said is clear and intelligible, for which there is no need for explanation. But all the same the learners today can not see his points, so I wrote those annotations by reading which they may save half their effort otherwise needed to understand them. But if a learner can not even get to understand those annotations, how can he figure out what the sage meant to say?" He continued, "Whenever you read something, you should sit up squarely and immerse yourself in the words. After a long time, in due course, there will naturally spurt smaller-worded annotations in the margin before you, so to speak. That means you have already gained a personal understanding of it. But if you only make up a shadow outside it and try to speak of it, it will be of no use to you. Peruse the sage's words and taste them, and you will see with some ease what he intended to say. If you devote all yourself to reading them, yet can not make out what his meaning is, can't it be said that he deceived you? Such scholars as Old Su, only by reading the words of Mencius and of Hanzi (i. e. Han Fei 韩非 [c. 280 – 233 BC]) and following them, were able to write many fine essays. Reading books is comparable to attacking a city. Though the city is well defended on all four sides, when you break through any one side of it, the city will become yours. It is not that you can not occupy the city until you grasp all its four sides. It is true that a beginner in learning should read the *Great Learning*, the *Analects*, and the *Mencius* first, but if he can gain a thorough understanding of the single book of the *Great Learning*, his reading of other books will be much easier and then whatever he touches, he will see it through with ease. " With a long sighing, he said, "That is true, as a matter of course, but when told that, they don't believe it. "

77 问:"近看论语精义,不知读之当有何法?"曰:"别无方法,但虚心熟读而审择之耳。"人杰。集义。

Question: Recently I have been reading your *Collected Meanings of the Analects*. What is the proper way of reading it?

Answer: No other way than perusing it with an open mind and discriminating prudently the opinions. [Renjie] The following several passages concern *Collected Meanings*.

78 因论集义论语,曰:"于学者难说。看众人所说七纵八横,如相战之类,于其中分别得甚妙。然精神短者,又难教如此。只教看集注,又皆平易了,兴起人不得。"振。

Thereupon the Master talked about his *Collected Meanings of the Analects*. He said, "It is hard to say how a learner should read it. Those various opinions collected in it appear untrammeled in a display of facility, opposing to one another like engaging in wars. By reading each of them, learners can taste its own forte, but it is hard to teach that to a learner short of mettle. If I let learners read *Collected Annotations* only, it will prove too plain and easy to be able to arouse their spirits. "［Zhen］

79 问:"要看精义,不知如何看?"曰:"只是逐段子细玩味。公记得书否? 若记不得, 亦玩味不得。横渠云: '读书须是成诵。'"又曰:"某近看学者须是专一。譬如服药, 须是专服一药, 方见有效。"干。

Question: I want to read your *Collected Meanings of the Analects*, but how should I do it?

Answer: You just taste it by poring over its paragraphs one by one. Have you learnt by heart the text of the *Analects*? If you have not, it is impossible for you to taste it well. As Henqü said, "To understand what a book means, one must recite it first. "

Further answer: Recently, I have got to know truly that a learner must be single-minded in reading. It is like taking medicine. An ill man must take only one medicine before it takes effect well. ［Gan］

80 问:"精义有说得高远处, 不知如何看。"曰:"也须都子细看, 取予却在自家。若以为高远而略之, 便卤莽了!"干。

Question: In your *Collected Meanings*, there are some opinions which sound far and high. How should I read them?

Answer: You must read them all carefully, but whether you take them or not depends on you. If you ignore them because they are far and high, you are reckless. ［Gan］

81 读书, 且须熟读玩味, 不必立说, 且理会古人说教通透。如语孟集义中所载诸先生语, 须是熟读, 一一记放心下, 时时将来玩味, 久久自然理会得。今有一般学者, 见人恁么说, 不穷究它说是如何, 也去立一说来捵说, 何益于事! 只赢得一个理会不得尔。广。

While reading a book, you should peruse and taste it, and just try your best to understand thoroughly what its ancient author says, refraining from conceiving your own opinion in concoction with it. For example, as regards the words said by those many preceding scholars, which are carried in *Collected Meanings of the Analects* and *Collected Meanings of Mencius*, you should read them carefully over and over again, learn them all by heart, and chew them from time to time, and in due course you will understand them naturally. Nowadays, there are a type of learners who, when they hear others air their opinions yet do not inquire what those opinions are, follow suit and put forth their own opinions on the book they are reading. What avail is that to? What they end up with is nothing but a failure to get a true understanding of the book. [Guang]

82 读书，须痛下工夫，须要细看。心粗性急，终不济事。如看论语精义，且只将诸说相比并看，自然比得正道理出来。如识高者，初见一条，便能判其是非。如未能，且细看，如看按款相似。虽未能便断得它按，然已是经心尽知其情矣。只管如此，将来粗急之心亦磨斦得细密了。横渠云："文欲密察，心欲洪放。"若不痛做工夫，终是难入。德明。

Reading calls for strenuous efforts for perusal. Any rashness and impatience entail no gain in reading. For example, when you read *Collected Meanings of the Analects*, you should study-read those many opinions comparatively, by which you will see the right principles naturally. If one is insightful, at the first sight of an opinion, he will be able to judge whether it is right or wrong. If one can not be that insightful, he should read it carefully first, just like examining a note. Even if he still can not say whether its conclusion is right or not, he has already pondered it and known what it is concerned with all over. A learner should do just in this way, and in the future even a mind rash and impatient by nature will get refined as being careful and prudent. As Hengqü remarked rightly, "The text should be scrutinized and the mind should be enlarged." Without making strenuous efforts, a learner will eventually go nowhere. [Deming]

83 看精义，须宽着心，不可看杀了。二先生说，自有相关透处，如伊川云："有主则实。"又云："有主则虚。"如孟子云："生于其心，害于其政；发于其政，害于其事。"又云："作于其心，害于其事；作于其事，害于其政。"自当随文、随时、随事看，各有通彻处。德明。

When reading *Collected Meanings*, you should keep a broadened and flexible mind and never get sluggish. The sayings of Master Cheng Hao and Master Cheng Yi are all related in one way or another. For example, Yichuan (i. e. Cheng Yi) said "With its master, (the mind) is substantial," and also said "With its master, (the mind) is empty." Mencius said, "(Their evils,) growing in the mind, do injury to government, and, displayed in the government, are hurtful to the conduct of affairs," (*Mencius*, 2A：2) and also said, "(Their delusions), springing up in the minds, do injury to their practice of affairs, and, shown in their practice of affairs, are pernicious to their government." (*Mencius*, 2A：2) So you should try to read their words in specific contexts, on specific occasions, and with regard to specific events, and in this way you will understand them coherently. [Deming]

84 读论语，须将精义看。先看一段，次看第二段，将两段比较孰得孰失，孰是孰非。又将第三段比较如前。又总一章之说而尽比较之。其间须有一说合圣人之意，或有两说，有三说，有四五说皆是，又就其中比较疏密。如此，便是格物。及看得此一章透彻，则知便至。或自未有见识，只得就这里挨。一章之中，程子之说多是，门人之说多非。然初看时，不可先萌此心，门人所说亦多有好处。蕫卿曰："只将程子之说为主，如何？"曰："不可，只得以理为主，然后看它底。看得一章直是透彻了，然后看第二章，亦如此法。若看得三四篇，此心便熟，数篇之后，迎刃而解矣。某尝苦口与学者说得口破，少有依某去着力做工夫者。且如'格物、致知'之章，程子与门人之说，某初读之，皆不敢疑。后来编出细看，见得程子诸说虽不同，意未尝不贯。其门人之说，与先生盖有大不同者矣。"骧。

The Master said, "While you read the *Analects*, you should meanwhile read *Collected Meanings of the Analects*. Peruse the first opinion and then the second opinion in it, and by comparing them, try to see the gain and loss of either and find which is right and which is wrong. And then turn to the third opinion and also compare it with the previous two. All the explanatory opinions in a chapter should be compared in that way. Of them, there must be one, or two, or three, or all that are in conformity with what the sage intended to mean. Then they should also be compared with regard to their rigorousness and completeness. Working in such a manner is the very process of investigating things. When you have got a thorough understanding of a chapter, it means knowledge has reached you. For those learners who are devoid of insights, they have to make strenuous efforts here in that way. In a chapter, generally speaking, most of those explanations of Master Cheng are right, while those of his disciples are often wrong. However, when you read them first, never get preoccupied by that idea, for even in those explanations said by his disciples are some good points. " Feiqing said, " How about reading Master Cheng's explanations only as the principal?" The Master replied, " Never do that. You should have to take the principle as the principal and thereby consider their explanations. After gaining a truly thorough understanding of the first chapter, you can take up the second by the same manner. When you have finished reading three or four pieces in *Collected Meanings of the Analects* that way, you will become conversant with them, and when you read all other pieces after them, they will turn a piece of cake to you. However, though I have taken great pains in instructing learners to read in that manner, few have made efforts to read as I told them. For example, as regards the chapter on investigation of things and extension of knowledge, when I read those explanations of Master Cheng and his disciples first, I did not dare to doubt them at all. But when I compiled them, I read them punctiliously and found that Master Cheng's explanations, though different in wording, were never inconsistent with one another, but those of his disciples distanced themselves quite far from their master's. " [Xiang]

85 读书考义理，似是而非者难辨。且如精义中，惟程先生说得确当。至其门人，非惟不尽得夫子之意，虽程子之意，亦多失之。今读语孟，不可便道精义都不是，都废了。须借它做阶梯去寻求，将来自见道理。知得它是非，方是自己所得处。如张无垢文字浅近，却易见也。问："如何辨得似是而非？"曰："遗书所谓义理栽培者是也。如此用工，久之自能辨得。"德明。

The Master said, "While reading a book, you should examine its meanings and principles, but it is hard to discriminate those specious explanations on them. For example, in *Collected Meanings*, only those explanations said by Master Cheng are accurate and to the point. As to those by his disciples, they not only fail to understand completely what Confucius intended to say but also deviate much from what their teacher wanted to convey. When you read the *Analects*, do not say that all the opinions gathered in *Collected Meanings* are unacceptable and thus discard them. You should take them as your ladder towards your true understanding of the truths. If you can penetrate their merits and demerits, it will be your gain from reading them. For example, the explanations put forth by Zhang Wugou 张无垢 (i. e. Zhang Jiucheng 张九成 [1092 – 1159]) are worded in too simple and plain a style, but his idea is easy to see. " Asked "How to discriminate the specious explanations?" The Master answered, "You can read carefully the part on *yili zaipei* 义理栽培 (cultivating meaning and principle) in *Er Cheng Yishu* 二程遗书 (Surviving Works of Two Chengs of Henan) for an advisable way. If you keep on making efforts that way, in due time, you will naturally be able to discriminate them. " (Deming)

86 论语中，程先生及和靖说，只于本文添一两字，甚平淡，然意味深长，须当子细看。要见得它意味，方好。淳。

In *Collected Meanings of the Analects*, as regards Master Cheng's and Hejing's (i. e. Yin Tun's) explanations, they only take the form of adding one or two words to the original, so they appear rather plain and simple, but what is meant by them is deep and profound, so you should peruse them. You should strive to see their true purpose and taste their true flavor. [Chun（淳）]

87 问："精义中，尹氏说多与二程同，何也？"曰"二程说得已明，尹氏只说出。"问："谢氏之说多华揜。"曰："胡侍郎尝教人看谢氏论语，以其文字上多有发越处。"敬仲。

Question: As carried in your *Collected Meanings*, most opinions said by Yin (i. e. Yin Tun) are the same as those of Two Chengs. Why?

Answer: What Two Chengs said is already clear, while what Yin said only cites theirs.

Further question: Xie's (i. e. Xie Liangzuo's) explanations tend to be obviously ornate and stretched. (How do you think?)

Answer: Assistant Minister Hu (i. e. Hu Yin) once instructed others to read Xie's interpretation of the *Analects* for the reason that, verbally, many parts in it were inspiring and revealing. [Jingzhong]

88 先生问："寻常精义，自二程外，孰得？"曰："自二程外，诸说恐不相上下。"又问萤卿。答曰："自二程外，惟龟山胜。"曰："龟山好引证，未说本意，且将别说折过。人若看它本说未分明，并连所引失之。此亦是一病。"又问仲思。答曰："据某，恐自二程外，惟和靖之说为简当。"曰："以某观之，却是和靖说得的当。虽其言短浅，时说不尽，然却得这意思。"顷之，复曰："此亦大纲偶然说到此，不可以为定也。"

The Master asked, "As regards those general explanations in *Collected Meanings*, excluding Two Chengs, who is the most insightful?" Someone answered, "Excluding Two Chengs, I'm afraid, all are about the same." He asked Feiqing that question, who answered, "Excluding Two Chengs, only Guishan (i. e. Yang Shi) is the most insightful." The Master said, then, "Guishan was keen on quotations from others. Unusually, he did not explain the original meaning of the text, but rather adapted what others had said of it.

When reading his words, we find his explanations of the original text are not clear, which, together with his quotations from others, are inadequate. That is a problem with him. " He asked Zhongsi the same question, who answered, "According to my understanding, excluding Two Chengs, only Hejing's explanations are terse and right. " The Master commented, "As I see it, it is Hejing indeed who is the most accurate and appropriate. In spite of his brevity and shallowness, and sometimes failure to be complete, his understandings are right. " After a while, he added, "This question occurred to me, which is concerned with the generality of the book, and you should not take what I said just now as a final conclusion. "

89 明道说道理，一看便好，愈看而愈好。伊川犹不无难明处，然愈看亦愈好。上蔡过高，多说人行不得底说话。杨氏援引十件，也要做十件引上来。范氏一个宽大气象，然说得走作，便不可晓。端蒙。

At first sight of Mingdao's (i. e. Cheng Hao's) elucidation of the principles, I know it is good and the more I read it, the better I think it is. Though Yichuan's (i. e. Cheng Yi's) has some points hard to understand, the more I read it, the better I feel it is, too. Shangcai's (i. e. Xie Liangzuo's) reads too high, which is prone to something that is impracticable. Yang's (i. e. Yang Shi's), when making ten citations, tends to match them with ten of his own ideas. That of Fan (i. e. Fan Zuyu 范祖禹 [1041 – 1098]) shows broadness, yet is troubled by affectation, so it is hard to understand. [Duanmeng]

90 上蔡论语解，言语极多。看得透时，它只有一两字是紧要。赐。

Shangcai's *Interpretation of the Analects* is extremely profuse with words, but when you see them through, you will know only one or two of the words count. [Ci]

91 问："谢氏说多过，不如杨氏说最实。"曰："尹氏语言最实，亦多是处。但看文字，亦不可如此先怀权断于胸中。如谢氏说，十分有九分过处，其间亦有一分说得恰好处，岂可先立定说。今且须虚心玩理。"大雅问:"理如何玩?"曰:"今当以小说明之:一人欲学相气色,其师与五色线一串,令入暗室中认之。云:'辨得此五色出,方能相气色。'看圣人意旨,亦要如此精专,方得之。到自得处,不从说来,虽人言亦不信。盖开导虽假人言,得处须是自得,人则无如之何也。孔子言语简,若欲得之,亦非用许多工夫不得。孟子之言多,若欲得之,亦合用许多工夫。孔子言简,故意广无失。孟子言多意长,前呼后唤,事理俱明,亦无失。若他人语多,则有失。某今接士大夫,答问多,转觉辞多无益。"大雅。

Someone said to the Master, "Most of Xie's explanations go beyond what is proper, not as substantial as Yang's." The Master replied, "What Yin's discourse is the most substantial and many opinions of his are also right. However, when you read something, you should not preoccupy your mind with such assertions first. For example, though nine tenths of Xie's explanations go a little too far, still there is one tenth which is to the point, so how can you deny everything of him? Now keep your mind open and 'play with' the principle." I asked, "How to 'play with' the principle?" The Master answered, "Now let me illustrate it with something from a story. Once upon a time, there was a man who wanted to learn how to practice fortune-telling by reading countenances. His teacher gave him a bundle of five-colored threads, and told him to identify the different colored threads in a dark room, saying, 'Only when you can identify the different colors will you be in a position to practice fortune-telling by reading countenances.' So when you try to figure out the idea purported by the words of the sage, only by such painstaking concentration can you make it. When you have gained a true understanding of the sage, even if you read another's explanation of him, yet find it inconsistent with your understanding, you will not be led away by it. Probably, in teaching and learning, though one has to borrow something said by others, so long as he can gain a personal understanding of the principles, no one else can shake him. What Confucius said is brief and concise, and without making much effort, you can not understand him. What Mencius said is much, but if you want to understand him, you have also to make much effort. Due to his brevity and conciseness, Confucius was wide-ranging, with nothing erroneous. With his length and load of meaning, calling at the beginning and responding in the end, Mencius is clear in both meaning and principle, also with nothing erroneous. By contrast, when others talk much, they err more or less. Recently, I received some scholar-officials and answered their many questions, but I have felt that talking too much is to little avail. "［Daya］

92 原父论语解，紧要处只是庄老。必大。诸家解。

In the interpretation of the *Analects* made by Yuanfu 原父（courtesy name of Liu Chang 刘敞［1019 – 1068］), what is crucial is but his discourse on Zhuang and Lao（i. e. Zhuangzi and Laozi）.［Bida］The following is concerned with various interpretations of the *Analects*.

93 先生问："曾文清有论语解，曾见否？"曰："尝见之，其言语简。"曰："其中极有好处，亦有先儒道不到处。某不及识之，想是一精确人，故解书言多简。"某曰："闻之，文清每日早，必正衣冠，读论语一篇。"曰："此所谓'学而时习之'，与今日学者读论语不同。"可学。

The Master asked, "Zen, Duke Wenqing, wrote an interpretation of the *Analects*. Have you read it?" I answered, "I once read it, which is plain and simple in language." He said, "But it contains some points very insightful, and something the previous Confucian scholars failed to see. I have not met him yet, but I think he must be a man keen on conciseness and accuracy, so on the whole his interpretation is terse in language." I replied, "I have heard of him that each day he got up in the morning and worn his cap and attire neat, and then read a passage in the *Analects*." The Master commented, "That is what is meant by 'learning with a constant perseverance and practicing frequently what is learned,' (*Analects*, 1: 1) a way different from that by which the learners at present read the *Analects*. " ［Kexue］

94 建安吴才老作论语十说，世以为定夫作者，非也。其功浅，其害亦浅。又为论语考异，其功渐深，而有深害矣。至为语解，即以己意测度圣人，谓圣人为多诈轻薄人矣！徐蕆为刊其书越州以行。方。

Wu Cailao 吴才老（i. e. Wu Yu 吴棫［c. 1100 – 1154］）in Jian'an（what is now Jian'ou, Fujian）made a ten-parted interpretation of the *Analects*, which has been taken widely for something written by Dingfu 定夫（courtesy name of You Cu 游酢［1053 – 1123］）, but actually not. When he began to study the *Analects*, he did not delve into it deep, so the harm his work brought about was also not deep. But later when he engaged in examining the textual differences in regard to the *Analects* and got deeper and deeper therein, what he did brought about deep harm. While interpreting the *Analects*, he tended to read too much of his conjecture into what the sage intended to say and even claimed that the sage was deceptive and made fool of people. Xu Chan 徐蕆（dates unknown）had his book published and circulated in Yuezhou（roughly in what is now Shaoxing, Zhejiang）. ①
［Fang］

95 学者解论语，多是硬说。须习熟，然后有个入头处。季札。

When scholars interpreted the *Analects*, most of them made forced and even far-fetched explanations. You have to read the book and get conversant with it before finding out an entry into its domain. ［Jizha］

96 孟子疏，乃邵武士人假作。蔡季通识其人。当孔颖达时，未尚孟子，只尚论语孝经尔。其书全不似疏样，不曾解出名物制度，只绕缠赵岐之说耳。璘。

The *Menzi Shu* 孟子疏（Sub-Annotation of the *Mencius*）is a work

---

① The translator suspects that in the last sentence of this passage the name Xu Dian 徐蕆 should be Xu Chan 徐蕆, for no information of the former is available, while the latter is the name of the writer of a preface for a book written by Wu Yu 吴棫, so Xu Chan was probably the publisher of the book mentioned in the passage; hence the change of the name in the translation.

fabricated by a scholar in Shaowu (what is now Shaowu, Fujian) and Cai Jitong (i. e. Cai Yuanding) knew him. In the time of Kong Yingda 孔颖达 (574 – 648), the *Mencius* was still unvalued and only the *Analects* and the *Classic of Filial Piety* were set stored by. That work does not read like a sub-annotation at all, for it did not unravel the names and descriptions of those things presented in the *Mencius*, but rather pestered only those opinions of Zhao Qi 赵岐 (c. 108 – 201) in his *Menzi Zhushu* 孟子注疏 (Annotation and Explanation of the *Mencius*). [Lin]

97 问伊川说"读书当观圣人所以作经之意，与圣人所以用心"一条。曰："此条，程先生说读书，最为亲切。今人不会读书是如何？只缘不曾求圣人之意，才拈得些小，便把自意硬入放里面，胡说乱说。故教它就圣人意上求，看如何。"问："'易其气'是如何？"曰："只是放教宽慢。今人多要硬把捉教住，如有个难理会处，便要刻画百端讨出来，枉费心力。少刻只说得自底，那里见圣人意！"又曰："固是要思索，思索那曾怎地！"又举"阙其疑"一句，叹美之。贺孙。集注读论孟法。

Someone asked about Yichuan's saying "While reading the books by the sages, a learner should ponder what they intended their books for and why they made that much mental effort." The Master answered, "This is Master Cheng's view of how to read books, which is very insightful. Why do people today not know how to read a book? That is only because they have never sought the sages' intentions and as soon as they touch something insignificant, they begin to force their own ideas into it and thus wind up talking nonsense, given to what is ungrounded. So he instructed learners to read and seek to know the sages' intentions." When asked "What is meant by 'reading with mental ease'?" he answered, "It means relaxing the mind so as to absorb what the sages meant little by little. Nowadays, people are inclined to grasp stiffly what they read and, if meeting something hard to understand, to force numberless explanations on it only to waste efforts. They do nothing but only displaying their own stuff, with no understanding of the sages' meaning to speak of. " He continued, "One needs, of course, to contemplate, but is that the way of contemplating?" He also cited Yichuan's saying "putting what one doubts in abeyance (rather than pretending to know it)" and sighed in praise of it. [Hesun]

98 先生尝举程子读论孟切己之说，且如"学而时习之"，切己看时，曾时习与否？句句如此求之，则有益矣。余正甫云："看中庸大学，只得其纲而无目，如衣服只有领子。"过当时不曾应。后欲问："谓之纲者，以其目而得名；谓之领者，以其衣而得名。若无目，则不得谓之纲矣。故先生编礼，欲以中庸大学学记等篇置之卷端为礼本。"正甫未之从。过。

The Master once cited Master Cheng as saying that one should read the *Analects* and the *Mencius* with regard to himself. He said, "When you read 'learning with a constant perseverance and practicing frequently what is learned,' (*Analects*, 1: 1) with regard to yourself, you should ask yourself 'Have I practiced frequently what I have learned?' If you can read every sentence and seek its true meaning in that way, you must benefit from it. " Yu Zhengfu 余正甫 (dates unknown, a scholar) said to me, "Reading only the *Doctrine of the Mean* and the *Great Learning* means getting only an outline but not its details, which is comparable to getting only the collar of a piece of clothing. " I did not say anything in response, but later I wanted to tell him, "An outline is called because there are the details for it and a collar is called because of the piece of clothing it belongs to. Without its details, the outline should not be called as an outline. Therefore, when moving to compile a new edition of the *Record of Rites*, my teacher wants to put the *Doctrine of the Mean*, the *Great Learning*, and *Xueji* 学记 (Record on the Subject of Education), etc. , as the first pieces respectively in different volumes of it, which can serve as the fundamental parts heading them. " Zhengfu did not take to this practice. [Guo]

99 问：“孔子言语句句是自然，孟子言语句句是事实。”曰：“孔子言语一似没紧要说出来，自是包含无限道理，无些渗漏。如云‘道之以政，齐之以刑；道之以德，齐之以礼’数句，孔子初不曾着气力，只似没紧要说出来，自是委曲详尽，说尽道理，更走它底不得。若孟子便用着气力，依文按本，据事实说无限言语，方说得出。此所以为圣贤之别也。孟子说话，初间定用两句说起个头，下面便分开两段说去，正如而今人做文字相似。”恻。

Question：Yichuan said, "In Confucius's discourse, every sentence is natural, while in Mencius's, every sentence is factual. "（Why is that?）

Answer：When Confucius said something, it seems that he did not say the essential explicitly and thus what he said naturally covers boundless truth, leaving out nothing. For example, as regards his "If the people be led by laws, and uniformity be sought in giving them punishments, ···If they be led by virtue, and uniformity be sought in giving them the rules of propriety···," (*Analects*, 2：3), he did not make conscious effort to lay bare the truth, so he seemed not to say out the essential, but those words are indirectly exhaustive in implying the principles, which are also impossibly productive of misunderstandings. By contrast, Mencius would, according to what he saw proper in writing something, exert himself to compose his text, where he poured out numerous words before completing his exposition of the principles. That is where the difference is between a sage and a worthy. In a piece of writing by Mencius, it would surely begin with two sentences as the starting point and then develop into two separate sections for their elaboration. His way of writing is rather similar to that prevalent among scholars today. [Xian]

100 论语之书，无非操存、涵养之要；七篇之书，莫非体验、扩充之端。盖孔子大概使人优游餍饫，涵泳讽味；孟子大概是要人探索力讨，反己自求。故伊川曰：“孔子句句是自然，孟子句句是事实。”亦此意也。如论语所言“居处恭，执事敬，与人忠”，“出门如见大宾，使民如承大祭"，"非礼勿视听言动"之类，皆是存养底意思。孟子言性善，存心，养性，孺子入井之心，四端之发，若火始然，泉始达之类，皆是要体认得这心性下落，扩而充之。于此等类语玩味，便自可见。端蒙。

What the *Analects* conveys is nothing but the essential for preserving personal integrity and cultivating oneself and what the seven pieces of writing clarify is nothing but the point from which to start experiencing and expanding oneself. Probably, what Confucius intended is to instruct others for a leisurely and carefree pursuit of extensive learning and a deep immersion therein to taste the flavor of it, while what Mencius meant is to urge others to exert themselves and probe into themselves. Therefore, Yichuan said, "In Confucius's discourse, every sentence is natural, while in Mencius's, every sentence is factual," which means also that. For example, "in retirement, to be sedately grave; in the management of business, to be reverently attentive; in exchange with others, to be strictly sincere," (*Analects*, 13: 19) "It is, when you go out, to behave to every one as if you were receiving a great guest; to employ the people as if you were assisting at a great sacrifice," (*Analects*, 12: 2) and "Look not at what is contrary to propriety; listen not to what is contrary to propriety; speak not what is contrary to propriety; make no movement which is contrary to propriety," (*Analects*, 12: 1) all these were meant to instruct people to preserve their personal integrity. When Mencius said such points as the goodness of human nature, preserving the mind and nourishing the nature, the feeling of sadness and commiseration for the child about to fall into a well, and the emanation of the four beginnings, like that of fire which has started to burn, or that of a spring which has started to find vent, he urged people to be aware of where the human mind and nature are and to give them all their development and completion. If a learner is able to taste such words well, he will see the principle therein naturally.

[Duanmeng]

101 问："齐景公欲封孔子以尼溪之田，晏婴不可。楚昭王欲封孔子以书社之地，子西不可。使无晏婴子西，则夫子还受之乎？"曰："既仕其国，则须有采地，受之可也。"人杰。集注序说。

Question: Duke Jing of Qi (? – 490 BC) wanted to confer the farm land of Nixi (in Shandong today) upon Confucius, but Yan Ying 晏婴 (? – 500 BC), a senior official of him, remonstrated with him, saying "Please do not." King Zhao of Chu (? – 489 BC) wanted to confer a large inhabited land upon Confucius, but Zixi 子西 (? – 479 BC), his prime minister, remonstrated with him, saying "Please do not." Without Yan Ying and Zixi, would Confucius have accepted the feoffments?

Answer: Since he took official positions of the two states, he should be conferred with fiefs, so it would be right for him to accept them. [Renjie]

102 楚昭王招孔子，孔子过陈蔡被围。昭王之招无此事。邹鲁间陋儒尊孔子之意如此。设使是昭王招，陈蔡乃其下风耳，岂敢围？张无垢所谓者非。

Zhang Wugou said, "King Zhao of Chu recruited Confucius and when Confucius went from Chen State to Cai State in his trip to Chu State, he and his disciples endured a siege." Actually, the so called event of King Zhao of Chu's recruiting Confucius did not occur at all. That was fabricated by some ignorant Confucians in Zou State (native place of Mencius) and Lu State (native place of Confucius) in a display of their esteem for Confucius. If King Zhao of Chu's recruiting Confucius had really happened, since both Chen and Cai were weaker states than Chu, how could they have dared to besiege Confucius? Obviously, what Zhang said is wrong.

卷第六十二 Book 62

中庸一

The *Doctrine of the Mean* I

纲领

Guideline

1 中庸一书，枝枝相对，叶叶相当，不知怎生做得一个文字齐整！方子。

The *Doctrine of the Mean* is highly symmetrical in its textual layout, with remarkably resonant composition among its different parts. I wonder how its writer made it appear so neat and well-balanced. [Fangzi]

2 中庸，初学者未当理会。升卿。

The *Doctrine of the Mean* is not a book suitable for beginners (in learning) to read. [Shengqing]

3 中庸之书难看。中间说鬼说神，都无理会。学者须是见得个道理了，方可看此书，将来印证。赐。夔孙录云"中庸之书，如个卦影相似，中间"云云。

The *Doctrine of the Mean* is hard to read. For this sentence, Kuisun's record reads, "The *Doctrine of the Mean* reads like a divinatory image (of the *Classic of Change*)." In its middle sections, something is said about ghosts and spirits, so beginners may as well neglect it. They'd better not turn to the book until they get adequate understanding of the principle, by which they can be in a position to verify whether what it says is right or not. [Ci]

4 问中庸。曰："而今都难恁理会。某说个读书之序，须是且着力去看大学，又着力去看论语，又着力去看孟子。看得三书了，这中庸半截都了，不用问人，只略略恁看过。不可掉了易底，却先去攻那难底。中庸多说无形影，如鬼神，如'天地参'等类，说得高；说下学处少，说上达处多。若且理会文义，则可矣。"问："中庸精粗本末无不兼备否？"曰："固是如此。然未到精粗本末无不备处。"淳。

Asked about the *Doctrine of the Mean*, the Master answered, "Now it is difficult for a beginner to read it with some true understanding. As I have advocated of the sequence for reading the Four Books, one should begin with the *Great Learning*, then the *Analects*, and then the *Mencius*. Given reading these three with true understanding of them, he will have seen, so to speak, half of what the *Doctrine of the Mean* intends to say and so a cursory look through it will be enough for him to gain a good understanding of that half, for which he will not need to consult others. It should be avoided to take up what is difficult before reading what is easy. That book is more about what is imperceptible, for example, gods and ghosts, and 'forming a ternion with Heaven and Earth. ' (*Doctrine of the Mean*, 23)[①] On the whole, it is concerned more with upward attainment than with down-to-earth studies. It is enough for a learner to start reading it by understanding only what its words say superficially. " When asked, "Is the *Doctrine of the Mean* complete with regard to the quintessential and coarse and to the root and consequence?" he replied, "It is, of course, but you are now not at the stage of learning for inquiring that. " [Chun (淳)]

5 问中庸大学之别。曰："如读中庸求义理，只是致知功夫；如慎独修省，亦只是诚意。"问："只是中庸直说到'圣而不可知'处。"

① The translation of the citations from the *Doctrine of the Mean* is based on the English version by J. Legge (see http://ctext.org/liji/zhong-yong), with some alterations, drawing on other translations such as that by Chan Wing-tsit (See Chan Wing-tsit. trans. and comp. , *A Source Book in Chinese Philosophy*. Princeton：Princeton University Press, 1963, pp. 95 – 114).

曰："如大学里也有如'前王不忘'，便是'笃恭而天下平'底事。"胡泳。

Someone asked about the difference between the *Doctrine of the Mean* and the *Great Learning*. The Master answered, "For example, pursuing the principle as said in the former means only making efforts to extend knowledge as said in the latter, and the 'being watchful over being alone,' (1) 'cultivating one's own character' (20) and 'examining one's own mind' (33) mean also only 'making intention sincere.' (*Great Learning*, 2)" Further asked, "But the *Doctrine of the Mean* says out straight 'What the sage is is beyond our knowledge' (*Mencius*, 7B: 71)," he replied, "The *Great Learning* also mentions 'The former kings are not forgotten,' (*Great Learning*, 4) which means what is said in '(The Superior Man) being sincere and reverential, the whole world is conducted to a state of happy tranquility' (33)." [1] [Hu Yong]

6 读书先须看大纲，又看几多间架。如"天命之谓性，率性之谓道，修道之谓教"，此是大纲。夫妇所知所能，与圣人不知不能处，此类是间架。譬人看屋，先看他大纲，次看几多间，间内又有小间，然后方得贯通。铢。

When reading a book, what a learner should do first is, as it were, to take a net by its head rope, and see how many parts there are within its framework. For example, the beginning sentence "What Heaven has conferred on humankind is called *xing* 性 (human nature); following this nature is called *Dao* 道 (the Way); cultivating this Way is called *jiao* 教 (education)" serves as a head rope if the *Doctrine of the Mean* is likened to a fishing net, and such as what the husband and wife know and be able to do and what the sage does not know and is not able to do pertains to its parts. It

---

① The translation of the citations from *Great Learning* is based on the English version by J. Legge (see http: //ctext. org/liji/da-xue), with some alterations.

is also comparable to one viewing a house. He should first look at its house arrangement and then at its rooms, including the small rooms in the big ones. With such looking, he will be thoroughly familiar with the layout of the whole house.［Zhu］

7 问："中庸名篇之义，中者，不偏不倚、无过不及之名。兼此二义，包括方尽。就道理上看，固是有未发之中；就经文上看，亦先言'喜怒哀乐未发之谓中'，又言'君子之中庸也，君子而时中'。"先生曰："他所以名篇者，本是取'时中'之'中'。然所以能时中者，盖有那未发之中在。所以先开说未发之中，然后又说'君子之时中'。"至。以下论名篇之义。

Someone said to the Master, "As regards the meaning of the title *Zhongyong* 中庸①, the *zhong* 中 means impartiality and being free from going beyond or falling short. A complete understanding of its meaning should cover these two sides. As far as the principle it concerns goes, it is true that *zhong* implies being in the state of unstirred feelings, but as far as its words are concerned, the text says first 'While there are no stirrings of pleasure, anger, sorrow, or joy, the mind may be said to be in the state of *zhong* 中（equilibrium）'（1）and then 'The Superior Man is embodying the course of *zhongyong* 中庸（the Mean）② because he is a Superior Man, and so maintains the Mean at any time.'（2）" The Master replied, "What is taken to entitle the piece of writing is originally the Mean in 'he is a Superior Man, and so maintains the Mean at any time.' But the reason why

---

① The name *Zhongyong* of that classic in Chinese is traditionally rendered into *The Doctrine of the Mean* in English. According to Zhu Xi's explanation, the *zhong* and *yong* in the name *Zhongyong* have different meanings. In the translated text, the name of the classic is still rendered into *The Doctrine of the Mean*, but the component sino-graphs of the name will be rendered in different ways in contexts.

② Either *zhong* 中 and *yong* 庸 in *zhongyong* 中庸 can be explained separately as they are in the text. The two sino-graphs, as a whole, are usually rendered into "the Mean," and as the name of the book, *zhongyong* 中庸 is traditionally translated into the *Doctrine of the Mean*.

a Superior Man maintains the Mean at any time probably also involves the *zhong* of the state when the feelings are unstirred. So it first states the *zhong* of the unstirred state and then the *zhong* of the Mean the Superior Man maintains. " ［Zhi］ The following several passages concern the meaning of the name of the piece of writing.

8 至之问："'中'含二义，有未发之中，有随时之中。"曰："中庸一书，本只是说随时之中。然本其所以有此随时之中，缘是有那未发之中，后面方说'时中'去。"至之又问："'随时之中，犹日中之中'，何意？"曰："本意只是说昨日看得是中，今日看得又不是中。然譬喻不相似，亦未稳在。"直卿云："在中之中，与在事之中，只是一事。此是体，彼是尾。"方子。与上条盖同闻。

Zhizhi said to the Master, "The *zhong* in the name of *Zhongyong* means both *weifa zhi zhong* 未发之中 (the state of equilibrium when the feelings are unstirred) and *suishi zhi zhong* 随时之中 (the state of the Mean maintained (by the Superior Man) at any time). " The Master replied, "The book entitled *Zhongyong* is originally concerned only with the latter. However, the reason why the Superior Man can maintain the Mean at any time lies in the state of unstirred feelings, and therefore 'maintaining the Mean at any time' is said after mentioning that unstirred state. " Zhizhi further asked, "What does 'The Mean maintained at any time is like the middle of the day' in your explanation of the book mean?" The Master replied, "The simile was intended to mean that what was regarded as the middle of the day yesterday is not necessarily regarded as the middle of the day today, yet that comparison between them is still not adequate for illustrating their dissimilarity. " Zhiqing said, "The *zhong* in the state of centrality and the *zhong* in events are concerned with the same, of which the former is the root, while the latter is the consequence. " ［Fangzi］ This latter record was probably made on the same occasion as the former.

9 "'中庸'之'中'，本是无过无不及之中，大旨在时中上。若推其中，则自喜怒哀乐未发之中，而为'时中'之'中'。未发之中是体，'时中'之'中'是用，'中'字兼中和言之。"直卿云："如'仁义'二字，若兼义，则仁是体，义是用；若独说仁，则义、礼、智皆在其中，自兼体用言之。"盖卿。

The Master said, "What the *zhong* of *Zhongyong* refers to originally is the state free from going beyond or falling short, and, in the title, is mainly the Mean (the Superior Man should maintain) at any time. To deduce their relation, the *zhong* begins from the equilibrium with no stirrings of pleasure, anger, sorrow, or joy and ends with the Mean the Superior Man maintains at any time. The the state of equilibrium when the feelings are unstirred is its substance and the Mean maintained at any time is its function. Thus, the *zhong* covers both *zhong* 中 (equilibrium) and *he* 和 (harmony)." Zhiqing responded, "It is like the two sino-graphs of *ren* 仁 (benevolence) and *yi* 义 (righteousness). If considered together, benevolence is the substance, and righteousness is the function, whereas, speaking of benevolence only, it covers all righteousness, propriety, and wisdom, so it is said as covering both substance and function." [Gaiqing]

10 "'中庸'之'中'，是兼已发而中节、无过不及者得名。故周子曰：'惟中者，和也，中节也，天下之达道也。'若不识得此理，则周子之言更解不得。所以伊川谓'中者，天下之正道'。中庸章句以'中庸'之'中'，实兼'中和'之义，论语集注以'中者，不偏不倚，无过不及之名'，皆此意也。"人杰。

The *zhong* in the name *Zhongyong* of the book means both the aroused feelings attaining their due measure and degree and the Mean state free from going beyond or falling short. Therefore, Master Zhou (i. e. Zhou Dunyi) said, "Only the Mean brings harmony, and it is the principle of regularity, and the universally recognized law." If you fail to understand this point, you will not see even what Master Zhou means to say. Thus, Yichuan (i. e. Cheng Yi) stated, "*Zhong* is the correct path of the world." In my *Zhongyong Zhangju* 中庸章句 (Interpretation of the *Doctrine of the Mean*, hereinafter, *Interpretation* for short in this Book 62), I explain the *zhong* in the name of *Zhongyong* as covering both equilibrium and harmony, and in my *Lunyu Jizhu* 论语集注（Collected Annotations of the *Analects*）I say that the *zhong* is the name of impartiality and the state free from going beyond or falling short. Both explanations of *zhong* mean the same. ［Renjie］

11 "'中庸'之'中'，兼不倚之中？"曰："便是那不倚之中流从里出来。"炎。

Asked "Does the *zhong* in the name *Zhongyong* also mean impartiality?" the Master answered, "Its meaning（pertaining to the state when the feelings are aroused）in the name stems from that meaning of impartiality（pertaining to the state when the feelings are not aroused）." ［Yan］

12 问："明道以'不易'为庸，先生以'常'为庸，二说不同？"曰："言常，则不易在其中矣。惟其常也，所以不易。但'不易'二字，则是事之已然者。自后观之，则见此理之不可易。若庸，则日用常行者便是。"僩。

Question：Mingdao（i. e. Cheng Hao）saw *yong* 庸 as meaning *buyi* 不易（being unchangeable），while you, sir, take *yong* as meaning *chang* 常（being ordinary）. Why are your explanations different?

Answer：When it is explained as being ordinary, it covers the meaning of being unchangeable. Only when there is being ordinary can there be being unchangeable. The "being unchangeable," however, implies that something has already become a fact, from which the principle of being unchangeable can be perceived. When it comes to *yong*, it refers to nothing but what is daily used and routinely practiced. ［Xian］

13 或问："'中庸'二字，伊川以庸为定理，先生易以为平常。据'中'之一字大段精微，若以平常释'庸'字，则两字大不相粘。"曰："若看得不相粘，便是相粘了。如今说这物白，这物黑，便是相粘了。"广因云："若不相粘，则自不须相对言得。"曰："便是此理难说。前日与季通说话终日，惜乎不来听。东之与西，上之与下，以至于寒暑昼夜生死，皆是相反而相对也。天地间物未尝无相对者，故程先生尝曰：'天地万物之理，无独必有对，皆自然而然，非有安排也。每中夜以思，不知手之舞之，足之蹈之也！'看得来真个好笑！"广。

Someone said to the Master, "As regards the two sino-graphs *zhong* and *yong*, Yichuan took the *yong* as meaning the definite principle, while you, sir, regard it as meaning ordinariness. Since *zhong*, though a single sino-graph, implies very much subtle meaning, if *yong*, as the other sino-graph in the name *Zhongyong*, is explained as ordinariness, the two sino-graphs, I'm afraid, are quite incoherent." The Master replied, "If you see them as being incoherent, it indicates, contrarily, they are coherent. It is just as we say that this thing is white, while that thing is black, and actually black and white are coherent." I thereupon said, "If not coherent, naturally they could not be spoken of as opposites." The Master responded, "But that is something hard to say. The day before yesterday, I talked with Jitong for a whole day, but it is a pity you were not present on that occasion. East and west, and top and bottom, as well as winter and summer, day and night, and life and death, all these are pairs of opposites, each with one relative to the other. Of all the things between heaven and earth, there is no one without its opposite. Thus Master Cheng Hao said, 'According to the principle of Heaven and Earth and all things, nothing exists in isolation but everything necessarily has its opposite. All this is naturally so and is not arranged or manipulated. [1]Every time when I thought over this at night, unconsciously I began to dance my feet and move my hands.' He appears to have been truly amused by that." [Guang]

14 "惟其平常，故不可易；若非常，则不得久矣。譬如饮食，如五谷是常，自不可易。若是珍羞异味不常得之物，则暂一食之可也，焉

---

① The translation of the part in the citation from Cheng Hao is based on a version by Chan Wing-tsit (see *A Source Book in Chinese Philosophy*. Princeton：Princeton University Press, 1963, p. 539).

能久乎！庸，固是定理，若以为定理，则却不见那平常底意思。今以平常言，则不易之定理自在其中矣。"广因举释子偈有云："世间万事不如常，又不惊人又久长。"曰："便是他那道理也有极相似处，只是说得来别。故某于中庸章句序中着语云：'至老佛之徒出，则弥近理而大乱真矣！'须是看得他那'弥近理而大乱真'处，始得。"广云："程子'自私'二字恐得其要领，但人看得此二字浅近了。"曰："便是向日王顺伯曾有书与陆子静辨此二字云：'佛氏割截身体，犹自不顾，如何却谓之自私得！'"味道因举明道答横渠书云："大抵人患在自私而用智。"曰："此却是说大凡人之任私意耳。"因举下文"豁然而大公，物来而顺应"，曰："此亦是对说。'豁然而大公'，便是不自私；'物来而顺应'，便是不用智。后面说治怒处曰：'但于怒时遽忘其怒，反观理之是非，则于道思过半矣。''忘其怒'，便是大公；'反观理之是非'，便是顺应，都是对说。盖其理自如此。"广因云："太极一判，便有阴阳相对。"曰："然。"广。

The Master said, "It is because of being ordinary that there is being unchangeable. If something is not ordinary, it will not last forever. For example, the five cereals are ordinary, so they are unchangeable. As for those rare foods and delicacies which are not available ordinarily, one can taste them occasionally, but how can he have them forever? It is true that *yong* refers to the definite principle, but that explanation tends to lead one to understand it as meaning that only, losing sight of its other meaning of ordinariness. By contrast, if it is explained as being ordinary, the unchangeable definite principle will be naturally implied therein. " Thereupon I cited a Buddhist verse as saying "The myriad things in the world keep changing, // Which is unsurprising and ever lasting. " The Master replied, "It indicates there is something that sounds very similar in the Buddhist doctrine, though different in essence. That is why I say in the preface to my *Interpretation* 'When Daoists and then Buddhists came on the scene, what they preached, respectively, sounded even closer to the principle and as a consequence it spoilt the truth to a greater extent. ' You should try to see that in its doctrine which sounds even closer to the principle and as a consequence it spoils the truth to a greater extent. " I said, "When Master Cheng said ' selfishness, ' I think, he was to the point, but others have failed to understand it deeply enough. " The Master responded, "An evidence is the letter written by Wang Shunbo 王顺伯（i. e. Wang Houzhi 王厚之, 1131 – 1204）some time ago to Lu Zijing（i. e. Lu Jiuyuan）for discrimination with regard to the word, saying ' Since Buddhists sever even their own bodies without any scruple, how can they be said as being selfish?' " Weidao thereupon cited Mingdao in his letter to Hengqü as saying "Generally, the trouble with everyone lies in resorting to selfishness and the exercise of cunning. "[①] The Master responded, "But what he meant by saying that is only that, in general, one is liable to indulging his selfish intention. " Then, citing "to become broad and extremely impartial and to respond spontaneously to all things as they come" in that letter, he said, "That is also said in an antithesis. The ' to become broad and extremely impartial ' points to unselfishness, while ' to respond spontaneously to all things as they come, ' to no exercise of cunning. After that, he said（in the same letter）, ' If in time of anger one can immediately forget his anger and look at the right and wrong of the matter according to principle, ⋯ he has gone more than halfway toward the Way. ' Here, ' forget his anger ' pertains to the great impartiality and ' look at the right and wrong of the matter according to principle, ' to the responding, which are presented also in an antithesis. Probably it is because, as he saw it, that is how the principle naturally was. " Then I said to him, "As soon as there occurred the Supreme Ultimate, there emerged the opposition between *yin* and *yang*. " He replied, "That is right. " ［Guang］

---

① The translation of the citations from Cheng Hao's letter is based on a version by Chan Wing-tsit（see *A Source Book in Chinese Philosophy*. Princeton：Princeton University Press, 1963, p. 526）.

15 "惟其平常，故不可易，如饮食之有五谷，衣服之有布帛。若是奇羞异味，锦绮组绣，不久便须厌了。庸固是定理，若直解为定理，却不见得平常意思。今以平常言，然定理自在其中矣。"公晦问："'中庸'二字，旧说依程子'不偏不易'之语。今说得是不偏不倚、无过不及而平常之理。似以不偏不倚无过不及说中，乃是精密切至之语；而以平常说庸，恰似不相粘着。"曰："此其所以粘着。盖缘处得极精极密，只是如此平常。若有些子咤异，便不是极精极密，便不是中庸。凡事无不相反以相成；东便与西对，南便与北对，无一事一物不然。明道所以云：'天下之物，无独必有对，终夜思之，不知手之舞之，足之蹈之!'直是可观，事事如此。"贺孙。

The Master said, "It is only because it is ordinary that it is unchangeable. It is like the five cereals to our food or the plain cotton and silk to our clothes. If we always eat those rare foods and delicacies and wear those brocades and embroideries, we will get bored before long. It is true that *yong* means the definite principle, but if it is explicated straight as the definite principle, it tends to close over its meaning of ordinariness. If it is explained as ordinariness, it will naturally imply the meaning of the definite principle." Gonghui asked, "The *zhong* and *yong* in the name of *Zhongyong* used to be taken as meaning 'impartial and unchangeable' respectively according to Master Cheng's explanation. At present, it is understood as meaning the impartiality and freedom from going beyond or falling short, and the principle of ordinariness. It seems that *zhong*, which says of the impartiality and freedom from going beyond or falling short, belongs to the discourse extremely subtle and penetrating, but *yong*, if explained as meaning ordinariness, does not go coherently with *zhong*." The Master replied, "That is the very reason why they can be seen as coherent with each other. Probably it is because what is the extremely subtle and quintessential appears rather ordinary. Whatever amazes you somewhat is not the extremely subtle and quintessential and thus does not pertain to the Mean. Of all things, no matter what it is, one thing is opposite to another thing, and meanwhile they are complementary to each other. For example, east is opposite to west, and north, to south. Such opposition is true of everything. That is why Mingdao said, 'Nothing exists in isolation but everything necessarily has its opposite. Every time when I thought over this at night, unconsciously I began to dance my feet and move my hands. ' That is easy to observe, for it is true of everything. ''〔Hesun〕

16　问：“中庸不是截然为二，庸只是中底常然而不易否？”曰："是。"淳。

Question：In the name of *Zhongyong*, the meaning of *zhong* and that of *yong* are not completely separate, for *yong* means only what is so ordinary as to be unchangeable which pertains to *zhong*. (Is this right?)

Answer：Right. 〔Chun（淳）〕

17　问："明道曰：‘惟中不足以尽之，故曰"中庸"。’庸乃中之常理，中自已尽矣。"曰："中亦要得常，此是一经一纬，不可阙。"可学。

Question：Mingdao said, "The *zhong* alone is not enough to convey the intended meaning, so *zhongyong* is used. " If *yong* is seen as meaning the principle of ordinariness which pertains to *zhong*, then *zhong* can convey all the intended meaning by itself. (How do you think about it?)

Answer：Despite *zhong*, *yong* is also indispensable, for they are like the warp and weft, either being necessary for making up a piece of fabric. 〔Kexue〕

18　蜚卿问："‘中庸之为德。’程云：‘不偏之谓"中"，不易之谓"庸"。’"曰："中则直上直下，庸是平常不差异。中如一物竖置之，常如一物横置之。唯中而后常，不中则不能常。"因问曰："不惟不中则不能常，然不常亦不能为中。"曰："亦是如此。中而后能常，此以自然之理而言；常而后能有中，此以人而言。"问："龟山言：‘高明则中庸也。高明者，中庸之体；中庸者，高明之用。’不知将体用对说如何?"曰:"只就'中庸'字上说,自分晓,不须如此说亦可。"又举荆公"高明处己,中庸处人"之语为非是。因言:"龟山有功于学者。然就他说,据他自有做工夫处。高明,释氏诚有之,只缘其无'道中庸'一截。又一般人宗族称其孝,乡党称其弟,故十项事其八九可称。若一向拘挛,又做得甚事!要知中庸、高明二者皆不可废。"宇。

Feiqing asked, " 'Zhongyong embodies the highest form of virtue.' (Analects, 6: 29) As Master Cheng explained, being impartial is referred to as zhong, and being unchangeable, to yong. (How do you think about it?)" The Master answered, "Zhong points to being upright, while yong, to being ordinary and free from deviation. Zhong is like something erected vertically, while the ordinary, like something else put horizontally on it. Only when there is zhong can there be the ordinary, and without zhong, there can be no ordinariness at all." Thereupon, Feiqing said, "Not only that, without zhong, there can be no ordinariness, but also that, without the ordinary, there can be no zhong." The Master responded, "That is also right. Only after there being zhong can there be the ordinary, which is said in the light of the natural principle; only after there being the ordinary can there be zhong, which is said from the viewpoint of humankind." Someone asked, "Guishan (i. e. Yang Shi) said, 'Gaoming 高明 (the high and brilliant) entails pursuing the course of the Mean. What is high and brilliant is the substance of the Mean, while the Mean is the function of what is high and brilliant.' What about speaking of the substance and function as a pair of opposites?" The Master replied, "What the name Zhongyong means is clear by itself, so they do not have to be spoken of that way." Then he cited Duke Jing (i. e. Wang Anshi) as saying "The high and brilliant is that which one cultivates in himself, while the Mean is that which one gets along with other people by," which he thought was not right. Thereupon he continued saying, "Guishan is a scholar who made contribution to learning.

As far as he is concerned, however, he seems to have had his own way of making efforts in pursuit of learning. The 'high and brilliant' is also found in the Buddhist discourse, indeed, but unfortunately it does not mention anything about the Way and the Mean. If an average man is praised by his clansmen as being filial and by his townsmen as being fraternal, then when he does ten things, he is able to finish eight or nine of them commendably. But if he sticks to a certain rule always rigidly, how can he do anything? You should know that neither the Mean nor the high and brilliant can be dispensable." [Yu]

19 或问："中与诚意如何?"曰："中是道理之模样,诚是道理之实处,中即诚矣。"又问："智仁勇于诚如何?"曰："智仁勇是做底事,诚是行此三者都要实。"又问"中、庸"。曰："中、庸只是一事,就那头看是中,就这头看是庸。譬如山与岭,只是一物。方其山,即是谓之山;行着岭路,则谓之岭,非二物也。方子录云:"问:'中庸既曰"中",又曰"诚",何如?'曰:'此古诗所谓"横看成岭侧成峰"也。'"中、庸只是一个道理,以其不偏不倚,故谓之'中';以其不差异可常行,故谓之'庸'。未有中而不庸者,亦未有庸而不中者。惟中,故平常。尧授舜,舜授禹,都是当其时合如此做,做得来恰好,所谓中也。中,即平常也,不如此,便非中,便不是平常。以至汤武之事亦然。又如当盛夏极暑时,须用饮冷,就凉处,衣葛,挥扇,此便是中,便是平常。当隆冬盛寒时,须用饮汤,就密室,重裘,拥火,此便是中,便是平常。若极暑时重裘拥火,盛寒时衣葛挥扇,便是差异,便是失其中矣。"

Someone asked, "How to distinguish the meaning of *zhong* and that of *cheng* 诚 (sincerity)?" The Master answered, "*Zhong* means what the principle looks like, and *cheng* means what is the substantial of the principle. So *zhong* can be understood as the same as *cheng*." The questioner further asked, "What about *zhi* 智 (wisdom), *ren* 仁 (benevolence), and *yong* 勇 (courage) in relation to sincerity?" The

Master replied, "The wisdom, benevolence, and courage pertain to the things that one does, while sincerity means that he should be sincere in conducting those three." When further asked about *zhong* and *yong*, he answered, "*Zhong* and *yong* are said of the same matter, which can be seen as *zhong* from this side and as *yong* from that side. They are comparable to *shan* 山 and *ling* 岭, which are both used to refer to the same thing. When you look at the mountain in the distance, you call it *shan*, and when you walk along a path on its ridge, you call it *ling*, but they do not refer to two different things. Fangzi's record for the foregoing several sentences read, 'When asked "Why does *zhongyong* refer to both *zhong* and *cheng*?" the Master answered, "It is a case, as a poem (by Su Shi) says, of 'Seen from its front, it is a mountain range, while seen from its side, it is a peak.'"' Both *zhong* and *yong* say of the same principle in that when its impartiality is given salience to, it is called *zhong*, while when its ordinariness and routine practicability are given salience to, it is called *yong*. There is never anything that is *zhong* but not *yong*, nor anything that is *yong* but not *zhong*. Whatever is *zhong* is ordinary. When Yao passed the throne to Shun and later Shun passed the throne to Yu, it was right and appropriate for them to do that and they did that properly on the right occasions. So what they did conforms to the principle of *zhong*. The *zhong* means nothing but being ordinary and whatever is extraordinary falls short of *zhong*. This is also true of Tang (founder of the Shang dynasty) and Wu (i. e. King Wu of Zhou, founder of the Zhou dynasty). For another example, in the hottest days of the midsummer, when one drinks something cool, dwells in a well-ventilated place, wears light clothes, and waves a fan, then what he does conforms to the principle of *zhong* and is ordinary. In the severe coldness of the midwinter, when one drinks something hot, dwells in a warm room, wears thick clothes, and keeps close to fire, then what he does conforms to the principle of *zhong* and is ordinary. If he keeps close to fire and wears thick clothes in midsummer or waves a fan and wears light clothes in midwinter, then what he does indicates his going against ordinariness, displaying his deviation from the principle of *zhong*."

20 问:"'中庸'之'庸',平常也。所谓平常者,事理当然而无诡异也。或问言:'既曰当然,则自君臣父子日用之常,以至尧舜之禅授,汤武之放伐,无适而非平常矣。'窃谓尧舜禅授,汤武放伐,皆圣人非常之变,而谓之平常,何也?"曰:"尧舜禅授,汤武放伐,虽事异常,然皆是合当如此,便只是常事。如伊川说'经、权'字,'合权处,即便是经'。"铢曰:"程易说大过,以为'大过者,常事之大者耳,非有过于理也。圣人尽人道,非过于理'。是此意否?"曰:"正是如此。"铢。

Question: The *yong* in the book name *Zhongyong* is explained (by you) as referring to ordinariness. By the so called ordinariness is meant the state of something as a matter of course according to its principle, free from any bizarreness. Your *Zhongyong Huowen* 中庸或问 (Questions and Answers on the *Doctrine of the Mean*, hereinafter *Questions and Answers* for short in this Book 62) says, "Since it is said of something as a matter of course, none of those things ranging from the daily matters in regard to sovereign and minister, and father and son, to the abdications of Yao and Shun and the punitive expeditions made by Tang and Wu, is not ordinary." In my humble opinion, the abdications by Yao and Shun and of the punitive expeditions by Tang and Wu are all extraordinary events brought about by those sages, so they should not be thought as being ordinary.

Answer: Despite the extraordinariness of the abdications made by Yao and Shun and the punitive expeditions launched by Tang and Wu, they happened as a matter of course, and in this sense they are only ordinary. Just as Yichuan said of the relationship between *jing* 经 (that which is unchangeable) and *quan* 权 (change for adaptation), whatever *quan* is done where it should be done under specific circumstances is *jing* itself.

I asked, "When Master Cheng Yi explicates 'Hexagram Daguo' 大过

(Preponderance of the Great)① in his *Explanation of the Classic of Change*, he says 'What Daguo refers to is nothing but the remarkable ones of the ordinary things and affairs, rather than going beyond what the principle stipulates. It concerns the fulfillment of the duty of humankind by the sage who does not go beyond the principle.' Is his explanation right?" The Master answered, "That is right." ［Zhu］

21 问道之常变。举中庸或问说曰:"守常底固是是。然到守不得处只着变,而硬守定则不得。至变得来合理,断然着如此做,依旧是常。"又问:"前日说经权云:'常自是着还他一个常,变自是着还他一个变。'如或问举'尧舜之禅授,汤武之放伐,其变无穷,无适而非常',却又皆以为平常,是如何?"曰:"是他到不得已处,只得变。变得是,仍旧是平常,然依旧着存一个变。"焘。

When I asked him about the ordinary and change with regard to the Way, the Master quoted his own *Questions and Answers* and said, "It is right of course to adhere to the ordinary, but, when such adherence can not be continued, change has to be made, for it will not do to stick rigidly to the definite rules. If the change is made for the better, which should be done flatly that way, it still remains on the track of the ordinary." I asked further "The day before yesterday when you talked about *jing* and *quan*, you said, 'The ordinary means naturally returning to the ordinary when such should be done, and the change also means naturally returning to the change when such should be done.' However, your *Questions and Answers* cites the abdications made by Yao and Shun and the punitive expeditions launched by Tang and Wu and says 'The change is inexhaustible and is made ultimately for the ordinary.' So you regard those events as being ordinary. Why?" The Master

---

① The translated names of the cited hexagrams are based on the English translation of *Yijing* by C. F. Baynes from the German translation of it by R. Wilhelm. (see C. F. Baynes ［trans.］ *The I Ching* or *Book of Changes* ［The Richard Wilhelm translation rendered into English］. New York: Penguin Group, Inc., 1950.)

replied, "When circumstances make change the only choice, change has to be done. If that change is done for the right, it remains what is the ordinary, but something is to be changed." [Tao]

22 有中必有庸，有庸必有中，两个少不得。赐。

There being *zhong* must entail there being *yong*, and vice versa. [Ci]

23 中必有庸，庸必有中，能究此而后可以发诸运用。季札。

Zhong must entail *yong*, and vice versa. When a learner has probed such relationship between them and has got conversant with it, he is in a position to apply it. [Jizha]

24 中庸该得中和之义。庸是见于事，和是发于心，庸该得和。侗。

Zhongyong (centrality and ordinariness) also means the meaning of *zhonghe* 中和 (equilibrium and harmony). *Yong* shows itself in events, while *he* (harmony) emanates from the mind. In meaning, *yong* is also harmony. [Xian]

25 问："'中庸'二字孰重?"曰："庸是定理，有中而后有庸。"问："或问中言：'中立而无依，则必至于倚。'如何是无依?"曰："中立最难。譬如一物植立于此，中间无所依着，久之必倒去。"问："若要植立得住，须用强矫?"曰："大故要强立。"德明。

Question: Of *zhong* and *yong*, which is more significant?

Answer: *Yong* pertains to the definite principle and when there is *zhong*, then there will be *yong*.

Further question: You, sir, say in your *Questions and Answers*, "If *zhong* is established upright yet with nothing to depend on, it will end up with partiality." How is there nothing to depend on?

Answer: It is most difficult to keep established upright. For example, if a thing stands here in isolation, yet without anything to lean on, it will wind up only with falling down after a long time.

Further question: If it is to keep standing upright, must it resort to support from something else?

Answer：Most probably it needs strong support from outside. ［Deming］

26 "向见刘致中说，今世传明道中庸义是与叔初本，后为博士演为讲义。" 先生又云："尚恐今解是初著，后掇其要为解也。" 方。诸家解。

The Master said, "I once heard Liu Zhizhong 刘致中 (dates unknown, a friend of Zhu Xi's father's) say that Mingdao's explanation of the *Doctrine of the Mean* in circulation among scholars today was recorded first by Yushu (i. e. Lü Dalin), and later it was extended by some *Boshi* 博士 (lit. Erudite Scholar, a scholar-official in the Imperial College) as a lecturing text." He added, "I'm afraid the explanation now was the earliest edition, and later the essentials of it were compiled as another text." ［Fang］ The passages below are about explanations of the *Doctrine of the Mean* by other scholars.

27 吕中庸，文滂沛，意浃洽。方。

Lü's (Lü Dalin's) *Zhongyong Jie* 中庸解 (Explanation of the *Doctrine of the Mean*) is verbally torrential and exuberant and ideologically coherent and thorough. ［Fang］

28 李先生说："陈几叟辈皆以杨氏中庸不如吕氏。" 先生曰："吕氏饱满充实。" 方。

Mr. Li (name unknown) said, "Chen Jisou 陈几叟 (i. e. Chen Yuan 陈渊 ［? – 1145］) and some other scholars all considered Yang's (Yang Shi's) *Explanation of the Doctrine of the Mean* inferior to Lü's." The Master replied, "Lü's is full and substantial." (Fang)

29 龟山门人自言龟山中庸枯燥，不如与叔浃洽。先生曰："与叔却似行到，他人如登高望远。" 方。

Guishan's disciples said themselves that their master's explanation of the *Doctrine of the Mean* was dull and dry, not as coherent and well-thought out as Yushu's. The Master said, "It is like a trip towards a destination. Yushu, so to speak, has already arrived at it, while others have only climbed a height and looked at it." ［Fang］

30 游杨吕侯诸先生解中庸，只说他所见一面道理，却不将圣人言语折衷，所以多失。

In their explanations of the *Doctrine of the Mean*, You 游（i. e. Yu Cu 游酢［1052 – 1123］），Yang 杨，Lü 吕，Hou 侯（i. e. 侯仲良［dates unknown］），and other scholars only presented what they each read out of it themselves but failed to synthesize the discourses of the ancient sages in regard to it, which results in many losses.

31 游杨诸公解中庸，引书语皆失本意。

In their explanations of the *Doctrine of the Mean*, when You, Yang, and others cited words from the *Classic of History*, they all missed their original meanings.

32 "理学最难。可惜许多印行文字，其间无道理底甚多，虽伊洛门人亦不免如此。如解中庸，正说得数句好，下面便有几句走作无道理了，不知是如何。旧尝看栾城集，见他文势甚好，近日看，全无道理。如与刘原父书说藏巧若拙处，前面说得尽好，后面却说怕人来磨我，且恁地鹘突去，要他不来，便不成说话。又如苏东坡忠厚之至论说'举而归之于仁'，便是不奈他何，只恁地做个鹘突了。二苏说话，多是如此。此题目全在'疑'字上。谓如有人似有功，又似无功，不分晓，只是从其功处重之。有人似有罪，又似无罪，不分晓，只得从其罪处轻之。若是功罪分明，定是行赏罚不可毫发轻重。而今说'举而归之于仁'，更无理会。"或举老苏五经论，先生曰："说得圣人都是用术了！"明作。

The Master said, "The learning of principle is the most difficult. It is a pity that, though so many words have been printed and circulated today, so big a number of them make no sense, a lot of which are even from the disciples of Two Chengs (founders of the Yiluo School of Neo-Confucianism). For example, in an *Explanation of the Doctrine of the Mean*, several sentences go well in their explaining work, but they are followed unexpectedly by several other sentences which make no sense. I do not know why. I once read *Luancheng Ji* 栾城集（Collected Works of Luancheng, by Su Zhe 苏辙

[1039 – 1112]), and only felt that its style of writing was very good. Recently, when I read it again, I felt what it said was completely unreasonable. For example, when he dwelt on ' hiding art and appearing stupid' in his letter to Liu Yuanfu (i. e. Liu Chang 刘敞 [1019 – 1068]), his first several sentences were insightful, but then he said that it meant that one pretends to be in confusion, for fear that others may come and pester him, so by that way he can keep them away. This is just unjustifiable. For another example, in Su Dongpo's (i. e. Su Shi's 苏轼 [1037 – 1101], elder brother of Su Zhe) *Xingshang Zhonghou Zhi Zhi Lun* 刑赏忠厚之至论 (On the Most Sincere and Considerate Treatment of Rewards and Punishments), he says '(when in doubt,) raise it and attribute it to benevolence. ' This indicates his lack of a true understanding, with a mere confusing saying like that. The discourses of the Two Sus (i. e. Su Shi and Su Zhe) are inclined to that style. Actually, for that topic, the key lies completely in the word 'doubt. ' When one seems to have done a deed of merit but also seems to have had not, and which is true can by no means be determined, then he should be treated as having done that deed of merit. When one seems to have committed a crime but also seems to have had not, and which is true can by no means be determined, then he should be treated as having not committed that crime. However, if whether one does a deed of merit or commits a crime is clear to determine, he should be rewarded or punished correspondingly, without any deviation from the established standards. Some scholars' interpretations of his '(when in doubt,) raise it and attribute it to benevolence' today are even more unreasonable. " When someone mentioned the "Wijing Lun" 五经论 (Treatise on Five Confucian Classics) by Su Xun 苏洵 (1009 – 1066, father of the two Su brothers), the Master commented on it, saying "It takes the ancient sages for employers of skills. " [Mingzuo]

33 游丈开问:"中庸编集得如何?"曰:"便是难说。缘前辈诸公说得多了,其间尽有差舛处,又不欲尽驳难他底,所以难下手,不比大学都未曾有人说。"雉。

You Zhangkai 游丈开（dates unknown, a disciple of Zhu's）asked, "How are things going with your compilation of the works on the *Doctrine of the Mean*?" The Master answered, "It is no easy job. It is because the previous scholars have presented many explanations about the book, and, though there are some problems with their opinions, I would not like to refute them completely. So I feel it hard to work on them. It is unlike the *Great Learning*, on which few scholars aired their opinions." ［Zhi（雉）］

34　先生以中庸或问见授，云："亦有未满意处，如评论程子、诸子说处，尚多粗。"僴

The Master taught us his *Questions and Answers*, saying "In this work, there are still some unsatisfactory places, such as my comments on Two Chengs and some other scholars, which are largely coarse." ［Xun］

35　问："赵书记欲以先生中庸解镂木，如何？"先生曰："公归时，烦说与，切不可！某为人迟钝，旋见得旋改，一年之内改了数遍不可知。"又自笑云："那得个人如此著述！"浩。

I asked the Master, "Zhao Shuji wanted to have your *Explanation of the Doctrine of the Mean* engraved for printing. How do you think, sir?" He answered, "When you return and see him, please tell him that it must not be done. I am a slow man, and whenever I get any new understanding, I will alter it somewhere. In this year, I have altered it many times, though I do not know exactly how many." Then he, smiling to himself, said "How can there be a man writing in that way?" ［Hao］

章句序

Preface to *Interpretation of the Doctrine of the Mean*

36　问："先生说，人心是'形气之私'，形气则是口耳鼻目四肢之属。"曰："固是。"问："如此，则未可便谓之私？"曰："但此数件物

事属自家体段上，便是私有底物；不比道，便公共。故上面便有个私底根本。且如危，亦未便是不好，只是有个不好底根本。"士毅。

Someone said to the Master, "You, sir, say that the human mind pertains to 'the private forms of his vital force,' and these forms refer to the mouth, nose, ears, limbs, and the like of a person." The Master replied, "Yes, of course." The former asked, "Then, how can it be said as private?" The Master answered, "Those human organs belong to a specific person, which are owned privately by him. They are different from the Way, which is shared by all. Therefore, underlying them is something fundamentally private. For instance, danger is not necessarily bad, but it is based on a foundation which is bad." [Shiyi]

37 问"或生于形气之私"。曰："如饥饱寒暖之类，皆生于吾身血气形体，而他人无与，所谓私也。亦未能便是不好，但不可一向徇之耳。"植。

Question: What do you mean by "perhaps (the human mind is) born of the private forms of his vital force"?

Answer: For example, such feelings as of hunger and satiety, warmth and coldness, all of which stem from the flesh and blood forms of the vital force in a person. They have nothing to do with other people and so they are private. One's capability of private feelings is not necessarily bad, but he should not always go all out in pursuit of them. [Zhi (植)]

38 问："人心本无不善，发于思虑，方始有不善。今先生指人心对道心而言，谓人心'生于形气之私'，不知是有形气便有这个人心否？"曰："有恁地分别说底，有不恁地说底。如单说人心，则都是好。对道心说着，便是劳攘物事，会生病痛底。"夔孙。

Question: There is originally nothing bad with the mind of humankind, but when a person deliberates things, he begins to give rise to something bad with his mind. Now you, sir, say that the mind of humankind is opposite to *daoxin* 道心 (the mind of the Way) and that "The mind of humankind is born of the private forms of vital force. " Can we say that, as soon as there occur the forms of the vital force, there will be the mind of humankind?

Answer: The mind of humankind and the mind of the Way may be said separately, or in relation to each other. If the mind of humankind is said separately, it is good all over. If it is said in relation to the mind of the Way, since it is disturbed by things and events, it will get troubled by diseases and pains. [Kuisun]

39 季通以书问中庸序所云"人心形气"。先生曰:"形气非皆不善,只是靠不得。季通云:'形气亦皆有善。'不知形气之有善,皆自道心出。由道心,则形气善;不由道心,一付于形气,则为恶。形气犹船也,道心犹柁也。船无柁,纵之行,有时入于波涛,有时入于安流,不可一定。惟有一柁以运之,则虽入波涛无害。故曰:'天生烝民,有物有则。'物乃形气,则乃理也。渠云'天地中也,万物过不及',亦不是。万物岂无中?渠又云:'浩然之气,天地之正气也。'此乃伊川说,然皆为养气言。养得则为浩然之气,不养则为恶气,卒徒理不得。且如今日说夜气是甚大事,专靠夜气,济得甚事!"可学云:"以前看夜气,多略了'足以'两字,故然。"先生曰:"只是一理。存是存此,养是养此,识得更无走作。"舜功问:"天理人欲,毕竟须为分别,勿令交关。"先生曰:"五峰云:'性犹水,善犹水之下也,情犹澜也,欲犹水之波浪也。'波浪与澜,只争大小,欲岂可带于情!"某问:"五峰云'天理人欲,同行而异情'却是。"先生曰:"是。同行者,谓二人同行于天理中,一人日从天理,一人专徇人欲,是异情。下云'同体而异用',则大错!"因举知言多有不是处。"'性无善恶',此乃欲尊性,不知却鹘突了它。胡氏论性,大抵如此,自文定以下皆然。如曰:'性,善恶也。性、情、才相接。'此乃说着气,非说着性。向吕伯恭初读知言,以为只有二段是,其后却云:'极妙,过于正蒙!'"可学。

Jitong wrote to the Master and asked about "the mind of humankind" and "the forms of the vital force" the Master dwelt on in his preface to his

Interpretation. The Master said, "It is not that the forms of the vital force are all bad, but that they are undependable. Jitong said in his letter to me, 'All the forms of the vital force possess goodness,' indicating his ignorance of the origination of all the goodness possessed by the forms of the vital force from the mind of the Way. If in compliance with the mind of the Way, the forms of the vital force will be good. Otherwise, whatever is turned into the forms of the vital force is evil. The forms of the vital force are comparable to a ship, while the mind of the Way, to its helm. Without a helm, when a ship sets on its trip, it sometimes enters a calm course, but sometimes bumps in rough waves, and that is uncontrollable. With a helm, it runs no risk even in surging billows. Thus, it is said in the *Classic of Poetry*, 'Heaven, in giving birth to the multitudes of the people, // To every thing annexed its law.' [①] Things are forms of the vital force, and laws are principles. Jitong said, 'Heaven and earth constitute *zhong* 中 (the centrality), while all other things go beyond it or fall short of it.' He was also not right, for how can the myriad things be devoid of their centrality? He also mentioned, 'The vast and flowing vital force is the upright vital force of Heave and Earth.' Actually, that is a statement made by Yichuan, which is concerned with nourishing the vital force. If one can nourish it, he will gain his vast and flowing vital force, or else he will get evil vital force, which he will end up with his inability of coping with it. Now, for example, the *yeqi* 夜气 (restorative effect of the night) (*Mencius*, 7A: 8). How much restorative effect can it produce? To nourishing the vast and flowing vital force, it is of little use to depend only on the restorative effect of the night." I said, "In the past, when I read the sentence where *yeqi* belongs, I paid little attention to the words 'not sufficient' after it. That is why I failed to understand its meaning well." The

---

① The translation of the citation is based on J. Legge's translation of *Shijing* (see http: // ctext. org/book-of-poetry).

Master responded, "Underlying preserving and nourishing is the same principle. The object of preserving and that of nourishing are the same vital force. With such an understanding, you will see it well. " Shungong asked, "The heavenly principle and the selfish human desire should, after all, be distinguished so that they do not get mixed with each other. (How do you think?)" The Master answered, "Wufeng (i. e. Hu Hong) said, 'The human nature is like water; the good, like what is below the water surface; the feelings, like the billows of the water; the selfish desire, like waves of the water. ' The billows and waves are different in terms of their sizes, so how can the selfish desire be confounded with the feelings?" I said thereupon, "But Wufeng was right when he said 'In the heavenly principle and the selfish human desire, (two people can) operate concurrently but with different feelings. '" The Master replied, "Yes. The 'operate concurrently' means that the two persons conduct themselves in the heavenly principle, but one pursues the heavenly principle each day, while the other seeks nothing but satisfying his selfish desire, so their feelings are different. However, when he continued to say 'They are the same in substance yet different in function,' he was wrong there all over. " Then the Master went on pointing out many wrong opinions in "Zhiyan" 知言 (Knowing Words) written by Hu Hong. He said, "When he claims 'As regards human nature, there is no good or evil to speak of,' his words indicate his inclination in favor of human nature, yet he is actually unaware of the confusion he incurs by them. This is the general style of him in his discourse concerned with human nature, and, actually, since Wending 文定 (posthumous title of Hu Anguo 胡安国 [1074 – 1138], father of Hu Hong), this trend has continued in their school of learning. For example, 'Human nature possesses good and evil, and human nature, feelings, and talent, all are interlinked. ' That is concerned with vital force rather than human nature. When Lü Bogong (i. e. Lü Zuqian) read Zhiyan for the first time, he thought only two sections in it were right, but later he claimed, 'Wonderful! Better than *Zhengmeng* 正蒙 (Correcting Youthful Ignorance, by Zhang Zai). '" [Kexue]

40 问："既云上智，何以更有人心？"曰："掐着痛，抓着痒，此非人心而何？人自有人心、道心，一个生于血气，一个生于义理。饥寒痛痒，此人心也；恻隐、羞恶、是非、辞逊，此道心也。虽上智亦同。一则危殆而难安，一则微妙而难见。'必使道心常为一身之主，而人心每听命焉'，乃善也。"偶。

Question: Since the wise of the highest class (*Analects*, 17：3) has been said, why is there furthermore human mind?

Answer: When pinched, one gets the feeling of pain, and when tickled, one gets the feeling of itch. If it is not human mind, what is it? A person possesses naturally the human mind and the mind of the Way. The former is born of the vital force of flesh and blood, and the latter, of the principle. The feeling of hunger, coldness, pain, and itch indicates the human mind, while the feeling of sadness and commiseration, shame and dislike, right and wrong, and deference and compliance manifests the mind of the Way. Though one is endowed with the wisdom of the highest class, he makes no exception in this regards. The mind of humankind is at risk and so hard to find ease, while the mind of the Way is subtle and so hard to be seen. By "Ensuring the mind of the Way to be the master of the entire body and the human mind always to be at its command," ("Preface" to *Interpretation*) there will be the good. [Xian]

41 "因郑子上书来问人心、道心，先生曰：'此心之灵，其觉于理者，道心也；其觉于欲者，人心也。'可学窃寻中庸序，以人心出于形气，道心本于性命。盖觉于理谓性命，觉于欲谓形气云云。可学近观中庸序所谓'道心常为一身之主，而人心每听命焉'，又知前日之失。向来专以人可以有道心，而不可以有人心，今方知其不然。人心出于形气，如何去得！然人于性命之理不明，而专为形气所使，则流于人欲矣。如其达性命之理，则虽人心之用，而无非道心，孟子所以指形色为天性者以此。若不明践形之义，则与告子'食、色'之言又何以异？
'操之则存，舍之则亡'，心安有存亡？此正人心、道心交界之辨，而
孟子特指以示学者。可学以为必有道心，而后可以用人心，而于人心之
中，又当识道心。若专用人心而不知道心，则固流入于放僻邪侈之域；
若只守道心，而欲屏去人心，则是判性命为二物，而所谓道心者，空虚
无有，将流于释老之学，而非虞书之所指者。未知然否？"大雅云：
"前辈多云，道心是天性之心，人心是人欲之心。今如此交互取之，当
否？"曰："既是人心如此不好，则须绝灭此身，而后道心始明。且舜
何不先说道心，后说人心？"大雅云："如此，则人心生于血气，道心
生于天理；人心可以为善，可以为不善，而道心则全是天理矣。"曰：
"人心是此身有知觉，有嗜欲者，如所谓'我欲仁'，'从心所欲'，
'性之欲也，感于物而动'，此岂能无！但为物诱而至于陷溺，则为害
尔。故圣人以为此人心，有知觉嗜欲，然无所主宰，则流而忘反，不可
据以为安，故曰危。道心则是义理之心，可以为人心之主宰，而人心据
以为准者也。且以饮食言之，凡饥渴而欲得饮食以充其饱且足者，皆人
心也。然必有义理存焉，有可以食，有不可以食。如子路食于孔悝之
类，此不可食者。又如父之慈其子，子之孝其父，常人亦能之，此道心
之正也。苟父一虐其子，则子必狠然以悖其父，此人心之所以危也。惟
舜则不然，虽其父欲杀之，而舜之孝则未尝替，此道心也。故当使人心
每听道心之区处，方可。然此道心却杂出于人心之间，微而难见，故必
须精之一之，而后中可执。然此又非有两心也，只是义理、人欲之辨
尔。陆子静亦自说得是，云：'舜若以人心为全不好，则须说不好，使
人去之。今止说危者，不可据以为安耳。言精者，欲其精察而不为所杂
也。'此言亦自是。今郑子上之言都是，但于道心下，却一向说是个空
虚无有之物，将流为释老之学。然则彼释迦是空虚之魁，饥能不欲食
乎？寒能不假衣乎？能令无生人之所欲者乎？虽欲灭之，终不可得而灭
也。"大雅。

Zheng Zishang 郑子上（i. e. Zheng Kexue 郑可学）wrote to the Master
and asked about the mind of humankind and the mind of the Way. In the

letter, he said, "You, sir, told me, 'The intelligence of the mind which can be conscious of the principle is the mind of the Way, while that which can be conscious of selfish desire is the mind of humankind.' I find that, in your own preface to your *Interpretation*, you say that the mind of humankind is born of the forms of the vital force, while the mind of the Way is born of human nature and destiny, and probably that which is consciousness of the principle is called the human nature and destiny, while that which is consciousness of the selfish desire is called forms of the vital force. Today, when I read once more the 'The mind of the Way is constantly the master of the entire body and the human mind is always at its command,' I was aware of my mistaken understanding before. I had thought that a person can possess the mind of the Way but not the mind of humankind, and now I know it is not right. Since one's mind of humankind is born of the forms of his vital force, how can he dispense with it? However, when he is ignorant of the principle of human nature and destiny but rather is at the mercy of the forms of the vital force, then he will be subject to his selfish desire. If he is fully aware of the principle of human nature and destiny, then whenever he applies his mind of humankind, it is always the functioning of the mind of the Way. That is why *Mencius* (7A: 38) says 'The bodily organs with their functions belong to our Heaven-conferred nature.' If one fails to understand the meaning of 'satisfying the design of his bodily organization,' (*Mencius*, 7A: 38) then how can he distance himself from Gaozi who claimed 'To enjoy food and delight in colors is human nature.' (*Mencius*, 6A: 4) 'Hold it fast, and it remains with you. Let it go, and you lose it.' (*Mencius*, 6A: 8) With regard to the mind, is there any 'remain' or 'lose' to speak of? But it is employed in an argument for the rectification of the boundary between the mind of humankind and the mind of the Way, and the *Mencius* points that out just for manifesting it to the learners. In my opinion, there must be the mind of the Way first and then the mind of humankind can be employed, while, in the mind of humankind, the mind of the Way should be identified. It is true that, if one employs the mind of humankind with ignorance of the mind of the Way, he will fall into the field of indulgence, perversity, vileness, and extravagance, but, if one seeks only to stick to the mind of the Way and reject the mind of humankind, he will end up with seeing human nature and destiny as two different things, and the so called mind of the Way, which is empty and vacuous, will fall down to the doctrines of Buddhism and Daoism rather than mean that which the 'Yü Xia Shu' 虞夏书 (Books of Yu and Xia, in the *Book of History*) refers originally to. Is this understanding of mine right?"

I said, "It was often said by the previous scholars that the mind of the Way is the mind of the human nature, while the mind of humankind is the mind of the selfish human desire. If their definitions are exchanged now, is it proper?" The Master answered, "If the mind of humankind is so bad, the body must be destroyed before the mind of the Way can be illuminant. And why did Shun not say the mind of the Way first before mentioning the mind of humankind (as recorded in 'Book of Yü and Xia' in the *Classic of History*)?" I replied, "In that way, the mind of humankind is born of the vital force of flesh and blood, and the mind of the Way, of the heavenly principle; The mind of humankind is capable of the good or otherwise, while the mind of the Way is the heavenly principle all over. " The Master said, "By the mind of humankind is meant the consciousness and selfish desire in the body. For example, 'I desire to be humane. ' (*Analects*, 7: 30) 'I follow what my heart desires. ' (*Analects*, 2: 4) and 'His activity shows itself as he is acted on by external things, and develops the desires incident to his nature. ' (*Record of Rites*, 17: 7) Therefore, how can one dispense with his desires? However, if one can not resist the temptation from materials and get indulgent of his desires, that will be harmful to him. Thus the sage regarded this as the mind of humankind with its consciousness and desire, which, without a master of them, would drift and forget to return. It could not be dependable for ease, so he saw it as being at risk. By contrast, the mind of the Way is the mind of principle which can serve as the master of the human mind and it can be depended on by the human mind as its criterion. Let us take having a meal for example. Whenever one feels hunger and thirst and desires to get food and drink, it is the function played by the mind of humankind. However, there must be the principle for a meal with regard to what can be eaten and drunk and what can not. When Zilu 子路 (courtesy name of Zhong You 仲由 [542 – 480 BC], a disciple of Confucius's) had meals offered by Kong Kui 孔悝 (dates unknown), it is a case illustrating what can not. For another example, a father is kind to his son and a son is filial to his father, and these are what ordinary people are capable of. They indicate the uprightness of the mind of the Way. If a father abuses his son, his son will go counter to his father ruthlessly, and this manifests why the mind of humankind is prone to running risks. But Shun was different, for though his father wanted to kill him, he never changed his mind of filial piety to his father. That is indicative of the mind of the Way. So the mind of humankind should be made always at the command of the mind of the Way. However, the mind of the Way is mingled in the mind of humankind, so subtle as to be hardly perceptible. Thus one should be concentrated on and focused on it so as to target and grasp it. Nonetheless, that does not mean there are two minds, for the mind of humankind and that of the Way are said as two only for distinguishing the principle and human desire. Lu Zijing was right when he said, 'If Shun had thought the mind of humankind as completely bad, he would have said it was bad and urged others to get rid of it. But he said of it only as being at risk and undependable for ease. When he mentioned refining, he expected others to examine carefully their mind and keep it from being mixed.' This is naturally right. Now what Zheng Zishang said is right except that he tended to take the mind of the Way for something empty and vacuous, which would lead to a fall into Buddhism and Daoism. But Shakjamuni, head of Buddhism, preaches emptiness and vacuity. When hungry, how can a person not eat? When feeling cold, how can he not clothe himself? How can he be made to get rid of all human desires? Though he desires to vanquish them, he will be ultimately unable to do that." [Daya]

章句

Interpretation of the Doctrine of the Mean

42 问中庸"始言一理，中散为万事，末复合为一理"云云。曰："如何说晓得一理了，万事都在里面？天下万事万物都要你逐一理会过，方得。所谓'中散为万事'，便是中庸。近世如龟山之论，便是如此，以为'反身而诚'，则天下万物之理皆备于我。万物之理，须你逐一去看，理会过方可。如何会反身而诚了，天下万物之理便自然备于我？成个甚么？"又曰："所谓'中散为万事'，便是中庸中所说许多事，如智仁勇，许多为学底道理，与'为天下国家有九经'，与祭祀鬼神许多事。圣人经书所以好看，中间无些子罅隙，句句是实理，无些子空缺处。"僩。

Someone asked about "(The book) first discourses one principle, next it spreads out to cover the myriad things, and finally returns and gathers them all under the one principle," and other statements. The Master answered, "How can it be said that, so long as a person understands the one principle, he can understand the myriad things and events? As for all the myriad things and events, he must understand them one by one. The so called 'next it spreads out to cover the myriad things' means the very Mean 中庸. Many scholars in the previous generation, such as Guishan, held that type of opinions, claiming that, by 'reflecting on one's self with sincerity,' one can be equipped with the principle covering the myriad things and events in the world. To get access to the principle underlying the myriad things and events in the world, one has to investigate them one by one for understanding each of them. How can he be equipped naturally with the principle merely by 'reflecting on one's self with sincerity'? What would that mean?" He continued, "The so called 'next it spreads out to cover the myriad things' refers to the many things expounded in the *Doctrine of the Mean*, for example, the wisdom, benevolence, and courage; the many principles for the pursuit of learning; 'All who have the government of the kingdom with its states and families have nine standard rules to follow' (21); the many events which have to do with sacrifices offered to ghosts and spirits. The classics made by the sages read well, for there are few crevices within their texts, which are made up all by substantial sentences, each with solid truth and no loophole. " [Xian]

43 问: "中庸始合为一理, "天命之谓性。" 末复合为一理。""无声无臭。""始合而开, 其开也有渐; 末后开而复合, 其合也亦有渐。"赐。

Question: The *Doctrine of the Mean* opens with one principle (i. e What Heaven has conferred is called the human nature) (1) and ends with the one principle (i. e. The doings of the Supreme Heaven have neither sound nor smell.) (33). (How do you think?)

Answer: It begins with closing, which leads to opening step by step, and it ends again with closing, which is made step by step. [Ci]

第一章
Chapter One of the *Doctrine of the Mean*

44 "天命之谓性", 是专言理, 虽气亦包在其中, 然说理意较多。若云兼言气, 便说 "率性之谓道" 不去。如太极虽不离乎阴阳, 而亦不杂乎阴阳。道夫。

The first sentence "What Heaven has conferred (on humankind and the myriad things) is called nature" is particularly said of the principle, which, though covering the vital force 气, is more concerned with the meaning of the principle. If it is considered as saying of the vital force concurrently, the next sentence "Following the nature is called the Way" is inexplicable coherently. It is like the Supreme Ultimate which, though inseparable from *yin* and *yang*, is not mingled with *yin* and *yang*. [Daofu]

45 用之问："'天命之谓性。'以其流行而付与万物者谓之命，以人物禀受者谓之性。然人物禀受，以其具仁义礼智而谓之性，以贫贱寿夭而言谓之命，是人又兼有性命。"曰："命虽是恁地说，然亦是兼付与而言。"贺孙。

Yongzhi 用之 (dates unknown, a disciple of Zhu's) asked, " 'What Heaven has conferred is called nature.' That which flows and gives endowments to humankind and the myriad things is called destiny 命 and that which is accepted by humankind and things is called nature. However, what is accepted by humankind and things, due to its benevolence, righteousness, propriety, and wisdom, is called nature, and, due to its wealth or poverty, longevity or premature death, is called destiny. Does this mean that humankind possesses both nature and destiny?" The Master answered, "Though destiny is defined in that way, it is also said with the meaning of giving endowments. " [Hesun]

46 问："'天命之谓性'，此只是从原头说否?"曰："万物皆只同这一个原头。圣人所以尽己之性，则能尽人之性，尽物之性，由其同一原故也。若非同此一原，则人自人之性，物自物之性，如何尽得?"又问："以健顺五常言物之性，如'健顺'字亦恐有碍否?"曰："如牛之性顺，马之性健，即健顺之性。虎狼之仁，蝼蚁之义，即五常之性。但只禀得来少，不似人禀得来全耳。"焘。

Question: Is "What Heaven has conferred is called nature" said only from the origin of nature?

Answer: All humankind and things share that same origin. The reason why the sage can attain the complete development of his nature and then, with that, can have the nature of humankind and that of things to develop to the utmost extent lies in their natures sharing the same origin. Or else, when a man possesses his own nature and a thing possesses its own nature, how can the sage have their natures develop to the utmost extent as he does?

Further question: If the vigorousness and compliance and the Five Constant Virtues are employed to talk about the nature of things, are the vigorousness and compliance, for example, a hindrance?

Answer: For example, the nature of the ox is compliance, while that of the horse is vigorousness, and these pertain to the nature of vigorousness and compliance. The benevolence of tigers and wolves and the righteousness of ants and mole crickets belong to the nature of the Five Constant Virtues, but they are endowed with much less than men, who are conferred on to the complete extent. [Tao]

47 问: "'天命之谓性', 章句云'健顺五常之德', 何故添却'健顺'二字?" 曰: "五行, 乃五常也。'健顺'乃'阴阳'二字。某旧解未尝有此, 后来思量, 既有阴阳, 须添此二字始得。" 枅。

Question: For "What Heaven has conferred is called nature," your *Interpretation* says "(It is of) the vigorousness and compliance and the Five Constant Virtues." Why do you say "vigorousness" and "compliance" in addition to the five virtues?

Answer: The Five Agents represent the very Five Constant Virtues. The "vigorousness" and "compliance" are what is meant by the very *yang* and *yin*, respectively. My previous version of the explanation did not contain these two words, but later I thought that since nature concerned also *yang* and *yin*, it was necessary to add the two words. [Ji]

48 问: "'木之神为仁, 火之神为礼', 如何见得?" 曰: "'神'字, 犹云意思也。且如一枝柴, 却如何见得他是仁? 只是他意思却是仁。火那里见得是礼? 却是他意思是礼。" 僩。古注。

Question: "The *shen* 神 of wood is benevolence and the *shen* of fire is propriety. ” (What does the *shen* mean?)

Answer: What the *shen* means is much like meaning. Take a stick of firewood for example. How can we know it is of benevolence? The meaning of it is but benevolence. How can we know the fire is of prosperity? But its meaning is propriety. 〔Xian〕 The following several passages are on ancient annotations.

49 "率性之谓道"，郑氏以金木水火土，从 "天命之谓性" 说来，要顺从气说来方可。泳。

As regards "Following the nature is called the Way," (1) Zheng's (郑 玄，127－200) explanation, on the basis of the Five Agents, i. e. metal, wood, water, fire, and earth, starts from "What Heaven has conferred is called nature." However, it should be explained from viewpoint of the vital force. 〔Yong（泳）〕

50 "率性之谓道"，"率" 字轻。方子。

In "Following (*shuai* 率) the nature is called the Way," (1) what the *shuai* means is less significant. 〔Fangzi〕

51 "率" 字只是 "循" 字，循此理便是道。伊川所以谓便是 "仁者人也，合而言之道也"。僩。

The *shuai* means only "go along," and to go along the principle is the Way. Therefore, Yichuan says it is what is meant by "Benevolence is the distinguishing characteristic of humankind. When embodied in the human conduct, it is called the Way." (*Mencius*, 7B：62) 〔Xun〕

52 "率性之谓道"，"率" 是呼唤字，盖曰循万物自然之性之谓道。此 "率" 字不是用力字，伊川谓 "合而言之道也"，是此义。僩。

In "Following (*shuai*) the nature is called the Way," (1) the *shuai* functions as a vocative sinograph, and the sentence probably means that going along the natural nature of things is called the Way. The *shuai* is not a word worth much attention. As Yichuan said, "When conforming to the human conduct, it is called the Way," (*Mencius*, 7B：62) which is its meaning.

[Xun]

53 安卿问"率性"。曰:"率,非人率之也。伊川解'率'字,亦只训循。到吕与叔说'循性而行,则谓之道',伊川却便以为非是。至其自言,则曰:'循牛之性,则不为马之性;循马之性,则不为牛之性。'乃知循性是循其理之自然尔。"伯羽。

Anqing asked about *shuai xing* 率性, the first two sino-graphs in the first sentences of the book. The Master answered, "The *shuai* is not the *shuai* (lead) in such sentence as 'Such and such person leads others.' Yichuan explained it only as meaning 'going along.' As for Lü Yushu's explanation of the sentence as 'Going along the nature and conducting oneself is called the Way,' however, Yichuan did not think it was right. In his own words, 'Going along the nature of the ox is not following the nature of the horse; going along the nature of the horse is not following the nature of the ox.' Thus, we know, his 'going along the nature' means following the natural being of the principle." [Boyu]

54 "率,循也。不是人去循之,吕说未是。程子谓:'通人物而言,马则为马之性,又不做牛底性;牛则为牛之性,又不做马底性。'物物各有个理,即此便是道。"曰:"总而言之,又只是一个理否?"曰:"是。"淳。

The Master said, "The *shuai* means going along (the nature), but it is not only a person going along (the nature). Lü's explanation is not right. Master Cheng said, 'It is said of both humankind and things. The horse possesses the nature of the horse, which is not the nature of the ox, while the ox possesses the nature of the ox, which is not the nature of the horse.' Everything possesses its principle, and it is the Way." When asked, "Is it, in a word, only the same principle?" The Master answered, "Yes." [Chun (淳)]

55 "率性之谓道",只是随性去,皆是道。吕氏说以人行道。若然,则未行之前,便不是道乎? 淳。

The "Following (*shuai*) the nature is called the Way" (1) means nothing but that whatever follows the nature is the Way. Lü thought, however, that it meant humankind conducting the Way. Were that true, before the conduct, would there not be the Way? [Chun (淳)]

56 问："'"率性之谓道"，率，循也。'此'循'字是就道上说，还是就行道人上说？"曰："诸家多作行道人上说，以率性便作修为，非也。率性者，只是说循吾本然之性，便自有许多道理。性是个浑沦底物，道是个性中分派条理。循性之所有，其许多分派条理即道也。'性'字通人物而言。但人物气禀有异，不可道物无此理。程子曰：'循性者，牛则为牛之性，又不做马底性；马则为马底性，又不做牛底性。'物物各有这理，只为气禀遮蔽，故所通有偏正不同。然随他性之所通，道亦无所不在也。"铢。

Question: "In 'Following (*shuai*) the nature is called the Way' (1), the *shuai* means going along." Here, is the 'going along' said in regard to the Way or to the man who conducts the Way?

Answer: Most scholars explain it as being said in regard to the man who conducts the Way, taking "following the nature" as meaning to pursue self-cultivation, but I do not think they are right. The "following the nature" means only that, so long as one follows his original nature, he will possess naturally many principles. The nature is something complete and the Way refers to the various veins in the nature. To follow what the nature possesses is to go along the various veins in it, which constitute the Way. The sino-graph *xing* 性 (nature) is said of both humankind and things, but though humankind and things are different in their endowments, it should not be said that things do not possess the principle. Master Cheng said, "As regards going along the nature, the horse goes along the nature of the horse, which is not the nature of the ox, while the ox goes along the nature of the ox, which is not the nature of the horse." Things each possess the principle, but because they each are beclouded by their own endowments, their penetrations into the principle are different in terms of their partiality. However, where their natures penetrate the principle, there is the Way. [Zhu]

57 问："率性通人物而言，则此'性'字似'生之谓性'之'性'，兼气禀言之否？"曰："'天命之谓性'，这性亦离气禀不得。'率，循也。'此'循'字是就道上说，不是就行道人说。性善只一般，但人物气禀有异，不可道物无此理。性是个浑沦物，道是性中分派条理，随分派条理去，皆是道。穿牛鼻，络马首，皆是随他所通处。仁义礼智，物岂不有，但偏耳。随他性之所通处，道皆无所不在。"曰："此'性'字亦是以理言否？"曰："是。"又问："鸢有鸢之性，鱼有鱼之性，其飞其跃，天机自完，便是天理流行发见之妙处，故子思姑举此一二以明道之无所不在否？"曰："是。"淳。

Question: Since the "following (*shuai*) the nature" is said of both humankind and things, this "nature" is similar to the "nature" in "Life is what we call nature" (said by Gaozi). (*Mencius*, 6A: 3) Does it also cover the meaning of endowment?

Answer: In "What Heaven has conferred is called nature," (1) the "nature" is inseparable with endowment. The *shuai* means going along, which is in regard to the Way rather than the man who conducts the Way. The nature is good, and this is true of everything. But it should not be said that things do not possess the principle because they are different from humankind in their endowment. The nature is something complete and the Way means the various veins in the nature. Going along each of the various veins therein is the Way. For example, an ox is led by a terret through its snout, while a horse is by a net on its head. Either is done by following where it penetrates the principle. As regards benevolence, righteousness, propriety, and wisdom, don't things possess them? But theirs are partial. Where their natures penetrate the principle, there is the Way.

Further question: Is that "nature" said in regard to the principle?

Answer: Yes, it is.

Further question: The glede has the nature of the glede and the fish has the nature of the fish. Their flying and leaping are furnished to them by Heaven's mystery, manifesting the fabulous flow of the principle of Heaven. Therefore, did Zisi 子思（483 BC – 402 BC, claimed as the author of the *Doctrine of the Mean*）just cite these two examples to illustrate that the Way is ubiquitous?

Answer: Yes.［Chun（淳）］

58 孟子说"性善"，全是说理。若中庸"天命之谓性"，已自是兼带人物而言。"率性之谓道"，性是一个浑沦底物，道是支脉。恁地物，便有恁地道。率人之性，则为人之道，率牛之性，则为牛之道，非谓以人循之。若谓以人循之而后谓之道，则人未循之前，谓之无道，可乎！砥。

When Mencius dwelt on the goodness of human nature, what he said is completely of the principle. In the *Doctrine of the Mean*, the "What Heaven has conferred is called nature"（1）is already said of both humankind and things. As for "Following the nature is called the Way"（1）, the nature is something complete and the Way is the veins therein. Such and such thing possesses such and such Way. To follow the nature of humankind is to go along the Way for humankind, and to follow the nature of the ox is to go along the Way for the ox. It does not mean that only when humankind follows it can there be the Way, for if it were true, before humankind follows it, can we say there would be no Way?［Di］

59 "天命之谓性"，指迥然孤独而言。"率性之谓道"，指着于事物之间而言。又云："天命之性，指理言；率性之道，指人物所行言。或以率性为顺性命之理，则谓之道。如此，却是道因人做，方始有也！"夔孙。

The Master said, "The 'What Heaven has conferred is called nature' （1）refers to that which is completely solitary, while 'Following the nature is called the Way' （1）refers to that which dwells in things and events. " He added, "The nature conferred by Heaven is said of the principle, while the Way of following the nature is said of what humankind and things do. Someone regards following the nature as setting up the principle complying with the conferred nature and calls that the Way. Then, this would mean that the Way did not come into being until humankind set about it. " [Kuisun]

60 万物禀受，莫非至善者，性；率性而行，各得其分者，道。端蒙。

What the myriad things each are endowed with, all of which is the supremely good, is their nature, while that they each go along their nature and accept what is due to them is the Way. [Duanmeng]

61 "天命之谓性，率性之谓道。"性与道相对，则性是体，道是用。又曰："道，便是在里面做出底道。"义刚。

The Master said, "In 'What Heaven has conferred is called nature. Following the nature is called the Way' (1), where the nature is opposite to the Way, the nature is the substance, while the Way is its function. " He added, "The Way is that which is caused in the nature. " [Yigang]

62 问："'天命之谓性，率性之谓道'，伊川谓通人物而言。如此，却与告子所谓人物之性同。"曰："据伊川之意，人与物之本性同，及至禀赋则异。盖本性理也，而禀赋之性则气也。性本自然，及至生赋，无气则乘载不去，故必顿此性于气上，而后可以生。及至已生，则物自禀物之气，人自禀人之气。气最难看。而其可验者，如四时之间，寒暑得宜，此气之正。当寒而暑，当暑而寒，乃气不得正。气正则为善，气不正则为不善。又如同是此人，有至昏愚者，是其禀得此浊气太深。"又问："明道云：'论性不论气，不备；论气不论性，不明。'"曰："论性不论气，孟子也；不备，但少欠耳。论气不论性，荀扬也；不明，则大害事！"可学问："孟子何不言气？"曰："孟子只是教人勇于为善，前更无阻碍。自学者而言，则不可不去其窒碍。正如将百万之兵，前有数万兵，韩白为之，不过鼓勇而进；至他人，则须先去此碍后可。"吴宜之问："学者治此气，正如人之治病。"曰："亦不同。须是明天理，天理明，则去。通书'刚柔'一段，亦须着且先易其恶，既易其恶，则致其中在人。"问："恶安得谓之刚？"曰："此本是刚出来。"语毕，先生又曰："'生之谓性'，伊川以为生质之性，然告子此语亦未是。"再三请益，曰："且就伊川此意理会，亦自好。"可学。

Question: As regards "What Heaven has conferred is called nature. Following the nature is called the Way" (1), according to Yichuan, it is said of both humankind and things. Then, it will be similar to what Gaozi said of the nature of humankind and things. (How do you think?)

Answer: As Yichuan saw it, the original nature of humankind and that of things are the same, but their endowments are different. Probably the original nature is the principle, while the nature of the endowments is the vital force. The nature is originally natural, but when its endowment is made, without the vital force, there would be nothing that could carry it. So the nature has to be loaded by the vital force before it can come into being. When it comes into being, things are endowed with it via the vital force of things, while humankind is endowed with it via the vital force of humankind. The vital force is the most difficult to perceive. What can be verifiable in it is, for example, during the four seasons, when the time for coolness or warmth is appropriate, it is cool or warm, and then the endowed vital force will be upright. But when it should be cold yet it is actually hot, or when it should be hot yet it is actually cold, then the endowed vital force will be surely not upright. The upright vital force means the good, while the not upright vital force means otherwise. Even for men of the same nature, some are utterly stupid and that is because they are endowed with too much turbid vital force.

Further question: Mingdao said, "When discussing nature, if one does not consider vital force, his discussion will be incomplete; when discussing vital force, if one does not consider nature, his discussion will be not clear."

（How do you think?）

Answer: Discussing nature without considering vital force is what Mencius did. Though it is incomplete, its deficiency is only a little. Discussing vital force without considering nature is what Xunzi and Yangzi did. Since it is not clear, it incurs tremendous harm.

I asked, "Why did Mencius not touch vital force?" The Master answered, "His purpose is only to instruct the learners to be brave to do good and, by that, to remove the obstacle in their way ahead. From the viewpoint of the learners, they must get rid of the obstacles against them. It is like a commander of a million troops who is faced with tens of thousand of enemy troops. If the commander was Han Xin 韩信（? – 196BC）or Bai Qi 白起（? – 257 BC）, either an ancient famous general, he would simply forge valiantly ahead as if that enemy did not exist. But for others, they would have to wipe out those enemy troops in order to advance." Wu Yizhi 吴宜之（dates unknown, a disciple of Zhu's）asked, "A learner treats the vital force just as a person treats his disease, doesn't he?" The Master replied, "They are different to some extent, for a learner should strive to be clear about the heavenly principle before he will be able to have the trouble with his vital force removed. The section on 'firmness and softness' in *Penetrating the Classic of Change*（by Zhou Dunyi）also says that one should strive first to transform his evil by himself and then, with that, it is up to him to arrive at the Mean." When asked, "How can the evil be referred to as firmness?" the Master replied, "Because it stems from the firmness." Then he added, "As for Gaozi's 'Life is what we call nature,'（*Mencius*, 6A: 3）Yichuan took it for meaning the physical nature, but what Gaozi said is not right, either." When I consulted him about that point for several times, the Master told me, "For the time being, you may as well try to understand what Yichuan said about that and it is also advisable." ［Kexue］

63 问"'天命之谓性,率性之谓道',皆是人物之所同得。天命之性,人受其全,则其心具乎仁义礼智之全体;物受其偏,则随其品类各有得焉,而不能通贯乎全体。'率性之谓道',若自人而言之,则循其仁义礼智之性而言之,固莫非道;自物而言之,飞潜动植之类各正其性,则亦各循其性于天地之间,莫非道也。如中庸或问所说'马首之可络,牛鼻之可穿'等数句,恐说未尽。所举或问,非今本。盖物之自循其性,多有与人初无干涉。多有人所不识之物,无不各循其性于天地之间,此莫非道也。如或问中所说,恐包未尽。"曰:"说话难。若说得阔,则人将来又只认'目之于色,耳之于声,鼻之于臭,四肢之于安佚'等做性;却不认'仁之于父子,义之于君臣,礼之于宾主,智之于贤者,圣人之于天道'底是性。"因言:"解经立言,须要得实。如前辈说'伊尹耕于有莘之野而乐尧舜之道',是饥食渴饮,夏葛冬裘,为乐尧舜之道。若如此说,则全身已浸在尧舜之道中,何用更说'岂若吾身亲见之哉'?如前辈说'文武之道未坠于地',以为文武之道常昭然在日用之间,一似常有一物昭然在目前,不会撅下去一般,此皆是说得不实。所以'未坠于地'者,只言周衰之时,文武之典章,人尚传诵得在,未至沦没。"先生既而又曰:"某晓得公说底。盖马首可络,牛鼻可穿,皆是就人看物处说。圣人'修道之谓教',皆就这样处。如适间所说,却也见得一个大体。"至。

方子录云:"至之问:'"率性之谓道",或问只言"马首之可络,牛鼻之可穿",都是说以人看物底。若论飞潜动植,各正其性,与人不相干涉者,何莫非道?恐如此看方是。'先生曰:'物物固皆是道。如蝼蚁之微,甚时胎,甚时卵,亦是道。但立言甚难,须是说得实。如龟山说"尧舜之道",只夏葛冬裘、饥食渴饮处便是。如此,则全身浸在尧舜之道里,又何必言"岂若吾身亲见之哉"?'黄丈云:'若如此说,则人心、道心皆是道去。'先生曰:'相似"目之于色,耳之于声,鼻之于臭,四肢之于安佚,性也"底,却认做道;"仁之于父子,义之于君臣,礼之于宾主,智之于贤者,有性焉"底,却认不得。如"文武之道未坠于地,在人",李光祖乃曰:"日用之间,昭然在是。"如此,则只是说古今公共底,何必指文武?孔子盖是言周家典章文物未至沦没,非是指十方常住者而言也。'久之,复曰:'至之却亦看得一个大体。'"盖卿同。

Question: As said in "What Heaven has conferred is called nature. Following the nature is called the Way" (1), both the nature and the Way are conferred to humankind and things. As regards the nature conferred by Heaven, humankind accepts it complete and thus the human mind possesses the entirety of the benevolence, righteousness, propriety, and wisdom. By contrast, things accept it partial, and different types of them get it to varying extent, so they each do not possess its entirety. As for the "Following the nature is called the Way," (1) if it is said in regard to humankind, that is, from the viewpoint of going along his nature of benevolence, righteousness, propriety, and wisdom, nothing of him does not pertain to the Way. If it is said in relation to things, the animals and plants everywhere each possess their right nature and each go along their nature between heaven and earth, and also nothing of them does not pertain to the Way. The several sentences you say in your *Questions and Answers*, that is, "A horse can be led by a net on its head, while an ox can be led by a terret through its snout," and others, I'm afraid, are not complete in explanation of that. The *Questions and Answers* from which the sentence is cited is not the edition in use at present. Probably, things follow their natures by themselves, and largely at first that has nothing to do with humankind. Many of them are not known to humankind, yet they each go along their own natures between heaven and earth. Therefore, nothing of them does not pertain to the Way. What you say in your *Questions and Answers*, I'm afraid, is not inclusive of them all.

Answer: It is so hard to say something. If the saying is broad, people may see only these things of "the mouth's desiring sweet tastes, the eye's desiring beautiful colors, the ear's desiring pleasant sounds, the nose's desiring fragrant odors, and the four limbs' desiring ease and rest," (*Mencius*, 7B: 70) as pertaining to nature, but not take such things as "the exercise of love between father and son, the observance of righteousness between sovereign and minister, the rules of ceremony between guest and host, the display of knowledge in recognizing the talented, and the fulfilling the heavenly course by the sage" (*Mencius*, 7B: 70) as pertaining to the nature. ①

Thereupon further answer: In explaining the classics and expounding ideas, what is the important is to be substantial. For example, a previous scholar, when explicating "Yi Yin was a farmer in the lands of the prince of Shen, delighting in the principles of Yao and Shun," (*Mencius*, 5A: 7) claimed that it meant Yi Yin's eating when hungry and drinking when thirsty, clothing himself with linens in summer and furs in winter, was his way of delighting in the principles of Yao and Shun. If that were true, it would mean Yi Yin was already completely immersed in the principles of Yao and Shun, then why would it be necessary to say "Had I not better in my own person see these things for myself?" (*Mencius*, 5A: 7) Another previous scholar, when explaining "The doctrines of King Wen of Zhou and King Wu of Zhou have not yet fallen to the ground," (*Analects*, 19: 22) said that the doctrines of Wen and Wu were always clear in daily activities just as if there was something clear before the eyes, which would not stumble down and get lost. Both explanations are devoid of substantiality. Actually, the so called "not yet fallen to the ground" means only that when the Zhou dynasty declined, the decrees and regulations established by Wen and Wu were still widely read and did not fall into oblivion.

Then, the Master continued, "I saw what you said just now. Probably, 'A horse can be led by a net on its head, while an ox can be led by a terret through its snout,' is said in relation to where humankind looks at things. It is in the same way as the sage saying 'Cultivating the Way is called education.' (1) What you said just now indicates that you were able to see

---

① The translation of the two citations from *Mencius* is based on a version by J. Legge (see http: //ctext. org/mengzi).

the basic idea. " [Zhi]

For this conversation, Fangzi's record reads as follows: Zhizhi (courtesy name of Yang Zhi) asked, " As regards ' Following the nature is called the Way, ' (1) your *Questions and Answers* mentioned only that ' A horse can be led by a net on its head, while an ox can be led by a terret through its snout ' is said in relation to where humankind looks at things. Nonetheless, of the animals and plants everywhere, which each possess their right nature and have nothing to do with humankind, who of them does not pertain to the Way? I'm afraid, it is the right way to see them. (How do you think?) " The Master said, " It is true that in everything dwells the Way. For example, even little things like mole crickets and ants, which, when they get pregnant and when they lay eggs, display the Way. But it is truly hard to use words to convey ideas about it and the saying with words must be substantial. For instance, when Guishan explained ' the principles of Yao and Shun, ' he only saw it in such matters as eating when hungry and drinking when thirsty, clothing oneself with linens in summer and furs in winter. If that was true, one would be immersed all over in the principles of Yao and Shun, and why would it be necessary to mention ' Had I not better in my own person see these things for myself? ' " Huang Zhang 黄丈 (i. e. Huang Gan) responded, " If in this way, the mind of humankind and the mind of the Way are both of the Way. " The Master replied, " Such as ' the mouth's desiring sweet tastes, the eye's desiring beautiful colors, the ear's desiring pleasant sounds, the nose's desiring fragrant odors, and the four limbs' desiring ease and rest, ' (*Mencius*, 7B: 70) are seen by some as the Way, but ' the exercise of love between father and son, the observance of righteousness between sovereign and minister, the rules of ceremony between guest and host, the display of knowledge in recognizing the talented, and the fulfilling the heavenly course by the sage ' (*Mencius*, 7B: 70) are not known by them as the Way. For another example, as regards the ' The doctrines of King Wen of Zhou and King Wu of Zhou have not yet fallen to the ground, for they are to be found among men, ' (*Analects*, 19: 22) Li Guangzu 李光祖 (i. e. Li Yu 李郁) explained it as ' (The doctrines of Wen and Wu are always) clear in daily activities just as if there was something clear before the eyes. ' Thus, that would be concerned with what is shared past and present, and why would Wen and Wu be mentioned? When Confucius said that, probably he meant that the decrees and regulations established by Wen and Wu were still widely read and did not fall into oblivion, so it was not said in relation to the multitudes of people with their daily activities. " After some time, he added, " But Zhizhi was able to see the basic idea. " (Gaiqing's record for this is the same.)

64　问: "伊川云: ' "天命之谓性，率性之谓道"，此亦通人物而言; "修道之谓教"，此专言人事。'" 曰: "是如此。人与物之性皆同，故循人之性则为人道，循马牛之性则为马牛之道。若不循其性，令马耕牛驰，则失其性，而非马牛之道矣，故曰'通人物而言'。"璘。

Question：Yichuan said，"The 'What Heaven has conferred is called nature. Following the nature is called the Way'（1）is said of both humankind and things；the 'Cultivating the Way is called education'（1）is concerned only with the matters of humankind."（How do you think？）

Answer：That is right. The nature of humankind and that of things are the same in that sense，so to go along the nature of humankind is the Way of humankind，and to go along the nature of the horse or the ox is the Way of the horse or the ox. Or else，to make the horse plough or make the ox gallop is to lose its nature，which is against its Way. That is why he said with regard to "both humankind and things." ［Lin］

65 问："'率性之谓道'，通人物而言，则'修道之谓教'，亦通人物。如'服牛乘马'，'不杀胎，不夭妖'，'斧斤以时入山林'，此是圣人教化不特在人伦上，品节防范而及于物否？"曰："也是如此，所以谓之'尽物之性'。但于人较详，于物较略；人上较多，物上较少。"砥。

Question：The "Following the nature is called the Way"（1）is said of both humankind and things and the "Cultivating the Way is called education"（1）is also said of both humankind and things. For example，"（They）used oxen（in carts）and yoked horses（to chariots），"（"Appended Remarks II" in the *Classic of Change*）"（They did）not kill pregnant animals，nor those which had not attained to their full growth，"（"Royal Regulations" in the *Record of Rites*）and "Let the axes and bills enter the hills and forests only at the proper time."（*Mencius*，1A：3）[1] Don't these mean that the sage intended education not only for fostering human relations but also for instructing observances to regulations towards things？

---

[1] The translations of the citations in the passage are based on J. Legge's versions（http：//ctext. org/）.

Answer: That is also right. So it is also said "to give the full development to the natures of things." (23) However, the book is more detailed in regard to humankind than to things, and more concerned with humankind than with things. [Di]

66 问："集解中以'天命之谓性，率性之谓道'通人物而言。'修道之谓教'，是专就人事上言否？"曰："道理固是如此。然'修道之谓教'，就物上亦有个品节。先王所以咸若草木鸟兽，使庶类蕃殖，如周礼掌兽、掌山泽各有官，如周公驱虎豹犀象龙蛇，如'草木零落然后入山林，昆虫未蛰不以火田'之类，各有个品节，使万物各得其所，亦所谓教也。"德明。

Question: As you, sir, said in your *Zhongyong Jijie* 中庸集解 (Collected Explanations of *The Doctrine for the Mean*) "The 'What Heaven has conferred is called nature. Following the nature is called the Way' (1) is said of both humankind and things." Is "Cultivating the Way is called education" (1) said only in regard to the matters of humankind?

Answer: It is true in reason, of course, but the "Cultivating the Way is called education" (1) also instructs observances to regulations towards things. The ancient kings were considerate of trees and grasses, birds and beasts, and took measures to ensure all kinds of them to multiply abundantly. For example, according to the records of the Zhou rites, officials were appointed in charge of animals, of mountains and lakes, etc; Duke of Zhou drove far away the tigers, leopards, rhinoceroses, elephants, pythons, and snakes; "When the plants and trees began to drop their leaves, they entered the hills and forests (with the axe). Until the insects had all withdrawn into their burrows, they did not fire the fields." ("Royal Regulations" in the *Record of Rites*) So there were observances to regulations towards things so that they each could be in their proper places. That is what is meant by that "education." [Deming]

67 问"修道之谓教"。曰："游杨说好，谓修者只是品节之也。明道之说自各有意。"去伪。

Asked about "Cultivating the Way is called education," (1) the Master answered, "You Cu's and Yang's explanations are tenable, saying that what is cultivated concerns only regulations of conducts and morals. Mingdao's explanation also has its point." [Quwei]

68 问:"明道曰:'道即性也。若道外寻性,性外寻道,便不是。'如此,即性是自然之理,不容加工。扬雄言:'学者,所以修性。'故伊川谓扬雄为不识性。中庸却言'修道之谓教',如何?"曰:"性不容修,修是揠苗。道亦是自然之理,圣人于中为之品节以教人耳,谁能便于道上行!"浩。

Question: Mingdao said, "The Way is the nature. It is not right to seek the nature outside the Way or the Way outside the nature." Then, it means that the nature is but the natural principle, allowing of no modification. Yang Xiong 扬雄 (53 – 18BC) once said "The learning is what the nature is modified (*xiu* 修) by." So Yichuan did not think Yang as one who knew the nature. However, in the *Doctrine of the Mean* is "Cultivating (*xiu* 修) the Way is called education." (1) How do you think of it?

Answer: The nature is admissive of no modification, or else it would be like pulling up a seedling to help it grow. The Way is also the natural principle. The purpose of the sage who formulated the regulations is only to instruct others about the Way. Who can impose modification on the Way? [Hao]

69 "修道之谓教"一句,如今人要合后面"自明诚"谓之教却说作自修。盖"天命谓性"之"性"与"自诚明"之性,"修道谓教"之"教"与"自明诚"之教,各自不同。诚明之性,"尧舜性之"之"性";明诚之教,由教而入者也。木之。

As for the "Cultivating the Way is called education (*jiao* 教)," (1) today many people, in an attempt to associate the *jiao* with the *jiao* 教 in the sentence "That sincerity results from enlightenment is due to education,"

(23) explain the *jiao* as meaning self-modification. Probably the nature in "What Heaven has conferred is called nature" (1) and the nature in "That enlightenment results from sincerity is due to the nature" (23) do not mean the same, nor do the education in "Cultivating the Way is called education" and the education in "That sincerity results from enlightenment is due to education." The nature in the latter sentence means the same as the nature in "(Benevolence and righteousness were) of the nature to Yao and Shun," (*Mencius*, 7A: 30) and the education in the latter sentence means entry through education. [Muzhi]

70 问:"中庸旧本不曾解'可离非道'一句。今先生说云'瞬息不存,便是邪妄',方悟本章可离与不可离,道与非道,各相对待而言。离了仁便不仁,离了义便不义。公私善利皆然。向来从龟山说,只谓道自不可离,而先生旧亦不曾为学者说破。"曰:"向来亦是看得太高。"今按:"可离非道",云"瞬息不存,便是邪妄",与章句、或问说不合,更详之。德明。

Someone said to the Master, "The old edition of your *Interpretation of the Doctrine of the Mean* did not explain the sentence 'If it (the Way) could be left, it would not be the Way.' (1) Now when I read in your explanation 'If it could not be preserved for even an instant, it would be vile and vain,' I have understood that 'could be left' and 'could not be left,' and 'the Way' and 'not the Way' said in that chapter of the book are said as opposites. If the benevolence could be left, it would not be the benevolence, and if the righteousness could be left, it would not be the righteousness. This is true of the public, the private, the good, and the profit. In the past, Guishan once only said that the Way naturally could not be left, and you did not lay bare that point for us learners, either." The Master replied, "I used to read it as something too aloft." (Note: The Master's new explanation of "If it could be left, it would not be the Way" as meaning "If it could not be preserved for even an instant, it would be vile and vain" is different from that in *Interpretation of the Doctrine of the Mean* and that in *Questions and Answers on the Doctrine of the Mean.*) ［Deming］

71 黻问:"中庸曰'道不可须臾离',伊川却云'存无不在道之心,便是助长',何也?"曰:"中庸所言是日用常行合做底道理,如'为人君止于仁,为人臣止于敬,为人子止于孝,为人父止于慈,与国人交止于信',皆是不可已者。伊川此言,是为辟释氏而发。盖释氏不理会常行之道,只要空守着这一个物事,便唤做道,与中庸自不同。"说毕又曰:"辟异端说话,未要理会,且理会取自家事。自家事既明,那个自然见得。"与立。

Fu 黻 (i. e. Yang Fu 杨黻, dates unknown, a disciple of Zhu's) asked, "The *Doctrine of the Mean* says 'The Way may not be left for an instant,' (1) whereas Yichuan claimed 'Preserving the mind for all dwelling in the Way is like pulling a seedling to help it grow.' Why?" The Master answered, "What is said in the *Doctrine of the Mean* refers to the principles which should be adhered to in daily conducts and routine activities. For example, 'As a sovereign, he rests in humaneness. As a minister, he rests in reverence. As a son, he rests in filial piety. As a father, he rests in kindness. In communication with his fellow countrymen, he rests in good faith.' (*Great Learning*, 7) All these principles should not be ignored. But what Yichuan said is driven at the doctrine of Buddhism. Probably it is because Buddhists neglect the principles over daily activities and conducts and instead they call that which they adhere to in vain 'the Way.' So he did not mean the same as the *Doctrine of the Mean*." After saying that, the Master added, "You do not need to heed those words said for breaking up heretic doctrines, and just focus on our own doctrine. When you are clear about our own doctrine, you will find those words easy to understand." ［Yuli］①

72 杨通老问:"中庸或问引杨氏所谓'无适非道'之云,则善

---

① Yuli 与立 is the courtesy name of Yang Fu 杨黻, according to Yang Yan 杨艳 (see Yang Yan, "Zhuzi Menren Zhi Pucheng Yangshi Jiazu Kao" 朱子门人之浦城杨氏家族考 ［A Biographical Study of the Disciples of Zhu Xi in Yang's Family in Pucheng］, *Guangxi Social Sciences*, 2013 ［12］).

矣，然其言似亦有所未尽。盖衣食作息，视听举履，皆物也，其所以如此之义理准则，乃道也。"曰："衣食动作只是物，物之理乃道也。将物便唤做道，则不可。且如这个椅子有四只脚，可以坐，此椅之理也。若除去一只脚，坐不得，便失其椅之理矣。'形而上为道，形而下为器。'说这形而下之器之中，便有那形而上之道。若便将形而下之器作形而上之道，则不可。且如这个扇子，此物也，便有个扇子底道理。扇子是如此做，合当如此用，此便是形而上之理。天地中间，上是天，下是地，中间有许多日月星辰，山川草木，人物禽兽，此皆形而下之器也。然这形而下之器之中，便各自有个道理，此便是形而上之道。所谓格物，便是要就这形而下之器，穷得那形而上之道理而已，如何便将形而下之器作形而上之道理得！饥而食，渴而饮，'日出而作，日入而息'，其所以饮食作息者，皆道之所在也。若便谓食饮作息者是道，则不可，与庞居士'神通妙用，运水搬柴'之颂一般，亦是此病。如'徐行后长'与'疾行先长'，都一般是行。只是徐行后长方是道，若疾行先长便不是道，岂可说只认行底便是道！'神通妙用，运水搬柴'，须是运得水，搬得柴是，方是神通妙用。若运得不是，搬得不是，如何是神通妙用！佛家所谓'作用是性'，便是如此。他都不理会是和非，只认得那衣食作息，视听举履，便是道。说我这个会说话底，会作用底，叫着便应底，便是神通妙用，更不问道理如何。儒家则须是就这上寻讨个道理方是道。禅老云'赤肉团上，有一无位真人，在汝等诸人面门上出入'云云。他便是只认得这个，把来作弄。"或问："告子之学便是如此？"曰："佛家底又高。告子底死杀了，不如佛家底活。而今学者就故纸上理会，也解说得去，只是都无那快活和乐底意思，便是和这佛家底也不曾见得。似他佛家者虽是无道理，然他却一生受用，一生快活，便是他就这形而下者之中，理会得似那形而上者。而今学者看来，须是先晓得这一层，却去理会那上面一层方好。而今都是和这下面一层也不曾见得，所以和那上面一层也理会不得。"又曰："天地中间，物物上有这个道理，虽至没紧要底物事，也有这道理。盖'天命之谓性'，这道理却无形，无安顿处。只那日用事物上，道理便在上面。这两个元不相离，凡有一物，便有一理，所以君子贵'博学于文'。看来博学似个没紧要物事，然那许多道理便都在这上，都从那源头上来。所以无精粗小大，都一齐用理会过，盖非外物也。都一齐理会，方无所不尽，方周遍无疏缺处。"又曰："'道不可须臾离，可离非道也。'所谓不可离者，谓道也。若便以日用之间举止动作便是道，则无所适而非道，无时而非道，然则君子何用恐惧戒慎？何用更学道为？为其不可离，所以须是依道而行。如人说话，不成便以说话者为道，须是有个仁义礼智始得。若便以举止动作为道，何用更说不可离得？"又曰："大学所以说格物，却不说穷理。盖说穷理，则似悬空无捉摸处。只说格物，则只就那形而下之器上，便寻那形而上之道，便见得这个元不相离，所以只说'格物'。'天生蒸民，有物有则。'所谓道者是如此，何尝说物便是则！龟山便只指那物做则，只是就这物上分精粗为物则。如云目是物也，目之视乃则也；耳物也，耳之听乃则也。殊不知目视耳听，依旧是物；其视之明，听之聪，方是则也。龟山又云：'伊尹之耕于莘野，此农夫田父之所日用者，而乐在是。'如此，则世间伊尹甚多矣！龟山说话，大概有此病。"僩。

Yang Tonglao 杨通老（Yang Ji 杨辑, with the courtesy name Tonglao, disciple of Zhu Xi）asked, "In your *Questions and Answers*, Yang（i. e. Yang Shi）is cited as saying 'There is nowhere without the Way,' which is right, but what he meant is still not complete. Probably, clothes and food, work and rest, hearing and seeing, and performing and fulfilling, all these are things and events, and the principles by which they are what they are constitute the Way.（How do you think?）"

The Master answered, "Clothes, food, and the actions are all things and events, and the principles governing them are the Way. But the things and events themselves should not be referred to as the Way. For example, this chair has four feet, and can be sat on. This is the principle of it. But if a foot of it is removed and thus it can not be sat on, then it will lose its principle.

'What exists before physical form (and is therefore without it) is called the Way. What exists after physical form (and therefore with it) is called a concrete thing.'[①] ('Appended Remarks' in the *Classic of Change*) It means that dwelling in the concrete things is the metaphysical Way. But the concrete things themselves can not be regarded as the metaphysical Way. Take this fan for example. It is a thing, where the principle of the fan inheres. The fan is made that way and should be used also that way. This illustrates the metaphysical principle. Take heaven and earth for another example. The heaven is the top and the earth is the bottom, between which are the sun, the moon, and numerous stars; and mountains, rivers, trees, and grasses; and humans, and birds, beasts. All these are concrete things, each possessing its principle which is the very metaphysical Way. The so called investigation of things means nothing but inquiring the metaphysical principles which dwell in concrete things. How can the concrete things be taken for the metaphysical principles? When feeling hungry and thirsty, one eats and drinks, and 'At sunrise I get up and work; at sunset I rest.' ('Miscellaneous Chapters' in *Zhuangzi*) All these are what they are because of the Way which dwells in them. But it should not be said that eating, drinking, working, and taking rest are the Way. That would be like 'In fabulous use is the transcendental power[②], // For hauling firewood and carrying water' in a Buddhist verse made by Pang (i. e. Pang Yun 庞蕴 [dates unknown]), the well known lay Buddhist in the Tang dynasty, which is troubled by the same problem. Though 'walking slowly and keeping behind one's elders' (*Mencius*, 7B: 22) and 'walking quickly and preceding one's elders' (*Mencius*, 7B: 22) are both walking, the former manifests the Way,

---

① The translation of the citation is based on the version rendered by Chan Wing-tsit (see *A Source Book in Chinese Philosophy*. Princeton: Princeton University Press, 1963, p. 267).

② The "transcendental power" is rendered from the *shentong* 神通, which is rendered from Sanskrit *abhijna*, meaning "to know, have special knowledge of, mastery over."

while the latter does not. Could it be said any walking manifests the Way? As for 'In fabulous use is the transcendental power, // For hauling firewood and carrying water,' only when it is capable of hauling firewood and carrying water can it be said as transcendental power in fabulous use. If not, how can it is that? This is also true of the 'Function and use manifest nature' said by Buddhism. It does not care right or wrong but rather only takes clothes and foods, work and rest, seeing and hearing, and conducting and performing, as the Way itself. From its point of view, whoever speaks, functions, and responses whenever called, is the transcendental power in fabulous use, and it never pays attention to asking where the principle is. But Confucianism is different in that it must seek out from those things the principle which it calls the Way. A certain Chan Buddhist①said such stuffs as 'On your lump of red flesh is a true man without rank, who is always going in and out of the face of every one of you.' That is what he knows only and plays with."

Someone asked, "Is it what Gaozi's learning is like?" The Master answered, "But the Buddhist learning is higher than Gaozi's learning, which is far less flexible than the·former. Nowadays, when learners try to understand what is on the old pieces of paper, their understanding can also be passable, only that they never find pleasure and joy therein, even like that which Buddhists get. Though there is little reasoning in the doctrine of Buddhism, the Buddhists enjoy it for life. That is because they get their understanding of what seems the metaphysical from the concrete things. When it comes to the learners today, they should try to understand the lower level of concrete things before turning to pursuing what is beyond that. However, in fact, they have not seen even the lower level, to say nothing of what is

---

① Referring to Linjin Yixuan 临济义玄 (? -867), a well known Chan Buddhist monk in the Tang dynasty.

beyond that. " He went on, "Everything between heaven and earth possesses the principle, and even the most trivial things also each have it. Probably, 'What Heaven has conferred is called nature,' but the principle is formless and gets nothing to inhere in but the daily things and events. They are never separated from each other, for whatever is possesses its principle. Therefore, the Superior Man sets store by ' extensively studying all learning. ' (*Analects*, 6: 27) Though extensive study seems something that is not urgent and important, many principles can be found thereby and it can serve therefore as their origin. Thus, things, whether coarse or fine, big or small, should be investigated in pursuit of understanding them, for they are not external. Only by making efforts to understand all of them can it be possible to ensure that everything is understood completely, without any oversight or omission. "

He continued saying, "In 'The Way may not be left for an instant, for if it could be left, it would not be the Way,' (1) what 'may not be left' is the Way. If the daily conducts and activities themselves were taken for the Way, then at any time there would be nothing which is not the Way. But why is the Superior Man in fear and watchful over himself when he is alone? Why is he necessary to pursue the Way through learning? Because the Way may not be left, one must go along it. For example, when one says something, what he says is not the Way, unless it conforms to the benevolence, righteousness, propriety, and wisdom. If any conduct or action is taken for the Way, why is it necessary to say 'may not be left'?"

He added, "The *Great Learning* discourses investigating things, but not inquiring the principle to the utmost. That is probably because talk about inquiring the principle to the utmost sounds merely something elusive and vacant. When it says of investigating things, it instructs learners to seek from the concrete physical things the metaphysical Way, who will, by that, know they two are never separable. That is why it discourses only investigating things. 'Heaven, in giving birth to the multitudes of the people, // To every faculty and relationship annexed its law. '① (*Classic of Poetry*) It is said of the Way, but never means things themselves are the law. According to Guishan, the things are the law, and the law is the result of distinguishing the quintessential and the coarse with regard to the things. For example, he said, the eye is a thing and the seeing of the eye is its law; the ear is a thing and the hearing of the ear is its law. He hardly realized that, when the eye sees and the ear hears, they are still things, while when the eye sees clearly and the ear hears acutely, these mean their laws. Guishan also said, 'When Yi Yin ploughed in the lands of the prince of Shen, he did what a farmer or husbandman did daily and delighted in that. ' If he were right there, there would be so many Yi Yins. Generally, Guishan's discourse is troubled by such a problem. " [Xian]

73 问："'道不可离'，只言我不可离这道，亦还是有不能离底意思否？"曰："道是不能离底。纯说是不能离，不成错行也是道！"时举录云："叔重问：'"道不可离"，自家固不可离，然他也有不能离底意。'曰：'当参之于心，可离、不能离之间。纯说不能离，也不得，不成错行了也是道！'"因问："龟山言：'饥食渴饮，手持足行，便是道。'窃谓手持足履未是道，'手容恭，足容重'，乃是道也；目视耳听未是道，视明听聪乃道也。或谓不然，其说云：'手之不可履，犹足之不可持，此是天职。"率性之谓道"，只循此自然之理耳。'不审如何？"曰："不然。桀纣亦会手持足履，目视耳听，如何便唤做道！若便以为道，是认欲为理也。伊川云：'夏葛冬裘，饥食渴饮，若着些私吝心，便是废天职。'须看'着些私吝心'字。"铢。

I asked, "Does the 'The Way may not be left' (1) only mean that I should not leave the Way, or, besides that, I can not leave the Way?" The

---

① The translation of the cited lines from the *Classic of Poetry* is based on the version by J. Legge (http: //ctext. org/book-of-poetry).

Master answered, "The Way can not be left. But when it is only said that the Way can not be left, if one does something wrong, could it be taken as the Way?" Shiju's record for this part reads: Shuzhong asked, "As for 'The Way may not be left,' (1) it is true that it should not be left, but it also means that one can not leave it, doesn't it?" The Master answered, "Think it over in your mind and you will know what it means is between that which can be left and that which can not be left. It will not do to say only that it can not be left, for if one does something wrong, could it be taken as the Way?"

Thereupon I continued asking, "Guishan said, 'One eats and drinks when hungry and thirsty, and uses his hands to carry something on and his feet to walk with. All these are the Way. ' However, I think that, when the hands carry something and the feet walk, they are not the Way, but when 'He did not move his feet lightly, nor his hands irreverently,' (*Record of Rites*) that is the Way. When the eye sees and the ear hears, they are not the Way, but when the eye sees clearly and the ear hears acutely, they are the Way. Someone else did not think so, and said 'Hands can not be used to walk by just as feet can not be used to carry things by. It is a matter of going against their bounden duty. "Following the nature is called the Way" (1) only means to go along the natural principle. ' I am not clear whether he was right. " The Master replied, "Not right. Jie of Xia and Zhou of Shang, both despots, could also use their hands to carry things with and their feet to walk with, with their eyes seeing and ears hearing, but how can they be called the Way? If they were taken for the Way, it would mean taking selfish desire for the principle. Yichuan said, 'One clothes himself with linens in summer and furs in winter, eats when hungry and drinks when thirsty. If he does those things with some selfish and miserly mind, it means he abandons his bounden duty. ' Here, read the 'some selfish and miserly mind' carefully. " [Zhu]

74 此道无时无之，然体之则合，背之则离也。一有离之，则当此之时，失此之道矣，故曰："不可须臾离"。君子所以"戒慎不睹，恐惧不闻"，则不敢以须臾离也。端蒙。

The Way is all the time. Nonetheless, to go with it is to conform with it, while to go against it is to leave it. Once the Way is left, at that time it is lost. Therefore, it is said "The Way may not be left for an instant." (1) That is why the Superior Man is "cautious over what he does not see and apprehensive over what he does not hear,"[①] (1) and dare not leave the Way for even an instant. 〔Duanmeng〕

75 "戒慎不睹，恐惧不闻"，即是道不可须臾离处。履孙。

That "(The Superior Man is) cautious over what he does not see and apprehensive over what he does not hear" (1) means that the Way may not be left for even an instant. 〔Lüsun〕

76 问："日用间如何是不闻不见处？人之耳目闻见常自若，莫只是念虑未起，未有意于闻见否？"曰："所不闻，所不见，不是合眼掩耳，只是喜怒哀乐未发时。凡万事皆未萌芽，自家便先怵地戒慎恐惧，常要提起此心，常在这里，便是防于未然，不见是图底意思。"徐问："讲求义理时，此心如何？"曰："思虑是心之发了。伊川谓：'存养于喜怒哀乐未发之前则可，求中于喜怒哀乐未发之前则不可。'"淳。寓录云："问：'讲求义理，便是此心在否？'曰：'讲求义理，属思虑，心自动了，是已发之心。'"

Someone asked, "How can it be not to hear and not to see in daily life? The ears and eyes of a man often hear and see of themselves. Could that mean only, since his idea or concern does not rise, he makes no conscious effort for hearing and seeing?" The Master answered, "His not hearing and seeing does not mean that he closes his eyes and covers his ears but rather means that he is in the mental state with no stirring of his pleasure, anger, sorrow, and joy. In any time before everything buds, it means, one becomes cautious and apprehensive of something by himself, and keeps his

---

① The translation of the citation is based on the version rendered by Chan Wing-tsit (see *A Source Book in Chinese Philosophy*. Princeton: Princeton University Press, 1963, p. 98).

mind always set up for that so as to prevent it before it emerges and guard against it before it is seen. " Xu (i. e. Xu Yu) asked, " When considering and pursuing the principle, what is the mind like? " The Master answered, " Thinking means the mind aroused. Yichuan said, ' to preserve and nourish oneself before his feelings of pleasure, anger, sorrow and joy are aroused will be right, while to seek equilibrium in the state before those feelings are aroused is not right. ' " [Chun (淳)] Xu Yu's record says, " Question: Does considering and pursuing the principle mean the mind present? Answer: Considering and pursuing the principle is thinking, which indicates the mind stirring of itself, so it is the mind present when the feelings are aroused. "

77 刘黻问:"不知无事时如何戒慎恐惧? 若只管如此, 又恐执持太过; 若不如此, 又恐都忘了。"曰:"也有甚么矜持? 只不要昏了他, 便是戒惧。"与立。

Liu Fu asked, " I do not know how one can keep being cautious and apprehensive when there is nothing cropping up. If he does nothing but it, I am afraid he will overdo it and stick to it with too much rigidity; if he does not do it, I am afraid he will forget it. How do you think, sir? " The Master answered, " How can there be any ' rigidity ' to speak of? So long as one prevents himself from getting befuddled, he is capable of being cautious and apprehensive. " [Yuli]

78 "戒慎乎其所不睹, 恐惧乎其所不闻", 这处难言。大段着意, 又却生病, 只恁地略约住。道着戒慎恐惧, 已是剩语, 然又不得不如此说。贺孙。

That " (The Superior Man is) cautious over what he does not see and apprehensive over what he does not hear " (1) is hard to explain. To grasp its general meaning only is productive of trouble, for that is only to get the rough idea conveyed therein, whereas to say " cautious " and " apprehensive " is to present something redundant, but that way of expressing has to be employed. [Hesun]

79 "戒慎恐惧是未发，然只做未发也不得，便是所以养其未发。只是耸然提起在这里，这个未发底便常在，何曾发？"或问："恐惧是已思否？"曰："思又别。思是思索了，戒慎恐惧，正是防闲其未发。"或问："即是持敬否？"曰："亦是。伊川曰：'敬不是中，只敬而无失即所以中。'‘敬而无失'，便是常敬，这中底便常在。"淳。

The Master said, "To keep being cautious and apprehensive refers to the state of mind when the feelings are not aroused, but to say that it is the state not aroused is still inadequate. That is why the state before the feelings are aroused needs preserving and nourishing. If being cautious and apprehensive is to be kept always alertly in the mind, the state not aroused will be always there. With that, has it ever been aroused?" Someone asked, "Does being apprehensive mean there having been thinking?" The Master answered, "Thinking is different, for it means pondering. The purpose of keeping being cautious and apprehensive is just to take precautions in the state when the feelings are not aroused. " Someone else asked "Does it mean the very adherence to seriousness?" The Master replied, "Yes, it is. Yichuan said, 'Seriousness is not equilibrium itself. But seriousness without fail is the way to attain equilibrium. ' Here 'seriousness without fail' means keeping serious always, and then, with that, there will be always the equilibrium. " [Chun（淳）]

80 问："戒慎恐惧，以此涵养，固善。然推之于事，所谓'开物成务之几'，又当如何？"曰："此却在博文。此事独脚做不得，须是读书穷理。"又曰："只是源头正，发处自正。只是这路子上来往。"德明。

Question: It is true that to keep being cautious and apprehensive by which to cultivate and nourish the mental state is good, but when that is deduced with regard to events, how to begin "to open up (the knowledge of the issues of) things and accomplish the undertakings (of men)"? ("Appended Remarks" in the *Classic of Change*)

Answer: That calls for extensive study, for it is impossible to do that only by something alone; rather what is important is to read books and inquire the principle to the utmost.

Further answer: So long as the origin is upright, wherever the arousing occurs, it is naturally upright. That is the only way from one end to the other. [Deming]

81 问：“中庸所谓‘戒慎恐惧’，大学所谓‘格物致知’，皆是为学知、利行以下底说否？”曰：“固然。然圣人亦未尝不戒慎恐惧。‘惟圣罔念作狂，惟狂克念作圣。’但圣人所谓念者，自然之念；狂者之念，则勉强之念耳。”闳祖。

Question: As regards the "(The Superior Man is) cautious over what he does not see and apprehensive over what he does not hear" in the *Doctrine of the Mean* and the "investigating things and extending knowledge" in the *Great Learning*, are they both said to instruct learners to study for knowledge and to benefit them in their conduct?

Answer: Right, of course. Nonetheless, the sage is never incautious over what he does not see and inapprehensive over what he does not hear. "The sage, through not thinking, becomes foolish, and the foolish, by thinking, becomes wise."① (*Book of History*) However, when the sage is thinking, he is doing it naturally, while when the foolish is thinking, he is doing it with effort. [Hongzu]

82 所谓“不睹不闻”者，乃是从那尽处说来，非谓于所睹所闻处不慎也。如曰“道在瓦砾”，便不成不在金玉！义刚。

The so called "not see" and "not hear" are said of the most profound rather than mean being incautious with regard to what is heard and what is seen. For example, to say that "the Way dwells in the rubble" does not mean that the Way does not dwell in the gold or jade. [Yigang]

---

① The translation of the citation from the *Book of History* is based on a version of it by J. Legge (see http://ctext.org/shang-shu).

83 问："'道也者，不可须臾离'与'莫见乎隐'两段，分明极有条理，何为前辈都作一段滚说去？"曰："此分明是两节事。前段有'是故'字，后段有'故'字。圣贤不是要作文，只是逐节次说出许多道理。若作一段说，亦成是何文字！所以前辈诸公解此段繁杂无伦，都不分明。"铢。

Question：Obviously, both the part beginning with "The Way may not be left for an instant" (1) and that with "There is nothing more visible than what is secret" (1) display separate conceptual veins. Why did the previous scholars tend to explain them as a whole?

Answer：They are clearly concerned with two ideas, as marked by the "Therefore" introducing the conclusion after the former and the "Therefore" introducing the conclusion after the latter. The sages and worthies, in writing such words, did not intend to compose a beautiful essay, but rather elucidate the principles one by one. If the two parts are treated as a whole concerned with a single idea, how can it serve that purpose? Consequently, the complex and diverse explanations made by the previous scholars of these parts are devoid of reasonable sequence and miss the point. [Zhu]

84 用之问："戒惧不睹不闻，是起头处，至'莫见乎隐，莫显乎微'，又用紧一紧。"曰："不可如此说。戒慎恐惧是普说，言道理偪塞都是，无时而不戒慎恐惧。到得隐微之间，人所易忽，又更用慎，这个却是唤起说。戒惧无个起头处，只是普遍都用。如卓子有四角头，一齐用着工夫，更无空缺处。若说是起头，又遗了尾头；说是尾头，又遗了起头；若说属中间，又遗了两头。不用如此说。只是无时而不戒慎恐惧，只自做工夫，便自见得。曾子曰：'战战兢兢，如临深渊！如履薄冰！'不成到临死之时，方如此战战兢兢。他是一生战战兢兢，到死时方了！"僩。

Yongzhi asked, "The '(The Superior Man is) cautious over what he does not see and apprehensive over what he does not hear' (1) indicates the starting point, while the 'There is nothing more visible than what is secret, and nothing more manifest than what is minute' (1) is meant to push forward what has been started. (Is this understanding right?)" The Master answered, "You should not understand it that way. The former says something universal, meaning that the principle is everywhere and so being cautious and apprehensive should be kept at any time. When it comes to the secret and the minute, since men tend to neglect them, more cautiousness is required, and this is to evoke attention. As for the 'cautious' and 'apprehensive,' there is no starting point to speak of, for it is universally applicable. It is like a square table which has four corners, each of which requires one to make effort so that none of them is left out. If we said only the front corners, we would miss out the rear ones; if we said only the rear corners, we would miss out the front ones; if we said only the middle between them, we would miss out the corners on both sides of it. So you should not say that way. It means only that one should be cautious and apprehensive at any time and so long as he makes efforts by himself, he will see the principle in due time. Zengzi (i. e. Zeng Shen) said, 'We should be cautious and apprehensive, as if on the brink of a deep gulf, as if treading on thin ice'① (*Analects*, 8：3) Could it be said that only when one is on his deathbed will he begin to be cautious and apprehensive? Actually, he is cautious and apprehensive in his life time until he dies. " [Xian]

85 问："旧看'莫见乎隐，莫显乎微'两句，只谓人有所愧歉于中，则必见于颜色之间，而不可揜。昨闻先生云'人所不知而己所独知处'，自然见得愈是分晓。如做得是时，别人未见得是，自家先见得是；做得不是时，别人未见得非，自家先见得非。如此说时，觉得又亲切。"曰："事之是与非，众人皆未见得，自家自是先见得分明。"问："'复小而辨于物。'善端虽是方萌，只是昭昭灵灵地别，此便是那不可

---

① The translation is based on the version of the *Analects* translated by J. Legge (see http：// ctext. org/analects).

揜处?"曰:"是如此。只是明一明了,不能接续得这意思去,又暗了。"胡泳。

Someone said to the Master, "In the past when I read 'There is nothing more visible than what is secret, and nothing more manifest than what is minute,' (1) I only understood it as meaning that whenever one feels shame or apology, it will show itself in his looks, for it can not be covered up. Yesterday when I heard you, sir, say 'It means that which is known only to oneself but not to others,' I see its meaning more clearly. If something right is done, when others do not see its rightness, one is the first to see it; if something wrong is done, when others do not see its wrongness, one is the first to see it. With such clarification, I feel closer to that sentence." The Master replied, "It means, with regard to the rightness or wrongness of something, when others fail to see it, one is the first to be aware of it." The former further asked, "The 'Appended Remarks' of the *Classic of Change* says, 'In Fu 复, we have what is small (at first), but there is in it a (nice) discrimination of (the qualities of) things.'① Though the beginning of the good just stirs, it is fairly fresh and manifest. Is this that which can not be covered up?" The Master answered, "That is right. But in that case, when the bright comes up, if it can not last and not continue that state, it will get dim again." [Huyong]

86 问:"'莫见乎隐,莫显乎微',程子举弹琴杀心事,是就人知处言。吕游杨氏所说,是就己自知处言。章句只说己自知,或疑是合二者而言否?"曰:"有动于中,己固先自知,亦不能掩人之知,所谓诚之不可揜也。"铢。

Question: As regards "There is nothing more visible than what is secret, and nothing more manifest than what is minute," (1) when Master Cheng

---

① Fu refers to "Hexagram Fu," the 24th hexagram in the *Classic of Change*. The translation is based on the version by J. Legge (see http://ctext.org/book-of-changes).

illustrated it by citing the story of Cai Yong 蔡邕 (133 – 192 BC) hearing the mind of killing from someone else's playing on the *qin* 琴 (ancient Chinese seven-stringed plucked musical instrument like the zither), he explained it in regard to that which was known to another man. What Lü, You, and Yang said about the sentence points to that which has been known to oneself. Your explanation in *Interpretation* is only concerned with that which has been known to oneself. I suspect that probably it is said with regard to those two. (How do you think?)

Answer: When there rises some stirring in one's mind, it is true that he is the first to know it, but it can not be hidden to prevent others from knowing it. That is what is meant by the saying that sincerity is impossible to be covered up. [Zhu]

87 问:"伊川以鬼神凭依语言为'莫见乎隐,莫显乎微',如何?"曰:"隐微之事,在人心不可得而知,却被他说出来,岂非'莫见乎隐,莫显乎微'?盖鬼神只是气,心中实有是事,则感于气者,自然发见昭著如此。"文蔚问:"今人隐微之中,有不善者甚多,岂能一一如此?"曰:"此亦非常之事,所谓事之变者。"文蔚曰:"且如人生积累愆咎,感召不祥,致有日月薄蚀,山崩川竭,水旱凶荒之变,便只是此类否?"曰:"固是如此。"文蔚。

I asked, "Yichuan regarded using words to convey *guishen* 鬼神 (lit. ghost and god) as what is meant by 'There is nothing more visible than what is secret, and nothing more manifest than what is minute.' (1) (How do you think?)" The Master answered, "What is the secret and the minute can not be known by the mind for it is inaccessible, but when one says it out, isn't it what is meant by 'There is nothing more visible than what is secret, and nothing more manifest than what is minute?' Probably the *guishen* is only vital force, and what is really in the mind is thing. Thus when it is inducted by the vital force, naturally, it will become clear and manifest." I went on and asked, "In the secret and the minute things with people today, there are too many ones that are not good. How can they each be clear and manifest like that?" The Master replied, "They are things extraordinary, the so called variants of events." I said to him, "For example, if a life accumulates faults and transgressions to the extent that the ominous is provoked, which causes eclipses of the sun and the moon, falls of mountains and dry-ups of rivers, floods and droughts, famines and disasters, do these belong to those variants of events?" The Master replied, "Yes, of course." [Wenwei]

88 戒慎恐惧乎其所不睹不闻，是从见闻处戒慎恐惧到那不睹不闻处。这不睹不闻处是工夫尽头。所以慎独，则是专指独处而言。如"莫见乎隐，莫显乎微"，是慎独紧切处。焘。

That (the Superior Man is) cautious and apprehensive over what he does not see and what he does not hear means that, by being cautious and apprehensive, he goes from what he sees and hears to what he does not see and hear. That which he does not see and hear indicates the end of the path of making efforts. That (the Superior Man must be) watchful carefully over solitude is said with special regard to his being alone. The "There is nothing more visible than what is secret, and nothing more manifest than what is minute" (1) says of what is the most demanding and pressing in his being watchful carefully over his solitude. [Tao]

89 黄灏谓："戒惧是统体做工夫，慎独是又于其中紧切处加工夫，犹一经一纬而成帛。"先生以为然。偶。

Huang Hao 黄灏 (dates unknown, courtesy name Shangbo 商伯, a disciple of Zhu's) said, "To keep cautious and apprehensive is concerned with the process of making efforts in a general sense, while to be watchful over solitude points to intensifying efforts where what is the most demanding and pressing lies. They are like the warp and weft which make up a piece of fabric." The Master agreed with him. [Xian]

90 问"慎独"。曰："是从见闻处至不睹不闻处皆戒慎了，又就其中于独处更加慎也。是无所不慎，而慎上更加慎也。"焘。

When asked about being watchful over solitude, the Master answered,
"It means that one not only keeps cautious and apprehensive in the path from
that which he sees and hears to that which he does not see and hear, but also
is more watchful over himself when he is alone. So it emphasizes that one
should be watchful wherever he is and, furthermore, ensure that he can not
be more watchful." [Tao]

91 问:"'不睹不闻'者,己之所不睹不闻也;'独'者,人之所
不睹不闻也。如此看,便见得此章分两节事分明。"先生曰:"'其所不
睹不闻','其'之一字,便见得是说己不睹不闻处,只是诸家看得自
不仔细耳。"又问:"如此分两节工夫,则致中、致和工夫方各有着落,
而'天地位,万物育'亦各有归着。"曰:"是。"铢。

I said to the Master, "The 'What he does not see and hear' means that
which one does not see and hear, while 'solitude,' that someone else does
not see and hear him. Thus, it is clear to see that the section where they
appear is concerned with two separate matters." The Master responded, "In
'What he does not see and hear,' the 'he' makes it clear that it is he
himself who does not see and hear, but the previous scholars have failed to
see it because they have not read it carefully enough." I asked, "Thus, it
is with such division of the efforts into two levels that those called for in
pursuit of equilibrium 中 and those for in pursuit of harmony 和 can each
have their destinations, and that each of 'Heaven and earth attain their
order, and all things will flourish' (1) can have its home. (Is my
understanding right?)" The Master answered, "Yes." [Zhu]

92 "戒慎"一节,当分为两事,"戒慎不睹,恐惧不闻",如言
"听于无声,视于无形",是防之于未然,以全其体;"慎独",是察之
于将然,以审其几。端蒙。

The section on "being cautious and apprehensive" should be divided
into two parts, each concerned with a matter. "(The Superior Man is)
cautious over what he does not see and apprehensive over what he does not

hear," which is like saying "He should be (as if he were) hearing when there is no voice, and seeing when there is no form there," (*Record of Rites*) means preventing something undesirable before it emerges so as to ensure his completeness. By contrast, "Watchful over his solitude" means keeping observant of what is to occur so as to be aware of its slightest possible sign. [Duanmeng]

93 问："'戒慎不睹，恐惧不闻'与'慎独'两段事，广思之，便是'惟精惟一'底工夫。戒慎恐惧，持守而不失，便是惟一底工夫；慎独，则于善恶之几，察之愈精愈密，便是惟精底工夫。但中庸论'道不可离'，则先其戒慎，而后其慎独；舜论人心、道心，则先其惟精，而后其惟一。"曰："两事皆少不得'惟精惟一'底工夫。不睹不闻时固当持守，然不可不察；慎独时固当致察，然不可不持守。"广。人杰录云："汉卿问云云。先生曰：'不必分"惟精惟一"于两段上。但凡事察之贵精，守之贵一。如戒慎恐惧，是事之未形处；慎独，几之将然处。不可不精察而慎守之也。'"

Question: As regards the two matters referred to by "(The Superior Man is) cautious over what he does not see and apprehensive over what he does not hear" and "Being watchful over solitude," (1) when I consider them broadly, I find they both concern the efforts called for "Be discriminating and be uniform (in the pursuit of what is right)" ("Counsels of the Great Yu" in *Book of History*). To be cautious and apprehensive and keep adherence without deviation is to make efforts for being uniform (in the pursuit of what is right); To be watchful over solitude and be observant of the first sign of the good or the evil with increasing insight is to make efforts for discriminating. When the *Doctrine of the Mean* discourses "The Way may not be left for an instant," (1) it says first being cautious and then being watchful over solitude. However, when Shun discourses the mind of humankind and the mind of the Way, he says first being discriminating and then being uniform (in the pursuit of what is right). (How do you think of this difference?)

Answer: Both of the two matters can not do without the efforts to be discriminating and be uniform. When one does not see and hear, he should, of course, keep adherence, but he should also strive to be observant; when he is watchful over his solitude, he should be observant, of course, but he should also keep adherence. 〔Guang〕 Renjie's record reads, "Hanqing (courtesy name of Fu Guang) asked the Master a question. The Master answered, 'It is not necessary to separate being discriminating and being uniform (in the pursuit of what is right) in correspondence to the two sections in the book. However, whatever it is, the more one is discriminating, the better, and the more he is uniform, the better. Being cautious and apprehensive refers to the state in regard to something before it takes shape, and being watchful over solitude, to the state when the first sign of something is to occur. So, one may not leave these states unobserved and discriminated, but rather should keep watchful over them adherently. '"

94 问："'戒慎不睹，恐惧不闻'与'慎独'虽不同，若下工夫皆是敬否？"曰："敬只是常惺惺法。所谓静中有个觉处，只是常惺惺在这里，静不是睡着了。"贺孙。

Question: Despite the difference between "(The Superior Man is) cautious over what he does not see and apprehensive over what he does not hear" and "Being watchful over his solitude," as far as making efforts is concerned, do they both mean seriousness 敬?

Answer: What the seriousness refers to is only the way of keeping wide awake, which means that in one's tranquility there is his consciousness by which to keep wide awake. The tranquility does not mean being asleep. 〔Hesun〕

95 问："'不睹不闻'与'慎独'何别？"曰："上一节说存天理之本然，下一节说遏人欲于将萌。"又问："能存天理了，则下面慎独，似多了一截。"曰："虽是存得天理，临发时也须点检，这便是他密处。若只说存天理了，更不慎独，却是只用致中，不用致和了。"又问："致中是未动之前，然谓之戒惧，却是动了。"曰："公莫看得戒慎恐惧太重了；此只是略省一省，不是恁惊惶震惧，略是个敬模样如此。然道着'敬'字，已是重了。只略略收拾来，便在这里。伊川所谓'道个"敬"字，也不大段用得力'。孟子曰：'操则存。'操亦不是着力把持，只是操一操，便在这里。如人之气，才呼便出，吸便入。"赐。

Question：What is the difference between "what one does not see and hear" and "being watchful over his solitude"?

Answer：The section with "what one does not see and hear" discourses preserving the original state of the heavenly principle and the next section with "being watchful over his solitude" concerns checking the selfish desire from budding.

Further question：Since the heavenly principle can already be preserved, it seems that the "being watchful over his solitude" after that is superfluous. (How do you think?)

Answer：Though one can make the preservation of the heavenly principle, when it is about to be aroused, he has to inspect it and this is something he does privately. If we said only the preservation of the heavenly principle yet did not touch being watchful over solitude, it would mean that we pursue only equilibrium but not harmony.

Further question：Pursuing equilibrium refers to the state before the feelings are aroused, but if being cautious and apprehensive is said of it, doesn't it mean their being aroused?

Answer：Do not lay too much importance on being cautious and apprehensive, for it is intended only to rouse one up a little rather than to keep him always in cautious and apprehensive in their usual sense. One should be somewhat in seriousness like that, but the word "seriousness" is already overemphatic. It only needs gathering up a little and that will be enough. Yichuan said, "Though speaking of 'seriousness,' it does not mean making too much effort." *Mencius* (7A：8) mentions "Hold it fast and it remains with you." "Hold" does not mean that one has to exert himself much to hold, but rather that, only by a little effort, one will make it. It is like our breathing, in that once you exhale, the air gets out, and once you inhale, it is taken in. 〔Ci〕

96 问"中庸戒惧慎独,学问辨行,用工之终始"。曰:"只是一个道理,说着要贴出来,便有许多说话。"又问:"是敬否?"曰:"说着'敬',已多了一字。但略略收拾来,便在这里。"夔孙。

Question: The *Doctrine of the Mean* discourses being cautious and apprehensive; being watchful over solitude; pursuing extensive study, accurate inquiry, clear discrimination, and earnest practice (of what is good), and all these indicate the beginning and end of making efforts. (How do you think?)

Answer: There is only one principle, but when it has to be said out, there are many words which have to be used.

Further question: Is it "seriousness"?

Answer: When you say "seriousness," there is a more word in addition to those ones. It means that one needs only to make a little effort to gather it up, and then he will get it. 〔Kuisun〕

97 问:"'不闻不睹'与'慎独'如何?"曰:"'独'字又有个形迹在这里可慎。不闻不见,全然无形迹,暗昧不可得知。只于此时便戒慎了,便不敢。"卓才。

Question: How is "what one does not see and hear" in contrast to "being watchful over his solitude"?

Answer: By the "solitude" is meant some trace which one can be watchful over. By contrast, "what one does not see and hear" points to something completely traceless, which is so beclouded that he can by no means know it. So long as one keeps cautious in the duration, he will not dare (to deviate from the Way). 〔Zhuocai〕[1]

98 问:"'慎独'是念虑初萌处否?"曰:"此是通说,不止念虑初

---

[1] Dates unknown, a disciple of Zhu's.

萌，只自家自知处。如小可没紧要处，只胡乱去，便是不慎。慎独是已思虑，已有些小事，已接物了。'戒慎乎其所不睹，恐惧乎其所不闻'，是未有事时；在'相在尔室，尚不愧于屋漏'，'不动而敬，不言而信'之时，'慎独'，便已有形迹了。'潜虽伏矣，亦孔之昭！'诗人言语，只是大纲说。子思又就里面剔出这话来教人，又较紧密。大抵前圣所说底，后人只管就里面发得精细。如程子横渠所说，多有孔孟所未说底。伏羲画卦，只就阴阳以下，孔子又就阴阳上发出太极，康节又道：'须信画前元有易。'濂溪太极图又有许多详备。"问："气化形化，男女之生是气化否？"曰："凝结成个男女，因甚得如此？都是阴阳。无物不是阴阳。"问："天地未判时，下面许多都已有否？"曰："事物虽未有。其理则具。"宇。可学录云："慎独已见于用。孔子言语只是混合说。子思恐人不晓，又为之分别。大凡古人说话，一节开一节。如伏羲易只就阴阳以下，至孔子又推本于太极，然只曰'易有太极'而已。至濂溪乃画出一图，康节又论画前之易。"

Question：Does the "being watchful over solitude" mean the consideration of the first signs of something?

Answer：That is said only in a general sense, which does not only mean one's consideration of the first signs of something and what he knows in himself. Even for what is trivial and insignificant, if he deals with it carelessly without discrimination, he is not watchful. Being watchful over solitude refers to that one has considered, that there have been some things insignificant, and that one has contacted things. "(The Superior Man is) cautious over what he does not see and apprehensive over what he does not hear" (1) refers to there being nothing. When "Looked at in your chamber, you ought to be equally free from shame before the light which shines in" and "(The Superior Man,) even when he is not moving, has a feeling of reverence, and while he speaks not, he has the feeling of truthfulness," (*Classic of Poetry*) if he is watchful over his solitude, there will have been some trace. "Although the fish sink and lie at the bottom, it is still quite clearly seen. " (*Classic of Poetry*)① When the poet discoursed, he said of only the generality. Thus, Zisi selected those lines by which to instruct learners, so the words are more compact. Generally, what ancient sages said would be elaborated more and more by later scholars. For example, what Master Chengs and Hengqü said contained many words Confucius and Mencius had not mentioned. When Fuxi drew the lines making up the eight trigrams, he illustrated only the *yin* and *yang*; Confucius, building on the *yin* and *yang*, pointed out the Supreme Ultimate; Kangjie (i. e. Shao Yong) said furthermore "It must be believed that before Fuxi drew the eight trigrams there had originally been *yi* 易 (i. e. the principle of change). " In his "Diagram of the Supreme Ultimate," Lianxi (i. e. Zhou Dunyi) was more detailed with regard to that.

Further question: As regards the transformation of vital force into forms, is the birth of a man or a woman is the result of that transformation of vital force?

Answer: It is the condensation (of vital force) which produces a man or a woman. Why does that occur? It is completely due to the *yin* and *yang*. There is nothing that is not from *yin* and *yang*.

Further question: Before heaven and earth were formed separately, had there been those things between them already?

Answer: Though the things had not come into being, their principles had already been. [Yu]

Kexue's record reads, "The 'being watchful over solitude' is already seen in use. What Confucius said is only some general discourse, and Zisi, for fear that others could not understand it, somewhat elaborated it. Generally speaking, in the discourse of the ancient sages and previous scholars, the later ones built on the preceding sayings one by one. For example, Fuxi's *yi* with his eight trigrams was indicative only of the *yin* and

---

① The translation of the citations from the *Classic of Poetry* is based J. Legge's version of the Chinese classic (see http: //ctext. org/book-of-poetry).

yang, and Confucius deduced from those trigrams back to the Supreme Ultimate, but he only mentioned simply 'In *yi*, there is the Supreme Ultimate.' ('Appended Remarks' in *Classic of Change*) Lianxi, going further, drew a 'Diagram of the Supreme Ultimate,' and Kangjie pointed further to the *yi* before Fuxi's eight trigrams."

99 问:"'慎独',莫只是'十目所视,十手所指'处,也与那闇室不欺时一般否?"先生是之。又云:"这独也又不是恁地独时,如与众人对坐,自心中发一念,或正或不正,此亦是独处。"椿。

I asked, "Does 'being watchful over solitude' (1) mean not only that, when one is alone, he should conduct as if 'Ten eyes are beholding and ten hands are pointing (to him),' (*Great Learning*, 3) but also that, when one is in a dark room, he should not do anything deceptive?" The Master answered affirmatively and then said, "That solitude refers to more than that. For example, when one sits together with some other people, an idea, upright or otherwise, occurs to his mind, and that is also what the solitude refers to." [Chun (椿)]

100 问:"'慎独'章:'迹虽未形,几则已动。人虽不知,己独知之。'上两句是程子意,下两句是游氏意,先生则合而论之,是否?"曰:"然。两事只是一理。几既动,则己必知之;己既知,则人必知之。故程子论杨震四知曰:'"天知、地知",只是一个知。'"广。

Question: As regards the section on "being watchful over solitude," (1) an explanation said "Despite no indication of something which occurs to one's mind, there has been the stirring of it therein. Though unknown to others, it is known to him alone." Master Cheng's idea is meant by the first sentence and You Cu's is by the second. By contrast, you, sir, combined them in your explanation.

Answer: Yes. Because the two are, actually, said of the same principle. When there is the stirring in one's mind, he must know it by himself, and, when he knows it, then others must know it. Therefore, Master

Cheng, when commenting on Yang Zhen's 杨震（? －124）"four knows,"① said, " 'Heaven knows' and 'Earth knows' are said of the same 'know.' " [Guang]

101 问："'迹虽未形，几则已动。'看'莫见、莫显'，则已是先形了，如何却说'迹未形，几先动'？"曰："'莫见乎隐，莫显乎微'，这是大纲说。"贺孙。

Question: As for "Despite no indication of something which occurs to one's mind, there has been the stirring of it therein," since the "visible" and "manifest" are said in "There is nothing more visible than what is secret, and nothing more manifest than what is minute," (1) why "no indication" before "the stirring"?

Answer: That sentence in the *Doctrine of the Mean* is concerned with the general principle. [Hesun]

102 "吕子约书来，争'"莫见乎隐，莫显乎微"，只管滚作一段看'。某答它书，江西诸人将去看，颇以其说为然。彭子寿却看得好，云：'前段不可须臾离，且是大体说。到慎独处，尤见于接物得力。'"先生又云："吕家之学，重于守旧，更不论理。"德明问："'道不可须臾离，可离非道'，是言道之体段如此；'莫见乎隐，莫显乎微'，亦然。下面君子戒慎恐惧，君子必慎其独，方是做工夫。皆以'是故'二字发之，如何滚作一段看？"曰："'道不可须臾离'，言道之至广至大者；'莫见乎隐，莫显乎微'，言道之至精至极者。"德明。

The Master said, "Lü Ziyue 吕子约 (i. e. Lü Zujian 吕祖俭 [? － 1200]) wrote to me and contended that the 'There is nothing more visible than what is secret, and nothing more manifest than what is minute' (1) and

---

① According to the biography of Yang Zhen in *Houhan Shu* 后汉书 (History of Later Han), Yang once recommended a man of talent to an official post. Later, when that man visited Yang one night, he tried to offer him some gold as a token of gratitude and urged him to accept it by saying "Nobody knows it." Yang refused it and said "Heaven knows it, spirits know it, I know it, and you know it. How can you say 'Nobody knows it'?" Later, Yang's "four knows" is also varied a little as "Heaven knows, Earth knows, I know, and you know."

words before it should have been read as a whole. When those scholars in Jiangxi read my reply to him, they must have thought his opinion was right, except Peng Zishou 彭子寿 (i. e. Peng Guinian 彭龟年 [1141 – 1206]), who said, 'The sentence of "The Way may not be left for an instant" (1) and others before it concern the generality, and the sentence of "being watchful over solitude" (1) after it is said particularly of the competent contact with things. '" He added, "Lü's pursuit of learning is conservative and even ignorant of the principle. " Deming asked, " 'The Way may not be left for an instant. If it could be left, it would not be the Way' (1) is said of the substance of the Way, and 'There is nothing more visible than what is secret, and nothing more manifest than what is minute' (1) is, too. But the 'Therefore, the Superior Man is cautious over what he does not see and apprehensive over what he does not hear' (1) after the former and the 'Therefore the Superior Man is watchful over his solitude' (1) after the latter are said of making efforts, and they are both introduced by 'therefore. ' How can all these be read as a whole?" The Master answered, " 'The Way may not be left for an instant' (1) says of the Way as the vastest and greatest, while 'There is nothing more visible than what is secret, and nothing more manifest than what is minute' (1) says of the Way as the most essential and the most ultimate. " [Deming]

103 "戒慎不睹，恐惧不闻"，非谓于睹闻之时不戒惧也。言虽不睹不闻之际，亦致其慎，则睹闻之际，其慎可知。此乃统同说，承上"道不可须臾离"，则是无时不戒惧也。然下文慎独既专就已发上说，则此段正是未发时工夫，只得说"不睹不闻"也。"莫见乎隐，莫显乎微，故君子必慎其独。"上既统同说了，此又就中有一念萌动处，虽至隐微，人所不知而己所独知，尤当致慎。如一片止水，中间忽有一点动处，此最紧要着工夫处！闳祖。

"(The Superior Man is) cautious over what he does not see and apprehensive over what he does not hear" (1) does not mean that he is not cautious and apprehensive over what he sees and hears. Rather, it means that, if he is cautious and apprehensive over what he does not see and hear, it is known how he is cautious and apprehensive over what he sees and hears. That sentence is said in regard to the generality and, put after "The Way may not be left for an instant," (1) it is emphatic that being cautious and apprehensive is kept all the time. By contrast, the "being watchful over solitude" after that is only concerned with the state when the feelings are aroused. That sentence concerns the efforts which should be made when there is no arousing, so it can only say "what he does not see" and "what he does not hear." Then, "There is nothing more visible than what is secret, and nothing more manifest than what is minute. Therefore the Superior Man is watchful over his solitude." (1) Since that sentence has said of the generality already, here these two turn to what is the stirring of something in the mind. As it is the most secret and minute that only one knows it but others do not, he should be watchful to the utmost extent. It is like an expanse of water still all over, but now suddenly some spot of it stirs. It is the stirring spot that is the crucial, calling for much effort. [Hongzu]

104 问："'道也者不可须臾离也'以下是存养工夫,'莫见乎隐'以下是检察工夫否?"曰:"说'道不可须臾离',是说不可不存。'是故'以下,却是教人恐惧戒慎,做存养工夫。说'莫见乎隐,莫显乎微',是说不可不慎意。'故君子'以下,却是教人慎独,察其私意起处防之。只看两个'故'字,便是方说入身上来做工夫也。圣人教人,只此两端。"大雅。

Question: Following the sentences "The Way may not be left for an instant. If it could be left, it would not be the Way" (1) is one sentence concerned with the effort called for preservation and nourishment. Are the sentences after "There is nothing more visible than what is secret, and nothing more manifest than what is minute" (1) said of the effort for retrospection?

Answer: "The Way may not be left for an instant" (1) means that one must preserve (the Way). The sentence introduced by "Therefore" after that is intended to instruct people to be cautious and apprehensive in making effort to preserve and nourish (the Way). The "There is nothing more visible than what is secret, and nothing more manifest than what is minute" (1) means that one has to be watchful. The sentence introduced by "Therefore" after that is intended to instruct people to be watchful over their solitude, vigilant of the stirring of their selfish intention, and guarding against it. The two words of "therefore" are meant to say that people should make efforts on themselves. Holding only two ends (preserving and nourishing the Way, and being watchful of solitude) is the way by which the sage instructed others. [Daya]

105　问："'戒慎乎其所不睹，恐惧乎其所不闻'，或问中引'听于无声，视于无形'，如何？"曰："不呼唤时不见，时常准备着。"德明指坐阁问曰："此处便是耳目所睹闻，隔窗便是不睹也。"曰："不然。只谓照管所不到，念虑所不及处。正如防贼相似，须尽塞其来路。"次日再问："'不睹不闻'，终未莹。"曰："此须意会。如或问中引'不见是图'，既是不见，安得有图？只是要于未有兆朕、无可睹闻时而戒惧耳。"又曰："'不睹不闻'是提其大纲说，'慎独'乃审其微细。方不闻不睹之时，不惟人所不知，自家亦未有所知。若所谓'独'，即人所不知而己所独知，极是要戒惧。自来人说'不睹不闻'与'慎独'，只是一意，无分别，便不是。"德明。

Someone asked, "As regards '(The Superior Man is) cautious over what he does not see and apprehensive over what he does not hear,' (1) in your *Questions and Answers*, what do you mean by citing 'One should be (as if he were) hearing when there is no voice, and seeing when there is no form' (*Record of Rites*)?" The Master answered, "Though he hears and sees nothing when there is no voice and form, he should keep ready for any voice and form." Deming, pointing to the things around in the room, said, "These are what my eyes and ears see and hear, but what is outside the window is that which I do not see. " The Master responded, "Not right. That only means what one does not look after and fails to consider. It is just like guarding against burglary, which requires every precaution be taken to prevent it from occurrence. " Next day, when I enquired, "As for 'cautious over what he does not see and apprehensive over what he does not hear,' (1) up to now I have still not fully understood what it means. " The Master replied, "Its meaning can only be felt. For example, in my *Questions and Answers*, I cite 'Before it is seen, it should be guarded against,' (*Classic of History*). Since it is 'before it is seen,' how can there be anything to guard against? But it actually means that one should keep cautious and apprehensive before there is any portent of any thing that can be seen and heard. " He added, "The 'being cautious and apprehensive over what he does not see and what he does not hear' is said of the generality, while 'being watchful over solitude' refers to being observant of what is subtle and minute of that. When something is not seen or heard by one, it is unknown not only to others, but also to himself. When it comes to the so called 'solitude,' it means that something is unknown to others but known only to himself, so he should be cautious and apprehensive to the utmost extent. It has always been said that 'being cautious and apprehensive over what he does not see and what he does not hear' and 'being watchful over solitude' mean the same meaning and there is no difference between them. But it is wrong. " [Deming]

106 问:"林子武以慎独为后,以戒惧为先。慎独以发处言,觉得也是在后。"曰:"分得也好。" 又问:"余国秀谓戒惧是保守天理,慎独是检防人欲。"曰:"也得。" 又问:"觉得戒慎恐惧与慎独也难分动静。静时固戒慎恐惧,动时又岂可不戒慎恐惧?"曰:"上言'道不可须臾离',此言'戒惧其所不睹不闻'与'慎独',皆是不可离。" 又问:"泳欲谓戒惧是其常,慎独是慎其所发。"曰:"如此说也好。" 又曰:"言'道不可须臾离',故言'戒慎恐惧其所不睹不闻';言'莫见乎隐，莫显乎微'，故言'慎独'。"又曰："'戒慎恐惧'是由外言之以尽于内，'慎独'是由内言之以及于外。"问："自所睹所闻以至于不睹不闻，自发于心以至见于事，如此方说得'不可须臾离'出。"曰："然。"胡泳。

Question: Lin Ziwu 林子武（i. e. Lin Kuisun 林夔孙）regards being watchful over solitude as posterior to being cautious and apprehensive, for being watchful over solitude is said in regard to where arousing occurs and the consciousness of it is also after that.（How do you think?）

Answer: His distinction is also good.

Further question: Yu Guoxiu 余国秀（i. e. Yu Songjie 余宋杰）said that to be cautious and apprehensive is to conserve the heavenly principle, while to be watchful over solitude is to check and guard against selfish human desire.（How do you think?）

Answer: He is also right.

Further question: To me, to be cautious and apprehensive and to be watchful over solitude are hard to distinguish in terms of activity and tranquility. When in tranquility, one should be cautious and apprehensive, and when in activity, could it be said that he does not need to be cautious and apprehensive?

Answer: The preceding sentence says "The Way may not be left for an instant"（1）and these ones dwell on "being cautious and apprehensive over what one does not see and hear" and "being watchful over solitude," but they all stress that the Way may not be left.

Further question: I want to say that the "being cautious and apprehensive" refers to what is constant, while "being watchful over solitude," to being watchful over what is aroused of it.（How do you think?）

Answer: Your opinion is also good.

Further answer: After "The Way may not be left for an instant" is said, therefore "being cautious and apprehensive over what one does not see and hear" follows; After "There is nothing more visible than what is secret, and nothing more manifest than what is minute" is said, therefore "being watchful over solitude" follows.

Further answer: The "being cautious and apprehensive" is said from the outside to refer to the inside to the utmost extent, while "being watchful over solitude" is said from the inside towards the outside.

Further question: Only when all is covered, from what one sees and hears to what he does not see and hear, and from origination in the mind to manifestation via things can the meaning of "The Way may not be left for an instant" be clarified. (How do you think?)

Answer: Right. [Hu Yong]

107 问:"中庸工夫只在'戒慎恐惧'与'慎独'。但二者工夫,其头脑又在道不可离处。若能识得全体、大用皆具于心,则二者工夫不待勉强,自然进进不已矣。"曰:"便是有个头脑。如'天命之谓性,率性之谓道,修道之谓教'。古人因甚冠之章首?盖头脑如此。若识得此理,则便是勉强,亦有个着落矣。"又问:"'费隐'一章云:'夫妇之愚,可以与知能行;及其至也,虽圣人有所不知不能。'先生尝云:'此处难看。'近思之,颇看得透。侯氏说夫子问礼,问官,与夫子不得位,尧舜病博施,为不知不能之事,说得亦粗。止是寻得一二事如此,元不曾说着'及其至也'之意。此是圣人看得彻底,故于此理亦有未肯自居处。如'所求乎子以事父未能'之类,真是圣人有未能处。又如说:'默而识之,学而不厌,诲人不倦,何有于我哉?'是圣人不敢自以为知。'出则事公卿,入则事父兄,丧事不敢不勉,不为酒困,何有于我哉?'此是圣人不敢以为能处。"曰:"夫妇之与知能行是万分中有一分,圣人不知不能是万分中欠得一分。"又问:"以实事言之,亦有可言者,但恐非立教之道。"先生问:"如何?"曰:"夫子谓'事君尽礼,人以为谄。'相定公时甚好,及其受女乐,则不免于行,是事君之道犹有未孚于人者。又如原壤登木而歌,'夫子为弗闻也者而过之',待之自好。及其夷俟,则以杖叩胫,近于太过。"曰:"这里说得却差。如原壤之歌，乃是大恶，若要理会，不可但已，且只得休。至于夷俟之时，不可教诲，故直责之，复叩其胫，自当如此。若如正淳说，则是不要管他，却非朋友之道矣。"人杰。

Question: The effort the *Doctrine of the Mean* focuses on is only "being cautious and apprehensive" and "being watchful over solitude." But the essential and foremost point of the two sorts of effort lies in "The Way may not be left for an instant." (1) If one is able to see its entirety and knows its main function inherent in his mind, he does not need to force himself in making that effort, for he can naturally keep gaining progress. (How do you think?)

Answer: There is such essential point as "What Heaven has conferred is called nature. Following the human nature is called the Way. Cultivating the Way is called education." (1) Why did the ancient writer put it at the beginning of the text? Because it is the essential point of the entire text. If one sees that point, even though he somewhat forces himself in his making that effort, he has something to aim at.

Further question: The twelfth chapter (of the *Doctrine of the Mean*) says "Men and women of simple intelligence can share the knowledge of it (the Way), yet in its utmost reaches, there is something which even the sage does not know. Men and women of simple intelligence can put it (the Way) into practice, yet in its utmost reaches, there is something which even the sage is not able to put into practice."[1] (12) You, sir, once said, "It is hard to read." Recently, when I thought it, I could see its meaning completely. Hou's (Hou Zhongliang 侯仲良) explanation is rather coarse when he says that, when Confucius enquired rites and official positions, it indicates his ignorance, and when Yao and Shun were still solicitous about extensively

---

[1] The translation of the citation is based on the English version by Chan Wing-tsit (1963, p. 100).

conferring benefits, it indicates their inability. He found only a few matters to illustrate that, and did not touch the meaning of "its utmost reaches. " The reason why the sage (confucius) said that in the book is that, though he saw the Way thoroughly, he was unwilling to consider himself that way in the regard. When it comes to "To serve my father, as I would require my son to serve me: to this I have not attained" (13) and the like, these manifest his inability indeed. When the sage said, "The silent treasuring up of knowledge; learning without satiety; and instructing others without being wearied—which one of these things belongs to me?" (*Analects*, 7: 2) this manifests that he dared not consider himself as being capable of them. "Abroad, to serve the high ministers and nobles; at home, to serve one's father and elder brothers; in all duties to the dead, not to dare not to exert one's self; and not to be overcome of wine—which one of these things do I attain to?" (*Analects*, 9: 16) also shows that he dared not consider himself as being capable of doing them. (How do you think?)

Answer: That "Men and women of simple intelligence can share the knowledge of it" and "put it into practice" mean that what they share and put into practice is one ten-thousandth, while that "even the sage does not know" and "is not able to put into practice" refer to only the deficiency of one ten-thousandth.

Further question: As far as actual events are concerned, there are some worth mentioning, yet, I am afraid, they do not manifest the way of conducting education. (The Master asked, "What are they?") Confucius said, "The full observance of the rules of propriety in serving one's prince is accounted by people to be flattery. " (*Analects*, 3: 18) When Confucius assisted Duke Ding of Lu, he did very well, but later when the people of Qi state sent to Lu a present of female musicians, it was accepted by the prime minister, and for three days no court was held. Then Confucius could not but take his departure. That indicates that there was still something that did not command public confidence in his conduct in serving his sovereign. For another example, Yuan Rang, an old friend of Confucius's, when his mother died, began singing, but Confucius acted as if he did not hear, and passed by him, expecting him to correct himself. However, when Yuan was squatting on his heels, and so waited the approach of Confucius, Confucius hit him on the shank with his staff. But here I think Confucius went a little too far in treating Yuan. [1]

Answer: What you said is not right. For example, actually, by that singing, Yuan Rang committed a major evil. Should he have been treated, not only his singing would have been stopped, but also the friendship with him would have been broken up. As for his squatting on his heels, he was hard to edify, so Confucius scolded him straight and hit him on the shank with his staff. That served him right. If, as you see it, Confucius had not been concerned about Yuan, he would not have conducted as the way of friendship requires. [Renjie] [2]

108 共父问"喜怒哀乐未发谓之中,发而皆中节谓之和"。曰:"'中'字是状性之体。性具于心,发而中节,则是性自心中发出来也,是之谓情。"时举。以下中和。

Gongfu 共父 (courtesy name of Liu Gong 刘珙 [1122 – 1178]) asked about "The state before the feelings of pleasure, anger, sorrow and joy are aroused is called equilibrium 中. When these feelings are aroused and each and all attain due measure and degree, it is called harmony 和." (1) The Master answered, "The word 'equilibrium' describes the substance of the nature. The nature dwells in the mind and the 'these feelings aroused and each and all attain due measure and degree' means that the nature emanates from the mind and gives rise to what is called 'feelings.'" [Shiju] The

---

① The stories in the two examples mentioned in the conversation are recorded in the *Analects*.

② The translation of the citations from the *Analects* is based on the version by J. Legge (see http://ctext.org/analects).

following concerns equilibrium and harmony.

109 答徐彦章问"中和",云:"喜怒哀乐未发,如处室中,东西南北未有定向,所谓中也。及其既发,如已出门,东者不复能西,南者不复能北。然各因其事,无所乖逆,所谓和也。"升卿。

In answering Xu Yanzhang 徐彦章(dates unknown, a disciple of Zhu's)who asked a question about equilibrium and harmony, the Master said, "When the feelings of pleasure, anger, sorrow, and joy are not aroused, they are like in a room, without definite orientation to north, south, east, or west. That is what is meant by the state of equilibrium. When they have been aroused, they are like going out of the room, and if they go towards the east, they can not change to the west and if they go towards the south, they can not change to the north. Nevertheless, no matter what direction they are oriented to, they take the due course as called for by the matter they are concerned with, free from any perversity and obstruction. That is what is meant by the state of harmony." [Shengqing]

110 问:"喜怒哀乐之未发,不偏不倚,固其寂然之本体。及其酬酢万变,亦在是焉,故曰'天下之大本'。发而皆中节,则事得其宜,不相凌夺,固感而遂通之和也。然十中其九,一不中节,则为不和,便自有碍,不可谓之达道矣。"曰:"然。"又问:"于学者如何皆得中节?"曰:"学者安得便一一恁地!也须且逐件使之中节,方得。此所以贵于'博学,审问,慎思,明辨'。无一事之不学,无一时而不学,无一处而不学,各求其中节,此所以为难也。"道夫。

Question: Before the feelings of pleasure, anger, sorrow, and joy are aroused, they are impartial, and so they are the quiet original state of them. When they are aroused to occur in innumerable forms for various social purposes, they are still rooted therein. Therefore, it is called "the great root from which grow all the human actings in the world."(1)When those feelings have been aroused and all act in their due degree, things can be dealt with appropriately, made free from any insulting and contending against one another. So they are in the state of harmony which penetrates forthwith all phenomena and events. However, of those feelings which have been aroused, even when one out of ten fails to act in its due degree, they will fall short of harmony and the state of harmony is still inaccessible, which is indicative of there being still obstruction. So it can not be called as having reached the Way. (How do you think?)

Answer: Right.

Further question: How can a learner strive to attain the state that all aroused feelings act in their due degree?

Answer: How can a learner attain that state all over at one fell swoop? He has to strive for their acting in their due degree in each one of the cases. That is why it is important to conduct "extensive study of what is good, accurate inquiry about it, careful reflection on it, and clear discrimination of it." (22) Therefore, a learner should strive for learning with regard to every affair, at any time, and in any place, and in each case try to ensure that his aroused feelings act in their due degree. So it is hard to do, indeed. [Daofu]

111 自"喜怒哀乐未发谓之中"至"天地位焉，万物育焉"，道怎生地？这个心才有这事，便有这个事影见；才有那事，便有那个事影见？这个本自虚灵，常在这里。"喜怒哀乐未发谓之中，发而皆中节谓之和。"须恁地，方能中节。只恁地黑淬淬地在这里，如何要得发必中节！贺孙。

From "While there are no stirrings of pleasure, anger, sorrow, or joy, the mind may be said to be in the state of equilibrium" (1) to "Heaven and earth will attain their order, and all things will flourish," (1) how does the Way come into being? Is it that, as soon as there occurs this thing to the mind, there appears this sign of it, and as soon as there occurs that thing to the mind, there appears that sign of it? Actually, the Way originates from the void and intelligent, and always dwells there. "While there are no stirrings of pleasure, anger, sorrow, or joy, the mind may be said to be in the state of equilibrium. When those feelings have been stirred and they act in their due degree, there ensues what is called the state of harmony. "（1）Only by his pursuing that therein can his aroused feelings act in their due degree. If one only keeps from the Way there, without making any effort to pursue it, how can his aroused feelings act in their due degree? [Hesun]

112 中和亦是承上两节说。闳祖。

Equilibrium and harmony are expounded on the basis of the preceding two sections. [Hongzu]

113 中，性之德；和，情之德。

Equilibrium is the virtue of the human nature, and harmony, the virtue of feelings.

114 喜怒是阴阳。发各有中节，不中节，又是四象。僣。

Pleasure and anger pertain to *yin* and *yang*. When they are aroused, they each can act in their due degree. Or else, there will appear *sixiang* 四象 (four images, i. e. *laoyin* 老阴 [greater *yin*], *shaoyin* 少阴 [lesser *yin*], *shaoyang* 少阳 [lesser *yang*], and *laoyang* 老阳 [greater *yang*]). [Xun]

115 "喜怒哀乐未发之中，未是论圣人，只是泛论众人亦有此，与圣人都一般。"或曰："恐众人未发，与圣人异否？"曰："未发只做得未发。不然，是无大本，道理绝了。"或曰："恐众人于未发昏了否？"曰："这里未有昏明，须是还他做未发。若论原头，未发都一般。只论圣人动静，则全别；动亦定，静亦定。自其未感，全是未发之中；自其感物而动，全是中节之和。众人有未发时，只是他不曾主静看，不曾知得。"淳。

The Master said, "The mental state of equilibrium when there are no stirrings of pleasure, anger, sorrow, or joy is said not only of the sage, but also of ordinary people in a general sense, who are the same as the sage in that regard. " Someone asked, "I'm afraid, before those feelings are aroused, the ordinary people are different from the sage. (Is this right?)" The Master answered, "When the feelings are not aroused, that is the original state before that arousing. Or else there would be no great root to speak of and there would be no principle at all. " The questioner continued, "I'm afraid, for the ordinary people, before their feelings are aroused, their original state is beclouded. (Is this right?)" The Master answered, "Here there is no matter of clearness or becloudedness, for that state is always the original one. When it comes to its origin, all men's states before their feelings are aroused are the same. As far as only the activity and tranquility of the sage are concerned, he is completely different, for whether in activity or tranquility, he is in a state of certainty; when he does not get any penetration from things, he is in an equilibrium with his feelings not aroused, and when he has penetration from things and enters into activity, he is in a state of feelings which act entirely in their due degree. As for ordinary people, before their feelings are aroused, they have fallen short of seeing them from the viewpoint of tranquility, ignorant of that state. " [Chun (淳)]

116 问:"恻隐羞恶,喜怒哀乐,固是心之发,晓然易见处。如未恻隐羞恶,喜怒哀乐之前,便是寂然而静时,然岂得皆块然如槁木!其耳目亦必有自然之闻见,其手足亦必有自然之举动,不审此时唤作如何?"宇录云:"不知此处是已发未发?"曰:"喜怒哀乐未发,只是这心未发耳。其手足运动,自是形体如此。"淳。寓录云:"其形体之行动则自若。"

Question: The feelings of sadness and commiseration, and dislike and shame, and the feelings of pleasure, anger, sorrow, and joy, are, of course, what is emanated from the mind, which are easy to understand. Nevertheless, before those feelings are aroused, one's mental state is absolutely quiet and tranquil, but how could it be said that it is there like a withered tree? His ears and eyes still hear and see naturally, and his hands and feet move naturally. Then I do not know how such can be referred to? Yu's record reads, "I do not know whether such state is one with the feelings aroused, or not?"

Answer: The state before one's feelings of pleasure, anger, sorrow, and joy are aroused refers only to his mind which does not make those emanations. As for the movements of his hands and feet, they are what his body does naturally. ［Chun（淳）］ Yu's record says, "The movements of his body occur naturally as he wants."

117 未发之前，万理备具。才涉思，即是已发动；而应事接物，虽万变不同，能省察得皆合于理处。盖是吾心本具此理，皆是合做底事，不容外面旋安排也。今说为臣必忠、为子必孝之类，皆是已发。然所以合做此事，实具此理，乃未发也。人杰。

Before the stirring of the feelings in the mind of one, the myriad principles are possessed by him. As soon as there is his thinking therein, it means there occurs his activity for their stirring. When he deals with things and events, though they vary in innumerable forms, he is capable of examining whether he conforms to the principles. That is probably because his mind possesses originally the principles and he does what he should do, admitting of nothing that is imposed from the outside. For example, when we say that a minister must be loyal to his sovereign and a son must be filial to his father, these pertain to the feelings that have been aroused. Nonetheless, they originally possess the principles requiring that those things should be done, which are in the state when their feelings are not aroused. ［Renjie］

118 "'喜怒哀乐未发谓之中'，只是思虑未萌，无纤毫私欲，自然无所偏倚。所谓'寂然不动'，此之谓中。然不是截然作二截，如僧家块然之谓。只是这个心自有那未发时节，自有那已发时节。谓如此事未萌于思虑要做时，须便是中是体；及发于思了，如此做而得其当时，便是和是用，只管夹杂相滚。若以为截然有一时是未发时，一时是已发时，亦不成道理。今学者或谓每日将半日来静做工夫，即是有此病也。"曰："喜怒哀乐未发而不中者如何？"曰："此却是气质昏浊，为私欲所胜，客来为主。其未发时，只是块然如顽石相似，劈斫不开；发来便只是那乖底。"曰："如此，则昏时是他不察，如何？"曰："言察，便是吕氏求中，却是已发。如伊川云：'只平日涵养便是。'"又曰：

"看来人逐日未发时少，已发时多。"曰："然。"端蒙。

The Master said, " ' While there are no stirrings of pleasure, anger, sorrow, or joy, the mind may be said to be in the state of equilibrium. ' (1) This means only that, before the stirring of any deliberation and consideration, the mind is free from any iota of selfish desire, so it is naturally not partial at all. The so called ' still and without movement' (' Appended Remarks' I in the *Classic of Change*) refers to the equilibrium. However, the state of equilibrium and that of no equilibrium are not two completely distinct states like that state called by Buddhism as ' sitting like a block' and the other states than that. It only means that the mind possesses naturally the period when the feelings are not aroused and the other period when they are aroused, and that before such and such thing occurs in consideration, it pertains to the equilibrium of the mental state and its substance, while when it is done in such and such way at the right time it pertains to the harmony and the function of the mind. The two states of the two periods are intermingled with each other. If they were regarded as two completely distinct periods, with one when the feelings are not aroused and the other when they are aroused, this would not make the principle. Nowadays, when some learners claim that they spend half a day in each day making efforts through tranquility, it indicates that problem with them. " I asked the Master, "What about one's state before pleasure, anger, sorrow, and joy are aroused, yet devoid of equilibrium?" He answered, "That is indicative of the turbidity of his physical nature, and that he is overcome by his selfish desire and is dominated by what comes from the outside. When his feelings are not aroused, his mind is, as it were, a block of rock, which can not be cleft open, and when they get aroused, they are only what is perverse. " I asked further, "Then, does he not introspect himself when he is in a beclouded state?" He replied, "Speaking of one introspecting himself, it is what was meant by Lü (Dalin) when he mentioned ' seeking the state of equilibrium,' but it pertains to the state when the feelings are already aroused. As Yichuan said, 'The only thing to do is to cultivate oneself everyday.'" He added, "It seems that, for one, in a day, the length of the period when feelings are not aroused is outweighed by that of the period when they are aroused." I responded, "Yes." 〔Duanmeng〕

119 已发未发，只是说心有已发时，有未发时。方其未有事时，便是未发；才有所感，便是已发，却不要泥着。慎独是从戒慎恐惧处，无时无处不用力，到此处又须慎独。只是一体事，不是两节。炎。

The "aroused" or "not aroused" refer only to the stirred or unstirred state of mind. The state when there is no stirring of anything is "not aroused," while as soon as there occurs penetration of something, it is "aroused," but one should avoid taking that distinction too rigidly. Being watchful over solitude means that, wherever one does not see or hear things, he makes effort all the time, and when he sees and hears things alone, he is watchful over his being alone. So the two states are essentially of the same thing rather than two distinct things. 〔Yan〕

120 大本用涵养，中节则须穷理之功。方。

The great root needs preserving and nourishing, while acting in due degree requires the effort to inquire into the principle to the utmost extent. 〔Fang〕

121 问："'发而皆中节'，是无时而不戒慎恐惧而然否？"曰："是他合下把捉，方能发而中节。若信口说去，信脚行去，如何会中节！"焘。

Question: Is "All one's feelings are aroused and act in their due degree" because of his being cautious and apprehensive all the time?

Answer: It is because of his effort for their grasp that all his feelings are aroused and act in their due degree. If he speaks thoughtlessly or walks casually, how can his feelings act in their degree? 〔Tao〕

122 问："中庸一篇，学者求其门而入，固在于'慎独'。至下文言中之已发未发者，此正根本处。未发之时，难以加毫末之功。当发之际，欲其中节，不知若何而用工？得非即其所谓'戒慎恐惧'，'莫见乎隐'之心而乃底于中节否？"曰："慎独是结上文一节之意。下文又自是一节，发明中与常行之道。欲其中节，正当加慎于欲发之际。"佐。

Question: As regards the book the *Doctrine of the Mean*, learners have tried to find its gate and enter it for a thorough understanding, and that gate is, of course, "being watchful over solitude." (1) The several sentences after that concern the state of mind when the feelings are aroused or not, and that is the fundamental. Before the state with the feelings aroused, it is hard for one to make any effort for it. When they begin to stir, if one wants to ensure that they can act in their due degree, how should he make effort? Could it be said that, only with the mind of the so called "being cautious and apprehensive" and "(There is) nothing more visible than what is secret" can he attain their acting in their due degree?

Answer: The "being watchful over solitude" serves to summarize what is meant by the preceding section, while the part after it makes up another section, which is meant to clarify the state of equilibrium and the Way which always works. If one wants his aroused feelings act in their due degree, he should intensify his effort to be watchful over the moment when his feelings are about to stir. [Zuo]

123 问："'浑然在中'，恐是喜怒哀乐未发，此心至虚，都无偏倚，停停当当，恰在中间。章句所谓'独立而不近四傍，心之体，地之中也'。"曰："在中者，未动时恰好处；时中者，已动时恰好处。才发时，不偏于喜，则偏于怒，不得谓之在中矣。然只要就所偏倚一事，处之得恰好，则无过、不及矣。盖无过、不及，乃无偏倚者之所为；而无偏倚者，是所以能无过、不及也。"铢。

Question: The "being completely in equilibrium" you say in your *Interpretation*, I think, means that before the feelings are aroused, the mind is vacuous to the utmost extent, free from any partiality, which is secure and right in the state of equilibrium. That is what is meant by "(The equilibrium) is independent and free from inclination to any of the four directions, which is the substance of the mind and the central of the earth" in your *Interpretation*. (Is my understanding right?)

Answer: The "(being) in equilibrium" refers to the just right state before the feelings stir, while the "(maintaining) the Mean at any time," to the just right state when the feelings have stirred. When one's feelings have just stirred, they have already either leant to pleasure or to anger, so his state of the mind should not be said as being in equilibrium. Nonetheless, so long as he can copy with that leaning just right, he will be able to be free from going beyond or falling short. Probably, being free from going beyond or falling short is what one who can be free from partiality is capable of, and his being free from partiality is the cause of his being free from going beyond or falling short. [Zhu]

124 问"浑然不待勉强而自中乎当然之节"。曰:"事事有个恰好处。因言荥阳王哀乐过人,以其哀时直是哀,才过而乐,亦直是乐。情性之变如此之易,'不恒其德'故也。"焘。

When asked about "One's feelings, completely without his any effort, act in their naturally due degree by themselves," the Master answered, "There is a due degree just right for everything. What is mentioned thereupon is the extraordinary display of sorrow and joy by the King of Xingyang (present day Xingyang, Henan), who was able actually to be sorrowful all over when he was sorrowful, and to turn joyful quickly after that was over. He changed his moods with so much ease, and so no wonder he 'does not continuously maintain his virtue.' ('Hexagram Heng' 恒 [Duration] in the *Classic of Change*)" [Tao]

125 问:"未发之中,寂然不动,如何见得是中?"曰:"已发之中,实时中也,中节之谓也,却易见。未发更如何分别?某旧有一说,谓已发之中,是已施去者;未发是方来不穷者,意思大故猛。要之,却是伊川说'未发是在中之义',最好。"大雅。

Question: In the state before the feelings are aroused are absolute quiet and inactivity, but how can we know it is equilibrium?

Answer: The state when the feelings have been aroused pertains actually to maintaining the Mean at any time, referred to as acting in their due degree, which is easy to see. But how to identify the state before the feelings are aroused? In the past I put forth an opinion, that is, "The state after the feelings are aroused points to what has been done, while that before they are aroused, to what is to come ceaselessly." Its meaning is broadly thrusting. Yet, in a word, Yichuan's saying is better, which is "Being in the state before the feelings are aroused is equilibrium." [Daya]

126 问:"伊川言'未发之中是在中之义',如何?"曰:"是言在里面底道理,非以'在中'释'中'字。"问:"伊川又云:'只喜怒哀乐不发,便是。'如何说'不发'?"曰:"是言不曾发时。"德明。

Question: Yichuan said, "Being in the state before the feelings are aroused refers to what is meant by being in equilibrium." How do you think of it?

Answer: It is said of the principle inherent in the state, rather than is meant to explain the "being in the state" by "being in equilibrium."

Further question: Yichuan also said, "Simply the state when the feelings of pleasure, anger, sorrow, and joy are not aroused is equilibrium." Why did he say "not aroused"?

Answer: It means the state when the feelings have not been emanated. [Deming]

127 伊川言:"'喜怒哀乐之未发谓之中',中也者,言'寂然不动'者也,故曰'天下之大本'。"喜怒哀乐未发,无所偏倚,此之谓中。中,性也;"寂然不动",言其体则然也。大本,则以其无不该遍,而万事万物之理,莫不由是出焉。"'发而皆中节谓之和',和也者,言'感而遂通'者也,故曰'天下之达道'。"喜怒哀乐之发,无所乖戾,此之谓"和"。和，情也；"感而遂通"，言其事则然也。达道，则以其自然流行，而理之由是而出者，无不通焉。先生后来说达道，意不如此。端蒙。

Yichuan said, "In 'The state before the feelings of pleasure, anger, sorrow, and joy are aroused is called equilibrium,' (1) the 'equilibrium' is said of 'being absolutely quiet and inactive,' so it is called 'the great root of from which grow all the human actings in the world.'" (1) In the state before the feelings of pleasure, anger, sorrow, and joy are aroused, there is no partiality, so it is called equilibrium. As regards the mind, the "equilibrium" pertains to its nature, and the "being absolutely quiet and inactive," to the natural state of its substance. The "great root" means that it is pervasive everywhere and all the principles over the myriad things and events issue from it. (Yichuan said,) "In 'The state when those feelings have been aroused and all act in their due degree is called harmony,' (1) the 'harmony' is said of that 'which penetrates forthwith all phenomena and events,' so it is said that '(Harmony is) the universal Way which they all should pursue.'" When the state after the feelings of pleasure, anger, sorrow, and joy are aroused is free from any perversity, it is called harmony. The "harmony" refers to the feelings, and that 'which penetrates forthwith all phenomena and events' is said of the natural state of all those things. The "universal Way" means that it flows naturally and is where the principles over those things come from, without any obstruction. But when the Master dwelt on "universal Way" later, he explained it in a different way. [Duanmeng]

128 喜怒哀乐未发，程子"敬而无失"之说甚好。闳祖。

As regards the state before the feelings of pleasure, anger, sorrow, and joy are aroused, Master Cheng's explanation of it with "seriousness without fail" is very good. [Hongzu]

129 "喜怒哀乐未发谓之中"，程子云："敬不可谓之中，敬而无失，即所以中也，未说到义理涵养处。"大抵未发已发，只是一项工夫，未发固要存养，已发亦要审察。遇事时时复提起，不可自怠，生放过底心。无时不存养，无事不省察。人杰。

As regards "The state before the feelings of pleasure, anger, sorrow, and joy are aroused is called equilibrium," (1) Master Cheng Yi said, "Seriousness is not equilibrium itself. Seriousness without fail is the way to attain equilibrium, but this does not touch the preservation and nourishment of the principle." Probably, whether it is the state when the feelings are not aroused or the state when they are, they call for the same effort, for the former needs, of course, preserving and nourishing, and the latter also requires retrospection. Whenever dealing with things, one should always remind himself of that, refrain from self-slacking, and avoid the idea of muddling along. Thus, one should keep on preserving and nourishing all the time and making retrospection of himself in regard to everything. [Renjie]

130 因论吕与叔说"中"字，大本差了。曰："他底固不是，自家亦要见得他不是处。"文蔚曰："喜怒哀乐未发之中，乃在中之义。他引虞书'允执厥中'之'中'，是不知'无过、不及之中'，与'在中'之义本自不同。又以为'赤子之心'，又以为'心为甚'，不知中乃喜怒哀乐未发而赤子之心已发。'心为甚'，孟子盖谓心欲审轻重，度长短，甚于权度。他便谓凡言心者，便能度轻重长短，权度有所不及，尤非孟子之意，即此便是差了。"曰："如今点检他过处都是，自家却自要识中。"文蔚曰："伊川云：'涵养于喜怒哀乐未发之前，则发自中节矣。'今学者能戒慎恐惧于不睹不闻之中，而慎独于隐微之际，则中可得矣。"曰："固是如此，亦要识得。且如今在此坐，卓然端正，不侧东，不侧西，便是中底气象。然人说中，亦只是大纲如此说，比之大段不中者，亦可谓之中，非能极其中。如人射箭，期于中红心，射在贴上亦可谓中，终不若他射中红心者。至如和，亦有大纲唤做和者，比之大段乖戾者，谓之和则可，非能极其和。且如喜怒，合喜三分，自家喜了四分；合怒三分，自家怒了四分，便非和矣。"文蔚。

Thereupon, the Master commented on Lü Yushu's explanation of *zhong*
中 that he missed the fundamental of it. He said, "True that his explanation
is not right, but you should try to know why he is not right. " I said, "Being
in the state before the feelings of pleasure, anger, sorrow, and joy are
aroused is what is meant by being in equilibrium. He cited *zhong* 中 from *Yun
zhi jue zhong* 允执厥中 (to keep to the centrality sincerely) ('Counsels of
the Great Yu' in *Classic of History*), yet neglected the *zhong* 中 which means
being free from going beyond or falling short. So his explanation is different
from the original meaning of 'being in equilibrium. ' He took it for 'The
mind of a newborn baby' (*Mencius*, 4B: 40) and for 'The mind is the most
important to estimate for its motions,' (*Mencius*, 1A: 7) yet ignorant of
their difference in that the *zhong* points to the state before the feelings are
aroused, while the 'mind of a newborn baby' pertains to the state after the
feelings are aroused. As for 'The mind is the most important to estimate for
its motions,' Mencius probably meant that when the mind desires to
discriminate significance and assessing merit and demerit, the most important
it is capable of is weighing. However, he said, 'Whatever is said of the mind
can be capable of assessing the significance, and merit and demerit, without
doing justice to its role of weighing. ' That deviates from Mencius's original
meaning. So what he said is not right. " The Master responded, "Now, what
you just said about his misunderstandings is right, but it is more important
that you yourself understand what is meant by *zhong*. " I replied, "Yichuan
said, 'One should make effort for preservation and nourishment before the
feelings of pleasure, anger, sorrow, and joy are aroused, and after a
sufficient period of time, the feelings will naturally attain due measure and
degree when they are aroused. ' Now, if a learner is able to be cautious and
apprehensive over what he does not see and hear and be watchful over his
being alone in seeing and hearing the secret and minute, he will be able to
attain the due measure and degree when his feelings are aroused. " The

Master answered, "It is of course right, and it is also important to understand that. For example, when you sit here upright, free from any inclination to the east or the west, your posture is an image illustrating equilibrium. Nonetheless, when we speak of it that way, we refer to its generality, and that which is in contrast to what is devoid of equilibrium can largely also be referred to as equilibrium, though it is not the equilibrium to the utmost extent. It is like one shooting an arrow in the hope of hitting the very center in the target. If he hits the area beside that, he can also be said as hitting the target, though not as good as hitting the center. When it comes to harmony, there is also the generality which can also be referred to as harmony, for it is contrastive largely to what is perverse, though it is not the harmony to the utmost extent. For example, as regards pleasure or anger, when it is due for one to have pleasure or anger in a three tenth degree but actually in a four tenth degree, it is not a case of harmony. " [Wenwei]

131 问："吕氏言：'中则性也。'或谓此与'性即理也'语意似同。铢疑不然。"先生曰："公意如何?"铢曰："理者，万事万物之道理，性皆有之而无不具者也。故谓性即理则可。中者，又所以言此理之不偏倚、无过不及者，故伊川只说'状性之体段'。"曰："'中'是虚字，'理'是实字，故中所以状性之体段。"铢曰："然则谓性中可乎?"曰："此处定有脱误，性中亦说得未尽。"铢因言："或问中，此等处尚多，略为说破亦好。"先生曰："如何解——嚼饭与人吃!"铢。

I said to the Master, "Lü said, 'The *zhong* refers to the nature. ' Someone else said that his explanation seemed similar to what is meant by (Master Cheng's) 'Nature is the same as principle. ' But I do not think so. " The Master asked, "How do you think?" I answered, "The principle underlies the myriad things and events, while the nature is endowed on everything. Therefore it is reasonable to say that nature is the same as principle. By contrast, the *zhong* says of the impartiality of the principle and its freedom from going beyond or falling short, so Yichuan only mentioned 'It describes the substantial being of nature.'" The Master replied, "The *zhong* is an empty sinograph, while the *li* (principle) is a substantial one, so the former serves as being descriptive of the substantial being of nature." Then I asked, "But is it right to say that nature is *zhong* (as you did in your *Questions and Answers*)?" The Master answered, "There must have been in it one word or two missed out from what I actually said, and my explanation of the nature and *zhong* falls also short of being complete." Thereupon I said to the Master, "In your *Questions and Answers*, there are some other cases like this. I think it would be better to lay bare what is meant by the words (in the *Doctrine of the Mean*) at greater length." The Master responded, "But how can I do it in a way like chewing everything and giving it to others for a meal?" [Zhu]

132 吕氏"未发之前，心体昭昭具在"，说得亦好。德明录云："伊川不破此说。"淳。

Lü's "Manifest before the feelings are aroused is all the substance of the mind" is also a good explanation. Deming's record reads, "Yichuan did not break that opinion." [Chun (淳)]

133 问："吕与叔云：'未发之前，心体昭昭具在；已发乃心之用。'南轩辨昭昭为已发，恐太过否？"曰："这辨得亦没意思。敬夫太聪明，看道理不子细。伊川所谓'凡言心者，皆指已发而言'，吕氏只是辨此一句。伊川后来又救前说曰：''凡言心者，皆指已发而言"，此语固未当。心一也，有指体而言者，"寂然不动"是也；有指用而言者，"感而遂通"是也，惟观其所见如何。'此语甚圆，无病。大抵圣贤之言，多是略发个萌芽，更在后人推究，演而伸，触而长，然亦须得圣贤本意。不得其意，则从那处推得出来？"

Question: Lü Yushu said, "Manifest before the feelings are aroused is all the substance of the mind, while that the feelings are aroused is the function of the mind." Nanxuan (style name of Zhang Shi) argued that the "manifest" should refer to the state after the feelings are aroused. Didn't he go too far?

Answer: His arguing is meaningless. Jingfu (courtesy name of Zhang Shi) was too intelligent to read carefully the words on the principle. Yichuan said "Whatever is said of the mind refers to the state when the feelings have been aroused," and Lü only tried to debate on that one sentence. But Yichuan, in an attempt to make up for what he had said before, explained "It is of course not right to say only that 'Whatever is said of the mind refers to the state when the feelings have been aroused,' for, though there is only one mind, it may be said in regard to its substance, for example, 'that which is absolutely quiet and inactive;' it may be said in regard to its function, for example, 'that which penetrates forthwith all phenomena and events.' So which is the case depends on which side is spoken of." This explanation is fully complete, free from any trouble. Generally, when the sages and worthies said something, they tended simply to make clear some germination of their ideas, which calls for later scholars' efforts to deduce therefrom, who should extend it by associating. But first of all they should know what the sages' and worthies' original meanings are. Without such knowing, where can they start to deduce?

问："心本是个动物，不审未发之前，全是寂然而静，还是静中有动意?"曰："不是静中有动意。周子谓'静无而动有'。静不是无，以其未形而谓之无；非因动而后有，以其可见而谓之有耳。横渠'心统性情'之说甚善。性是静，情是动。心则兼动静而言，或指体，或指用，随人所看。方其静时，动之理只在。伊川谓：'当中时，耳无闻，目无见，然见闻之理在，始得。及动时，又只是这静底。'"

Question: The mind is essentially an active thing. It is not clear to me whether, before (feelings) are aroused, the mind is completely quiet and tranquil, or whether its tranquility contains within it a tendency toward activity.

Answer: It is not that tranquility contains within it a tendency toward activity. Master Zhou Dunyi said, "When tranquil, it is in the state of non-being. When active, it is in the state of being." Tranquility itself is not non-being as such, for it is because it has not assumed physical form that we call it non-being. It is not because of activity that there is being. It is because (activity makes) it visible that we call it being. Hengqü's theory that "The mind commands human nature and feelings" is excellent. The nature is tranquil, while feelings are active, and the mind involves both tranquility and activity. Whether it refers to its substance or its function depends on one's point of view. While it is in the state of tranquility, the principle of activity is already present. Yichuan said, "In the state of equilibrium (before the feelings are aroused), although the ear hears nothing and the eye sees nothing, the principles of hearing and seeing must be already there before hearing and seeing are possible. When activity takes place, it is the same tranquility that becomes active."[1]

淳举伊川以动之端为天地之心。曰:"动亦不是天地之心,只是见天地之心。如十月岂得无天地之心? 天地之心流行只自若。'元亨利贞',元是萌芽初出时,亨是长枝叶时,利是成遂时,贞是结实归宿处。下梢若无这归宿处,便也无这元了。惟有这归宿处,元又从此起。元了又贞,贞了又元,万古只如此,循环无穷,所谓'维天之命,于穆不已',说已尽了。十月万物收敛,寂无踪迹,到一阳动处,生物之心始可见。"曰:"一阳之复,在人言之,只是善端萌处否?"曰:"以善言之,是善端方萌处;以德言之,昏迷中有悔悟向善意,便是复。如睡到忽然醒觉处,亦是复底气象。又如人之沉滞,道不得行,到极处,忽少亨达,虽未大行,已有可行之兆,亦是复。这道理千变万化,随所在无不浑沦。"淳。

---

① The English translation of the conversation is based on a version by Chan Wing-tsit (see *A Source Book in Chinese Philosophy*. Princeton: Princeton University Press, 1963, p. 629).

I cited Yichuan as saying the beginning of activity as the mind of Heaven and Earth. The Master replied, "The activity is not the mind of Heaven and Earth, for it only indicates the mind of Heaven and Earth. For example, don't Heaven and Earth in the tenth month of the year have their mind? The mind of Heaven and Earth flows along its own course. As regards *yuan heng li zhen* 元亨利贞 said in 'Hexagram Qian' 乾 (The Creative) of the *Classic of Change*, *yuan* refers to the time when germination begins; *heng*, to the time when branches and leaves grow; *li*, to the time when fruits ripen; *zhen*, to the place where the fruits return. Therefore, without the place for the return, there would be no germination to speak of. Only with the place for the return can germination begin once more therefrom. Thus, from germination to return, from return to germination, that is the endless circulation for eons. That is elucidated to the utmost extent by 'The ordinances of Heaven, how profound are they and unceasing!' (*Classic of Poetry*) The tenth month of the year witnesses the retraction of the myriad things which finally get silent and traceless. It is not until when the first sign of *yang* starts to appear again that the mind of Heaven and Earth for generating things begins to indicate itself once more." I asked, "Does the return (*fu* 复) of the first sign of *yang*, in regard to humankind, show the beginning of the good?" The Master answered, "To speak from the viewpoint of the good, it is the first sign showing the beginning of the good; to speak from virtue, when there appears in the becloudedness the intention of repentance and orientation to the good, it is what is meant by the return. For example, when one awakens suddenly from his state of slumber, it is an indication of return; when one was bogged down in a state of stagnation where the Way could not work, yet when that state has gone to an extreme and he has experienced suddenly a little thriving, showing a portent of the prevalence of the Way, it is also an indication of return. Though the principle undergoes myriads of changes, it is always complete and thorough wherever it is." [Chun (淳)]

134　先生问铢曰："伊川说：'善观者，却于已发之时观之。'寻常看得此语如何？"铢曰："此语有病。若只于已发处观之，恐无未发时存养工夫。"先生曰："杨吕诸公说求之于喜怒哀乐未发之时，伊川又说于已发处观，如此则是全无未发时放下底。今且四平着地放下，要得平帖，湛然无一毫思虑。及至事物来时，随宜应接，当喜则喜，当怒则怒，当哀乐则哀乐。喜怒哀乐过了，此心湛然者，还与未发时一般，方是两下工夫。若只于已发处观，则是已发了，又去已发，展转多了一层，却是反鉴。看来此语只说得圣人之止，如君止于仁，臣止于敬，是就事物上说理，却不曾说得未发时心，后来伊川亦自以为未当。"铢曰："此须是动静两下用工，而主静为本。静而存养，方始动而精明。"曰："只为诸公不曾说得静中未发工夫。如胡氏兄弟说得已发事大猛了。"铢曰："先生中和旧说，已发其义。"先生因言当时所见次第云云。铢。

The Master asked me, "Yichuan said, 'Whoever is good at observing observes at the time when the feelings are aroused.' How do you usually understand this saying by him?" I answered, "There is some problem with that saying by him. If one only observes at the time when the feelings are aroused, I'm afraid, he will make no effort at the time before they are aroused." In reply, the Master said, "Yang, Lü, and some other scholars advocated that the pursuit should be made before the feelings are aroused, while Yichuan said that observation should be made when they are aroused. What he said touches nothing of what is put down at the time before the feelings are aroused. Now, suppose that one puts down everything in his mind, and that flat squarely and completely, clearly free from an iota of deliberation. When something comes up, he receives it appropriately and feels joyful when he should be joyful, angry when he should be angry, or sorrowful when he should be sorrowful. If he goes beyond what he should feel, but his mind is still as clear as when the feelings are not aroused, it will indicate that he has made two separate types of efforts. If one makes observation only at the time when the feelings are aroused, since his feelings have been aroused and now he goes to observe the state after his feelings have been aroused, so this indirectness gives rise to a more layer, which is actually retrospection. It seems that saying by him is only concerned with the resting discoursed by the sage, for example, 'As a sovereign, he rested in benevolence. As a minister, he rested in reverence,' (*Great Learning*, 7) which expounds the principle with regard to concrete things yet without regard to the mind when the feelings are not aroused. Later, Yichuan himself admitted that his saying that was not right." I responded, "One must make efforts in respect of both activity and tranquility, where it is the fundamental to take the tranquility as the master. Only by preservation and nourishment in tranquility can he be acute in activity." The Master said then, "It is because those scholars, in their discourse, did not touch on the effort called for at the tranquility before the feelings stir. For example, the Hu brothers attached too much emphasis on the state when the feelings are aroused." I responded, "In your early explanations of the equilibrium and harmony, you already clarified their meanings." Thereupon the Master talked about his early opinions of them and so on. [Zhu]

135 龟山说"喜怒哀乐未发",似求中于喜怒哀乐未发之前。方。

When Guishan explained "the state before the feelings of pleasure, anger, sorrow, and joy are aroused," he seemed to have sought equilibrium before the state when the feelings of pleasure, anger, sorrow, and joy are aroused. [Fang]

136 尝以所论湖南问答呈先生。先生曰:"已发未发,不必大泥。只是既涵养,又省察,无时不涵养省察。若戒惧不睹不闻,便是通贯动静,只此便是工夫。至于慎独,又是或恐私意有萌处,又加紧切。若谓已发了更不须省察,则亦不可。如曾子三省,亦是已发后省察。今湖南诸说,却是未发时安排如何涵养,已发时旋安排如何省察。"必大录云:"存养省察,是通贯乎已发未发功夫。未发时固要存养,已发时亦要存养。未发时固要省察，已发时亦要省察。只是要无时不做功夫。若谓已发后不当省察，不成便都不照管他。胡季随谓譬如射者矢傅弦上始欲求中，则其不中也必矣。某谓'内志正，外体直'，觑梁取亲所以可中，岂有便闭目放箭之理！"。賀

I presented my opinion to the Master on the first letter he wrote to the scholars in Hunan on equilibrium and harmony. The Master commented, "As regards the distinction between the state before the feelings are aroused and that after they are aroused, you need not stick to it rigidly. What is important is to preserve and nourish and at the same time to retrospect yourself, and to do them all the time. To be cautious and apprehensive over what one does not see and hear is to interconnect his activity and tranquility, and only that is the effort one should make. As for being watchful over your solitude, it refers to one being afraid of the occurrence of selfish intention and thus making exigent effort to guard against it. It should not be said that one is unnecessary to make retrospection of himself when his feelings have been aroused. For example, Zengzi said, 'I daily examine myself on three points.' (*Analects*, 1: 4) His examination was conducted after his feelings had been aroused. By contrast, according to the theories held by those scholars in Hunan, preservation and nourishment should be manipulated before the feelings are aroused and as soon as the feelings are aroused self-examination should be made." Bida's record reads, "To preserve and nourish and to retrospect are the efforts interconnecting the state before the feelings are aroused and that after they are aroused. It is necessary, of course, to preserve and nourish in the former, and it is also necessary to preserve and nourish in the latter. It is necessary, of course, to retrospect in the former, and it is also necessary to retrospect in the latter. What is important is to make effort at any time. If it is said that it is not necessary for one to retrospect after his feelings are aroused, doesn't that mean he needs not to take care of that state? Hu Jisui 胡季随 (i. e. Hu Dashi 胡大时, dates unknown) cited shooting an arrow for an example, and said 'If one does not consider how to hit the target until he fits his arrow on the string, then he is sure to miss the target.' I once said, 'Whoever is upright in his internal intent is upright in his external body. ' It is due to *Qu liang qu qin* 觑梁取亲 (seeing clearly the target before shooting)① that he can hit the target. How can there be such a principle that one closes his eyes and shoots an arrow?" [Xun]

137 再论湖南问答，曰："未发已发，只是一件工夫，无时不涵养，无时不省察耳。谓如水长长地流，到高处又略起伏则个。如恐惧戒慎，是长长地做；到慎独，是又提起一起。如水然，只是要不辍地做。又如骑马，自家常常提掇，及至遇险处，便加些提控。不成谓是大路，便更都不管他，恁地自去之理！"正淳曰："未发时当以理义涵养。"曰："未发时着理义不得，才知有理有义，便是已发。当此时有理义之原，未有理义条件。只一个主宰严肃，便有涵养工夫。伊川曰：'敬而无失便是，然不可谓之中。但敬而无失，即所以中也。'"正淳又曰："平日无涵养者，临事必不能强勉省察。"曰："有涵养者固要省察，不曾涵养者亦当省察。不可道我无涵养工夫后，于已发处更不管他。若于发处能点检，亦可知得是与不是。今言涵养，则曰不先知理义底涵养不得；言省察，则曰无涵养，省察不得。二者相捱，却成担阁。"又曰："如涵养熟者，固是自然中节。便做圣贤，于发处亦须审其是非而行。涵养不熟底，虽未必能中节，亦须直要中节可也。要知二者可以交相助，不可交相待。"瑩。

When revisiting his first letter to the scholars in Hunan on equilibrium and harmony, the Master said, "The state before the feelings are aroused and that after they are aroused call for effort as a whole. It is nothing but conducting preservation and nourishment and making retrospection all the time. It is just like a long river, in which, when it flows to some place higher, there rise some bigger waves. Being cautious and apprehensive over what one does not see and hear is a long term task, and when it comes to

---

① According to a note in the original work, the meaning of the four sino-graphs 觑梁取亲 is unknown. Separately, the *qu* 觑 means "look (at); see," *liang* 梁, "beam," *qu* 取, "take," and *qin* 亲, "clearly." Taken as a whole, in the context, the four sinographs may mean "seeing clearly the target before shooting." This expression indicates Zhu's disagreement with Hu in regard to the example of shooting an arrow.

being watchful over his solitude he becomes more cautious and apprehensive. It is like a river, which keeps flowing for ever. It is also comparable to one riding a horse. He should pick up the checkrein on it and when meeting some dangerous place he must manipulate it with more effort. Could it be said that since the way ahead is all wide one can release the checkrein on his horse and let it go as it pleases?" Zhengchun responded, "In the state before the feelings are aroused, one should make preservation and nourishment by the principle and righteousness." The Master replied, "How can you find the principle and righteousness before your feelings stir? As soon as you know there being the principle and righteousness, your feelings have already been aroused. Though there is the origin of the principle and righteousness before your feelings are aroused, there are not the conditions for your being conscious of them. So long as there is the seriousness as the master in you, you are making effort for preservation and nourishment. Yichuan said, 'Seriousness without fail is equilibrium, yet seriousness is not equilibrium itself. But seriousness without fail is the way to attain equilibrium.'" Zhengchun further said, "Whoever makes no daily effort for self-cultivation is sure to be incapable of conducting well self-examination when one thing or another comes up." The Master said then, "It is true that those who have made effort for self-cultivation should examine themselves, but those who have not made that effort should also examine themselves. It should not be said that since one has not made effort for self-cultivation he can ignore the state after his feelings are aroused. If he can conduct self-examination in that state, he can also know whether something is right or not. Nowadays, when speaking of self-cultivation, they say that without knowing the principle and righteousness one would not be able to make self-cultivation, and when speaking of self-examination, they say without self-cultivation one would not be able to make self-examination. Thus, with these two sides in discordance, procrastination is caused." He further said, "For those who are mature in their self-cultivation, their feelings, of course, act naturally in their due measure and degree. Even for the sages and worthies, when their feelings have been aroused, they should also discriminate between right and wrong of something before doing it. For those who are not mature in their self-cultivation, though their feelings act not necessarily in their due measure and degree, they should strive in pursuit of that. It is because that maturity and that due measure and degree are mutually conducive and they should not be kept waiting for each other." [Xun]

138 论中：〇五峰与曾书。〇吕书。〇朱中庸说。〇易传说"感物而动"，不可无"动"字，自是有动有静。〇据伊川言："中者，寂然不动。"已分明。〇未发意，亦与戒慎恐惧相连，然似更提起自言。此大本虽庸、圣皆同，但庸则愦愦，圣则湛然。某初言此者，亦未尝杂人欲而说庸也。〇如说性之用是情，心即是贯动静，却不可言性之用。〇"在中"，只言喜怒哀乐未发是在中。如言一个理之本，后方就时上事上说过与不及之中。吕当初便说"在中"为此"时中"，所以异也。方。

On equilibrium：

〇 Letter of Wufeng (style name of Hu Hong) to Zeng (i. e. Zeng Ji)

〇 Letter of Lü (i. e. Lü Zuqian)

〇 Zhu's explanation of *The Doctrine of the Mean*

〇 The *Explanation of the Classic of Change* (*Yizhuan* 易传) says "The activity of the mind is due to penetration from things (external to it)," and the word "activity" is indispensable, for there is naturally both activity and tranquility.

〇 As Yichuan said, "The equilibrium means the mind is absolutely quiet and inactive." He made that very clear.

〇 The meaning of one's feelings not aroused is also related to that of one being cautious and apprehensive (over what one does not see and hear). Nevertheless, it seems said particularly of oneself. As regards their great *root*, *yong* 庸 (being ordinary) and *sheng* 圣 (being sagely) are the same, but the former refers to the state of being muddleheaded, while the latter, to clear-minded. In my early explanation of the book in this regard, I did not discourse on *yong* by blending the selfish human desire into it.

○ If the function of the nature can be said as the feelings, then the mind is that which penetrates both activity and tranquility, but it should not be said that it is the function of the nature.

○ "Being in equilibrium" is said only of the state when the feelings of pleasure, anger, sorrow, and joy are not aroused. If it is spoken of the root of the principle, then only after that is the equilibrium of not going beyond or falling short said with regard to the time and events. But Lü said at first that the "being in equilibrium" was the "(maintaining) the Mean at any time," so his explanation changed later. [Fang]

139 "在中"之义，大本在此，此言包得也。至如说"亭亭当当，直上直下"，亦有不偏倚气象。方。

The meaning of "being in equilibrium" can contain that of the great root. As for speaking of it as being "well-settled and upright straight," this also gives a display of impartiality. [Fang]

140 问："中庸或问曰：'若未发时，纯一无伪，又不足以名之。'此是无形影，不可见否?"曰："未发时，伪不伪皆不可见。不特赤子如此，大人亦如此。"淳曰："只是大人有主宰，赤子则未有主宰。"曰："然。"淳。

I asked, "You, sir, said in your *Questions and Answers*, 'Before the feelings are aroused, the state of the mind is purely one, free from any fakeness, but that is insufficient to name it.' Do you mean that, since there is no form of it, it can not be seen?" The Master answered, "In the state before the feelings are aroused, whether there is any fakeness or not can not be seen. This is true of not only a new born baby but also an adult." I asked further, "Only that the adult has his master in him, while the newborn baby has not. " The Maser responded, "Yes. " ［Chun（淳）］

141 问：“中庸或问说，未发时耳目当亦精明而不可乱。如平常着衣吃饭，是已发，是未发？”曰：“只心有所主着，便是发。如着衣吃饭，亦有些事了。只有所思量，要恁地，便是已发。”淳。

Question：You, sir, said in your *Questions and Answers* that, in the state when one's feelings are not aroused, his ears and eyes should also be kept acute and sharp, and from being confused. Take clothing and having a meal in our daily life for example. Do they pertain to the state when the feelings are aroused or not?

Answer：Whenever the mind is oriented to something, it is in the state when the feelings are aroused. In the case of clothing and having a meal, they are also concrete matters. Whenever the mind makes any deliberation of anything, it enters the state when the feelings have been aroused. ［Chun（淳）］

142 问：“或问中‘坤卦纯阴不为无阳’之说，如何？”曰：“虽十月为坤，十一月为复，然自小雪后，其下面一画，便有三十分之一分阳生，至冬至，方足得一爻成尔。故十月谓之‘阳月’，盖嫌于无阳也。自姤至坤亦然。”曰：“然则阳毕竟有尽时矣。”曰：“剥尽于上，则复生于下，其间不容息也。”广。

Question：In your *Questions and Answers*, sir, what is meant by the "In spite of all the six *yin* lines of 'Hexagram Kun' 坤 (The Receptive) (in the *Classic of Change*), it is not that there is completely no *yang* therein"?

Answer：Though the tenth month (in the Chinese lunar calendar) pertains to "Hexagram Kun" and the eleventh month to "Hexagram Fu" 复 (Return), since the solar term Xiaoxue 小雪 (Slight Snow), the bottom *yang* line of "Hexagram Fu" begins with one thirtieth *yang*, and when it reaches the solar term Dongzhi 冬至 (Winter Solstice) the line emerges to its full extent. Therefore, the tenth month is called *yangyue* 阳月 (*yang* month) probably because the name is thought as making up for the lack of *yang*. This is also true of the change from "Hexagram Gou" 姤 (Coming to Meet) to "Hexagram Kun."

Further question: But ultimately there is the time when *yang* comes to an end. (How do you think?)

Answer: The *yang* ends at the top line of "Hexagram Bo" 剥 (Splitting Apart), while it begins at the bottom line of "Hexagram Fu." During the period between the two ends, there is no time when there is any cease of the change. [Guang]

143 问"喜怒哀乐未发谓之中"。曰:"喜怒哀乐如东西南北,不倚于一方,只是在中间。"又问"和"。曰:"只是合当喜,合当怒。如这事合喜五分,自家喜七八分,便是过其节;喜三四分,便是不及其节。"又问:"'达'字,旧作'感而遂通'字看,而今见得是古今共由意思。"曰:"也是通底意思。如喜怒不中节,便行不得了。而今喜,天下以为合当喜;怒,天下以为合当怒,只是这个道理,便是通达意。'大本、达道',而今不必说得张皇,只将动静看。静时这个便在这里,动时便无不是那底。在人工夫却在'致中和'上。"又问"致"字。曰:"而今略略地中和,也唤做中和。'致'字是要得十分中、十分和。"又问:"看见工夫先须致中?"曰:"这个也大段着脚手不得。若大段着脚手,便是已发了。子思说'戒慎不睹,恐惧不闻',已自是多了,但不得不恁地说,要人会得。只是略略地约住在这里。"又问:"发须中节,亦是倚于一偏否?"曰:"固是。"因说:"周子云:'中也者,和也,天下之达道也。'别人也不敢恁地说。'君子而时中',便是恁地看。"夔孙。以下"致中和"。

When asked about "The state before the feelings of pleasure, anger, sorrow and joy are aroused is called equilibrium," (1) the Master answered, "Pleasure, anger, sorrow and joy are like north, south, east, and west, and equilibrium means being in the center, free from inclination to any one of the four directions." When asked further about "harmony," the Master answered, "It means only that one is joyful when he should be joyful and is angry when he should be angry. For example, if one should be joyful to a five tenth extent, yet he actually is joyful to a seven or eight tenth extent, then he goes beyond what is due in that regard, while, when he is joyful to a three or four tenth extent, he falls short of what is due. " When asked further, "The *da* 达 was explained in the past as meaning that 'which is acted on and penetrates forthwith immediately all phenomena and events,' but at present is understood as meaning being universal, that is, that which is shared by present and past," the Master answered, "It also means unimpeded penetration. For example, if the feelings of pleasure and anger do not act in their due degree, there will be impedance. Now if one feels pleasure when all other people think he should feel pleasure, and he feels anger when all other people think he should feel anger, then that is only the principle at work in unimpeded penetration. As for the 'great root' and 'universal Way,' now you need not see them as something imposing and even frightening, and just see them as referring to tranquility and activity. In tranquility, it dwells there, and in activity, there is no other thing than it that dwells there. However, what calls for your efforts is what is referred to by *zhi zhong he* 致中和 (realizing equilibrium and harmony to the highest degree). (1) " When asked further about the "realize" 致, the Master answered, "Nowadays, the state of a little equilibrium and harmony is also referred to as the state of equilibrium and harmony. But what the 'realize' requires is the full extent of equilibrium and harmony. " When asked further "Should I realize equilibrium to the highest degree before making efforts on what I see and hear?" the Master answered, "In this regard, you should not set about it by making much efforts, for that would mean that your feelings have already been aroused. When Zisi put forth, 'Being cautious over what one does not see and apprehensive over what he does not hear,' (1) he already said too much, but he could not but say that way so that others could understand him. So you can only stick to the state of equilibrium to a little extent. " When asked further "Does 'the feelings must act in their due degree' mean they are inclined to one side?" the Master answered, "Yes, of course." Thereupon the Master added, "Master Zhou Dunyi said, 'The equilibrium is harmony, which is the universal way in the world.' Other scholars dared not say in that way. 'The Superior Man maintains the Mean at any time' (2) can be understood that way." [Kuisun] The following conversations concern "realizing equilibrium and harmony to the highest degree. (1)

144 "致中和"，须兼表里而言。致中，欲其无少偏倚，而又能守之不失；致和，则欲其无少差缪，而又能无适不然。铢。

The "realizing equilibrium and harmony to the highest degree" (1) should be understood as referring to both the outside and the inside. As regards realizing equilibrium to the highest extent, that means one should strive to make sure that it is not only free from any partiality but also is maintained without any fail. As regards realizing harmony to the highest extent, one should strive to make sure that it is not only free from any discordance but also pervasive anywhere. [Zhu]

145 "致中和。"所谓致和者，谓凡事皆欲中节。若致中工夫，如何便到？其始也不能一一常在十字上立地，须有偏过四旁时。但久久纯熟，自别。孟子所谓"存心、养性"，"收其放心"，"操则存"，此等处乃致中也。至于充广其仁义之心等处，乃致和也。人杰。

With regard to "realizing equilibrium and harmony to the highest degree," (1) the so called "realizing equilibrium to the highest extent" means that one's feelings for everything are able to act in their due degree, and as for the effort to realize harmony to the highest extent, how to make it? In the beginning, it is impossible for one to be always able to establish himself to the complete extent in regard to everything, for he must experience some inclination to one or another of the four sides. But after a long time when he gets complete maturity, he will be different naturally. Mencius's "preserve the mind and nourish the nature," (*Mencius*, 4B: 56) "seek for the lost mind," (*Mencius*, 7A：11) "hold onto it fast and it will remain," (*Mencius*, 7A：8), and so on are for realizing equilibrium to the highest extent, while his sayings on enlarging and extending the mind of benevolence and righteousness are concerned with realizing harmony to the highest extent. ［Renjie］

146 周朴纯仁问"致中和"字。曰："'致'字是只管挨排去之义。且如此暖阁，人皆以火炉为中，亦是须要去火炉中寻个至中处，方是的当。又如射箭，才上红心，便道是中，亦未是。须是射中红心之中，方是。如'致和'之'致'，亦同此义。'致'字工夫极精密也。"自修。

Zhou Pu 周朴 (courtesy name Chunren 纯仁, dates unknown, a disciple of Zhu's) asked about "realizing equilibrium and harmony to the highest degree," (1) the Master answered, "The 'realize' means going further degree by degree towards something. For example, for this warm room, you all take the stove as the center, but you have to find the most central point in the stove, so that you can say it is the center in the true sense. Take shooting an arrow for another example. If the arrow hits just a point in the peripheral of the heart marked on the target, it is not proper to say that the arrow hits the center of the target, for only when it gets the center of the heart marked on the target can it be said as hitting the center. The 'realize' in 'realizing harmony to the highest extent' can be understood this way. That 'realize' calls for one making the subtlest effort." ［Zixiu］

147 问："未发之中是浑沦底，发而中节是浑沦底散开。'致中和'，注云：'致者，推而至其极。''致中和'，想也别无用工夫处，只是上戒慎恐惧乎不睹不闻，与慎其独，便是致中和底工夫否？"曰："'致中和'，只是无些子偏倚，无些子乖戾。若大段用倚靠，大段有乖戾底，固不是；有些子倚靠，有些子乖戾，亦未为是。须无些子倚靠，无些子乖戾，方是'致中和'。"至。

Question: The equilibrium before the feelings stir is completely one, while when the feelings stir and act in their due degree the oneness of equilibrium is dispersed (to be many). You, sir, say in your annotation of "realizing equilibrium and harmony to the highest degree," (1) that "The 'realizing' means deducing to the highest extent," I think, there is nowhere for one to make effort, except being cautious and apprehensive over what he does not see and hear and being watchful over his solitude, as said before that in the book. (Is this understanding right?)

Answer: The "realizing equilibrium and harmony to the highest degree" means only that one should keep away from partiality and from perversity. If there is much partiality and much perversity with him, he has not, of course, realized equilibrium and harmony to the highest degree. If there is a little partiality and a little perversity with him, he has not realized equilibrium and harmony to the highest degree, either. Only when he is free from any partiality and perversity can he be said as having realized equilibrium and harmony to the highest degree. [Zhi]

148 存养是静工夫。静时是中，以其无过不及，无所偏倚也。省察是动工夫。动时是和。才有思为，便是动。发而中节无所乖戾，乃和也。其静时，思虑未萌，知觉不昧，乃复所谓"见天地之心"，静中之动也。其动时，发皆中节，止于其则，乃艮之"不获其身，不见其人"，动中之静也。穷理读书，皆是动中工夫。祖道。

To preserve and nourish is to make effort while in tranquility. When there is tranquility, the state is equilibrium, for it is free from going beyond or falling short and from partiality. To retrospect is to make effort while in activity. When there is activity, the state is harmony, for the moment there occurs thinking, there appears activity, and when the feelings are aroused and act in due degree, free from any perversity, they are in harmony. While in tranquility, one does not have any thinking or deliberation, with his consciousness not beclouded, so he can, as "Hexagram Fu" says, "see the mind of Heaven and Earth," which indicates the activity in the tranquility. While in activity, his feelings are aroused and all act in their due degree, which rest in abiding by their rules, so, as "Hexagram Gen" 艮 (Keeping Still, Mountain) says, "He no longer feels his body" and "He does not see his person," indicating the tranquility in the activity. To inquire the principle and read books is to make effort while in activity. [Zudao]

149 问："中有二义：不偏不倚，在中之义也；无过不及，随时取中也。无所偏倚，则无所用力矣。如吕氏之所谓'执'，杨氏之所谓'验'、所谓'体'，是皆欲致力于不偏不倚之时，故先生于或问中辨之最详。然而经文所谓'致中和，则天地位焉，万物育焉'，'致'之一字，岂全无所用其力耶？"曰："致者，推至其极之谓。凡言'致'字，皆此意。如大学之'致知'，论语'学以致其道'，是也。致其中，如射相似，有中贴者，有中垛者，有中红心之边晕者，皆是未致。须是到那中心，方始为致。致和亦然，更无毫厘丝忽不尽，如何便不用力得！"问："先生云：'自戒慎而约之，以至于至静之中，无所偏倚，而其守不失，则天地可位。'所谓'约'者，固异于吕杨所谓'执'、所谓'验'、所谓'体'矣，莫亦只是不放失之意否？"曰："固是不放失，只是要存得。"问："孟子所谓'存其心，养其性'，是此意否？"曰："然。伊川所谓'只平日涵养底便是也'。"枅。偁录云："问'致'字之义。曰'致者，推至其极之谓'云云。问：'吕氏所谓"执"，杨氏所谓"验"、所谓"体"，或问辨之已详。延平却云："默坐澄心，以验夫喜怒哀乐未发之时气象为如何。""验"字莫亦有吕杨之失否？'曰：'它只是要于平日间知得这个，又不是昏昏地都不管也。'"

Question: The *zhong* has two meanings: being impartial, which refers to being in equilibrium (*zai zhong* 在中); being free from going beyond or falling short, which refers to taking the Mean at any time (*shi zhong* 时中). Being impartial is making no exertion. Lü's *zhi* 执 (holding), Yang's *yan* 验 (experiencing) and *ti* 体 (embodying) are all intended to expound the time of impartiality. That is why you, sir, make discrimination of its meanings at the greatest length in your *Questions and Answers*. However, as regards the "When equilibrium and harmony are realized to the highest degree, Heaven and Earth will attain their proper order and all things will flourish"[①] (1) in the text of the book, could it be said that what is referred to by the "realize" calls for no effort at all?

Answer: The "realized" means (being) deduced to the extreme extent. Whenever the word is mentioned, it means that meaning. For example, the *zhi* in *zhizhi* 致知 (extending knowledge) said in *Great Learning* (2) and the *zhi* in *xue yi zhi qi dao* 学以致其道 (learning in order to reach to the utmost of the Way) said in *Analects* (19:7). Realizing equilibrium to its highest degree is akin to shooting an arrow. It may hit the peripheral area of the heart marked on the target, the margin of the target, or the mount where the target is erected. But in all such cases the arrow misses the center of the heart. Only when it gets the central point of the heart can it be said as hitting the center. This is true of realizing harmony, too. They call for making effort without the slightest deficiency. How can it be said that the "realize" calls for no effort at all.

Further question: You, sir, said "One should restrain (*yue* 约) oneself by beginning with being cautious and apprehensive (over what he does see and hear) and strive towards the equilibrium in the supreme tranquility, being free from any partiality and without fail in sticking to it. Then 'Heaven and Earth can attain their proper order.' (1)" The so called *yue* is of course different from Lü's *zhi* and Yang's *yan* and *ti*. Does it only mean not to release and lose?

Answer: It means of course not to release and lose, and to preserve without fail.

---

① The translation of the citation is based on the version of it by Chan Wing-tsit (see *A Source Book in Chinese Philosophy*. Princeton: Princeton University Press, 1963, p. 98).

Further question: Does *Mencius* mean the same when it says "preserve the mind and nourish the nature"?

Answer: Yes. That is also meant by Yichuan when he said "The only thing to do is to cultivate oneself everyday." [Ji]

Xian's record says, "Someone asked about the meaning of the 'realize.' The Master answered, 'The "realized" means (being) deduced to the extreme extent,' and so on. The questioner further asked 'As regards Lü's so called *zhi* and Yang's so called *yan* and *ti*, you make discrimination of them at great length in your *Questions and Answers*. However, Yanping (Li Tong) said, "Sit in silence and keep the mind clear in concentration, and experience what the state is like when the feelings of pleasure, anger, sorrow, and joy are not aroused." Is his "experience" also troubled by the same problem with Lü and Yang?' The Master answered, 'It means only that one should strive to know the state in his daily life rather than be muddleheaded and pay no attention to it.' "

150 或问："致中和，位天地，育万物，与喜怒哀乐不相干，恐非实理流行处。"曰："公何故如此看文字！世间何事不系在喜怒哀乐上？如人君喜一人而赏之，而千万人劝；怒一人而罚之，而千万人惧；以至哀矜鳏寡，乐育英才，这是万物育不是？以至君臣、父子、夫妇、兄弟、朋友、长幼相处相接，无不是这个。即这喜怒中节处，便是实理流行，更去那处寻实理流行！"子蒙。

Someone asked, "The 'When equilibrium and harmony are realized to the highest degree, Heaven and Earth will attain their proper order and all things will flourish,' (1) has nothing to do with the feelings of pleasure, anger, sorrow, and joy. I'm afraid, that is not where the substantial principle flows. (How do you think?)"

The Master answered, "How can you read the sentence that way? What on earth has nothing to do with the feelings of pleasure, anger, sorrow, and joy? For example, when a sovereign feels liking for someone and rewards him, who serves as a model for tens of thousands of others, and when he feels angry against someone else and punishes him, who serves as a warning for tens of thousands of others. Aren't the compassion for widows and widowers and the delight for educating talents part of 'all things will flourish'? Aren't the contacts between sovereign and minister, between father and son, between husband and wife, between brothers, between friends, between old and young, all of whom get along with each other, part of ' all things will flourish'? Where there are feelings of pleasure and anger which act in their due degree, there is the substantial principle flowing. Or else, where can you go and find the flowing substantial principle?" [Zimeng]

151 问："'致中和，天地位焉，万物育焉。'只'君君、臣臣、父父、子子'之分定，便是天地位否?"曰："有地不得其平，天不得其成时。"问："如此，则须专就人主身上说，方有此功用?"曰："规模自是如此。然人各随一个地位去做，不道人主致中和，士大夫便不致中和!"学之为王者事。问："向见南轩上殿文字，多是要扶持人主心术。"曰："也要在下人心术是当，方可扶持得。"问："今日士风如此，何时是太平?"曰："即这身心，亦未见有太平之时。"三公燮理阴阳，须是先有个胸中始得。德明。

Question: As regards "When equilibrium and harmony are realized to the highest degree, heaven and earth will attain their proper order and all things will flourish," (1) if only the proper order of "The sovereign is sovereign, and the minister is minister; the father is father, and the son is son" (*Analects*, 12：11) is established, then can Heaven and Earth be said as attaining their proper order?

Answer: But there is the time when Earth does not get level and Heaven does not get completion.

Further question: Then, is it that, unless it is said only of the sovereign, its function is not that meaningful?

Answer: That is naturally the required scale. Nevertheless, when everyone strives for equilibrium and harmony in his own capacity, it should not be said that only the sovereign can realize them to the highest degree, while the scholar-officials can not realize them to the highest degree. To pursue learning of them (equilibrium and harmony) is to engage in the sovereign's service.

Further question: I once read the words Nanxuan wrote to the throne, most of which were intended to aid the sovereign's intention. (How do you think?)

Answer: Only when the subjects are proper in their intention can they aid their sovereign's intention.

Further question: Nowadays, the common spirits and practices among scholars are in such style. When can there be prevalence of peace and placidity?

Answer: Even in this mind and body, there has never been a time prevalent with peace and placidity. (As said in the *Classic of History*,) the *San Gong* 三公, i. e. *Taishi* 太师 (Grand-Master), *Taifu* 太傅 (Grand-Assistant), and *Taibao* 太保 (Grand-Guardian), were appointed to harmonize (also) and regulate the operations (in nature) of *yin* and *yang*. But unless they, first of all, had a well-thought out order in their mind, they could not fulfill their duties. [Deming]

152 "天地位，万物育"，便是"裁成辅相"，"以左右民"底工夫。若不能"致中和"，则山崩川竭者有矣，天地安得而位！胎夭失所者有矣，万物安得而育！升卿。

The "Heaven and Earth will attain their proper order and all things will flourish" (1) means the efforts to "fashion and complete (the regulations) after the Way of Heaven and Earth and assist the application of them in order to benefit the people." ("Hexagram Tai" 泰 [Peace] in the *Classic of Change*) If equilibrium and harmony can not be realized to the highest degree, there will appear disastrous landslides of mountains and dry-ups of rivers. Then how can Heaven and Earth attain their proper order? And there will be fetal deaths and homeless people. How can all things flourish? [Shengqing]

153 元思问："'致中和，天地位，万物育'，此指在上者而言。孔子如何？"曰："孔子已到此地位。"可学。

Yuansi 元思 (Cai Yuansi 蔡元思, with the courtesy name Niancheng

念成〔dates unknown〕, a disciple of Zhu's) asked, " 'When equilibrium and harmony are realized to the highest degree, Heaven and Earth will attain their proper order and all things will flourish' （1） refers to those top-positioned. How about Confucius?"

The Master answered, "Confucius reached that status. " 〔Kexue〕

154 问："'致中和，天地位，万物育'，此以有位者言。如一介之士，如何得如此?"曰："若致得一身中和，便充塞一身；致得一家中和，便充塞一家；若致得天下中和，便充塞天下。有此理便有此事，有此事便有此理。如'一日克己复礼，天下归仁'。如何一日克己于家，便得天下以仁归之? 为有此理故也。"赐。

Question：The "When equilibrium and harmony are realized to the highest degree, heaven and earth will attain their proper order and all things will flourish" （1） is said with regard to those with high positions. What about one in a low position? How can he realize that?

Answer：If one realizes equilibrium and harmony in himself, he will be imbued with them；if a family realizes equilibrium and harmony in itself, it will be imbued with them；if the world realizes equilibrium and harmony in itself, it will be imbued with them. Where there is such principle, there is such thing, and where there is such thing, there is such principle. For example, "Once a man subdues himself and returns to propriety, all under heaven will ascribe benevolence to him. " （*Analects*, 12：1） Why is it possible that once a man subdues himself so that his family returns to propriety, all under heaven will ascribe benevolence to him? It is because there is such principle. 〔Ci〕

155 "致中和，天地位，万物育"，便是形和气和，则天地之和应。今人不肯恁地说，须要说入高妙处。不知这个极高妙，如何做得到这处。汉儒这几句本未有病，只为说得迫切了，他便说做其事即有此应，这便致得人不信处。佐。

"When equilibrium and harmony are realized to the highest degree,

heaven and earth will attain their proper order and all things will flourish. "
(1) This means, as the Han Confucians said, "To the harmony in form and in vital force, the harmony in Heaven and Earth corresponds. " Nowadays, people are unwilling to say it that way, but rather to claim it as a high and elusive state. However, to that high and elusive state, I do not know how one can make access. Though there is no trouble with the above which the Han Confucians said, the way they put it feels exigent, for their words have been taken for meaning that the moment such and such thing is done there will be such and such response immediately. That is why they have not been believed by later people. [Zuo]

156 问："'静时无一息之不中，则阴阳动静各止其所，而天地于此乎位矣。'言阴阳动静何也？"曰："天高地下，万物散殊，各有定所，此未有物相感也，和则交感而万物育矣。"问："未能致中和，则天地不得而位，只是日食星陨、地震山崩之类否？"曰："天变见乎上，地变动乎下，便是天地不位。"德明。

Question: (In your *Questions and Answers*, you say) "If, in the state of tranquility, there is equilibrium all the time, *yin* and *yang*, activity and tranquility, will rest where it is proper for them to rest, and then Heaven and Earth will attain their proper order. " What is said with regard to the *yin* and *yang*, activity and tranquility in this sentence?

Answer: Heaven is high and Earth is low, and the myriad things take different manifestations, each having its fixed position. In such state, they do not get interacted, but when harmony is realized in them, interaction works among them and they will flourish.

Further question: If equilibrium and harmony are not realized, then Heaven and Earth can not attain their proper order. Is it indicated by such phenomena as the eclipse of the sun and fall of stars, and the earthquakes and landslides?

Answer: The change of Heaven appears in the high and the change of

Earth occurs in the low, and they indicate Heaven and Earth not in their proper order. [Deming]

157 问："'善恶感通之理，亦及其力之所至而止耳。彼达而在上者既日有以病之，则夫灾异之变，又岂穷而在下者所能救也哉？'如此，则前所谓'力'者，是力分之'力'也。"曰："然。"又问："'但能致中和于一身，则天下虽乱，而吾身之天地万物不害为安泰。'且以孔子之事言之，如何是天地万物安泰处？"曰："在圣人之身，则天地万物自然安泰。"曰："此莫是以理言之否？"曰："然。一家一国，莫不如是。"广。

Question: (In your *Questions and Answers*, you say) "The operation of the principle over the good and evil and over things being acted upon mutually and penetrating each other is also subject to the extent which the potency of each of them can reach. If those who are advanced to dignity in the high commit this or that fault daily, which causes disastrous changes, then how can those who are impoverished in the low set them right?" Then, does the so called "potency" mean what an individual is capable of?

Answer: Yes.

Further question: (You also say,) "But if I realize equilibrium and harmony in myself, though the world may be in turmoil, it does not spoil the peace and placidity of Heaven, Earth, and myriad things in me." Take Confucius for example, and how could he illustrate the peace and placidity of Heaven, Earth, and myriad things?

Answer: Since he is a sage, there is naturally the peace and placidity of Heaven, Earth, and myriad things illustrated in him.

Further question: Is it said with regard to the principle?

Answer: Yes. That is true of either a state or a family. [Guang]

158 问："或问所谓'吾身之天地万物'，如何？"曰："尊卑上下之大分，即吾身之天地也；应变曲折之万端，即吾身之万物也。"铢。

Question: In your *Questions and Answers*, you, sir, say "Heaven,

Earth, and myriad things in me." What do you mean?

Answer: The major distinction I make between the honorable and the humble, and between high and low, means the Heaven and Earth in me, while the multifarious cases I handle with their tremendous complexity means the myriad things in me. [Zhu]

卷第一百二十五 Book 125

老氏附庄列
Laozi, with Zhuangzi and Liezi

老子
Laozi

1 康节尝言"老氏得易之体，孟子得易之用"，非也。老子自有老子之体用，孟子自有孟子之体用。"将欲取之，必固与之"，此老子之体用也；存心养性，充广其四端，此孟子之体用也。广。

When Kangjie (posthumous title of Shao Yong) said, "Laozi gained the *ti* 体 (substance) of *yi* 易 (*Classic of Change*), while Mencius gained the *yong* 用 (function) of *yi*," he was wrong, for either Laozi or Mencius gained his own substance and function of it. "When one is going to despoil another, he will first have made gifts to him,"[1] (*Laozi*, 36) indicates the substance and function in the possession of Laozi, while preserving the mind and nourish the nature, and extending and enlarging the four beginnings (of benevolence, righteousness, propriety, and wisdom) manifest the substance and function in the possession of Mencius. [Guang]

2 老子之术，谦冲俭啬，全不肯役精神。闳祖。

In Laozi's pursuit, he kept himself modest and stingy, completely

---

① The translation of the citations from *Laozi* (also named *Dao De Jing* 道德经) in this fascicle is based on the version rendered by J. Legge (seehttp://ctext.org/dao-de-jing), with some alterations.

unwilling to give play to his spirits. [Hongzu]

3 老子之术，须自家占得十分稳便，方肯做；才有一毫于己不便，便不肯做。闳祖。

When Laozi pursued something, he would not engage in doing it unless he would take all the benefits therefrom, and he would be unwilling to do it if he found an iota of inconvenience to him therein. [Hongzu]

4 老子之学，大抵以虚静无为、冲退自守为事。故其为说，常以懦弱谦下为表，以空虚不毁万物为实。其为治，虽曰"我无为而民自化"，然不化者则亦不之问也。其为道每每如此，非特"载营魄"一章之指为然也。若曰"旁月日，扶宇宙，挥斥八极，神气不变"者，是乃庄生之荒唐；其曰"光明寂照，无所不通，不动道场，遍周沙界"者，则又瞿昙之幻语，老子则初曷尝有是哉！今世人论老子者，必欲合二家之似而一之，以为神常载魄而无所不之，则是庄释之所谈，而非老子之意矣。偶。

In his learning, Laozi, largely speaking, emphasized *xu* 虚 (void), *jing* 静 (quietness), and *wuwei* 无为 (doing nothing), and was given to humility and self-conservation. Therefore, his theory was inclined to feature cowardice and lowliness on its surface and void and restraint from detriment of the myriad things in its essence. As for the way of ruling, though he claimed "I will do nothing (of purpose), and the people will be transformed of themselves," (57) he was not concerned about them when they were not transformed. That is the way he always took to, which is not shown only in the tenth chapter opened with *zai ying po* 载营魄 (When the intelligent and animal souls are held together). (10) If it is said that "(The Perfect Man) flies close to the sun and the moon, keeping the universe up, and soars untrammeled among the eight ultimate ends, without any change coming over his spirit or his breath," it exposes the sort of preposterousness Zhang Zhou 庄周 (i. e. Zhuangzi) was known for, and if it is said that "The light and bright permeates in stillness everything, never obstructed in any way, and the immovable seat of Daoism pervades all places, countless like sand,"① it is nothing but illusory images described by Gautama's words. However, was there anything like these in *Laozi* at first? Nowadays when people talked about *Laozi*, they were eager to mix up the doctrine of Buddhism with *Laozi* and made *Laozi* seem to contain it as one, but when one claims that the spirit holds the soul and goes everywhere, he merely reiterates something talked about often by Zhuangzi and Buddhists, rather than what was originally meant by Laozi. 〔Xian〕

5 伯丰问："程子曰'老子之言窃弄阖辟'者，何也?"曰："如'将欲取之，必固与之'之类，是它亦窥得些道理，将来窃弄。如所谓'代大匠斫则伤手'者，谓如人之恶者，不必自去治它，自有别人与它理会。只是占便宜，不肯自犯手做。"曶曰："此正推恶离己。"曰："固是。如子房为韩报秦，撺掇高祖入关，及项羽杀韩王成，又使高祖平项羽，两次报仇皆不自做。后来定太子事，它亦自处闲地，又只教四老人出来定之。"曶。

Bofeng (courtesy name of Wu Bida) asked, "Why did Master Cheng Hao say 'What Laozi said is playing with the closing and opening of words'?" The Master answered, "For example, when Laozi said, 'When one is going to despoil another, he will first have made gifts to him' (*Laozi*, 36) and the like, they indicate he peeped at some truths, yet he took them over and played with them. His 'Seldom is it that one who undertakes the hewing, instead of the masterly carpenter, does not cut his own hands!' means that if one sees some evil on the part of another, he should never bother himself with redressing it, for there will naturally be someone else who will set it right. So he only intended to profit from things in one way or another, rather than was willing to set about taking trouble to do things

---

① In terms of Buddhism, the sentence may read, "The light and bright permeates in stillness everything, never obstructed in any way, and the immovable Bodhimanda pervades all places, countless like the sand of the Ganges".

personally. " I said, "What he did is pushing evils away from himself. " The Master responded, "It is, of course. For example, Zifang 子房 (courtesy name of Zhang Liang 张良, 250 – 186 BC), in order to get revenge against the state of Qin 秦 for the state of Han 韩, incited Liu Bang, the later Emperor Gaozu of Han 汉, to attack Qin troops via Wuguan Pass, and then, after Xiang Yu 项羽 (232 – 202 BC) killed Cheng, King of Han 韩, he urged Liu to attack Xiang. He was a successful avenger in these two cases, yet he got revenge by leveraging rather than by doing it himself. Later, when dealing with the matter of the crown prince, Zhang did not get himself involved therein, but rather advised that the four aged worthies Liu admired yet had failed to recruit be enquired and entrusted for that. " [Xun]

6 老子不犯手，张子房其学也。陶渊明亦只是老庄。

Laozi did not get involved in doing things, and Zhang Zifang followed his way. Tao Yuanming 陶渊明 (i. e. Tao Qian 陶潜 [352 – 427]) was also only a follower of Laozi and Zhuangzi.

7 问：“杨氏爱身，其学亦浅近，而举世宗尚之，何也？”曰：“其学也不浅近，自有好处，便是老子之学。今观老子书，自有许多说话，人如何不爱！其学也要出来治天下，清虚无为，所谓‘因者君之纲’，事事只是因而为之。如汉文帝曹参，便是用老氏之效，然又只用得老子皮肤，凡事只是包容因循将去。老氏之学最忍，它闲时似个虚无卑弱底人，莫教紧要处发出来，更教你枝梧不住，如张子房是也。子房皆老氏之学。如峣关之战，与秦将连和了，忽乘其懈击之；鸿沟之约，与项羽讲和了，忽回军杀之，这个便是他柔弱之发处。可畏！可畏！它计策不须多，只消两三次如此，高祖之业成矣。”僴。

When asked, "Yang Zhu 杨朱 (dates unknown) treasured only himself and his learning was also plain and shallow, yet he was adored and followed across the kingdom. Why?" the Master answered, "His learning was not shallow, for it had its own merits, a continuation of Laozi's learning. Now, when we read *Laozi*, we can find many insightful sayings in it, so why has it not been popular among people? His learning is also intended to aid ruling the country, which advocates pure void 清虚 and non-action 无为, and it is the so called 'to make the best of it is the basic rule for a ruler to abide by,' meaning, in doing anything, one should guide himself along the natural course of its development. For example, Emperor Wen of Han and Cao Can 曹参（? –190BC）adopted the principles advocated by Laozi, yet they applied only the superficial of them, for they did nothing but carrying on old rules and practices in doing things. What the learning of Laozi sets store by is forbearance, and a follower of him would appear weak and humble at ordinary times, but when he breaks out at some critical moments, he is hard to cope with. A typical follower of Laozi is Zhang Zifang, who pursued nothing but the learning of Laozi. In the Yaoguan Pass warfare（207 BC）, Liu Bang entered into collusion with the Qin general keeping the pass, yet he had his troops to attack the general when his men were slack. In 203 BC when Liu Bang made peace with Xiang Yu, he broke their agreement later and attacked Xiang when Xiang was in a precarious condition. In both cases, Liu adopted Zhang's ideas, which illustrates the outbreak of his seemingly weakness. How awful! How horrible! He did not need many stratagems, for by using only a couple of them he helped Liu Bang to be Emperor Gaozu of Han!" [Xian]

8 问："杨朱似老子，顷见先生如此说。看来杨朱较放退，老子反要以此治国，以此取天下。"曰："大概气象相似。如云'致虚极，守静笃'之类，老子初间亦只是要放退，未要放出那无状来。及至反一反，方说'以无事取天下'，如云'反者道之动，弱者道之用'之类。"㑇。

Question: Yang Zhu resembled Laozi. You, sir, said that just now. It seems that Yang was more detached from statecraft, whereas Laozi drove at the rule of a state and thereby taking over the whole kingdom. (How do you think?)

Answer: They are similar in their miens. For example, as regards "The (state of) vacancy should be brought to the utmost degree and that of stillness, guarded with unwearying vigor" (16) and the like, they indicate Laozi's inclination only to detachedness at first, manifesting nothing of that kind of scheme. It is only in the later parts of the text that he mentioned "taking over the whole kingdom by freedom from action and purpose," (57) and such things as "The movement of the Way // By contraries proceeds; // And weakness marks the course // Of the Way's mighty deeds." (40) [Xian].

9 杨朱之学出于老子，盖是杨朱曾就老子学来，故庄列之书皆说杨朱。孟子辟杨朱，便是辟庄老了。释氏有一种低底，如梁武帝是得其低底。彼初入中国，也未在。后来到中国，却窃取老庄之徒许多说话，见得尽高。新唐书李蔚赞说得好。南升。

Yangzhu's learning issued from Laozi. Since he was probably a student of Laozi, he was talked about in both *Zhuangzi* and *Liezi*. When Mencius negated him, it means he denied *Zhuangzi* and *Laozi*. Buddhism held a low doctrine and Emperor Wu of Liang (464 – 549) learned that low doctrine. When Buddhism came to the central kingdom (*Zhongguo* 中国), its theory did not go well, but later it stole much discourse from the followers of *Laozi* and *Zhuangzi* and blended it with its original theory, so the Buddhists' doctrine appears much insightful. The section "Eulogy" of "Biography of Li Wei" presented in *Xin Tangshu* 新唐书 (New Book of Tang) says that well. [Nansheng]

10 人皆言孟子不排老子，老子便是杨氏。

They all say Mencius did not reject Laozi, yet Laozi was Yang (in terms of their learnings).

11 问：“老子与乡原如何?”曰：“老子是出人理之外，不好声，不好色，又不做官，然害伦理。乡原犹在人伦中，只是个无见识底好人。”淳。

Question：What is the difference between Laozi and *xiangyuan* 乡原?

Answer：Laozi was outside the human principles, with neither liking for good sounds and good looks, nor going after any official post, but to the detriment of human ethic relations. As for *xiangyuan*, it refers to a type of people, good yet ignorant. [Chun（淳）]

12 老子中有仙意。

Laozi smacks of some celestial sense.

列子

Liezi

13 列子平淡疏旷。方子。

Liezi reads plain, distant, and broad. [Fangzi]

庄子

Zhuangzi

14“庄周曾做秀才，书都读来，所以他说话都说得也是。但不合没拘检，便凡百了。”或问：“康节近似庄周？”曰：“康节较稳。”焘。

The Master said，“When young，Zhuang Zhou was a talented learner and read all the classic works in his time，so when he talked about something，he was also right. However，he should not have conducted himself with little self-restraint，and detached himself from everything.” Someone asked，“Does Kangjie resemble Zhuang Zhou?” The Master answered，“Kangjie is steadier.” [Tao]

15 庄子比邵子见较高，气较豪。他是事事识得，又却蹴踏了，以为不足为。邵子却有规矩。方子。

Zhuangzi manifests more vision in his views and more boldness in his mien than Shaozi（Shao Yong）. He sees through everything，yet treads it away, thinking that it is not worth doing. By contrast, Shaozi has his own rules (over his doing things). [Fangzi]

16 李梦先问：“庄子孟子同时，何不一相遇？又不闻相道及，林作：‘其书亦不相及。’如何？”曰：“庄子当时也无人宗之，他只在僻处自说，然亦止是杨朱之学。但杨氏说得大了，故孟子力排之。”义刚。

Li Mengxian 李梦先（dates unknown, a disciple of Zhu's）asked, "Zhuangzi and Mencius were contemporaries, and why did they not meet? And they were never heard mentioning each other? Why?" The Master answered, "In his time what Zhuangzi did is forming his doctrine while staying at some secluded place, with no one else following him as his student. His doctrine, however, was only built on that of Yangzhu. When Yang's doctrine got influential widely, Mencius tried hard to repudiate it." [Yigang]

17 问：“孟子与庄子同时否？”曰：“庄子后得几年，然亦不争多。”或云：“庄子都不说着孟子一句。”曰：“孟子平生足迹只齐鲁滕宋大梁之间，不曾过大梁之南。庄子自是楚人，想见声闻不相接。大抵楚地便多有此样差异底人物学问，所以孟子说陈良云云。”曰：“如今看许行之说如此鄙陋，当时亦有数十百人从他，是如何？”曰：“不特此也，如庄子书中说惠施邓析之徒，与夫‘坚白异同’之论，历举其说。是甚么学问？然亦自名家。”或云：“他恐是借此以显理？”曰：“便是禅家要如此。凡事须要倒说，如所谓‘不管夜行，投明要到’；如‘人上树，口衔树枝，手足悬空，却要答话’，皆是此意。”广云：“通鉴中载孔子顺与公孙龙辩说数话，似好。”曰：“此出在孔丛子，其它说话又不如此。此书必是后汉时人撰者。若是古书，前汉时又都不见说是如何。其中所载孔安国书之类，其气象萎薾，都不似西京时文章。”广。

Someone asked, "Were Mencius and Zhuangzi contemporaries?" The Master answered, "Zhuangzi was later for a number of years, but not many." Someone else asked, "Zhuangzi did not mention anything of Mencius.

（Why？）" The Master replied, "In his life, Mencius moved in the region where the states of Qi, Lu, Teng and Song, and Daliang, the capital of the state of Wei were（in the Warring States period）, but he never went as far as the south to Daliang. Zhuangzi was a native from the state of Chu, to the south of that region. It is easy to imagine that what they said and heard were quite far from each other. Probably, in the region of Chu, there were many people like Zhuangzi, who pursued a different learning. That is why Mencius mentioned Chen Liang 陈良① and so on. " The latter questioner asked further, "Today, we see the theory of Xu Xing 许行（372 – 289 BC）as so mean and coarse, but in his days he had almost a hundred followers. Why?" The Master answered, "His was not the only case in that period of time. *Zhuangzi* mentions Hui Shi 惠施（370 – 310 BC）, Deng Xi 邓析（545 – 501 BC）, and the like, and the debate on 'the sameness of and difference between the hardness and the whiteness of a white rock,' and states their theories one by one. What kinds of learning were theirs? Nonetheless, they each earned their names and fames. " Someone else asked, "Did they, I'm afraid, intend to make clear the truth by that?" The Master answered, "That is the way Buddhists choose to take. For example, whatever they say, they must bring it forth in inverse order, like their 'One is not allowed to walk at night, but required to reach his destination at daybreak,'② and 'One is made to clime a tree and use his mouth to hold a branch of it, with his hands and feet hanging in the air, but required to answer a question verbally. '" I said, "In the *Zizhi Tongjian* 资治通鉴（Comprehensive Mirror to Aid in Government, compiled by Sima Guang）is recorded the debate between Kong Zishun 孔子

---

① As said in the *Mencius*（3A: 4）, "Chen Liang was a native of Chu. Pleased with the doctrines of Duke of Zhou and Confucius, he came northwards to the Middle Kingdom and studied them. "

② As regards the Buddhist sense of the sentence, see Cheng Xun, "Chanyu shidu: buxu yexing, touming xudao" 禅语释读: 不许夜行, 投明须到. *Journal of Southeast University*, 2010（S1）.

顺（dates unknown, sixth generation grandson of Confucius）and Gongsun Long 公孙龙（320 – 250 BC）, which seems good. " The Master replied, " It came from *Kongcongzi* 孔丛子, which reads stylistically different from other parts in the book. *Kongcongzi* must have been written by someone in Eastern Han Dynasty（25 – 220）, and it was not an ancient book before that period, for it had never been mentioned in Western Han Dynasty（206 BC- AD 24）. That can be further evidenced by the parts of Kong Anguo 孔安国（156 – 74 BC, eleventh generation grandson of Confucius）in it, which smack of much lethargy, quite different from the writings composed in the Western Capital period（i. e. the period of Western Han Dynasty）. " ［Guang］

老庄

Laozi and Zhuangzi

18 老子犹要做事在。庄子都不要做了，又却说道他会做，只是不肯做。广。

Laozi still went in for some affairs, whereas Zhuangzi did nothing whatsoever, yet claimed he was capable of everything, though unwilling to do it. ［Guang］

19 "庄周是个大秀才，他都理会得，只是不把做事。观其第四篇人间世及渔父篇以后，多是说孔子与诸人语，只是不肯学孔子，所谓'知者过之'者也。如说'易以道阴阳，春秋以道名分'等语，后来人如何下得！它直是似快刀利斧劈截将去，字字有着落。"公晦曰："庄子较之老子，较平帖些。"曰："老子极劳攘，庄子得些，只也乖。庄子跌荡。老子收敛，齐脚敛手；庄子却将许多道理掀翻说，不拘绳墨。方子录云："庄子是一个大秀才，他事事识得。如天下篇后面乃是说孔子，似用快刀利斧斫将去，更无些碍，且无一句不着落。如说'易以道阴阳'等语，大段说得好，然却不肯如此做去。老子犹是欲敛手齐脚去做，他却将他寰宇一齐踢翻了！"庄子去孟子不远，其说不及孟子者，亦是不相闻。今亳州明道宫乃老子所生之地。庄子生于蒙，在淮西间。孟子只往来齐宋邹鲁，以至于梁而止，不至于南。然当时南方多是异端，如孟子所谓'陈良，楚产也，悦周公仲尼之道，北学于中国'；又如说'南蛮鴃舌之人，非先王之道'，是当时南方多异端。"或问：'许行恁地低，也有人从之。"曰："非独是许行，如公孙龙'坚白同异'之说，是甚模样？也使得人终日只弄这个。"汉卿问："孔子顺许多话却好。"曰："出于孔丛子，不知是否？只孔丛子说话，多类东汉人文，其气软弱，又全不似西汉人文。兼西汉初若有此等话，何故不略见于贾谊董仲舒所述？恰限到东汉方突出来？皆不可晓。"贺孙。

The Master said, "Zhuang Zhou was highly talented, and he understood everything well, but he did not do anything. When we read the 'Man in the World' in the fourth chapter and 'The Old Fisherman' in the 'Miscellaneous Chapters' of *Zhuangzi*, we find they are mainly concerned with what Confucius and some others said, yet he was unwilling to take Confucius for an example. That is what is meant by 'The knowing goes beyond it.' (*Doctrine of the Mean*, 4) For example, he said 'The *Yi* 易 (*Classic of Change*) is intended to show the action of the *yin* and *yang*; and *Chunqiu* 春秋 (*The Spring and Autumn Annals*), to display names and the duties belonging to them.' Who of the later scholars could say that? His style is like a sharp knife or axe cutting something neat and tidy, and in his writing, every sino-graph is well-positioned." Gonghui said, "In contrast to Laozi, Zhuangzi is steadier and more appropriate." The Master responded, "Laozi is rather laborious and fidgety, while Zhuangzi is a little more moderate, yet only quick-witted. Laozi is more self-restraining, and stands straight, holding his hands and feet back, while Zhuangzi is more unconventional, and overturns many truths when talking about them in a unrestrained manner. Fangzi's record reads, 'Zhuangzi was a great talent, who knew everything. For example, when he talked about Confucius in the later sections of "Under the Heaven" (in the "Miscellaneous Chapters" of *Zhuangzi*), his style reads like a sharp knife or axe cutting something well, with little obstruction, and every one of his sentences is well positioned. For example, his sayings such as "The *Yi* is intended to show the action of the *yin* and *yang*," are made very well, but he is unwilling to do anything as he says. By contrast, Laozi seems to do something yet hold his hands and feet back, while Zhuangzi, so to speak, kicks over all those conventions. ' Zhuangzi was only a little later than Mencius, yet he did not mention anything about Mencius in his writings, and it is probably because they did not hear about each other. The area where Mingdao (Daoist) Temple sits today is the birthplace of Laozi (in the Spring and Autumn period). Zhuangzi was born in Meng (in the Warring States period), which is located now in western Huainan (in Anhui at present). Mencius spent his life in the region of the Qi, Song, Zou, and Lu states, and never went beyond Liang and reached the south of it (in the Warring States period). At that time, there were many heresies in the south, and as said in *Mencius* (3A: 4), 'Chen Liang was a native of Chu. Pleased with the doctrines of Duke of Zhou and Confucius, he came northwards to the Middle Kingdom and studied them,' and 'Now there are those shrike-tongued barbarians of the south, whose doctrines are not those of the ancient kings. ' Thus, the south then was replete with heresies. " Someone asked, "Xu Xing's theory was rather base, but there were still many followers of him. (Why?)" The Master answered, "His theory was only one of those in that type. For example, Gongsun Long's discourse 'sameness and difference' and 'hardness and whiteness,' and what theory it is? That, actually, attracted many people who set their mind to it. " Hanqing asked, "Much of what Kong Zishun said reads well. (Why?)" The Master answered, "I do not know for sure whether it is cited from *Kongcongzi*. But the verbal style of *Kongcongzi* reads like that languidness prevalent among the scholars in Eastern Han Dynasty, completely different from that style characterizing Western Han Dynasty. Besides, if it was written in the beginning years of Western Han, why was it never mentioned in the writings by Jia Yi 贾谊

(200 – 168 BC) or Dong Zhongshu 董仲舒 (179 – 104 BC), and why did it happen that it was given salience to only in Eastern Han? We can by no means answer such questions. " [Hesun] The 17th conversation afore-presented was probably recorded by Guang on the same occasion as this one.

20 问："老子与庄子似是两般说话。"曰："庄子于篇末自说破矣。"问："先儒论老子，多为之出脱，云老子乃矫时之说。以某观之，不是矫时，只是不见实理，故不知礼乐刑政之所出，而欲去之。"曰："渠若识得'寂然不动，感而遂通天下之故'，自不应如此。它本不知下一节，欲占一简径言之；然上节无实见，故亦不脱洒。今读老子者亦多错。如道德经云'名非常名'，则下文有名、无名，皆是一义，今读者皆将'有、无'作句。又如'常无欲，以观其妙；常有欲，以观其窍'，只是说'无欲、有欲'，今读者乃以'无、有'为句，皆非老子之意。"可学。

Question: Laozi and Zhuangzi seem quite different in their verbal styles. (How do you think?)

Answer: In the ending part of his writing, Zhuangzi revealed his own point by himself.

Further question: When the previous Confucians commented on Laozi, they tended to vindicate him, saying his book as a work for rectifying the problems in his time, but in my opinion it is not for that purpose, but rather for abolishing all the rites, music, punishment and governance because he did not see the substantial principle and thus was ignorant of the reason why those institutions were practiced. (How do you think?)

Answer: If he had known "It is still and without movement; but, when acted on, it penetrates forthwith all phenomena and events in the world," ("Appended Remarks" I of the *Classic of Change*) he would not have been like that naturally. Though he did not know originally what would come in the next section, he desired to take a whole bamboo slip to write it on directly, but due to the preceding section devoid of any substantial opinion, his writing here was not easy. Nowadays when people read his book, they have misunderstood it often, too. For example, *Dao De Jing* 道德经 (Classic of the Way and Its Power, i. e. *Laozi*) says, "Ming fei chang ming" 名非常名, and the *youming* 有名 and *wuming* 无名 after that mean the same meaning, but the readers today all have taken the sino-graphs *you* and *wu* for the markers of two separate clauses. For another example, his "Chang wu yu, yi guan qi miao; chang you yu, yi guan qi qiao" (常无欲, 以观其妙; 常有欲, 以观其窍)① says only of *wuyu* 无欲 (having no desire) and *youyu* 有欲 (having desire), but the readers all have seen *wu* and *you* as markers of separate clauses. However, what they have got is not what Laozi intended to say at all. [Kexue]

21 庄子老子不是矫时。夷惠矫时, 亦未是。可学。

Neither Zhuangzi nor Laozi wrote their words to set right the problems in their times. To say Yi (Boyi 伯夷, dates unknown) and Hui (Liuxia Hui 柳下惠, 720 – 621 BC), both men of integrity, as setting the problems in their times, is not right, either. [Kexue]

庄列
Zhuangzi and Liezi

22 孟子庄子文章皆好。列子在前, 便有迂僻处。左氏亦然, 皆好高而少事实。人杰。

Both Mencius and Zhuangzi were good at writing. Liezi, who was earlier than them, was somewhat pedantic and eccentric. So was Zuo (i. e. Zuo Qiuming 左丘明, 502 – 422 BC). They both were liable to have their heads

---

① The *qiao* 窍 (aperture) is *jiao* 徼 (outer fringe) according to the more often adopted edition of *Dao De Jing*, where the 常無欲, 以觀其妙; 常有欲, 以觀其徼 is rendered by J. Legge into "Always without desire we must be found, // If its deep mystery we would sound; // But if desire always within us be, // Its outer fringe is all that we shall see." (See https: //ctext. org/dao-de-jing)

in the clouds and fell short in factuality. 〔Renjie〕

23 因言，列子语，佛氏多用之。庄子全写列子，又变得峻奇。列子语温纯，柳子厚尝称之。佛家于心地上煞下工夫。贺孙。

Thereupon the Master said, "What Liezi had said was often cited in Buddhists' writings. Zhuangzi wrote completely on Liezi, yet his style became aloof and peculiar. Liezi's writing style is mild and pure, and Liu Zihou 柳子厚（i. e. Liu Zongyuan 柳宗元, 773 – 819）once praised it. The Buddhists tend to make tremendous effort in the heart-mind. " 〔Hesun〕

24 列庄本杨朱之学，故其书多引其语。庄子说："子之于亲也，命也，不可解于心。"至臣之于君，则曰："义也，无所逃于天地之间。"是他看得那君臣之义，却似是逃不得，不奈何，须着臣服他。更无一个自然相胥为一体处，可怪! 故孟子以为无君，此类是也。大雅。

Liezi and Zhuangzi followed the learning of Yangzhu, so in their writings, they often quoted Yang. Zhuangzi said, "The love of a son for his parents is the implanted requirement, and can never be separated from his heart-mind. " and with regard to a minister in relation to his sovereign, he said, "The service of his sovereign by a minister is what is required by righteousness, and from its obligation, there is no escaping anywhere between heaven and earth. " ("Man in the World" in *Zhuangzi*) As he saw it, the righteousness between a minister and his sovereign is inescapable and the minister can not but serve his sovereign, and furthermore, there is no naturally interactive union between them. That is bizarre, indeed! Therefore, when Mencius criticized his want of acknowledgement of the sovereign, he pointed to that type of his discourse. 〔Daya〕

老庄列子
Laozi, Zhuangzi, and Liezi

25 庄子是个转调底。老子列子又细似庄子。

Zhuangzi switched his writing style from those before him. Both Laozi and Liezi were more exquisite than Zhuangzi in their writing styles.

26 "雷击所在，只一气滚来，间有见而不为害，只缘气未揪裂，有所击者皆是已发。"蔡季通云："人于雷所击处，收得雷斧之属，是一气击后方始结成，不是将这个来打物。见人拾得石斧如今斧之状，似细黄石。"因说道士行五雷法。先生曰："今极卑陋是道士，许多说话全乱道。"蔡云："禅家又胜似他。"曰："禅家已是九分乱道了，他又把佛家言语参杂在里面。如佛经本自远方外国来，故语音差异，有许多差异字，人都理会不得；他便撰许多符咒，千般万样，教人理会不得，极是陋。"蔡云："道士有个庄老在上，却不去理会。"曰："如今秀才读多少书，理会自家道理不出，他又那得心情去理会庄老！"蔡云："无人理会得老子通透，大段鼓动得人，恐非佛教之比。"曰："公道如何？"蔡云："缘他带治国、平天下道理在。"曰："做得出，也只是个曹参。"蔡云："曹参未能尽其术。"曰："也只是恁地，只是藏缩无形影。"因问蔡曰："公看'道可道，非常道；名可名，非常名；无名天地之始，有名万物之母'，是如何说？"蔡云："只是无名是天地之始，有名便是有形气了。向见先生说庚桑子一篇都是禅，今看来果是。"曰："若其它篇，亦自有禅话，但此篇首尾都是这话。"又问蔡曰："庄子'虚无因应'，如何点？"曰："只是恁地点。""多有人将'虚无'自做一句，非是。他后面又自解如何是无，如何是因。"又云："庄子文章只信口流出，煞高。"蔡云："列子亦好。"曰："列子固好，但说得困弱，不如庄子。"问："老子如何？"曰："老子又较深厚。"蔡云："看庄周传说，似乎庄子师于列子。云先有作者如此，恐是指列子。"曰："这自说道理，未必是师列子。"蔡问："'皆原于道德之意'，是谁道德？"曰："这道德只自是他道德。"蔡云："人多作吾圣人道德。太史公智识卑下，便把这处作非细看，便把作大学中庸看了。"曰："大学中庸且过一边，公恁地说了，主张史记人道如何？大凡看文字只看自家心下，先自偏曲了，看人说甚么事，都只入这意来。如大路看不见，只行下偏蹊曲径去。如分明大字不看，却只看从罅缝四旁处去。如字写在上面不看。却就字背后面看。如人眼自花了，看见眼前物事都差了，便说道只恁地。"蔡云："不平心看文字，将使天地都易位了。"曰："道理只是这一个道理，但看之者情伪变态，言语文章自有千般万样。合说东，却说西；合说这里，自说那里；都是将自家偏曲底心求古人意。"又云："如太史公说话，也怕古人有这般人，只自家心下不当如此。将临川何言江默之事观之，说道公羊谷梁是姓姜人一手做，也有这般事。尚书序不似孔安国作，其文软弱，不似西汉人文，西汉文粗豪；也不似东汉人文，东汉人文有骨肋；也不似东晋人文，东晋如孔坦疏也自得。他文是大段弱，读来却宛顺，是做孔丛子底人一手做。看孔丛子撰许多说话，极是陋。只看他撰造说陈涉，那得许多说话正史都无之？他却说道自好，陈涉不能从之。看他文卑弱，说到后面，都无合杀。"蔡云："恐是孔家子孙。"曰："也不见得。"蔡说："春秋吕氏解煞好。"曰："那个说不好？如一句经在这里，说做褒也得，也有许多说话；做贬也得，也有许多说话，都自说得似。"又云："如史记秦纪分明是国史，中间尽谨严。若如今人把来生意说，也都由他说，春秋只是旧史录在这里。"蔡云："如先生做通鉴纲目，是有意？是无意？须是有去取。如春秋，圣人岂无意？"曰："圣人虽有意，今亦不可知，却妄为之说，不得。"蔡云："左氏怕是左史倚相之后，盖左传中楚事甚详。"曰："以三传较之，在左氏得七八分。"蔡云："道理则谷梁及七八分。或云，三传中间有许多骩处，都是其学者后来添入。"贺孙。

The Master said, "When a thunder strikes somewhere, it is a ball of material force 气 rolling fleetingly down to hit it. But sometimes it is seen, yet without striking, which does no harm. It is only because the ball of material force does not break up. Whenever there is striking, it is caused by its breaking up before that." Cai Jitong replied, "Some people have found 'thunder axes' and the like in the places struck by thunders. They are formed after a place is hit by a ball of material force, rather than used to strike things. I once saw the stone axe found by someone, which appeared like the shape of the axe we use today, and its texture is like that of fine yellow stone. " Thereupon, they talked about the Daoists' practice of the Five Thunder Magic. The Master said, "Nowadays, the most vulgar and abject are the Daoists, much of whose discourse is completely nonsensical. " Cai replied, "The Chan Buddhists are more so. " The Master said then, "The Chan Buddhists have already been nonsensical to the nine-tenth extent, yet the Daoists have gone so far as to mix the Buddhists' discourse into theirs. The Buddhist sutras came from distant foreign lands and their words are pronounced differently. Their translated versions contain many words too weird to be understood. Drawing on them, the Daoists concoct many figures in multifarious forms, inscrutable to other people, which are monstrously shabby. " Cai said, "Laozi and Zhuangzi are the founders of the Daoists' doctrine, but the Daoists do not try to understand well what they said. " The Master responded, "Nowadays, how many books have the *Xiucai* 秀才 (scholars who passed the imperial examination at the county level) read? They have not read out even the principles they should have understood. How can they be expected to turn to Laozi and Zhuangzi?" Cai said, "None of them have understood *Laozi* thoroughly, and since it is quite inciting, I'm afraid, it is incomparable to Buddhist sutras. " The Master, "Why do you think so?" Cai answered, "Because it contains the principles for ruling a state and bringing peace to the empire. " The Master replied, "Even if Laozi could have done it, he would, at best, have been a Cao Can who followed the established rules. " Cai responded, "Cao Can failed to give full play to his competence. " The Master said, "He could only do that much, hiding himself and leaving no trace of his own. " Thereupon the Master asked Cai, "How do you understand the opening sentences of *Dao De Jing*, that is, 'Dao ke dao, fei chang dao; ming ke ming, fei chang ming; wu ming tian di zhi shi, you ming wan wu zhi mu' (道可道，非常 ming; wu ming tian di zhi shi, you ming wan wu zhi mu'（道可道，非常

道；名可名，非常名；无名天地之始，有名万物之母）①?" Cai answered, "It says that *wuming* 无名 is the beginning of heaven and earth, while *youming* 有名 indicates the form and material force coming into being. I once heard you say that the whole piece of 'Gengsangzi' 庚桑子 (written by Gengsangzi 庚桑子 [dates unknown], believed as a disciple of Laozi) in *Zhuangzi* is filled with the meaning of Buddhist Chan 禅. Seen today, it is, indeed." The Master went on saying, "The other pieces in *Zhuangzi* also contain more or less meaning of Chan, but this piece reads like that from its beginning to its end." The Master further asked Cai, "How do you punctuate *xu wu yin ying* 虚无因应② of *Zhuangzi*?" Cai answered, "It can only be taken as a sentence." The Master responded, "Many take *xuwu* 虚无 as a separate sentence, who are not right. After the four sino-graphs, Zhuangzi goes on to explain by himself what the *wu* 无 and *yin* 因 mean respectively." He continued, "The words of Zhuangzi just flew casually from his mouth, but they were indicative of quite a master-hand." Cai said, "*Liezi* is also well-written." The Master replied, "True that *Liezi* is also well-written, but its style is languid, not as good as *Zhuangzi*." When asked, "What about *Laozi*?" the Master answered, "*Laozi* is more profound." Cai said, "According to the biography of Zhuang Zhou, it seems that Zhuangzi was a student of Liezi. The biography says that there might be such and such writer before him, and, I'm afraid, the writer refers to Liezi." The Master replied,

---

① There are hundreds of English translations of *Laozi*. For the translation of the opening sentences of the book, Wang Hongyin 王宏印 compares several versions by both Chinese and English translators, and proposes an interpretive rendering, which reads, "Ontologically, *Dao* is inexpressible. Whatever we say about it, it is not the *Dao* as it is. Whatever we name it, it isn't, either, nor are all other things or concepts, for not all things or concepts could be properly named, and names are not what they name." (See *Xin Yixue Lungao* 新译学论稿 [Fresh Explorations into New Translation Studies], China Renmin University Press, 2011, pp. 82–96)

② The speaker might have made a mistake in giving the source of the quoted *xu wu yin ying* 虚无因应, which is not found in the text of *Zhuangzi* and that of *Laozi*. It is found in *The Records of the Grand Historian*.

"That says of the possibility, but the writer does not necessarily refer to Liezi." Cai asked, "As regards ' All is originated from the meaning of *Dao De*' said in *Shiji* 史记 (*The Records of the Grand Historian*), whose *Dao De* does it refer to?" The Master answered, "The *Dao De* refers naturally to Laozi's *Dao De Jing.* " Cai then said, " Many have understood that as referring to the *Daode* 道德 (morality) of the sage we Confucians adore. The Grand Historian was low in his insight and wisdom so that he did not consider that carefully and took it for being concerned with the *Great Learning* and the *Doctrine of the Mean.* " The Master said, "Now put aside the *Great Learning* and the *Doctrine of the Mean.* Since you have said that, how do you think about the discourse on the Way of humankind in *The Records of the Grand Historian*? Generally, if one, while reading something, sees it only from what is in his own mind, he will be biased. Whatever is said by others, he will understand it only from himself. It is like a walker who, despite the broad way in front of him, does not see it but rather chooses to take the winding byway. He does not see the clear big words but rather looks for something through the crevices around them, neither does he see the words facing him, but rather turns to the backside of them. It is as if one whose eyes become farsighted fails to see the things just in front of him clearly and gets some blurred images, but says they are what those things actually are. " Cai then replied, "If one does not read words objectively, he will have heaven and earth upside down. " The Master responded, "The principle is only the same principle, but when the people with various attitudes and different sincerity see and write about it, they will produce just as various and different understandings of it. For some, when they should say the east, they actually say the west and when they should say here, they actually say there. All such is caused by their biased mind, distorting what was meant by the ancients. " The Master continued, "When the Grand Historian wrote something, he also feared that, of those ancients, there had been that type of people, and tried to avoid that sort of distortion. If we take into consideration the affairs of Linchuan 临川 (i. e. Wang Anshi), He Yan 何言 (dates unknown), and Jiang Mo 江默 (courtesy name Degong 德功 [dates unknown]), when they said *Gongyang* and *Guliang* (two explanations of *The Spring and Autumn Annals*) had been made by the same person named Jiang 姜, they were also doing that sort of thing. And it seems that the preface to *Classic of History* was not composed by Kong Anguo, for its writing style is rather flabby. It is not like the style prevalent in Western Han Dynasty, which was robust and forthright, nor is it like the style popular in Eastern Han Dynasty, which was strong in character, nor is it like the style favored by Eastern Jin, illustrated by the memorials to the throne written by Kong Tan 孔坦 (285 – 335, twenty fifth grandson of Confucius), which were characterized by their own features. That preface is largely languid, yet it reads somewhat smooth, which was composed by the same writer of *Kongcongzi*. When reading *Kongcongzi*, we feel much of the discourse made up in it is outrageously vulgar. Just read the story of Chen She 陈涉 (i. e. Chen Sheng 陈胜 [? – 208 BC]) made up therein, and you will ask, ' Why are many words said by him not found in the official history? ' But the writer felt good about himself in saying them, yet Chen She would not have accepted that. His writing reads low and weak, and when reaching the ending part of a piece of writing, he gave no ending at all. " Cai said, "I'm afraid, the writer was a descendant of Confucius. " The Master responded, "Not necessarily. " Cai then said, "Lü's *Explanation of The Spring and Autumn Annals* reads very good. " The Master said in reply, "Who says it is not good? For a sentence from the classic, when it is explained as laudatory, that will do, for there is much reasoning for that, and when it is explained as derogatory, that will also do, for there is also much reasoning for it. The reasoning on either side is similar. " He continued, "For example, the ' Records of Qin ' in *The Records of the Grand Historian* is obviously a history of the state, where the narration is made with much rigor.

If some people today make speculation of its purport, they will have their way at will in doing that. As for *The Spring and Autumn Annals*, it is only ancient history recorded there." Cai said, "When you, sir, wrote your *Tongjian Gangmu* 通鉴纲目 (Outline of the Comprehensive Mirror), you had to choose between there being its original purport or not. In the case of *The Spring and Autumn Annals*, could it be said the sage who wrote it had no purport?" The Master answered, "Though the sage had his purport, when it is unknowable to us today, we should not make groundless speculation on it." Cai said, "Zuo (Qiuming), I'm afraid, was an offspring of Yixiang 倚相, the *Zuoshi* 左史 (Historian on the Left [for recording sayings]) of the Chu state, probably for the matters of Chu are stated at very great length in Zuo's *Explanation of The Spring and Autumn Annals*." The Master said, "In comparison, of the three explanations of the classic, Zuo's gets seven or eight points, if ten is the full." Cai then said, "With regard to the principles, Guliang's can get seven or eight points. Someone said, 'In the three explanations, there are many places which read rather dull and dry, and they were added by later scholars.'" [Hesun]

27 儒教自开辟以来，二帝三王述天理，顺人心，治世教民，厚典庸礼之道；后世圣贤遂著书立言，以示后世。及世之衰乱，方外之士厌一世之纷拏，畏一身之祸害，躭空寂以求全身于乱世而已。及老子倡其端，而列御寇庄周杨朱之徒和之。孟子尝辟之以为无父无君，比之禽兽。然其言易入，其教易行。当汉之初，时君世主皆信其说，而民亦化之。虽以萧何曹参汲黯太史谈辈亦皆主之，以为真足以先于六经，治世者不可以莫之尚也。及后汉以来，米贼张陵、海岛寇谦之之徒，遂为盗贼。曹操以兵取阳平，陵之孙鲁即纳降款，可见其虚缪不足稽矣。僩。

As for the tradition of Ruism, since the world came into being, the two emperors (i. e. Yao and Shun) and three kings (i. e. Yu of Xia, Tang of Shang, and King Wen of Zhou) stated the heavenly principle and rectified the human mind, brought peace and prosperity to the world and educated the people, and fostered the Way by forming laws and regulations and setting up the rites as conventions, which the later sages and worthies elucidated by words to instruct the generations to come. When the decadence started and the turmoil cropped up, those outside the common ways of the world, who had got disgusted with the chaotic state and feared to recur disaster on themselves, turned to the vacuous and quiet in the hope of nothing but keeping themselves safe and sound from the troubled times. The first of them was Laozi and followed by Lie Yukou 列御寇 (name of Liezi), Zhuang Zhou, Yang Zhu, and so on. Mencius once criticized them as sovereign-deniers and father-deniers and likened them as beasts. Nonetheless, their teachings were easily accessible and their doctrine was easily practicable. In the beginning period of the Han dynasty, the emperors and ministers were attracted by their theory and the people were also transformed by it. Those high-positioned officials such as Xiao He 萧何 (257 – 193 BC), Cao Can, Ji An 汲黯 (? – 112 BC), and Sima Tan 司马谈 (165 – 110 BC, Grand Historian before Sima Qian, his son) advocated it, believing it was more important than the Six Classics, which the rulers should carry forward. Since Eastern Han began, Zhang Ling 张陵 (? – 156), the rice thief[①], and Kou Qianzhi 寇谦之 (365 – 448), who went to an sea island and sought Daoism, and their kind, turned thieves and brigands. When the troops of Cao Cao 曹操 (155 – 220) moved to attack the Yangping Pass of Zhang Lu 张鲁 (? – 216), grandson of Zhang Ling, Zhang surrendered immediately. That shows the theory of the Zhangs was empty and fallacious, which is not worth examination. [Xian]

---

① Zhang Ling, also called Zhang Daoling 张道陵, was an Eastern Han Dynasty Daoist, who was credited with founding the Way of the Celestial Masters Sect of Daoism, which is also known as "Wudoumi Dao" 五斗米道 (The Way of the Five Pecks of Rice), because each person wishing to join was required to donate five pecks of rice.

老子书

Laozi

道可道章第一
Chapter One

28 问："老子'道可道'章，或欲以'常无''常有'为句读，而'欲'字属下句者，如何?"曰："先儒亦有如此做句者，不妥帖。"问："'三十辐共一毂，当其无，有车之用。'无，是车之坐处否?"曰："恐不然。若以坐处为无，则上文自是就辐毂而言，与下文户牖埏埴是一例语。某尝思之，无是毂中空处。惟其中空，故能受轴而运转不穷。犹伞柄上木管子，众骨所会者，不知名何。缘管子中空，又可受伞柄，而辟阖下上。车之毂亦犹是也。庄子所谓'枢始得其环中，以应无穷'，亦此意。"侗。

Question: In the first chapter of *Laozi*, perhaps punctuation should be made after *changwu* 常无 and *changyou* 常有 respectively, and thus in either case the following *yu* 欲 should belong to the following clause. How do you think?

Answer: Some previous scholars punctuated the two sentences that way, too. But I do not think it is appropriate.

Question: In the sentence "San shi fu gong yi gu, dang qi wu, you che zhi yong" 三十辐共一毂，当其无，有车之用 (The thirty spokes unite in the one nave; but it is on the *wu* 无 that the use of the carriage wheel depends) in the eleventh chapter, does the *wu* 无 mean the place where one sits on a carriage?

Answer: I'm afraid not. If you regard the seat as what is meant by *wu*, the preceding words in the sentence are said naturally of the spokes and the nave of a carriage, and it is the same kind of example as the "clay" and "the door and windows" in the following sentences. I once considered what it meant and thought that it referred to the empty space in the nave. It is only due to the empty space there that the axle can be carried for its ceaseless revolution. It is like the wood tube in the umbrella handle where its ribs meet, the name of which I do not know. Since the tube is empty inside, which can case the handle, and thus it can move up and down, enabling the ribs to open and close. This function is also true of the nave of a carriage. That is also meant by Zhuangzi's "As soon as one finds this pivot, he stands in the centre of the ring (of thought), where he can respond without end to the changing views." ("Qiwu Lu" 齐物论 [On the Equality of All Things] in *Zhuangzi*) [Xian]

谷神不死章第六
Chapter Six

29 正淳问"谷神不死,是谓玄牝"。曰:"谷虚。谷中有神,受声所以能响,受物所以生物。"䚪。

Zhengchun asked about "Gu shen bu si shi wei xuan pin" 谷神不死,是谓玄牝 (The valley spirit dies not, aye the same // The female mystery thus do we name). The Master answered, "The *gu* 谷 (valley) is vacuous. In it there is the spirit, which gives sound when it receives sound and produces things when it receives things." [Xun]

30 问"谷神"。曰:"谷只是虚而能受,神谓无所不应。它又云:'虚而不屈,动而愈出。'有一物之不受,则虚而屈矣;有一物之不应,是动而不能出矣。"问:"'玄牝',或云,玄是众妙之门,牝是万物之祖。"曰:"不是恁地说。牝只是木孔承笋,能受底物事。如今门臼谓之牝,镮则谓牝;锁管便是牝,锁须便是牡。雌雄谓之牝牡,可见。玄者,谓是至妙底牝,不是那一样底牝。"问:"老子之言,似有可取处?"曰:"它做许多言语,如何无可取?如佛氏亦尽有可取,但归宿门户都错了。"夔孙。

When asked about *gus hen* 谷神 (valley spirit), the Master answered,

"*The gu* is empty so that it is capable of receiving, and the *shen* means giving response whenever it receives. The fifth chapter also says, 'It is emptied, yet it loses not its power // And the more it is moved, the more it sends forth.' If there is anything it does not receive, it is empty, yet it loses its power. If there is anything it gives no response to, it moves, yet it does not send forth." When asked, "Regarding *xuan pin* 玄牝, someone said that *xuan* refers to *zhong miao zhi men* 众妙之门 (the gate of all that is subtle and wonderful) (1), while *pin*, to *wan wu zhi zu* 万物之祖 (the ancestor of all things)," (1) the Master answered, "His is not right. The *pin* refers only to the hole in the wood piece which can carry the tenon, something that receives. For example, today, the door catch is called *mu* 牡 and the ring of it is called *pin*. The bar of a lock is referred to as *mu*, and the lock, *pin*. The female and the male are called *pin* and *mu* respectively and this is clear. The *xuan* 玄 means the most subtle *pin*, not the ordinary." When asked, "Is there anything to draw on from what Laozi said?" the Master answered, "He said so many words, so how can there be nothing to draw on from them? Even the Buddhists' discourse contains something worth drawing on; however, they take a wrong gate and go to a wrong destination." [Kuisun]

31 问"谷神不死"。曰:"谷之虚也,声达焉,则响应之,乃神化之自然也。'是谓玄牝'。玄,妙也;牝,是有所受而能生物者也。至妙之理,有生生之意焉,程子所取老氏之说也。"人杰。

When asked about "The valley spirit dies not," the Master answered, "The valley is vacuous, so when sound reaches it, it gives back sound as a response. It is its natural being like the spirit. As for 'The *xuan pin* thus do we name,' *xuan* means mystery and *pin* refers to that which can receive and then produce things. That is the subtlest principle, with the meaning of producing life. Master Cheng's view draws on the theory of Laozi." [Renjie]

32 玄牝盖言万物之感而应之不穷,又言受而不先。如言"圣人执左契而不责于人",契有左右,左所以衔右。言左契,受之义也。方子。

The *xuan pin* speaks probably of being acted upon by the myriad things and responding to them unceasingly, and also of receiving but not acting first. It is like saying "The sage keeps the left-hand portion of *qi* 契 (the record of the engagement) with the other party, and does not insist on the (speedy) fulfillment of it by the party." (*Laozi*, 79) The *qi* has its left-hand portion and its right-hand portion, of which the former (held by the creditor) engages with the latter (held by the debtor). The "left-hand portion" mentioned in the sentence means reception. [Fangzi]

33 沈庄仲问："'谷神不死,是谓玄牝',如何?"曰:"谷神是那个虚而应物底物事。"又问:"'常有欲以观其徼',徼之义如何?"曰:"徼是那边徼,如边界相似,说那应接处。向来人皆作'常无''常有'点,不若只作'常有欲''无欲'点。"义刚问:"原壤看来也是学老子。"曰:"他也不似老子,老子却不恁地。"庄仲曰:"却似庄子。"曰:"是。便是夫子时已有这样人了。"庄仲曰:"庄子虽以老子为宗,然老子之学尚要出来应世,庄子却不如此。"曰:"庄子说得较开阔,较高远,然却较虚,走了老子意思。若在老子当时看来,也不甚喜他如此说。"庄仲问:"'道可道'如何解?"曰:"道而可道,则非常道;名而可名,则非常名。"又问"玄"之义。曰:"玄,只是深远而至于黑窣窣地处,那便是众妙所在。"又问"宠辱若惊,贵大患若身"。曰:"从前理会此章不得。"义刚。

Shen Zhuangzhong 沈庄仲 (i. e. Shen Xian 沈僩) asked, "How to understand 'The valley spirit dies not, aye the same // The female mystery thus do we name' (6)?" The Master answered, "The valley spirit means the thing-event which is empty and gives responses to whatever it receives." Shen further asked, "In 'Chang you yu yi guan qi jiao' 常有欲以观其徼, what is meant by the *jiao* 徼?" The Master answered, "It means something like the boundary, referring to where things are dealt with. The punctuation in the sentence has been made usually after *changwu* 常无 and *changyou* 常有 respectively, but it is more reasonable to make it after *chang you wu* 常

有欲 and *wu yu* 无欲 . " Yigang asked, "It seems that Yuan Rang 原壤 (dates unknown, a contemporary of Confucius) followed Laozi in his learning. (How do you think?)" The Master answered, "He is not like Laozi, for Laozi is not like that. " Zhuangzhong said, "But he is like Zhuangzi. " The Master responded, "Yes. That means in the time of Confucius there was already the sort of men. " Zhuangzhong further asked, "Though Zhuangzi followed Laozi as his master, Laozi's learning was still intended to deal with affairs in the world, but Zhuangzi's was not. (How do you think?)" The Master said, "Zhuangzi's discourse is more lofty, broad-ranging and far-reaching, yet sounds more empty, going astray from the track of Laozi. If Laozi had read his words, he would have had little liking for them. " Zhuangzhong further asked, "How to understand his 'dao ke dao' 道可道 (1)?" The Master answered, "The *Dao* which can be expressed is not the constant *Dao*; The name which can be defined is not the constant name. " [1] When asked further about the meaning of *xuan*, the Master answered, "The *xuan* means only what is the profound, a reach towards the dark, which is where all that is subtle and wonderful lies. " When further asked about "chong ru ruo jing gui da huan ruo shen" 宠辱若惊，贵大患若身 (lit. Favor and disgrace seem to be alarming; honoring great trouble seem as honoring one's person) (13), the Master replied, "The chapter which it belongs to has not been understood well. " [Yigang]

34 张以道问 "载营魄" 与 "抱一能无离乎" 之义。曰："魄是一，魂是二；一是水，二是火。二抱一，火守水；魂载魄，动守静也。" 义刚。

Zhang Yidao 张以道 (dates unknown, a disciple of Zhu's) asked about the meaning of *zai ying po* 载营魄 and *bao yi neng wu li hu* 抱一能无离乎

---

① The translation of the sentence draws on a version in *Tao Te Ching*, London: Unwin Paperbacks, 1982.

(10). The Master answered, "The *po* 魄 is one, while *hun* 魂 is two; One is water, while two is fire. Two embracing one indicates fire guarding water; *hun* carrying *po* indicates activity guarding tranquility." [Yigang]

35 "专气致柔"，只看他这个甚么样工夫。专，非守之谓也，只是专一无间断。致柔，是到那柔之极处。才有一毫发露，便是刚，这气便粗了。偶。

The Master said, "As for *zhuan qi zhi rou* 专气致柔 (lit. When one gives all his attention to the vital breath and brings it to the utmost degree of pliancy) (10), you should know what effort it refers to. The *zhuan* 专 does not mean 'guard,' but rather means being concentrated without interruption. The *zhi rou* 致柔 means getting to the utmost degree of pliancy. As soon as there appears an iota devoid of pliancy, it means hardness and that the vital breath 气 gets coarse." [Xian]

36 "老子之学只要退步柔伏，不与你争。才有一毫主张计较思虑之心，这气便粗了。故曰'致虚极，守静笃'；又曰：'专气致柔，能如婴儿乎？'又曰：'知其雄，守其雌，为天下溪；知其白，守其黑，为天下谷。'所谓溪，所谓谷，只是低下处。让你在高处，他只要在卑下处，全不与你争。他这工夫极离。常见画本老子便是这般气象，笑嘻嘻地，便是个退步占便宜底人。虽未必肖他，然亦是它气象也。只是他放出无状来，便不可当。如曰'以正治国，以奇用兵，以无事取天下'，他取天下便是用此道。如子房之术，全是如此。峣关之战，啖秦将以利，与之连和了，即回兵杀之；项羽约和，已讲解了，即劝高祖追之。汉家始终治天下全是得此术，至武帝尽发出来。便即当子房闲时不做声气，莫教他说一语，更不可当。少年也任侠杀人，后来因黄石公教得来较细，只是都使人不疑他，此其所以乖也。庄子比老子便不同。庄子又转调了精神，发出来粗。列子比庄子又较细腻。"问："御风之说，亦寓言否？"曰："然。"偶。

The Master said, "Laozi's learning drives at nothing but regression and compliancy, shunning competition against others. According to him, as soon as one set an iota of his mind to concern, consideration, or deliberation, his vital breath would get coarse, so he said, ' The (state of) vacancy should be brought to the utmost degree and that of stillness, guarded with unwearying vigor. ' (1) He also said, ' When one gives undivided attention to the (vital) breath and brings it to the utmost degree of pliancy, can he become as a (tender) baby? ' (10) He also said, ' Who knows his manhood's strength, // Yet still his female feebleness maintains; // As to one channel (*xi* 溪) flow the many drains, // All come to him, yea, all beneath the sky···. // Who knows how white attracts, // Yet always keeps himself within black's shade, ··· // Behold his presence in a spacious vale 谷 // To which men come from all beneath the sky. ' (28) The so called channel and the vale are but low places. He lets you be on the high, while he keeps himself on the low, avoiding contending with you completely. The effort he makes is extremely odd. He is often portrayed as an image with that air, grinning, who takes regressing as gaining advantage. Though the image is not necessarily close to him, the air is surely his. But when he let out his scheme, he would be irresistible. He says, ' A state may be ruled by (measures of) correction; weapons of war may be used with crafty dexterity; (but) the kingdom is made one's own (only) by freedom from action and purpose. ' (57) That is his way of making the kingdom his own. For example, Zifang's stratagems were all based on it. In the Yaoguan Pass warfare (207 BC), as he suggested, Liu Bang enticed the Qin general keeping the pass by substantial benefits and feigned to enter into collusion with him, and then he had his troops to attack the general when his men were slack. In 203 BC, Liu Bang made peace with Xiang Yu, but as he suggested, Liu broke their agreement later and attacked Xiang when Xiang was in a precarious condition. That is also the way by which the early emperors of Han ruled the empire and in the reign of Emperor Wu of Han the way was applied to the full extent. When Zifang was unoccupied, he kept silent, and not even a word could be heard from him, but he would be more irresistible. When young, in a display of chivalrousness, he attempted to assassinate Emperor Shihuang of Qin. Later, he met Huangshi Gong 黄石公 (lit. Mr. Yellow Rock; c. 292-c. 195 BC), who was said to have taught him by giving him a book. Later he taught himself very carefully, and was able to make himself under no suspicion. That is why he was shrewd. Zhuangzi distanced himself from Laozi, and changed the spirit of Daoism in him, which was given off coarse. By comparison Liezi was more exquisite than Zhuangzi. " When asked " Is (Liezi) riding on the wind also a parable?" the Master answered, " Yes. " [Xian]

古之为善士章第十五
Chapter Fifteen

37 甘叔怀说："先生旧常谓老子也见得此个道理，只是怕与事物交涉，故其言有曰：'豫兮若冬涉川，犹兮若畏四邻，俨若容。'"广因以质于先生。曰："老子说话大抵如此。只是欲得退步占奸，不要与事物接。如'治人事天莫若啬'，迫之而后动，不得已而后起，皆是这样意思。故为其学者多流于术数，如申韩之徒皆是也。其后兵家亦祖其说，如阴符经之类是也。他说'以正治国，以奇用兵，以无事取天下'。据他所谓无事者，乃是大奇耳。故后来如宋齐丘遂欲以无事窃人之国。如今道家者流，又却都不理会得他意思。"广。

Gan Shuhuai 甘叔怀 (dates unk own, a disciple of Zhu's) said, "Our teacher used to say that Laozi also saw some truth, only that he feared to get involved in things and events. So, Laozi said, ' Shrinking looked they like those who wade through a stream in winter; irresolute like those who are afraid of all around them; grave like a guest (in awe of his host). ' (15)" Thereupon, I asked the Master about that. The Master answered, " What Laozi said is largely emphatic of that inclination. He desired to step back craftly, refraining from contacting things and events. For example, ' For ruling humans and rendering the (proper) service to the Heaven, there is nothing like *se* 嗇 (moderation). ' (59) And only when one is forced will he take action and only when he has no other choice will he rise up. All these mean the same thing. Thus, most of those followers of him in learning degenerated to divination, such as Shen (i. e. Shen Buhai 申不害 [420 – 337 BC]) and Han (i. e. Han Fei 韩非 [280 – 233 BC]). After him, the School of the Military (*Bingjia* 兵家) also took his doctrine as their theoretical source, like its *Yinfu Jing* 阴符经 (Classic of the Secret Talisman) and so on. In his ' A state may be ruled by (measures of) correction; weapons of war may be used with crafty dexterity; (but) the kingdom is made one's own (only) by freedom from action and purpose, ' (57) the so called 'freedom from action and purpose' is actually a strategy of great crafty dexterity. Thereby, later, Song Qiqiu 宋齐丘 (887 – 959) intended to steal the state power by freedom from action and purpose. However, nowadays, the so called Daoists can not understand what Laozi meant to say. ” [Guang]

将欲噏之章第三十六
Chapter Thirty Six

38 问老氏柔能胜刚，弱能胜强之说。曰：“它便拣便宜底先占了。若这下，则刚柔宽猛各有用时。”德明。

When asked about Laozi's theory of "The soft overcomes the hard, and the weak, the strong," (36; 78) the Master answered, "By that, he takes the advantageous first. If with that, then for the hard and the soft, the lenient and the harsh, there is time for the use of each. ” [Deming]

上德不德章第三十八
Chapter Thirty Eight

39 郭德元问：“老子云：‘夫礼，忠信之薄而乱之首。’孔子又却问礼于他，不知何故？"曰："他晓得礼之曲折，只是他说这是个无紧要底物事，不将为事。某初间疑有两个老聃，横渠亦意其如此。今看来不是如此。他曾为柱下史，故礼自是理会得，所以与孔子说得如此好。只是他又说这个物事不用得亦可，一似圣人用礼时反若多事，所以如此说。礼运中'谋用是作，而兵由此起'等语，便自有这个意思。"文蔚。

Guo Deyuan 郭德元 (dates unknown, a disciple of Zhu's) asked, "*Laozi* said, 'Now, propriety is the attenuated form of loyalty and sincerity, and is also the commencement of disorder,' (38) However, Confucius went and asked him about propriety. I do not know why?" The Master answered, "Laozi understands the ins and outs of propriety, only that he says it is something insignificant and that does not need taking seriously. When I read him at first, I suspected there had been two persons named Lao Dan 老聃 (i. e. Laozi) , and Hengqü had suspected that, too. But now I know it was not right. Since he acted as an official in the imperial archives for some time, he naturally knew the propriety prevalent in his time. That is why he talked about it so well with Confucius. But he also said that it could as well be abolished, for it seemed that, when the sage practiced propriety, it would cause trouble which could be avoided otherwise. The sayings such as 'It is due to the seeking constantly for schemes and enterprises that recourse is had to arms' (*Record of Rites*) convey that sort of meaning. " [Wenwei]

反者道之动章第四十一
Chapter Forty One

40 问"反者，道之动；弱者，道之用"。曰："老子说话都是这样意思。缘他看得天下事变熟了，都于反处做起。且如人刚强咆哮跳踯之不已，其势必有时而屈。故他只务为弱。人才弱时，却蓄得那精刚完全；及其发也，自然不可当。故张文潜说老子惟静故能知变，然其势必至于忍心无情，视天下之人皆如土偶尔。其心都冷冰冰地了，便是杀人也不恤，故其流多入于变诈刑名。太史公将他与申韩同传，非是强安排，其源流实是如此。"广。

Asked about "The movement of the Way // By contraries proceeds // And weakness marks the course // Of the Way's mighty deeds," (41) the Master answered, "When Laozi says something, his meaning is always like that. It is because, since he could see the vicissitudes in the world with penetration, he chose to start from the contrary side of things. For example, if one strives to keep unyielding, roaring, treadling, and kicking, there will surely some time when he discontinues. Thus, he always kept himself on the weak side. If one keeps a weak appearance, yet stores up his complete firmness and energy, when he bursts out, he is naturally irresistible. Therefore, Zhang Wenqian 张文潜（i. e. Zhang Lei 张耒［1054 - 1114］）said that only by tranquility could Laozi know the changes, but the consequence is inevitably that he was hardhearted and merciless, seeing all people under heaven as figures made from soil. So when one's heart got hard, he would be relentless to kill others, and the followers of Laozi tended to degenerate into ones who were given to fickleness and deception, and to infliction of various punishments. When the Grand Historian put the biography of Laozi and those of Shen Buhai and Han Fei under the same title, he did not make some forced juxtaposition, for that is their origin and development, indeed. " ［Guang］

41 易不言有无。老子言"有生于无"，便不是。闳祖。

Yi 易 (Classic of Change) does not say of *you* 有 (being) and *wu* 无 (non-being). When Laozi said *you sheng yu wu* 有生于无 (Being sprang from non-being) (40) he was not right. ［Hongzu］

道生一章第四十二
Chapter Forty Two

42 一便生二，二便生四。老子却说"二生三"，便是不理会得。

One produced two, and two produced four. But Laozi said, "Two produced three," (42) which indicates he did not understand that.

43 "道生一，一生二，二生三。" 不合说一个生一个。方。

"The Way produced one; one produced two; two produced three." (42) It should not be said that one produces another. [Fang]

名与身章第四十四
Chapter Forty Four

44 多藏必厚亡，老子也是说得好。义刚。

"The more one loves large stores, the more probably he incurs disaster." (44) Laozi said it very well. [Yigang]

天下有道章第四十六
Chapter Forty Six

45 "天下有道，却走马以粪车" 是一句，谓以走马载粪车也。顷在江西见有所谓 "粪车" 者，方晓此语。今本无 "车" 字，不知先生所见何本。偲。

"When the Way prevails in the world, (they) send back (their) horses for the dung carts." (46) This is one sentence, which refers to having war horses to draw the dung carts. I did not know what the so called "dung cart" looked like until I once saw it in Jiangxi (roughly the present day Jiangxi).

According to the accepted edition of *Laozi*, the relevant sentence from its text does not contain the sinograph for "carts." I do not know where the Master cited the sentence from. [Xian]

治人事天章第五十九
Chapter Fifty Nine

46 老子言："治人事天，莫若啬。夫惟啬，是谓早服；早服，谓之重积德。重积德，则无不克。" 他底意思，只要收敛，不要放出。友仁。

Laozi said, "For ruling humans and rendering the (proper) service to the Heaven, there is nothing like moderation. It is only by this moderation that there is effected an early return (to man's normal state). That early return is what I call the repeated accumulation of the virtues (of the Way). With that repeated accumulation of those virtues, there comes the subjugation (of every obstacle to such return)." (59) What that means is only taking back but not giving out. 〔Youren〕

47 俭德极好。凡事俭则鲜失。老子言："治人事天，莫若啬。夫惟啬，是谓早服；早服，是谓重积德。"被它说得曲尽。早服者，言能啬则不远而复，便在此也。重积德者，言先已有所积，复养以啬，是又加积之也。如修养者，此身未有所损失，而又加以啬养，是谓早服而重积。若待其已损而后养，则养之方足以补其所损，不得谓之重积矣。所以贵早服。早服者，早觉未损而啬之也。如某此身已衰耗，如破屋相似，东扶西倒，虽欲修养，亦何能有益耶！今年得季通书说，近来深晓养生之理，尽得其法。只是城郭不完，无所施其功也。看来是如此。偪。

The virtue of frugality is very good. Whatever it is, so long as one is frugal in it, he seldom suffers loss. Laozi said, "For ruling humans and rendering the (proper) service to the Heaven, there is nothing like moderation. It is only by this moderation that there is effected an early return (to man's normal state). That early return is what I call the repeated accumulation of the virtues (of the Way)." (59) All that is made clear by him indirectly. The "early return" means that if one can be moderate he will be able to return, before he goes too far, to man's normal state. The "repeated accumulation of the virtues" says that, if one has already made some accumulation, when he goes on and fosters it by his moderation, it is his further accumulation. For example, for one engaged in self-cultivation, if he has not lost anything, when he fosters it by moderation, he can be said as having "early return" and "repeated accumulation of the virtues." However, if he has already suffered some loss, when he fosters it then, he can only make up for the loss, so he should not be called as having "repeated accumulation of the virtues." That is why "early return" is set store by. By "early return," one can be aware of avoiding loss and fostering by moderation. If one's body has already declined and been consumed, like a broken house on the verge of collapse, though he wants to cultivate it, how can he make it? This year, I received a letter from Jitong, in which he said, "Recently, I have got to know the principle of keeping in good health deeply and the method for it completely, only that, since the walls of the city (in my self-cultivation) is incomplete, I can by no means apply them (i. e. the principle and the method) well." It seems that is true. [Xian]

48 老子："治人事天莫如啬。"啬，养也。先生曰："啬，只是吝啬之'啬'。它说话只要少用些子。"举此一段，至"莫知其极。"僴。

As regard Laozi's "For ruling humans and rendering the (proper) service to the Heaven, there is nothing like *se* (moderation) ," (59) the Master said, "The *se* refers to nourishment. It is only the same *se* as that in *lin se* 吝啬 (miserliness). In his discourse, he was liable to use sinographs as few as possible." Then he talked about the section from the beginning to *mo zhi qi ji* 莫知其极 (we know not what shall be the limit) in the chapter. [Xian]

庄子书
Zhuangzi

内篇养生第三
Chapter Three Nourishing the Lord of Life
(in Inner Chapters)

49 "'因者，君之纲。'道家之说最要这因。万件事，且因来做。"因举史记老子传赞云云："虚无因应，变化于无穷。"曰："虚无是体，与‘因应’字当为一句。盖因应是用因而应之之义云尔。”植。

The Master said, "(The Grand Historian wrote) 'yin 因 (to adapt) is the cardinal principle for the sovereign.' In the doctrine of Daoism, to adapt is valued most. The myriad matters, according to it, can be done by adapting to their changing conditions." Thereupon, he cited from the eulogy in the biography of Laozi in the *Records of the Grand Historian*, the *xu wu yin ying bian hua yu wu qiong* 虚无因应变化于无穷①, and said "The 'xu wu' 虚无 (void and non-being) is the substance and the two sinographs and the following *yin ying* 因应 (to adapt to changing conditions) should be regarded as making one part in the sentence. Probably it means making adaptation to cope with things." [Zhi (植)]

50 因论“庖丁解牛”一段，至“恢恢乎其有余刃”，曰：“理之得名以此。目中所见无全牛，熟。”㣽。

Thereupon, the Master talked about the section on *pao ding jie niu* 庖丁解牛 (The cook cut up an ox), from the beginning to *hui hui hu qi you yu ren* 恢恢乎其有余刃 (When the knife which is so thin enters where the interstice is, how easily it moves along!) (3), and said, "That is the way on which account the principle gains its name. In the eyes of the cook, there was not the whole ox (but rather every part of it), and so familiar was he with the ox." [Xian]

外篇天地第十二
Chapter Twelve Heaven and Earth (in Outer Chapters)

51 “庄子云：‘各有仪则之谓性。’此谓‘各有仪则’，如‘有物

---

① In the *Records of the Grand Historian*, the *wu qiong* 无穷 is *wu wei* 无为. The sentence, according to Zhu's explanation, reads *Xu wu yin ying, bian hua yu wu qiong* 虚无因应，变化于无穷，meaning "The void and non-being make adaptations (to cope with things) under changing conditions in inexhaustible ways."

有则'，比之诸家差善。董仲舒云：'质朴之谓性，性非教化不成。'性本自成，于教化下一'成'字，极害理。"可学。

Zhuangzi says, "(That shape was the body preserving in it the spirit, and) each had its peculiar manifestation, which we call its nature." (12) The "each had its peculiar manifestation" here, as "(Heaven) to every faculty and relationship annexed its law," (*Classic of Poetry*) means, is not good in comparison with other doctrines. Dong Zhongshu said, "The plainness and simplicity are called the nature, and it can not be shaped unless by education and transformation." The nature is shaped by itself, so what he said is very destructive to knowing the truth. [Kexue]

52 问："'野马也，尘埃也，生物之以息相吹也'，是如何？"曰："他是言九万里底风，也是这个推去。息，是鼻息出入之气。"节。

Question: What does "Ye ma ye chen ai ye sheng wu zhi yi xi xiang chui ye" 野马也，尘埃也，生物之以息相吹也① (1 in Inner Chapters) refer to?

Answer: It says of the wind whirling 90 thousands *li* (1 *li* is 1/2 kilometer) mentioned before that sentence. The wind was also formed by the *xi* 息, which means the breathing air of living things. [Jie]

53 问："庄子'实而不知以为忠，当而不知以为信'，此语似好。"曰："以实当言忠信，也好。只是它意思不如此。虽实，而我不知以为忠；虽当，而我不知以为信。"问："庄生他都晓得，只是却转了说。"曰："其不知处便在此。"僩。

Question: *Zhuangzi* says "There was honesty, yet not knowing that it was loyalty; there was appropriateness, yet not knowing that it was faithfulness." (13 in Outer Chapters) This saying seems good.

---

① In the cited sentence, which is metaphorical, *ye ma* 野马 means literally wild horses or the horses in the open fields, and actually refers to the vapor in the open fields. The sentence can be understood as meaning that the vapor in the fields and the dusts are caused by living things as they are blown against one another by the air.

Answer：It is good to speak of loyalty and faithfulness in terms of honesty and appropriateness. However, that is not what he actually meant to say. He intended to mean that, though it is honesty, I do not know it is loyalty, and though it is appropriate, I do not know it is faithfulness.

Further question：Zhuangzi knew that well, but he said that indirectly. (Right?)

Answer：But it is where he did not know. ［Xian］

外篇天运第十四
Chapter Fourteen The Revolution of Heaven
（in Outer Chapters）

54 先生曰："'天其运乎，地其处乎，日月其争于所乎。孰主张是？孰纲维是？孰居无事而推行是？意者，其有机缄而不得已邪？意者，其运转不能自止邪？云者为雨乎？雨者为云乎？孰能施是？孰居无事淫乐而劝是？'庄子这数语甚好，是他见得，方说到此。其才高。如庄子天下篇言'诗以道志，书以道事，礼以道行，乐以道和，易以道阴阳，春秋以道名分'，若见不分晓，焉敢如此道！要之，他病，我虽理会得，只是不做。"又曰："庄老二书解注者甚多，竟无一人说得他本义出，只据他臆说。某若拈出，便别，只是不欲得。"友仁。

The Master said, "*Zhuangzi* says 'How (ceaselessly) heaven revolves! How (constantly) earth abides at rest! And do the sun and moon contend about their (respective) places? Who presides over and directs these (things)? Who binds and connects them together? Who is it that, without trouble or exertion on his part, causes and maintains them? Is it, perhaps, that there is some secret spring, in consequence of which they cannot be but as they are? Or is it, perhaps, that they move and turn as they do, and cannot stop of themselves? (Then) how the clouds become rain! And how the rain again forms the clouds! Who diffuses them so abundantly? Who is it that, without trouble or exertion on his part, produces this elemental enjoyment, and seems to stimulate it?' (1, in 14 of Outer Chapters) He said these several sentences very well, because he saw those points truly, manifesting his remarkable talent. In the 'Tian Xia' 天下 (Under Heaven) included in the 'Miscellaneous Chapters,' he says 'The *Shi* 诗 (referring to the *Classic of Poetry*) describes what should be the intent of the mind; the *Shu* 书 (referring to the *Classic of History*), the course of events; the *Li* 礼 (referring to the *Record of Rites*) is intended to direct the conduct; the *Yue* 乐 (referring to the *Record of Music*), to set forth harmony; the *Yi* 易 (referring to the *Classic of Change*), to show the action of *yin* and *yang*; and the *Chun Qiu* 春秋 (referring to the *Spring and Autumn Annals*), to display names and the duties belonging to them. ' If he had not understood them well, how could he have said that? In a word, his trouble is that though I know everything I do not do anything. " He added, "There have been a great number of annotators of *Laozi* and *Zhuangzi*, but actually no one of them have pointed out their original meanings, for they have only made groundless speculations on their meanings. If I reveal their meanings, they will be different, but I do not want to do that. " [Youren]

55 "烈风",庄子音作"厉风"。如此之类甚多。节。

The *lie feng* 烈风 (fierce gusts) is pronounced as *li feng* 厉风 in *Zhuangzi*. There are many such cases of pronunciation changes found in it. [Jie]

参同契

Cantong Qi (The Kinship of the Three)①

56 先生以参同契示张以道云:"近两日方令书坊开得,然里面亦难晓。"义刚问:"曾景建谓参同本是龙虎上经,果否?"曰:"不然。

---

① Its full title is *Zhouyi Cantong Qi* 周易参同契 (The Kinship of the Three in Accordance with the *Classic of Change*).

盖是后人见魏伯阳传有'龙虎上经'一句，遂伪作此经，大概皆是体参同而为，故其间有说错了处。如参同中云'二用无爻位，周流行六虚'。二用者，即易中用九、用六也。乾坤六爻，上下皆有定位，唯用九、用六无位，故周流行于六虚。今龙虎经却错说作虚危去。盖讨头不见，胡乱牵合一字来说。"义刚。

The Master, showing *Cantong Qi* to Zhang Yidao, and said, "I just got this copy from a bookshop the other day, but what it says is hard to understand." I asked, "Zeng Jingjian 曾景建 (dates unknown) once said *Cantong Qi* was originally the very *Longhu Shangjing* 龙虎上经 (or simply *Longhu Jing* 龙虎经 [The Dragon and Tiger Classic]). Is that true?" The Master answered, "No. That was said probably because someone later found the mention of *Longhu Shangjing* in the biography of Wei Boyang 魏伯阳 (dates unknown, in Eastern Han, author of *Cantong Qi*) and then fabricated that book perhaps by imitating *Cantong Qi*. Therefore, there are some mistakes in it. For example, *Cantong Qi* says 'Er yong wu yao wei, zhou liu xing liu xu' 二用无爻位，周流行六虚①, the *er yong* 二用 refers to the *yong jiu* 用九 in 'Hexagram Qian' and *yong liu* 用六 in 'Hexagram Kun.' In either hexagram, every one of the six lines has its fixed position, but neither *yong jiu* nor *yongliu* has its fixed position. Thus they are said as flowing about into the *liu xu* 六虚 (any one of the six places of the hexagram), respectively. However, the *Longhu Shangjing* says them wrongly as *xu* 虚 and *wei* 危, two of the Twenty-eight Constellation Deities 二十八

---

① The cited sentence means "The two *yongs* (i. e. *yong jiu* and *yong liu*) have no position of their own, so they flow about into any one of the six places of either hexagram." In "Hexagram Qian," there is an extra unbroken line called *yong jiu*, besides the six unbroken lines (each being *yang*, represented by the number of *jiu* i. e. nine) in its image, and in "Hexagram Kun," there is an extra broken line called *yong liu*, besides the six broken lines (each being *yin*, represented by the number of *liu* i. e. six). There have been various explanations of the meaning and function of the two extra lines. All other sixty two hexagram images each are made of six lines, broken or unbroken, which do not contain such extra lines.

宿. Probably the fabricator could not know the origination of them, but rather simply made some far-fetched interpretation, with no justification at all. "〔Yigang〕

57 参同契所言'坎、离、水、火、龙、虎、铅、汞'之属，只是互换其名，其实只是精气二者而已。精，水也，坎也，龙也，汞也；气，火也，离也，虎也，铅也。其法：以神运精气结而为丹，阳气在下，初成水，以火炼之则凝成丹。其说甚异。内外异色如鸭子卵，真个成此物。参同契文章极好，盖后汉之能文者为之，读得亦不枉。其用字皆根据古书，非今人所能解，以故皆为人枉解。世间本子极多。其中有云：'千周粲彬彬兮，万遍将可睹；神明或告人兮，魂灵忽自悟。'言诵之久，则文义要诀自见。"又曰："'二用无爻位，周流行六虚'，二用者，用九、用六，九、六亦坎、离也。六虚者，即乾坤之初、二、三、四、五、上六爻位也。言二用虽无爻位，而常周流乎乾、坤六爻之间，犹人之精气上下周流乎一身而无定所也。世有龙虎经，云在参同契之先，季通亦以为好。及得观之，不然，乃隐括参同契之语而为之也。"偁。卓录云："'铅、汞、龙、虎、水、火、坎、离皆一样是精气。参同契尽被后人胡解。凡说铅汞之属，只是互换其名，其实只一物也。精与气二者，而以神运之耳'云云。'"千周兮粲彬彬，用之万遍斯可睹；鬼神将告予，神灵忽自悟。"言诵之久，则文义要诀自见。'又云："'二用无爻位，周流遍六虚"，言二用虽无爻位，常周流乎乾、坤六爻之间，犹人身之精气常周流乎人之一身而无定所也。'又云：'"往来无定所，上下无常居"，亦此意也。世有龙虎经，或以为在参同契之先。尝见季通说好。及观之，不然，尽是隐括参同契为之。如说"二用六虚"处，彼不知为周易之"二用六虚"，尽错解了，遂分说云，有六样虚，尽是乱说！参同契文章极好，念得亦不枉。其中心云，汝若不告人，绝圣道罪诛，言之着竹帛，又恐漏泄天机之意。故但为重复反复之语，令人子细读之自晓。其法皆在其中，多不晓。'"

The Master said, "The '*kan* 坎（symbol of water）, *li* 离（symbol of fire）, *shui* 水, *huo* 火（fire）, *long* 龙（dragon）, *hu* 虎（tiger）, *qian* 铅（lead）, *gong* 汞（mercury）' mentioned in *Cantong Qi* are only alternative names of, actually, the two of *jing* 精（essence; energy of the physical body） and *qi* 气 (vital force ; natural energy of the universe). The *jing* is referred to as *shui*, *kan*, *long*, or *gong*, while the *qi*, to *huo*, *li*, *hu*, or *qian*. Its method (of internal alchemy), according to the book, goes like : To operate *jing* and *qi* by spirit so that they condense as internal *dan* 丹 (elixir), because the *yang qi* 阳气 (positive energy) starts from below and becomes water first, which can be refined by fire to condense as *dan*. Its theory is rather weird. As it says, the external and the internal can be made different in color, like those of a duck egg, and that difference can be really cultivated in the human physical body. As far as its writing style is concerned, *Cantong Qi* is very good, which was probably composed by someone with high talent of writing in the Eastern Han period. Reading it is also not a waste of time and energy. Its use of words is based on the far more ancient books, hardly interpretable to people today, so the explanations of it all are groundless. There have been many different editions and in one of them there is ' Qian zhou can bin bin xi, wan bian jiang ke du ; shen ming huo gao ren xi, hun ling hu zi wu ' 千周粲彬彬兮，万遍将可睹；神明或告人兮，魂灵忽自悟 (Provided one for thousand rounds seeks after the resplendence, // From reciting ten thousand times he will see its issuance ; // The deity and spirit may come down him to enlighten, // But with his own soul he understands that all of sudden). It means so long as one recites the text long enough its essential meaning will dawn on him naturally. " He went on and said, " In ' Er yong wu yao wei, zhou liu xing liu xu, ' the *er yong* refers to the *yong jiu* in ' Hexagram Qian ' and *yong liu* in ' Hexagram Kun. ' The *jiu* 九 (nine) and *liu* 六 (six) represent *li* 离 (symbolic of fire) and *kan* 坎 (symbolic of water), respectively. The *liu xu* points to the positions of the six lines, from the bottom, second, third, fourth, and fifth, to the top in the images of ' Hexagram Qian ' and ' Hexagram Kun, ' respectively. That sentence means that, though neither *yong jiu* nor *yong liu* has a fixed position of its own, it flows about into any one of the six places of either hexagram, respectively, like the vital energy of a man, which flows throughout his entire body, without staying at a fixed location in it. The *Longhu Jing* was said to be prior to *Cantong Qi*, and Jitong thought it better than the latter. When I got it, my reading it did not agree to his judgment, for it was made by varying and adapting what was said in the latter. ”［Xian］Zhuo's record reads, “The Master said, ‘The *qian* and *gong*, *long* and *hu*, *shui* and *huo*, *kan* and *li*, all refer to the essential energy（*jing*）and the vital force（*qi*）of the physical body. Later explanations of *Cantong Qi* have been reckless completely. In it, whenever *qian* and *gong*, and the like, are mentioned, they are only different names of the same things. The *jing* and *qi* are operated only through the spirit. ’ He continued, ‘As for the “Provided one sticks to seeking after the resplendence, // From reciting ten thousand times he will see its issuance; // The deity and spirit may come down him to enlighten, // But with his own soul he understands that all of sudden, ” it means if you read it and recite it for long enough, its meaning will naturally be accessible to you. ’ He went on and said, ‘The “Er yong wu yao wei, zhou liu xing liu xu” means, though neither *yong jiu* nor *yong liu* has a fixed position of its own, it flows about into any one of the six places of either “Hexagram Qian” and “Hexagram Kun,” respectively, like the vital energy of a man, which flows throughout his entire body, without staying at a fixed location in it. ’ He also said, ‘The “Wang lai wu ding suo, shang xia wu chang ju” 往来无定所，上下无常居（To and fro, it has no fixed position, and up and down, it has no constant stay）also means that. The *Longhu Jing* was said to be prior to *Cantong Qi*, and I once heard Jitong say it was better than the latter. When I got it, my reading it did not agree to his judgment, for it was made by varying and adapting what was said in the latter. For example, when speaking of *er yong* 二用 and *liu xu* 六虚, it betrays its ignorance of their reference to the *Classic of Change*, and misunderstands them. Consequently it explains them as meaning six separate types of *xu* 虚（void）, which is nonsense all over. The use of language in *Cantong Qi* is very good, so reading it is not a waste of time. The central meaning of it goes like that, if you do not tell it to them, you will commit a sin for which you should be put to death, for you discontinue the Way of the sage; if you write it on bamboo slips and silks, you run the risk of divulging Heaven's secret. It employs only such tautology, and what it is intended to say can be understood naturally by reading it over and over again. The method of self-cultivation is also implied therein, but it is hardly understandable. ’”

58 参同契为艰深之词，使人难晓。其中有“千周万遍”之说，欲人之熟读以得之也。大概其说以为欲明言之，恐泄天机，欲不说来，又却可惜！人杰。

The words of *Cantong Qi* tend to be abstruse and hardly understandable. When it says "thousand rounds" and "ten thousand times," it intends to tell its readers to read it carefully over and over again so as to understand it ultimately. That is probably because, as its authors thought, if he made clear what he intended to say, he would fear divulging Heaven's secret, but if he did not say that, he would feel pity for it. [Renjie]

论修养
On Self-Cultivation

59 人言仙人不死。不是不死，但只是渐渐销融了，不觉耳。盖他能炼其形气，使渣滓都销融了，唯有那些清虚之气，故能升腾变化。汉书有云："学神仙尸解销化之术。"看得来也是好则剧，然久后亦须散了。且如秦汉间所说仙人，后来都不见了。国初说锺离权吕洞宾之属，后来亦不见了。近来人又说刘高尚，过几时也则休也。广。

It is said that a *xian ren* 仙人 is immortal. It is not that he is immortal, but that he melts away gradually and is unconscious of that. That is because he can refine his form and vital force so that, when the dross in him melts away, what is left is only the pure and vacuous vital force, by which he is capable of ascension and transformation. As said in the *History of Han* (by Ban Gu 班固 [32−92]), "(They) learn how to transcend into an immortal by transformation via death." Obviously, it is also quite a sporting play. Nonetheless, after a long time, that pure and vacuous force would end up dispersing. For example, all those immortals often mentioned in the hearsays during Qin and Han period vanished later. Zhongli Quan 锺离权 (c. 168−c. 256), Lü Dongbin 吕洞宾 (798−?), and the like, who were often heard talked about among people in the beginning years of our country, all disappeared later. In recent years, Liu Gaoshang 刘高尚 (dates unknown, a Daoist) has often been spoken of, but after some time he is sure to sink into oblivion. [Guang]

60 长孺说修养、般运事。曰："只是屏气减息，思虑自少，此前辈之论也。今之人传得法时，便授与人，更不问他人肥与瘠，怯与壮。但是一律教他，未有不败、不成病痛者。"

Changru 长孺（i. e. Yang Changru 杨长孺［1157 – 1236］, a disciple of Zhu's）talked about the matters of self-cultivation and internal alchemy. The Master said thereupon, "It meant only that one held his breath and reduced it, and then his deliberation would decrease naturally. That was explained by the previous scholars. Nowadays, when a master of the method (of self-cultivation and internal alchemy) gets some chance to instruct it to someone else, he does that indiscriminately, without enquiring whether the learner is fat or lean, strong or weak. Consequently, the learner is liable to wind up with failure and physical trouble."

61 因论道家修养，有默坐以心缩上气而致闭死者。曰："心缩气亦未为是。某尝考究他妙诀，只要神形全不挠动。故老子曰：'心使气则强。'才使气，便不是自然。只要养成婴儿，如身在这里坐，而外面行者是婴儿。但无工夫做此。其导引法，只如消息，皆是下策。"淳。

Thereupon the Master talked about the Daoist self-cultivation, mentioning that there had been deaths caused by reducing breath by the mind while sitting in silence. He said, "The practice of reducing breath by the mind is not right, either. I once examined the knack it employed, which stresses but keeping the mind and body free from exertion. Therefore, Laozi said, 'Where the mind makes the vital force to burn, the strength is false.' (*Laozi*, 55) The moment one exerts his vital force, it deviates from naturalness. What such a Daoist seeks after is only becoming as a baby. For example, while his flesh body sits here, the actor outside there is the baby of him. However, no way has been proposed of making effort to that end. The Daoist ways of *daoyin* 导引 (internal breath exercises), only like rising and falling, are all unwise moves." ［Chun（淳）］

62 "阴符经，恐皆唐李筌所为，是他着意去做，学他古人。何故只因他说起，便行于世？某向以语伯恭，伯恭亦以为然。一如麻衣易，只是戴氏自做自解，文字自可认。"道夫曰："向见南轩跋云：'此真麻衣道者书也。'"曰："敬夫看文字甚疏。"道夫。

The Master said, "The *Yinfu Jing* 阴符经（i. e. *Huangdi Yinfu Jing* 黄帝阴符经，Yellow Emperor Classic of Secret Talisman），I'm afraid, was made completely by Li Quan 李筌（dates unknown）in the Tang dynasty. It is a work he wrote purposely in imitation of his ancestor（Li Er, i. e. Laozi）. But why did the work get popular just after he mentioned it? I once said that to Bogong（courtesy name of Lü Zuqian），who agreed with me. It is like the case of *Mayi Yi* 麻衣易（Sackcloth *Classic of Change*, i. e. *Zhengyi Xinfa* 正易心法 [Mental Cultivation Method on the Basis of *Classic of Change*]），which was nothing but concocted by Dai Shiyu 戴师愈（dates unknown, a contemporary of Zhu Xi）and also interpreted by himself, and this can be evidenced by the use of words in them." I said then "I once read a postscript Nanxuan（style name of Zhang Shi）wrote for it, which says 'This is truly the work written by the Sackcloth Daoist.'" The Master replied, "Jingfu（courtesy name of Zhang Shi）is rather careless while reading something." [Daofu]

63 闾丘主簿进黄帝阴符经传。先生说："握奇经等文字，恐非黄帝作，池本作"因闾丘问握奇经，引程子说，先生曰"云云。唐李筌为之。圣贤言语自平正，都无许多嶢崎。"池本此下云："又，诗序是卫宏作，好事者附会，以为出圣人。其诗章多是牵合，须细考可也。"因举遗书云："'前辈说处或有未到，池本作"有到，有不到处。"不可一概定。'横渠寻常有太深言语，如言'鬼神二气之良能'，说得好。伊川言'鬼神造化之迹'，却未甚明白。"问良能之义。曰："只是二气之自然者耳。"因举"明则有礼乐，幽则有鬼神"。"鬼自是属礼，从阴；神自是属乐，从阳。池本云：""'鬼神即礼乐。'又云：'前辈之说如此。当知幽与明之实如何。鬼自从阴，属礼；神自从阳，属乐。'因举'乐者敦和，率神而从天；礼者别宜，归鬼而从地'云云。"易言'精气为物，游魂为变'，此却是知鬼神之情状。'魂气升于天，体魄归于地'，是神气上升，鬼魄下降。不特人也，凡物之枯败也，其香气腾于上，其物腐于下，此可类推。"

Subprefectural Registrar Lüqiu 闾丘 (i. e. Lüqiu Cimeng 闾丘次孟 mentioned below, dates unknown, a disciple of Zhu's) presented *Explanation of Huangdi Yinfu Jing* to the Master. The Master said, "The *Woji Jing* 握奇经 (Classic of Strategies within a Military Commander's Tent, assumed as made by Huangdi) and the like are, I'm afraid, not composed by Huangdi. For this direct speech, Chi's edition is: 'Since Lüqiu asked about the *Woji Jing*, the Master cited Master Cheng as saying such and such.' It is Li Quan in the Tang dynasty who made it. The discourses of the sages and worthies are naturally even and upright, devoid of that much bizarreness. " After this sentence, Chi's edition says, "By the way, the preface of the *Classic of Poetry* was written by Wei Hong 卫宏 (dates unknown) in Eastern Han, but by their strained interpretation, some officious men claimed it had been out of the hands of the sage. Its chapters are more farfetched than not, which can be evidenced by scrutinizing them. " Thereupon the Master cited *Yishu* 遗书 (i. e. 二程遗书 [Surviving Works of Two Chengs]) as saying "There are points not insightful enough with the preceding scholars' opinions, Chi's edition is 'There are insightful points and not enough insightful ones in the preceding scholars' opinions.' so they should not be accepted without question. " Then he said, "Hengqü usually uttered some phrases deep and profound. For example, he says it very well that 'The *gui shen* 鬼神 (the positive and negative spiritual forces) are the spontaneous activity of the two vital forces (i. e. *yin* and *yang*) .' But when Yichuan said 'The negative and positive spiritual forces are traces of natural creation,' it is not quite understandable. " When asked about the meaning of "spontaneous activity," the Master answered, "It means only the natural operation of the *yin* and *yang* vital forces. " Thereupon he cited "In the visible sphere there are ceremonies and music; in the invisible, the positive and negative spiritual forces (*gui shen* 鬼神)" from the "Record of Music" (12) in the *Record of Rites*. He explained, "Naturally, the *gui* pertains to the rites, which is *yin* in nature, while *shen* pertains to the music, which is *yang* in nature. Chi's edition says, 'The Master said, "The *gui* and *shen* are the rites and music." He went on, "That is the opinion of the previous scholars, who should have known what the substantial sides of the visible and invisible are. Naturally, the *gui* pertains to the rites, which is *yin* in nature, while *shen* pertains to the music, which is *yang* in nature." He thereupon cited from the "Record of Music" (17) in the *Record of Rites* that "Harmony is the thing principally sought in music—it therein follows Heaven, and manifests the spirit-like expansive influence characteristic of it. Normal distinction is what is aimed at in ceremonies—they therein follow Earth, and exhibit the spirit-like retractive influence characteristic of it," and so on. ' The 'Appended Remarks' I of the *Classic of Change* says '(He perceives how the union of) essence and breath forms things, and the (disappearance or) wandering away of the soul produces the change (of their constitution), ' which indicates knowing the characteristics of the *gui* and *shen*. 'The intelligent spirit returns to Heaven and the body and the animal soul return to the Earth,' ('Jiao Te Sheng' 郊特牲 [The Single Victim at the Border Sacrifices] in the *Book of Rites*) which means the vital force of the *shen* ascends, while the animal soul of the *gui* descends. That is not necessarily only limited to humankind. Whenever a thing withers and decays, its fragrance transpires over its top, while its body gets rotten at its root. This can be understood by analogy. "

64 闾丘次孟谓："阴符经所谓'自然之道静，故天地万物生；天地之道浸，故阴阳胜；阴阳相推，变化顺矣'。此数语，虽六经之言无以加。"先生谓："如他闾丘此等见处，尽得。"今按阴符经无其语。道夫。

Lüqiu Cimeng said, "The *Yinfu Jing* says, 'The Way as being what it is is of tranquility, and thereby Heaven, Earth, and the myriad things come into being; The Way of Heaven and Earth penetrates everything, and thereby the *yin* and *yang* prevail. The *yin* and *yang* interact with each other, and thereby the course of change becomes smooth. ' These several sentences can not be bettered even by using the language of the Six Classics. " The Master commented, "Such understandings as that of Lüqiu are all right." (Note: Currently, the Master's comment is not found in his *Yinfu Jing Zhu* 阴符经注 [Classic of Secret Talisman Annotated]). [Daofu]

65 阴符经云："天地之道浸。"这句极好。阴阳之道，无日不相胜，只管逐些子挨出。这个退一分，那个便进一分。道夫。

Yinfu Jing's saying "The Way of Heaven and Earth penetrates everything" is very good. The Way of *yin* and *yang* does not lose its prevalence for even one day, and it issues out simply little by little on things. When it retreats a degree here, it advances a degree there simultaneously. [Daofu]

66 问："阴符经云：'绝利一源。'"曰："绝利而止守一源。"节。

When asked about *jue li yi yuan* 绝利一源 (lit. severing all benefits and having one source) said in *Yinfu Jing*, the Master answered, "It means getting away from all those distractions and keeping only one focus." [Jie]

67 问："阴符经'三反昼夜'是如何?"曰："三反，如'学而时习之'，是贯上文言，言专而又审。反，是反反覆覆。"节。

When asked about the meaning of *san fan zhou ye* 三返昼夜 said in *Yinfu Jing*, the Master replied, "The *san fan* 三返①, with the meaning like that of 'To learn and practice frequently what one has learned' (*Analects*, 1：1), is said coherently after the words before it, which means being focused and careful. The *fan* 返 means 'over and over again.'" [Jie]

68 "三反昼夜"之说，如修养家子午行持。今日如此，明日如此，做得愈熟，愈有效验。人杰。

What the *san fan zhou ye* said in *Yinfu Jing* means is like a self-cultivator's diligent practice of cultivation by adhering conscientiously to the required rules day and night. While practicing that way day after day, the

---

① The *san fan* 三返 has been understood as referring to one's not using his eyes 眼, ears 耳, and mouth 口 externally (that is, not seeing, hearing, and saying), or to one's not using his essence 精, breath 气, and spirit 神 internally.

more he is diligent and persistent, the more efficacious the effect of his self-cultivation is on him. [Renjie]

论道教
On Daoism

69 老氏初只是清净无为。清净无为，却带得长生不死。后来却只说得长生不死一项。如今恰成个巫祝，专只理会厌禳祈祷。这自经两节变了。贺孙。

At first Laozi's doctrine was only concerned with discarding all desires and worries from one's mind, and doing nothing. Associated with this doctrine, however, was the belief of the possibility of living forever. Later what was talked about is only living forever. Nowadays, that has been transmuted as merely concerning sorcery and sacrifice, doing nothing but averting disasters by prayers. Thus, it underwent these two changes (in the history of Daoism). [Hesun]

70 道家有老庄书，却不知看，尽为释氏窃而用之，却去仿效释氏经教之属。譬如巨室子弟，所有珍宝悉为人所盗去，却去收拾人家破瓮破釜！必大。

Though Daoists own *Laozi* and *Zhuangzi*, they do not know to read them. The contents of the two books have been completely pilfered and used by Buddhists, but the Daoists went out of the way and turned to the Buddhist sutras, instructions, and the like. That is like a son of a rich family, whose gems and treasures are all pilfered by someone else, but who goes to pick up the used urns and pots of the pilferer. [Bida]

71 道教最衰，儒教虽不甚振，然犹有学者班班驳驳，说些义理。又曰："佛书中多说'佛言'，道书中亦多云'道言'。佛是个人，道却如何会说话？然自晋来已有此说。"必大。

The Master said, "Daoism is more devoid of vitality today than Confucianism which, though not very prosperous itself, is now stuck up for by some Confucian disciples who exert themselves somewhat to advocate its doctrine. " He added, "The reporting clause *fo yan* 佛言 (The Buddha says) is often used in Buddhist sutras and the *dao yan* 道言 (The *Dao* says) is also often employed in the Daoist books. The Buddha is a person, but how can the *Dao* speak? Since the Jin dynasty, it (i. e. *dao yan*) has been in use. "

[Bida]

72 道家之学，出于老子。其所谓"三清"，盖仿释氏"三身"而为之尔。佛氏所谓"三身"：法身者，释迦之本性也；报身者，释迦之德业也；肉身者，释迦之真身，而实有之人也。今之宗其教者，遂分为三像而骈列之，则既失其指矣。而道家之徒欲仿其所为，遂尊老子为三清：元始天尊，太上道君，太上老君。而昊天上帝反坐其下。悖戾僭逆，莫此为甚！且玉清元始天尊既非老子之法身，上清太上道君又非老子之报身，设有二像，又非与老子为一，而老子又自为上清太上老君，盖仿释氏之失而又失之者也。况庄子明言老聃之死，则聃亦人鬼尔，岂可僭居昊天上帝之上哉？释老之学尽当毁废。假使不能尽去，则老氏之学但当自祀其老子关尹列庄子徒，以及安期生魏伯阳辈。而天地百神自当领于天子之祠官，而不当使道家预之，庶乎其可也。僩。

The doctrine of Daoism originated from Laozi. Its so called *Sanqing* 三清 (Triple-purity) is probably only a creation by imitating the *Sanshen* 三身 (li. Triple-body; Trikaya in Sanskrit)[①] of Buddhism. The *Sanshen* of Buddhism refers to *fashen* 法身 (truth-body; Sanskrit dharmakaya), referring to the true nature of Shakyamuni; *baoshen* 报身 (enjoyment-body; Sanskrit samboghakaya), to the virtue and worldly achievement of him; and *roushen* 肉身 (activity body, Sanskrit nirmanakaya), to the real body of him.

---

① Trikaya, a Sanskrit word used in the Buddhist context to refer to the levels of manifestation or activity, is a concept concerning three levels of buddhahood. Shakyamuni, the historical Buddha who is generally considered one of many buddhas to have come to the help of sentient beings, is understood to be accessible in various ways, which are called the dharmakaya, samboghakaya, and nirmanakaya. These three terms have been rendered into English as truth-body, bliss or enjoyment-body, and activity body, respectively.

Nowadays, the Buddhists divide the triple body into three separate bodies and put the three bodies side by side, losing its original reference. The Daoists imitated their practice and adored Laozi as Triple-purity, or the Three Pure Ones, that is, Yuanshi Tianzun 元始天尊 (Lord of Primordial Beginning, also known as Yuqing 玉清 [Jade Pure One]), Taishang Daojun 太上道君 (Lord of the Way of the Highest Loftiness, also so known as Lingbao Tianzun 灵宝天尊 [Lord of the Numinous Treasure] or Shangqing 上清 [Supreme Pure One]), and Taishang Laojun 太上老君 (Old Lord of the Greatest Loftiness, also known as Daode Tianzun 道德天尊 [Lord of the Way and its Virtue] or Taiqing 太清 [Grand Pure One]). But the Haotian Shangdi 昊天上帝 (Great Heaven Emperor)① is lower in the Daoist hierarchy. There is nothing more perverse and authority-overstepping than that. Furthermore, Yuqing is not the *fashen* of Laozi, nor is Shangqing the *baoshen* of Laozi. The two images are not identified with Laozi, while Laozi himself serves as Taiqing. This is probably the trouble with its imitating the Buddhist Triple-body, with yet another trouble with the result of that imitation. Besides, Zhuangzi said definitely that Laodan (i. e. Laozi) died, and this means Laodan was only a ghost and how could he get higher than Great Heaven Emperor? Both the learning of Laozi and of Buddhism should be abolished completely. If they can not be thrown away completely, as far as the former is concerned, it should offer sacrifices only to Laozi, Guanyin 关尹② , Liezi, and Zhuangzi, as well as such later famous Daoists as Anqi Sheng 安期生 (dates unknown, in the Qin and early Han period) and Wei Boyang. As for the various temples for offering sacrifices to Heaven and Earth, they should be

---

① The Haotian Shangdi 昊天上帝 (Great Heaven Emperor) had been proclaimed as the supreme sovereign of all before the Song dynasty. He was redefined by Daoists in the Song dynasty and usually called Yuhuang Dadi 玉皇大帝 (Great Emperor of Jade).

② Guanyin refers literally to the official keeping a pass and actually to the Pass Keeper named Xi 喜, who was said as the receiver of the book now known as *Laozi* or *Dao De Jing* left by Laozi when he passed the so called Hangu Pass (in Henan today) and went westwards.

put in the charge of the sacrificial officials appointed by the Son of Heaven
(the Emperor), for it is improper for them to be handled by Daoists, so that
things can be set right. [Xian]

73 论道家三清，今皆无理会。如那两尊，已是诡名侠户了。但老
子既是人鬼，如何却居昊天上帝之上？朝廷更不正其位次？又如真武，
本玄武，避圣祖讳，故曰"真武"。玄，龟也；武，蛇也；此本虚、危
星形以之；故因而名。北方为玄、武七星；至东方则角、亢、心、尾象
龙，故曰苍龙；西方奎、娄状似虎，故曰白虎；南方张、翼状似鸟，故
曰朱鸟。今乃以玄武为真圣，而作真龟蛇于下，已无义理。而又增天蓬
天猷及翊圣真君作四圣，殊无义理。所谓"翊圣"，乃今所谓"晓子"
者。真宗时有此神降，故遂封为"真君。"义刚。

When it comes to the Three Pure Ones of Daoism, there has been no
right understanding of them today. The names of the first two, that is, the
Lord of Primordial Beginning and Lord of the Numinous Treasure, are eerie
and weird, and, furthermore, since Laozi was said to have died, so he is a
ghost, then how can he be positioned above the Great Heaven Emperor? Why
has the imperial court not have their mistaken positions set right? For another
example, *Zhenwu* 真武, which was originally called *Xuanwu* 玄武. The
renaming was caused by using *xuan* instead of *zhen* which was avoided as
taboo. [1]The *xuan* refers to the turtle and the *wu*, to the snake. Originally
they were names for the *Xu* 虚 (Emptiness) and *Wei* 危 (Rooftop), two of
the seven mansions (positions of the moon) within the *Xuanwu*
Constellation. [2]In the north are the seven stars or mansions including *Xuan*

---

① The royal family name of the Song dynasty is Zhao, and Emperor Zhenzong of Song took Zhao
Xuanlang 赵玄朗, a god of Daoism, as the ancestor of the royal family, who was adored as Emperor
Shengzu of Song.

② Xuanwu 玄武 (the Black Turtle of the North) is one of the four symbols of Chinese
constellations, the other three being Qinglong 青龙 (the Azure Dragon of the East), Zhuque 朱雀 (the
Vermilion Bird of the South), and Baihu 白虎 (the White Tiger of the West). Despite its English
name "Black Turtle," it is usually depicted as a turtle entwined together with a snake.

and *Wu*; In the east are seven mansions including *Jiao* 角, *Kang* 亢, *Xin* 心, and *Wei* 尾, which look like the shape of a dragon, hence the name *Qinglong* 青龙 (Azure Dragon); In the west are seven mansions including *Kui* 奎 and *Lou* 娄, which appear like a tiger, hence the name *Baihu* 白虎 (White Tiger); In the south are seven mansions including *Zhang* 张 and *Yi* 翼, which takes the shape of a bird, hence the name *Zhuniao* 朱鸟 (Vermilion Bird). At present, *Xuanwu* has been regarded as a true deity, depicted with his feet on a real turtle entwined with a real snake, and those original meaning and principle have already been lost. Beside him, the other three deities are also added, i. e. *Tianpeng* 天蓬 (Heavenly Canopy), *Tianyou* 天猷 (Heavenly Scheme), and *Yisheng Zhenjun* 翊圣真君 (Sage-Assisting True Lord), to make the *Sisheng* 四圣 (Four Sages), for which there is no meaning and principle to speak of at all. The so called *Yisheng* 翊圣 refers to what is like the *Xiaozi* 晓子 (lit. knower; roughly, wizard) today. It is said that, during the reign of Emperor Zhenzong 真宗 (968 – 1022), the god descended, who was then conferred with the title *Zhenjun* 真君 (True Lord).

[Yigang]

74 "道家行法，只是精神想出，恐人不信，故以法愚之。太史迁。吕与叔集记一事极怪。旧见临漳有孙事道巡检亦能此。"可学云："天下有许多物事，想极，物自入来。"曰："然。"可学。

The Master said, "As regards the Daoists' practice of their occult techniques, their arts are only to think out something, but they fear others do not believe it, so they use those techniques to fool them. In *Lü Yushu Ji* 吕与叔集 (Collected Works of Lü Yushu)[①] is recorded something (practiced by Daoists) very weird. I once saw a routing inspection official Sun Shidao 孙事道 (dates unknown) in Linzhang (roughly present day Linzhang, Hebei) who was also able to do that." I said thereupon, "There are many things and

---

① Probably referring to *Yuxi Ji* 玉溪集 (Collected Works by Yuxi) by Lü Dalin.

events in the world which, if one thinks over them extremely hard, will naturally seem as if they came up to him really. " The Master responded, "Yes. " [Kexue]

75　道家说仙人尸解，极怪异。将死时，用一剑，一圆药，安于睡处。少间，剑化作自己，药又化作甚么物，自家却自去别处去。其剑亦有名，谓之"良非子"。良非之义，犹言本非我也。"良非子"好对"亡是公"！

The Daoist saying of the process of someone turning to be an immortal through death is extremely weird. As they describe, when he is dying, he has a sword and a round medicine put where he lies, and soon the sword transforms into him. But what does the medicine transform into? Not caring it, he goes to somewhere else for himself. The sword is called Liangfeizi 良非子 (lit. Truly-Not Master). The meaning of it is like that of "being originally not me." Liangfeizi is antithetic well to Wushigong 亡是公 (No Such Duke). [1]

---

[1]　A fictional character in "Zixu Fu" 子虚赋 (Master Void Rhapsody) by Sima Xiangru 司马相如 (179 – 127 BC). Zhu Xi borrowed the name to refer to the person under description.

参考文献
Cited Translations of Chinese Classics

[1] Baynes, C. F. *The I Ching or Book of Changes* (The Richard Wilhelm translation rendered into English). New York: Penguin Group, Inc. , 1950.

[2] Chan, Wing-tsit. *A Source Book in Chinese Philosophy*. Princeton: Princeton University Press, 1963.

[3] Legge, James. *Analects* (http: //ctext. org/analects)

[4] Legge, James. *Book of Filial Piety* (http: //ctext. org/xiao-jing)

[5] Legge, James. *Book of History* (http: //ctext. org/shang-shu)

[6] Legge, James. *Book of Changes* (http: //ctext. org/ book-of-changes)

[7] Legge, James. *Book of Poetry* (http: //ctext. org/ book-of-poetry)

[8] Legge, James. *Laozi* (http: //ctext. org/dao-de-jing)

[9] Legge, James. *Mencius* (http: //ctext. org/mengzi)

[10] Legge, James. *Record of Rites* (http: //ctext. org/liji)

[11] Legge, James. *Zhuangzi* (http: //ctext. org/zhaungzi)

[12] Lin, Wusun. *Getting to Know Confucius: A New Translation of the Analects*. Beijing: Foreign Language Press, 2010.

[13] Lynn, Richard. *The Classic of Changes: A New Translation of the I Ching as Interpreted by Wang Bi*. New York: Columbia University

Press, 1994.

[14] Wang, Xiaonong. *Selections from Classified Conversations of Zhu Xi*. Guilin: Guangxi Normal University Press, 2014.

术 语 表
Glossary

an	安	tranquil repose
baixing	百行	hundred conducts or activities
Bingjia	兵家	School of the Military
ceyin	恻隐	sadness and commiseration
Chan	禅	Chan Sect of Buddhism；dhyana
Chanyuan Qinggui	《禅苑清规》	*Rules in the Buddhist Monasteries*
chang	常	being ordinary；constant
cheng	诚	sincerity
chengque	诚悫	honesty and guilelessness
chengyi	诚意	making intention sincere
Chunqiu	《春秋》	*Spring and Autumn Annals*
cixun	辞逊	deference and compliance
cunxin	存心	preserving the mind
daxue	大学	imperial academy；great learning
Daxue	《大学》	*Great Learning*
Daxue Huowen	《大学或问》	*Questions and Answers on the Great Learning*
Daxue Zhangju	《大学章句》	*Interpretation of the Great Learning*
Dao	道	the Way

daoxin	道心	the mind of the Way
Daoxue	道学	Learning of the Way, the Neo-Confucianism in the Song dynasty
de	德	virtue
de	得	the attainment (of the desired end)
di	弟	fraternity
Dizi Zhi	《弟子职》	*Pupils' Rules and Regulations*
ding	定	determined
dong	动	activity
dongjing	动静	activity and tranquility
du	独	being alone; solitude
Dushi Guanjian	《读史管见》	*Humble Opinions on Histories*
Er-cheng Yishu	《二程遗书》	*Surviving Works of Two Chengs*
er-wu zhi qi	二五之气	two-five (i. e. *yin* and *yang*, and the Five Agents) vital forces
fangcun	方寸	heart (thought as the human organ of thinking)
fangxin	放心	lost mind
Fayan	《法言》	*Exemplary Sayings*
fu	孚	confidence-inspiring
gewu zhizhi	格物致知	investigating things and pursuing perfection of knowledge
gongfu	工夫	effort
haoran zhi qi	浩然之气	flowing vast vital force
he	和	harmony
hua	化	transformation
Huangji Jingshi	《皇极经世书》	*Supreme Principles Governing the World*

gaoming	高明	the high and brilliant
Guanzi	《管子》	*Writings of Master Guan*
ji	几	the minutest springs (of things)
ji xiong hui lin	吉凶悔吝	auspicious, inauspicious, regret, trouble
Jiafan	《家范》	*Family Precepts*
jian' ai	兼爱	loving all equally
jin	谨	being solemnly careful
jin	矜	complacency
jinxin	尽心	exerting the mind to the utmost
jing	敬	respectfulness; seriousness
jing	静	unperturbedness
jing quan	经权	that which is unchangeable, and change for adaptation
jiujing fa	究竟法	paramattha dhamma
jiyi	集义	accumulating righteousness
Junzi	君子	Superior Man; man of true honor
Kongzi Jiayu	《孔子家语》	*Confucius's Family Discourse*
li	理	principle
li	礼	propriety
Liji	《礼记》	*Record of Rites*
liandan	炼丹	Daoist external alchemy
liangneng	良能	intuitive ability
liangzhi	良知	intuitive knowledge
Lienü Zhuan	《列女传》	*Biographies of Famous Women*
liuji	六极	six occasions of suffering
Liujing	六经	Six Confucian Classics, i. e. the *Classic of Poetry*, *Classic of History*, *Record of Rites*, *Classic of*

		Change, Spring and Autumn Annals, and Classic of Music
liuyi	六艺	six arts, i. e. rites, music, archery, driving a chariot, writing, and mathematics
longhu	龙虎	lt. dragon and tiger, referring metaphorically to spirit and essence
Longhu Shangjing	《龙虎上经》	*The Dragon and Tiger Classic*
Luancheng Ji	《栾城集》	*Collected Works of Luancheng*
Lunyun	《论语》	*Analects*; *The Analects of Confucius*
Lunyu Jiyi	《论语集义》	*Collected Meanings of the Analects*
Lunyu Jizhu	《论语集注》	*Collected Annotations of the Analects*
Lunyu Luejie	《论语略解》	*Brief Explanation of the Analects*
lü	虑	deliberation
Lü Yushu Ji	《吕与叔集》	*Collected Works of Lü Yushu*
Mao Shi	《毛诗》	*Maos' Edition of the Classic of Poetry*
Mengzi	《孟子》	*Mencius*
MengziJizhu	《孟子集注》	*Collected Annotations of the Mencius*
Menzi Zhushu	《孟子注疏》	*Annotation and Explanation of the Mencius*
ming	命	destiny; what is conferred by Heaven
mingde	明德	illustrious virtue
mingshan	明善	clarifying what is good
Nüjie	《女戒》	*Lessons for Women*

ren	人	humankind; human beings
ren	仁	benevolence; humanity
renwu zhi xing	人物之性	the nature of humankind and things
pian	偏	partiality
qi	气	vital force; material force
qiangong	铅汞	lit. lead and mercury; fig. destiny and nature
qinse	琴瑟	ancient Chinese plucked music instruments, like zithers and lutes
qing	情	feeling
qingxu	清虚	pure void
qiongli	穷理	inquiring the principles to the utmost
qipian	七篇	seven pieces of writing, i. e. *Mencius*
qizhi	气质	physical nature; physical constitution
qizhi zhi xing	气质之性	physical nature
sandai	三代	three dynasties , i. e. the Xia, Shang, and Zhou dynasties
sanli	三礼	three ancient books on rites, i. e. *The Rites of Zhou*, *Ceremonial Etiquettes*, and *Record of Rites*
shan	善	good; goodness
Shangdi	上帝	Topmost Master; Supreme Being
Shangshu	《尚书》	*Book of History* (i. e. *Shujing* 书经 *Classic of History*)
shen	神	the inscrutable; god; spirit; deity

shendu	慎独	being watchful over being alone or solitude
sheng	圣	sage; being sagely
shengde	盛德	complete virtue
shengzhi	生质	born quality
shifei	是非	right and wrong
Shijing	《诗经》	*Classic of Poetry*
Shiwen	时文	prescribed essay for the imperial examinations
shi zhong	时中	taking the Mean at any time
siduan	四端	four beginnings, i. e. the feelings of sadness and commiseration, shame and dislike, deference and compliance, and right and wrong
Sishu	四书	Four Books, i. e. the *Great Learning*, *Analects*, *Mencius*, and *Doctrine of the Mean*
Shuoyuan	《说苑》	*Garden of Anecdotes*
suishi zhi zhong	随时之中	the state of the Mean maintained at any time
Taiji	太极	Great Ultimate; Supreme Ultimate
Taiji Tu	"太极图"	"Diagram of the Great Ultimate"
Taiji Tu Jie	《太极图解》	*Explanation of the Diagram of the Great Ultimate*
Taixu	太虚	Great Void
ti	体	substance; body; embodying
tian	天	Heaven; Nature; heaven; nature
tiande	天德	heavenly virtue
Tiangan Dizhi	天干地支	Heavenly Stems and Earthly

		Branches
Tianming	天命	Mandate of Heaven; that which Heaven confers
tiaoli	条理	veins; orderliness
Tongjian Gangmu	《通鉴纲目》	*Outline of the Comprehensive Mirror*
Tongshu	《通书》	*Penetrating the Classic of Change*
weifa zhi zhong	未发之中	the state of equilibrium when the feelings are unstirred or not aroused
wen	文	form and beauty
wenbian	问辨	inquiry and discrimination
Woji Jing	《握奇经》	*Classic of Strategies within a Military Commander's Tent*
wu	物	thing(s)
wuchang	五常	five constant virtues
wufu	五福	five sources of happiness
wushi	物事	thing-event
wuwei	无为	non-action; doing nothing
wuxing	五行	five agents, i.e. metal, wood, water, fire, and earth
xiao	孝	filial piety
Xiaojing	《孝经》	*Classic of Filial Piety*
xiaoren	小人	petty man
xiaoxue	小学	primary school; primary learning
Xiaoxue	《小学》	*Primary Learning*
Ximing	"西铭"	"The Western Inscription"
xin	心	mind; heart-mind
xin	信	faithfulness
Xin Tangshu	《新唐书》	*New Book of Tang*
xing	性	nature; humanity

xiuwu	羞恶	shame and dislike
xiuxing	修省	cultivating one's own character and examining one's own mind
xu jing	虚静	void and quietness
xu wu	虚无	void and non-being
Xueji	《学记》	*Record on the Subject of Education*
xueju	学聚	accumulation of learning
yan	验	experiencing
yang	阳	positive cosmic force
yeqi	夜气	restorative effect of the night
yi	义	righteousness
yi	易	change; the principle of change
yi	意	intention; meaning
yifa zhi zhong	已发之中	the state of equilibrium when the feelings are stirred or aroused
Yijing	《易经》	*Classic of Change*
yili	义理	principle
yin	阴	negative cosmic force
Yinfu Jing	《阴符经》	*Classic of the Secret Talisman*, i. e. *Huangdi Yinfu Jing* 黄帝阴符经 *Yellow Emperor Classic of Secret Talisman*
Yinfu Jing Zhu	《阴符经注》	*Classic of Secret Talisman Annotated*
Yixue Qimeng	《易学启蒙》	*Rudimentary Knowledge of Learning on the Classic of Change*
Yizhuan	《易传》	*Explanations of the Classic of Change*
yong	庸	being ordinary

yong	勇	courage
yong	用	function
yuan heng li zhen	元亨利贞	origination, prosperity, advantage, and firmness
Yuan Xing	"原性"	"The Origin of Nature"
yue	约	restraining
zaizhong	在中	being in equilibrium
zaohua	造化	creation and transformation in nature
zeshan	择善	choosing what is good
zhenshi fa	真实法	sacca-dhamma
zheng	正	impartiality; correctness
zhi	知	knowledge; wisdom
zhi	执	holding
zhi	智	wisdom
zhi	志	bent; intent
zhi	质	essence; substance
zhidao	至道	supreme Way
zhide	至德	supreme virtue
zhishan	至善	supreme good
zhixing	知行	knowledge and action
zhixing	知性	understanding humanity; understanding
zhizhi	知止	knowing the point where to rest
zhong	忠	loyalty
zhong	中	equilibrium; centrality
zhonghe	中和	equilibrium and harmony
zhongjie	中节	acting in the due degree
zhongshu	忠恕	loyalty-forbearance, i. e.

		cultivating to the utmost the principles of one's nature and exercising them on the guideline of reciprocity
zhongxin	忠信	loyalty and faithfulness
zhongyong	中庸	centrality and ordinariness; the Mean
Zhongyong	《中庸》	*Doctrine of the Mean*
Zhongyong Huowen	《中庸或问》	*Questions and Answers on the Doctrine of the Mean*
Zhongyong Jie	《中庸解》	*Explanation of the Doctrine of the Mean*
Zhongyong Zhangju	《中庸章句》	*Interpretation of the Doctrine of the Mean*
Zhouyi Cantong Qi	《周易参同契》	*The Kinship of the Three in Accordance with the Classic of Change*
Zizhi Tongjian	《资治通鉴》	*Comprehensive Mirror to Aid in Government*
Zuozhuan	《左传》	*Zuo's Explanation of the Spring and Autumn Annals*

译 后 记

  《朱子语类》（黎靖德编本）是南宋理学大师朱熹（1130—1200）与门人的对话录，凡 140 卷，内容丰富，析理精密，是后人研究朱熹思想的主要文献之一。该书尚无英文全译本出版，仅有少量内容散见于英文版的中国哲学论著。2010 年至 2012 年，王晓农选译了《朱子语类》九卷，包括"理气上"、"理气下"、"学四"、"自论为学工夫"、"论治道"、"论取士"、"论兵刑"、"论民财"和"论官"，于 2014 年以《朱子语类选》为题，作为"大中华文库"之一种由广西师范大学出版社出版。该译著是世界范围内第一部英文《朱子语类》选译本。

  这本汉英对照《朱子语类选译》是该译著的继续。本书选译了《朱子语类》（黎靖德编，中华书局，1986）十卷，分别是"卷四性理一"、"卷五性理二"、"卷六性理三"、"卷七学一"、"卷八学二"、"卷九学三"、"卷十四大学一"、"卷十九论语一"、"第六十二中庸一"、"卷一百二十五老氏附庄列"，反映了朱子在哲学、治学方法、四书学和道家论等方面的思想。译者对原文的理解参考了国内外学者相关的研究成果，力求准确认识所选章节的概念系统，把握朱子思想的原貌。在英译过程中，译者根据典籍外译的基本理论，结合对英译文本目标读者的分析，延续了《朱子语类选》（2014）英译采用的文献性翻译为主、艺术性翻译为辅的策略。在操作过程中，重点关注了两方面的问题：一方面，如何保持原有表述的价值观念、信念体系、理论形态、义理框架和表述方式；另一方面，如何为与异域视野产生亲和力而添加内容，调整评论角度，以期能够向西方学术过渡和表述，与其进行有效沟通。在词、句、篇和文体风格等层面的英译策略和方法主要涉及了准确、有序地英译术语和词语，以句子为基本单位、语义明晰而行文晓畅地英译句子，为实现适合性对篇章进行必要的调整，以体现不同文体和表达功能的灵活翻译方法，以及文献性翻译策略为主兼顾艺术性和诗学功能的辩证综合的翻译策略和方法。对于涉及的术语，根据具体术语的内涵，对现有庞杂的英译文进行了甄别研究，以确立本书的术语英译系统；在具体上下文中基于对术语语源、定义、搭配、语境和系统的考虑采用了适当的处理方法来明确有序地处理术语。根据对汉语原文的阐释和对一些专名、术语、典故和某些词句的解释，结合对英语读者背景知识的大致预测，建立了本书的英译注释系统。其中，显性注释部分主要包括文本内部夹注和副文本的脚注，对较重要的术语则给出了综合注释，以有助于读者理解译文。在确立英译文的过程中，译者借鉴了一些相关的汉籍英译文本，也参阅了不少网上资源，例如维基百科的相关英语词条。

全书英译由王晓农、赵增韬完成。具体分工如下，王晓农英译了"性理一"、"性理二"、"性理三"、"学一"、"大学一"和"中庸一"，以及"序"和"译后记"，赵增韬英译了"学二"、"学三"、"论语一"、和"老氏附庄列"，全部译文由王晓农统稿。两位译者分别是鲁东大学和浙江外国语学院全职教师，本书翻译工作是在繁重的教学、科研工作之余，锱铢积累地完成的。翻译过程艰苦，存在不少困难，却也实是一桩乐事。我们希望本译本能够和"大中华文库"的汉英对照《朱子语类选》一起，为帮助英语读者了解朱子思想以及中国传统思想做出贡献，也希望通过读者和朋友们的积极合作，本书能够幸运地获得英语世界一定程度的认可。

本书的英译工作得到了中国典籍翻译研究会会长、南开大学教授王宏印先生的指导，中国历史文献研究会前会长、华东师范大学终身教授朱杰人先生热情为本书作序，在此向两位先生表示由衷谢意。译者特别感谢本书的责任编辑、中国社会科学出版社刘艳女士为本书的出版付出的辛劳。译者感谢鲁东大学外国语学院 2017 级翻译方向研究生于涤非、石英在搜集资料和译稿校对方面所做的工作。也借此机会向关心、支持、帮助本书翻译工作的领导、同事、家人和同学一并表示感谢。我们虽尽最大努力，但囿于学识、译笔，译文中必有谬误之处，责任全在译者，衷心希望各位专家、同仁斧正。

译　者

2018 年 6 月 15 日

Translators' Postscript

Zhuzi Yulei (Li Jingde's edition), a voluminous Confucian classic of 140 *juan* (fascicles or books), records the classified conversations of Zhu Xi (1130 – 1200), the great Neo-Confucian scholar in the Southern Song Dynasty (1127 – 1279), with his disciples. Carrying Zhu's thought in an encyclopedic way, it is one of the main references for those scholars engaging in studies of Zhuzi, or Master Zhu, as he has been called respectfully by generations after him. Up to now, there has been no English translation of the entire classic the available, though there are a few translated conversations which can be found in some works on Chinese philosophy published in English.

From 2010 to 2012, Wang Xiaonong selected nine books from it and translated them into English, including "Book 1 *Li* and *Qi*, Part I," "Book 2 *Li* and *Qi*, Part II," "Book 10 On Learning, Part Four," "Book 104 Master Zhu's Account of His Pursuit of Learning," "Book 108 On the Way of Ruling," "Book 109 On Enlisting Civil-Service Scholar Officials," "Book 110 On the Military and Penal Affairs," "Book 111 On the Populace and Revenues," and "Book 112 On Officialdom." 2014 saw the publication of that translation with the title *Selections from Classified Conversations of Zhu Xi* as a contribution to the bilingual series of "Library of Chinese Classics," a key state-sponsored publishing project of China. It is the world's first English translation of selections from the Chinese classic published in book form.

Getting to Know Master Zhu Xi: *English Translation of Selections from Zhuzi Yulei* is a continuation of that translation. This new translation by Wang Xiaonong and Zhao Zengtao in collaboration includes the English version of ten more books selected from *Zhuzi Yulei* (compiled. by Li Jingde and published by Zhonghua Book Company, 1986), i. e. "Book 4 Nature and Principle I," "Book 5 Nature and Principle II," "Book 6 Nature and Principle III," "Book 7 Learning I," "Book 8 Learning II," "Book 9 Learning III," "Book 14 *Great Learning* I," "Book 19 *Analects* I," "Book 62 The *Doctrine of the Mean* I," and "Book 125 Laozi, with Zhuangzi and Liezi," which concern Zhuzi's philosophy, way of pursuing learning, thoughts on the Four Books, and comments on Daoism.

Making reference to available research achievements by scholars at home and abroad, we strove to grasp the conceptual system of those books within the frame of reference of the entire work and to understand the thoughts of Zhuzi accurately. Drawing on the experience from translating *Selections from Classified Conversations of Zhu Xi* (2014) and taking into account the target readership, our English translation features a primary documentary orientation complemented by some secondary literary and artistic considerations in the light of the basic theory over translating Chinese classics into other languages. We paid attention to both sides of our coin: for one, retaining as much as possible the original values, beliefs, theoretical conceptions, argumentation frameworks, and the Chinese ways of conveying them, and for the other, creating affinity with the English readership by means of compensation in information and readjustment of perspectives, so as to render our English version intelligible to the West academic community for effective communication. Our linguistic operations on the lexical, syntactic, and textual levels aimed to emphasize accurate and systematic rendering of the terms, of the sentences for conveying ideas in a semantically faithful, syntactically sound, and stylistically readable way, and of the text with proper and flexible restructuring for a better textual effect. Our pursuit was for highlighting the original features in content and form, yet without losing sight of the artistic and the poetic function of the translated text. Regarding the Chinese terms, we, after analyzing their English translations by other translators past and present, adopted some of them and, by considering such factors as etymology, definition, and system, created some new ones, or rendered the same Chinese term in different ways in contexts, all of which constitute the system of terms in our English version. Considering the target English readership, we constructed our noting system which is composed of intra-textual and para-textual annotations of some Chinese proper names, terms, and allusions, and those concepts and expressions which, we thought, need background information. For some important cultural terms in the original text, we provided their comprehensive explanations to facilitate readers' efforts to understand our translation. Our English version makes some citations from the widely accepted English translations of relevant Chinese classics as well as many on-line resources, such as those English materials presented by such websites as Wikipedia.

As regards our division of work, Wang from Ludong University translated "Book 4 Nature and Principle I," "Book 5 Nature and Principle II," "Book 6 Nature and Principle III," "Book 7 Learning I," "Book 14 *Great Learning* I," and "Book 62 The *Doctrine of the Mean* I," as well as the "Foreword" and the "Translators' postscript," and Zhao from Zhejiang International Studies University, "Book 8 Learning II," "Book 9 Learning III," "Book 19 *Analects* I," "Book 125 Laozi, with Zhuangzi and Liezi." Wang was responsible for the work of finalizing the entire English version. As full-time teachers, we devoted much of our spare time to our translation work, submerging ourselves in translating and emerging with our English versions, and cooperatively completed the task on schedule. We hope that our translation, together with *Selections from Classified Conversations of Zhu Xi*, will contribute to the English readers' getting to know Master Zhu better and understanding his thought and thereby the Chinese culture at large deeper, and with active cooperation of our readers and friends, this translation will be lucky enough to gain some popularity in the English speaking world.

Many people, with or without their knowing, have had a hand in carrying out this translation project, to whom we are indebted. We express our gratitude to Mr. Wang Hongyin, Professor of Nankai University and President of Chinese Association of Classics Translation, for his insightful suggestions and guidance over our translating work, and Mr. Zhu Jieren, Lifetime Professor of East China Normal University and former President of Chinese Association of Historical Documents, who wrote a foreword in Chinese for our translation. Special thanks are due to Ms. Liu Yan, editor of China Social Sciences Publishing House, for her hard work on editing our manuscript. We are thankful also to Yu Difei and Shi Ying, two 2017 grade MA students majoring in translation studies in Ludong University, for their help in proofreading.

Even with so much good will and generous assistance from so many people, there are bound to be some problems and infelicities with our translation and even errors left in it. For these we take full responsibility. Any criticism of and suggestion for our translation are welcome!

Wang Xiaonong & Zhao Zengtao

June 15, 2018